COMPETITIVE DIALOGUE IN EU PROCUREMENT

Competitive dialogue is a procedure introduced into the EU procurement system in 2004 to provide an improved method for awarding complex contracts, such as those for public infrastructure and major IT systems. This book provides a critical examination of the legal rules on this new procedure, focusing in particular on grey areas such as availability of the procedure and the scope for negotiations after 'final tenders'. It considers both the EU-level rules and the way in which those rules have been applied in national systems. The examination draws on extensive evidence of the way in which the procedure has been operated and interpreted across Europe, including from several studies commissioned specifically for this volume. It also includes an extensive chapter co-authored by the volume editors which provides a thorough analysis of the EU-level rules, a comparative reflection on national experiences, and significant critical commentary and recommendations.

SUE ARROWSMITH is Achilles Professor of Public Procurement Law and Policy at the University of Nottingham, where she is also Director of the Public Procurement Research Group and of the postgraduate Executive Programme in Public Procurement Law and Policy.

PROFESSOR STEEN TREUMER is Professor of Procurement Law and Privatization Law at the University of Copenhagen. He is also a consultant in public procurement law and a member of the Danish Complaints Board for Public Procurement.

COMPETITIVE DIALOGUE IN EU PROCUREMENT

Edited by

SUE ARROWSMITH

and

STEEN TREUMER

CAMBRIDGE
UNIVERSITY PRESS

CAMBRIDGE UNIVERSITY PRESS
Cambridge, New York, Melbourne, Madrid, Cape Town,
Singapore, São Paulo, Delhi, Mexico City

Cambridge University Press
The Edinburgh Building, Cambridge CB2 8RU, UK

Published in the United States of America by Cambridge University Press, New York

www.cambridge.org
Information on this title: www.cambridge.org/9781107023833

First published 2012

Printed and bound in the United Kingdom by the MPG Books Group

A catalogue record for this publication is available from the British Library

Library of Congress Cataloging-in-Publication Data

Competitive dialogue in EU procurement / edited by
Sue Arrowsmith and Steen Treumer.
p. cm.
Includes index.
ISBN 978-1-107-02383-3 (Hardback)
1. Government purchasing–Law and legislation–European Union countries.
I. Treumer, Steen.
II. Arrowsmith, Sue, 1962– III. Title: Competitive dialogue in
European Union procurement.
KJE5632.C63 2012
342.240′4–dc23
2012018199

ISBN 978-1-107-02383-3 Hardback

CONTENTS

FIGURES

TABLES

CONTRIBUTORS

PROFESSOR SUE ARROWSMITH is Achilles Professor of Public Procurement Law and Policy at the University of Nottingham, where she is also Director of the Public Procurement Research Group and of the School's postgraduate Executive programme in Public Procurement Law and Policy. Her numerous publications have been extensively cited by courts and legislators in North America, Asia and Africa as well as Europe. Authored books include *The Law of Public and Utilities Procurement* (2nd edn, 2005); (with Linarelli and Wallace) *Regulating Public Procurement; National and International Perspectives* (2000); and *Government Procurement in the WTO* (Kluwer, 2003). In 1992, she launched the first international academic procurement journal, *Public Procurement Law Review*. In 2007, she was awarded the CIPS Swinbank Medal for thought innovation in purchasing and supply. She has taught university modules on procurement since 1995 and from 2009 to 2011 was Project Leader of the EU-funded Asia Link project for developing a global academic network on procurement regulation, which included setting up the global Procurement Law Academic Network (PLAN, www.planpublicprocurement.org). She has been a member since 1997 of the European Commission's independent Advisory Committee on public procurement; is a member of the UNCITRAL Experts Group on Procurement; and has been consultant and trainer for, *inter alia*, the UK Office of Government Commerce, UN, WTO, European Commission, OECD, EU, European Central Bank, ILO and Law Commission of England and Wales.

PROFESSOR STEEN TREUMER is Professor of Procurement Law and Privatisation Law, in the Faculty of Law, Centre for Enterprise Liability (CEVIA), University of Copenhagen. He is a graduate in law and wrote his prize-winning doctoral thesis on the principle of equal treatment of tenderers in the EC public procurement rules. He is currently Professor of Procurement Law and Privatisation Law at the University of Copenhagen and Director of Studies. He has published widely on public procurement law, including numerous international publications on public procurement law. His publications in 2011 include *Enforcement of the EU Public Procurement Rules* (Copenhagen: DJØF Publishing) (co-editor Professor François Lichère, Aix-Marseille III). Since 2006, he has been Assistant Editor of the international academic journal, *Public Procurement Law Review* and one of the Editors of the *European Procurement Law Series* established in 2009 (co-editor, Professor Roberto Caranta, Turin). He is also a consultant in public procurement law and has been involved as such in many public procurement procedures and has assisted practising lawyers in several disputes. Steen Treumer has organised more than thirty international conferences and seminars on EU law. About fifteen of these have concerned public procurement law. He was the conference programme director, together with Professor Sue Arrowsmith, for the global public procurement conference, 'Public Procurement: Global Revolution V', and also for the 1st Interdisciplinary Symposium on Public Procurement organised in 2011 together with Professor Gustavo Piga, Rome. In 2000, he was awarded the Spar Nord Foundation's Research Prize for his doctoral thesis. The prize is awarded to a researcher at Aalborg University who has concluded a particularly excellent project at the university. He is also Chairman and co-founder of the Danish Association for Public Procurement Law.

PROFESSOR DR MARTIN BURGI is Professor of German and European Public Law (since 1999) and Director of the only research institute in Germany for the Modernisation of Administrative Law and Government Procurement Law, at the Ruhr-University Bochum (since 2004). He is a member of the board of directors of the Institute for Mining and Energy Law at the Ruhr-University Bochum and a Research Fellow at the George Washington University Law School in Washington DC. His areas of expertise are: modernisation and privatisation of the state, administration and local governments and privatisation in the international context; privatisation in Europe; government procurement law; protection of fundamental rights of enterprises; legal protection at international courts; and the role of regions and municipalities in the global change. He is an official expert for parliamentary institutions and legal consultant for stock exchange enterprises, states and local municipalities. Furthermore, he is the scientific supervisor of the 'Düsseldorfer Vergaberechtstag', which is one of the leading annual conferences on government procurement law in Germany. He has written numerous books and articles (more than 10 books and over 100 essays) on all his research areas, for example: 'Small and Medium-Sized Enterprises and Procurement

Law – European Legal Framework and German Experiences' (2007) 16 *Public Procurement Law Review* 284; *Kommunalrecht* (2nd edn, Munich: Verlag C. H. Beck, 2008); 'Die Bedeutung der allgemeinen Vergabegrundsätze Wettbewerb, Transparenz und Gleichbehandlung' (2008) NZBau 29; 'Tagungsband zum 10. Düsseldorfer Vergaberechtstag' (2009); 'The Policy on Regulating Electronic, Communications in Germany', in S. Arrowsmith (ed.), *Reform of the UNCITRAL Model Law on Procurement: Procurement Regulation for the 21st Century* (2009), pp. 305–27; 'Die Modernisierung des Vergaberechts als Daueraufgabe' (2009) DÖV 829; 'Federal Republic of Germany', in N. Steytler (ed.), *Local Government and Metropolitan Regions in Federal Systems* (2009), pp. 136–65; and *Damages as an Effective Remedy? German Perspective* (2010).

DR DARIO CASALINI is Assistant Professor of Public Law at the Faculty of Economics, University of Turin, where he teaches public law for economists and EU public procurement law. He is a lawyer at the Bar of Turin, and was visiting researcher at King's College London in 2008–2009. He has taken part in several research projects focused on European public procurement law and has published various articles on the issues arising in the national implementation of EU procurement law, including a book on the notion of a body governed by public law and in-house provision, *L'organismo di diritto pubblico e l'organiszazione in house* (Jovene, 2003). He has presented papers at international conferences (IGU 2009, IPPC 2010, PLPR 2011) and his research interests lie in the area of public and administrative law, public procurement, public utilities, NHS, public service, water and natural resources law, and public ownership in a comparative perspective.

RICHARD CRAVEN is a PhD candidate at the University of Nottingham. His research explores the operation of competitive dialogue in the UK, combining a socio-legal analysis of the legal rules with qualitative interviews with key actors (contracting authority procurement officers and internal legal advisors, external legal advisors, and policy-makers). The research is supervised by Professor Sue Arrowsmith, Professor David Fraser and Susie Smith (Bevan Brittan LLP), and is funded by the Economic and Social Research Council and Bevan Brittan LLP.

ANNA GORCZYNSKA holds the Chair of European Economic Law in the Faculty of Law and Administration, University of Lodz, Poland. She read law at the University of Lodz, where she prepared her masters thesis titled

'Direct investments of the foreign capital in Poland'. In 2005, she prepared her dissertation titled 'Public procurement in the European law' and she is now preparing her habilitation on public–private partnerships. She was previously a law student at the German universities of Muenster, Giessen and Bonn. She was a postgraduate student at the International Law and Business Law School organised by the Catholic University in Washington in co-operation with Jagiellonian University (1994, 1996). In 1999, she participated in the Internationale Parlaments Praktika in Bundestag, Germany, and from 2000 to 2002 worked in regional lobbying offices in Brussels. She was also a guest professor at the Freie University in Berlin and University in Giessen. In 2010, she was invited as a guest speaker at the International Public Procurement Congress in Beijing. She directs postgraduate studies on European structural funds in the Faculty of Law and Administration. She is also a member of the European Law Association. Her main scientific interests and publications concern public procurement law, public–private partnership, European economic law, competition law, regional policy and the structural funds of the EU. Parallel to her academic work she has been working for regional self-government as head of the unit responsible for international co-operation of the Lodz Region (since 1999). She is also involved in the legal practise in Eurokancelaria.

DR SYLVIA DE MARS is a Lecturer in Law at the Newcastle Law School, Newcastle University. She obtained a Bachelor in Social Science from University College Utrecht and thereafter specialised in international law, obtaining an LLM and a PhD at the University of Nottingham. She is currently lecturing in the fields of public procurement law, international trade law, EU internal market law, and financial regulation. Her main research interests include comparative EU procurement law, regulatory theory, and general EU internal market law.

MRS JACOBIEN MUNTZ-BEEKHUIS is senior counsel for the Professional and Innovative Procurement Network for Contracting Authorities (PIANOo), an expertise centre for public procurement which is part of the Ministry of Economic Affairs, Agriculture and Innovation in the Netherlands. From 2005 to 2008, she was a senior counsel within the PPP Unit of the Government Building Agency. She holds a law degree in civil law and a law degree in notarial law from the University of Amsterdam (1994). She is specialised in procurement law, having gained experience as a licensed attorney for Trenité van Doorne, and as a legal counsel for Siemens. Previous publications include 'The Competitive Dialogue', a guide based on the experience of the Rijksgebouwendienst, Rijkswaterstaat and the Ministry of Defence.

MS MARIJKE NAGELKERKE is a senior consultant on legal affairs with the Ministry of Infrastructure and Environment, Department of Water Management and Public Works in the Netherlands. From 2007 to 2011, she was a senior consultant with the PPP Unit of the Department of Water Management and Public Works. Currently, she is a senior legal consultant with the Service Organisation Infrastructure of the same department. She holds a law degree in civil law from the University of Tilburg (2000). Her field of expertise is procurement and contract law. Recently, she has started her dissertation research, focused on PFI contracts in the Netherlands for her doctoral degree with the Delft University of Technology. She has extensive experience of contract and procurement law, both during her career with the Ministry of Infrastructure and with the Ministry of Defence. Previous publications include 'The Competitive Dialogue', a guide based on the experience of the Rijksgebouwendienst, Rijkswaterstaat and the Ministry of Defence.

MRS FRÉDÉRIQUE OLIVIER has been a Partner at DS Avocats in Paris since 2005. She advises public authorities and private economic operators on national and international public procurement and litigation matters. She specialises in public contracts and especially in public–private partnerships. Previously, she was the head of the legal department of ADEME, a French public organisation in the field of environment, energy and sustainable development, from 1982 to 1990. She was then part of the legal department of Cité des Sciences et de l'Industrie from 1990 to 1996 and the legal department of Federation Française du Bâtiment, a French professional building federation, from 1996 to 2005.

PROFESSOR GABRIELLA M. RACCA is Professor of Administrative Law, Deputy Dean at the Faculty of Economics, University of Turin and Member of the Scientific Board of the Master of Science in Public Procurement Management for Sustainable Development jointly organised by the International Training Centre of the International Labour Organisation and the University of Turin. She led several national and European research projects on the contractual autonomy of health authorities (PRIN 2005 and PRIN 2007) and on educational paths regarding collaborative public procurement financed by the Region of Piedmont (European Social Fund). She is responsible for the Procurement Contract topic of the Ius

Publicum Network, founded in Madrid by the Editorial Boards of *Die Verwaltung, Diritto amministrativo, International Journal of Constitutional Law, Public Law, Revista de Administración Pública* and *Revue française de droit administratif*. Her research interests include public services, public contracts and public procurement, PPP, collaborative procurement and central purchasing bodies particularly in European healthcare systems, and sustainability (environmental and social considerations) in public procurement; public liability and compensation for damages; and accountability of public administrations. She has presented papers at international conferences (Paris 2010, Symposium international des acheteurs publics et privés de la santé; New York University 2010, The New Public Law in a Global (Dis)Order; George Washington University 2010; IPPC 2010, Seoul; and WP Carey Law School, Arizona University 2011). She recently published in *Public Procurement Law Review* ('Collaborative Procurement and Contract Performance in the Italian Healthcare Sector: Illustration of a Common Problem in European Procurement' (2010) 19 *Public Procurement Law Review* 119), and in European Procurement Law Series, in Quaderni Consip – Consip website with R. Cavallo Perin and G. L. Albano on competition in the execution phase of public procurement.

DR DEIVIDAS SOLOVEIČIKAS is a lecturer at Vilnius University Faculty of Laws where he teaches courses on public procurement law and EU public procurement law. He received the degree of Master of Laws at Vilnius University (2001). He also studied at the Faculty of Law of Lund University, Sweden (1999), continuing his studies at the University of Essex, England, where he obtained the degree of Master of Laws (LLM) in European Community Law (2004). From 2001 to 2005, he was a PhD candidate and studied at the Faculty of Laws of the University of Vilnius. In 2005, he successfully defended his PhD dissertation on the subject of comparative aspects of corporate criminal liability, on the basis of which the degree of Doctor of Law was received. He is a member of the Lithuanian Bar Association and a managing partner of the MAQS law firm's Vilnius office. In 2011, he became a Member of the Chartered Institute of Arbitrators.

DR PEDRO TELLES is a Lecturer in Law at Bangor University, Wales, teaching procurement-related modules and media law. He is a member of the team for the Winning in Tendering project, a €3.7 million INTERREG-funded project assessing different aspects of procurement in Wales and Ireland. Within the project, Pedro is leading the research on low-value procurement with the aim of improving participation by small and medium-sized enterprises (SMEs) and experience in this type of procurement without overburdening contracting authorities. Pedro joined Bangor in January 2011 after concluding his PhD in the University of Nottingham with a thesis on the implementation of competitive dialogue in Portugal and Spain, under the supervision of Professors Sue Arrowsmith and David Fraser. For his thesis, Pedro conducted qualitative analysis through semi-structured interviews with lawyers, contracting authorities and law-makers as to assess competitive dialogue use in practice. Previously, after graduating from the University of Lisbon in 2003, he practised law in Lisbon and Barcelona until 2007, working mostly in public procurement and international contracts. He has been a member of the Portuguese Bar Association since 2005.

DIEDERIK VAN DER STAAY has been active within the Dutch Government Buildings Agency for thirteen years. From the very first pilot DBFMO project starting in 2003, he has experienced the development of DBFMO at the Government Buildings Agency. He has developed himself to become a dedicated trainer in this field. His main tasks now are helping anyone who is at the beginning of an integrated project to learn the skills before trying them out for real.

PREFACE

The introduction of competitive dialogue into the EU's legal regime on public procurement was indisputably one of the most important elements of the latest revision of this regime in 2004. Competitive dialogue was introduced in order to improve on the procedures previously available for realising complex projects, such as privately financed infrastructure projects, complex IT systems, and new types of services. Prior to this, many stakeholders considered that the award procedures for such projects were either too inflexible or were not sufficiently widely available in law, and competitive dialogue was added to fill the gap. The complex contracts to which it applies are significant both because they often involve considerable public expenditure and because they concern vital public services and infrastructure, and a suitable legal regime for awarding such contracts is therefore of utmost importance.

The main aim of this book is to provide a critical examination of the legal regime on competitive dialogue, in light of its objective of providing a procedure for complex procurement across the diverse Member States of the EU. This involves considering both the legal rules at EU level and the way in which those rules have been implemented and applied at national level, the latter being essential for a full perspective on the EU rules themselves. Through this analysis, the book also, significantly, aims to contribute towards the sound future development of the rules on competitive dialogue, both at EU level and in its implementation in national law and practice – whether that be through legislative change, judicial development, government guidance or simply application by contracting authorities. The work also offers an interesting case study of the way in which EU public procurement law has been received in national law and practice, and has influenced, and been influenced by, national approaches to regulating public procurement.

Enhancing the simplicity of the EU's legal regime and the flexibility of the procurement procedures it offers are also at the top of the agenda in the current process of modernising the EU procurement regime. A first proposal for a new basic Directive on public procurement was forwarded by the European Commission in December 2011, after the text of this book was completed. The outcome of the legislative process is by its very nature uncertain. However, it is notable that it will become much easier to access the competitive dialogue procedure if the European legislator follows the proposal of the European Commission. As this book demonstrates, its current scope is very uncertain, and this is one of the main reasons for the remarkable variation in the frequency of its use between Member States; but the Commission has proposed that the procedure should in future become more generally available, eliminating this uncertainty and the legal risks that may arise in choosing this procedure.

To increase the value of this book we have conducted several empirical studies. These studies have examined the way in which the legal rules 'in the books' have been applied and interpreted in practice by those responsible for operating and/or advising on competitive dialogue – mainly lawyers, procurement practitioners and policy-makers – in several of the Member States covered. This information is supplemented with information from other empirical studies, mostly from national governments. It is our hope that this element of the book will be a source of inspiration for practitioners, as well as informing policy-makers of the practical difficulties and concerns that need addressing in relation to this relatively novel procedure.

Many persons contributed to the production of this book or otherwise provided necessary support. Early versions of some of the papers incorporated in this volume were included in a workshop, held at Copenhagen Business School in September 2009. Subsequent versions and some additional papers included in the volume were presented at the conferences, Public Procurement: Global Revolution IV in Nottingham in April 2010, and Public Procurement: Global Revolution V in Copenhagen in September 2010, both of which were organised jointly by the University of Nottingham and the University of Copenhagen. We are grateful to all those who made presentations at these events, as well as to the delegates who provided interesting feedback on the papers presented there. We would also like to record our thanks to those assisting with the organisation of these events, in particular Justine Goodenough and Paula Faustino at the Nottingham event and Tina Futtrup Borg at the Copenhagen event.

At the School of Law of the University of Nottingham, thanks are due to all those who worked on technical aspects of the manuscript, in particular to Richard Craven and Gabor Soos for their very efficient contributions. Sue Arrowsmith would like also to express her great appreciation to the sponsors of the Public Procurement Research Group, in particular to Achilles Information for funding and support for many aspects of the project, including the empirical studies on Spain and Portugal, and to Bevan Brittan for co-funding the empirical research on UK practice. We are also grateful to the ESRC for the funding that it provided for this UK project under the CASE studentship scheme. The editors would also like to express their great appreciation to the many practitioners and policy-makers who were willing to take part in the empirical study on competitive dialogue in the UK, Denmark, France, Spain and Portugal.

At Cambridge University Press, we are grateful to Kim Hughes for both her encouragement and her patience and to Richard Woodham for his able assistance in readying the manuscript for production.

We also record our very sincere thanks to the authors/co-authors of all the chapters of the book, who freely gave of their time and insights and whose contributions made the book possible.

The information in this book is in general up to date as of July 2011. However, it has also been possible to a limited extent to note some important later developments, including, in Chapter 3, a change of policy on use of competitive dialogue announced in the UK in November 2011.

PART I

Competitive dialogue in the EU

1

Competitive dialogue in EU law: a critical review

SUE ARROWSMITH AND STEEN TREUMER

1. Introduction

Competitive dialogue is a relatively novel award procedure in EU procurement law, which was introduced in 2004[1] as part of a major overhaul of the EU's procurement regime.[2] Its purpose is to provide a suitable method for awarding the 'complex' contracts that have become increasingly important throughout the EU – for example, contracts for infrastructure projects, transport networks and major information technology systems. These are significant not only because of the high level of government expenditure that is often involved, but also because of their importance in securing effective public services and infrastructure. A suitable legal regime for awarding such contracts is therefore of great importance. Prior to 2004, some stakeholders considered that the existing award procedures in EU law were either inadequate for all complex contracts or – in the case of the flexible negotiated procedure – insufficiently available; and competitive dialogue was introduced to fill this gap.

The main aim of this book is to provide a critical examination of the legal regime on competitive dialogue, in light of its objective of providing a procedure for complex contracts across the diverse Member States of the EU.[3] This will involve considering both the

[1] In Directive 2004/18/EC of the European Parliament and of the Council of 31 March 2004 on the co-ordination of procedures for the award of public works contracts, public supply contracts and public service contracts [2004] OJ L134/114 ('Public Sector Directive').

[2] See generally S. Arrowsmith, 'An Assessment of the New Legislative Package on Public Procurement' (2004) 41 *Common Market Law Review* 1.

[3] For further legal analysis in English, see S. Arrowsmith, *The Law of Public and Utilities Procurement* (2nd edn, London: Sweet & Maxwell, 2005), Ch. 10; P. Trepte, *Public Procurement in the EU: A Practitioner's Guide* (Oxford University Press, 2007), pp. 404–9 and 445–53; M. Burnett (with M. Oder), *Competitive Dialogue – A Practical Guide* (European Institute of Public Administration, 2009); S. Treumer, 'Competitive Dialogue' (2004) 13 *Public Procurement Law Review* 178; S. Treumer, 'The Field of

legal rules at EU level and the way in which those rules have been implemented and applied at national level, the latter being essential for a full perspective on the EU rules themselves. At EU level we are concerned, in particular, to explain the key features of the legal rules; to identify areas of legal uncertainty; to evaluate possible interpretations; and to highlight any problems with the rules. This information should be of value to those who operate the rules in practice throughout the EU. Through this analysis the book also, significantly, aims to contribute towards the sound future development of the rules on competitive dialogue, both at EU level and in its implementation in national law and practice – whether that be through legislative change, judicial development, government guidance or simply application by contracting authorities. Further, as well as providing an analysis of the specific subject of competitive dialogue, this work also offers an interesting case study of the way in which EU public procurement law has been received in national law and practice, and has influenced, and been influenced by, national approaches to regulating public procurement. It should be emphasised, however, that the book does not elucidate all aspects of practice of competitive dialogue or serve as a comprehensive practical guide to the procedure:[4] it considers questions of practice only to the extent that these are relevant to the legal critique.

Application of Competitive Dialogue' (2006) 15 *Public Procurement Law Review* 307; A. Brown, 'The Impact of the New Directive on Large Infrastructure Projects: Competitive Dialogue or Better the Devil You Know?' (2004) 13 *Public Procurement Law Review* 160; M. Burnett, 'Conducting Competitive Dialogue for PPP Projects – Towards an Optimal Approach?' (2009) 4 *European Public Private Partnership Law Review* 190; M. Burnett, 'Developing a Complexity Test for the Use of Competitive Dialogue for PPP Contracts' (2010) 4 *European Public Private Partnership Law Review* (2010) 215; P. Delelis, 'The Competitive Dialogue' (2007) 3 *Revue du Tresor* 279; M. Farley, 'Directive 2004/18/EC and the Competitive Dialogue Procedure: A Case Study on the Application of the Competitive Dialogue Procedure to NHS LIFT' (2007) 2 *European Public Private Partnership Law Review* 60; C. Kennedy-Loest, 'What Can Be Done at the Preferred Bidder Stage in Competitive Dialogue?' (2006) 15 *Public Procurement Law Review* 316; A. Rubach-Larsen, 'Competitive Dialogue', Ch. 5 in R. Nielsen and S. Treumer (eds.), *The New EU Public Procurement Directives* (Copenhagen: DJØF Publishing, 2005), p. 67; S Verschuur, 'Competitive Dialogue and the Scope for Discussion after Tenders and Before Selecting the Preferred Bidder – What Is Fine-Tuning Etc.?' (2006) 15 *Public Procurement Law Review* 327.

4 For practical guidance and proposals, see, in particular, Burnett, *Competitive Dialogue*, n. 3 above, and the guidance issued by national governments referred to in other chapters of this volume, in particular Ch. 3 (UK) and Ch. 12 (Netherlands).

The book draws on several empirical studies. First, several studies not published elsewhere have been conducted by, or under the supervision of, the editors, that look in detail at the practical operation of the legal rules in the first few years. These studies, covering the UK, Denmark, Spain and Portugal, have examined the way in which the legal rules 'in the books' have been applied and interpreted in practice by those responsible for operating and/or advising on competitive dialogue – mainly lawyers, procurement practitioners and policy-makers – and also the perceptions which those stakeholders have of the applicable legal rules. This information is also supplemented, both for some of these Member States and some others, with information from other empirical studies, mostly from national governments; such studies are available, in particular, for the Netherlands and UK. In addition, the editors commissioned a detailed statistical analysis of the use of competitive dialogue in several Member States which shows, in particular, the precise types of projects for which the procedure has been used; and the results of this are presented in Chapter 2. A more detailed methodology for some of these studies as well as their key findings is described in the relevant chapters.

In this first chapter we present a detailed analysis and critique of the EU rules and some reflections on their implementation and application at national level. This analysis draws throughout on the more detailed analysis of Member State systems that are provided in the later chapters, as well as on other published information on the procedure.

As already mentioned, Chapter 2 offers a statistical analysis of the use of competitive dialogue in several Member States, looking in detail at the precise type of projects for which the procedure is used, and also the kinds of contracting authorities that use the procedure.

The remaining chapters then present a detailed analysis of the experience of selected Member States, which informs the analysis in the current chapter. These cover the UK (Chapter 3), France (Chapter 4), Germany (Chapter 5), Denmark (Chapter 6), Portugal (Chapter 7), Spain (Chapter 8), Poland (Chapter 9), Lithuania (Chapter 10), Italy (Chapter 11) and the Netherlands (Chapter 12). In each case the relevant chapter examines the way in which the EU rules have been transposed into national legislation; national jurisprudence – although this is currently quite limited; and any soft law in the form of guidance. As noted above, for some Member States this doctrinal information is supplemented also by empirical evidence on the operation of the procedure, in particular regarding the application and interpretation of the legal provisions. These chapters have been written to a common template to allow for comparison across a number of key themes, and the organisation of these chapters is paralleled in the structure of the EU-wide analysis in the current chapter. The Member States chapters differ significantly in length, however, reflecting factors such as the extent of the hard and soft law that exists, the actual extent of use of competitive dialogue and – in particular – the extent of empirical information available.

The choice of Member States for study in these individual country chapters was influenced by several considerations.

First, it was considered essential to include France and the UK, since they are by far the most significant users of competitive dialogue in terms of absolute numbers, as well as two of the five largest EU states by population. It was also considered appropriate to include the other three of the five largest Member States, Germany, Italy and Spain, in order to cover a significant proportion of the EU. At the same time, it was necessary to provide a perspective from some smaller Member States, and this has been done by including, in particular, Lithuania and Denmark. It was also considered useful to include a perspective from states which, whilst they have made the procedure available, have used it little in practice: this is the case with Portugal and Lithuania.

It was decided also to include some Member States which have only relatively recently been subject to EU law, and some that have only recently made the transition from centralised to market economies. Both of these situations throw up special problems that might not be experienced elsewhere, such as limited expertise in EU law and limited experience of operating competitive public procurement procedures on both the demand and supply side. Lithuania and Poland (both of which acceded to the EU in 2004) fall into both these categories.

It was desirable also to study both states that have a long tradition of legal rules of public procurement – the case with most of the countries in the sample (and indeed the EU generally) – and states whose procurement law is limited largely to that required by EU membership, as with the UK and Denmark, to examine whether this tradition is reflected in the approach to competitive dialogue. The sample also includes countries with a Civil Law tradition, including those with a separate system of administrative courts (such as France and Italy), and the Common Law jurisdiction of the UK.

Finally, it was decided at a late stage to add a chapter on the Netherlands. This was because significant information became available in that state on the practical application of the procedure, which could make a valuable contribution to the study.[5]

The analysis of the ten selected Member States appears likely to give a reasonably broad picture of competitive dialogue in the EU that highlights many key issues raised by the regulatory regime without excessive duplication or an unduly lengthy analysis. Nevertheless, given that the book covers in depth only ten of twenty-seven Member States, it clearly does not present a comprehensive picture and needs to be read with this limitation in mind.

The present chapter begins, in section 2, with the relevant background. This covers: the EU procurement rules in general; the approach to complex procurement prior to competitive dialogue; the reasons for introducing the new procedure and the legislative history; and a brief overview of the key rules. Section 3 then explains the extent to which the new procedure has been introduced into the legal systems of Member States and the manner in which this has been done, and also offers reflections on the implications of this for the relationship between EU and national procurement law and the development of a harmonised approach.

Section 4 then looks in detail at the scope of competitive dialogue, and in particular at the conditions for its use. In this section we make a number of concrete proposals regarding the interpretation of the procedure which should serve to ensure that the procedure is available and used as intended to give flexibility to Member States. In addition, this section also considers the use of a competitive dialogue-type of procedure for contracts *outside* the Directive.

Section 5 then looks at the operation of the different phases of the procedure. After a brief introduction this section considers in turn preparation and planning (5.2), confidentiality requirements (5.3), advertising (5.4), the selection phase (5.5), the dialogue phase (5.6), the final tender phase (5.7), the 'preferred bidder' phase (5.8) and the issue of payments to participants (5.9). In these sections we again consider both the legal rules at EU level and their application at national level, and make some proposals for addressing the issues that arise in interpreting the EU rules.

[5] The empirical studies initiated by the authors for the UK, Denmark, Spain and Portugal were undertaken for the purpose of the project, rather than these states being included – as with the Netherlands –*because of* the availability of information.

Section 6 concludes by reviewing the key areas of concern and uncertainty that we identify in our detailed study of the legal rules and our proposals for interpretation. It will be argued that in addressing these areas a balanced approached is needed that takes account of the principles of proportionality and competition as well as considerations of equal treatment and transparency; and that further guidance from the European Commission which reflects this balanced approach would be useful for the future development and use of competitive dialogue.

2. Background: the EU procurement rules, complex procurement prior to competitive dialogue and the introduction of competitive dialogue

2.1. The EU procurement rules

Competitive dialogue is one of the contract award procedures provided for in the main Directive governing public sector procurement in the EU, namely, Directive 2004/18/EC ('Public Sector Directive'). This Directive regulates the award of major contracts by public bodies in the EU with the aim of ensuring a level playing field in competition for public procurement as part of the EU's internal market. The Treaty on the Functioning of the European Union (TFEU) itself prohibits discrimination in public procurement and also certain other restrictions on access to government markets through, in particular, Article 34 TFEU on free movement of goods, Article 49 on freedom of establishment, and Article 56 on freedom to provide services, all of which apply to public procurement as well as to the government's regulatory activity.[6] However, these provisions were considered insufficient alone to open procurement markets; in particular, it was considered necessary also to require transparent award procedures so that public bodies could not conceal discriminatory behaviour under a cloak of discretion. Thus, through Directives dating back to 1970,[7] the EU has regulated public contract procedures to ensure transparency.[8] Under these Directives covered authorities must use specified procedures, which generally involve, *inter alia*, a competition publicised in the *Official Journal of the European Union* (OJEU), and use pre-disclosed selection and award criteria. The Directives also contain other provisions to

[6] See further Arrowsmith, n. 3 above, Ch. 4; Trepte, n. 3 above, pp. 3–27.
[7] For a historical account, see Arrowsmith, n. 3 above, Ch. 3.
[8] For details, see Arrowsmith, n. 3 above; and Trepte, n. 3 above.

improve market access such as minimum time limits for key phases of tendering procedures, and rules on drafting specifications to remove obstacles to participation.

The current Public Sector Directive 2004/18 is the main Directive for public sector bodies. It applies to the state (for example, government departments), regional and local authorities, and also 'bodies governed by public law' – a term defined to include all other bodies that are mainly financed or appointed by other public bodies or are subject to supervision by them[9] (for example, state-financed universities). These bodies are collectively referred to as 'contracting authorities'. It applies only to contracts above certain financial thresholds set – in light of the Directive's objective of opening up markets to trade – to identify contracts that are of interest to tenderers from other Member States. For 2010–11, the main thresholds were €4,845,000 for all works contracts, €125,000 for the supply and services contracts of central/federal bodies, and €193,000 for the supply and services contracts of other authorities.[10]

Subject to a few exclusions all works, supply and services contracts above the thresholds are regulated. However, contracts for some types of services ('Part B' services) are not covered by the full rules but are subject only to very limited obligations, notably those on technical specifications.[11] It was decided to make this distinction when services were first brought into the regime in 1992 because of the novelty and sensitivity of regulating services in some Member States. Services were selected for full regulation on the basis of the potential scope for cross-border trade, potential savings, and the availability of information. Services covered by the full rules are specified in Annex IIA and include, for example, services relating to the maintenance of vehicles and refuse collection, as well as professional services such as accountancy, IT services, and consultancy; all those not listed, which includes, for example, legal services, medical services and many social services, escape this full regulation.

It is important also to mention that the Directive does not fully regulate concessions – that is, arrangements under which the economic operator is remunerated not by the contracting authority but by third parties, and takes the economic risk involved in the activity.[12] In this

[9] Directive 2004/18, Art. 1(9).

[10] Directive 2004/18, Art. 7, as amended by Commission Regulation 1177/2009 [2009] OJ L314/64.

[11] See Directive 2004/18, Arts. 20–21.

[12] Directive 2004/18, Art. 1(3); and Case C-382/05, *Commission* v. *Italy* [2007] ECR I-6657.

respect, works concessions are subject merely to an obligation to advertise the arrangement and to give a minimum time for response,[13] whilst services concessions are wholly excluded from the Directive.[14]

Whilst many important contracts are thus outside the Directive, it is important to note that advertising obligations, as well as certain other transparency requirements, may apply under the TFEU itself. This is because the CJEU has interpreted the Treaty's free movement provisions not merely as prohibiting discrimination and certain other 'negative' restrictions on access to public markets, but also as implying a positive principle of transparency to support non-discrimination.[15] However, it can be noted that the CJEU now appears to be adopting a relatively cautious approach towards imposing procedural requirements for these contracts excluded from the Directive.[16] This Treaty obligation is relevant for present purposes in that a number of the contracts excluded wholly or in part from the Directive's rules, in particular as concessions or Part B contracts, are particularly complex contracts of a kind for which competitive dialogue might be suitable. Whilst the procedure is not formally relevant for these contracts, nothing precludes states from adopting a procedure of a similar kind to award them, including to satisfy transparency obligations of the Treaty, and, as we will see below, this has in fact happened in some cases.[17]

For those contracts that *are* covered by its full regime, the Public Sector Directive requires contracts to be awarded by one of a number of specified procedures.

The position prior to the introduction of competitive dialogue was that contracting authorities were generally required to use one of two procedures, which Member States may allow for any type of procurement without conditions. One is the open procedure, a formal

[13] Directive 2004/18, Arts. 56–61. [14] Directive 2004/18, Art. 17.

[15] Case C-324/98, *Telaustria* v. *Telekom Austria and Herold Business Data* [2000] ECR I-10745. For a recent review, see A. Brown, 'EU Primary Law Requirements in Practice: Advertising, Procedures and Remedies for Public Contracts outside the Procurement Directives' (2010) 19 *Public Procurement Law Review* 169; and, for the European Commission's views, see Commission, *Commission Communication on the Community law applicable to contract awards not or not fully subject to the provision of the Public Procurement Directives* (hereinafter 'Communication on non-covered contracts') [2006] OJ C179/2.

[16] Case C-95/10, *Strong Segurança SA* v. *Município de Sintra*, judgment of 17 March 2011; Case C-226/09, *Commission* v. *Ireland*, judgment of 18 November 2010.

[17] Section 4.6.2 below.

tendering procedure that must be advertised in the OJEU, and in which any interested economic operator may submit a tender.[18] The contracting authority must select the winner using as the basis of the award either the lowest price or the most economically advantageous tender[19] (although it may, of course, exclude the tenders of those who do not have the financial or technical capability to perform the contract, or do not meet other conditions of participation). The second is the restricted procedure:[20] again, under this procedure, the contract must be advertised in the OJEU and potentially open to any interested economic operator, but, in contrast with the open procedure, the contracting authority need not allow submission of tenders by all interested parties: it can invite to tender only those that meet the requirements for participation *and*, further, choose to invite only a limited number of those who meet the requirements, provided that the selection is made using objective criteria contemplated in the Directive.[21]

In addition, the Directive provides for another procedure, the negotiated procedure. In contrast with the open and restricted procedures, this is available only in specified circumstances,[22] and is defined in Article 11 (d) of the Public Sector Directive: '"Negotiated procedures" means those procedures whereby the contracting authorities consult the economic operators of their choice and negotiate the terms of contract with one or more of these.' Whilst the Directive formally refers to just one procedure in this regard, however, there are actually two distinct and very different variations of the negotiated procedure.

One, the 'negotiated procedure with prior publication of a contract notice' (hereinafter 'negotiated procedure with a notice'), requires the contracting authority to advertise the contract in the OJEU, hold a competition and consider all interested parties (although with the restricted procedure it may invite only a limited number of them); and it must also follow many of the other rules that govern open or restricted procedures, such as those on how to select firms to invite and on award criteria. However, the form of the competition is flexible and the contracting authority may simply hold discussions to determine the best offer.

[18] Defined in Directive 2004/18, Art. 1(11)(a). [19] Directive 2004/18, Art. 53.

[20] Defined in Directive 2004/18, Art. 1(11)(a).

[21] As to which, see further section 5.5 below.

[22] Currently set out in Directive 2004/18, Arts. 30–31.

The second type of negotiated procedure is the 'negotiated procedure without publication of a contract notice' (abbreviated here to 'negotiated procedure without a notice'). Under this procedure, the authority may simply negotiate a contract with one or more economic operators, without any advertisement and, usually, without a competition.

The procedures above must all be conducted in accordance with detailed rules laid down in the Directive. In addition, the Directive expressly sets out in Article 2 three principles, namely, transparency, equal treatment and non-discrimination (probably a specific aspect of equal treatment referring to non-discrimination on grounds of nationality) that contracting authorities must apply. These serve both as an aid to interpreting other express provisions and to impose additional obligations which are *not* expressly stated in the Directive.[23] An example of the latter – referred to in section 5.6 below – is a requirement under the transparency principle for authorities to disclose sub-criteria that they set for assessing tenders, even though not required by the explicit rules on disclosure.

Competitive dialogue was added to the list of permitted award procedures as part of a new comprehensive 'legislative package' adopted in 2004. As discussed in section 2.3 below, this replaced the pre-existing EU procurement Directives with new Directives, including Public Sector Directive 2004/18, which consolidated into a single Directive what were previously three separate Directives on public sector procurement.[24] As well as consolidating the existing rules, Directive 2004/18 included significant changes to give more flexibility to contracting authorities, of which the introduction of competitive dialogue was one.

It is important to highlight that this Directive – as well as the other Directives on award procedures outlined below – does not provide a comprehensive system for regulating public procurement in the Member States. Rather, the Directives merely provide a minimum framework with which Member States must comply, and Member States remain free within the scope of that a framework to adopt rules and practices to implement their own national policies. This framework nature of the

[23] See Arrowsmith, n. 3 above, pp. 424–32.

[24] Directive 93/36/EEC [1993] OJ L199/1 (on public supply contracts); Directive 93/37/EEC [1993] OJ L199/54 (on public works contracts); Directive 92/50/EEC [1992] OJ L209/1 (on public services contracts).

Directive was emphasised in the early case law of the CJEU.[25] Thus Member States may choose whether or not to make available the different award procedures provided under the Directives;[26] whether to allow their procuring entities the full flexibility that the Directive allows – for example, as regards the reasons for excluding firms from a procurement – or to impose stricter requirements;[27] and whether to supplement the Directives with additional requirements that do not contravene the rules or principles in the Directives themselves. This general principle of the framework nature of the Directive is expressed, for example, in Article 28 of the Public Sector Directive, which states that 'In awarding their public contracts, contracting authorities shall apply the national procedures adjusted for the purposes of the Directive' – contemplating the existence of a body of national procurement law that co-exists with the Directive's rules. We will consider in section 3 below the extent to which Member States have supplemented the Directive's framework in the specific context of competitive dialogue. As a general rule, we consider that the flexibility mentioned is important, both because of the different factual circumstances of different states – such as different levels of corruption, nature of markets, or skills of procurement officers – and because of different values and policies (such as differing emphasis on issues of public accountability) that need to be reflected in national procurement rules.[28] It can be noted that Burnett has proposed that in practice a standardised approach be adopted to competitive dialogue for PPP projects within this flexible legal framework;[29] but, whilst clearly there is scope for a degree of standardisation to reflect good practice in some areas, we consider that the above differences between Member States (as well as the differences between different projects) limit the potential for

[25] Joined Cases 27–29/86, *S. A. Construction et Entreprises Industrielles and others* v. *Société Cooperative 'Association Intercommunales pour les Autoroutes des Ardennes' and others* ('*CEI and Bellini*') [1987] ECR 3347; Case 31/87, *Gebroeders Beentjes BV* v. *Netherlands* ('*Beentjes*') [1988] ECR 4635, para. 20. See also, for example, Joined Cases C-226/04 and C-228/04, *La Cascina and others* v. *Ministero della Difesa and others* [2006] ECR I-1347, confirming Member States' discretion in applying certain exclusions permitted by the Directives.

[26] See section 3 below. [27] *La Cascina*, n. 25 above.

[28] See, for example, S. Arrowsmith, 'The EC Procurement Directives, National Procurement Policies and Better Governance: The Case for a New Approach' (2002) 27 *European Law Review* 3.

[29] Burnett, *Competitive Dialogue*, n. 3 above; Burnett, 'Conducting Competitive Dialogue for PPP Projects', n. 3 above.

standardisation, and certainly that there should be no move as yet towards removing legal flexibility in this respect.

In addition to the Public Sector Directive, procurement in the EU is also regulated by Utilities Directive 2004/17.[30] This covers contracts connected with various activities in the energy, water, transport and postal services sectors, both when carried out by public sector bodies and – in certain cases – where carried out by private sector bodies that present a risk of discrimination (for example, because of governmental influence over the award of their licences).[31] The award procedures in this Directive are more flexible, with procuring entities having a free choice for all procurements between the open procedure, restricted procedure and negotiated procedure with a prior call for competition.[32] Competitive dialogue has not been included in this Directive as it is unnecessary: the utilities rules already provide for the flexibility that competitive dialogue entails given that the utilities have free use of the negotiated procedure for all contracts, since utilities can choose to operate their award procedures in accordance with the approach of competitive dialogue within the parameters of the negotiated procedure.[33] Further, given the non-comprehensive nature of the rules in the Directives as outlined above, it also appears that Member States could adopt national regulatory procedures akin to those for competitive dialogue to be used by their utilities.

The EU has also recently adopted Directive 2009/81,[34] the Defence and Security Directive, governing procurement related to the fields of defence and security. Its principles and rules follow the same general model of those in the other Directives, with the most important difference being that the two freely available award procedures are the restricted procedure and negotiated procedure with a notice.[35] Even

[30] Directive 2004/17/EC of the European Parliament and of the Council of 31 March 2004 co-ordinating the procurement procedures of entities operating in the water, energy, transport and postal services sectors [2004] OJ L134/1.

[31] For full details, see Arrowsmith, n. 3 above, Ch. 15.

[32] On the differences, see Arrowsmith, n. 3 above, Ch. 16.

[33] A view stated also in footnote 2 of Commission, *Explanatory Note – Competitive Dialogue – Classic Directive*, available at http://ec.europa.eu/internal_market/publicprocurement/docs/explan-notes/classic-dir-dialogue_en.pdf.

[34] Directive 2009/81/EC of the European Parliament and of the Council of 13 July 2009 on the co-ordination of procedures for the award of certain works contracts, supply contracts and service contracts by contracting authorities or entities in the fields of defence and security [2009] OJ L216/76.

[35] Defence and Security Directive, Art. 25.

though, as stated, the negotiated procedure is capable of accommodating a competitive dialogue-type approach, competitive dialogue *has* nevertheless been made available under this Directive,[36] in contrast with the position under the Utilities Directive. However, it is not freely available but may be used only for particularly complex contracts, as under the Public Sector Directive.[37] According to recital 48 of the Defence and Security Directive, use of either the negotiated procedure or the restricted procedure is not feasible in certain cases where competitive dialogue applies because it is not possible to define the contract with enough precision to allow candidates to draw up their offers. This, in fact, seems questionable in the case of the negotiated procedure since the negotiations allowed by that procedure can be used to that end, if necessary – including by following the same kind of approach as with competitive dialogue within the rules of a negotiated procedure. This view also seems inconsistent with the omission of competitive dialogue from the Utilities Directive:[38] the reasoning in recital 48 of the Defence and Security Directive would, if correct, imply that certain complex contracts cannot be awarded at all under the Utilities Directive because of the absence of a feasible award procedure! However, although based on false reasoning, it remains the case that competitive dialogue is a formal procedure available for procurements falling under the Defence and Security Directive. This Directive was not required to be transposed in Member States until 21 August 2011, just before this book was completed, and is not considered further here.

As regards enforcement of EU law, aggrieved economic operators have a right to bring proceedings before an independent national review body. For contracts covered by the procedural Directives described above, detailed rules on remedies and related matters[39] are set out in Remedies Directive 89/665/EEC (for contracts governed by the Public Sector Directive and the Defence and Security Directive) and Utilities Remedies Directive 92/13/EEC.[40] These remedies were recently

[36] Defence and Security Directive, Art. 25.

[37] Defence and Security Directive, Art. 27 and also Art. 1(21) defining particularly complex contract.

[38] As well as with the approach sometimes adopted in practice to awarding contracts under the negotiated procedure: see section 2.2 below.

[39] See generally S. Treumer and F. Lichère (eds.), *Enforcement of the EU Public Procurement Rules* (Copenhagen: DJØF Publishing, 2011).

[40] Council Directive 92/13/EEC [1992] OJ L76/7.

strengthened by extensive amendments introduced by Directive 2007/66.[41] For contracts outside the Directives, remedies are available in accordance with general rules on remedies in EU law, although these remedies are not as strong as those for contracts covered by the Directives.[42] The European Commission as 'guardian' of the EU Treaties also plays a significant role in enforcing the rules, including through actions in the CJEU against Member States.[43]

We can finally note that the EU procurement regime is currently undergoing a general review with a view to modernisation, with some proposals for reform expected towards the end of 2011.[44] Whilst the review extends in general terms to the suitability of the 'procedural toolbox' available for contracting authorities, there is no specific indication in the Green Paper that formed the basis of the consultation on reforms that the competitive dialogue procedure is a specific target for amendment.[45] However, the introduction of more flexibility to negotiate within award procedures, which is one possibility mooted in the Green Paper, could have significant implications for the role of competitive dialogue in the system. Any reforms are, however, some years away.

2.2. *Complex procurement prior to competitive dialogue and the justification for introducing competitive dialogue*

The pressure for introducing a procedure like competitive dialogue arose from the fact that pre-2004 procedures for awarding complex contracts were not perceived universally as adequate for this purpose. This was combined with the fact that contracts of a complex nature were becoming increasingly important in practice in some Member States, apparently due to several factors. One was developments in IT and the consequent use of IT in delivering and supporting government services. A second was the increasing outsourcing of services previously provided

[41] Directive 2007/66/EC of the European Parliament and the Council of 11 December 2007 amending Council Directives 89/665/EEC and 92/13/EEC with regard to improving the effectiveness of review procedures concerning the award of public contracts [2007] OJ L335/31.

[42] See, in particular, Case C-91/08, *Wall AG* v. *Stadt Frankfurt am Main* [2010] ECR I-2815.

[43] On this, see A. Delsaux, 'The Role of the Commission in Enforcing EC Public Procurement Rules' (2004) 13 *Public Procurement Law Review* 130.

[44] *Green Paper on the Modernisation of EU Public Procurement Policy: Towards a More Efficient European Procurement Market*, COM (2011) 15 final.

[45] *Ibid.*, section 2.2.

by government, often involving the conclusion of relatively long-term arrangements with the private sector. A third and very important point was the development of new approaches to procurement, notably the use of private financing for building and operating public infrastructure in novel areas – including for projects not classified as 'concessions' under the Directives and which thus could not use the flexible approach allowed by EU law for concessions.[46] The increased use of non-contractual forms of partnership with the private sector[47] also contributed to the complexity of some of these arrangements. These trends could be seen, for example, in the UK, which was one of the Member States to argue strongly for a new procedure.[48] All these trends increased the use of contracts with outside providers that were either inherently complex or were complex because of their novelty at the relevant time.

One possibility for awarding complex contracts in these and other areas was to use open or restricted procedures, which, as we have seen above, could be used for any procurement, including complex procurement, without conditions.

These procedures were, and still are in fact, used in practice in some Member States for many complex procurements covered by the Directives. Thus, in Poland and Portugal, both open and restricted procedures have been widely used; in Lithuania, following a general government preference for open procedures, the open procedure has been favoured;[49] and Denmark has often used the restricted procedure.[50] As described in Chapter 4, France, which as we will see is now a major user of competitive dialogue, used a procedure that was intended as a version of the restricted procedure in the sense of EU law, but provided for a specific variation of the restricted procedure within domestic law. This procedure, the *l'appel d'offres sur performances* ('call for tenders on performance') was, as Chapter 4 explains, available on similar grounds to the current EU competitive dialogue procedure and has clearly inspired the drafting of the grounds for using that procedure.[51] Italy, likewise, also developed special procedures in national law – the *appalto concorso* and,

[46] See section 2.1 above.

[47] See Commission, *Interpretative Communication on the Application of Community Law on Public Procurement and Concessions to Institutionalised Public–Private Partnerships (IPPP)* C (2007) 6661.

[48] See Ch. 3.

[49] Although there has also been significant use of the negotiated procedure without a notice: see Ch. 10.

[50] See Ch. 6, section 2.

[51] See Ch. 4, section 2.

later (and still applicable), the *appalto integrato* – that are a version of EU procedures (in this case open or restricted procedures), and were used for projects that were complex because of the involvement of both planning/design and execution.[52] The former procedure was repealed as it allowed the award of the execution element without full specification and, hence, competition of this element, contrary to EU law; the newer procedure corrects this defect. In the UK, also, the other major user of competitive dialogue along with France, the restricted procedure was sometimes used to award the kind of contracts now awarded through competitive dialogue, including for major IT projects; however, it seems that the restricted procedure was not considered entirely satisfactory for the purpose and, in addition, was operated in a flexible manner that in some respects might not have been compliant with EU law[53] – and the competitive dialogue procedure has now largely replaced that approach for many of the relevant contracts. It is not surprising that two of the main states that struggled to find a satisfactory way to award complex contracts within the old 'standard' procedures of the Directives, France and the UK, should have now turned to competitive dialogue as a solution and become the main users of that procedure.

One approach used extensively in some Member States has been to separate the study, design and planning elements of projects into several contracts, thus reducing the complexity of the project as a whole and facilitating use of the Directive's other procedures for various parts of the project. Thus Member States might first award a services contract for a study to establish relevant specifications, followed by separate contracts for (possibly) completing the design and for execution of the project. One possible approach to the initial planning and design stage when the work is split in this way is to hold a design contest whereby several firms submit designs or plans, with payments being made for the best design or designs. Such competitions are regulated by explicit rules, currently in Articles 66–74 of Directive 2004/18. This approach is facilitated by the fact that the Directive allows use of a negotiated procedure without a notice for the award of a further contract to finalise a design based on a winning entry in a design contest (although not a contract for the execution stage) where awarded to the winner(s) of the design contest.[54] Italy and Portugal have both used this approach,[55] for example, and also

[52] On these procedures, see Ch. 11, section 2. [53] See Ch. 3, section 2.
[54] Directive 2004/18, Art. 31(3).
[55] See respectively Ch. 11, section 2 and Ch. 7, section 2.

made extensive use of design contests, whilst Denmark, for example, has used design contests to a limited extent for public works and IT projects.

There are various advantages and disadvantages of this approach compared with using a single award procedure for both the development and execution of a project in the manner of competitive dialogue. Thus using two award procedures might be more time consuming; there may be difficulty in securing sufficient participation in both design and execution stages given the potential for conflicts of interest that arise from participation in both stages; it may be difficult to choose a winning design in isolation from full costing of that design in the same award process in which the design is chosen; and it may simply not be possible to separate design and execution because of special or exclusive rights held by the relevant persons. When a design contest is used, it can also be perceived as a problem that in a design contest held under the Directives the jury must be autonomous in its decisions, so that the contracting authority loses some control over the award decision. On the other hand, it has been suggested that separating the different elements can better ensure protection of rights to confidentiality of information than a single award procedure[56] (an issue that explicit provisions on confidentiality in competitive dialogue are designed to address);[57] and it can be argued that separating different elements allows easier use of procedures (in particular, open and restricted procedures) that are more transparent.

It should be emphasised that open and restricted procedures, in some cases preceded by service contracts for the design of the project and/or design contest, continue in fact to be used by most of the Member States considered in this book as the primary procedure for awarding contracts for complex projects. In the case of Portugal and Lithuania, for example, as mentioned above, the old practice has changed very little or not at all (see section 4 below) despite the availability of competitive dialogue for several years in national legislation, and in Italy the procedure was until very recently formally suspended, and hence not used at all, it being considered that existing award procedures were adequate. To a limited extent, this might be explained by the fact that some states – such as

[56] Communication of the European Commission to the Council, to the European Parliament, to the Economic and Social Committee and to the Committee of the Regions on Public Private Partnerships in Trans-European Network Projects, COM (97) 453, section 2.1.

[57] See section 5.3 below.

Lithuania – have only recently seen some of the major developments that have led to the demand for competitive dialogue elsewhere in Europe, notably use of private finance for infrastructure procurement. However, this is only a small part of the picture and it is clear that the 'traditional' award procedures have not in practice been displaced for the kind of procurement now potentially covered by competitive dialogue.

On the other hand, a few other Member States have considered the traditional 'standard' open and restricted procedures as inadequate for certain complex procurement for various reasons – and this has led in some cases to use of competitive dialogue as an alternative.

That these traditional procedures were not wholly adequate for many complex procurement was the view taken in the UK. As Chapter 3 will explain, empirical evidence shows that in undertaking privately financed infrastructure procurement during the 1990s, including in many novel areas, entities developed a standard practice of using the negotiated procedure with a notice. As explained there,[58] this was done, however, not simply through negotiations, but by a formal competitive process – generally involving interim offers, discussions and then final offers – that retained some of the advantages of a restricted procedure in terms of competition and transparency, but was more flexible in certain respects, rejecting some of the features of the restricted procedure (and, *a fortiori*, of the open procedure) perceived as ill-suited to complex procurement. Thus, in particular, under this approach[59] the number of bidders could potentially be limited below five, the minimum for the restricted procedure[60] (important in light of the procedural costs); there was the possibility for discussions throughout the procedure to enable bidders to propose and adjust different solutions; there was a possibility of reducing the number of participants further on the basis of outline submissions, further reducing participation costs; and it was considered unnecessary for all participants to submit full, final tenders – again, reducing the costs involved. It is notable that almost all these flexibilities have now been incorporated into competitive dialogue, the major exception being the possibility of completing tenders after bidding and extensive post-bid negotiations or amendments, as discussed at 5.7 and 5.8 below. As Chapter 3 explains, since the advent of competitive dialogue, that new procedure seems

[58] See Ch. 3, section 2. [59] See further Ch. 3, section 2.
[60] Rather than three for the negotiated procedure with a notice: see now Directive 2004/18, Art. 44(3).

to have displaced the negotiated procedure in the UK for complex infrastructure projects previously let through the negotiated procedure.[61] Further, although (as we have seen) the restricted procedure was ostensibly used for some other projects, such as complex IT contracts, this was problematic, and arguably procedures were not always legally compliant; and competitive dialogue has now to some extent displaced the restricted procedure, also, in the UK.

Similarly to the UK, so in Germany also, according to Burgi in Chapter 5, was the negotiated procedure with a notice used to a significant extent in awarding complex contracts prior to 2004.[62]

Despite these practices in the UK and Germany, use of the negotiated procedure was not, however, considered by all stakeholders as a satisfactory solution for awarding complex contracts under the Directives.

First, there has been much debate over the legal availability of the procedure for some of the situations in which it has been used. As Chapter 3 explains, UK entities generally relied on the grounds that overall pricing was not possible (applicable to works and services contracts) and that it was not possible to set a specification (applicable to services contracts).[63] The same grounds are also relied on in Germany for using negotiated procedures for some complex contracts.[64] However, the meaning of these provisions is rather unclear,[65] and the European Commission has taken a narrow view of their scope, expressing doubts over the availability of the negotiated procedure for general use for privately financed infrastructure contracts and initiating discussions

[61] See Ch. 3, section 4.2.

[62] Ch. 5, section 4.6. It is also interesting that in Poland a version of the negotiated procedure with a notice that applies in Polish law to lower-value contracts – but on wider grounds than the procedure is available in Directive 2004/18 and its predecessors – has been widely used for complex contracts below the Directives' thresholds. However, it has not been used in Poland for above-threshold contracts. In Lithuania, the negotiated procedure has been widely used for awarding complex contracts, including the negotiated procedure *without* a notice, purportedly justified by the absence of satisfactory bids when attempting to award contracts by open or restricted procedures; however, rather than the negotiated procedure used because it is suitable, the above practice has been seen as highly unsatisfactory by government policy-makers, who have taken steps to prevent it: see Ch. 10, section 2.

[63] Grounds found respectively in Council Directive 93/37/EEC [1993] OJ L199/547(2)(c) (Works Directive) and Art. 11(2)(b) of Council Directive 92/50/EEC [1992] OJ L209/1 (Services Directive); and Art. 11(2)(c) of Directive 92/50. See the discussion in Ch. 3, section 2.

[64] Ch. 5, sections 2 and 4.

[65] For a detailed discussion, see Arrowsmith, n. 3 above, pp. 562–9.

with the UK on this subject.[66] Whilst case law in the UK itself followed the flexible approach of UK practice, which was also supported by government guidance and some academic literature,[67] clearly there was legal uncertainty on this point. This appears to be one reason for the shift from negotiated procedures to competitive dialogue in the UK.[68] There are perhaps even more doubts over a broad interpretation of the negotiated procedure since 2004, given the existence of competitive dialogue.[69] However, despite this legal uncertainty, which has been debated also in the German literature,[70] Germany has continued to use the negotiated procedure extensively for complex projects and uses the competitive dialogue procedure much less, even in absolute terms (although its economy is the largest of the Member States) in comparison with France and the UK[71] – in contrast with the UK the new competitive dialogue procedure has not substantially displaced the previous approach.[72]

Secondly, it seems that the Commission did not consider use of the negotiated procedure necessary from a commercial perspective for many of the cases to which it was applied, on the basis that something more transparent could be devised. Thus in formulating the proposals for the new legislative package the Commission did not accept merely extending the scope of the negotiated procedure as it existed under the previous Directives,[73] but instead developed a new and more transparent procedure.

Competitive dialogue was thus introduced to meet the legitimate need of some Member States for a procedure that had sufficient flexibility to maximise value for money for complex projects, whilst at the same time ensuring an appropriate balance between flexibility and transparency. From this perspective, competitive dialogue provides a kind of half-way house between the restricted procedure – involving less flexibility but

[66] See Ch. 3, section 2. A narrow interpretation of the conditions for using negotiated procedure in this respect is stated in the Commission's Explanatory Note, n. 33 above, section 1.

[67] See Arrowsmith, n. 3 above, pp. 562–9.

[68] Along with the fact that the competitive dialogue has been considered a more suitable procedure.

[69] See section 4 below. [70] See Ch. 5, section 4. [71] See Ch. 2.

[72] See Ch. 5, section 4.

[73] As explained later below, an initial proposal of 2000 for giving more flexibility for complex contracts was in fact formulated in theory as extension of the negotiated procedure but in practice was a more detailed and transparent procedure.

more transparency than competitive dialogue – and the negotiated procedure with a contract notice – involving more flexibility but less transparency. An expected and related consequence of this reform was that Member States would no longer use restricted and negotiated procedures in a manner that the Commission considered did not comply with the Directives, either by conducting the restricted procedure in a way that might be considered to violate the Directives or invoking the negotiated procedure in cases in which it might be considered not to apply. Thus the introduction of competitive dialogue can also be seen as a tool to remedy circumvention of the EU public procurement rules or at least a tool to stop a trend in practice whereby the boundaries of these procedures were stretched.[74] Seen from this perspective, it is interesting that the UK and France, two of the countries engaged in such conduct, subsequently have become the most frequent users of competitive dialogue as outlined in Chapter 2.

Some comments are appropriate here on the suitability of the open and restricted procedures, especially given the divergent approaches of different Member States under both the previous and current Directives. These are relevant to the legal analysis of the legal scope of competitive dialogue in section 4 below.

The first is that the 'suitability' of the open or restricted procedure, as opposed to a more flexible approach, for awarding complex contracts cannot properly be considered an objective concept but is heavily dependent on the overall context. In this respect, the context is different for different Member States. As Arrowsmith has emphasised previously, the appropriate balance between transparency and flexibility from the point of view of achieving *national* procurement objectives, including value for money, varies greatly between states according to both the factual context – such as extent of corruption and the extent of training and skills of public procurement officers – and the nature of national procurement objectives and the balance between different objectives selected by each Member State.[75] Thus, whilst a minimum degree of transparency is specified by the Public Sector Directive for all Member States, provided that that threshold level is reached Member States may choose how to further balance transparency and discretion within the area of national discretion. We have already suggested above that

[74] The testing of the boundaries of these procedures in previous practice is stressed by Burnett, *Competitive Dialogue*, n. 3 above, pp. 20–1.

[75] Arrowsmith, n. 28 above.

national differences explain and justify the 'framework' nature of the Directives more generally; and such differences not only justify different national approaches to *conducting* competitive dialogue (and hence to retaining the current flexibility in the legal regime) as mentioned above, but also to the *use* of competitive dialogue. The question of whether an open procedure, restricted procedure or competitive dialogue is more appropriate for a particular procurement in a particular Member State is, in fact, one issue that will depend on the particular national situation. To give an example, a state with a high level of corruption may find that using competitive dialogue for a complex procurement will not provide the best approach because of the risk of corruption, which might outweigh or indeed negate any potential benefit from discussions with economic operators in an iterative tendering phase; whilst a state that considers that there is a low risk of corruption may benefit greatly from negotiations in terms of improved solutions and contract terms. Such national differences can perhaps explain the differing perceptions in Member States of the need for a more flexible procedure for complex procurement, and the very different reception given to competitive dialogue in different Member States of the EU. It is interesting, for example, that – as Chapter 11 on Italy explains – Italy at first suspended the competitive dialogue procedure after providing for it in national legislation apparently because of a concern that the degree of discretion involved might not be appropriate for Italy and that existing award procedures were adequate in the Italian context.

A second point is that the suitability of open and restricted procedures for certain complex procurements will depend on how these procedures are interpreted. There is in fact considerable uncertainty on the flexibility of these procedures in some key areas that are relevant for complex procurement including in the areas that, prior to 2004, were the basis of some of the 'flexible' practice as mentioned above. There is surprisingly little case law of the CJEU to help resolve this uncertainty. Relevant areas in this respect include the scope for correcting errors or ambiguities in tenders;[76] the scope for discussions with providers at the pre-tender stage;[77] the possibility of ever including a second stage of formal

[76] See section 5.7 below.

[77] See S. Treumer, 'Technical Dialogue and the Principle of Equal Treatment – Dealing with Conflicts of Interest after Fabricom' (2007) 16 *Public Procurement Law Review* 99; S. Treumer, 'Technical Dialogue Prior to Submission of Tenders and the Principle of Equal Treatment of Tenderers' (1999) 8 *Public Procurement Law Review* 147.

tendering in these procedures;[78] the possibility for completing contractual detail after tenders;[79] and requirements for certainty in the content of contractual obligations awarded by these procedures.[80] It may be that the Court's interpretation of the flexibility availability in these procedures – as well as, possibly, the scope of the negotiated procedure as discussed in section 4 below – will be affected by the existence of competitive dialogue as an alternative: the Court might take a stricter view of open and restricted procedures now they are no longer needed for more complex procurement – but that may in turn have the effect of widening the scope of competitive dialogue itself.

We have so far considered complex procurement that is covered by the full rules of the Directives, but we should also note that much complex procurement takes place outside this context – notably through the procurement of concessions and Part B services, which we saw in section 1 above are wholly or mainly excluded from the Directives' rules, though subject to limited obligations under the TFEU. Given the limited degree of EU regulation of these contracts, it might be expected that Member States would take divergent approaches, perhaps sometimes using procedures wholly unique to the Member State but sometimes using procedures that take some inspiration from those in the Directives. Examples of various different approaches are given in the later chapters of the book. For example, in Portugal projects outside the Directives are often awarded using an open procedure with a negotiated phase, which involves submission of tenders, followed by negotiations on those tenders and then a best and final offer;[81] whilst, in the UK, prior to competitive dialogue, privately financed infrastructure projects outside the Directives, such as services concessions, were awarded in the same way as similar projects covered by the Directives, as described above.[82]

2.3. *The introduction and development of competitive dialogue*

Competitive dialogue, as we noted above, was introduced into the EU procurement regime in 2004 in Directive 2004/18. This Directive was the culmination of extensive review of the EU's procurement Directives that commenced with a 1996 Green Paper from the European Commission,

[78] See Arrowsmith, n. 3 above, pp. 544–5. [79] See section 5.8 below.
[80] See section 5.8 below. [81] See Ch. 7, section 2. [82] See Ch. 3, section 2.2.

Public Procurement in the European Union: Exploring the Way Forward,[83] launching a general debate on EU procurement policy. The Green Paper itself did not envisage significant legal changes, but, on the contrary, contemplated 'a period of stability',[84] and focused mainly on the need to apply the rules and to enable firms to take advantage of them. However, the subsequent consultations suggested a strong desire for enhanced legal flexibility, both in the procedures for awarding complex contracts and in other areas. Thus the follow-up Communication of 1998[85] concluded that changes were needed, including to provide a new award procedure permitting greater dialogue with providers.[86] After a legislative process of nearly four years, the EU finally adopted the new 'legislative package' – much amended from the original Commission proposals – in the form of Public Sector Directive 2004/18/EC and Utilities Directive 2004/17/EC which, as we have seen, essentially replaced the previous Directives, and added the competitive dialogue procedure to the award procedures available for public bodies.

In its 1998 Communication which first formally mooted a new procedure for complex contracts, the Commission had already labelled the procedure 'competitive dialogue' – although without providing details of the intended procedural rules.[87] The Communication's stated justification for the new procedure was simply the need for dialogue *during* the procedure because of the purchaser's inability to know in all cases the best solution for its needs, which the Commission considered was not adequately provided for under open and restricted procedures:

> Many contributions confirmed the Commission's finding that, especially in the case of particularly complex contracts in areas that are constantly changing, such as high technology, purchasers are well aware of their needs but do not know in advance what is the best technical solution for satisfying those needs. Discussion of the contract and dialogue between

[83] Commission, Green Paper, *Public Procurement in the European Union: Exploring the Way Forward*, COM (96) 583 final.

[84] E.g. *ibid.*, para. 6: 'A period of stability in this framework is desirable and it is not therefore intended to make any fundamental change.'

[85] Commission, Communication, *Public Procurement in the European Union*, COM (98) 143.

[86] *Ibid.*, section 2.1.2.2.

[87] *Ibid.*, section 2.1.2.2. This document envisaged that the new procedure would actually *replace* the negotiated procedure with a notice, operating as a standard procedure, in the sense that it would not be treated as exceptional and interpreted strictly, although available only on limited grounds (broader than those for the negotiated procedure with a notice): see again, *ibid.*, section 2.1.2.2.

> purchasers and suppliers are therefore necessary in such cases. But the standard procedures laid down by the 'traditional' Directives leave very little scope for discussion during the award of contracts and are therefore regarded as lacking in flexibility in situations of this type.[88]

Likewise, the Explanatory Memorandum to the 2000 proposal for the new Directive emphasised the need for dialogue during the award procedure itself as the justification for change: this document put forward an even stricter view on the possibilities for dialogue, namely, that this is 'not allowed' during an open or restricted procedures, but only prior to the launch of the procedure.[89] This document also suggested that the use of a design contest might not be adequate to find the best solution because of the problem that the threat to competition from prior involvement might prevent the design contest winner from bidding for the execution work.[90] The Explanatory Memorandum also reiterated clearly the view of the Commission that the negotiated procedure was narrow in scope and thus did not cover the situations for which greater flexibility was demanded.

Regarding the applicable procedural rules, the original proposal of 2000 envisaged a procedure that differed in important ways from competitive dialogue as adopted.[91] Detailed analysis of the proposal is not needed here, but two key points are worth highlighting about this proposal.

First, it was much more limited in its flexibility than the adopted version in that it envisaged a dialogue solely for the purpose of, and leading to, the drafting of specifications to form a common basis for all tenders.[92] In contrast, as we will see,[93] the procedure as adopted now allows also for an approach whereby bidders tender based on their own, possibly quite different, solutions. On the other hand, the procedure in the proposal did display some of the important features found in the

[88] *Ibid.*, section 2.1.2.2.

[89] Commission, *Proposal for a Directive of the European Parliament and of the Council on Co-ordination of Procedures for the Award of Public Works Contracts, Public Supply Contracts and Public Service Contracts*, COM (2000) 275 final/2, Explanatory Memorandum, at 3.2 and 3.4.

[90] *Ibid.*, section 3.4.

[91] *Ibid.*, Arts. 29 and 30. See also S. Arrowsmith, 'The European Commission's Proposal for New Directives on Public and Utilities Procurement' (2000) 9 *Public Procurement Law Review* NA 126.

[92] See *ibid.*, Art. 30(6) and (7), and the explanation of the Commission at 3.5 in the Explanatory Memorandum.

[93] Section 5.6 below.

adopted version of competitive dialogue that distinguish it from the restricted procedure and go beyond simply providing expressly for dialogue, namely, in allowing for a more limited number of participants than in restricted procedures,[94] obtaining outline tenders,[95] and reducing the number of participants during the award phase.[96] However, requiring development of a common solution for all tenders at the end of the procedure would have made it quite a different procedure from the one known today and one that would certainly not have fitted the practice of some of many users, as we will see in section 5.6 below.

Secondly, in the original proposal the procedure was presented not as a distinct award procedure but as a version of the negotiated procedure with a notice – it was provided that the negotiated procedure with a notice would be available based on new grounds of the inability of purchasers to define the solution to their needs, but also that when the negotiated procedure was used on these grounds special procedural rules would apply.[97] The explanation offered was 'to avoid having a multiplicity of procedures'.[98] However, clearly this was a fiction since it was in substance an additional procedure, albeit disguised as a negotiated procedure – and this approach was later dropped, as explained below.

Following further analysis of the subject, the original proposal was wholly redrafted. A revised draft published by the Commission of 31 May 2001[99] was quite different from the original, and fairly closely resembles the current competitive dialogue procedure. This provided for competitive dialogue as a distinct award procedure, based on similar grounds for use as apply in the adopted version;[100] contemplated tenders based on tenderers' own solutions; and contained many of the procedural rules found in the adopted provisions – although further additions and alterations were made prior to final adoption.

[94] Art. 30(7) of the draft provided for a minimum of three final bids, two fewer than in restricted procedures (although two seem possible under the adopted version of competitive dialogue: see section 5.7 below).

[95] See Commission, Proposal, n. 89 above, Art. 30(2) and (5).

[96] *Ibid.*, Art. 30(1).

[97] *Ibid.*, Art. 30.

[98] *Ibid.*, section 3.6 (Explanatory Memorandum).

[99] DG C II, *Proposal for a Directive of the European Parliament and of the Council on the Co-ordination of Procedures for the Award of Public Supply Contracts, Public Service Contracts and Public Works Contracts*, Working Document, SN 2325/1/01 REV 1 (MAP), Art. 30.

[100] *Ibid.*, Art. 30(1). An additional condition that use of a design contest would not be appropriate, not included in the final version, is also included.

As with other provisions in the procurement Directive, the provisions finally adopted on competitive dialogue clearly show the influence of laws and practices of some Member States. In particular, as Chapter 4 explains, the grounds for using the procedure show significant similarities with those for using the old French *l'appel d'offres sur performances* – the variation of the restricted procedure previously used for some complex procurement in France. The structure of competitive dialogue, on the other hand, is largely consistent with the UK's previous practice for awarding privately financed infrastructure projects and, as Chapter 3 explains, appears to have been influenced heavily by this practice.[101] Thus competitive dialogue not only allows for dialogue during the award procedure – the main justification for its introduction – but also for other features found in the UK's pre-2004 practice, notably the possibility for fewer participants in the award phase (a minimum of three at the outset rather than the five in restricted procedures), the possibility of phases (including different tender stages) in the award stage, and the possibility of reducing the number of participants during this phase. These features of the award procedure are related to the wide scope for dialogue provided in the procedure, in the sense that they are designed to reduce costs that arise from a dialogue process – but these features were not an *inevitable* consequence of the acceptance of dialogue.

2.4. *The current rules in outline*

In the Directive as adopted, the main special rules governing the scope and operation of the procedure are found in Article 29, a special Article devoted to competitive dialogue, and also in Article 1(11), setting out the definition of the various award procedures. Apart from this, the applicable rules appear in many other Articles, which apply to some or all of the other award procedures, as well as to competitive dialogue.

So far as scope is concerned, competitive dialogue is available for contracts governed by the full rules of the Directive where contracting authorities are not objectively able to define the technical means of satisfying their needs or objectives and/or are not objectively able to specify the legal and/or financial make up of a project.[102] It is also necessary as a further condition that the contracting authority considers

[101] See Ch. 3, section 2.

[102] Directive 2004/18, Art. 29(1), read with Art. 1(11)(c) (defining a particularly complex contract).

Table 1.1 *Outline of the competitive dialogue procedure*

1. ADVERTISING Phase	Contract notice in OJEU
2. Phase of SELECTION OF PARTICIPANTS IN THE DIALOGUE Articles 44–52	Suitability
	Selection of candidates to tender from suitable ones
3. DIALOGUE Phase Article 29(3)–(5)	Identification of solution(s) and possible reduction in number of participants
4. FINAL TENDER Phase Article 29(6)	Submission of full tenders and selection of the most economically advantageous tender
5. POST-TENDER Phase Article 29(7)	Clarification and confirmation of commitments; notification and standstill; and contract award notice

that the open or restricted procedure will not allow award of the contract.[103] An analysis of both the legal requirements for use and of the way that the procedure has actually been used in practice is provided in section 4 below, drawing on the more detailed analysis of use found in Chapter 2, as well as on the chapters on specific Member States.

So far as the operation of procedure is concerned, this can be divided into five distinct phases under the legal regime, summarised in Table 1.1 and examined separately in section 5 below.

The first phase mentioned specifically in the legal rules is the launch of the procedure with the publication of a notice advertising the contract – a 'contract notice' – in the OJEU. This is discussed in section 5.4 below. In practice, this should be preceded by a phase of careful planning and preparation, something that is discussed in section 5.2 below – a phase which is not subject to any special legal rules in Article 29 but is, of course, subject to equal treatment and to the other general principles of the Directive.

The second phase comprises the selection of those economic operators who will be invited to participate in the dialogue phase. This selection involves two aspects. First, it is necessary to make at least a provisional assessment of which of those interested meet the requirements for participation – for example, in terms of relevant experience – and to

[103] Directive 2004/18, Art. 29(1).

limit participation to those economic operators. This is referred to as assessing suitability. Secondly, as with restricted or negotiated procedures with a notice, if there are considered to be too many who are suitable, the contracting authority may then select only a limited number of these to actually participate. This phase, which is governed by Articles 44–52 of the Directive, is analysed in section 5.5 below.

The remaining three phases all concern what may be described in terms of the decision stages of the Directive as the award stage of the procedure. This involves obtaining information on what the different candidates can offer, and applying the award criteria to determine the most economically advantageous tender. During the first part of this period, the contracting authority may also fix on a possible solution or solutions for the project within the (often broad) parameters set by the notice and descriptive document.

The first of these three 'award' phases in time, and the third phase in the overall five-phase process referred to above, is what the Directive refers to as the 'dialogue' phase. This is the phase that precedes the submission of final tenders, during which contracting authorities can engage with the economic operators they have selected to address all aspects of the contract. In this phase, they can both seek to identify a suitable solution or solutions (from a technical, legal and/or financial perspective) *and* consider the terms (including the price and other financial terms) on which those solutions can be provided. During this phase, the contracting authority can, based on the suitability of the solutions and/or the terms available, reduce the number of participants still further. Member States have considerable flexibility in structuring this process and numerous variations are possible: it can involve both discussions *and* one or more tendering phases, including the possible submission of interim tenders that can be used as the basis for discussions and/or to reduce the number of participants or solutions considered. To some extent, the term 'dialogue' can be misleading since this phase can involve tenders as well as discussions, and arguably need even not involve any actual discussions. This phase is regulated by Article 29 (3)–(5) of the Directive and is discussed in section 5.6 below.

The dialogue phase is followed by a fourth phase, which is the submission of complete final tenders by those still participating in the process, and the selection of the most economically advantageous tender. As mentioned above, tendering may be on the basis of a specific solution, or may involve each tenderer offering its own solution. It is a key feature of competitive dialogue that the selection must be made on the basis of these tenders, and that they must be relatively complete. This phase is governed primarily by Article 29(6) of the Directive and is examined in section 5.7.

A fifth phase referred to in the Directive is the post-tender phase – the phase after selecting the most economically advantageous tender in the final tender stage. This stage involves the possibility of what the Directive refers to as 'clarification and confirmation' of commitments, governed by Article 29(7), and also involves (as with other procedures) a requirement for a notification of the award and a standstill notice to losing parties, as well as publication of a contract award notice. Issues relating to this part of the procedure are considered at sections 5.8 and 5.9 below.

3. Legal implementation of the competitive dialogue procedure: the general picture and reflections on harmonisation

Competitive dialogue is an award procedure that is optional for Member States. This is confirmed in recital 16 of Directive 2004/18, which provides expressly that 'Member States should be allowed to choose whether contracting authorities may use' competitive dialogue, along with other mechanisms introduced explicitly for the first time such as electronic auctions and framework agreements. This seems merely to make explicit for new procedures and mechanisms a more general principle that Member States may decide which procedures to make available: as explained in section 2, the Directives merely lay down *minimum* standards of transparency and access, and Member States may generally choose whether or not to make available to their contracting authorities the full flexibilities allowed by the Directives.

In practice, however, Member States have all provided in their legislation for use of competitive dialogue.[104] This includes countries that did not perceive there to be any particular need for this addition to the Directive and which have since used the procedure only in a very few cases, such as Portugal and Lithuania, or which have not used it at all.[105] To take advantage as soon as possible of the increased *flexibility* offered by competitive dialogue some Member States, notably France and Germany, in fact introduced this procedure before the deadline for

[104] See EPEC (European PPP Expertise Centre), *Procurement of PPP and the Use of Competitive Dialogue in Europe – A Review of Public Sector Practices across the EU* (2011), available at www.eib.org/epec/resources/epec-ppp-procurement-and-cd.pdf.
[105] See section 4 below.

transposing the new *obligations* of the Directive and prior to transposing those obligations.[106]

As well as having a discretion on whether to allow for use of competitive dialogue at all, in light of the framework character of the Directive discussed above it appears that Member States may also choose to limit regulation of the procedure solely to what is necessary to ensure compliance with the rules in the Directive itself, or may supplement the rules with further requirements designed better to promote their national procurement objectives when operating the competitive dialogue procedure.

In practice, it is striking that Member States have almost unanimously chosen largely simply to copy out the text of the Directive without supplementing its requirements, thus leaving to contracting authorities the full flexibility allowed by the Directive itself: this applies both to the issue of whether to use the competitive dialogue procedure at all and to the issue of how to operate it. As will be seen in subsequent chapters, this is to a very large extent the case with all the countries studied for this book with the sole exception of Portugal; and it is also the approach adopted by nearly all other Member States.[107]

There are some exceptions and qualifications to this general approach, however. Thus Member States sometimes apply some general requirements of their procurement systems to competitive dialogue. This is often the case with requirements to advertise in national publications or on national websites, which are widely applied to competitive dialogue as well as to other award procedures: of the countries studies in this book, France, Italy, the Netherlands, Poland, Lithuania and Spain all have such requirements which are extended also to competitive dialogue.[108] Another example of applying general rules to competitive dialogue is the application of the general requirement in Spain for use of a jury in the evaluation (where there is also an additional requirement for competitive dialogue in the form of an obligation for the jury to possess special expertise).[109] There are also a few other areas in which Member States have supplemented the Directive's rules to an extent.

[106] See section 3 of Chs. 4 and 5, respectively. [107] EPEC, n. 104 above, Annex II.

[108] As reported in each case in section 5.4 of the respective chapters. Portugal also has a requirement for national publication, along with many other special national rules, as discussed further below.

[109] See Ch. 4, section 2.

Thus in Italy the legislation contains some additions such as provisions that define and limit the scope of application of the procedure, define the contents of the descriptive document issued at the start of the procedure, and require submission of a feasibility study with offers in the first part of the dialogue phase.[110] In Poland, there is a requirement for an absolute minimum of five participants in the dialogue, as opposed to the three required by the EU rules and also – although the law is unclear – a suggestion that the legislation may not allow reduction of numbers in phases during the dialogue[111] – features that combined would make the procedure more costly and less flexible than in most other Member States. There are also provisions in France and Germany for payment of certain bid costs for tenderers in certain cases.[112] However, for the most part Member States have not sought to regulate through enforceable regulatory provisions the approach taken to key aspects of competitive dialogue – for example, how the very flexible dialogue phase is to be structured.

It is striking that this approach of merely repeating the requirements of the Directives without substantial supplementary regulation has been adopted not only in countries where this is the traditional approach to EU procurement obligations, such as the UK and Denmark, but also in countries where traditionally EU obligations have been implemented simply as one part of a much more extensive national regulatory framework on procurement which goes beyond EU law requirements. This 'minimal' approach to competitive dialogue has been adopted, for example, in France, where the extensive Code des Marchés Publics has previously regulated public procurement in much more detail than the Directives, both before and after France's EU membership.[113] An example of that is the award procedure used for many complex contracts prior to competitive dialogue, *l'appel d'offres sur performances*, a version of the EU restricted procedure but with many detailed additional rules, which competitive dialogue has now replaced. It is interesting to observe, however, that, although the current public procurement system in France still maintains many rules going beyond the procurement Directives, this is becoming increasingly less the case, and that France has moved towards a more minimal approach to regulation when dealing with other innovations of the 2004 Directives as well (for

[110] See Ch. 11, section 3. [111] See Ch. 9, sections 5.5 and 5.6.
[112] See section 5.10 below. [113] See Ch. 4, section 1.

example, framework agreements).[114] Other Member States with extensive regulatory systems that have likewise confined themselves largely to copying the Directive's provisions where competitive dialogue is concerned include Spain, Poland and Lithuania.[115] The explanation for this approach might possibly be found to some extent in the novelty of the competitive dialogue concept, with lack of experience making it difficult to know how to regulate the procedure,[116] and also in the risks of legal challenge of provisions that go beyond EU law as being incompatible with EU legal requirements – particularly in light of uncertainty and the unpredictability of EU case law.[117]

As stated above, Portugal provides a notable exception to this general trend of merely repeating the Directive's provisions. As Chapter 7 describes, Portugal requires contracting authorities to operate competitive dialogue in a specific way set out in legislation that does not offer all the flexibilities provided in the Directive, including by precluding any possibility of reducing the number of candidates or solutions in the dialogue stage, and by requiring all tenderers to submit final offers based on a common approach, rather than their own solutions. In both respects, this is very different from the way that competitive dialogue is often operated in other Member States.[118]

The general approach to legal transposition, along with the very fact that a more specific and common award procedure has been introduced for complex contracts, has created a greater degree of legal harmonisation of public procurement procedures than existed previously, and a degree of harmonisation that from a legal perspective goes beyond what is actually required by EU law. However, it cannot be assumed that the absence of legal rules makes for a more harmonised regime *de facto* rather than simply *de jure* since legal rules additional to those in the

[114] See L. Folliott-Lalliot, 'The French Approach to Regulating Frameworks under the New EC Directives', Ch. 4 in J. Tilipman and S. Arrowsmith (eds.), *Reform of the UNCITRAL Model Law on Procurement* (Thomson Reuters/West, 2010), p. 193.

[115] See respectively Chs. 8, 9 and 10.

[116] The UK, on the other hand, had had extensive experience of applying an approach similar to that of competitive dialogue but its traditional approach is not to limit legal rules to those required by the Directive and to address additional matters of policy only by government guidance: see Ch. 3, section 2.

[117] See S. Arrowsmith, 'The Past and Future Evolution of EC Procurement Law: From Framework to Common Code?' (2006) 35 *Public Contract Law Journal* 337.

[118] See the account in sections 5.5 and 5.6 of this chapter; though recall that, as noted above, it has been argued that the Polish legislation also precludes eliminating economic operators or solutions during the dialogue.

Directive can serve to co-ordinate the practices of contracting authorities within a Member State.

As Arrowsmith has previously explained, another way in which EU procurement law has exerted an influence in favour of a common approach to procurement in Member States is through the application of rules equivalent to those in the Directives to procurements that are not fully regulated by those Directives.[119] From this perspective, it is worth highlighting that, as discussed in section 4 below, the competitive dialogue procedure has influenced procurement that is not fully regulated by the Directives: as that section explains, formal or informal versions of competitive dialogue have been applied in law and/or in practice to these procurements to a degree. Since the procedure for these procurements is regulated formally only to a limited extent by EU law, it may be that use of a competitive dialogue-type approach in this context has increased, or could increase, the degree of harmonisation for complex contracts outside the Directives, *de facto* and/or *de jure*. However, this depends on factors such as the degree of divergence in law and practice prior to 2004 and actual use of the procedure, and requires further study for definitive conclusions to be drawn.

From the perspective of harmonisation, it is also appropriate to mention that some evidence emerged from this study of competitive dialogue that Member States are taking into consideration each other's law and policy in regulating public procurement.[120] For example, in Denmark the practice of using competitive dialogue in the UK and France was presented to a Danish review body to argue for a flexible approach to the scope of the procedure,[121] whilst the UK standard contract and approach for certain kinds of privately financed infrastructure procurement is used in the Netherlands for certain transport projects, with adjustments for the Dutch legislation.[122]

4. Scope of the competitive dialogue procedure[123]

4.1. Introduction

In considering the scope of competitive dialogue, it is pertinent to start by observing that there is considerable uncertainty on this issue, and it

[119] Arrowsmith, n. 117 above. [120] On this again, see Arrowsmith, n. 117 above.
[121] See Ch. 6, section 4. [122] See Ch. 12, section 5.7.
[123] See also, in particular, Arrowsmith, n. 3 above, pp. 632–5; Treumer, 'The Field of Application of Competitive Dialogue', n. 3 above; Burnett, 'Developing a Complexity Test', n. 3 above.

seems that this uncertainty inhibits the use of the procedure in at least some Member States – for example, in Germany and Denmark.[124] Essentially, the wording of the rules on the scope of competitive dialogue in the Directive is rather ambiguous, and clarity is not helped by the fragmentation of the relevant legal provisions across several provisions and a recital. Further, the wording of the Articles and the content of the recital are only two elements to consider: due account must also be taken to the purpose of introducing the procedure, possible case law from the CJEU, the Court's style of interpretation, the tendency in the Court's other case law on procurement, case law at national level, use of the procedure in the Member States, national implementing law, and European Commission guidance and enforcement proceedings. It is important to bear in mind here that the procedure was introduced to achieve procedural simplification and to make the EU regime more flexible, as well as to prevent alleged abuse of existing procedures – that is, over-use of the negotiated procedure with a notice, and the flexible conduct of the restricted procedure, as discussed in section 2 above.[125]

4.2. *The Directive's provisions on scope*

As we have mentioned, competitive dialogue is not freely available for all contracts but may be used only in special circumstances as specified in the Directive. In this respect, Article 28 provides that contracting authorities may use competitive dialogue in the specific circumstances expressly provided for in Article 29. This Article in turn provides that, in the case of 'particularly complex' contracts, Member States may provide that, where contracting authorities consider that the use of the open or restricted procedure will not allow the award of the contract, these authorities may use competitive dialogue in accordance with that Article. 'Particularly complex' is defined in Article 1(11)(c) of the Directive as referring to the case in which contracting authorities are not objectively able to define the technical means in accordance with Article 23(3)(b), (c) or (d) capable of satisfying their special needs or objectives, and/or are not objectively able to specify the legal and/or financial make-up of a project.

[124] See respectively Ch. 5 and Ch. 6, section 4. This contrasts with the position in the UK where the risk of challenge to use of competitive dialogue is considered to be low: see Ch. 3, section 4.2.

[125] Stressed in the Commission Communication, n. 85 above, section 2.

Recital 31 to the Directive reads as follows:

> Contracting authorities which carry out particularly complex projects may, without this being due to any fault on their part, find it objectively impossible to define the means of satisfying their needs or of assessing what the market can offer in the way of technical solutions and/or financial/legal solutions. This situation may arise in particular with the implementation of important integrated transport infrastructure projects, large computer networks or projects involving complex and structured financing, the financial and legal make-up of which cannot be defined in advance. To the extent that use of open or restricted procedures does not allow the award of such contracts, a flexible procedure should be provided which preserves not only competition between economic operators but also the need for the contracting authorities to discuss all aspects of the contract with each candidate.

It can be noted that this recital, unlike the text of the Directive itself, refers to the fact that competitive dialogue is available when it is objectively *impossible* to define the means for satisfying the authority's needs or assess solutions. It should be recalled that, whilst a statement in a recital may cast light on the interpretation to be given to a legal rule, it can not in itself constitute a legal rule.[126]

4.3. *The approach of the CJEU*

The above provisions establish the fundamental basis for interpreting the scope of the procedure. However, as pointed out above the wording of the relevant Articles and recital is only one of several elements to consider, one other of which is the case law of the CJEU. The Court has in fact not yet considered this particular issue – or indeed any of the legal provisions on competitive dialogue – in its case law, and to our knowledge there are also no pending cases. This is remarkable as the procedure was introduced more than five years ago and has been applied in practice thousands of times.

It is important to stress that the Court is known for its *purpose-oriented* and *dynamic* interpretation of EU law, and that the background to the introduction of the competitive dialogue procedure was to ensure a more flexible approach for complex contracts in general, and for 'important integrated transport infrastructure projects, large computer

[126] Case C-215/88, *Casa Fleischhandels* v. *Bundesanstalt für Landwirtschaftliche Marktordnung* [1989] ECR I-2789.

networks or projects involving complex and structured financing' in particular, as indicated by recital 31 set out above. In the face of any arguments that the Directive's wording could justify a restrictive interpretation, this legislative history and purpose must also be considered, and supports a flexible and pragmatic approach. Further, it needs noting that the current tendency of the CJEU is to interpret the procurement rules in a more flexible and pragmatic manner than previously – and that the Commission has recently lost several cases that it might have expected to win based on the stricter approach of earlier case law.[127]

4.4. *The approach of the European Commission*

The European Commission plays the role of 'the guardian of the Treaties', including by bringing infringement proceedings before the CJEU, and also had the leading role in the drafting of the Public Sector Directive. Thus it is of obvious relevance to consider the Commission's interpretation and approach to the enforcement of the rules on competitive dialogue. It is notable that there is a general lack of enforcement activity in this area; the authors have been unable to find any references to concrete cases where the Commission has questioned the application of competitive dialogue procedures. It therefore seems possible that the Commission has accepted the approach adopted towards the use of competitive dialogue in the Member States.

Written material from the European Commission also supports a flexible approach. A few examples are worthy of note.

First, a key element in delimiting the field of application of the competitive dialogue procedure is the definition of 'particularly complex'. A possible clarification of the phrase 'without this being due to any fault on their part' in recital 31 and the meaning of 'objectively' in Article 11(1)(c) ('contracting authorities are not objectively able to define the technical means ... and/or are not objectively able to specify the legal and/or financial make-up of a project') can be found in the preparatory works to the Public Sector Directive. The preparatory works contain the following remarks:

> [T]he complexity must be established and able to be objectively justified by the contracting authority. This does not therefore concern subjective

[127] Case C-480/06, *Commission* v. *Germany* [2009] ECR I-4747; and Case C-250/07, *Commission* v. *Greece* [2009] ECR I-4369. See also the cases on the TFEU, n. 16 above.

> impossibility i.e. due to deficiencies on the part of the contracting authority itself. The authority may not simply affirm that it is unable to provide a definition or an evaluation. On the contrary, the contracting authority must prove that this is objectively impossible, given the nature of the specific contract. Depending on the case, this might mean that the contracting authority would be required to prove that there are no precedents for the project, *or that disproportionate time or money would be required to acquire the necessary knowledge.*[128]

Of particular interest is the indication that the condition of not being objectively able to define the means or make-up of a project could be fulfilled where 'disproportionate time or money would be required to acquire the necessary knowledge'.

The Explanatory Note on Competitive Dialogue from the European Commission[129] is also relevant, although it is important to mention that this does not reflect the official position of the Commission. On various points this document interprets the field of application in a flexible manner.

A first example relates to the remarks on when competitive dialogue may become relevant due to legal or financial complexity in the context of public–private partnerships. The Commission has stated that such a situation arises 'very, very often in connection with projects of Public Private Partnerships'.[130] As the Commission rightly points out, calling something a 'PPP project' does not in itself entail legal or financial complexity,[131] and it is notable that the examples given by the Commission all concern projects involving private finance implying that the Commission may have in mind this particular (common) type of PPP only when making this statement. Nevertheless, the invitation to apply competitive dialogue in connection with a significant category of public–private partnerships is very obvious, and the formulation used indicates a wide scope for the procedure in this context.

Secondly, the Commission seems to adopt a flexible approach on what is meant by being unable 'objectively able to define the technical means', apparently endorsing the view that the question is not whether the authority may establish *some* appropriate technical specification but whether it can define the *best* means for meeting its needs. The

[128] Explanatory Memorandum, n. 89 above, p. 26 (emphasis added).

[129] Explanatory Note, n. 33 above.

[130] *Ibid.*, section 2.3. See also Commission, *Green Paper on Public–Private Partnerships and Community Law on Public Contracts and Concessions*, COM (2004) 327 final, pp. 8–11, on the *suitability* of competitive dialogue for public–private partnerships.

[131] *Ibid.*, section 2.3.

Explanatory Note[132] refers to the example of a contracting authority wanting to create a connection between the shores of a river where it might be that the authority cannot determine whether the *best* solution would be a bridge or a tunnel. Although it would be able to establish the specifications for both the bridge and the tunnel, the Commission suggests that competitive dialogue can be justified on the basis that the authority may not be able to establish which provides the best solution. In fact, it seems highly unlikely that a contracting authority would not be able to determine which of several possible solutions would be best suited to satisfying its needs after investigation where the solutions are as diverse in nature as in this example and it is unlikely that that competitive dialogue would be suitable to do so – but the general point of interpretation endorsed here, that competitive dialogue may be used to establish the *best* solution, is important (and, we will argue below, is correct). It might also be argued that the use of this particular (extreme) example also indicates a flexible attitude to the *application* of the test.

Thus, to sum up, the Commission appears implicitly to have accepted a flexible approach to interpreting the scope of competitive dialogue.

4.5. Interpreting the scope of competitive dialogue: some concrete propositions

It is submitted that the considerations discussed above, along with further specific arguments set out below, support several propositions (to some extent related) regarding the scope of competitive dialogue:

Proposition 1: competitive dialogue is not an exceptional procedure

The first proposition is that the procedure is not to be considered as an 'exceptional' one *in the legal sense in which that concept is used in the context of the negotiated procedure without a notice.*[133] In the context of the negotiated procedure without a notice, the CJEU has concluded that, since that procedure[134] provides an exception to general principles of EU

[132] *Ibid.*, section 2.2. [133] See also Arrowsmith, n. 3 above, at p. 632.

[134] The relevant cases do not even concern the negotiated procedure with a notice but only the negotiated procedure without any notice, and it could even be argued that the former is not an exceptional procedure: Arrowsmith, n. 3 above, pp. 560–1.

law, it must be interpreted strictly[135] and the burden of proving the existence of exceptional circumstances lies on the person seeking to rely on those circumstances.[136]

It is submitted that, despite the requirement for specific grounds for its use, competitive dialogue is not an exceptional procedure in the same sense. This is based on the fact that awarding a contract with neither a public advertisement nor competition – as is permitted under the negotiated procedure without a notice – involves a complete departure from the basic principle of transparency in the Directive and hence of the possibility of ensuring compliance with equal treatment, including non-discrimination. Competitive dialogue, on the other hand, involves a high degree of transparency, particularly in the requirement for a competition, use of objective criteria in selection, and the need for the choice of the winner to be based on complete final tenders. In these respects, it is very much closer to open and restricted procedures than to the negotiated procedure without a notice. Although it does involve more discretion than those procedures in the dialogue stage, it does not involve any substantial derogation from the Directive's basic principles, but rather a more limited application of those principles during part of the process, to take account of the specific needs of complex procurement. It can be pointed out also that, when the Commission first proposed a new procedure for complex contracts, it explicitly contemplated that it would be a 'standard' procedure like the open and restricted procedures, rather than an exceptional procedure.[137] The mere fact that the procedure is not generally available does not *per se* render it a limited one: the principle of 'exceptionality' developed by the CJEU in the context of the negotiated procedure without a notice is properly based on the exceptional nature of the *content* of the procedural rules in question – in that this content derogates from basic principles of EU law – and not by the decision of the legislature to limit the availability of the procedure *per se*.

[135] Case 199/85, *Commission* v. *Italy* [1987] ECR 1039, para. 14; Case C-71/92, *Commission* v. *Spain* [1993] ECR I-5923, para. 36; Case C-328/92, *Commission* v. *Spain* [1994] ECR I-1569, para. 15; Case C-57/94, *Commission* v. *Italy* [1995] ECR I-1249; Case C-318/94, *Commission* v. *Germany* [1996] ECR I-1949; Case C-385/02, *Commission* v. *Italy* [2004] ECR I-8121, paras. 19 and 37.

[136] *Ibid.*, Case 199/85, para. 14; Case C-328/92, para. 16; Case C-57/94; Case C-318/94; Case C-385/02, para. 19.

[137] But also, however, as replacing the negotiated procedure with competition: see Explanatory Note, n. 85 above, section 2.1.2.2.

The Directive's wording clearly leaves room for this interpretation – even if the negotiated procedure with a notice, as well as without a notice, is to be treated as exceptional[138] – since the Directive treats competitive dialogue separately from both forms of negotiated procedure. This is the case both in Article 28, setting out the procedures, and in that the procedural rules on competitive dialogue (Article 29) and negotiated procedures (Articles 30 and 31) are set out in separate Articles.

The consequence of this, it is submitted, is that the rules of interpretation laid down for the negotiated procedure without a notice cannot be applied automatically. It is submitted that it is, in fact, appropriate that the basic burden of proving the grounds for the existence of the procedure be placed on the party relying on them,[139] since this party will have access to the relevant facts. However, we consider that it is appropriate to allow a relatively wide margin of discretion to be afforded to the contracting authority in judging whether the conditions are actually met (such as lack of suitability of the open and restricted procedures).

Further, it is submitted that it is *not* appropriate to apply at all the principle that the grounds for using the procedure must be very narrowly interpreted, as is the case for exceptional procedures: this interpretation must take an equal and balanced approach to all interests involved, including the considerations discussed in section 2 above regarding the need for flexibility to accommodate legitimate national differences.

If, in accordance with the above arguments, the procedure is not considered exceptional in the sense in which this concept is used in relation to the negotiated procedure without a notice, then this will provide additional support for the principles suggested below. These principles do not, however, necessarily depend on the non-exceptional nature of the procedure, since they are also clearly supported by other arguments.

Proposition 2: competitive dialogue can be used when contracting authorities cannot define the best technical means for meeting their needs or the best legal or financial make-up for the project

[138] As to which, see n. 133 above.

[139] Also the view of, for example, Burnett, *Competitive Dialogue*, n. 3 above, p. 27. For practical considerations regarding the justification for use, see Burnett, *Competitive Dialogue*, n. 3 above, pp. 27–8.

A second, and more specific, proposition of interpretation that we put forward is that the test of whether the contracting authority is objectively unable to define the technical means capable of satisfying its objectives, or to specify the best legal and/or financial make-up of the project, as referred to in Article 1(9) of Directive 2004/18, refers not only to the case in which the authority is unable to define or specify any solution but also where it is not able to define or specify the *best* technical, legal and/or financial solution available.[140]

This can be deduced, first and foremost, from the purpose of the dialogue as stated explicitly in Article 29(3): this provides that the aim of the dialogue shall be 'to identify and define the means *best* suited to satisfying [the contracting authorities'] needs' (emphasis added). The principles of interpretation used by the CJEU require that legal provisions be interpreted in the context of the legislation as a whole, and this context very clearly favours this second proposition of interpretation.

The argument is bolstered further by recital 31: this refers to the fact that entities may find it objectively impossible to define 'the means of satisfying their needs *or assessing what the market can offer in the way of technical solutions and/or financial/legal solutions*' (emphasis added again). This very specifically ties the concept of inability to define the means to inability to assess the various possibilities available in the market.

Further, this interpretation is strongly supported by the historical circumstances of the introduction of competitive dialogue as a wider procedure for complex contracts than the negotiated procedure with a notice. As section 2 explained, in the context of use of the negotiated procedure in the UK for privately financed infrastructure contracts, the European Commission disputed the availability of the grounds relied on, namely, that overall pricing was not possible (applicable to works and services contracts) and that it was not possible to set a specification (applicable to services contracts) – and competitive dialogue was introduced to provide a procedure for awarding these kinds of contracts that would be available in wider circumstances than the negotiated procedure (as supported also by the references to these kinds of projects in recital 31). If a contract is considered particularly complex only when it

[140] Again, see also Arrowsmith, n. 3 above, pp. 633–4; and Treumer, 'The Field of Application of Competitive Dialogue', n. 3 above, p. 312.

is not possible to specify the technical means at all, this, however, seems to limit competitive dialogue to the same circumstances that apply for using the negotiated procedure on the basis of inability to set a specification – contrary to the very reasons for introducing the procedure. Even apart from this historical perspective, consideration of the grounds for using competitive dialogue in the context of the text of Directive 2004/18 as a whole supports our proposed interpretation: there is no point in having competitive dialogue if the negotiated procedure can be used in the same circumstances (since the competitive dialogue process can be accommodated within the latter procedure): thus the text taken alone indicates that the scope of the two procedures is different.

We can also note, as was discussed in section 4.4 above, that this interpretation seems also to be endorsed in the Commission's Explanatory Note on competitive dialogue.

This second proposition of interpretation is not dependent on the first principle above since, as we have explained, it appears clearly justified on the basis of the textual provisions and by the historical context, even if a narrow interpretation must be adopted on the basis that competitive dialogue is an exceptional procedure.

Proposition 3: competitive dialogue can be justified by the disproportionate time and/or cost that a different approach would involve

Our third proposition is that use of competitive dialogue can be justified by the fact that disproportionate time and/or cost would be involved in establishing the technical, financial and/or legal make-up of the project without using this procedure. Similarly, it is submitted that difficulties other than time and cost – notably the difficulty of attracting sufficient competition where design and execution elements are separated in view of potential conflicts of interest of participating in both, as mentioned in section 2 – are also relevant. In other words, it can be said that, for the purpose of Article 1(11) defining a particularly complex contract, a contracting authority may be considered 'not objectively able' to define the (best) technical legal or financial composition of a project because of the problems of doing so rather than simply because of absolute impossibility. We have already seen in section 4.4 that this approach finds support in the preparatory works for Directive 2004/18. It is interesting to note that the French legislator appears to have interpreted the condition of complexity based on the same assumption.[141] The French implementing legislation on this point is of general interest as the pre-2004 French legislation appears heavily to have inspired the formulation of the grounds for using competitive dialogue.[142] Further, what is a disproportionate cost needs to be judged in light of the different policies and values of different Member States, as discussed in section 2. Thus a design contest may, for example, not involve the same costs in one state as in another because of different circumstances or different legal rules on conflicts of interest.[143]

It might be argued that the reference in recital 31 to objective *impossibility* in defining the means or assessing what the market can offer may indicate that the requirement that the authority is not able to define the (best) means for meeting its needs or the (best) make-up of a project is to be interpreted strictly. However, a recital is not conclusive as to the meaning of the text and the other points made above point in the opposite direction. In any case, 'impossibility' may reasonably be interpreted as existing when circumstances make a particular course of action exceptionally difficult.

> Proposition 4: in deciding whether an authority is 'objectively' able to define the technical, financial or legal composition of the contract it is to be judged against a 'reasonable' contracting authority of the same size and nature

Our fourth proposition concerns the use in Article 1(11) of the word 'objectively' to qualify the ability of the contracting authority to define the technical, financial or legal composition of the contract. It is suggested that this requires that the contracting authority be judged against the position of a 'reasonable' contracting authority *of the same size and nature* but, on the other hand, that its specific position – in particular, past experience – is not wholly irrelevant to the assessment of its ability

[141] According to the French legislation, the contract is considered particularly complex when the contracting authority is unable to define the specifications 'alone and in advance': 'est objectivement dans l'impossibilité de définir seule et à l'avance'; cf. Art. 36 of the Code des Marchés Publics, modified by Art. 4 of Décret No. 2008-1355 of 19 December 2008 and Art. 5 of the Ordonnance of 17 June 2004 sur les contrats de partenariat.

[142] See Ch. 4, section 2.

[143] Some states exclude those participating in a design contest from participating in execution of the project whilst others do not.

to define the project (and may preclude use of competitive dialogue). It can also be noted that the Commission also states in its Explanatory Note that the contracting authority has an obligation of diligence and that it is necessary to examine on a case-by-case basis the nature of the market in question *taking into consideration the capacity of the contracting authority concerned*[144] – thus also endorsing the view that the characteristics of the authority are relevant to some degree.

Proposition 5: a contracting authority enjoys discretion in determining whether open or restricted procedures could be used instead for the contract

Finally, a fifth proposal for interpretation is that the contracting authority enjoys a degree of discretion in determining the application of the conditions stated in Article 29(1), namely, 'that the use of the open or restricted procedure will not allow the award of the contract'. It can be recalled that it is a condition according to Article 29(1) 'that the use of the open or restricted procedure will not allow the award of the contract' and there is a reference in recital 31 to objective *impossibility* in defining the means or assessing what the market can offer; and the approach in Danish case law on the issue has been to suggest that the contracting authority only enjoys a limited discretion in this respect, with complainants arguing that this reference to objective impossibility indicates a strict interpretation.[145] However, the relevance of the recital here is clearly contradicted by the wording of the Directive itself which uses subjective language, referring to whether the *contracting authority considers* that these other procedures will allow the award of the contract. Clearly, any discretion must, of course, be exercised in accordance with minimum standards required by EU law for the review of commercial judgments of contracting authorities as indicated by Advocate General Jacobs in *SIAC*[146] (which was concerned with the discretion to judge what is the most economically advantageous tender). However, the subjective language used indicates that the decision is predominantly

[144] Explanatory Note, n. 33 above, section 2.1. [145] See Ch. 6, section 4.

[146] Case C-19/00, *SIAC Construction Ltd* v. *County Council of the County of Mayo* [2001] ECR I-7725, para. 53 of the Opinion. The degree of intensity of legal scrutiny that is applied to commercial judgments will in practice vary between Member States, within the area of procedural autonomy that Member States enjoy under EU law.

one for the contracting authority, even if subject to scrutiny by the courts to prevent any abuse.

Thus, again, even if competitive dialogue is an exceptional provision, a broad ambit for the provision is justified in this particular respect by the explicit wording.

Such an approach is further supported by the considerations discussed in section 2 above regarding the justifications for a different approach to complex contracts in Member States with different circumstances and values, and reinforced by recital 3 stating that the co-ordinating provisions of the Directives 'should comply as far as possible with current procedures and practices in each of the Member States'. It is clear from this that the fact that open or restricted procedures are considered appropriate for awarding a particular type of contract in one Member State does not necessarily make them so in another Member State.

More generally, it needs to be stressed that the application of the concept of a particularly complex contract is, inevitably, closely dependent on the facts of each case. Thus, even if it were clearly established that the above principles of interpretation represent the law, uncertainty would remain over its availability in specific cases. However, endorsement of such principles by the courts, preferably, and in the interim in clear formal guidance from the European Commission, would certainly encourage and facilitate use of the procedure for the purposes for which it was intended – to the benefit of greater flexibility in some Member States and perhaps with the opposite effect – reduced reliance on the negotiated procedure – in others.

In contrast with the flexible approach advocated above for competitive dialogue, it can be pointed out that the same principles of interpretation, including the historical context of competitive dialogue, may incline the CJEU towards a more restrictive approach towards the availability of the negotiated procedure with a notice for contracts than it might have done before 2004. It is conceivable that prior to the adoption of the 2004 Directive the Court might have allowed use of the negotiated procedure for a wide range of complex contracts, contrary to the arguments of the Commission. However, now that competitive dialogue has been introduced, this is perhaps less likely. In this respect, the Court might interpret the scope of the grounds for using the negotiated procedure in a narrow, rather than broad, fashion, ruling that they do not cover many situations. Alternatively, the Court might preclude use of the negotiated procedure where the grounds overlap with those of competitive dialogue and the latter procedure would have been suitable, extending the 'hierarchy' of procedures that is arguably already seen in the requirement to consider the suitability of open and restricted procedures before using competitive dialogue. On the other hand, it may be that, in line with its recent more general tendency towards a flexible approach[147] and the acknowledgment in the Commission's 2011 Green Paper that the procurement regime may still lack sufficient flexibility, the Court will interpret all award procedures in a flexible manner.

4.6. *The approach in the Member States*

4.6.1. Implementation

Reflecting the general approach towards transposing the legal rules on competitive dialogue of simply repeating the provisions of the Directive (see section 3 above), the majority of the Member States studied in this book have made the procedure available to their contracting authorities simply on the exact grounds stated in the Directive, without limiting its use and without elaborating further on the grounds for its application.

There are, however, some exceptions. The most notable innovation is in Spain, where competitive dialogue has been made the automatic procedure for certain types of public–private partnership arrangements – possibly contrary to the Directive (although under EU law the provisions must be *interpreted* in line with the requirements of the Directive where this is possible).[148] In addition, in France the legislator has elaborated on the meaning of 'particularly complex' by stating that there is technical complexity where the contracting authority is not objectively capable of establishing *alone and in advance* the technical specifications.[149] This interpretation evidently makes it relatively easy to fulfil the condition and indicates a wide field of application. As previously mentioned, the European Commission has in its Explanatory Note indicated public–private partnerships contracts as an area where competitive dialogue could typically be used. It is therefore surprising that, on the other hand, the current Portuguese legislation possibly rules out the application of the procedure for this type of

[147] See section 4.3 above. [148] See Ch. 8, section 4.

[149] '[E]st objectivement dans l'impossibilité de définir seule et à l'avance'; cf. Art. 36 of the Code des Marchés Publics, modified by Art. 4 of Décret No. 2008-1355 of 19 December 2008 and Art. 5 of the Ordonnance of 17 June 2004 sur les contrats de partenariat.

contract because of specific provisions in its legislation on public–private partnerships that some consider are incompatible with using competitive dialogue.[150] It is also noteworthy that the Portuguese legislation appears to limit the use of the procedure to those situations where defining the specifications is objectively impossible, deliberately choosing a strict approach.[151] Italy has also narrowed down the scope of the procedure in its legislation: the most important limitation is that the most complex works, such as strategic infrastructure projects and production plants, are excluded.[152]

4.6.2. Public procurement practice in the Member States

4.6.2.1. Contracts fully regulated by the Public Sector Directive

Although, as we have seen, all Member States have now included competitive dialogue in their legislation for contracts covered by the Public Sector Directive, and many provide for the same broad scope of use as the Directive itself, use in practice varies very widely between Member States.

To give a broad figure of current usage, Table 1.2 shows the total number of notices in the OJEU for the year 1 April 2010 to 31 March 2011,[153] and is presented in order of frequency of use of the procedure. However, the procedure is currently in what may be termed an experimental phase,[154] and current use may reflect this.

Chapter 2 of this book provides a detailed analysis of use of the procedure between 1 January 2006 and 31 December 2009 in six of the countries covered by the present volume – France, Germany, the Netherlands, Portugal, Spain and the UK – and also in Ireland. That chapter looks not merely at the number and broad category of contracts (works, supplies or services) but also at what types of contracting authorities have been using competitive dialogue; the market sectors in which it is used; the precise types of projects involved; and what proportion of projects involves private finance. This information is supplemented by further, though briefer, statistical information on covered contracts in the specific country chapters, including on Denmark, Lithuania, Poland and Italy, which are not covered in Chapter 2. The following remarks will

[150] See Ch. 7, section 4.4. [151] See Ch. 7, section 4.1. [152] See Ch. 11, section 4.

[153] It is assumed that these are wholly, or very largely, for contracts within the Public Sector Directive. Note that competitive dialogue was not included in the legislation of Belgium during the relevant period whilst in Italy it was not in force.

[154] See Burnett, *Competitive Dialogue*, n. 3 above, p. 19.

Table 1.2 *Contract notices in the OJEU relating to competitive dialogue: 1 April 2010 to 31 March 2011*

Member State	Number of contract notices
France	452
United Kingdom	356
Poland	48
Finland	25
Germany	19
Netherlands	19
Estonia	17
Spain	16
Sweden	16
Ireland	15
Slovenia	13
Denmark	8
Czech Rep	7
Italy	6
Romania	5
Greece	4
Hungary	2
Luxembourg	2
Slovakia	2
Austria	1
Lithuania	1
Belgium	0
Bulgaria	0
Cyprus	0
Latvia	0
Malta	0
Portugal	0
Total	1,034

merely briefly highlight key points regarding use of the procedure, based on the information from the above sources.

Following the approach taken in Chapter 2, users can be divided into heavy, regular and irregular. In this respect, there are two (very) heavy users, namely, the UK and France: in the three-year period (2006–9) covered by Chapter 2, the number of notices for competitive dialogue procedures recorded were 1,380 and 1,430 respectively. This is many times the number from all other Member States combined – and it can be seen from Table 1.2 that the same trend has continued strongly in the past year. Regular users, as classified in Chapter 2, in terms of total number of notices, with between 50 and 200 notices in that same three-year period, were Poland,[155] Ireland, the Netherlands, Denmark[156] and Germany – although it is perhaps questionable to describe Germany as a truly regular user given that it has the largest economy in the EU.[157] Irregular users, with fewer than 50 notices in the three-year period, were Portugal, Spain, Lithuania, Belgium and Italy[158] (although it should be noted that in the latter two cases legislation allowing use of the procedure for contracts covered by Directive 2004/18 either had not been adopted or was not in force in the relevant period).

The very high number of procedures in the UK and France perhaps points towards a reasonably flexible interpretation of the conditions for the use of competitive dialogue in those states.

As discussed in section 4.4 above, the Commission's Explanatory Note indicates that public–private partnerships – at least those involving private sector finance – will 'very, very often' be of sufficient financial/legal complexity to give grounds for using competitive dialogue. The high level of use in the UK and France might to some extent reflect a high use of privately financed arrangements. However, this cannot be the whole explanation: Chapter 2 shows that the number of such projects in the UK at most represents only 35 per cent of all purchases made with competitive dialogue covered by the study and about 13 per cent in France.[159] It is interesting that – as reported in further detail in Chapter 3 – a recent assessment by the UK government's Cabinet Office itself suggested that in 30 per cent of cases analysed use of competitive dialogue as opposed to other procedures was 'neither necessary nor helpful'[160] (although this conclusion is not tied expressly to the legal grounds for using the procedure, but based on practical needs). On the other hand, it can be highlighted that infrastructure and ICT contracts represented the majority of competitive dialogue purchases in the UK and that both types are used as examples of 'particularly complex contracts' allowing use of competitive dialogue in recital 31 of the Public Sector Directive. Certainly, it seems, therefore, that very many of the

[155] See Ch. 9, section 4. [156] See Ch. 6, sections 3 and 4.
[157] This point is stressed in Ch. 5, section 4.5.
[158] See Ch. 2 and, on Lithuania and Italy, Chs. 10 and 11.
[159] See Ch. 2, sections 6.4.1 and 6.4.2. [160] See Ch. 3, section 4.5.

projects for which competitive dialogue is used in the heavy user countries are of precisely the kind for which the procedure was introduced.

As regards the kind of authorities using the procedure, the study in Chapter 2 covering eight Member States shows that local government bodies have been the most frequent users of competitive dialogue, and that the health sector also is a very heavy user in the UK, France and Germany.[161]

Another issue to consider is how the new procedure has impacted on use of other types of award procedure. In practice, the introduction of competitive dialogue has had a significant impact in the high user Member States of France and the UK.

So far as France is concerned, section 4 above explained that a tender procedure named *l'appel d'offres sur performances* was introduced at the start of the 1990s as a variant of the EU's restricted procedure to introduce flexibility and thereby to make the restricted procedure suitable for complex contracts.[162] This procedure was wholly repealed following the introduction of competitive dialogue.[163] In other words, in France the introduction of competitive dialogue entailed the total disappearance of a national procedure that bore some similarities to competitive dialogue and was available in similar circumstances. Another interesting phenomenon is that use of the negotiated procedure with a notice has been strongly declining in France from 2006 onwards. As pointed out in Chapter 4, this is possibly related to the introduction of competitive dialogue, although other explanations might also be relevant – one being that the conditions for using the negotiated procedures have become more restrictive in view of changes to the legislation and case law.[164]

In the UK, the figures suggest that competitive dialogue is now being used for many projects that would previously have been procured under the negotiated procedure, including privately financed infrastructure projects which previously were generally awarded using the negotiated procedure with a notice.[165] This is in line with a strong policy steer of the UK government towards the use of competitive dialogue for these and

[161] See Ch. 2, section 4.3.3. [162] See Ch. 4, section 2.

[163] However, it should be noted that competitive dialogue was made available very early in France in anticipation of the Public Sector Directive. The relevant French legislation entered into force on 10 January 2004 before the Directive was finally adopted on 31 March 2004. See Ch. 4, section 3.

[164] See Ch. 4, section 4.5. [165] See Ch. 3, section 4.2.

other complex projects in cases where the negotiated procedure with a notice would previously have been used.[166]

On the other hand, it is clear that the introduction of competitive dialogue has so far had little or no impact in most EU Member States. Clearly, its impact is negligible in those countries – the majority of Member States, as indicated in Table 1.2 above – that can be considered as irregular users of the procedure. The same can also generally be said of those countries defined as regular users, since the total number of competitive dialogue procedures involved in each state (50–200 over several years) is still insignificant in the context of the overall number of procedures advertised in the OJEU.[167]

It is also worth reiterating that there is considerable uncertainty as to the scope of the procedure, as mentioned in section 4.2, and also much uncertainty over many of the rules governing its operation (as will be explored in section 5 below). This appears in general to inhibit its use, with contracting authorities fearing legal challenge. This appears to be the case in Denmark and also in Germany, the largest economy of the EU, where a fear of challenge to the use of the procedure, as well as to its operation, means that contracting authorities stick to the well-known and flexible negotiated procedures.[168] This seems to suggest that in Germany use of the negotiated procedure with a notice may be perceived as safer than use of competitive dialogue despite the Commission's narrow view of the scope of the negotiated procedure. It is interesting also that in the Netherlands disputes have arisen in more than 15 per cent of competitive dialogue procedures compared with only about 3.5 per cent of other tender procedures.[169] It might be expected that such a high level of disputes, perhaps attributable to uncertainty over the scope and/or operation of the procedure, would inhibit use of competitive dialogue there. It has been suggested that fear of litigation because of the uncertainty of the legal rules and the phased and discretionary nature of the competitive dialogue procedure will also significantly deter its use in Italy,[170] although the procedure has only just entered into force there so that the level of actual use cannot yet be established.

[166] *Ibid.*

[167] It is interesting also that, in the Netherlands, use of both competitive dialogue and the negotiated procedures with a notice increased until 2010. There was then a sudden drop in negotiated procedures, which possibly was caused by Commission infringement proceedings: see Ch. 12, section 4.

[168] See respectively Ch. 6, section 4, and Ch. 5, section 6.

[169] See Ch. 12, section 3.

[170] See Ch. 11.

The position is quite different in the UK. There – in contrast with the position in Germany – the negotiated procedure is used significantly less since competitive dialogue was introduced, possibly because of the risk of challenge to use of the negotiated procedure but also clearly because of a steer by central government away from the negotiated procedure towards use of competitive dialogue (itself apparently influenced by the Commission's approach). On the other hand, the risks of legal challenge in the UK to the use of competitive dialogue as an alternative to open or restricted procedures is considered to be relatively low, in part because the market does not generally wish to challenge the decision to use the procedure at the time that decision is made and often cannot challenge later because of the time limits for challenge.[171]

4.6.2.2. Contracts that are not fully regulated by the Public Sector Directive We have seen in section 2.1 that many public sector contracts are outside the EU Directives altogether or only partly regulated. Many of these contracts, especially many concessions and some Part B services contracts, are complex in nature and thus potentially suitable for awarding by a competitive dialogue approach. Indeed, as we saw in section 3, the practices in the UK in awarding privately financed infrastructure contracts prior to 2004 on which competitive dialogue is modelled in part were applied equally to concessions as to contracts covered by the Directive. Further, we can note that the fact that the TFEU applies to contracts outside the Directives that are of cross-border interest can provide an incentive to the use of procedures similar to those of the Directive for awarding contracts even when not required by the Directives themselves, since this provides a low-risk approach to Treaty compliance. It is perhaps not surprising, therefore, to find that in both the laws and/or practices of Member States a procedure akin to the competitive dialogue procedure of Directive 2004/18 has been adopted also for contracts that are not regulated, or not fully regulated, by that Directive.

Many of the states covered in this book have made competitive dialogue available as a formal procedure in law for contracts that are

[171] See Ch. 3, section 4.2. The rules on use of the procedure are, however, considered uncertain and capable of giving rise to challenge in the UK, something that influences behaviour in the conduct of the procedure, particularly in the award stage: see Ch. 3, section 5.

not covered, or not fully covered, by Directive 2004/18 itself. Thus in Italy an informal award procedure akin to competitive dialogue, which bears the name 'competitive dialogue' in the national law, has been included in the law for awarding public sector contracts that are outside the Directive or its full rules, including for concessions and other forms of privately financed arrangements and public–private partnerships.[172] This procedure has been used in practice in these cases: as Chapter 11 explains, there were thirty-four such procedures advertised in the OJEU, for example, between 2006 and 2010.[173] In Portugal,[174] also, competitive dialogue is an award procedure that is made formally available for public contracts in general, including for below-threshold contracts[175] and, in principle, for concessions, provided that the general conditions for using competitive dialogue in Portugal (stricter than those of the Directive itself)[176] are met – although possibly it cannot be used for PPP contracts, its use arguably being inconsistent with specific Portuguese legislation on PPPs.[177] Poland makes a competitive dialogue procedure available in its law for contracts below the thresholds, with conditions for use similar to those of the Directive. In France, also, for many public bodies competitive dialogue is made available as a formal procedure in the law beyond the Directive itself – there it is available for contracts below the thresholds on the same conditions as for above-threshold contracts, namely, for 'particularly complex' contracts.[178] However, competitive dialogue has not been made available in France as a formal procedure for concessions, which historically have been governed by their own flexible type of award procedures. In Spain, competitive dialogue is again available – and has been used – for below-threshold contracts where the usual grounds for use concerned with complexity of the contract are met.[179] It is also the *required* award procedure for contracts designated as 'public–private co-operation contracts' that might include some contracts outside the Directives – but this type of

[172] See Ch. 11, section 3. [173] Ch. 11, section 3. [174] See Ch. 7, section 4.2.
[175] Ch. 7, section 4.4. [176] Ch. 7, section 4.2. [177] See Ch. 7, section 4.2.
[178] For certain other public bodies, that are not within the Code des Marchés Publics, it is not formally available, but a similar approach can be followed within the rules of the informal procedures that are available for below-threshold contracts; and the same also applies for certain types of contract, *contrats de partenariat*, which are below the thresholds, for which negotiated procedures can be used that could be structured like competitive dialogue: see Ch. 4, section 4.
[179] Ch. 8, section 4.3.

contract is little used. It is not used in Spain for most concession-type arrangements: concessions, as in France, historically are regulated by different procedures which remain applicable and are widely used.[180]

Some other states, on the other hand, have not made any formal provision for competitive dialogue for contracts not fully regulated by the Directive. This is the case, for example, in Denmark,[181] the UK[182] and Lithuania.[183]

However, when there is no formal legal provision for competitive dialogue or an equivalent procedure, there is evidence of at least occasional use of an approach equivalent to, or based on, competitive dialogue, where this is not actually ruled out by the legal framework that does exist. Thus, in the UK, where such contracts are generally not subject to any domestic legal rules but are governed only by EU-level requirements under the TFEU, use of a competitive dialogue-type procedure is clearly not ruled out by law, and has been seen for some Part B services and concession contracts: some of these were advertised in the OJEU as competitive dialogue procedures, whilst others were not advertised as such but structured in the same manner as competitive dialogue.[184] An example has also been observed in Denmark.[185]

4.6.3. Legal challenges to the use of competitive dialogue in the Member States

As contracting authorities appear to interpret the conditions for the use of the competitive dialogue procedure in a flexible manner in some Member States and have an obvious interest in access to the procedure with a high degree of dialogue, one could expect that there would be challenges to the use of competitive dialogue in the Member States.

However, in practice Denmark is the only Member State studied that has significant case law of this type. As explained in section 4 of Chapter 6, the use of competitive dialogue was considered justified in some of the Danish cases but the Danish interpretation is in general rather restrictive. It can be added that in Denmark it is possible for tenderers to challenge the use of the procedure after the award of the contract.[186] In the UK, the absence of case law, despite high use of the procedure, could be explained by the limited interest of economic

[180] Ch. 8, section 4.3. [181] Ch. 6, section 4. [182] Ch. 3, section 4.2.
[183] Ch. 10, section 4. [184] Ch. 3, section 4.2. [185] Ch. 6, section 4.
[186] See Ch. 6, section 4.

operators in challenging use of a procedure that they themselves consider appropriate, combined with the short time limits that encourage challenges to be brought once the defect in the procedure becomes known, rather than waiting for the outcome of the award process, as noted above, the costs of litigation, and the absence of a significant culture of litigation.[187] It is not clear why there is yet no case law in France, the other very heavy user of the procedure which also has a tradition of procurement litigation.

4.7. Conclusion on the scope of the competitive dialogue procedure

For contracts covered by Public Sector Directive 2004/18, there is considerable uncertainty as to the scope of competitive dialogue, and this uncertainty appears to inhibit its use in at least some Member States. However, the uncertainty has not led to case law from the CJEU, European Commission infringement proceedings or – with the exception of Denmark – legal challenges before national review bodies. Thus little guidance on use is provided by these sources.

We have argued, in light of the legislative history of the procedure and the principles of interpretation adopted by the CJEU, that the procedure is not in fact to be very narrowly interpreted. We have above offered several propositions for interpretation which we consider should guide the future development of the procedure. The procedure has been found to be one of significant value in Member States that have used it, and endorsement of the proposed propositions in future case law or in guidance from the Commission or national authorities could assist considerably in promoting competitive dialogue as a useful approach for the award of complex contracts in those states for which it is suitable (bearing in mind that other states may always decline to allow it or may restrict its use).

It is also interesting that, as we have seen, the introduction of competitive dialogue has to a degree influenced award procedures outside the Public Sector Directive as well as those within it, demonstrating the potential harmonisation role of the EU procurement regime even beyond its formal scope of application.

[187] On the last two points, see D. Pachnou, 'Bidders' Use of Mechanisms to Enforce EC Procurement Law' (2005) 14 *Public Procurement Law Review* 256.

5. Operation of the competitive dialogue procedure

5.1. Introduction

Having considered the scope of the competitive dialogue procedure, we now turn to consider the operation of that procedure, looking again both at the legal rules at EU level and at the way they have been applied in the Member States in law and (where information is available) in practice. The key stages of the procedure as envisaged in Directive 2004/18 have already been outlined briefly in section 2.4 above; here we will focus on the detail of those stages. As with the legal provisions on scope of the Directive, we will see that most Member States studied have transposed the Directive largely by merely repeating the wording of Directive 2004/18 itself, and thus allowing their contracting authorities the full flexibilities permitted under the Directive. These flexibilities are quite significant, giving scope for significant divergence in practice, and we will see that in fact there are many different ways in which competitive dialogue is actually operated. As we have already mentioned, Burnett has proposed that a significantly standardised approach be adopted to improve value for money but, whilst there is indeed much scope for this, different approaches may clearly be justified to many issues in some cases in light of the specific nature of the project and circumstances concerned.

5.2. The planning stage and drafting of the descriptive document

The legal rules of the Directive do not deal specifically with the planning stage. As regards the launch of the procedure they merely provide that the contract must be advertised by a contract notice in the OJEU setting out the authority's needs and requirements (Article 29(2), and also Article 35(2) on contract notices generally: see section 5.4 below); and that these needs and requirements must be defined in a 'descriptive document'. This descriptive document must be made available to candidates at latest at the time that they are invited to participate in the dialogue, since this document – or information on how to access it – must be sent to candidates with the invitation (Article 40(2), and see further section 5.5 below).

However, although planning is not a subject for EU regulation, and in general not an appropriate subject for the Directive to address, it is clear that it is a very important phase: the need for careful planning, including to ensure proper drafting of a useful descriptive document, is in fact one of the most important lessons to have been learned so far from experience with competitive dialogue.[188]

Thus, in the UK, one of the two very heavy users of the procedure, reports from both government and the private sector, as well as a recent academic study, all put great emphasis on the importance for success of planning prior to the contract notice.[189] These UK studies have identified careful planning as essential to keep down the costs for both sides and also to attract bidders to the procedure: as explained in Chapter 3, there is significant evidence that bidders assess the level of preparation made by contracting authorities before becoming involved and may be unwilling to participate without evidence that this is adequate. They have also indicated that such planning often has not been given the attention that it deserves.[190] The same point regarding the importance of adequate planning is made strongly in Chapter 7 on Spain, where a study by Telles found a strong correlation between the level of planning and success in outcomes.[191] It is also relevant here to point to the experience of Denmark, reported in Chapter 6, where there has generally been both a high level of preparation, with high quality and detailed descriptive documents, and satisfaction with the outcomes.

Crucial in this planning process, of course, is identification of the actual requirement and the degree of specification of that requirement. It is essential from the perspective of value for money and an efficient procedure that the contracting authority should undertake adequate research to determine its requirement and to draft the parameters of the project in an appropriate manner. The aim in this respect should be to minimise the time and costs for those involved in the dialogue from both sides whilst at the same time ensuring that the authority is able to benefit from innovations and different approaches available in the market.[192] Burnett has drawn a distinction between two main approaches in this respect – which are in fact specifically recognised and distinguished in the Recommendations issued by the Public Procurement Office in Lithuania.[193] One is the 'consultative approach' to

[188] See also Burnett, *Competitive Dialogue*, n. 3 above, pp. 83–96, who discusses in detail the practical considerations that need to be addressed.

[189] See Ch. 3, section 5.2. [190] Ch. 3, section 5.2. [191] See Ch. 7, section 5.2.

[192] Burnett, *Competitive Dialogue*, n. 3 above, p. 108.

[193] *Ibid.*, pp. 107–8; and Ch. 10, section 5.6.

dialogue, whereby the authority sets out a preferred solution at the start of the dialogue based on its own prior investigations (although perhaps also considering alternative approaches proposed during the dialogue),[194] with competition being based on the detail of how those solutions will be implemented and on financial aspects. Under this approach, for example, the basic site and design of a building – such as a school – will be specified and competition might occur based on materials used and the means of ensuring delivery. The other approach is an 'investigative' approach, according to which the contracting authority sets out a very broad description of a project, and the solutions emerge through the dialogue itself. For example, in a privately financed project for the provision of improved school facilities for an existing school, an extreme version of this approach would involve setting out the need for a school for a certain number of pupils without specifying the site or design, leaving economic operators to propose different ways of meeting the requirement. This could potentially involve, for example, refurbishing the existing school; demolishing the existing school and constructing a new one on the same site (with various different designs being submitted by different participants); or demolishing the existing school and using the land for commercial purposes whilst erecting a new school on a different site (with, again, the possibility of various different designs and sites). Obviously, these are shades on a spectrum and there are numerous possibilities in between. It can be noted that Burnett generally favours an approach that lies significantly towards the 'consultative' end of the spectrum as offering best value for money overall, even though this involves more work and cost for the contracting authority at the start of the process.

Another issue that UK practical experience has highlighted as crucial in the planning stage is identification of issues that are to be open to discussion in the dialogue – whilst the legislation expressly *permits* discussion of all aspects of the contract, in practice confining the dialogue to limited issues identified in advance is perceived as making a significant contribution to reducing costs when compared with an approach that potentially leaves open all contractual issues for discussion in the dialogue phase.[195] As Burnett has observed, however:[196]

[194] As to recommendations for the matters that should be addressed in the preferred solution, see Burnett, *Competitive Dialogue*, n. 3 above, p. 113.

[195] See Ch. 3, section 5.2.

[196] Burnett, *Competitive Dialogue*, n. 3 above, p. 39.

> This is far from being an easy judgment – at one extreme lies a provisionally preferred solution which is absolutely prescriptive and, at the other, a set of objectives, performance standards and operating constraints but no preferences between the means of achieving the desired outcomes.
>
> The extent to which scope should be allowed for variation, and what kind of variations should be permitted, within its provisionally preferred *solution is a key judgment for the contracting authority.* [Emphasis added.]

Other issues identified by practitioners and studies in the UK as calling for early planning (and not always addressed in the past, according to those studies) include organisational preparation within an authority (including governance and resourcing for negotiations); planning of the procedure itself (number, nature and timing of the phases etc.); and development of documentation and criteria (selection and award criteria).[197]

The importance of the planning phase is clearly one of the key lessons to be learned by countries intending to use competitive dialogue, which may wish to study the experiences of other EU Member States and to draft guidance or even legislation to guide their own contracting authorities. It is interesting that even prior to any actual experience with competitive dialogue, Lithuania, through its Public Procurement Office, drafted detailed Recommendations which included much precise guidance on the planning stage, including a detailed checklist and guidance on evaluating the state of the market prior to the procedure.[198] The UK government is in the process of drafting further significant material on planning to avoid future problems experienced by some contracting authorities and there is also, for example, material on this subject produced in Germany, including by the PPP task forces set up there.[199]

One reason for careful planning that needs some attention in a book focused on legal issues is its importance for avoiding legal difficulties. It appears that the equal treatment principle prohibits, at the very least, any material change to either the nature of a project or the stated rules of the procedure without 'rewinding' the procedure to the extent necessary to allow all relevant parties to participate on the changed terms.[200] For example, if the content of a project as advertised is changed, the change will be material in this sense if there are economic operators who were

[197] Ch. 3, section 5; and see also Burnett, *Competitive Dialogue*, n. 3 above, pp. 83–96.

[198] See Ch. 10, section 5.2. [199] See Ch. 5, section 5.2.

[200] By analogy with Case C-454/06, *pressetext Nachrichtenagentur* v. *Austria* [2008] ECR I-4401, concerning changes to concluded contracts.

not interested in the original project but might have been interested in the revised project – and it will then be necessary to re-advertise the changed project to allow them to participate on the revised terms. Similarly, if minimum technical or financial requirements are stated in the contract notice but later deemed unnecessary, they probably cannot be removed without giving a new opportunity to participate – through a new notice – if there might be economic operators who failed to respond to the original notice because of those particular previous conditions. In some cases, the rules against change might be even stricter, precluding even changes that are not material in the above sense, where allowing change might give the contracting authority an opportunity to manipulate the situation in favour of a particular bidder (as discussed, for example, in section 5.6 below in the context of award criteria). Without careful planning, there is thus a danger of a potentially costly and time-consuming rewinding of the procedure. This issue is discussed further in section 5.2 below in the specific context of changes to the contract notice; in section 5.6 in relation to changes to the contract award procedure; and in section 5.8 in relation to changes to the project after appointment of the preferred bidder. However, it is a wider issue that could potentially affect many aspects of the procedure.

Although there are no specific legal rules on the preparatory stage, equal treatment and transparency apply. The application of the equal treatment principle has given rise to some issues in the UK in the context of consultations with the market in advance of the contract notice. As explained in section 5.2.2 of Chapter 3, such consultations are used widely in the UK. They are considered relevant to decide whether to use competitive dialogue in the first place, to gauge interest and also to help develop the initial technical requirements. As explained in Chapter 3, a 2010 government review found that both public and private sectors felt that these were essential and that earlier and more extensive consultations would improve competitive dialogue still further. Consultations are also undertaken in other Member States – such as Germany – although not all have experience of this (they were not held in any of the three competitive dialogues undertaken in Portugal at the time of the study).[201] However, as Chapter 3 explains,[202] use of consultations in an effective way is considered to

[201] See Ch. 7, section 5.2.

[202] See further Ch. 3, section 5.2.2, on these points.

give rise to legal risk for contracting authorities in the UK: whilst it is considered easier to obtain helpful information through detailed dialogue with a limited number of participants than in a very broad consultation, contracting authorities also fear that doing this might violate the equal treatment principle. As a result, practitioners take very different approaches to this issue: those that do engage in detailed dialogue with a few economic operators do so as transparently as possible, documenting discussions carefully and making the documentation publicly available; but others shy away from such detailed dialogue.

5.3. *Confidentiality of information and solutions*

Article 29(3) of Directive 2004/18 states that contracting authorities may not reveal to the other participants solutions proposed or other confidential information[203] communicated by a candidate participating in the dialogue without the candidate's agreement. Furthermore, Article 29(6) provides that the contracting authority shall ask the participants in the procedure to submit their final tenders on the basis of the solution or solutions presented and specified during the dialogue. From this it follows that the practice of selecting all or some of the aspects of different candidates' solutions and including them as the basis for the final tender of other candidates – a practice sometimes referred to as 'cherry-picking' – is not permitted unless the participant agrees. In the absence of such agreement, each participant must submit a bid based on its own proposal for a solution. In this respect, Article 29(3) supplements the general provision in Article 6 of the Directive, which is a general provision on confidentiality in award procedures under the Directive.[204]

In line with the general approach adopted to transposing competitive dialogue into national legislation, Member States' legislation on this points corresponds essentially to the wording of Article 29 itself, and typically does not clarify what should be considered as confidential or establish procedures for classification of the information as such. The Portuguese and Lithuanian rules are interesting exceptions

[203] It is not clear how other confidential information should be defined. See on this point Ch. 12, section 5.3.

[204] This provision concerns information forwarded to the contracting authority which has been designated as confidential, in particular technical or trade secrets and the confidential aspects of tenders.

as they state that the contracting authority must treat information as confidential if the participant has classified it as such.[205] This solution has an apparent flaw as it does not open up for the assessment of the contracting authority of the confidential nature of the information. Nevertheless, this approach forces the participant to consider the issue and to take action to safeguard its interests. The common practice developed in the UK[206] has some of the same features, but differs in important respects. According to this practice, the participants must mark up any specific information they regard as confidential if they want to be sure that it is not shared with other bidders. If a contracting authority disagrees with the classification of the information as confidential, it will warn the bidder before sharing it and, if agreement cannot be reached, give the participant the option of withdrawing the information.[207] Similar procedures have been developed by Dutch procurement agencies.[208]

The approach in France appears to be fundamentally different as the perception is that it is the contracting authority that must take active measures to respect confidentiality.[209] The German approach appears to be similar to the French, and the German implementation goes a step further as it is specified that solutions shall not be communicated to other participants or passed to third parties. The German legislation thereby ensures that the proposed solutions are not communicated to and used in other projects by third parties.[210]

As we discuss in section 5.6, a frequent practice in Member States is for the contracting authority to conduct the dialogue with all qualified candidates or a selection of candidates shortlisted, and subsequently to allow all participants to bid after revising the documentation. It appears that many tenderers fear in this situation that contracting authorities will not respect the confidentiality of information and solutions, or at

[205] See Ch. 7, section 5.3; and Ch. 10, section 5.3 (which indicates that all information in bids is often classified as confidential by the participants in Lithuania to cut off third parties' access to the information).

[206] Ch. 3, section 5.3. [207] Ch. 3, section 5.3.

[208] See Ch. 12, section 5.3, for details of the procedure. However, this procedure does not appear to be used for the solutions as any information relating to proposed solutions will automatically be considered confidential.

[209] French contracting authorities will generally ask the participants to sign a non-disclosure agreement. Where the contracting authority aims at drafting a common solution on the basis of the proposed solutions, this must be done with candidates' permission: Ch. 4, sections 5.2 and 5.5.

[210] Ch. 5, section 5.3.

least initially feared that this would not be the case.[211] On the other hand, as emphasised in section 5.6 below, there have been thousands of competitive dialogue procedure and these have not led to any case law on the issue.[212]

It is an unsettled and frequently debated issue whether a contracting authority can insert a tender condition in the contract notice or descriptive document to the effect that the participants must accept that the contracting authority may share its solution with the other participants.[213] One point of view is that this is excluded since it essentially undermines the protection given to bidders in Article 29(3).[214] However, it is submitted that the better view is that this is permitted if the contracting authority considers it a useful commercial approach in the circumstances,[215] and a similar view is expressed in the European Commission's Explanatory Note on competitive dialogue.[216] A contracting authority using such a tender condition from the very outset of the procedure risks, however, a failure of the procedure if potential tenderers oppose the sharing of solutions and know-how; and such tender conditions do not appear to be common.[217] As discussed in section 5.10 below, contracting authorities can specify prices and payments to the participants in the dialogue, a practice that can facilitate agreement to information-sharing. However, as section 5.10 explains, it is not common in most Member States studied for payment to be used for this purpose.

5.4. *Advertising requirements (contract notice etc.)*

The first formal step of the award procedure is the publication in the OJEU of a notice advertising the contract, to inform the market of the

[211] See, for example, Ch. 3, section 5.3 (UK); Ch. 8, section 4.4 (Spain); Ch. 6 (Denmark); and Ch. 5, section 5.3 (Germany).

[212] Note that tenderers in Denmark have generally not considered that the confidentiality rules have been violated in procedures in which they have participated: see Ch. 6, section 5.3.

[213] See further Ch. 12, section 5.3 (Netherlands); Ch. 9 (Poland); Ch. 5 (Germany); Ch. 6 (Denmark); and Ch. 3 (UK).

[214] See also Ch. 5, section 5.3, on Germany, where it is stated that such a tender condition would run counter to the purpose of the confidentiality rules which is to protect bidders from having their solutions revealed; also Ch. 9, section 5.6, on Poland.

[215] See also Ch. 12, section 5.3, on the Netherlands; and Ch. 6 on Denmark.

[216] See the Explanatory Note, n. 33 above, p. 7, footnote 21.

[217] However, it has been seen in at least one Danish case by Treumer; and there are a few examples from the UK: see Ch. 3, section 5.3.

contract and to allow economic operators to express their interest. This is required for all competitive dialogue procedures by Article 35(2) of the Directive, as well as for open and restricted procedures and for negotiated procedures with a notice.[218]

The Directive expressly envisages that notices may also be published at national level, although not before the date on which they are sent to the Commission, and national notices must not contain additional information (Article 36(5)). As mentioned in section 3, many Member States do supplement the EU obligation with requirements to advertise in national publications or on national websites: this is the case, for example, with France, Italy, the Netherlands, Poland, Lithuania and Spain, which have general requirements of this kind and apply them to competitive dialogue.[219] In the UK, advertising on a national website is also required of some contracting authorities – although (in accordance with the UK's regulatory tradition) by government policy rather than legal rules.[220]

The main legal issue on notices that was highlighted in the studied countries is the need for – and difficulty of – drafting a notice that provides for sufficient flexibility for a competitive dialogue procedure, but also gives an adequate indication of the subject-matter of the contract, both to meet the Directive's legal requirement for a description in the notice[221] and to attract the right bidders. As noted in section 2, EU law probably requires a new notice if any change made to the description in the notice is a material one,[222] making it important to get the notice right to avoid the cost and delay of a new notice. As Chapter 3 explains,[223] the difficulty of drafting suitable notices in these circumstances has been highlighted by UK practitioners, and in 2008 the European Commission commenced infraction proceedings in relation to a situation of this kind – leading the UK government to issue specific advice to contracting authorities on this matter.[224]

[218] And, for competitive dialogue, see also Art. 29(2) stating that authorities must publish a contract notice which must set out their needs and requirements.

[219] As reported in section 5.4 of Chs. 4, 11, 10, 9, 12 and 8, respectively. Portugal also has a requirement for national publication, along with many other special national rules, as discussed below.

[220] See Ch. 3 at 5.4.

[221] Case C-423/07, *Commission* v. *Spain*, judgment of 22 April 2010.

[222] *pressetext*, n. 200 above. This applies also for contracts outside the Directives: Case C-91/08, *Wall*, n. 42 above.

[223] Ch. 3, section 5.4.2. [224] Ch. 3, section 5.4.2.

5.5. *The selection phase: choosing the candidates to participate in the dialogue*

Once the procedure has been advertised, interested economic operators will contact the contracting authority to indicate their interest. The authority then needs to decide which of these are to be invited to participate in the next phase – the 'dialogue' phase – in which (as described in section 5.6) it will begin to discuss with the participants the possible solutions and the terms on which those solutions can be offered.

In competitive dialogue procedures, as with restricted procedures and negotiated procedures with a notice, but in contrast with open procedures, authorities are not required to invite all interested economic operators, and need not even invite all qualified firms; they may limit below this the number to be invited into the dialogue, provided that a sufficient number of suitable candidates is available (Article 44(3)). Doing this can significantly reduce the costs of procedures for both the government and supply side.

As regards the numbers to be invited, Article 44(3) of the Public Sector Directive provides that the authority must take a minimum of three qualifying firms through to the dialogue, and in any event sufficient to ensure genuine competition.

The rules on how the selection is to be made can be found in Articles 44–52 of the Public Sector Directive. In brief,[225] they allow authorities to choose based on the same kinds of criteria that may be used to *exclude* suppliers, in particular financial and technical criteria. One view is that these selection criteria for exclusion are exhaustive of the criteria that may be used, whilst another view, however, is that certain other criteria may also be considered, provided that they are objective and non-discriminatory as is explicitly required by Article 44(3).[226]

Following their general approach to implementing competitive dialogue, national legislation on the number to be selected typically simply

[225] See further Arrowsmith, n. 3 above, pp. 462–73; S. Treumer, 'The Selection of Qualified Firms to be Invited to Tender under the EC Procurement Directives' (1998) 7 *Public Procurement Law Review* 147; D. Triantafyllou and D. Mardas, 'Criteria for Qualitative Selection in Public Procurement: A Legal and Economic Analysis' (1995) 4 *Public Procurement Law Review* 145.

[226] For the former view, see, for example, Arrowsmith. n. 3 above; for the latter, see, for example. Treumer, n. 220 above, and Ch. 6, section 5.5, on Denmark; and see also Ch. 5, section 5.5, where Burgi reports a division of views amongst German scholars.

repeats the Directive. However, a couple of countries deviate from this approach, requiring a higher number of invitees. Thus in Italy the number of participants may only be limited if required for 'justified needs of good administration'[227] and the number invited must not be less than six.[228] This reflects the fact that in Italy selecting only a limited number from those qualified is a relative novelty, and case law relating to all other tendering procedures obliges contracting authorities to invite all qualified economic operators.[229] In addition, in Poland authorities must invite five participants where the contract value meets the thresholds of the Public Sector Directive.[230]

As regards application of the legal provisions in practice, it is common in states whose legislation allows this for authorities to limit the number of invitees, rather than to invite all those qualified. Typically, contracting authorities select three to five candidates.[231] In Spain and Portugal, the approach is different, however: authorities avoid restricting the numbers of candidates in advance. In Spain, the consequence is that twenty or more candidates have been invited to take part in the dialogue in some instances, straining the resources of contracting authorities and failing to ensure effective dialogue.[232] In the handful of competitive dialogue cases that have occurred in Portugal, authorities so far have preferred to invite all of the qualified candidates.[233]

It is interesting that Burnett suggests four – a common number in the practice of Member States – as the general optimum number of candidates to ensure both compliance with the Directive's requirements for genuine competition and efficient procurement, on the basis that this allows three to remain even if one drops out, but also keeps costs proportionate.[234] However, we suggest that, whilst this is indeed often an appropriate number, the optimum will vary, both according to the values and circumstances of the Member State, as discussed in section 2, and the circumstances of the procurement and market (such as the actual likelihood of drop-outs).

[227] Ch. 11, section 5.5. [228] *Ibid.* [229] *Ibid.*

[230] Or three when the procedure is used for below-threshold contracts: Ch. 9, section 5.5.

[231] In France, contracting authorities normally fix the maximum of candidates at five: Ch. 4, section 5.4; in Germany, it is typically three to five: Ch. 5, section 5.5; in Denmark, it is normally three to four: Ch. 6, section 5.5; and, in the Netherlands, three to five: Ch. 12, section 5.5. In the UK, for PPP projects, the number typically ranges from three to seven: Ch. 3, section 5.5.

[232] See Ch. 8, section 4.6. [233] See Ch. 7, section 2.5.3.

[234] Burnett, *Competitive Dialogue*, n. 3 above, pp. 97–8.

In practice, the criteria for selecting between qualified candidates correspond frequently to the Directive's criteria for choosing which candidates are qualified. This is the case, for example, in France, Germany, the UK and Poland.[235] These criteria typically are applied in a relative manner in the sense that the contracting authority selects the best qualified, based on their experience, financial standing etc.[236] (It is not necessarily the case, however, that the contracting authorities look at exactly the same financial/technical issues at the exclusion stage and when making the selection; one approach is to consider as qualified firms that have adequate general technical experience, but then to select amongst them based on which have the most experience relevant to the project in question). However, the approach of using only the 'qualification' criteria has not been followed universally. Thus in Denmark – following the view that authorities are *not*, in making the selection limited to the criteria expressly listed in the Public Sector Directive criteria for exclusion – a method is seen in practice according to which the authority aims at composing a field of prospective tenderers resulting in the best possible competition: it will aim at the best blend taking account of a variety of elements such as the experience and size of the company, such as by choosing a mix of experienced firms and newcomers.[237] In Germany there is a debate over whether the selection criteria are limited to the same criteria as are permitted by the Directive for qualification.[238] However, it can be noted that reserving invitations to dialogue for a certain number of SMEs that meet the selection criteria has been considered as contrary to the principle of equal treatment by the French courts.[239]

Finally, Member States' experience suggests that it is often important to keep qualification and selection decisions under review throughout the procedure. Competitive dialogue procedures tend to be of longer duration than open procedures or restricted procedures and the chances of changes potentially impacting upon selection decisions are therefore higher.[240] This is relevant not only from the perspective of value for

[235] See respectively, Ch. 4, section 5.5, Ch. 5, section 5.5, Ch. 4, section 5.5, and Ch. 9, section 5.5.

[236] *Ibid.* It appears to be obligatory to apply the relative method in Poland: see Ch. 9, section 5.5.

[237] See Ch. 6, section 5.5. [238] See Ch. 5, section 5.5. [239] See Ch. 4, section 5.4.

[240] See Ch. 3, section 5.5, on the UK. In France, there is full room in the legislation (and support from guidance) for the composition of a consortium to change during the competitive dialogue procedure: cf. Ch. 4, section 5.4.

money but also from a legal perspective: the principle of equal treatment[241] may require that, if any change occurs that would render a participant unqualified or would have meant that that participant was not selected to participate in the dialogue, the decision to qualify or select will need to be changed. This could result, for example, from a change to membership in a bidding consortium[242] – a not infrequent occurrence in competitive dialogue procedures.

5.6. *The dialogue phase*

5.6.1. Introduction

Once the participants have been selected as described at section 5.5 above, the contracting authority will then commence the 'dialogue' phase of the procedure. In this respect, Article 29(3) states:

> Contracting authorities shall open, with the candidates selected in accordance with the relevant provisions of Articles 44 to 52, a dialogue the aim of which shall be to identify and define the means best suited to satisfying their needs. They may discuss all aspects of the contract with the chosen candidates during this dialogue.

The Directive does not contain explicit rules on how this dialogue is to be structured, except for the fact that it explicitly *confirms* a certain flexibility in this by stating in Article 29(4) that (if indicated in the contract notice or descriptive document) the dialogue may take place 'in successive stages' and that these may result in the number of solutions considered being reduced (by applying the award criteria) before the final tender stage. Apart from this provision, and from reiterating the need for equal treatment, particularly with regard to provision of information and stating rules on confidentiality (which are discussed at section 5.3 above), the Directive does not regulate this stage of the process.

This leaves Member States or (if allowed by national legislation) their contracting authorities free to design the process in various different ways. Again following the general approach towards competitive dialogue, national legislation has in fact generally conferred upon contracting authorities the full freedom allowed by the Public Sector Directive

[241] By analogy with the material change doctrine applying to, for example, changes to concluded contracts: see section 5.2 above.

[242] Such changes are permitted in principle: Case C-57/01, *Makedoniko Metro and Michaniki* v. *Elliniko Dimosio* [2003] ECR I-1091.

itself as regards the organisation of the dialogue phase in the above respects.[243] The major exception to this is Portugal which, as Chapter 7 explains, requires contracting authorities to adhere to a very specific structure and approach.

5.6.2. Models for developing the project in the dialogue phase

We have seen in section 5.2 that the descriptive document issued at the start of competitive dialogue may differ in the degree of flexibility left to candidates, according to whether an approach towards the 'consultative' or 'investigative' end of the spectrum is to be adopted. As regards further development of the project *during the dialogue stage itself*, again different approaches, or 'models', are seen in European practice. As with the approach to specifying the project's initial parameters, the differences are again a matter of degree – they are shades on a spectrum rather than distinct concepts – but again are nevertheless valuable for descriptive purposes. These different models are outlined below.

It should be noted that each model can apply regardless of whether the initial approach is a consultative one with a relatively detailed initial specification or an investigative one in which the project's parameters are set only in broad outline – in either situation the initial project description and terms can be refined either hardly at all (as with Model 1, the 'own-solutions' model, below) or to a significant degree using the participants' proposals (Model 3, the designated solution model, below). The models referred to say nothing about the degree of detail in the final tender documentation – an 'own-solutions' approach where the initial parameters are narrowly set could result in broader terms for final tendering than a 'designated solution' approach that is used to narrow what were initially broad project terms.

Model 1: The 'own-solutions model' At one end of the spectrum is what may be called the 'own-solutions' model[244] (a similar model being referred to in relation to Italy as the 'Chinese walls'

[243] Only the legislation in Portugal appears to deviate from this pattern as it follows from the analysis in this section.

[244] This name is applied in Ch. 3 on the UK (section 5.6.1) and in Ch. 8 on Spain to a model falling broadly within our 'own-solutions' model, although the author of the latter chapter rules out by definition a set of common technical specifications within which different solutions are presented.

model).[245] In this model, tenders propose their own solutions based on the initial project description and discuss these with the contracting authority on a confidential basis. The final tenders are revisions of the solutions developed during the dialogue by the individual tenderers that submit them. The contracting authority does not designate a single specific solution at the end of the dialogue phase nor refine or develop the tender documentation using elements of the proposed solutions.

An example might be where an authority tenders a project for an automatic parking facility in a country where this type of project has no precedent. In such a facility, the car is picked up by computerised lifting machinery that places it inside the parking facility on a shelving system (making it unnecessary for the driver to find a parking space and taking up much less space than a conventional car park). The facility is to be situated near a shopping centre close to the city centre with heavy traffic, meaning that both capacity and the speed with which the cars can be handled are important. The authority initially identifies the qualified applicants and chooses five of them to invite to the dialogue. It then opens the dialogue and proceeds with strict emphasis on confidentiality and observance of a stated ban on cherry-picking elements from the different solutions. It carries out the dialogue in stages to eliminate participants whose solutions are of no interest due to their pricing, capacity or speed. Two participants are formally eliminated in this way because of low capacity and because it takes too long to retrieve the cars. The remaining three tenderers are invited to submit their final bids on the basis of the individual solutions developed during the dialogue. The solution offered in the tender selected as the most economically advantageous offers important benefits in terms of both capacity and speed, as well as a competitive price. The tenderer offering this solution has previously provided parking facilities in urban areas where speed and capacity have been important, whereas the business concept of the two other tenderers is based on their facilities outside city centres where price and operation costs are typically more significant.

This is arguably an approach that was expected by the European Commission to become standard, either in a pure form or at least as part of a hybrid approach (as to which see Model 3 below): thus the

[245] Ch. 11, section 5.6.

Commission's Explanatory Note states that 'generally speaking these final tenders are based on the solution (or possibly solutions) of each of their participants'.[246] An approach based at least in part on tenderers' own solutions is also perhaps the first one that comes to mind when reading the Public Sector Directive. This approach appears to be applied frequently in some of the largest Member States: thus it is found, for example, in the UK, France, Germany and Italy.[247] A potential drawback of a pure form of this model is that the contracting authority must accept one solution even though this might not be as good as a solution drawn from a combination of offered solutions that draws on the collective know-how and innovation of all participants. It is also possible that the tenderer that originally proposes the solution is not the one that can provide it on the best terms. Effective and transparent comparison between the solutions can also sometimes be difficult, although this depends on how different the solutions are in practice. However, a major advantage of this model is that competing firms can be expected to be fully motivated to submit innovative and original solutions. To protect their commercial interests, candidates may hold back on their ideas for creative and innovative solutions during the dialogue[248] and this can lead to shortcomings in the final tender – but this does depend on all the circumstances and how the procedure is operated (in the UK, for example, it is common to hold a full dry-run of tenders in the dialogue stage in which in practice tenderers do fully disclose their proposed solutions prior to close of dialogue). It may also be that certain solutions can only be provided by one firm – for example, because they depend on ownership of specific land or intellectual property rights.

Model 2: The designated solution model At the other end of the spectrum is what we call the 'designated solution' model. In this model, the contracting authority, openly and without keeping the solutions confidential, picks the best solution(s) as the foundation for the final tender conditions. This may involve quite substantial refinement and development from the original descriptive document, from a relatively

[246] Explanatory Note, n. 33 above, section 3.3. See also Ch. 5, section 5.5 on France, where it is stated that this model is most in line with the 'spirit' of competitive dialogue.

[247] See respectively Ch. 3, section 5.6.1, Ch. 4, section 5, Ch. 5, section 5.6, and Ch. 11, section 5.6.

[248] See, for example, Ch. 12, section 5.3.

broad description to a much more precisely specified solution.[249] This model appears to have been applied in its pure form by a few contracting authorities. For example, it appears to have been used in Spain in at least fifteen procedures.[250] A variation of this model is obligatory in Portugal where the objective of the dialogue stage is the drafting of a specified single solution at the end[251] – although contracting authorities in Portugal must treat information as confidential if it is classified as such by the candidates, creating potential difficulties in including such information in drafting the specified solution.[252]

Under this model, the designated solution could potentially use elements from a number of proposals or could be based wholly or mainly on one suggested solution. Of course, if the solution is based significantly on the proposals of one or a limited number of participants, and this gives these participants a competitive advantage, this could potentially threaten the level of competition and the contracting authority must keep this in mind. This kind of model has been labelled in the chapter on Spain as the 'common-trunk' model;[253] where solutions are taken from several tenders, it has been referred to as the 'crowd-sourced' model[254] and in the chapter on Italy as the 'patchwork' model;[255] and, where the solution is based on one particular proposal, the label of the 'promoter model' has been applied (Italy).[256]

An example of this approach might be where a contracting authority tenders out the construction of a highway. The route is particularly challenging because it runs through the mountains and there are many considerations to take into account to limit damage to the habitat of several endangered species. The authority outlines a fairly basic description of the project in the contract notice and descriptive document, in which it highlights these environmental challenges. As it will be time-consuming to participate in the dialogue, the authority offers payments for participation in the various stages. At the same time, it reserves the right to integrate elements from the suggested solutions into the designated solution that the final bids must adhere to. It also specifies in the initial tender documents that the dialogue might result in a revised and

[249] Here, the authority must take care not to introduce any *changes* that are material without following the appropriate rules – for example, a material change to the project advertised could lead to a need to re-advertise (see section 5.2 above).

[250] See Ch. 8, section 5.6.3.3. [251] See Ch. 7, in particular section 5.3. [252] *Ibid.*

[253] See Ch. 8, section 5.6.3.3, on Spain. [254] Ch. 8, section 5.6.3.3.

[255] See Ch. 11, section 5.6, on Italy. [256] Ch. 11, section 5.6.

expanded project description. The notice provides that the authority will select a minimum of three and a maximum of six for the dialogue phase and that the procedure will take place in stages. However, it does not reserve the right to reduce the number of participants during dialogue as it wishes to obtain tenders from as many of the participants as possible. Ten economic operators apply and six are selected to participate in the dialogue. However, three later withdraw because the contracting authority does not integrate any elements of their suggested solutions. The remaining three submit bids on the basis of a designated solution that contains elements taken from all their suggestions. One important element taken from one of the tenderers relates to a novel method for removing rock by the use of explosives, which is less costly than other methods in particular because it ensures better control of what is removed by the explosion. Another tenderer has developed a system of small bridges that ensures that certain species of wildlife can pass from one side of the highway to another without any risk of being killed in traffic, and this is also included as a requirement. The designated solution also includes two elements proposed by the third tenderer, namely, use of a new 'everlasting' blend of asphalt developed by an Austrian professor and the use of a thin concrete railing along the road with a core of steel, that can be delivered at low cost. As the final bids are based on a single designated solution, they are in general very similar. The bidder that originally suggested the new blend of asphalt and the thin concrete railing offers good financial terms, in part because of its cost advantage in providing these elements of the designated solution, and is chosen as the most economically advantageous bidder.

The procedure for the automatic car parking facility referred to under Model 1 above could also be operated through a designated-solutions rather than an own-solutions approach. In that case, the contracting authority would again make it clear that it reserves the right to use elements proposed by the various bidders when it draws up the basis for the final tenders. Assume, for example, that 2,000 square metres of the land intended for the parking facility cannot be built on because of an obstacle on the ground – for example, a technical installation such as a transformer station. All tenderers but one propose a facility with a ground surface covering all of the land apart from this 2,000 square metre area. However, one tenderer proposes a construction that is extended over the 2,000 square metre area which exceeds the height of the obstacle, thus providing a much greater capacity for the facility. This innovation is then integrated into the designated solution.

Model 3: The hybrid model A third model that appears to be common in practice is what may be referred to as the 'hybrid model' – a mix of the first and second models. In this model, as a starting point a dialogue takes place with all invited participants under conditions of confidentiality. The dialogue ends with the production of tender specifications and conditions that have been developed from the initial descriptive documents. The formulation of the tender specification for the final tenders, however, ensures that all the solutions that have been discussed and that remain in the dialogue are covered by the specification, and refinements to and changes from the draft documents are in practice often minor. All tenderers submit their bid on the basis of the revised common specifications and conditions.

This may be illustrated by referring again to the example of the mountain highway project discussed under Model 2 above. We may assume that the contracting authority commences with a fairly basic description of the envisaged project in the notice and descriptive document, in which it highlights the environmental challenges. It also specifies that the dialogue will take place under conditions of confidentiality. The contract notice provides that the authority will select a minimum of three and a maximum of six to take part in the dialogue and that the procedure will take place in stages. Seven companies apply to participate, and four are selected. One of the participants withdraws, and the contracting authority therefore does not make use of its right to reduce numbers. The remaining three tenderers submit their bids on the basis of revised terms applicable to all tenderers. The specifications remain essentially unchanged with regard to the content of the works, which are still for the most part described in the original broad terms based on functionality. However, the authority has now in addition specified that the solution must ensure that wildlife can pass from one side of the road to another without disturbing traffic and being at risk from traffic. This adjustment was inspired by the solution of small bridges for wildlife proposed by one of the tenderers, as set out under model 2 above. The tenderer that proposes the new blend of asphalt and use of a thin concrete railing with a core of steel, as described under Model 2 above, is, however, chosen as providing the most economically advantageous tender. A part of its winning solution is a combination of tunnels under the highway and bridges above the highway that enable wildlife to pass from one side to the other.

This general approach has been seen in the UK, the Netherlands and Denmark (it being the predominant approach in Denmark), occasionally in Spain (where two instances were found in the research for the chapter on Spain) and also in France, where it is used in addition to the own-solutions model.[257]

It can be noted that cherry-picking can to some extent take place when the hybrid model is applied and could potentially lead to issues over the incorporation of confidential information or solutions[258] (although this is not necessarily the case: for example, the issue may not arise at all since modification and development of the tender specifications might cover matters that are not confidential). Given this fact, and the fact[259] that practitioners frequently fear that authorities will not respect confidentiality, one might expect a developed case law at national level on confidentiality and organisation of the dialogue. However, it appears that this does not exist.[260] It is also noteworthy, as stated in section 5.3, that interviewed tenderers in general considered that confidentiality had been respected. One explanation for this may be that authorities are fully aware of the potential pitfalls and in general balance the conflicting interests in a manner that is considered appropriate by tenderers. However, another explanation might be that tenderers' interests differ fundamentally depending on the model used.[261] As is pointed out in Chapter 8 on Spain, where elements of the solution are taken from different tenders they have an interest in influencing the drafting of the solution as this may give them a competitive advantage;[262] thus they may be willing to submit highly detailed information on their solution and may hesitate to challenge the organisation of the procedure. Under the own-solutions model, on the other hand, tenderers will wish to prevent the contracting authority from transmitting their innovative ideas to competitors to their own competitive disadvantage.

[257] See Ch. 3, section 5.6.1 (UK), Ch. 12, section 5.6.4 (Netherlands), Ch. 6 (Denmark) (where this model has been applied in the majority of cases), Ch. 4, section 5.5 (France); and Ch. 8 (Spain) (where the model labelled 'common specifications' appears similar to this 'hybrid' approach).

[258] Compare also with Ch. 8, section 4.3, where the author is sceptical of the assurances of various Spanish contracting authorities that they fully ensured confidentiality of information and solutions when they have created common trunk solutions.

[259] See section 5.3 of this chapter.

[260] Based on, section 5.3 above on confidentiality, and the fact that case law on organisation of the dialogue was not reported in the countries studied for the book.

[261] See Ch. 8, section 4.7.3.3, on Spain.

[262] See Ch. 8, section 5.6.3.

5.6.3. The structure of the dialogue phase

5.6.3.1. General As well as affording flexibility in the approach towards defining the final requirement, as discussed above, the limited rules of the Directive and the general lack of further restrictions in national legislation also entail significant flexibility for contracting authorities in the way that the dialogue is structured in moving towards the final tender stage.

As mentioned earlier, this can involve discussions on all or some aspects of the contract: Article 29(3), as we have seen, specifically provides that authorities may discuss all aspects of the contract with chosen candidates. Thus the dialogue stage may address not only the technical solutions available, but also any of the terms on which those solutions might be provided, including financial terms, allocation of risks under the contract etc. These are all, of course, relevant to the basic purpose of the dialogue as stated in Article 29(3) which is to determine which is the best means of meeting the contracting authority's requirements. We should recall from section 5.2 above, however, that, whilst discussion of all aspects of the contract is allowed, it is not necessarily appropriate (and is certainly not legally *required*); and authorities need to plan carefully which precise aspects of the project should in practice be opened up for discussion in the dialogue stage.[263]

As seen above, the dialogue process in the sense of the Directive can also include various bidding stages.[264] These bidding stages do not necessarily involve complete tenders, but they are often tenders in outline form or dealing only with certain limited aspects of the project.[265] Such bidding stages are sometimes used to reduce the number of participants, as discussed later below. However, bidding phases are also often important, even when the numbers are not reduced, as an important tool for developing the project terms and the submitted solutions, as discussed in the paragraph below. Indeed, Burnett has suggested that interim bids should not be used at all for eliminating participants but

[263] See the further discussion in section 5.2.

[264] See also Explanatory Memorandum, n. 89 above, section 3.2, noting that, during the dialogue, authorities 'may ask the participants to specify their proposals in writing, possibly in the form of progressively completed/refined tenders, as implicitly assumed in Art. 29(5)'.

[265] As pointed out by the Commission in its Explanatory Memorandum, n. 89 above, section 3.2.1, it is clear that, even if considered to be 'tenders', they cannot be required to contain 'all the elements required and necessary for the performance of the project' given that this requirement only applies to final tenders (see section 5.7 below).

only for these other purposes[266] – for which they are considered 'a key element of the management of the process by the contracting authority'.[267]

Such discussions and bidding phases may be used, first, to help the authority determine the basis of final tenders – that is, to refine both the technical requirements and the contract terms, such as financial and contractual requirements. In this respect, they may be used, for example, to identify a designated solution based on the ideas put forward by one or more participants under the designated solution approach outlined in section 5.6.2 above; to refine draft contract terms that were designated as open to negotiation, based on what is acceptable to participants or on what will provide the best value for money; or to test whether the project is in fact affordable. They are also relevant to enable the bidders to understand the contracting authority's needs better and to incorporate these into their own final tenders. This may serve simply to ensure affordability and acceptability of the technical aspects of proposals – if these are unacceptable the participant might either be excluded or choose to withdraw, as discussed below, or might amend its proposal – or to enhance value for money (for example, a tenderer might decide to remove from its proposal a feature that is expensive but does not offer proportionate benefits for the contracting authority).

UK experience is illustrative, showing that the level of detail of proposals often increases as the dialogue progresses. As Chapter 3 explains,[268] the dialogue typically starts with outline proposals with no or limited financial information. The contracting authority will then frequently choose a limited number of participants to submit further proposals that then subsequently are developed in further detail and followed up by detailed proposals on both financial and technical matters. In some cases, there is even a 'dry-run' of the final tenders. These dry-run tenders are in content equivalent to the final tenders but are not treated as final tenders under Directives/national regulations. Their purpose is to ensure that no problems emerge in the final tenders, given that the lawful scope for adjustment after the formal final tender stage is both limited and uncertain.[269] Finally, the authority will then formally close the dialogue and call for final tenders, which are the fully detailed and costed proposals in binding form.[270] Likewise, in the

[266] See the discussion further below.
[267] Burnett, *Competitive Dialogue*, n. 3 above, p. 41. [268] Ch. 3, section 5.6.
[269] See sections 5.7 and 5.8 below. [270] See Ch. 3, section 5.6.1.

Netherlands, following a general initial kick-off meeting, the contracting authority will typically intensify the dialogue focusing on a limited range of solutions. One approach seen in Dutch practice (typical also in the UK and elsewhere) is to invite the remaining participants to submit final tenders considering all elements of the tender at the same time, whilst another (particularly for larger projects)[271] is to require participants to submit the finalised elements of the tender in parts during the discussion phase followed by a concluding submission of a tender in a final bidding phase.

5.6.3.2. Reducing the number of participants and solutions Article 29(3) of Directive 2004/18, as we have seen, expressly states that authorities may provide for the procedure to take place in successive stages 'in order to reduce the number of solutions to be discussed during the dialogue stage' by applying the pre-stated award criteria. This indicates that authorities can use initial tenders and/or discussions to eliminate certain proposed *solutions* from consideration before the final tender stage – for example, proposed solutions that are unaffordable, which do not adequately meet the authority's needs, or which contain unacceptable features such as excessive adverse environmental impact. Contracting authorities might also at this stage seek to eliminate not just proposals that do not meet acceptability thresholds, but also those that appear unlikely to succeed at final tender stage.

Whilst Article 29(3) refers to eliminating 'solutions', it is clear, looking at the provision in its context in the Directive, that it envisages the possibility of excluding candidates if the candidate's proposed solution is to be eliminated: it is not necessary to allow the candidate to continue in the process bidding against the solutions offered by others. This approach of eliminating candidates based on their solutions is relevant in those procedures in which tenderers will bid at least to some extent against their own solution, namely, under the 'own-solutions' or hybrid models.

The fact that such elimination is envisaged by the Directive is supported by Article 44(4), stating that '[i]n the final stage, the number arrived at shall make for genuine competition insofar as there are enough solutions or suitable candidates'; the reference to solutions here envisages that economic operators may be bidding only against their

[271] See Ch. 12.

own solutions. Further support for this view is found in recital 41, stating that authorities should be allowed to make provision for stages in the procedure in order gradually to reduce 'the number of tenders': a reduction in the number of tenders implies a reduction in the number of participants. This is also the point of view of the European Commission expressed in its Explanatory Note: this states that in the majority of cases, participants will only have developed one solution each, and the elimination of the solution therefore also entails the elimination of the participant.[272] The idea that reduction of participants is not possible is also incompatible with the confidentiality provisions and with other practical considerations: it is frequently impossible to allow tenderers whose solution have been eliminated to bid on the basis of solutions submitted by others because of either the confidentiality rules or exclusive rights, such as a bidder's ownership of suitable land. It should also be borne in mind that the details of competitive dialogue have been heavily inspired by UK practices on complex contracts prior to competitive dialogue, which often involved reducing the number of participants on the basis of outline submissions judged according to the contract award criteria.[273]

That the Directive indeed allows for reducing the number of participants on the basis of their proposals as well as for reducing the number of solutions themselves is the dominant interpretation in European legal theory.[274] It is also assumed in the practice of several Member States – for example, the UK, Germany, Spain, the Netherlands and Denmark.[275] It is noteworthy that many contracting authorities in these countries appear to have provided for the procedure to take place in successive

[272] Explanatory Note, n. 33 above, section 3.2.1, in particular footnote 29.

[273] See section 2.2 above and Ch. 3, section 2.

[274] Brown, n. 3 above, p. 174; Treumer, 'Competitive Dialogue', n. 3 above, p. 180; and Arrowsmith, n. 3 above, pp. 644–6. For literature in Danish, see Rubach-Larsen, n. 3 above, p. 75; S. Troels, S. Poulsen and S. E. Kalsmose-Hjelmborg, 'Hvor meget konkurrence skal der være i konkurrencepræget dialog? Om afvejningen af markedsåbning om offentlige ordregiveres behov inden for rammerne af EU's udbudsdirektiv' (2007B) *Ugeskrift for Retsvæsen* 34; M. Steinicke and L. Groesmeyer, *EU's udbudsdirektiver med kommentarer* (2nd edn, Copenhagen: Jurist- og Økonomforbundets Forlag, 2008), p. 329; R. Offersen, *Udbudsprocessen* (Copenhagen, 2010), p. 28; S. T Poulsen, P. S. Jakobsen and S. E. Hjelmborg, *EU Udbudsretten* (2nd edn, Copenhagen, 2011), p. 364. For a contrary point of view, see J. Fejø, in J. Fejø and S. Treumer (eds.), *EU's Udbudsregler – implementering og håndhævelse i Norden, J* (2006), p. 25.

[275] See respectively Ch. 3, section 5.6.1, Ch. 5, section 5.5, Ch. 8, section 4.7.2, Ch. 6, section 5.6 6 and Ch. 12, section 5.6.

stages with exclusion of participants[276] and participants are often excluded in practice on the basis of their solutions in the UK, Germany and the Netherlands.[277] Indeed, for the practical reasons noted, this possibility is fundamental to the way in which competitive dialogue is operated in many of these countries. Until recently, there has been no jurisprudence, but a German court has now confirmed that reduction in numbers in this way is possible.[278]

It is noteworthy that the possibility of stages in the procedures has not been introduced explicitly in Poland,[279] however, leading to doubts over whether this possibility is available there at all, and that the Portuguese legislation clearly and explicitly precludes reducing the number of participants[280] (although it is interesting – and perhaps significant – that the legislation does not address the problems that may arise with this in the context of the confidentiality rules, and the procedure is not actually used in Portugal in practice).

It is also interesting that in some countries, such as Spain and Denmark, contracting authorities also frequently abstain from reducing the number of participants, even though – as mentioned above – they reserve the right to do so and consider themselves entitled to do this.[281] Many contracting authorities have also deliberately chosen not to provide for reducing the number of participants at all. The decision not actually to reduce numbers, or even not to provide for the possibility in the first place, may be made for a variety of reasons. Thus, the practice of reducing numbers is sometimes perceived as very difficult, as lacking in transparency and as exposing the contracting authority to the risk of legal challenge.[282] It may also involve a risk of eliminating candidates without being sure that the candidate cannot offer the best value; this may be a concern where the number of candidates is reduced simply to limit the numbers participating, rather than because the candidates' solutions do not meet minimum acceptability limits; and where elimination takes place only on the basis of limited information (an issue discussed further in section 5.6.4 below). Furthermore, contracting authorities sometimes prefer not to limit competition more than strictly

[276] In Denmark, the *possibility* has been provided for in more than 50 per cent of procedures: see Ch. 6, section 4.
[277] See respectively Ch. 3, section 5.6.1, Ch. 5, section 5.6 and Ch. 12, section 5.6.
[278] Ch. 5, section 5.6. [279] Ch. 9, section 5.6. [280] Ch. 8, section 5.6.
[281] See respectively Ch. 8, section 4.7.2 and Ch. 6, section 5.6.
[282] See also Burnett, *Competitive Dialogue*, n. 3 above, pp. 127, who considers this is inadvisable from a value-for-money perspective as well as legally risky.

necessary, either because the number of qualified applicants fairly often turns out to be relatively low or because the authority has an interest in holding on to serious and competitive participants even though their number might be higher than anticipated.

Of course, if certain solutions are considered unacceptable or unlikely to succeed, but the contracting authority does not want to eliminate them formally (for example, because of the legal risk or because this judgment may turn out to be difficult to make definitively until a full tender is submitted), the authority might wish to provide feedback and then to leave the participant to decide whether or not to proceed. It may also wish to establish or clarify requirements that may be very difficult for certain participants to meet, but not to exclude them formally from the final tender stage.[283]

In some circumstances, especially where there is a high level of interest, reducing the numbers of participants in the dialogue stage can, however, play an important role in ensuring that costs are kept to a proportionate level both for the contracting authority and for the supply market. So far as the latter is concerned, competitive firms may also be discouraged from participating if the costs are too high in comparison with the likelihood of success, which is affected by the number of competitors. These have been important concerns in, for example, the UK, and explain the widespread practice of reducing numbers in the dialogue stage when adequate competition is available.[284]

5.6.4. Closure of the dialogue

Article 29(6) of the Directive provides that at the end of the dialogue the contracting authority must declare that the dialogue is concluded and inform the participants of this fact.

With regard to the formal closure of the dialogue, it is worth noting that an important point to emerge from experience is that the flexibility of the procedure enables all issues to be addressed fully during the dialogue stage, and that if this is done it can prevent difficulties arising at the final tendering stage as a result of errors or misunderstandings, insufficient information in tenders, or the desire to improve tenders. A useful practice to ensure the full benefit of this possibility is the UK practice mentioned above of holding a 'dry-run', whereby remaining

[283] See Ch. 8, section 4.7.2 (Spain) and Ch. 6, section 5.6 (Denmark). [284] See Ch. 3.

participants submit full tenders before the formal closing of the dialogue. This ensures that any remaining difficulties of this kind can be addressed before the final tender stage, whilst it is clear that this is still legally possible – important given the legal uncertainty over what kinds of discussions, corrections and amendments are allowed in the final tender stage itself (see section 5.7 below).

5.6.5. Award criteria

As noted in the outline of competitive dialogue in section 2.4, following the selection of the candidates to participate in the dialogue, both the dialogue phase and the final tender phase are mainly directed at choosing the best offer from amongst the selected candidates by applying the pre-stated award criteria. The basic rules in the Directive appear straightforward but, as will be seen below, there are some uncertainties in applying them, including some of particular relevance or importance for competitive dialogue; and the rules have also been supplemented by judge-made requirements based on the general transparency principle that add further uncertainty. The academic research in the UK has found that legal uncertainty in the area of award criteria is a major concern of those operating and advising on competitive dialogue in the UK, particularly in view of the high risk of legal challenge at this stage of the process and the serious consequences of such a challenge.[285] The existence of uncertainty in this area is reinforced by the fact that much of the – so far rather limited – case law in Member States on competitive dialogue has concerned issues relating to award criteria. These rules will be considered at this point in the chapter, since they are relevant for the dialogue stage; the discussion here will, however, cover points relevant for the application of the award criteria throughout the 'award phase', including the final tender stage discussed in section 5.7 below.

The subject of award criteria is governed, in particular, by Article 53 of the Public Sector Directive. For open, restricted or negotiated procedures[286] that do not involve variants, this requires the contracting authority to choose the winning tender based on either the lowest price or what the Directive refers to as 'the most economically advantageous tender' basis for the award (Article 53(1)). However, in the case of competitive dialogue the contracting authority *must* use the most economically advantageous tender basis (a rule stated in Article 29(1)), it being

[285] See Ch. 3, section 5.11.1.
[286] This applies only to negotiated procedures with a notice.

considered that price alone is not an appropriate basis for awarding contracts under competitive dialogue since (as also with any award procedures involving variants) the differences between the merits of solutions must be taken into account in evaluating bids.[287]

Article 53(1)(a) lists various factors which could be used, such as quality, running costs, after-sales service and delivery date, as well as price, but the list is not exhaustive: authorities may use other factors (as was previously established in the cases[288] and is now made clear in the text of the Directive). The criteria for choosing the most economically advantageous tender must be linked to the subject-matter of the contract, as stated expressly in Article 53(1)(a) (for example, they cannot generally concern matters relating only to the tenderer itself, such as whether it is an SME).

There are also important rules on the disclosure of the way in which the award will be made, which derive either from the explicit rules of the Directive or from the transparency principle as developed by the CJEU.

First, the contract notice itself must state whether the award will be based on lowest price or most economically advantageous tender.[289]

Secondly, when – as is required for competitive dialogue – the authority proposes to use the most economically advantageous criterion for award, Article 53(2) of the Directive requires the authority to state the criteria to be used, either in the contract notice or (for competitive dialogue) in the descriptive document.

Further, also under Article 53(2), the authority must state in the contract notice or descriptive document the 'relative weighting' of these award criteria – a requirement introduced for the first time in the 2004 Directive. The same provisions also state that this weighting may be expressed as a range, with a minimum and maximum weighting, where the authority considers this appropriate. There is an exception to the requirement for weighting when, 'in the opinion of the contracting authority', it is not possible to provide weightings on objective grounds (again stated in Article 53(2)); however, even here, the entity must indicate the criteria in descending order of importance. In this respect, it is relevant to note that recital 46 of the Directive suggests that cases in

[287] This neglects the fact that the final tenders could in fact be based on a common solution.

[288] Case C-19/00, *SIAC Construction Ltd* v. *County Council of the County of Mayo* [2001] ECR I-7725; Case C-513/99, *Concordia Bus Finland* v. *Helsinki* [2002] ECR I-7213.

[289] Directive 2004/18, Art. 36(1) and Annex VIIA, Contract Notice, point 23.

which weighting cannot be established in advance may exist 'in particular on account of the complexity of the contract'. Since competitive dialogue is available only for particularly complex contracts, this may indicate that an exception to the weighting requirement may exist for contracts awarded by competitive dialogue. The Commission's Explanatory Note on competitive dialogue goes even further in this respect, stating:

> Given that recourse to competitive dialogue presupposes that the contract is 'particularly complex', it seems almost tautological that the conditions for not weighting the award criteria should therefore be met when the contract is awarded by this award procedure – contracting authorities may instead limit themselves to mentioning the criteria in decreasing order of importance.[290]

This perhaps goes too far and certainly it is not possible to conclude, as the Commission seems to do, that the fact that the condition for the exception is met 'in particular' for complex contracts entails that it is met for such contracts *in general*. However, one might expect this sometimes to be the case at the start of the procedure when the contracting authority has limited understanding of the possible solutions to its needs that may make it difficult to judge what the weightings of the criteria should be. Further, the Note may at least be useful in being indicative of the fact that the Commission is unlikely to challenge authorities that invoke this exception in the Directive for competitive dialogue procedures.

In addition to these explicit requirements, recent case law of the CJEU has established that authorities are not merely required to disclose the 'headline' criteria that they propose to use, as referred to expressly in the Directives (quality, running costs, after-sales service, etc.) but also – under the transparency principle – any formal sub-criteria that they intend to use and the weightings of those sub-criteria whenever these sub-criteria and weightings 'may affect' preparation of tenders.[291] For example, where 'quality' is stated as a criterion and is then formally divided into different quality elements for the purpose of evaluation, these elements, and any weightings attached, must also be disclosed. In procedures for complex contracts it is, of course, particularly likely that a

[290] Explanatory Note, n. 33 above, section 3.1.

[291] Case C-532/06, *Emm. G. Lianakis* v. *Dimos Alexandroupolis* [2008] ECR I-251; Case C-331/04, *ATI EAC Srl e Viaggi di Maio Snc* v. *ACTV Venezia SpA* [2005] ECR I-10109.

detailed and formal mechanism will be used for making the award, and many of the details of this may need to be disclosed to tenderers under this principle. This principle has already been applied in case law in the UK on competitive dialogue where it was held that the contracting authority had not disclosed all the required material.[292] As that experience illustrates, the principle causes some uncertainty because of the difficulty sometimes of determining what matters are to be treated as subject to disclosure in principle and what material may be considered to affect tenders. Research in the UK has revealed that, even prior to the case law on competitive dialogue just referred to, the uncertainty over disclosure requirements has been one important source of concern in practice for those running competitive dialogues.[293]

As we have noted above, candidates may be eliminated during the dialogue stage by reference to the award criteria that have been stated in accordance with the above principles, and we have seen that this is done in practice in some Member States, often by considering formal outline solutions. The above rules will also apply in choosing between the tenders finally submitted at the final tender stage discussed in section 5.7 below.

Within the framework of these rules as stated in the Directive and elaborated in specific case law of the CJEU, there are a number of further important grey areas that are of particular concern in the context of competitive dialogue, which have not yet been the subject of clear CJEU jurisprudence, and contribute to the general state of uncertainty in this field. These questions are sometimes confused in case law and analysis and need to be carefully distinguished.

A first issue, which arises from the 'iterative' nature of the award phase of competitive dialogue as opposed to open and restricted procedures (and which is thus relevant also for negotiated procedures, which can also have an iterative award phase) is the timing of disclosure. The issue is whether all criteria and weightings to be used at different points[294] must be drafted and disclosed fully before the dialogue begins, or whether such material may be developed and then disclosed *during* the dialogue and the later stages of the procedure. For example, may a contracting authority use broad award criteria, such as

[292] See Ch.3, section 5.11.2. [293] See Ch.3, section 5.11.2.

[294] This assumes that some further specification of detail and/or variation is possible, either in the headline award criteria to be used, as discussed below, in the weightings, or in the detailed application of sub-criteria etc.

simply 'quality of the solution', for outline submissions and then develop and add more detailed sub-criteria (for example, sub-criteria for how quality is to be assessed) for the purpose of judging final tenders (or other formal submissions that are used to eliminate solutions later in the process)?

In this respect, the Directive expressly provides in Article 29(4) – dealing with the dialogue phase – that solutions may be eliminated by reference to the award criteria stated in the contract notice or descriptive document, and Article 29(7) likewise provides that final tenders are to be assessed based on the award criteria in the notice or descriptive document; but the Directive is silent on the specific question of whether there is room for further specification within the scope of the stated criteria later in the process. It seems very clear that if this is possible transparency will require that any detail that may affect tenders is disclosed to tenderers at least in good time for them to take this into account in their tenders: this follows from the general case law referred to above requiring disclosure in award procedures in general of any sub-criteria or weightings that the authority decides to use that may affect tenders. However, this case law does not necessarily indicate that information beyond the award criteria and weightings referred to expressly in Article 53 must be stated in the contract notice or specifications/descriptive document. To the contrary, the judgments in those cases appear deliberately to refrain from stating that as a requirement, indicating merely that tenderers must be aware of the relevant information for the purpose of preparing their tenders, and implying that this could be done at a later point in the process.[295]

We will see in the later chapters that this has arisen as a practical issue in several Member States. In France, it has arisen before the Conseil d'Etat, which concluded that the Local Authorities Code did not violate the Directives in allowing authorities to clarify how they would apply the award criteria after the dialogue phase, so long as the award criteria themselves and their weightings were not altered from those announced in the contract notice and, of course, that the clarifications were

[295] Case C-331/04, *ATI EAC Srl e Viaggi di Maio Snc* v. *ACTV Venezia SpA* [2005] ECR I-10109, para. 24, when addressing disclosure of the sub-criteria, as opposed to the main award criteria, merely stated that tenderers must be 'aware of the features that are to be taken into account', without stating when disclosure is required. This is repeated in Lianakis, n. 291 above, para. 36, which also adds that they must be able to ascertain the information when preparing their tenders (para. 37) and that the information must be 'brought to the tenderers' attention' (para. 38).

communicated to tenderers.[296] Similarly, in Denmark the Complaints Board for Public Procurement has indicated explicitly that development of the criteria is permitted in principle, upholding the specification of sub-criteria for both economic and technical aspects, which occurred when this occurred during the dialogue process and in a final version of the criteria after the conclusion of the dialogue.[297] In Italy, on the other hand, a different approach has been taken: whilst the original rules on competitive dialogue explicitly allowed contracting authorities to specify award criteria in further detail at the final tender stage to adapt them to the solution(s) chosen during the dialogue, this provision was later repealed following an infraction procedure against Italy[298] and the Italian law now requires the criteria for both the dialogue phase *and* final tenders stage to be stated in the contract notice or descriptive document without later development. In the UK, the issue has not been addressed in either legislation or case law, but academic research has found that in the context of PPP projects the practice is fairly evenly divided between the approach of specifying in full at the start, and the approach of developing the criteria and their application further during the award phase approaches in the context of PPP projects, with a slight majority favouring the latter approach and considering also that this practice is permitted by law.[299] In both Germany and the Netherlands, the practice is also seen of developing the assessment material for commercial reasons during the award phase.[300]

In favour of the view that further development of award criteria and/or their application is allowed after they have been stated in the notice or descriptive document, and during the award phase itself, is the fact that this is considered a useful commercial practice in Member States to ensure appropriate assessment of bids in light of the developments that may occur in the dialogue phase – thus allowing Member States to take full advantage of the improved value for money that may be obtained through dialogue. This is an important consideration in favour of a flexible approach. In favour of a less flexible view under EU law it could be suggested that allowing any development of criteria after the contracting authority has become aware of the likely nature of tenders allows the opportunity to develop the criteria in such a way as to favour specific bidders. This is an issue that does not arise with open or restricted procedures involving only one round of tendering, where any

[296] See Ch. 4, section 5.5, and Ch. 12, section 5.6.5. [297] See Ch. 2, section 5.6.
[298] See Ch.7, section 5.2. [299] See Ch. 3, section 5.11. [300] See Ch. 5, section 5.7.

development of the criteria is done before any indication is given to the authority of the nature of the different tenders, but arises potentially in competitive dialogue or negotiated procedures where the award phase is iterative.[301] However, it can be pointed out that the case law does not require authorities to specify sub-criteria. Thus the authority is even *less* constrained in its ability to favour particular tenderers by not further specifying the original award criteria at all than it is by specifying and disclosing them part way through the award procedure. From this perspective any argument for prohibiting further specification during the award procedure based on the potential for discrimination seems flawed – indeed it positively discourages the structuring of discretion that would in fact bring a more transparent approach than leaving it unstructured as at least some monitoring of the decision would be possible against the pre-stated sub-criteria etc. The better view thus appears to be that further specification is indeed permitted.

Another area of debate is the extent to which award criteria and other matters, such as sub-criteria, or the weightings of criteria and sub-criteria, may be *changed* once they have already been set and disclosed in accordance with the Directive (a different question from whether *more detailed* methodology may be developed within the scope of the originally stated criteria or weightings, which we have just considered above). The need for changing the basis of assessment seems not so pressing as the need to allow further development, since the former can be avoided to a great extent by planning in advance for the possibility of developing and completing the assessment material so that change is not needed. (The need for change is perhaps more likely to arise as a practical issue if the contracting authority tries to develop all the rules governing the award at the start of the award phase, rather than taking advantage of any opportunities for further specifying the basis of the assessment later, as discussed above.) Nevertheless, flexibility to introduce changes may be valuable in competitive dialogue to allow the contracting authority to deal with unforeseen circumstances – particularly important with lengthy award procedures – or to allow corrections in what is a complex or difficult process. Again, such flexibility can be important to allow contracting authorities to fully exploit

[301] It can be noted that, if greater limits are to be placed on changing award criteria in competitive dialogue than open and restricted procedures for the reason given, these limits will not be relevant in the phase prior to the start of the dialogue.

the potential benefits of competitive dialogue, without the unreasonable costs and delay that may be caused by re-opening the procedure.

So far as the legal position is concerned, we can first note that the possibility for ever changing the award criteria could be interpreted as ruled out for procedures in general based on statements by the CJEU that the criteria cannot be changed.[302] However, the better view is that, based on a broader assessment of the legal sources, changes can be permitted in certain circumstances (although, as explained below, Professors Treumer and Arrowsmith differ on what these circumstances are, with Professor Arrowsmith taking a more flexible view). It should be noted that the statements of the CJEU that change is not permitted were in fact made in cases in which the change in question violated the Directives' principles of equal treatment and transparency and are limited to that context. Thus in the case of *EVN*, for example, the CJEU commented that changes to award criteria are not possible[303] – but that specific case concerned changes to criteria *after* the tenders had been submitted and without any notification to participants, which would clearly violate both equal treatment and transparency.

Another argument for ruling out changes of the award criteria in competitive dialogue procedures[304] is the danger of changing the criteria in a manner that discriminates in favour of particular tenders that have been presented – at least in outline form – in an iterative procedure. The possibility for changing the criteria set may be seen to give more scope for abuse of discretion than simply developing criteria that have already been stated as applicable. This is the view put forward in the Commission's Explanatory Note on competitive dialogue:[305]

> It should be stressed that the award criteria (and the order of their importance) may not be changed during the award procedure (that is, at the latest after the transmission of invitations to participate in the dialogue) for obvious reasons of equal treatment; in fact, any changes to the award criteria after this stage in the procedure would be introduced at a time when the contracting authority could have obtained knowledge of the solutions that are proposed by the different participants.

[302] Case C-448/01, *EVN AG and Wienstrom GmbH* v. *Austria* [2003] ECR I-14527, para. 93; Case C-226/09, n. 16 above, para. 60.

[303] *EVN*, n. 302 above, para. 93. Case C-226/09, n. 16 above, was also a case where the conditions set out below were violated when making the change, as it occurred after submission when there was no chance for bidders to adjust their bids to the change.

[304] And also negotiated procedures.

[305] Explanatory Note, n. 33 above, section 3.1.

The view that criteria cannot generally be changed in competitive dialogue once they have been set and disclosed also finds some support in the history of the Directive. A previous draft provision explicitly assumed that the award criteria could be amended during the procedure where they were 'no longer appropriate to the subject-matter of the contract as defined in the contract documents after the negotiations phase',[306] but this was omitted in the adopted version of the Directive. It is also relevant to note that in Case C-226/09, *Commission* v. *Ireland*,[307] concerning a Part B services contract under the TFEU, the CJEU clearly ruled out any changes to the award criteria after the evaluation had commenced. However, this case is not conclusive of the position in competitive dialogue as it concerned a non-iterative procedure in which the justification for change is lower, and change after the submission of tenders that were intended to be final, which clearly presents a higher risk of manipulating the outcome.

Deciding whether to allow changes depends on the appropriate balance between the commercial need for flexibility for good procurement in situations of complexity and the need to limit the risk of abuse. Given the wide margin of discretion available anyway in competitive dialogue through the actual application of award criteria to complex situations (including the possibility of comparing widely different solutions), the fact that weightings might not be applied, and the possibility for developing the criteria – so that the risk of abuse may in practice be increased only marginally or not at all by allowing *changes* to criteria – it can be argued that commercial needs should take precedence here to admit the possibility of change in principle, provided that they meet certain conditions to ensure equal treatment. These include the fact that they must be disclosed to tenderers in sufficient time for them to be taken into account in tenders (as demonstrated by *EVN* and *Commission* v. *Ireland*) and that they must not be material in the sense that had they been introduced earlier they might have affected the outcome of the competition (for example, where they might have affected who would have been eliminated in an earlier tendering stage). This is the view of Professor Arrowsmith. On the other hand, it might be argued that the risk of abuse is too high to contemplate permitting changes (as opposed merely to developments of the criteria) and that these are largely excluded based on CJEU case law and the history of the Directive as

306 Commission proposal, n. 89 above, Art. 30(4).
307 Case C-226/09, n. 16 above, para. 60.

mentioned above. This appears to be even more so for reasons of equal treatment where the dialogue phase is conducted in stages and this leads to reduction of participants based on different versions of the award criteria. This is the view of Professor Treumer. However, even if changes to the criteria are not allowed in principle in *all* types of circumstances, it can be argued that they are (again subject to the limiting conditions below) permitted where the contracting authority can show good reason for the change – such as an unforeseeable change in circumstances – by analogy with other situations where a change to the rules or content of a procurement is allowed.[308]

Of course, if there is indeed no scope for *developing* the pre-set criteria in competitive dialogue after the start of the award procedure, there is also *a fortiori* no scope for actually changing those criteria – but we have suggested above that development is in fact allowed.

Again, different approaches to this legal issue can be found. In Lithuania and Italy, for example, the law expressly provides that no changes are permitted to the award criteria stated in the contract notice or descriptive document,[309] whilst in Germany it is the view of academic writers, at least, that the criteria cannot be changed.[310] It is suggested also in Chapter 4 on France that, although the case law does not directly address the issue, it is indicated in the judgment of the Conseil d'Etat, mentioned above, on the possibility for developing the award criteria, that, whilst the criteria may be developed during the award process, they may not actually be changed. In Denmark, research has found that in practice contracting authorities have generally refrained from changing the criteria, considering the legal risks of this to be too high (even though not covered by case law) – although this had been done occasionally.[311] On the other hand, academic research on the UK – where the issue is not regulated expressly by law – found that a majority of practitioners considered that there was some scope for variation in the criteria, sub-criteria and/or weightings provided that the variation was not 'material'.[312]

Another issue that arises with award criteria is the extent to which different criteria or sub-criteria, and weightings for these, may be applied during different phases of the award, where this possibility is

[308] See the discussion in section 5.8 below.
[309] See respectively Ch. 10, and Ch. 11, sections 5.2 and 5.6. [310] See Ch. 5, section 5.7.
[311] See Ch. 6, section 5.6.
[312] That is, would not have affected the outcome at any stage of the process.

laid down in advance in the contract notice or descriptive document. In Italy, legislation expressly provides for this possibility, provided that the criteria to be applied at the different stages are stated in the contract notice.[313] As Chapter 2 explains, although not regulated expressly, the same issue also arises in practice in the UK, in particular in the context of consideration of financial criteria, which are considered difficult to apply on a comparative basis until technical solutions are fully developed. As Chapter 3 explains, government guidance takes the view that applying different criteria and/or weightings in different phases is potentially lawful and also efficient procurement practice in some cases. Research shows that this view is followed by most practitioners by leaving significant consideration of financial aspects until late in the award process, eliminating some solutions without significant regard to these aspects.

It is difficult to see that there is any policy of the Directive that would preclude such an approach, provided that it is a reasonable approach on the facts of the case to identifying the most economically advantageous tender. It is true that such an approach involves some risk of eliminating at an earlier stage an economic operator that may turn out to be the most economically advantageous. However, this is a risk that applies in many types of procurement processes – for example, all procedures that involve selecting only a limited number of firms to tender, or framework agreements that involve placing only a limited number of suppliers on the framework – and is considered justified by the need to balance wide competition with procedural efficiency. Given the very high costs potentially involved in operating and competing in competitive dialogue procedures, these procedures in particular require a sensitivity to this balance, and this can justify applying different award criteria at different stages.

5.7. *Final tender stage*

5.7.1. Introduction

As already noted in section 5.6.4 above, Article 29(6) requires that at the end of the dialogue stage the contracting authority must formally declare the dialogue to be concluded and inform the participants of this. The same provision also states that the authority then 'shall ask [the participants] to submit their final tenders on the basis of the solution or

[313] Ch. 11, section 5.2.

solutions presented and specified during the dialogue', and that '[t]hese tenders shall contain all the elements required and necessary for the performance of the project'.

5.7.2. Number of bidders

As regards the number of tenderers to be invited at the final tender stage, the Directive merely provides, in Article 44(4), that, 'In the final stage, the number arrived at shall make for genuine competition insofar as there are enough solutions or suitable candidates'. In contrast with the position regarding the number to be invited to commence dialogue, when three is always the minimum number when three are available, no specific minimum number is mentioned. Following the usual approach to transposition of the competitive dialogue rules, many Member States have simply copied out the Directive's wording in this respect. However, this is not universal: in Lithuania, the legislation elaborates by specifying three as an absolute minimum,[314] whilst in Portugal all candidates whose solutions were admitted to the dialogue must be invited to tender[315] (even though, as we saw, the final tender in Portugal will take place on a common basis rather than based on candidates' own proposals).

The actual number invited varies very significantly in practice, both because of the different policies of Member States and – not surprisingly – because of the very different circumstances of different procurements: here relevant factors may include such matters as the cost of tendering, and the likelihood of all invited suppliers actually submitting a final tender. In Spain, for example, there is, as we saw above, a policy of inviting all qualified parties to the dialogue, sometimes leading to twenty or so participants (although it is acknowledged that this does not lead to an efficient outcome), and the dialogue phase is not used formally to reduce the number (although reduction may result from other factors).[316] This could potentially lead to a significant number of final tenders. Likewise, in Portugal, the requirement to invite to tender all whose solutions have been admitted could lead to a large number of tenders – although limited use of competitive dialogue there means an absence of experience of how this might operate in practice. At the other end of the scale, inviting only two or three participants to submit final tenders is very common. Thus empirical research suggests that this is the most common number invited in public–private partnership projects in

[314] Ch. 10, section 5.7. [315] Ch. 7, section 5.7.3. [316] Ch 8, section 5.6.2.

the UK;[317] in the Netherlands it is the standard policy of central government agencies to invite three (who will have been selected in an early stage of the dialogue phase from five to seven candidates initially invited);[318] and guidance in France also suggests that three is an appropriate *maximum* number[319] (although there is no empirical evidence available to us on the practice in France). We have also seen that the legislation in Lithuania stipulates three, but there is as yet no practice on this issue given that use of competitive dialogue there is so far negligible. In Denmark, we saw that in general only four or five are invited into dialogue and further formal reduction generally does not take place, often leaving the same four or five at final tender stage also, although sometimes there may be fewer since bidders may drop out. However, it is far from unknown to invite more than three even when numbers are reduced in the dialogue. Thus in the UK, whilst a smaller number is very common, a 2010 Treasury review found that 15 per cent of the survey respondents had taken six bidders to the final tender stage (although it should be said that this has been criticised by a government review as wasteful);[320] and there have also been several Danish procedures with about five tenderers at the final tender stage.[321]

The Directive appears to allow the contracting authority to choose to invite only two firms to submit final tenders, even if more potential bidders (qualified bidders with acceptable solutions) are available.[322] In some procedures this is an important issue because of the very high cost of submitting final tenders – which as we will see below must be complete tenders, even for the most complex procedures. These costs may amount to hundreds of thousands and even millions of euros. This cost is of great concern to many tenderers and in some procedures it may be difficult to get a competitive field if more than two must be invited in the final stage,[323] as well as leading to a significant waste of resources which must be paid for directly or indirectly by tenderers and/or contracting authorities. The view that two may sometimes be a sufficient number seems clearly indicated by the fact that the Directive expressly requires a minimum of three to be invited alongside the general requirement for genuine competition at dialogue stage, but does *not* apply such an express minimum for the final tender stage, indicating that such a

[317] Ch. 3, section 5.7.2. [318] Ch. 12, section 5.6. [319] Ch. 4, section 5.7.
[320] Ch. 3, section 5.7.2. [321] Ch. 6, section 5.7.
[322] See also Arrowsmith, n. 3 above, pp. 649–50.
[323] See the discussion of the UK experience in Ch. 3, section 5.7.2.

minimum does not apply. That two is a sufficient number of final offers to invite in a negotiated procedure seems to have been accepted in the Commission Decision on state aid in *London Underground*;[324] and the same principle should apply for competitive dialogue, where the need for complete tenders means that it may be even more justified to limit numbers to two, because of the potentially much higher costs. This approach of inviting only two tenderers in appropriate circumstances is endorsed in UK government guidance, and all interviewees in a study of UK practitioners considered this legally acceptable.[325] It is also interesting that guidance in France from the Mouvement des Entreprises de France (French Confederation of Business Enterprises) (MEDEF) refers to the fact that 'foreign experience' suggests that retaining two candidates is possible – although it does not go so far as to recommend using two, merely mentioning three as a *maximum*. This does not, of course, mean that two should be invited in every case: what is sufficient for genuine competition depends on the facts (such as whether those invited are likely to tender), as the UK guidance stresses,[326] and will vary with the nature of the project.

It seems clear that when fewer suitable candidates than the normal minimum remain at the end of the dialogue or have presented acceptable solutions, that the contracting authority can continue with only those candidates, even when that leaves only one candidate (as is accepted in the Commission's Explanatory Note):[327] whilst the authority is obliged to seek to ensure competition throughout the process it is obviously not possible to guarantee this. At least this will be the case if the rules on sufficient numbers of tenderers have been complied with in previous stages. The possibility of proceeding with fewer than the general minimum for processes in the Directive is generally accepted – it is specifically stated in Article 44(3) in the context of issuing invitations to participate in the award phase. Should the authority decide that such an

[324] Decision of the Commission of the European Communities in Case N 264/2002, *London Underground Public Private Partnership*, Decision of 2 October 2002, on the Utilities Directive. In two of the three projects in that case, only two bids had been solicited at the final bid stage and there is no suggestion in the Decision that this was unlawful.

[325] See Ch. 3, section 5.7.2. [326] See *ibid*.

[327] Explanatory Note, n. 33 above; section 3.2 states that: 'Reduction by application of the award criteria might therefore show that there is only one appropriate candidate or solution which does not prevent the contracting authorities from continuing with the procedure.'

approach would not be satisfactory because of the absence of competitive pressure, however, the Directive allows for it to recommence the award procedure or terminate the project[328] – a possibility that might induce the one remaining tenderer to submit a tender on reasonable terms even in the absence of competition.[329]

5.7.3. Completeness of final tenders[330]

As noted above, Article 29(6) requires that final tenders contain all the elements 'required and necessary' for the performance of the project. This indicates that the award should not be made on the basis of limited commitments, leaving scope for negotiation of the substance of the deal after selecting the winner. This was widely done in the UK in awarding PPP contracts under the negotiated procedure with a notice prior to competitive dialogue – substantial issues affecting the commercial value of the deal (such as allocation of substantial risks) were often left unresolved at the point at which the preferred bidder was selected but finalised *before* conclusion of the contract[331] – and it seems that Article 29(6) was targeted at this practice. In terms of both legal principle and practical application, however, the provision raises difficult legal questions and its exact implications are unclear.[332]

From the point of view of legal principle, the historical context just mentioned as well as the wording that the provision indicates that it is aimed at the very least at controlling what can be done between choosing the winner and concluding the contract; and the literature and guidance has focused on this perspective. To illustrate, the combination of the final tender documents and the content of the offer could lead to contract terms stipulating a building design in varying degrees of detail – at one (extreme) end of the spectrum simply as a hospital with certain facilities for a certain number of patients and at the other (extreme) end a specific hospital design with every design detail and individual fitting of every room specified fully. Article 29(6) potentially limits the design

[328] On the width of discretion to terminate an award procedure, see, in particular, Case C-27/98, *Metalmeccanica Fracasso* [1999] ECR I-5697; Case C-244/02, *Kauppatalo Hansel* v. *Imatran Kaupunk* [2003] ECR I-12139.

[329] Note also the possibility of switching to the negotiated procedure without a further notice on the grounds in Art. 30(1)(a) of the Directive where *all* offers are irregular or unacceptable.

[330] See also Arrowsmith, n. 3 above, pp. 650–2; and Kennedy-Loest, n. 3 above.

[331] See Ch. 3, section 5.7.

[332] The legislative history does not reveal any substantial discussions of this provision.

detail that can be developed between choosing the winner and concluding the contract. The reason for such a limitation from the perspective of EU law is to ensure that bidders' proposals relating to the full detail of the project are taken into account in selecting the most economically advantageous tender, and under conditions of transparency, reducing the possibilities for favouring certain bidders by allowing them to agree favourable terms in a non-competitive environment. In this respect, the provision represents one dimension of the EU's efforts to shift the award of complex contracts into a more competitive and transparent process than was often applied when awarding these contracts under negotiated procedures. From a national perspective in ensuring value for money including the detail in the competitive phase will help secure the best possible offers: terms negotiated without the pressure of competition are likely to be less favourable to the contracting authority than those determined during a competitive process. On the other hand, the more detailed that final tenders must be, the higher the process costs for both bidders and contracting authorities; and high costs may deter good firms from participating, may lead contracting authorities to limit the number of firms invited at the final tender stage, or may cause contracting authorities to shun competitive dialogue in favour of otherwise less suitable procedures. The rules on the content of final tenders must clearly be fashioned to balance these various interests.

Although the focus of discussion in the literature and guidance has been on the phase between final tenders and conclusion of the contract, Article 29(6) is likely, however, to go a step further, limiting also the parties' ability to complete contractual detail *after* the contract is signed. There do not appear, in fact, to be strong reasons for limiting what can be done between the final tenders and contract award if similar limitations do not apply in the contract execution stage. For example, if Article 29(6) precludes the parties from settling certain aspects of the design detail between award and final tenders, it is not clear why it is justified to allow the parties to complete those details after the contract is signed, when the same problems of potential abuse and absence of competition to secure value for money will be as relevant as at the 'preferred bidder' stage.[333]

[333] Perhaps the key difference between the two stages is that the process of reaching agreement in the latter case is more likely to be governed by contractual mechanisms, such as third party adjudication, that can provide a solution in the absence of agreement; but the presence or absence of such mechanisms cannot be assumed in either case.

The question also arises as to how far the level of detail required in final tenders is governed by an objective test, in the sense that it does not depend solely on the choice of the parties as to how much detail will be contractually specified (at whatever point this is done) but involves some universal requirement for a minimum level of the completeness and certainty of the agreement as a matter of EU law[334] to ensure that the most economically advantageous tender is selected. Some element of objectivity follows from requirements of completeness and certainty in concluded contracts under national contract law: Article 29(6) seems to entail that the agreement contemplated in the final tenders should (once confirmed) be sufficiently detailed and certain to constitute a legally binding contract under national law. However, such national requirements are variable and are often quite limited – for example, they may allow parties simply to provide for a 'reasonable' price for the work, or may allow for a contract to be concluded for construction of a work with only very limited details of the design specified at the time of the contract. It seems likely that Article 29(6) in fact imposes both a subjective requirement, for completing the detail that the parties intend to include in the contract, and an objective requirement, imposing a minimum standard of certainty and completeness. The use of the words 'required' and 'necessary' in the English version of the Directive, if they are to be given different meanings, might suggest that both types of requirement apply, with the concept of an element being 'required' bearing the subjective meaning of required by the parties – although the words themselves could also carry an identical meaning.

Whatever the correct legal test, the question then arises as to its application – that is, as to the precise degree of completeness and certainty envisaged, and the way in which the general approach will be applied to specific situations.

In this respect, it seems clear, first, that the requirement to include in the final tender the terms 'required and necessary' for the performance of the project does not necessarily rule out completion of *any* detail at

[334] To leave the level of completeness to the contract law of Member States (or any parallel concepts of Member States' rules on the award of public contracts) could not ensure that the purpose of the provision is achieved, and also is not consistent with the general approach of EU law of interpreting concepts in the Directive as self-contained rather than referring to definitions of similar concepts that occur in the national law of the Member State applying the provision (see, for example, Case C-373/00, *Adolf Truley* v. *Bestattung Wien* [2003] ECR I-1931).

later stages. That it does not do so is indicated by Article 29(7) stating that, after the entity has identified the most economically advantageous tender,

> [a]t the request of the contracting authority the tenderer identified as having submitted the most economically advantageous tender may be asked to clarify aspects of the tender or confirm commitments provided that this does not have the effect of modifying substantial aspects of the tender or the call for tender and does not risk distorting competition or causing discrimination.

This implies some scope for completing tenders later: it appears that the words 'clarify' and 'confirm' are to be given a broad meaning since the prohibition on measures that modify *substantial* aspects of the tender or call for tender implies that even measures that involve some actual modification are permitted when not substantial (see the discussion in section 5.8 below); and if modifications are permitted when not substantial then *a fortiori* completion of detail under the concept of 'clarification' is also potentially possible when not 'substantial'. Thus it may be argued that, whatever interpretation is adopted of Article 29(6), there is scope for leaving out certain detail – such as a certain level of design detail – from final tenders, and completing this either prior to concluding the contract or during contract execution. This allows the courts to develop an appropriate balance between the costs and benefits of full tenders.

It should also be mentioned that, whatever the position with competitive dialogue, it seems likely that parallel obligations on completeness and certainty in tenders apply also for other award procedures based on the Directive's general principles and/or the rules on contract award, since the policy considerations are the same.[335] However, this issue has not been addressed in CJEU case law and the degree of completeness and certainty, if any, required under EU law is thus unclear. It would appear that the scope for completing the details of the project after the final tender stage may – as with other rules of

[335] The inclusion of an explicit requirement for competitive dialogue procedure reinforces, by analogy, the existence of such a general requirement for completeness under the EU Directives, rather than excludes it, given that the same policy in this respect is relevant for all procedures: the inclusion of the explicit provision in the competitive dialogue rules is explained by the need to indicate specifically that certain practice adopted previously in the context of complex contracts are not acceptable under the new procedure.

the Directive – vary between award procedures in recognition of the different nature of the procurement covered, with more flexibility applying at this point in those procedures that show more flexibility in general.[336]

It is beyond the scope of this chapter on competitive dialogue to explore fully these difficult and unresolved legal questions, but, as explained below, it is necessary to appreciate this background when considering the way in which this issue is treated in Member States.

In this respect, we can note that the interpretation and application of Article 29(6) has given rise to considerable debate and concern in the UK. There is, on the other hand, little evidence of concern in the other Member States covered in this book.

That the provision should be of major interest in the UK is not surprising given the potential impact of Article 29(6), and also Article 29(7), on the UK's previous practice under the negotiated procedure in completing, or sometimes amending, the contract terms prior to the contract. Given this historical background, the focus of discussion has been on the impact of Article 29 on the preferred bidder stage, rather than on contract execution. As Chapter 3 explains, this has in fact been one of *the* major concerns in the UK over competitive dialogue, with a fear that a restrictive approach could lead to an increase in tendering costs – and the adverse consequences that may follow, as outlined above – to an extent that is disproportionate to any benefit.

As Chapter 3 explains, guidance documents from the UK government accept that Article 29 leaves some room for work with the preferred bidder, and suggest that this may be justified by the practical impossibility of addressing certain matters earlier *or* by concerns of cost-effectiveness, whilst also, however, recognising that the scope for such work is very much less than under negotiated procedures.[337] This guidance suggests that areas that might be addressed at the preferred bidder stage include details of sub-contracts, detailed planning applications, financial swap rates, design detail[338] and completion of the performance

[336] For example, Verschuur, n. 3 above, p. 330, has suggested that clarification in the context of open and restricted procedures is limited to supplying detail that is already likely to exist; but it is submitted below that any such limit does not exist in competitive dialogue, but may in principle extend to detail such as design detail that has not yet been developed.

[337] Ch. 3, section 5.7.3.

[338] See also Arrowsmith, n. 3 above, p. 651; and Kennedy-Loest, n. 3 above, p. 324, noting a 'consensus' in the UK on the possibility of fleshing out the design after tendering.

mechanism.[339] Empirical evidence on UK practice[340] indicates a divergence amongst practitioners both as regards the interpretation of what is allowed at this stage as a matter of legal principle and what is done in practice. Regarding the former, a significant majority of practitioners have suggested that a very high degree of development of tenders is needed, allowing for a contract to be concluded immediately after choosing a winner (a 'strict' view); however, a minority prefer a more flexible legal test that allows the completion of detail that is not likely to affect the ranking of bids. On the other hand, even though the strict approach is reasonably prevalent, most practitioners do not actually follow such a strict approach in their practice even when they consider this to be required as a matter of law: most leave open the kind of matters referred to in the government guidance above either because of the perceived balance of costs and benefits because of factors such as time or (internal) cost pressures necessitating a premature closure of the dialogue.

As Chapter 3 explains, many involved in the process in the UK consider that the change in practice that has resulted from a shift from the negotiated procedure to competitive dialogue has led to improved value for money in the terms of public–private partnership arrangements as a result of greater competitive pressure in agreeing project terms; and this was a key finding of a recent government review.[341] However, despite the relatively flexible approach adopted in practice (if not in law), as discussed above, costs have, as predicted, increased dramatically, more than doubling from those incurred when awarding similar projects through negotiated procedures.[342] A significant number of UK practitioners interviewed for an empirical study considered that any benefits were outweighed by these higher costs,[343] whilst research from both the Confederation of British Industry and national government have concluded that the approach adopted to final tenders results in disproportionate costs. In the light of this, Chapter 3 suggests that 'a strict legal interpretation [of Article 29(6)] is very much out of line with the practicalities of effective procurement in complex projects; and that even the more pragmatic approach applied in the UK practice does not adequately meet the commercial concerns of bidders'.

339 *Ibid.* 340 Ch. 3, section 5.7.3.

341 Ch. 3, section 5.7.3 (and see also the views of Burnett, *Competitive Dialogue*, n. 3 above, pp. 54–70). However, some practitioners interviewed did not share the view that the new approach has enhanced value for money: Ch. 3, section 5.7.3.

342 Ch. 3, section 6. 343 Ch. 3, section 5.7.3.

There is little information available on how Article 29(6) is interpreted in this respect in many of the Member States covered by this volume, and no specific indication that this provision has given rise to significant debate: in general, legislation merely repeats the Directive *verbatim* and there is as yet no case law. However, there are some exceptions to this that suggest that a certain level of detail is addressed after tendering in the same way as in the UK. Thus in Italy there is specific legislation that supplements the Directive by providing that the offer is to be accompanied merely by the preliminary plan and that the winner is to draft the final and executive plan only once chosen, this being done *after* the contract is concluded;[344] this plan includes the kind of elements, such as the detail of design, that are left until after selection of the winner in the UK (but completed there *before* the contract is concluded). Likewise, in France guidance issued by Mouvement des Entreprises de France (French Confederation of Business Enterprises, MEDEF) contemplates that *full* detail of the project is not required at the final tender stage, giving the example of design detail as a possible area for later completion.[345] Further, Chapter 6 on Denmark reports, based on interviews with practitioners, that with ICT contracts, at least 'elements of a more technical nature are sometimes deliberately left for the final stage between award and conclusion of the contract in order not to waste the time of all bidders'.[346] Thus it seems that the practice of a number of Member States accepts that it is appropriate to leave some detail to be fleshed out after tendering.

It needs to be stressed, however, that the current project has not investigated the actual practices followed in the covered Member States regarding the level of detail fixed in final tenders, nor examined the interpretations of the provisions applied by practitioners. It is thus not possible to draw any general conclusions on how the provision is interpreted and applied, on the level of detail actually obtained from tenderers in most states, or on how different interpretations could impact on existing Member State practice except, as noted above, to observe that completion of some limited detail after tendering appears to be widespread and uncontroversial. It is possible that the absence of significant debate over completing the project details between final tenders and the contract's conclusion could in some states reflect a practice of completing all detail at the former

[344] Ch. 11, section 5.7. [345] Ch. 4, section 5.7. [346] Ch. 6, section 5.8.

stage. Equally, however, it could be explained by a practice (as in Italy, for example) of completing some detail during the contract execution stage combined with a perception that Article 29(6) does not address that stage, especially if that is merely a continuation of practice prior to competitive dialogue.

In light of the problems experienced in the UK – one of the two major users of competitive dialogue and where there is significant evidence of practice – it can be argued that an unduly rigid interpretation of Article 29(6) must be avoided, both to make competitive dialogue workable in light of external constraints such as planning procedures, and to control the costs of tendering and the adverse consequences that might flow from such high costs. There is, it is submitted, a need for greater flexibility than for open and restricted procedures in view of the complex nature of the procurement covered by competitive dialogue which results, *inter alia*, in particularly high participation costs.[347] It was suggested above that the wording of Article 29(6) allows for an interpretation that leaves some matters to be developed after final tenders. In this respect, it can be further argued that an interpretation should be adopted that allows for the flexibility to complete at any point – including between the final tender stage and conclusion of the contract, as well as during contract execution – *any matters that are unlikely to impact on the decision of selecting the winner.* Thus, for example, as regards building design it can be argued that it is necessary at final tender stage merely for tenderers to submit design detail to a level that is reasonably likely to impact on the value of the offer in such a way as to differentiate one tenderer from another, but not beyond that level. In this situation, both the risk of abuse and the possibility of the contract's completion undermining the competitive process are by definition low; and the relevance of this point is reinforced by analogy by Article 29(7) which limits the possibility of post-tender modifications to cases in which the conduct in question 'does not risk distorting competition or causing discrimination'.[348] On the other hand, there is value in such an approach in reducing costs and thereby also potentially widening competition. In these circumstances, it would, in fact, contravene the principle of proportionality to require all detail of the contract to be complete in final tenders. It can also be pointed out that the precise threshold of risk of

[347] Arrowsmith, n. 3 above, p. 655; Kennedy-Loest, n. 3 above, p. 318.

[348] The relevance of a test of whether competition might be distorted is also supported by the general reference to this in recital 31 of Directive 2004/18.

abuse or distortion of competition when applying the suggested test needs to be set at a reasonable level in light of the proportionality principle – completion of detail cannot be ruled out altogether merely because of a slight possibility of affecting the competition.[349]

Nevertheless, it also seems clear from the Directive's[350] wording that there is a much more limited scope for leaving matters to be resolved with a preferred bidder than applies under the negotiated procedure with a notice, where the degree of flexibility that appears to have been accepted by the Commission (and also applied in UK practice) does not provide for all elements that are required and necessary for performance. In terms of legal principle this difference might be reflected in a different threshold level under the different procedures for the likelihood of the matter in question having an actual impact on the choice of winner (with a greater likelihood of impact being tolerated under the negotiated procedure than competitive dialogue).

Finally, UK experience on this issue suggests that, in the absence of significant available information on this subject, it would be useful to undertake further research on the subject of completeness of bids in other Member States.

5.7.4. Clarification, specification and fine-tuning of tenders[351]

Once final tenders have been submitted the issue then arises, as with other award procedures, as to what may be done in relation to tenders between submission of these final tenders and choosing the winner based on the tenders. Many different questions potentially arise at this stage concerning the possibility for completing, clarifying and amending tenders, as noted below. It is noteworthy that the legal position on these issues still remains to a large extent unclear in the context of other award procedures under the Directive, with few CJEU cases, making it even more difficult than it might be to determine how they will be resolved in the context of competitive dialogue.

[349] A different view seems to be taken by Burnett, *Competitive Dialogue*, n. 3 above, p. 162, who argues for a 'restrictive' approach, manifested in the lists set out on pp. 58–70 of the book which take a narrow approach to issues that may never be addressed at preferred bidder stage.

[350] And, as noted above, is recognised in UK government guidance.

[351] See also Arrowsmith, n. 3 above, pp. 652–9; and Verschuur, n. 3 above.

For competitive dialogue, in contrast with other procedures, this stage of the procedure is governed by an explicit provision, Article 29(6), which states as follows:

> [Final] tenders may be clarified, specified and fine-tuned at the request of the contracting authority. However, such clarification, specification, fine-tuning or additional information may not involve changes to the basic features of the tender or the call for tender, variations in which are likely to distort competition or have a discriminatory effect.

This provision is based on the similar, although not identical, Council and Commission Declaration dealing with the post-tender stage in open and restricted procedures and stating the equal treatment principle in that context;[352] and, similarly, Article 29(6) may be regarded as an articulation of equal treatment in competitive dialogue. A narrow view, based on the similarities between this provision and the Declaration (which refers to 'clarifying' and 'supplementing' tenders or requirements), is that it merely states expressly the same principle as applies in open and restricted procedures. Another view, however – and the one preferred by the present authors – is that Article 29(6) must be read in light of the fact that competitive dialogue deals with complex contracts involving greater need for further submissions, and thus as permitting greater flexibility, as elaborated below.[353] This is consistent with the generally variable content of equal treatment in different award procedures given their differing nature, which is partly accounted for by the different circumstances in which they apply.[354] However, resolving this issue of principle does not take us very far towards applying the provision to specific issues, especially given the limited case law on open and restricted procedures. The European Commission in its Explanatory Note on competitive dialogue merely concludes that 'the room for manoeuvre that contracting authorities have after the submission of

[352] Council and Commission Statement concerning Art. 7(4) of Public Works Directive 93/37 [1994] OJ L111/114, referred to with approval in Case C-243/89, *Commission* v. *Denmark ('Storebaelt')* [1993] ECR I-3353, para. 19 of the Opinion. The Commission's Explanatory Note, n. 33 above, section 3.3, states that this provision in the Directive is based on this.

[353] Arrowsmith, n. 3 above, p. 655, whose statement on this subject is endorsed also by Kennedy-Loest, n. 3 above, p. 318 and (for the specific issue of correction of errors in tenders) Burnett, *Competitive Dialogue*, n. 3 above, p. 154.

[354] Seen, for example, in the fact that open procedures but not others require that all interested firms can submit a tender.

the final tenders is fairly limited',[355] thus indicating a narrow interpretation but throwing no further light on its precise application to different problems.

One key question is whether a contracting authority may request amendments that will improve tenders. Generally it violates equal treatment to allow one tenderer, but not others, to improve its tender (for example, lowering the price or enhancing the service offered) when this affects the outcome of the competition;[356] this is a change to the basic feature of the tender that distorts competition. For open and restricted procedures, it appears to be prohibited to negotiate generally for tenderers to improve their tenders, even if all are treated equally.[357] Is this the case also for competitive dialogue, however? Different interpretations could be adopted. The first is that (in accordance with the general principle above) competitive dialogue offers more flexibility than open or restricted procedures, and that 'fine-tuning' (which the Council and Commission Declaration on open or restricted procedures does not refer to) 'could be interpreted as covering minor improvements – for example, pressing a tenderer to improve its cost structure for one particular facilities management service in a PFI contract'.[358] If this is possible in principle, opportunities for improvement could be offered to all tenderers, where appropriate, or to one or a limited number of tenderers where the contracting authority can justify distinguishing between them. A different interpretation, however, is based on the fact that competitive dialogue specifically envisages tendering rounds that are followed by discussions and possible improvements in the dialogue phase, making it unnecessary after final tenders. (Contracting authorities can even, for example, adopt the UK practice of a 'dry-run' before final tendering.) It is in this dialogue phase that the complexity of the contracts can be taken into account and consequently there is perhaps *less*, rather than more, need for final improvements at the final tender stage than in open or restricted procedures. Arguably a combination of flexibility in the dialogue stage and a strict approach that prohibits improvements at the final tender stage provides an appropriate balance between transparency and flexibility; thus, it may

[355] Explanatory Note, n. 33 above, section 3.3. [356] *Storebaelt*, n. 352 above.

[357] See Arrowsmith, n. 3 above, pp. 540–7.

[358] Arrowsmith, n. 3 above, p. 655. Even if that is the case, however, 'fine-tuning' may imply qualitative and quantitative limitations to any changes, even when these do not affect the 'basic features of tenders' or have the potential to distort competition.

be argued that Article 29(6) should be interpreted strictly as regards the scope for improvements.[359]

Another question is whether amendments are allowed for the purpose not of improvement but correction of error, even when the amendment might enable the tenderer to introduce improvements and/or present opportunities for abuse (including by the procuring entity supplying information on other tenders). This may occur, for example, when the tenderer has submitted a non-compliant offer, perhaps because of error in understanding the specification, and wishes now to bring the offer into compliance and to make corresponding adjustments (for example, to price); or where there are inconsistencies or errors in the tender, but the correct content of the tender is not clear on its face.[360] Even if the contracting authority cannot permit such amendments in open or restricted procedures (which is not clear),[361] it is submitted that it may do so in competitive dialogue within the concept of 'clarification' under Article 29(6) or 'fine-tuning' (in the case of non-compliant tenders), on the basis that the complexity of the procurement and hence the greater potential for error warrants a more flexible approach.

Contracting authorities may also wish to seek from tenderers more detailed information about specific points or additional information, and the provision of such information (including for the purpose of elaborating contractual commitments) will often fall within the concepts of 'clarification' or 'specification' under Article 29(6).[362] Regardless of the position in open or restricted procedures (where again there is a remarkable absence of EU-level case law) the complexity of procurement falling within competitive dialogue means that significant flexibility should arguably be afforded – for example, to allow the contracting

[359] This does not make the concept of fine-tuning redundant, as it may be given other meanings, for example a broader right of correction than applies in open or restricted procedures that perhaps extends to correcting mistakes even when the intended content of the tender is not clear on the face (as discussed below).

[360] Where the error and intended content *is* clear, it seems that correction *must* be allowed under the proportionality principle, at least in some cases: Case T-211, *Tideland Signal* v. *Commission* [2002] ECR II-3781.

[361] See Arrowsmith, n. 3 above, pp. 540–4.

[362] These concepts seem analogous to the concepts of clarifying and supplementing the tender referred to in the Council and Commission statement, n. 351 above, which have been elaborated by Advocate General Lenz in Case C-87/94, *Commission* v. *Belgium (Walloon buses)* [1996] ECR I-2043, as concerning 'the communication of details which describe the object in question more clearly and precisely' and 'the addition of details previously not available': para. 37 of the Opinion.

authority to seek further information to verify whether the bid is realistically deliverable.[363] It is more questionable, however, whether further information may be sought where this would have the effect of improving a bidder's scoring – for example, further information on service quality.[364] It may be argued that this is no different from the case of improvements resulting from amendment and should be treated the same way and prohibited: it presents risks of abuse without being necessary for commercial reasons, given the flexibility that exists at the dialogue stage.

Under Article 29(6), any fine-tuning, etc. must be at the authority's request. However, this condition seems merely to indicate that it is within the authority's discretion to permit fine-tuning, etc. and that the tenderer has no right to this (subject, however, to the general principle of proportionality which may, for example, require that a tenderer be allowed to make certain corrections).[365] There seems to be no reason why a request might not be made because a tenderer draws the authority's attention to a problem.[366]

As regards the Member States' experience, this provision has again in general not been modified in transposition, with national laws in general merely repeating the Directive.[367] However, by way of exception, the legislation in both Germany and Portugal[368] appears to preclude fine-tuning.[369] The Portuguese law also explicitly adopts a strict approach to

[363] *London Underground*, n. 324 above.

[364] Verschuur, n. 3 above, p. 330, rules out any conduct that could affect the outcome in this sense. For a more flexible approach, see Brown, n. 3 above; Burnett, *Competitive Dialogue*, n. 3 above, p. 341, whilst generally advocating a restrictive approach after selection of the winner, suggests that at the stage of evaluating final tenders it may be possible under the concept of fine-tuning for the authority to obtain additional information that brings about 'minor' improvements to tenders.

[365] *Tideland Signal*, n. 360 above.

[366] Arrowsmith, n. 3 above, p. 658; Treumer, 'Competitive Dialogue', n. 3 above, p. 183, proposing an interpretation in accordance with the common interpretation of the general ban on negotiations as also allowing tenderers to seek fine-tuning etc.

[367] See Ch. 3, section 5.7 (UK), Ch. 4, section 5.7 (France), Ch. 5, section 5.7 (Germany), Ch. 6, section 1 (Denmark), Ch. 9, section 5.7 (Poland), Ch. 10, section 5.7 (Lithuania), and Ch. 11, section 5.7 (Italy).

[368] See Ch. 7, section 5.7.6.

[369] The precise significance of this is, however, unclear, given the uncertainty that exists over the meaning of this and the other terms used in Art. 29(6). See also Ch. 12, section 5.7, where it is explained that the wording of this provision has a slight change in the Netherlands.

solicitation of additional information, applying the same provision of the Public Contracts Code that applies in other award procedures.[370]

National legislation also generally has not sought to interpret the boundaries of engagement that is permitted under the concepts of clarification, specification and fine-tuning, and their meaning also does not seem to have been considered in national case law. There is also little guidance issued by Member States, a position which in most Member States merely reflects the limited or non-existent role played by guidance more generally. An exception, however, is the UK where, as we have seen, government guidance often plays a significant role and offers substantive interpretations of EU law. Here, however, it is interesting that the guidance from the Treasury/Office of Government Commerce deliberately avoids addressing specific issues and scenarios, or giving a general definition of fine-tuning etc., stating that this is a matter for the CJEU and that the domestic guidance could be misleading.[371] However, at a general level it seems to endorse a narrow approach which equates the final tendering stage in competitive dialogue with the tendering phase of the open and restricted procedures in this respect;[372] and, more specifically, it rules out the possibility of calling for improvements once final tenders are submitted. On the other hand, guidance issued under the UK Partnerships for Schools programme suggests that there *is* more flexibility than for open and restricted procedures, and specifically contemplates both a flexible approach to correcting errors and to introducing minor improvements.[373] The differing approaches to this issue reflect neatly the uncertainties over the meaning of Article 29(6) – and, as noted below, are also mirrored in UK practice.

Such evidence as exists suggests that the provision is perceived as unclear, and also that in general a narrow approach is adopted in applying it, at least in relation to improvements. Thus Chapter 5 on Germany reports briefly that views differ on how limited contact with tenderers may be, but that most tend to avoid it in practice.[374] Chapter 8 on Spain indicates that Spanish contracting authorities in practice are divided, with some not using the provision at all and others using it to some extent but only for minor points such as the brand of equipment supplied (where irrelevant to functionality) or to clarify compliance with the specifications.[375] In Denmark, contracting authorities interviewed indicated that the provision has been used only to a limited extent and in

370 Ch. 7, section 5.7.6.
371 Ch. 3, section 5.7.4.
372 Ch. 3, section 5.7.4.
373 Ch. 3, section 5.7.4.
374 Ch. 5, section 5.7.
375 Ch. 8, section 5.7.

line with the same approach as in open and restricted procedures –not necessarily because they considered a more flexible approach to be excluded by law, but because of the risk of legal challenge or because broader engagement after final tenders was unnecessary given the flexibility at the pre-tender stage.[376] In the UK,[377] a majority of practitioners interviewed endorsed a narrow legal interpretation in line with the Treasury/Office of Government Commerce guidance referred to above, confining engagement within the limits found in open and restricted procedures, but a significant minority considered that more flexibility than this exists in law. There was also divergence in the practical application of the provision in the UK – whilst, as in Denmark, many simply considered that substantial engagement at this stage was not needed (reflecting in part the widespread practice in the UK of holding a 'dry-run' of the final tender stage before closing dialogue), a similar number reported that conduct sometimes does go beyond mere clarification, including to allow amendments to improve tenders. The lack of clarity in the provision was also highlighted by a significant number of UK interviewees, who reported that the approach adopted in practice consequently often depended on practical considerations, such as the risk of legal challenge.

However, whilst there can be clearly seen to be (i) a perceived lack of clarity of the provision and (ii) a general tendency towards rejecting the possibility of improvements, in the absence of more detailed information it is not possible to know more precisely how this provision is applied, including in the context of issues such as correction of errors and collection of additional information to supplement tenders.

5.7.5. Variants

As elaborated below, it is not obvious that variants are permitted in competitive dialogue; and it might be argued that there is no need of variants since under Article 29(3) of the Public Sector Directive contracting authorities 'may discuss all aspects of the contract with the chosen candidates during this dialogue'. It is therefore interesting that it is common to allow variants in competitive dialogue in some Member States.[378] In Denmark, the Danish Complaints Board for

[376] Ch. 6, section 5.7. [377] See Ch. 3, section 5.7.

[378] See Ch. 5, section 5.7 (Germany), stating that approximately 50 per cent of the contracting authorities allow variants in competitive dialogue; Ch. 6, section 5.7 (Denmark), stating that variants are frequently seen in practice; Ch. 3, section 5.6.1 (UK); Ch. 4,

Public Procurement has specifically ruled that variants are not precluded in competitive dialogue.[379]

It is not evident that variants may be authorised given that Article 29(6) of the Directive states that 'contracting authorities shall ask them [the tenderers] to submit their final tenders *on the basis of the solution or solutions presented and specified during the dialogue*' (emphasis added). This suggests that the possibility of variants in competitive dialogue was not foreseen when drafting the provisions. It may also be argued that allowing variants is not compatible with equal treatment, in that, if the competitive tender procedure takes place in successive stages and this leads to a reduction of the number of both solutions and participants,[380] tenderers eliminated during the various stages of the procedure, unlike those participating in the final tender stage, will not enjoy a chance of being awarded the contract by submitting a variant bid.

However, the fact that variants apparently were not foreseen does not automatically rule out such an approach. Furthermore, nothing in the wording of the Directive expressly prohibits variants. A very important argument in favour of allowing variants is the fact that this approach can turn out to be advantageous for the contracting authority, since a variant may be the most economically advantageous tender. Further, the possibility is apparently accepted in a lengthy and frequently overlooked footnote in the Commission's Explanatory Note on Competitive Dialogue – although the Commission also suggests that the need to have recourse to variants will be limited.[381] It is submitted that variant bids can, in fact, be authorised in competitive dialogue,[382] but not where the contracting authority has eliminated participants during the dialogue.

5.7.6. Selection of the winning tender (or preferred bidder)

Once tenders are fully finalised and any clarifications etc. fully complete, the contracting authority will then select the most economically

section 5.6 (France), were variants are not, however, common; and Ch. 8 (Spain), citing one instance of variants being authorised. In the Netherlands, it is stated in the Procurement Regulations on Tender Procedures for Works (ARW) that variants are not allowed (see Ch. 12, section 5.7), although note that the ARW is not legislation as such.

379 Ch. 6, section 5.7.

380 On this, see section 5.6 above.

381 Explanatory Note, n. 33 above, p. 5, footnote.

382 S. Treumer, 'Implementation of Competitive Dialogue – Danish Legislation and Case Law: The Experience so far', paper presented at the conference Public Procurement: Global Revolution V, 9 September 2010, Copenhagen.

advantageous tender: this is provided by the first paragraph of Article 29(7), which states as follows:

> Contracting authorities shall assess the tenders received on the basis of the award criteria laid down in the contract notice or the descriptive document and shall choose the most economically advantageous tender in accordance with Article 53.

The winner selected at this stage is sometimes referred to as the preferred bidder, since (as discussed below) in some Member States a period of time may follow in which certain matters are further finalised before the final contract is signed (see further section 5.8 below).

5.8. Procedure following the selection of the winning tender (or preferred bidder)[383]

Like the phase that occurs after the final tenders are submitted and before selecting the winner, so with the phase after selecting the preferred bidder, for which the Directive contains a provision for competitive dialogue which has no explicit parallel for other award procedures, which seeks to control engagement with the winner. In particular, this limits the possibility of changes to the terms set in the final tendering phase. This provision is Article 29(7), which states:

> At the request of the contracting authority, the tenderer identified as having submitted the most economically advantageous tender may be asked to clarify aspects of the tender or confirm commitments contained in the tender provided this does not have the effect of modifying substantial aspects of the tender or of the call for tender and does not risk distorting competition or causing discrimination.

What, if anything, may then be done in competitive dialogue between selecting the winner and actually concluding the contract?

We have already suggested in section 5.7 that – in contrast with the negotiated procedure – in competitive dialogue the requirement for complete final tenders limits the scope for engaging with the preferred bidder after that preferred bidder is selected, by limiting the scope for *completing* the terms of the project at this time. This results from the requirement of Article 29(6) for final tenders to be complete. However, it was suggested that there remains some scope for the detail of the

[383] See also Arrowsmith, n. 3 above, pp. 660–3; and Kennedy-Loest, n. 3 above.

contract to be completed after final tenders within the scope of the 'clarification' permitted by Article 29(7) where this is unlikely to affect the outcome of the competition.

In addition, the question arises as to whether any *changes* may be made to what has been agreed. The issues of completion and change are linked, in that when key elements of the contract are left open the parties may wish, as part of the bargaining process, to re-open the provisional agreement on other matters; thus a requirement for complete final tenders may reduce the perceived need for changes after tendering. However, there are still several reasons why the parties may wish to make changes. Various reasons for seeking changes are, for example, identified in Chapter 3 based on research into the practical experience of UK practitioners.[384] The most common reason given for seeking changes in the UK was the need to meet requirements imposed by lenders in the due diligence process, which lenders have recently (particularly since the advent of the recession) been willing to undertake only once a preferred bidder is identified. Further, lenders' willingness to adhere to funding terms may change. The research also suggested that strategies adopted to avoid the need for change due to lenders' requirements have not generally succeeded, often leaving contracting authorities with the choice of making changes or (given the state of the funding market) losing the bid. Another common reason external to the authority was the need to address planning issues, often arising from the fact that planning authorities will not consider detailed planning applications for the same site from more than one applicant. Other reasons included the fact that matters were not sufficiently covered during dialogue; costing and other errors in tenders; mistaken assumptions by bidders (for example, in relation to ground conditions); and changed requirements due to new circumstances, such as political change or spending cuts.

As regards the possibility of change, Article 29(7) is ambiguous, possibly deliberately so to reflect a difference of opinion between Member States. Thus: 'On the one hand, the statement that clarification or confirmation must not have the effect of modifying "substantial" aspects implies that there *is* room for modifying non-substantial aspects. On the other hand, the words "clarify" and "confirm" do not naturally allow room for actual change.'[385]

[384] On all the points below, see Ch. 3, section 5.8.

[385] Arrowsmith, n. 3 above, p. 661.

We will first consider the reported experience of Member States in operating these provisions and then consider some proposals for interpretation.

As regards Member States' approach, it can first be noted that, following the general pattern of implementation of competitive dialogue, legislation transposing the EU rules has again not sought to elucidate the meaning of the provision and – again as with many other areas – the position has not yet been addressed in national case law; nor has national legislation generally sought to elaborate on the provision with additional national rules.[386] A limited exception did, however, apply for a period in France, where legislation on certain types of contract (*contrats de partenariat*) expressly endorsed changes to funding arrangements and certain other financial aspects of tenders as a response to the recession.[387] In addition, an exception in this respect, as in a number of others, is Portugal, which applies in its legislation the same rules on discussions with the winning bidder as apply under other award procedures; thus, even if the Directive itself allows for greater flexibility than in some other procedures, that flexibility may not be enjoyed by Portuguese authorities.

As Chapter 3 elaborates, in the UK the question of what adjustments can be made at the preferred bidder stage has been the subject of particular debate. As with the issue of filling in the detail of the contract at this stage, this has been relevant in determining how far the practice adopted for privately financed infrastructure projects under the negotiated procedure could continue under competitive dialogue. More generally, it has significant implications for costs for all parties (given the expense and delay caused by reopening the procedure or aspects of it) and – even more fundamentally – for the possibility of concluding a contract at all in some cases.

As in other areas, the government has issued guidance on this subject.[388] The main guidance documents take the view – unsurprisingly and uncontroversially – that scope for amendments is less than under the negotiated procedure.[389] Guidance from the Treasury/Office of

[386] See section 5.8 of each of Ch. 3 (UK), Ch. 4 (France – although here, see also the qualification in the text below), Ch. 6 (Denmark), Ch. 9 (Poland), Ch. 10 (Lithuania) and Ch. 11 (Italy).

[387] Ch. 4, section 5.8.

[388] For fuller discussion of and references to the points made below, see Ch. 3, section 5.8.

[389] See Ch. 3, section 5.8.

Government Commerce also suggests that authorities cannot make changes where these could have been anticipated and dealt with at the dialogue stage or on matters directly under the authority's control. Other than this, however, the guidance generally shies away from offering specific legal interpretations but merely gives practical advice on addressing legal uncertainty in a way that takes account of the kind of commercial constraints outlined above: it is phrased in terms of reducing the *risk* of challenge – by reference to factors such as using transparent mechanisms to handle change in a pre-agreed manner – rather than definitive legal statements. Guidance issued by Partnerships for Schools suggests more categorically, citing Arrowsmith's *The Law of Public and Utilities Procurement*,[390] that change for good external reasons *is* permitted, subject to the conditions regarding modifying substantial aspects of the tender or risking distorting competition or causing discrimination.[391]

As regards UK practice, government research in 2010 found that both the time period at the preferred bidder stage and the practice of making changes was (in accordance with its guidance) much reduced, and that the introduction of competitive tension had led to better value for money and reduced delay at this stage[392] (although it should perhaps be noted that this was against a background of concern over the value-for-money aspects of the old practices in negotiated procedures and also greater standardisation of projects, so that it is hard to determine the precise extent to which the change in practice is caused by the switch to competitive dialogue).

However, both government research and an empirical study of practitioners undertaken for Chapter 3 revealed that some changes to the agreement made with the preferred bidder are still made. As to the approach taken to the legal rules,[393] interviewees tended to emphasise the uncertain nature of the rules and took different views on the applicable legal principles as discussed in this section – but generally indicated that they determined the issue of whether to actually make or advise in favour of change in practice in light of the perceived legal risks balanced with commercial and other considerations. Relevant factors included the degree of the change and reasons for it (the existence of good external reasons for change was – as in the government guidance – considered significant in reducing the legal risk); the likelihood of

[390] Arrowsmith, n. 3 above. [391] See Ch. 3, section 5.8. [392] See Ch. 3, section 5.8.
[393] Again, see the detailed discussion in Ch. 3, section 5.8.

challenge; the possibility of restarting or otherwise rewinding the process; the legal risks in rewinding the process; the costs, delay and political and professional embarrassment of restarting or rewinding the procedure; and personal relationships with bidder teams. In view of its convenience, and practical and legal difficulties associated with other options (notably restarting the procedure or rewinding it back to the dialogue or final tender stage), in most circumstances a contracting authority was likely to go ahead with a change that was considered essential, and conclude the contract with the preferred bidder. It can also be noted that government research found that a significant number of practitioners perceived that the limited room for manoeuvre under the legislation at the preferred bidder stage creates 'difficulties' for conducting competitive dialogue (without indicating, however, how wide these different respondents perceived the room for manoeuvre to be).

Information on practice in other Member States that have experience of competitive dialogue is more limited; in particular, there is no scientific information available on operation of this phase in France. Interviews with representatives of contracting authorities in Denmark reveal, as reported in Chapter 6,[394] a general perception of both sides that the legal rules are complied with in that 'substantial' changes are not made, despite, often, a considerable timespan between choosing the winner and concluding the contract. However, no more precise information is available on what is understood by substantial or the precise nature of changes actually made. Based on anecdotal evidence, Chapter 5 reports that in Germany practitioners generally reject negotiations on the contents of tenders, and at this stage are mainly concerned with confirming funding commitments and necessary authorisations – but, however, accept 'small' changes that are not relevant for choosing the winner as these do not affect competition or cause discrimination.[395] Thus in Germany, as in the UK, it appears that not all change is considered as precluded, although there is no specific information in Germany on the kind of changes that are made or the reasons for them. (It should also be mentioned here that there appears to be significant use of the negotiated procedure for complex contracts in Germany that may reduce the need for changes in projects that use competitive dialogue.) In the Netherlands, it is reported that, as in the UK and Denmark, the preferred bidder phase may be lengthy (several months) but that in general this

[394] See Ch. 6, section 5.8. [395] Ch. 5, section 5.8.

is limited to activity concluding the financial arrangements and preparing the final contractual documents. In Spain, it appears that contracting authorities refrain from entering into any discussions but, as already mentioned in section 5.7, run the post-tender stage of the procedure in the same way as an open procedure.

We can also note that the Lithuanian Public Procurement Office has issued guidance that identifies certain types of changes – such as changes to the payment mechanism and payment schedule, and to the scope of the contract – as prohibited, but as yet Lithuania has negligible experience of operating the procedure.

We may now return to the interpretation of Article 29(7) and consider various proposals for interpretation.

In this respect, although there is some uncertainty in its meaning, it at least seems clear that the starting point for interpretation is that the preferred bidder stage cannot be used to renegotiate the terms established by the tender process. This position is encapsulated in the comment on Article 29(7) in the Commission's Explanatory Note:[396] 'It must be emphasised that this does not entail any negotiations solely with this economic operator – amendments aimed at authorising such negotiations were proposed and rejected by the Community legislative process.' As we have seen above, such limited evidence as exists indicates that this interpretation is accepted as the correct one in Member States in guidance and by practitioners.

On the other hand, however, it can be argued that Article 29(7) does not preclude *any* possibility of changes, in that the prohibition on 'substantial' change implies that at least some changes that are non-substantial are possible. Further, a strong argument can be made that this is an appropriate interpretation given the realities of many of the complex procurement situations for which competitive dialogue is useful, and in which it may be disproportionately costly, difficult or even impossible for practical reasons to finalise all aspects of the procurement at the final tender stage. Such an interpretation is also strongly reinforced by the analogy of the position of concluded contracts; in this context, the CJEU has accepted that there is some scope for change without re-tendering,[397] and it would be anomalous to wholly discount all change merely because the contract has not yet been signed. This is particularly the case in the context of complex procurement that

[396] Explanatory Note, n. 33 above, section 3.3.

[397] *pressetext*, n. 200 above.

necessitates relatively lengthy award procedures; it may, in fact, be easier to make amendments to a concluded contract by holding a new open or restricted procedure than it would be to adjust a proposed contract by re-opening a nearly complete competitive dialogue award procedure, or parts of that procedure, *before* signing the contract. In both cases, the proportionality principle entails some scope for adjustments where required for good reason. As we saw above, this possibility of *some* change is accepted in the government guidance in the UK and Lithuania, and we have seen that changes are made in practice in a number of Member States – although, with the exception of the UK, there is limited information on the details and on the perceived limits of change.

Recognition of the possibility of change can be based in part on an interpretation of the concept of confirmation and clarification. Thus, it is submitted that use of the power of *clarification* can in some cases lead to amendment. For example, discovery of an error, ambiguity or contradiction in a tender might necessitate a correction no less than if this is discovered during examination of tenders or after concluding the contract. Indeed, correction before concluding the contract may be greatly preferable to entering a contract based on an error, which may give rise to significant practical difficulties.[398] It is also arguable that adjustment is possible on the basis of the scope for *confirmation* of tenders when the tenderer is unable to obtain confirmation of commitments due to external circumstances such as funders' refusal to accept the terms.[399] (If, however, confirmation does not embrace this possibility, many such changes still seem possible under the principles discussed below allowing for change as a result of external events.)

It can also be argued that further scope for change exists by analogy with the case of concluded contracts. In this respect, it can be suggested that Article 29(7) does not contain an exhaustive statement of the rules applicable to the preferred bidder stage. Rather, it contains a positive statement that clarification and confirmation are possible – subject to the stated limits that such conduct does not have the effect of modifying substantial aspects of the tender or of the call for tender and does not risk distorting competition or causing discrimination – and also implies

[398] The position will depend on the national law on the effect of errors on contractual obligations.

[399] For a contrary view, see Burnett, *Competitive Dialogue*, n. 3 above, pp. 145–6, arguing that commitments must be definitive and thus not dependent on, for example, funder approval.

that the parties do not have a general freedom to renegotiate terms, but it does not regulate the issue of adjustments exhaustively, including the possibility of adjustment to deal with unforeseen circumstances. This issue is left – as in other award procedures and at other points of time, such as after conclusion of the contract – to the general principles of the Directive.

Drawing on the analogy of concluded contracts, what are the limits on change?

Consistently with the basic principle that the terms of the agreement cannot be negotiated at the post-tender stage, it can be argued that in defining the scope for change the reason for the change is relevant: in particular, any change must be the justified outcome of some external factor, change in circumstances or unforeseen situation. Examples of this based on practical experiences (from the UK) might include refusal of funders to commit to the project; refusal of planning permission for the details of the tendered design; or the 'September 11' terrorist attack, which occurred during the 'preferred bidder' stage of the project to upgrade and maintain the London Underground and significantly affected the risks involved in the project, entailing renegotiation of some terms.[400] This approach of focusing on the reason for change is reflected in the UK government guidance referred to above. Of course, there is room for debate as to what should qualify as sufficient reason. For example, if parties could realistically require funders' approval or obtain planning approvals before final tendering, it might be argued that failure to obtain approval might not be considered a sufficient reason for change. There may also be some debate over whether it is permitted for cost reasons to leave tenderers' own site surveys until after selection of the preferred bidder and to adjust the terms of the agreement if the results of the surveys were wholly unanticipated and thus not addressed in any prior agreement.[401] However, it is submitted that the mere fact that it is not totally impossible to address the issue prior to the preferred bidder stage will not *per se* preclude change to the agreement – this will be permitted when to address it would involve disproportionate costs, in accordance with the proportionality principle. This is consistent with the suggestion made earlier that costs of alternatives are relevant to the *use*

[400] An example given in UK government guidance as a permitted reason for change: see Ch. 3, section 5.8.

[401] See Arrowsmith, n. 3 above, p. 651, who considers that this is permitted; and Kennedy-Loest, n. 3 above, p. 324.

of competitive dialogue and to interpreting the requirement for complete tenders.[402] In considering this issue it needs to be kept in mind that, as discussed below, even changes that are permitted in principle are subject to important limiting conditions, that substantially limit any risks of undermining the objectives of the EU procurement rules – from this perspective, a strict approach to what changes are permitted *in principle* would very clearly be disproportionate. The proportionality principle requires a flexible approach to, in particular, changes (such as inability to obtain planning approvals) that would actually prevent the project going ahead with the preferred bidder, rather than those that make new terms more appropriate (for example, adjusting the terms to new risks), given the high costs of possible alternatives to adjusting the preferred bid: it may be impossible in practice to proceed without a new final tender or – where other tenderers are no longer interested (as UK experience shows is often the case)[403] – even without a new award procedure, which could take significant time.

For all changes that are permitted in principle, however – whether as a result of clarification or confirmation or for other reasons – certain important limits apply, either under Article 29(7), by analogy with Article 29(7), or under general principles of equal treatment.

One important general limit seems to be that any change must not be such that, had it been made earlier, it would have affected the outcome. Such a limit applies in delimiting permitted changes to a concluded contract as articulated in *pressetext* where the CJEU stated that an amendment constitutes a new contract when it 'introduces conditions which, had they been part of the original award procedure, would have allowed for the admission of different tenders or acceptance of a tender other than the one accepted';[404] and the same limit is relevant by analogy to pre-contract changes. Such a limit was apparently accepted in relation to changes at preferred bidder stage in a negotiated procedure, in the *London Underground* state aid case.[405] An example of a prohibited change would be where a pricing error entails adjusting the price upwards to a figure that, if included at the time of evaluation, would have meant that that tender was not the most economically advantageous tender. Another would be where a design feature crucial to the success of the tender is dropped because planning permission is refused.

[402] See section 5.7 above. [403] See the discussion later below.
[404] *pressetext*, n. 200 above, para. 35. [405] *London Underground*, n. 324 above.

However, in practice often it is not wholly clear whether or not the preferred bidder would have remained. For example, if changes are made to the scope of the contract it will not always be clear what terms other tenderers would have offered and thus how the changes would have affected their relative positions. In this case – based on the statement on Article 29(7) that changes must not risk distorting competition – it seems that the change will be prohibited if there was a *risk* of a different outcome. How significant this risk must be is not clear, but the principle of proportionality again seems to require a reasonably flexible approach recognising, in particular, the practical difficulties of reopening a competitive dialogue procedure.[406] Precisely the same issue may arise in the context of a change to a concluded contract and similar principles would appear to be relevant – but the jurisprudence on concluded contracts does not provide any guidance as yet.

A second limit can also possibly be deduced based on the analogy of concluded contracts, which is that any change must not alter the economic balance of the contract in favour of the tenderer,[407] even if it would not have affected the choice of winner. Changes that have this effect may possibly be permitted in negotiated procedures to a limited extent, recognising that this may be necessary to secure agreement when renegotiation is required or negotiation is incomplete.[408] However, in view of the complete nature of tenders in competitive dialogue and the general prohibition on renegotiating matters already agreed, such changes arguably are not permitted in that procedure, the situation being more analogous to that of a concluded agreement than to the preferred bidder stage of a negotiated procedure.

In addition, the requirement in Article 29(7) that changes may not be 'substantial' may also imply an independent qualitative and quantitative limit on permitted changes even when they do not violate the limits discussed above. Again, this would be consistent with the CJEU's approach to changes to concluded contracts: the court has stated that a change is prohibited when it 'extends the scope of the contract considerably to encompass services not initially covered'.[409]

406 Ch. 5 on Germany reports that some German authors favour a broad view in this respect: Ch. 5, section 5.8.

407 *pressetext*, n. 200 above, para. 37. A different view is stated in Arrowsmith, n. 3 above, p. 662, but needs to be revised in light of *pressetext*.

408 See *London Underground*, n. 324 above.

409 *pressetext*, n. 200 above, para. 36.

In Case C-160/08, *Commission* v. *Germany*,[410] an extension to a contract for providing ambulance services in one region of Germany to cover a new ambulance station was characterised by the CJEU as a new contract under this rule. In this respect, the court simply noted that the contract was 'considerably above' the relevant threshold[411] – but it appears (as indicated by Advocate General Trstenjak)[412] that a relevant test for a 'considerable' increase from a quantitative perspective is the increase in size in proportion to the contract (in that case, a 15 per cent increase in value and a 25 per cent increase in the area covered) (although it is submitted that a requirement for additional work to be above the threshold to be unlawful may also be an additional requirement).[413]

In deciding whether the principles above apply to limit changes it is important to determine what constitutes an actual change and what is merely an *application* of agreed terms. With a concluded contract, the fact that a potential adjustment or alternative approach to a project is contemplated and addressed in the agreement itself is relevant to whether it is a change[414] but is not conclusive[415] – this depends on several factors. It is submitted that the same basic approach is to be adopted to defining change for the purpose of the rules governing the preferred bidder stage in competitive dialogue – especially when it is borne in mind that it may depend simply on the choice of the parties whether a particular issue (such as the effect of refusal of certain permissions) is addressed at pre-contract or post-contract stage, making it illogical to take a different approach to the two stages. Based on principles of equal treatment and transparency, whether or not a measure constitutes a change arguably depends on factors such as the degree of precision with which the contract specifies the circumstances of the measure occurring and the

410 Case C-160/08, *Commission* v. *Germany*, judgment of 29 April 2010.
411 *Ibid.*, para. 99 of the judgment.
412 See Opinion of Advocate General Trstenjak delivered on 4 June 2009, Case C-536/07, *Commission* v. *Germany*, paras. 132–4.
413 It is submitted that the transparency requirements of the TFEU are met for below-threshold work by their award to the winner of a transparent procedure for the rest of the work.
414 *pressetext*, n. 200 above, paras. 64–9 and 84 of the judgment.
415 It would provide *carte blanche* to evade the Directive if the parties could, for example, simply agree to raise prices or increase quantities 'by agreement' in future. See further Arrowsmith, n. 3 above, pp. 287–90.

consequences for the parties' obligations;[416] where precision is not possible, whether there is a mechanism for external and objective verification and approval of the need for the measure and the manner of adjustment of the parties' obligations[417] (such as the amount of any price increase); normal commercial practice (such as whether mutual annual renewal of contract over a period of years, as with insurance, is common commercial practice); and the extent to which the impact of the possible adjustments was considered when evaluating the original tenders.[418] It is submitted that it is from this perspective that – as suggested in UK government guidance discussed above – agreed provision at the final tender stage for dealing with foreseen circumstances may affect the legality of the measures taken at the preferred bidder stage. For example, if an alternative to proposed elements of a design in the event of planning permission being refused are provided for expressly in the final tendering process, adoption of the alternative may (depending on all circumstances) be regarded as an application of agreed terms rather than as a change to the project.

If it is not possible to reach agreement within the above constraints, the contracting authority's options may be, depending on the circumstances, to re-tender the project (often costly and time-consuming); to rewind the procedure to some other earlier point, such as by holding a new round of tendering with previous bidders (where some or all are still prepared to participate); or to award the contract to another bidder based on that bidder's final tender (for example, if that bidder is now the most economically advantageous as the result of the change). It can be noted that recital 31 of Directive 2004/18 states that competitive dialogue: 'must not be used in such a way as to restrict or distort competition . . . by involving any tenderer other than the one selected as the most economically advantageous', possibly suggesting that discussion after the entity has identified the most advantageous tender cannot be used as part of the process of choosing the winning tender. However, even if this statement (found in the recital only) has that effect, it does not appear to preclude awarding

[416] As with a price index for changing the prices as referred to in *pressetext*, n. 200 above, paras. 64–9; and Case C-337/98, *Commission* v. *France* ('*Rennes Railway*') [2000] ECR I-8377, para. 53; and see *London Underground*, n. 324 above.

[417] See *London Underground*, n. 324 above.

[418] Case C-340/02, *Commission* v. *France* [2004] ECR I-9845.

the contract to the second best tenderer or re-tendering when the best tenderer is no longer in the competition.[419]

However, whilst UK guidance endorses the last two options above as legal possibilities,[420] UK practical experience shows that these options are often not feasible as the rejected bidders are no longer available. It is not clear whether or not there are potential workable solutions to this issue in the UK or elsewhere – for example, how far measures can be taken that will induce other bidders to stay engaged until the contract is finally signed. However, in view of the resources that must be kept committed for many of the kind of projects awarded by competitive dialogue, it would not be surprising if this were not practicable. If the bidders whose equal treatment is in issue have been given the opportunity to participate again but are genuinely no longer interested or available, then an argument could be made that it does not violate equal treatment to make the change without rewinding the procedure if the contracting authority considers that the best course of action. A rule that allows this may in fact enhance transparency by making it more likely that the contracting authorities will deal with this situation openly after consulting other bidders, rather than make the change behind closed doors for fear of violating the law. However, the position at present seems unclear.

To sum up, it is suggested that some changes to the agreement made at the final tender stage are possible at preferred bidder stage, but that these are generally subject to certain conditions that can be deduced by analogy with the rules applying to concluded contracts: they must be justified by external factors, a change of circumstances or some unforeseen situation; they must be such that they would not have changed the outcome if made earlier (although a reasonably flexible approach should be applied to deciding whether there is a risk of a different outcome); they must not change the economic balance of the contract; and they must not exceed certain quantitative and qualitative limits. In addition, parties may include in the agreement reached at final tender stage mechanisms for adjusting the details of the agreement on certain eventualities, and these adjustments will not necessarily be regarded as changes at all; whether this is so depends on several factors, such as the use of an objective and

[419] There is nothing in the Directive to preclude this for other award procedures and it may be needed for many reasons – for example, because the winning tenderer is unqualified or refuses to sign the contract; and it would be highly anomalous if the position were different under competitive dialogue.

[420] See Ch. 3, section 8.

transparent change mechanism. These conditions can adequately ensure that equal treatment is respected and that any real risk of discrimination is avoided – and, given that this is the case, any stricter approach to change is ruled out by the principle of proportionality, in light of the significant and related interests of Member States in ensuring value for money and limiting the costs of participation.

5.9. *The standstill period*[421]

For competitive dialogue, as for other competitive award procedures under Directive 2004/18, there is a requirement in Remedies Directive 89/665 for a 'standstill' period between notification of the result of the award decision to participants and the conclusion of the contract.[422] In this respect, Article 2a(2) of the Remedies Directive states:

> A contract may not be concluded following the decision to award a contract falling within the scope of Directive 2004/18/EC before the expiry of a period of at least ten calendar days with effect from the day following the date on which the contract award decision is sent to the tenderers and candidates concerned if fax or electronic means are used or, if other means of communication are used, before the expiry of a period of either at least 15 calendar days with effect from the day following the date on which the contract award decision is sent to the tenderers and candidates concerned or at least ten calendar days with effect from the day following the date of the receipt of the contract award decision.

The purpose of this standstill period is to allow unsuccessful participants an effective opportunity to challenge the award decision before the contract is actually concluded. To ensure such an effective opportunity, the notification must be accompanied by certain information concerning the reason for the award decision.[423] This explicit provision in the Directives gives effect in a more concrete and certain form to a standstill obligation that the CJEU had already held to exist under the Remedies Directive's general requirement for effective remedies,[424] in jurisprudence originating in the *Alcatel* case.[425] It is an important obligation

[421] See further A. Brown, 'Applying Alcatel in the Context of Competitive Dialogue' (2006) 15 *Public Procurement Law Review* 332.

[422] Directive 89/665, n. 41 above, Art. 2a, as inserted by Directive 2007/66/EC, n. 41 above.

[423] Directive 89/665, n. 41 above, Art. 2a(2).

[424] Directive 89/665, n. 41 above, Art. 1(1).

[425] Case C-81/98, *Alcatel Austria* v. *Bundeministerium für Wissenschaft und Verkehr* [1999] ECR I-7671; Case C-444/06, *Commission* v. *Spain* [2008] ECR I-2045 (concluding that a standstill must be applied even when a concluded contract can be challenged).

since failure to observe the standstill must under certain conditions give rise to the ineffectiveness of the subsequent contract.[426]

In the context of competitive dialogue, the minimum period of the Directive as stated above (for example, ten calendar days from notification by email or fax) is relatively short and thus need not cause undue delay. Member States appear generally to have applied the same period to competitive dialogue as to other award procedures, and to have used the minimum period allowed by the Directive – although in some cases with minor tweaks or minor extensions.[427] An exception to this latter approach, however, is found in Italy, where in general a thirty-five-day standstill period is provided for all award procedures.[428] It is suggested in Chapter 11 that this long standstill period, along with the legal risks faced by contracting authorities there in operating competitive dialogue, may discourage use of the procedure in Italy.[429]

The question has been debated in the UK as to what exactly is the 'award' decision for the purpose of Article 2a(2) above, as this is the point at which the explicit obligation to send a notification and observe a standstill will arise. It can be noted that there is no formal definition of the concept of 'award' for the purpose of any UK domestic law. Even if this were the case, as in some Member States, it would not provide an answer to the current question as the concept of an award here is an EU-level concept that probably does not depend on domestic definitions.[430] The issue is whether, given a time period of several months between selecting a winner based on final tenders and actually concluding the legal agreement that may involve some scope for completing immaterial detail or the possibility of change to the terms, the award occurs when the choice is originally made, just before the contract is concluded when all details are fixed, or at some point in between. As Chapter 3 explains in detail, practitioners in the UK (where the domestic law does not elaborate on the Directive's requirements) vary significantly in their approach both to interpreting and applying the standstill in this respect in competitive dialogue, with notices being sent sometimes on initial identification of the preferred bidder, sometimes once formal approval has been given to the appointment (which usually occurs close to the conclusion of the contract), sometimes just prior

[426] Directive 89/665, n. 41 above, Art. 2d(1)(b).

[427] See section 5.9 of each of Ch. 3 (UK), Ch. 4 (France), Ch. 5 (Germany), Ch. 9 (Poland), Ch. 10 (Lithuania) and Ch. 8 (Spain).

[428] Ch. 11, section 5.9. [429] Ch. 11, section 5.9. [430] See n. 234 above.

to contract conclusion, and sometimes both at the time the preferred bidder is identified and sometimes at a later stage.[431] The UK government guidance indicates that a standstill should be applied not necessarily immediately a preferred bidder is identified but once 'there will be no further changes that will modify the terms under which the contract will be concluded'.[432]

One view of the law, preferred by Professor Treumer, is that an award for the purpose of the standstill obligation always takes place at the time of the original choice. This is based on the fact that the presumption of all parties in the procedure and the typical outcome of such a choice is that the contract will be concluded with the so-called preferred bidder and it is therefore relevant to send a notification already at this point; and this will also ensure that a challenge can be made at an early stage in accordance with the purpose of the Remedies Directive.

Another possible view, however, is that a notice is required only once it is definitively decided to conclude the contract with a particular bidder on particular terms, as indicated in the UK guidance referred to above. On this latter view, it does not violate the Remedies Directive to send a formal standstill notice *only* just prior to concluding the contract. However, if this view is correct, it would seem also to be compliant with the Remedies Directive to choose instead to send the formal notice at the earlier point when the preferred bidder is chosen as an alternative. Sending a notification at this point can help ensure that challenges are made in practice at an early stage, as well as satisfying bidders' expectations of receiving information about their position at this stage. (Indeed, it can be argued that there is an obligation at least to keep bidders informed at this stage, even if not to send the formal notice under the Remedies Directive, on the basis that transparency requires bidders to be informed of their status.)[433]

However, whichever of these two views is adopted, it would seem that when a notice is not sent just prior to the conclusion of the fully agreed contract (either because it must be sent at this point by law or – under the second view of the law – where the contracting authority chooses to send it at this point) it would seem that a second notice and standstill period is needed whenever there has been a change to, or completion of,

[431] See Ch. 3, section 5.9. [432] See Ch. 3, section 5.9.
[433] *Embassy Limousines and Services* v. *European Parliament* [1998] ECR II-4239.

the agreement *that would affect the information required or given in the earlier standstill notice.*[434] Should the actual choice of contractor change between the sending of the original notice and the signing of a contract – for example, because the winner drops out – then arguably a new notice is always needed in any award procedure.

As we have noted above, although the Remedies Directive does not apply to contracts outside Directive 2004/18, effective national remedies must be provided for violations of EU law – such as violations of TFEU obligations – in awarding contracts outside the Directive under general Treaty principles. The CJEU has not yet clarified whether a standstill obligation applies to contracts outside the scope of the procurement Directives and it might be argued that is the case based on the Treaty principle of effectiveness, by extension of the reasoning in *Alcatel* which, as we have seen, based a standstill obligation on the general effectiveness principle of the Directive. However, this seems less likely since the case of *Wall*[435] which, as we mentioned in section 2.1, has made it clear that the effectiveness principle under the Treaty does not entail such strong remedies principles as are found under the Remedies Directives.

5.10. *Payments for costs of participation*

Article 29(8) of Directive 2004/18 states expressly that: 'The contracting authorities may specify prices or payments to the participants in the dialogue.' The reference to 'prices' apparently refers specifically to the concept of a prize or award that is won,[436] for example, for submitting an innovative design (without that economic operator necessarily being awarded the contract or the design even being used), whilst payment refers to any type of payment – for example, this could be payment for the costs of preparing a bid.

This possibility is not limited to competitive dialogue. As the Commission's Explanatory Note clarifies, there is nothing else in the Directive to prevent Member States from specifying such payments etc. in other

[434] Brown, n. 421 above, p. 335, suggested prior to the introduction of the explicit provision on standstill in the Remedies Directive that a later notice was necessary only upon a material change – that would amount to an admission of a violation and be unlikely to be complied with; but, whether or not that was the case, the introduction of the explicit provision justifies the suggestion given here in the text.

[435] Case C-91/08, *Wall AG* v. *Stadt Frankfurt am Main* [2010] ECR I-2815.

[436] See Explanatory Note, n. 33 above, footnote 25 in, section 3.2 of the Note.

types of award procedures,[437] and Article 29(8) was not intended to change this position. Rather, it was included in order to signal that such payments may be particularly appropriate in the context of competitive dialogue.[438] This is, first, because of the significant costs that were envisaged for those participating in competitive dialogue – and which have been confirmed by the experiences of Member States.[439] As we have mentioned, there is perceived to be a danger that high costs are a deterrent to participation, and it was envisaged that this issue might possibly be addressed by compensating participants for some of these costs. In addition, it was envisaged that it might be appropriate to use prizes or payments as a means of facilitating the agreement of participants to use of their ideas or other confidential information, where contracting authorities wish to use some kind of designated solution or hybrid model for the competitive dialogue procedure. As discussed in section 5.3, Article 29(3) of the Directive states that the contracting authorities may not reveal to the other participants solutions proposed or other confidential information[440] communicated by a candidate participating in the dialogue without the candidate's agreement and, whilst we suggested that agreement to use of such information might be made a condition of participation, payments might be needed as a means to induce participation under such a condition, or to ensure that participants are actually willing to put forward their innovative ideas during the procedure.

Experience with this provision so far reveals a very different approach in different Member States – whilst in one group such payments etc. are non-existent or extremely rare, another group of states uses them extensively, with payments being required by law in some cases.

As regards the first group, in Member States the legislation essentially simply repeats the permissive provision of the Directive itself, in most cases in the same (or almost same) form, leaving the choice of whether to make payments etc. to contracting authorities themselves; and those contracting authorities rarely, if at all, use this possibility. This is the case in the UK, Portugal, Spain and Denmark. In the UK, such payments

437 Explanatory Note, n. 33 above, section 3.2, which also points out that Art. 9(1) concerning inclusion of prizes and payments when calculating the value of contracts for threshold purposes is not expressly limited to competitive dialogue.

438 Explanatory Note, n. 33 above, section 3.2.

439 See, for example, Ch. 3, section 6.

440 It is not clear how other confidential information should be defined. See on this point Ch. 12, section 5.3.

were very rare in the context of complex contracts awarded under the negotiated procedure. The main government guidance suggests a strong presumption against such payments under competitive dialogue also,[441] and this is reflected in actual practice with competitive dialogue: empirical research on the experience of practitioners which was undertaken for this book revealed only one instance of such a payment, and that of a tiny 'token' amount.[442] Research on Spain and Portugal reported in Chapters 7 and 8 did not uncover any instances of such payments being made.[443] In Denmark,[444] payments appear rare – the research done for Chapter 6 found no tradition of, or expectation of, payments in the IT field, and few other cases of payments being made. However, it did find occasional payments being made in projects for public works, of around €337,000 in one case and €135,000 in two others – estimated at less than 10 per cent of the costs incurred but nevertheless (according to the contracting authorities) considered to be worthwhile by the recipients. These, it may be noted, were payments for the costs of participation, rather than for the use of tenderers' ideas – as we will see is the case also in some other states that make payments. In Poland, the legislative provision refers to payment for those proposing a solution which subsequently becomes the basis for the submission of tenders, but Chapter 9 reports that such payments are 'very rare'.[445]

By contrast with this group of Member States, in France, Germany and the Netherlands – all with significant experience of competitive dialogue – payments are often made. In France, legislation not only provides for payments but *requires* their use for certain types of contract, when the demands of the contracting authority require a significant investment by the participant in the award procedure; and payments are very commonly made in general for the purpose of compensating for participation costs, to encourage participation and better-quality solutions.[446] In Germany, also, certain payments are required by law for certain matters: a contracting authority is obliged to 'appropriately' compensate participants asked to submit sketches, drafts, drawings, calculations, diagrams or building plans (but not for the value of their ideas or solutions nor for the handling and mere processing of the tenders).[447] In the Netherlands, although the legislation is purely permissive for contracting authorities, it is common in practice to

[441] See Ch. 3, section 5.10. [442] See Ch. 3, section 5.10.
[443] Section 5.10 of Chs. 7 and 8 respectively. [444] See Ch. 6, section 5.10.
[445] See Ch. 9, section 5.10. [446] See Ch. 4, section 5.10. [447] See Ch. 5, section 5.10.

compensate for part of the costs of participation, although not where candidates must merely calculate a price or when a small amount of additional effort is required.

It can also be noted that the approach of providing for the possibility of payment but leaving the issue mainly to authorities themselves, is found also in Italy and Lithuania – but, as we have seen, there is in these two cases no practical experience to draw on as yet on how the provisions might operate. The Italian legislation elaborates slightly on how the provision is to be used, providing, *inter alia*, that, whenever payments of prizes or awards are provided for, they *must* bring about the transfer of the property of the preliminary plan submitted during the dialogue[448] – indicating a specific role of payments in ensuring that proposals can be used as the basis of the project by other tenderers. As Chapter 8 explains and as we noted above[449] in considering other approaches to complex procurement, Italy – in contrast with, for example, the UK – has a past practice of awarding prizes and other payments for a comparable purpose in the context of design contests used there for complex projects, and this might affect their use in competitive dialogue also. In Lithuania, the possible use of payments is elaborated in guidance from the Public Procurement Office rather than legislation, with its Recommendation stating that prizes and payments shall compensate at least part of the costs incurred in preparing proposals – indicating a potential focus on compensating for costs rather than purchasing ideas.

We can see that practice shows that a number of Member States never, or rarely, appear to make payments to participants, considering them either unnecessary or inappropriate to ensure adequate participation or to obtain relevant ideas; whilst others use them to a significant extent to compensate firms for the costs of participating in award procedures, although apparently less so for the purchase of ideas to use in a project. It is not clear whether such payments improve the overall efficiency of outcomes for contracting authorities or whether the best approach varies between states (according, for example, to the nature of local markets or the expectations of participants), or what are the reasons for the differences in approach. Relevant considerations in deciding whether and how to use payments may be the extent to which this approach improves participation and/or the quality of input in practice, the extent to which different approaches help or hinder the control of costs of participation

[448] See Ch. 11, section 5.10. [449] See section 2.2 above.

(which may depend on which party is better placed to control certain costs, or whether making payments encourages inefficient participation simply as a source of income for firms) and the extent to which costs are passed on to contracting authorities. This may be a useful area for further research.

6. Conclusions

Our key aim in this chapter has been to provide some critical reflections on the legal rules on competitive dialogue, based on experience of the procedure in its first few years. At the outset it may be said that two related themes have been prominent in the chapter and are reflected in the conclusions below.

The first is that it is important not to place undue emphasis on transparency and formal equality at the expense of other considerations. Of course, the principles of transparency and equal treatment are fundamental to competitive dialogue, as they are to the other award procedures under Directive 2004/18, and play a central role. However, it must be kept in mind that their content is variable according to the nature of the different award procedures, and that other principles such as proportionality and competition also come into play in interpreting the legal rules. These last two principles are particularly relevant for competitive dialogue given the need to keep the costs of the procedure to a reasonable level, with participation costs being relevant for attracting competition. A balanced approach in applying all these different principles is essential for ensuring adequate consideration is given to the interests of the diverse Member States in achieving their own procurement goals in a manner suitable to their particular circumstances and values – whilst some Member States place transparency and formal equality very high on the agenda in their domestic values or as a means of achieving domestic goals, such as value for money, this is not true in all cases, as we have explained. A balanced approach is also important, however, for the EU's own objectives, the need to manage costs to promote competition being a key illustration of this.

The second theme is the need to deal with the considerable uncertainty in the legal rules, which affects both use and operation of competitive dialogue, and seems to deter its use to a significant degree in some Member States, particularly in light of the high risks of legal challenge that exist in some of those states. We consider that addressing the grey areas of the law through guidance that promotes a balanced approach as described above could play an important role in encouraging use of competitive dialogue where it is suitable. In this respect, the European Commission will need to play a primary role, especially given the limited or non-existent role of national guidance in some Member States and the general reluctance to provide formal guidance that may risk contravening the Commission's approach.

In light of these general points, what, then, are the key findings and conclusions?

As regards the reception of the procedure in the Member States, we have seen first, in section 3, that, although it is optional, the new procedure has been included in the legal regimes of *all* Member States. In this regard, it is noteworthy that, for the most part, the Member States studied have transposed the procedure simply by copying out the wording of the Directive itself, neither adding to the EU-level rules nor elaborating their meaning to any significant extent (although Portugal provides a significant exception). This is true even of those Member States that have a strong tradition of regulating public procurement and in other areas tend to regulate in a way that goes beyond the requirements of Directive 2004/18. In this way, Member States have provided for their contracting authorities all the flexibilities allowed by the Directive itself – and also maintained the uncertainties of the EU legislation. It is relevant, however, to reiterate that recognition at EU level of the *possibility* of certain approaches does not mean that they must necessarily be made available to contracting authorities, even if that has occurred so far. This is relevant to the point made above concerning the need for a balanced approach towards transparency and formal equality – Member States that place great weight on these matters in their own systems and prefer greater transparency than is required by the Directive can always provide for this on a national level, and their preferences should not affect the endorsement of a more flexible approach at an EU level.

We have seen also, however, in section 4, that, although competitive dialogue has been formally adopted throughout Europe, it has been actually used to a significant extent only in the UK and France, the two countries that most perceived a need for this procedure prior to 2004, and on whose past experiences in law and practice the procedure is most closely modelled. Elsewhere, its use has been quite limited – although (as in Poland and Denmark, for example) not necessarily insignificant or without importance; and in some countries its impact has been negligible. However, the use that the procedure *has* seen justifies its inclusion in the Directive bearing in mind, as we have discussed, the diverse nature of Member States and the Directive's principle of accommodating national practices. It is clear that the procedure has in part at least achieved its aims in that it has significantly reduced reliance on the negotiated procedure for complex contracts in the UK, thus improving transparency, whilst at the same time providing a more flexible option for other complex contracts.

Further, we consider that the procedure could be useful elsewhere (including to reduce continued over-use of the negotiated procedure with a notice) and that a flexible approach should be adopted in interpreting the grounds for use in order to facilitate this and to give effect to the intention of the legislator. In section 4.5 we proposed five key principles of interpretation, namely, that competitive dialogue is not an exceptional procedure in the sense that this concept is used in the context of the negotiated procedure without a notice, and that thus it must not be very narrowly interpreted; that it is available when contracting authorities cannot define the *best* technical means for meeting their needs or the *best* legal or financial make-up for the project; that its use can be justified by the disproportionate time and/or cost involved in a different approach; that whether an authority is 'objectively' able to define the technical, financial or legal composition of the contract is to be judged by the standard of a 'reasonable' contracting authority of the same size and nature; and that a contracting authority enjoys a margin of discretion in determining whether open or restricted procedures could be used instead of competitive dialogue. As noted in section 4, it seems that the uncertainty over the procedure's availability in law is a factor that deters its use in some Member States, at least, and it would be appropriate to address this through clear guidance at the EU level that mandates a flexible approach. Whilst, as section 4.4 explained, the Commission's current 'unofficial' guidance in its Explanatory Note does address the issue to some extent and exhibits a flexible approach in many respects, more formal and detailed guidance that endorses the propositions set above, and perhaps gives practical examples of appropriate use based on actual experience, would be very useful. Given that use of the procedure also appears to be influenced in part by familiarity with its approaches, appropriate use might be further encouraged by disseminating information on practices in Member States – and this could also, of course, be important to help avoid pitfalls in operating the procedure. In this respect, many valuable lessons are available from countries such as the UK, Spain and the Netherlands, where use of the procedure has been analysed in various studies referred to in Chapters 3, 8 and 12, respectively.

As regards the operation of the procedure, we have seen in section 5 that a main difference from the restricted procedures lies in the flexibility of the dialogue phase – that is, the phase leading up to final tenders that will form the basis of the award decision. In this phase, Member States enjoy a significant degree of discretion in structuring the dialogue, which, as we have seen, they have tended to pass on to their individual contracting authorities. Many different approaches are seen both within and between Member States in terms of the numbers invited, numbers taken through to final tendering, use of the dialogue stage to reduce numbers, use of one or more interim tendering stages, the approach to conducting meetings, and the extent to which the dialogue is used merely to develop the solutions of individual candidates as a basis for their own tenders or to identify a specific solution. Some of these variations may reflect inefficiencies and bad planning – but many appear to reflect valid differences in the values and circumstances of different Member States or between projects. For example, the numbers invited to various stages and the decision on whether or not to reduce numbers in the dialogue might properly vary according to the expected costs of participation and the nature of the market for particular services (that may affect the drop-out rate); whilst, as section 5.6 shows, this decision is also clearly affected by Member States' general approach in their public procurement systems to the balance between discretion and other considerations (such as procedural costs and transparency). There is no indication that the legal rules – or absence thereof – on structuring the dialogue in general present any difficulties, and the current flexible approach seems appropriate. From a practical point of view, however, there seems to be much to be learned by sharing the experiences and lessons from the Member States that have used competitive dialogue on issues such as the importance of advance planning of the dialogue and the need for a clearly established focus to meetings in the dialogue stage, so that Member States can make optimum use of the desirable flexibility provided by Directive 2004/18. (It is interesting that a number of common points emerged in this respect from different countries – such as the UK and Spain – that have used competitive dialogue.) This could, of course, lead to national regulation of and/or guidance on the way in which the dialogue is structured in different Member States – something which could perhaps again encourage use of competitive dialogue in those states.

There is, however, one legal point relating to the structure of the dialogue which might usefully be clarified – and that is the fact that the Directive allows not only for the reduction of solutions considered in the dialogue but also for the elimination of *candidates* whose solutions are rejected. As we explained in section 5.6.3, it seems very clear from the provisions of the Directive in context that this is possible and, indeed, that such an approach has always been envisaged as a primary approach in the operation of the procedure, especially given the rules on confidentiality. However, given that Article 29(3) refers to the reduction of 'solutions', clarification of this point would be helpful to ensure legal certainty; and this is also a matter on which amendment to the wording of the Directive might be warranted.

Another area of law that affects the dialogue phase, amongst others, and which could usefully be addressed at EU level, is that of award criteria. As we have seen in section 5.6.5, there is some uncertainty over several questions relating to the flexibility of award criteria, and these are important given the risk and consequences of legal challenge at the award stage. Again, we have suggested that a reasonably flexible approach is needed to recognise the practical realities of complex procurement. A first issue is whether all criteria, weightings and other methodology to be used during the dialogue and final tender phases must be drafted and disclosed (so far as required by the disclosure rules) *before* the dialogue begins, or whether such material may be developed and disclosed later in the process. We have suggested that there are strong arguments to support the legality of later development within certain parameters, and that not to allow this could in fact discourage authorities from structuring discretion, thus reducing transparency overall. A second and more controversial question is whether the award criteria may ever be *changed* once they have already been set and disclosed. Whilst the Commission in its informal guidance seems to preclude altogether any changes, we have argued that a more flexible approach is needed that admits some possibility of change under certain conditions (including that the change is not material), although we differ on the extent of this possibility (with Professor Arrowsmith supporting a general possibility of change and Professor Treumer confining this to where unforeseen circumstances occur). A third issue is whether a different methodology for the award may be applied at different stages (such as the interim and final tendering stages) and here again we suggested that this is possible in certain circumstances where commercially justified.

We have also seen in section 5.7 that some important legal issues arise around the final tender stage which occurs once the flexible dialogue phase is complete and provides the basis for choosing the most economically advantageous tender. This clearly has a significant resemblance to the tendering stage of open and restricted procedures, and one possible view of this stage of competitive dialogue is that it is governed by precisely the same rules that apply to the tendering stage in open and restricted procedures. We have suggested, however, that, whilst there are substantial similarities between the tendering stages in competitive dialogue and open/restricted procedures, it is erroneous to equate them completely.

A first issue at this final tendering stage concerns the degree of certainty and completeness required in tenders under Article 29(6) of the Directive, which requires that final tenders contain all the elements 'required and necessary' for the performance of the project. This is another area of legal uncertainty – and one which is potentially important because of its possible impact on the costs of participation. We have suggested that this raises interesting broader questions concerning the extent of EU law requirements of completeness and certainty in public contracts in general, concerning the scope for completing the details of a project both before and after the contract is concluded with the winning bidder – questions which have not yet been addressed at all by the CJEU. These questions could not be considered in detail in the present study, but a number of general principles were suggested. First, it is clear that the above requirement of Article 29(6) is a very substantial one which requires a much greater degree of completeness and certainty in offers before the winner is selected than is required in negotiated procedures. Not only is the substantial nature of this requirement an important aspect of competitive dialogue for ensuring transparency in support of EU objectives, but the experience of the UK – an extensive user of competitive dialogue – tends to suggest that it also supports national value-for-money objectives by ensuring that the commercial terms of the procurement are negotiated under conditions of competitive pressure. On the other hand, it was suggested also that the requirement may not be as rigid as the rules applicable on this subject in open or restricted procedures, particularly in view of the potentially high participation costs. Thus it was suggested that the principle of proportionality entails that it is permitted to omit details of the project from final tenders when this is unlikely to impact on the decision of selecting the winner, with the level of risk of impact that is acceptable not being set too low in light of the same principle of proportionality.

A second area of legal uncertainty concerning the final tendering stage relates to the meaning of the provision in Article 29(6) which allows final tenders to be 'clarified, specified and fine-tuned'. In this respect, it was again suggested that the requirement is not necessarily to be equated very rigidly with the parallel rules that apply in open and restricted procedures, and that flexibility (which may possibly be greater than in those procedures) is needed in some areas – for example, correction of errors. On the other hand, it was also suggested that – as in open and restricted procedures – the provision probably does not offer scope for negotiating improvements to tenders: this is unnecessary since the possibility is already provided for in the flexible dialogue stage, and is thus probably ruled out in the interests of transparency.

Once the winning bidder has been identified in the final tender stage, further legal uncertainty arises over the question of scope for change in the agreement reached, which is governed by Article 29(7) of the Directive. Again, this is important because of the potential impact of the legal rules on the costs of the procedure. In this respect, it is again clear that the room for manoeuvre is significantly less than in the negotiated procedure. However, as discussed in section 5.8, it is suggested that some scope for change does exist when the particular change is justified by an external event, by a change of circumstances or by an unforeseen situation – provided that certain conditions are met, which are derived to a large extent from those applicable in the context of concluded contracts. The first is that any change must not be such that, had it been made earlier, it would have affected the outcome. When it is not clear whether or not the outcome would have been affected, the change may be ruled out on the basis that changes must not risk distorting competition, but the principle of proportionality again requires that the acceptable threshold of risk not be set at too low a level. A second probable limit is that any change must not alter the economic balance of the contract in favour of the tenderer; and a third is that any change must not be 'substantial' in a qualitative and quantitative sense. It has also been explained that adjustments provided for in advance will often not be seen as changes at all for this purpose, although this depends on a number of different factors.

These issues relating to the final tender stage and to the stage after identifying the winner or preferred bidder are touched on only briefly in the Commission's Explanatory Note, the tenor of which is towards a rather strict interpretation, although the Note is neither clear nor specific on this subject. Again, a formal document that endorses a more flexible approach could be useful in boosting the use of competitive dialogue – bearing in mind again that states that favour less flexibility may provide for this for their own contracting authorities.

It is finally worth highlighting here two related legal provisions which are of general relevance for the conduct of competitive dialogue.

One is Article 29(3) of Directive 2004/18 which provides that contracting authorities must not reveal solutions or other confidential information without the consent of the relevant participant. This is important for, in particular, those approaches towards competitive dialogue which involve taking elements from one or more solutions proposed during the dialogue and incorporating these into the final specification, which we have seen is done in practice under the 'designated solution' and 'hybrid' models of competitive dialogue (discussed in section 5.6.3 above). The other relevant provision is Article 29(8), which explicitly draws attention to the possibility of making payments to participants for their solutions (as well as for their participation costs). It is interesting that, given the concerns that were raised about possible inappropriate sharing of information when the Directive was adopted, in the (admittedly limited) number of Member States where some information is available (such as the UK, Spain and Denmark), there is little evidence of concerns over the way in which information is treated in actual competitive dialogue procedures, whilst at the same time there has also been very little recourse to the option of 'buying' solutions from the participants. Possibly this is because of tenderers' interests in having elements of their solution included in the final mandatory specifications under the designated solution and hybrid models, as this provides them with a competitive advantage. On this subject we can also mention that it remains a grey area of law as to whether contracting authorities may require sharing of information as a condition of participation (that is, whether they can properly stipulate that mere participation implies consent to information-sharing) but this does not seem to have caused problems in practice.

In conclusion, we may observe that, whilst competitive dialogue has been perceived as a valuable addition to the toolbox of public procurement procedures – and has been widely used – in some Member States, in most it has so far played a rather limited role. Whilst the procedure is not necessarily suitable for all Member States, in others there is clearly some potential both to extend and to improve its use. In this chapter we have suggested that a balanced approach to interpreting the rules of the procedure combined with efforts to address some of the current legal uncertainty that affects both its scope and operation, could assist in facilitating its future development and supporting its use in appropriate cases. We have suggested that, in the short term, guidance from the European Commission could play an important role both in promoting such a balanced approach and in reducing current uncertainties. However, in the longer term, it is hoped that the suggestions made will also provide a useful basis for other hard- or soft-law development of the procedure, including through judicial fora.

2

An analysis of use of competitive dialogue in the EU

SYLVIA DE MARS AND RICHARD CRAVEN*

1. Introduction

This chapter presents the results of a quantitative comparative research project into the use of the competitive dialogue procedure across the EU conducted between 2007 and 2010. The project gathered data from contract notices published in the OJEU for the period between 1 January 2006 and 31 December 2009 in Belgium, France, Germany, Ireland, the Netherlands, Portugal, Spain and the UK. The research conducted sought to answer the following set of questions in order to provide a general picture of the use of competitive dialogue in the EU:

(1) What types of 'contracting authority' have been using competitive dialogue?
(2) In what market sectors is competitive dialogue being used?
(3) What types of project is competitive dialogue being used to procure?
(4) What proportion of projects procured by way of competitive dialogue involves private finance?

This chapter will, first, in section 2, describe the methodology and methods adopted by the authors in order to answer the above questions. In sections 3 to 7, the findings from the research will be presented. The chapter concludes in section 8 with some final observations on the research conducted and its findings in relation to the use of competitive dialogue.

* The authors would like to thank Dr Pedro Telles and Dr Pamela Hölbling for the data they collected for Spain, Portugal and Germany, as well as clarifications they offered on the collected data, where requested.

2. Methodology

2.1. Nature of the research

The research project was designed to be quantitative in nature; that is, it sought to measure the use of competitive dialogue in a manner that could be reduced to numerical data. Collected data could then be subjected to statistical analysis, so that trends and patterns in behaviour could be identified. The research was also designed to be comparative: data was gathered from different EU Member States, and findings on use of the procedure were compared and contrasted between subject countries where appropriate.

Data were collected from a study of contract notices published in the series S supplement to the OJEU. Contracting authorities awarding contracts governed by Directive 2004/18/EC[1] must have a contract notice published in the OJEU for those contracts that are covered by the Directive (Article 35, Directive 2004/18/EC). The notice ensures that economic operators throughout the EU are aware of the competition for the contract and should provide them with sufficient information to decide whether to bid. Article 36 of the Directive stipulates what information must be contained in a contract notice.

In addition to publishing notices where required under Article 35, contracting authorities may publish 'voluntary' notices for contracts not covered by the Directive (Article 37), using the same publication process outlined in Article 36. It should be noted that this research project did not investigate whether notices were 'mandatory' or 'voluntary', which does not need to be specified in the submitted contract notice;[2] instead, all notices published in the OJEU were incorporated into the research project.

Since 1998, the S series supplement to the OJEU has been available online at the Tenders Electronic Daily (TED) website.[3] Here, registered users are permitted free access to search within the TED archives and view full contract notices. Using the TED search facilities, it was possible

[1] Directive 2004/18/EC of the European Parliament and of the Council of 31 March 2004 on the co-ordination of procedures for the award of public works contracts, public supply contracts and public service contracts [2004] OJ L134/114.

[2] The standard forms for publication are identical in both cases, and the only clear means through which to identify if contracts are 'voluntary' is by examining the value of the advertised contract. This was not part of the current research project.

[3] http://ted.europa.eu.

to view all notices advertising contracts to be awarded by competitive dialogue in individual Member States. The TED website therefore presented the ideal data collection tool; it allowed for a comprehensive analysis of advertised use of competitive dialogue throughout the EU. The research is acknowledged, however, to be completely reliant on the accuracy of the TED searches.

2.2. *Subject countries*

Available resources did not allow for examination of use of competitive dialogue in all twenty-seven Member States, and those selected for examination were Belgium, France, Germany, Ireland, the Netherlands, Portugal, Spain and the UK. These states were chosen, first, to ensure coverage of the two states that are by some margin highest users of competitive dialogue as ascertained from a purely numerical consideration of use of the competitive dialogue procedure each year (UK and France, see further section 3 below). To these states were added others to provide coverage of a reasonable number of other Member States that was manageable given the language competence and resources available to the researchers. It is acknowledged that the pattern of use found in Member States not analysed, however, may well be different.

2.3. *Categories*

2.3.1. Introduction

The quantitative data collection method adopted for the project was 'content analysis'.[4] Bryman explains that content analysis is '[a]n approach to the analysis of documents and texts that seeks to quantify content in terms of predetermined categories and in a systematic and replicable manner'.[5] In accordance with this method, at the outset of the research, it was decided that data for the following categories would be collected:

(1) type of public body;
(2) name of public body;
(3) type of document;
(4) category of contract;

[4] A. Bryman, *Social Research Methods* (3rd edn, Oxford: Oxford University Press, 2008), p. 182.
[5] *Ibid.*, p. 183.

(5) type of contract;
(6) subject-matter of the contract;
(7) whether or not private finance was used for the procurement; and
(8) any other matters arising that appeared to be of significance or interest.

Data collection proved taxing. Not only was the process laborious, but it also proved to be a challenge objectively to categorise the contract data found. The primary reason a contracting authority is using the competitive dialogue procedure may be that it cannot say with precision what it wants to procure, but can merely express it in terms of outputs (see Chapter 1). In addition, a well-drafted contract notice, particularly one involving a complex contract to be procured by way of competitive dialogue, is drafted to cater for a degree of change to contract scope. Further, as will be explained later below, contract notices are often not drafted with adequate clarity even taking into account the inherent difficulties involved. Consequently, the researchers were called upon to interpret what was in some cases vague text. Judgment calls on the parts of researchers resulted in the burgeoning of categories and sub-categories titled 'other' and 'unclear', used when the content of the notice could not be recorded with confidence.

2.3.2. Category 1: type of public body

In relation to the first category, type of public body, the OJEU notice asks that contracting authorities classify themselves into one of the following categories:

(a) body governed by public law;
(b) ministry or any other national or federal authority;
(c) armed forces;
(d) regional or local authority;
(e) utilities;
(f) European institution/agency or international organisation;
(g) other;
(h) not applicable;
(i) national or federal agency/office; or
(j) regional or local agency/office.

Where this information was provided, it was recorded by the researchers. It should be noted that where an authority has failed to specify a category, it is automatically classified by TED as 'other'.

2.3.3. Category 2: name of public body

For the second category, the actual name of the authority was recorded. When it became clear that data in Category 1 was not providing a clear picture (see section 4 below), the researchers grouped authorities into their own more meaningful classifications, using the name of the public body as a primary means of categorisation. The following classification of types of public bodies was adopted:

(a) local government;
(b) central government (including sub-divisions);
(c) health authorities;
(d) educational authorities;
(e) housing and other local development/regeneration authorities;
(f) emergency services;
(g) waste; and
(h) miscellaneous.

It should be noted that, in Germany, 'state authorities' also constitute a category; this encompasses all authorities operating at the 'state' or 'länder' level. Central government authorities in Germany were defined as those working at the 'national' ('federal') government level.

2.3.4. Category 3: type of notice

A full TED search of all documents concerning competitive dialogue competitions was carried out. The number of contract notices was recorded, as was the number of additional information notices (which could be used to notify cancellations of procurements) and corrigenda notices. These additional information and corrigenda notices were filtered out of the research as they concern identical procedures to those already included, and including data on them would duplicate findings.

The number of cancellations was observed during data collection; however, the information on this is not presented in the findings below as it is highly likely that further cancellations of advertised contracts would take place after the data collection process for this project was concluded that could not be recorded here. The research therefore only provides an overview of competitive dialogue contract notices *advertised*; it does not necessarily follow that these procedures were successfully completed.

2.3.5. Category 4: type of contract

In the contract notice, contracts are classified as works, services, or supplies. This classification was recorded.

2.3.6. Category 5: contract category

The following sub-categories were identified in order to classify the type of contract being advertised:

(a) Advertising and public relations. This sub-category includes contracts relating to, *inter alia*, national advertising campaigns or general communications strategy consultancy.
(b) Business services. This sub-category includes contracts relating to, *inter alia*, management consultancy or infrastructure project management contracts.
(c) Defence. This sub-category includes all contracts issued by national ministries of defence that were specifically *military* in nature.[6]
(d) Energy. This sub-category includes all contracts related to the acquisition or distribution of energy (i.e. gas, electricity, solar/wind energy),[7] including the construction of energy infrastructure.
(e) Financial services. This sub-category includes all contracts related to financial service provision, in the areas of, *inter alia*, banking, loans and credit.
(f) Health services and supplies. This sub-category includes all health-related purchasing apart from health infrastructure.
(g) Information and communication technologies (ICT). This sub-category combines all contracts that relate to IT purchases as well as telecommunications purchases.
(h) Infrastructure and building construction. This sub-category includes any contract involving building and construction, with the exception of 'energy' and 'waste' infrastructure.
(i) Insurance.
(j) Other. The 'other' sub-category is made up of types of contract that did not occur frequently enough to justify a separate sub-category. Frequency was determined both on a per-country basis, and an EU-wide basis: if a specific type of purchase was made reasonably regularly in one country but not in others, it was not given its own category.
(k) Waste. This sub-category includes all contracts related to waste collection and treatment, including the construction of any waste infrastructure.

[6] E.g. catering at an army base was excluded as the subject-matter of the contract was not inherently military.

[7] Included in France are also 'heating distribution' contracts, as they require the establishment of an energy source and then subsequent heating installation in housing.

2.3.7. Category 6: specific subject of contract

In this category, the specifics of the contract were recorded. Data will only be presented in relation to contracts falling into the most significant Category 5 sub-categories that emerged: 'Infrastructure and building construction' and 'ICT'.

The 'Infrastructure and building construction' sub-category is broken down as follows:

(a) Education infrastructure. This category includes schools, further education colleges, and university buildings.
(b) Health infrastructure. This category includes hospitals as well as hospital wings and clinics.
(c) Housing and accommodation. This category includes housing, care/social housing and student halls of residence.
(d) Mixed use area developments. This category includes town regeneration projects that requested new residential infrastructure but also retail and other non-residential infrastructure.
(e) Non-residential area developments. This category includes town regeneration projects which did not contain a residential element.
(f) Offices.
(g) Other. As with the 'other' section in Category 5, this category contains any building construction projects that do not fit into the above categories but were not of a sufficient number to warrant their own separate category.

The 'ICT' sub-category was broken down into the following:

(a) Call centre.
(b) Hardware.
(c) Mixed (combining software and hardware).
(d) Networking (telephony and Internet).
(e) Other. See above.
(f) Software.
(g) Web services.

2.3.8. Category 7: private finance

For each contract notice it was recorded whether the authority intended the advertised project to be privately financed, left this option open, or did not intend private finance to be part of the arrangement. The investigation into the use of private finance proved difficult, as authorities did not always state explicitly how they intended to finance projects.

For this reason, it was also recorded whether it was unclear whether or not private finance was intended to be part of the arrangement (see section 6 below for details).

Where the contract notice stated explicitly that it would be following an established private finance arrangement or clearly described the arrangement (for example, the UK Private Finance Initiative (PFI), the Dutch *publiek private samenwerking* (PPS) or the French *contrat de partenariat* (CDP)) this was recorded.

2.3.9. Category 8: other matters of significance or interest

Finally, where contracts were considered to raise particular points of interest, for example if they seemed inappropriate for use of competitive dialogue, or represented a very interesting project, these findings were recorded.

It is worth mentioning that there were several contract notices identified where the level of complexity was questioned by the researchers. However, the number of questionably complex contracts identified was not sufficient to support a general argument of over-use, and, in any case, it would not be appropriate to make such a judgment on the basis of the limited information presented in the contract notice.

3. General observations: number and type of contract notices

3.1. Number and type of contract notices for subject countries

Table 2.1 summarises use of competitive dialogue in two ways: how many OJEU notices mentioning 'competitive dialogue' as the procedure to be used were published in the OJEU in the years 2006–9? And, what type of contracts did these notices concern: works, services, or supply contracts?

3.2. Use by numbers

In Table 2.1, the bracketed numbers refer to the total number of documents (i.e. contract notices, additional information documents etc.) the research turned up for that particular year or total of years. The figure next to the bracketed number represents the number of contract notices published that were not cancelled at a later date, so as to accurately reflect the actual number of competitive dialogue procedures that took place in the subject countries over the studied period. The findings presented below are on the basis of the information provided by contract notices only.

Table 2.1 *Number and type of contract notices for subject countries*

Member State		2006	2007	2008	2009	Total
Portugal	Supply	–	–	–	0	0
	Works	–	–	–	0	0
	Services	–	–	–	2	2
	Total	–	–	–	2 (5)	2 (5)
Belgium	Supply	0	1	2	0	3
	Works	0	1	1	1	3
	Services	5	5	7	1	18
	Total	5 (7)	7 (12)	10 (13)	2 (2)	24 (34)
Spain	Supply	–	2	2	11	15
	Works	–	0	7	3	10
	Services	–	0	0	5	5
	Total	–	2 (2)	9 (10)	19 (24)	30 (36)
Ireland	Supply	5	9	2	2	18
	Works	4	7	2	6	19
	Services	6	12	11	14	43
	Total	15 (15)	28 (33)	15 (17)	22 (31)	80 (96)
Netherlands	Supply	0	0	5	1	6
	Works	15	12	6	17	50
	Services	2	4	10	12	28
	Total	17 (20)	16 (20)	21 (29)	30 (47)	84 (116)
Germany	Supply	7	9	10	11	37
	Works	11	4	13	13	41
	Services	21	11	13	6	51
	Total	39 (47)	24 (31)	36 (49)	30 (46)	129 (173)
United Kingdom	Supply	53	57	49	46	205
	Works	65	73	74	54	266
	Services	162	237	252	258	909
	Total	280 (322)	367 (437)	375 (475)	358 (464)	1,380 (1,698)
France	Supply	89	96	100	104	394
	Works	46	75	62	94	277
	Services	171	182	220	191	764
	Total	306 (351)	353 (381)	382 (460)	389 (499)	1,430 (1,691)

Table 2.1 reveals that there was wide variance in the frequency of use of the competitive dialogue procedure among the countries examined in this chapter. Three different categories of 'user countries' can at this point be identified:

(a) Irregular users: Portugal, Belgium, Spain (fewer than 50 notices each in total). These countries are all typified by very slight frequency of use, making it impossible to make generalisations on how the procedure is used.
(b) Regular users: Ireland, the Netherlands, Germany (between 50 and 200 notices in total). This category is entitled 'regular' users primarily because competitive dialogue has been used regularly enough in these Member States for some general analysis to be made of the types of purchases made using the procedure; however, as will be seen, there is a significant difference between 'regular' use and 'heavy' use in the field of competitive dialogue.
(c) Heavy users: the UK, France (more than 1,000 notices in total). These two countries used the procedure extensively; with more than 1,000 contract notices for competitive dialogue procedures each, they will form the basis of most of the detailed discussion in the rest of this chapter.

3.3. *Type of contract*

On the subject of type of contract, Table 2.1 reveals that the majority of all contracts being advertised were services contracts; this is especially easy to see in the heavy-use nations of France and the UK, but a similar trend also reveals itself in most of the other countries studied.[8]

The use of the procedure for works as against supply contracts was more variable, and (as will be explored in section 5) depended primarily on the amount of infrastructure that was being procured by competitive dialogue in the subject countries.

Even though these data were easy to extract from the contract notices, the statistics are not informative: the classification of a contract as a works contract rather than a services contract within the meaning of the Directive, as is required for the contract notice, very often does not reveal anything about what types of purchases are actually sought. For

[8] Exceptions to this are Spain and the Netherlands, where more supply contracts and works contracts were advertised.

example, many large infrastructure projects that involve both construction of works and the subsequent management and operation of the works over a period of time are considered as services contracts on the basis that the services are the main objective of the contract in accordance with the test in Article 1(d) of Directive 2004/18/EC for classification of contracts (and the services are also often the major part of the value). These findings thus prompted the further investigation that follows in sections 4–6 below.

4. Types of public authorities using competitive dialogue

4.1. Introduction

As discussed in sections 2.3.1 and 2.3.2 above, the OJEU collects data on the type of public authority that advertises a given contract. However, it is up to contracting authorities themselves to properly identify which of the OJEU's categories they fall into. The research found that this results in questionable data in nearly every country, with an abundance of bodies classified as 'other'; a more subjective approach was thus adopted by the researchers so as to provide a clearer picture. The researchers thus opted to organise the contracting authorities into categories defined by *sector* in which the contracting authorities conduct their business rather than using the TED classification. Authorities which clearly and exclusively operated within the health sector were thus classed as 'health' authorities; conversely, local government authorities that purchased requirements relating to a variety of functions were considered as 'local government' authorities.

4.2. Light use countries

As we have seen, for light use there are very limited instances available of use altogether. However, it can be noted that, in Spain, the most regular users were local and city councils and regional public health service providers (fifteen out of thirty contracts) whereas in Belgium, most contracts (fourteen out of twenty-four in total) originated from European institutions. This can be explained by the fact that, as of 1 January 2010, Belgium had not yet introduced competitive dialogue into its national legislation. It is not clear, however, how *other* uses materialised in Belgium at this time. Both purchases made in Portugal originated from the same local authority.

4.3. 'Regular' use countries

4.3.1. Ireland

As we have seen, medium-use countries were Ireland, the Netherlands and Germany. Figure 2.1 shows use of the competitive dialogue procedure in Ireland. Unfortunately, however, the figure is not very illuminating due to the large number of contracting authorities that could not be categorised as local government, central government, education, health or waste – though it can be noted that, as in all other countries, a significant proportion of contracts were advertised by local government authorities (seventeen contracts out of eighty). The miscellaneous category included authorities such as the Commission for Taxi Regulation (five notices), Coillte Teoranta (three notices), Irish Greyhound Board (two notices), Radio Telefis Eireann Network Limited (four notices), Tourism Ireland (six notices) and the National Roads Authority (three notices).

4.3.2. The Netherlands

Figure 2.2 shows use of the competitive dialogue procedure in the Netherlands. In the Netherlands, the Dutch national service for 'road and water transport' construction (Rijkswaterstaat) was responsible for nearly all contracts in 2006 and at least two in all subsequent years, thus accounting for the large amount of purchases made by central government authorities. Other frequent users were local councils; significantly

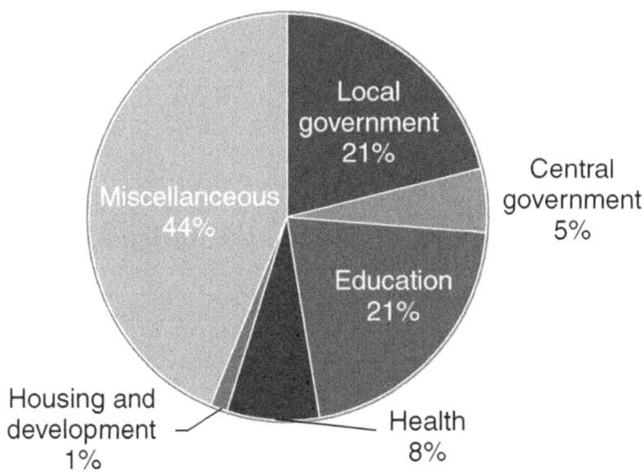

Figure 2.1 Ireland: purchasers by sector

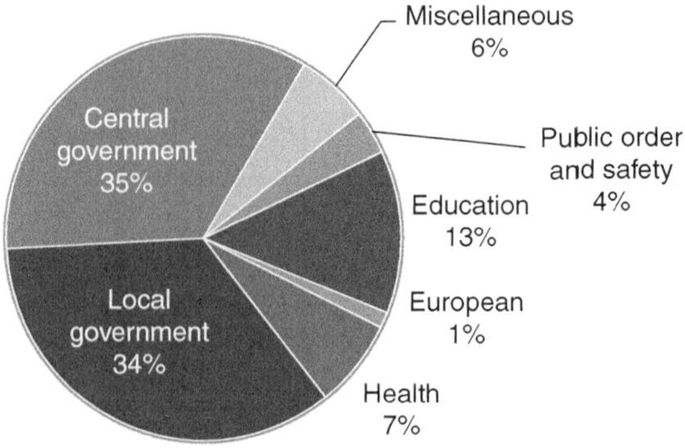

Figure 2.2 The Netherlands: purchasers by sector

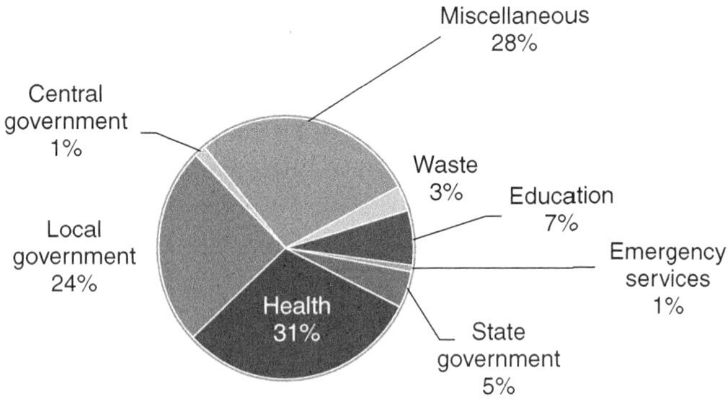

Figure 2.3 Germany: purchasers by sector

less frequently, educational bodies (such as universities), and health purchasers (such as hospitals) also used the procedure.

4.3.3. Germany

Figure 2.3 shows use of the competitive dialogue procedure in Germany. What can be observed in Germany, and will be found in the UK and France as well (see section 4.4), is that the health sector is a very heavy user of competitive dialogue, although, in Germany, local (rather than state or national) government also used the procedure very regularly.

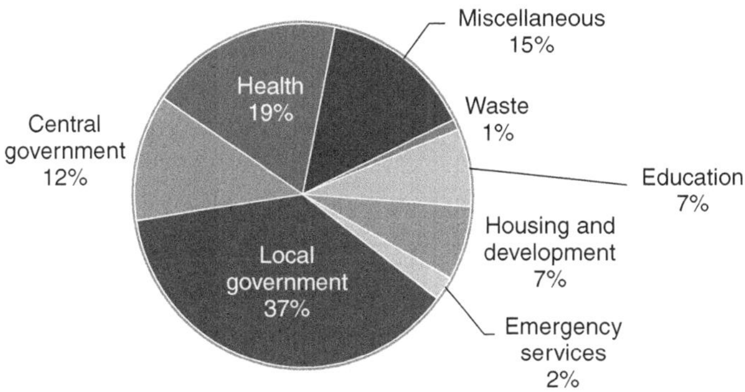

Figure 2.4 United Kingdom: purchasers by sector

Other frequent users, filed under 'miscellaneous', were bodies governed by public law that deal with either community development (building of public infrastructure) or research. It is interesting to note that in Germany only *two* instances of central government use of competitive dialogue were recorded, and only *six* uses took place at the state level; while central governments in other Member States were rarely the most frequent users of competitive dialogue, this is a particularly low usage statistic in comparison to the other countries in this project.

4.4. *Heavy users*

4.4.1. The UK

Figure 2.4 shows use of the competitive dialogue procedure in the UK. This figure shows that local government was by far the most common user of competitive dialogue in the UK. It is worth noting that, in addition to general local authority purchasing (i.e. infrastructure requirements for local government), the UK local government sector is also responsible for the bulk of all waste and educational purchases in the UK; for instance, local authorities are responsible for managing the 'Building Schools for the Future' investment programmes and the OJEU notice for such contracts will also be in their name.

It can be further noted that the education sector was made up mainly of UK universities, whereas the primary users of competitive dialogue in the health sector were local NHS trusts. In the

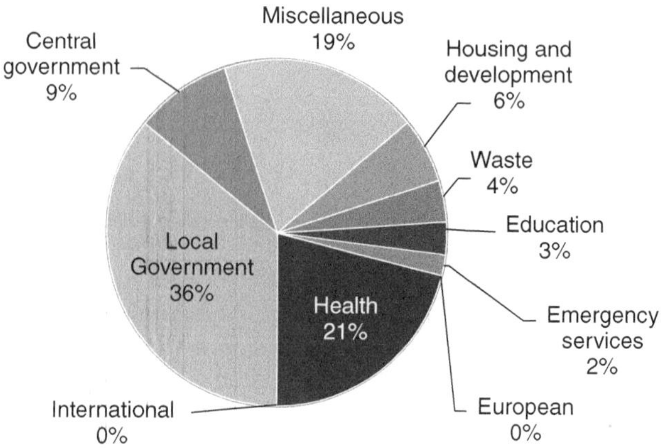

Figure 2.5 France: purchasers by sector

miscellaneous category, bodies such as the BBC, the British Library, Transport for London and the Equality and Human Rights Commission were found. It should be mentioned that, in the UK, in particular, shared services purchasing (i.e. a local authority purchasing services on behalf of itself and other authorities) was a relatively common occurrence. It was recorded whether or not the contract notice was advertised on behalf of other contracting authorities. This was the case with 376 (27 per cent) notices (68 in 2006, 103 in 2007, 86 in 2008 and 119 in 2009). In 806 (58 per cent) notices the authority signalled that it was procuring for itself only (173, 217, 231 and 185), and in the remaining 198 (14 per cent) this section of the contract notice was left blank (39, 47, 58 and 54).

4.4.2. France

Figure 2.5 shows use of the competitive dialogue procedure in France. As can be seen in Figure 2.5, a variety of sectors have in fact been using competitive dialogue in France, though – as in most other countries – local and regional authorities and health sector purchasers, such as hospitals and health authorities, were the most frequent users in the years examined. A striking point is that, unlike in the UK, the educational sector did not use competitive dialogue to a significant degree; this will be commented on further when examining the type of infrastructure built in France (section 5.4.2 below).

The 'miscellaneous' category does contain several varieties of repeat purchasers specific to France; for instance, local and national chambers of commerce use competitive dialogue quite frequently, as do a variety of national research centres and agencies. Bodies tasked with managing museums or heritage sites also used the procedure on a regular basis; beyond this – as was observed in the UK – a wide variety of other bodies granted supervisory or management power through French law have relied on the procedure for their purchases.

5. Main subject areas of contracts

5.1. Introduction

As explained in section 2.3.5 above, in order to provide a global overview of the types of purchases made, the researchers agreed on ten main categories of purchase. Also used was a residual category titled 'other', used for notices that did not fit any of the ten main categories. Findings in each of the subject countries are discussed below.

5.2. Light users

Since there are a limited number of instances of use in the light-user countries, it is difficult to generalise the findings, but the following observations can be made.

Portugal used competitive dialogue to buy one ICT software package, and for a contract regarding public-use bicycles as a method of inner-city transportation. Most of the contracts in Belgium, on the other hand, related to on-site assistance at nuclear power plants in Russia; other contracts were for financial services (credit and loan services), business services (consultancy), advertising and PR (information campaigns on the European Union) and infrastructure (EU delegation office buildings).

In Spain, there was a fairly balanced division of ICT, infrastructure, and health services and supplies contracts. Beyond this, there were also notices for interesting one-off purchases such as the development of a fire-safety boot[9] for the fire services and an astrophysics telescope.

[9] According to Dr Pedro Telles, this contract notice has been cancelled without award, though the OJEU does not reflect this.

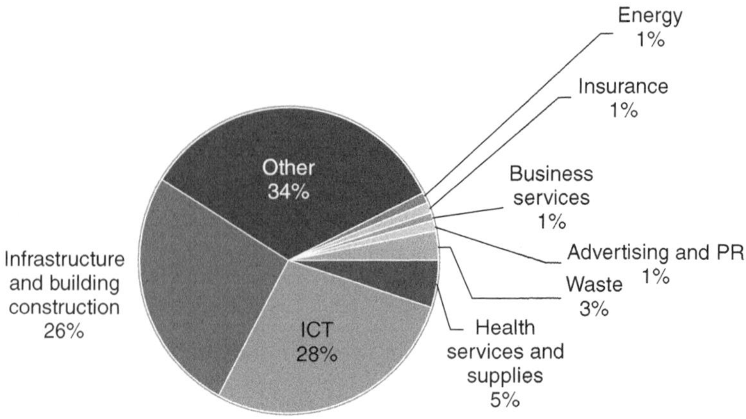

Figure 2.6 Ireland: contract subject areas

The light-use countries thus indicate a wide variety of uses for competitive dialogue. This is a trend that is also seen in the countries in which it is used more regularly.

5.3. *'Regular' users*

5.3.1. Ireland

Figure 2.6 illustrates the types of purchases being made with competitive dialogue in Ireland, whilst Figure 2.7 breaks down further the types of purchases found within the category of infrastructure and building construction.

Interestingly, in Ireland the largest number of competitive dialogue advertisements fell within the 'other' contract subject category. A variety of projects has been classified as 'other'; some of the more interesting of these one-off complex projects included the supply of library books, the production of rooted sitka spruce cuttings (two notices), the provision of admissions tests for the selection of students for undergraduate medical programmes, the design and build of a vehicle to travel from Ireland to Turin for the City of Science event 2010, the naming rights for a new stadium, and the supply of evidential breath alcohol testing equipment.

ICT purchases were regular and, as in all Member States, primarily involved software purchases. The 'infrastructure' category is also well

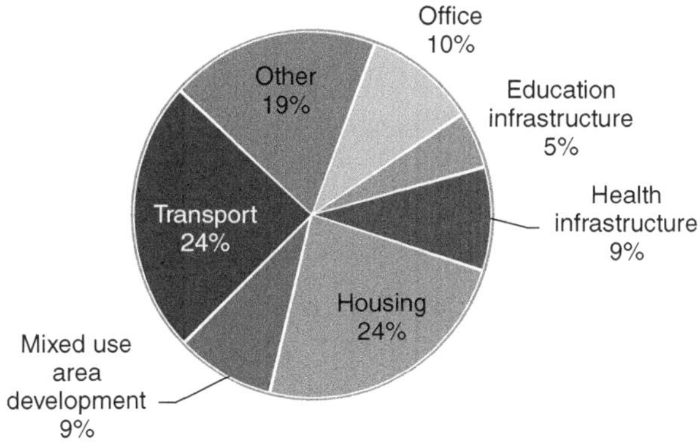

Figure 2.7 Ireland: types of infrastructure

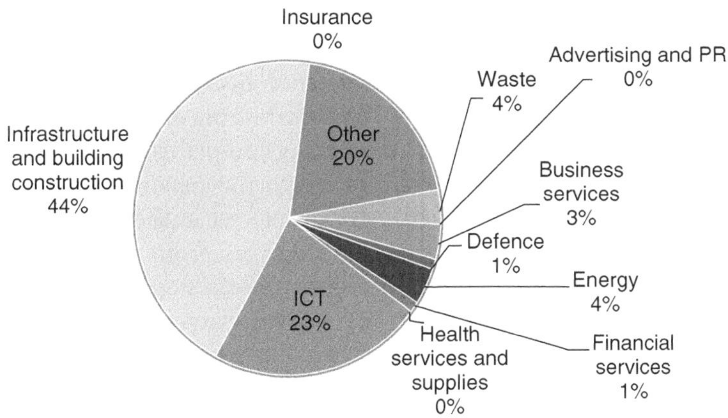

Figure 2.8 The Netherlands: contract subject categories

represented in Ireland. As can be seen in Figure 2.7, the different sub-categories within the infrastructure category are reasonably evenly distributed, which is unusual; other countries demonstrated a clear stand-out category within this category, as is explained below.

5.3.2. The Netherlands

In the Netherlands, infrastructure and ICT purchases were also very common, as were 'other' category contracts, as shown in Figure 2.8:

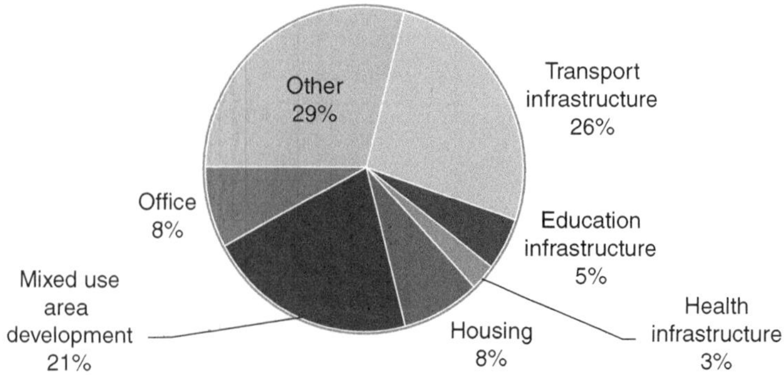

Figure 2.9 The Netherlands: types of infrastructure

Figure 2.9 reveals that, while many infrastructure contracts related to either road works or urban development that included a mixture of housing and commercial properties, there were also a substantial number of interesting one-off purchases; for instance, in 2007, a fission research reactor was purchased, and in 2009, the refurbishing of prison facilities at Schiphol airport was put up for award using competitive dialogue.

Regarding contracts in the ICT category, the majority of contracts once again were software-related. Also of interest in the Netherlands is the 'other' category. While space restricts us from discussing this category in detail, some interesting contract notices can be highlighted; one of these is the KOSMOS project, which relates to the design and maintenance of roadside artwork in all provinces of the Netherlands, and which accounts for five notices. Another example of a very rare purchase was a contract notice for a 'research laser' by a university; less unusual, but not fitting into any particular category, were contract notices related to tram and train exploitation (through a concession), the provision of assisted living to the elderly, and a research project into rush-hour traffic on certain highways in the Netherlands.

5.3.3. Germany

Figure 2.10 reveals that there were four main categories of contract subject areas found in Germany. Unsurprisingly, infrastructure, ICT and 'other' also covered the majority of the contract notices in Germany, as they did in the Netherlands and Ireland – but, with 14 per cent, a significant proportion of the notices related to health services and supplies:

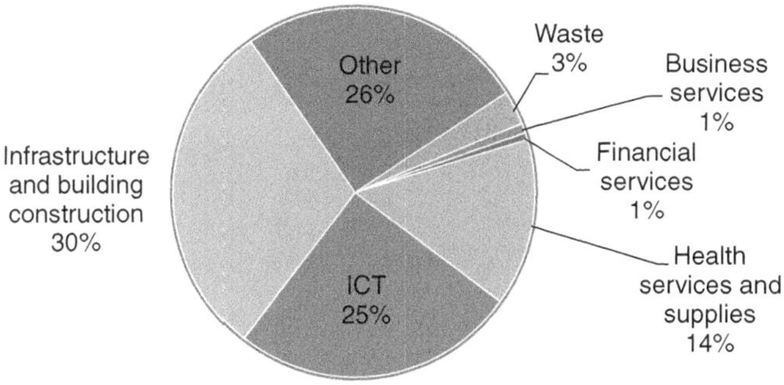

Figure 2.10 Germany: contract subject categories

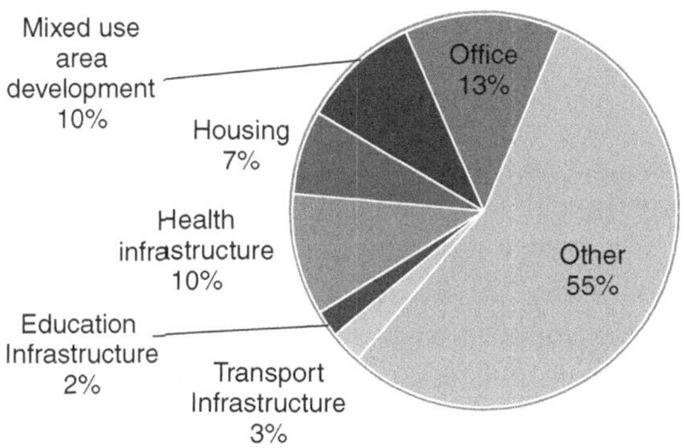

Figure 2.11 Germany: types of infrastructure

As we can see in Figure 2.11, the majority of German infrastructure contracts fell into the 'other' category. This is in large part due to the fact that seven contracts were advertised for the construction of swimming pools and spas, which was not a sufficiently common type of project in any other country to warrant its own mention, and thus these were included in the category of 'other'. Also in the 'other' category were construction projects relating to infrastructure for a nationwide garden show, and the provision of various public buildings such as a town hall and a new site for parliament.

The ICT category again primarily involved software purchases. There was also a variety of interesting purchases in the 'other' category; for

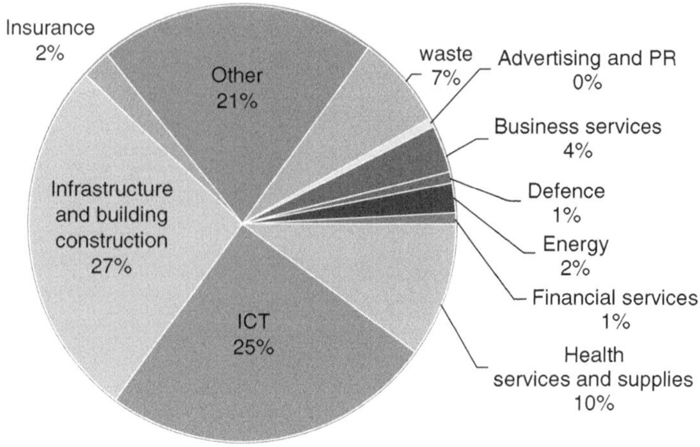

Figure 2.12 United Kingdom: contract subject categories

example, competitive dialogue was used to award contracts as disparate as the supply of an organ, construction of an exhibition for a museum, service provision to asylum seekers by means of a smart-card system for food and clothing supplies, and the restoration of a historic medical fence. This once again illustrates the wide variety of uses that competitive dialogue has as a contract award procedure.

5.4. *Heavy users*

5.4.1. The UK

The UK is second only to France in terms of the number of competitive dialogue contract notices published over the period studied and is a higher user in terms of number of contracts per annum. Figure 2.12 clearly shows that the majority of contracts advertised fell into the infrastructure, ICT and 'other' categories:

The breakdown of the infrastructure category can be seen in Figure 2.13. Here, housing, which includes residential accommodation such as student halls of residence, is the largest sub-category (at 28 per cent). The education sector is also well represented. In part, this may be down to the UK Government's major schools investment programme, 'Building Schools for the Future', in which the UK's pre-2010 Labour government committed

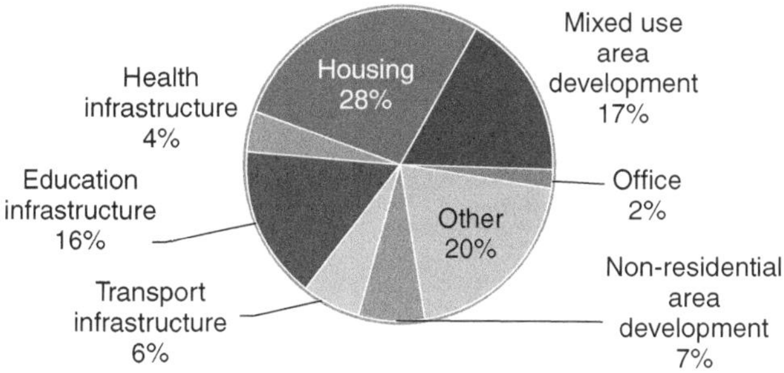

Figure 2.13 United Kingdom: types of infrastructure

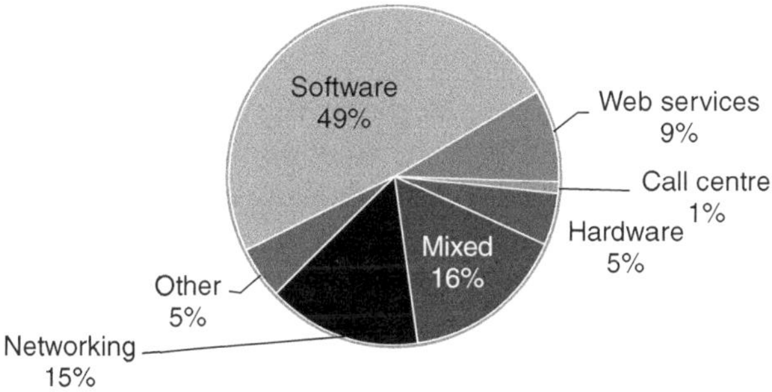

Figure 2.14 United Kingdom: types of ICT

itself to replace, rebuild or renovate every secondary school in England (around 3,500 in total).[10] Construction work on university buildings also fell within this sub-category.

There was also a significant number of ICT competitive dialogue contract notices. A breakdown of this category can be seen in Figure 2.14. Here, it can be seen that software purchases account for nearly half of all ICT notices. As is discussed further in Chapter 3, there is anecdotal evidence pointing to dissatisfaction amongst practitioners with the procurement of complex ICT projects under the restricted procedure prior

[10] See www.partnershipsforschools.org.uk/about/aboutbsf.jsp. The BSF programme was cancelled on 5 July 2010 (see www.education.gov.uk/news/news/bsf-review/a0061486/overhaul-to-englands-school-building-programme for further details).

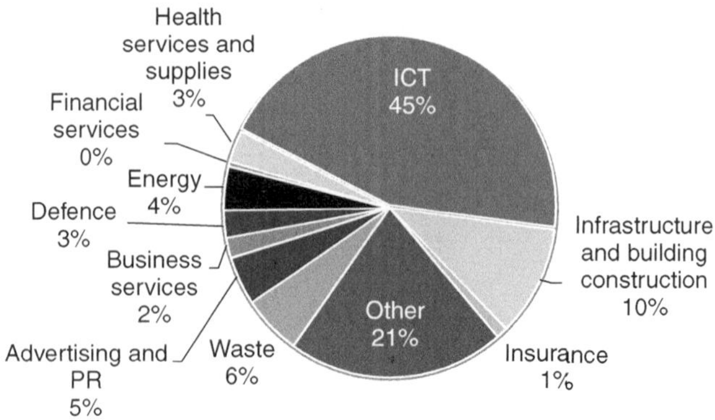

Figure 2.15 France: contract subject categories

to the introduction of competitive dialogue, and it is possible that many of the more complex ICT projects that would have been carried out under the restricted procedure are now being procured under competitive dialogue. In that sense, it would seem that competitive dialogue has achieved its objective of bringing greater flexibility.

The substantial 'other' category covers an array of different projects: examples include nursery services, provision of fairground attractions, bar and catering services, printing and mailing services, double glazing, design and production of UK passports, the supply of low-carbon and electric-powered vans, and the supply of bullet-proof vests. It should be noted that there were several facilities management contracts and other maintenance-type projects advertised; however, they were not numerous enough to warrant separate categories.

5.4.2. France

In Figure 2.15, we see that, unlike in the UK, the majority of uses of competitive dialogue in France were for ICT purchases rather than infrastructure. In fact, infrastructure only ranks third in terms of regularity of use; the 'other' category represents nearly a quarter of all notices.

Figure 2.16 shows clearly that nearly half of all ICT contracts purchased had software as their main component; this is unsurprising given findings in other Member States. What is interesting, however, is that, with this much use, repeat purchases in the 'software' category can be

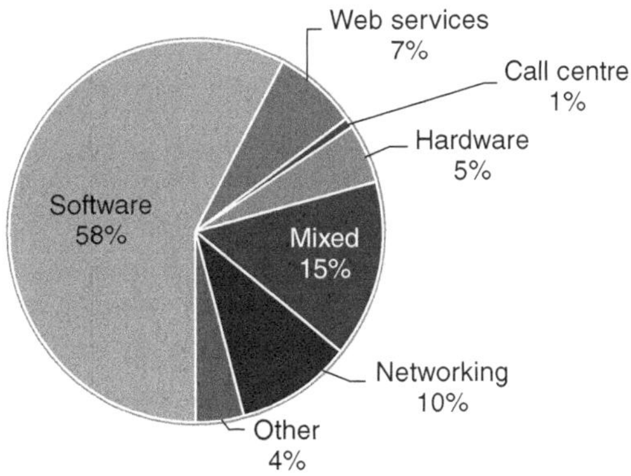

Figure 2.16 France: types of ICT

found. It was already observed in section 4 that the health sector is a heavy user of competitive dialogue. The vast majority of all ICT software purchased was in fact for hospital ICT requirements to enable digital patient files.

It is nearly impossible to chart the 'other' contracts category in France, where there were far too many varied contract notices (306 over the entire period, versus 152 for infrastructure, to illustrate); much as in the light- and medium-user countries, however, competitive dialogue was used for a wide variety of purchases, only a few of which occur more than once in the same year.

What can be highlighted here is that there were two types of repeat 'other' purchases common in, and also mainly limited to, France. The first is public lighting, a category that covers all sorts of urban activity dealing with the installation, operation and maintenance of outdoor lighting on a municipal level, but also unrelated requirements, such as the installation and maintenance of road signage. The other category – urban furniture – is broader, and relates to any sort of 'structure' that a municipality can build outdoors, but that does not amount to a building; this includes contracts for bus shelters, public benches, multimedia kiosks, and even public bicycles. Both of these types of contracts recurred regularly over the examined period, but only in France.

Figure 2.17 reveals that, in terms of the different sub-categories under infrastructure contracts, most contract notices were found in the 'other'

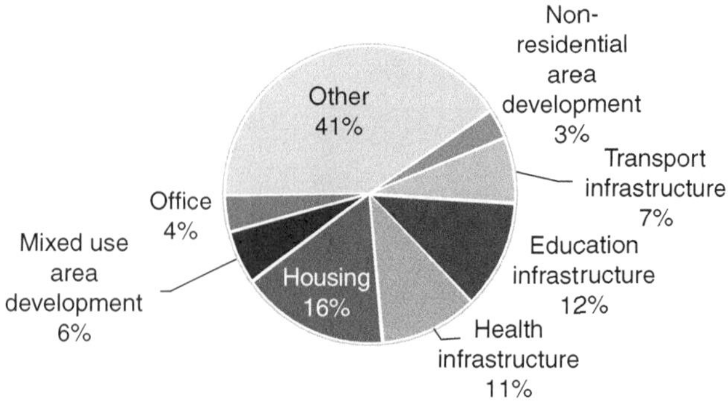

Figure 2.17 France: types of infrastructure

category. As in Germany, these involved country-specific purchases that did not surface often enough in other countries to warrant their own category. Specific to France were purchases of bases/barracks for the *gendarmerie* (a police force that is part of the military), which recurred several times over the period examined, and contracts relating to redevelopment or renovation of zoos, football stadiums and velodromes (cycling arenas) and various conference/exhibition centres, for either general or specific purposes.

The other types of infrastructure projects that were frequently advertised using competitive dialogue in France related to housing, health and education. It can be highlighted here that housing and school renovation projects using the procedure were far more common in the UK, whereas hospital construction using competitive dialogue was more common in France. However, health infrastructure in France usually related to the building of specific wards within an existing hospital, but not the entire redevelopment or construction of a hospital as it frequently would in the UK; similarly, education infrastructure in France was more commonly concerned with the redevelopment of university buildings than with the building of entire schools, as occurs under the 'Building Schools for the Future' projects in the UK.

Lastly, it is notable that area development, whether mixed use or non-residential, did not figure heavily among the notices published in 2006–9 in France; the position in this respect can be contrasted with the UK, where competitive dialogue was quite frequently used for area development contracts.

6. Competitive dialogue and private finance: a murky picture

6.1. *What is private finance?*

The phrase 'public–private partnership' (PPP) is not defined in EU law. The phrase has different meanings when used, and its definition is often dependent on context. In the UK, the government defines PPP broadly, covering 'a range of business structures and partnership arrangements, from the Private Finance Initiative (PFI) to joint ventures and concessions, to outsourcing and the sale of equity stakes in state-owned businesses'.[11] The term is not therefore limited to instances of private sector finance.

In the European Commission's Explanatory Note on Competitive Dialogue, it is stated that PPPs will 'very, very often' be of sufficient financial/legal complexity to satisfy the grounds for using competitive dialogue.[12] This is not to say, however, that a PPP project will automatically qualify. The Commission goes on to give examples of PPP projects where the financial/legal complexity condition would in its opinion be satisfied; all of the examples involve private sector financing. It was felt that an assessment of the proportion of competitive dialogue procured contracts involving private financing would be of particular interest in light of this and also because the UK's perceived use of the competitive negotiated procedure for the award of PFI contracts and the need for an alternative seems to have been a key reason behind the introduction of competitive dialogue (see Chapter 3).

6.2. *Light users*

Even in the countries that rarely used competitive dialogue over the course of the four years studied, it was common for contract notices to be found that required private financing. In Belgium, for instance, both contracts purchased by the Commission in order to build new delegation buildings in foreign countries required private financing; but no specific type of financing structure was identified. Similarly, in Portugal,

[11] HM Treasury, *Public Private Partnerships: The Government's Approach* (2000), available at http://archive.treasury.gov.uk/docs/2000/ppp.html, p. 8.

[12] European Commission, *Explanatory Note – Competitive Dialogue – Classic Directive*, available at http://ec.europa.eu/internal_market/publicprocurement/docs/explan-notes/classic-dir-dialogue_en.pdf, p. 3.

one of the two contracts advertised contained an option for private finance – but not under any specific name.

Spain is a slightly different case; the notices that required private finance there generally referred to a *contrato de colaboración entre el sector público y privado* (CPP), which is a specific *type* of PPP contract, defined in Article 11 of the Spanish Public Procurement Code.[13] Beyond this, there was one notice for a concession contract as well. These findings on the whole indicate that private finance is a common element to many contracts purchased using competitive dialogue, even where the procedure is used very infrequently.

6.3. *'Regular' users*

6.3.1. Ireland

In Ireland, out of the eighty notices, it was felt that only seventeen could be said to definitely involve private sector financing. The vast majority of the seventeen notices described a design-build-finance-operate (DBFO) structure. There was one contract notice where the decision to use private financing for the project was to be left open to be discussed during dialogue. Thirteen of the advertisements considered to be definitely notifying of a private finance arrangement were concerned with infrastructure and building construction. It should also be mentioned, however, that there were fourteen contract notices where the researcher could not decipher whether private finance was intended to form part of the project, for reasons outlined in section 2.3.7.

6.3.2. The Netherlands

In the Netherlands, a distinction can be drawn between *publiek private samenwerking* or PPS contracts, which are a generic type of PPP contracts that the central government uses primarily to fund infrastructure projects, and other 'private finance' projects, which do not use this name. Examination of the contract notices revealed thirteen privately financed contracts in total, of which seven were PPS contracts and six were other private finance contracts.

The general assumption about contracts classified as PPS is that they operate on a DBFM(O) basis, which is to say that the private partner usually designs, builds, finances, maintains (and sometimes operates)

[13] Ley 30/2007, de 30 de octobre 2007, de Contratos del Sector Público (BOE 261/2007).

the infrastructure being purchased. Despite its being difficult to define a PPS contract beyond indicating that it is a *type* of public–private partnership, these contracts are mentioned specifically here because the central government has issued specific guidance on using competitive dialogue for these PPS contracts[14] – meaning there was, at the start of the research, an expectation of finding that PPS contracts were awarded using this procedure.

As stated, other types of private finance arrangements can, however, also be used in the Netherlands; for instance, concession agreements with a financing element, or a contract notice that just very generally mentioned a 'transfer of risk' to the private sector without indications of a specific framework for said risk transfer were thus also found. Lastly, there were also instances of DBFM(O) contracts being advertised *without* the PPS label – indicating once again that PPP terminology is applied irregularly, even within the context of just one Member State.

6.3.3. Germany

In total, in Germany, twenty-eight privately financed contracts of a variety of types were found.

In Germany, it is not possible to properly identify any specific type of public–private partnership setup as being dominantly used or encouraged by government. In contrast with the Netherlands and the UK, there is no legislation or policy that identifies one particular type of new-style PPP arrangement;[15] while the term *öffentlich-privaten Partnerschaft* (OPP) is occasionally used by contracting authorities, this is merely the German term for 'PPP' – but not any specific type of PPP arrangement.[16] Ten contract notices, however, explicitly used the phrase 'PPP' or 'OPP', either as a requirement or an option for financing.

Aside from notices advertising an interest in OPP, there were also various contract notices that required private finance in the form of concession agreements, long-term leaseholds, and, interestingly, privatisation contracts; one of these involved a sale of a 49 per cent stake in the airport as well as its daily operation. As in the Netherlands, there were

[14] Rijksoverheid, *De Concurrentiegerichte Dialoog* (2009), available at www.ppsbijhetrijk.nl/dsresource?objectid=709&type=org.

[15] To be contrasted with traditional PPP arrangements such as concessions and long-term leaseholds.

[16] See the EU Internal Market: Public Procurement website in German, available at http://ec.europa.eu/internal_market/publicprocurement/partnerships/public-private/index_de.htm.

also a few contracts that just generally required 'finance' or 'funding', but without any specific mention of the establishment of public–private partnerships for that funding; and, like Ireland, Germany also advertised several contracts that required 'private partners' but did not specifically mention finance.

6.4. *Heavy users*

6.4.1. The UK

The UK showed the most frequent use of private finance in competitive dialogue procedures out of every country examined, with 467 notices referring to projects that potentially involved some element of private finance. However, it must be stressed that this is still, at most, only 35 per cent of all purchases made with competitive dialogue over the relevant period.

In the UK, the Private Finance Initiative (PFI) was formally commenced in 1992 to encourage the use of private finance for major capital investment projects. Essentially, a PFI arrangement is a long-term contract (typically 15–30 years duration) whereby a private sector partner will finance the design and construction of a capital asset and recoup its costs and make a profit by charging for services provided over the duration of the contract. A typical model for such contracts is the DBFO model.

A range of projects have been procured by way of PFI, including roads (motorways) and bridges, schools, hospitals, prisons, waste treatment plants and major ICT systems. Because of the importance of PFI in the UK at the time of research, it was decided that PFI projects clearly stating they are being procured under the PFI would be recorded in a separate category to other private finance arrangements. Although UK authorities have been advised to specify in the contract notice the fact that a contract is being procured under the PFI,[17] the authors were not certain that this always happened in practice and so projects clearly describing a DBFO structure, even though not specifically referring to PFI, were grouped into this category as well.

Only 8 per cent of the contract notices examined could clearly be said to be for PFI projects; however, this is to be expected considering it

[17] See Treasury Taskforce, *Technical Note No. 2: How to Follow the EC Procurement Procedure and Advertise in the OJEC* (Treasury Taskforce Technical Note, May 1998), p. 10.

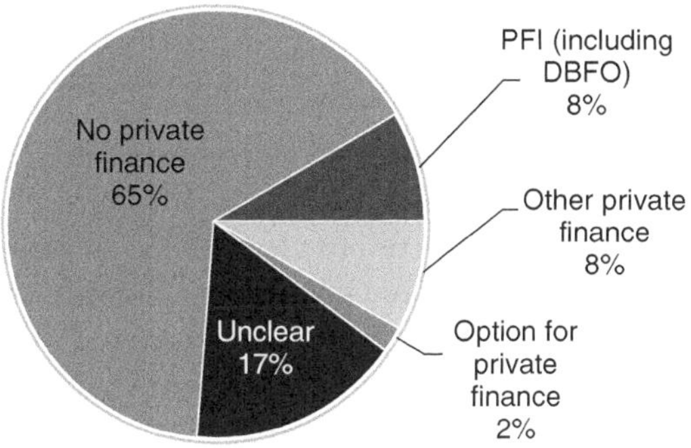

Figure 2.18 United Kingdom: private finance

is an arrangement for infrequent major capital investments. It was projects in the areas of infrastructure and building construction and also waste (for example, for the construction of a waste treatment plant) that employed the PFI method. In particular, there were several Building Schools (and colleges) for the Future projects and also many housing and town regeneration projects that adopted this finance arrangement.

In 8 per cent of the notices it was clear that private finance was involved, but this was not necessarily under PFI; for example, non-PFI joint ventures involving private finance found their way in to this category.[18]

UK government guidance for PPP projects in the market conditions of 2009 advises authorities to 'draft the OJEU notice and other tender documents as widely as possible to ensure that alternative financing solutions can be accommodated'.[19] This advice notice was issued quite late in the data collection period for this project (August 2009); however, in the view of the authors, this was a welcome instruction, as only 2 per cent of notices over the entire period examined were drafted in such a manner to leave financing options open.

[18] School projects procured under the BSF programme and National Health Service (NHS) Local Improvement Finance Trust schemes, although not strictly speaking PFI, were, for the purposes of the research classified as PFI in line with similar Partnerships UK categorisations (see www.partnershipsuk.org.uk/PUK-Projects-Database.aspx).

[19] HM Treasury, *Application Note – PPP Projects in the Current Market Conditions* (28 August 2009), available at www.hm-treasury.gov.uk/d/market_dislocation_280809.pdf, p. 2.

It can be seen that in 17 per cent of cases the authors did not feel sufficiently confident to classify a contract as requiring private finance or not. This commonly occurred where, for example, an authority made no mention of private finance but used a phrase such as 'partnering arrangement'. Such phrases may mean more to those involved with procurement in practice but were not clear to the authors.

The data supports UK Office of Government Commerce and Treasury claims that authorities in the UK have steadily moved away from use of the competitive negotiated procedure for PFI and other private finance projects, which prior to 2006 was viewed as the procedure of choice for such procurement,[20] to use of the competitive dialogue.[21] This may be down to the clear guidance from the UK government, published in 2006, that the negotiated procedure should only be used in 'very exceptional circumstances'.[22] According to the Office of Government Commerce (OGC), overall use of the negotiated procedure has declined from 2006 onwards, suggesting that the above policy statement has had an impact.[23]

6.4.2. France

In France, only 180 contract notices indicated a need for private finance. One reason that the number is lower than for the UK may be because there were significantly fewer 'unclear' contracts in France than there were in the UK. This greater clarity may be because the legal framework for PPP-type contracts in France is quite different from that in most other Member States, as the types of PPPs commonly concluded by contracting authorities are all subject to specific legislation, rather than

[20] See P. Braun, 'Strict Compliance versus Commercial Reality: The Practical Application of EC Public Procurement Law to the UK's Private Finance Initiative' (2003) 9(5) *European Law Journal* 575, at 580.

[21] M. Wynne (OGC), 'Competitive Dialogue: Keeping up the Momentum on Best Practice', Achilles Conference: Operating Competitive Dialogue, 29 April 2009. See also HM Treasury, *HM Treasury Review of Competitive Dialogue* (November 2010), available at www.hm-treasury.gov.uk/d/ppp_competitive_dialogue.pdf, p. 10. A detailed discussion of this trend is provided by Arrowsmith and Craven in Ch. 3 below.

[22] OGC, *Competitive Dialogue Procedure: OGC Guidance on the Competitive Dialogue Procedure in the New Procurement Regulations* (January 2006), available at http://webarchive.nationalarchives.gov.uk/20110822131357/www.ogc.gov.uk, p. 3. A brief scan of contract notices for negotiated procedures advertised by UK contracting authorities gives the impression that the process is now mostly used to procure insurance or financial services; however, the researchers have no data to substantiate this claim.

[23] Wynne, n. 21 above.

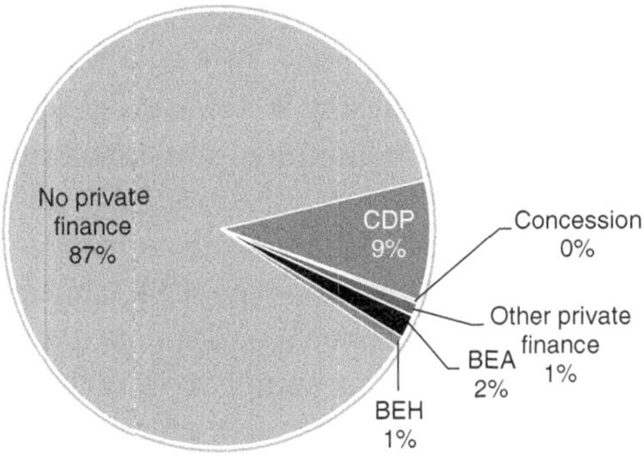

Figure 2.19 France: private finance

just the general procurement rules.[24] This has the consequence that the various types are readily identified in contract notices and are easy to separate for the purposes of this study.

As can be seen in Figure 2.19, one particular type of PPP contract was dominant in France. This is the so-called *contrat de partenariat* (CDP), a type of PPP that follows a DBFM(O) structure. Award of these contracts is regulated in a specific ordinance that entered into force in 2004.[25] CDPs can be used in all sectors and have been used particularly often with regard to the urban furniture/public lighting-type contracts discussed in section 5.4.2 above – however, they were also used for general infrastructure contracts, waste contracts and transport infrastructure.

Beyond this, several specific sectors in France have been given the right to conclude PPP-type contracts separately. The public health sector can use a specific type of long-term leasehold agreement called a *bail emphytéotique hospitalier* to build new public health-related infrastructure.[26] Until 2008, local contracting authorities dealing with public order and security could use long-term leasehold structures to build their necessary infrastructure; thus, for example, police stations, military barracks, courts and prisons could all be constructed using a type of PPP leasehold entitled a *bail emphytéotique administratif* (BEA).[27] Until

[24] For a complete outline of the types of PPP contracts regulated by law in France, see www.ppp.minefi.gouv.fr/tableau_comparatif.pdf.

[25] Ordonnance No. 2004-559 of 17 June 2004.

[26] Arts. L.6148-1 *et seq.* of the Code de la santé publique (Public Health Code).

[27] More specifically, public order and safety construction is usually purchased using a so-called AOT-LOA (Autorisation d'occupation temporaire assortie d'une location

2010, the BEA setup could also be used to build infrastructure related to the fire services;[28] and, more generally, BEA is still available for public authorities when they are purchasing in order to carry out their public services or (more specifically) in building sports infrastructure.[29] As well as being used in the indicated sectors, BEAs were also commonly used to purchase swimming pools and local authority offices.

Beyond these leaseholds and new-type PPP contracts, concession agreements were also found in France – although these appear not to be concluded very regularly using competitive dialogue, as they only sparingly surfaced in the search (see Figure 2.19 above). This finding may be explained by the fact that, under the French procurement rules, concession agreements can be concluded using more flexible procedures than competitive dialogue (see also Chapter 4 on France) and in any event do not have to be advertised in the OJEU under Article 35 of the Directive, as concession agreements are not covered by the Directives. Any concession agreements advertised were thus voluntarily advertised.

As with other jurisdictions, there were also a number of contract notices that only mentioned 'finance' or 'partnering' as a necessity, but without reference to any of the specific contract types highlighted above.

7. Observations on the clarity and utility of EU notices

Although not an initial issue for study in the project, it can finally be mentioned that it was discovered that there are significant problems with the supply of information in OJEU notices. Some of the information is not helpful, where it was expected to be informative; other information is highly contingent on contracting authorities filling it in correctly which – as was discovered – is done with highly variable degrees of accuracy.

More generally, it is a substantial problem that the specific requirements – technical or financial – for any given contract can only be

avec option d'achat) setup; this refers to a situation whereby a temporary right to occupy and operate is granted to the leaseholder, who concludes the lease with an option to buy. For more detail, in English, see T. Laloum and A. Jahanguiri, 'Chapter 5: France', in the *International Comparative Legal Guide to PFI/PPP Projects 2007*, available at www.iclg.co.uk.

[28] See Art. L.1311-2 of the Code général des collectivités territoriales (Local Authorities Code).

[29] The latter inserted by Loi No. 2009-179 du 17 février 2009 pour l'accélération des programmes de construction et d'investissement publics et privés.

obtained in the original language that the OJEU notice was posted in. Only very basic information about contracts is available in languages other than the originally submitted language, and the title of the contract, for instance, only rarely accurately describes that which is actually being purchased. If the 'real' information is only available in local languages, be it through TED or – quite commonly – on the authority's website, there are obviously real limits to the utility of OJEU notices.

8. Conclusions

In conclusion, from the above specific findings we can draw out some general trends in the use of competitive dialogue prior to 2010. In terms of number of contracts placed using this procedure, local government was the most regular competitive dialogue user, with the health sector following closely behind. Furthermore, the infrastructure and ICT categories together represented the majority of regular purchases being made using competitive dialogue; this is unsurprising as complex infrastructure and IT systems were used as examples of 'particularly complex contracts' that would warrant use of competitive dialogue.[30] It is quite difficult to generalise findings beyond this, however, as the 'other' categories proved to be substantial in many of the subject Member States; this demonstrates that many interesting non-regular purchases are also made using competitive dialogue – some of which are country specific, and some of which only occurred once in the entire EU during the time investigated.

Finally, research on private finance highlighted primarily that there are significant drawbacks to the non-existence of an agreed definition of 'PPP', as the statistics collected on private financing arrangements were not comparable between Member States. Furthermore, many of the contract notices were deliberately drafted in vague terms in countries where there are no set legal frameworks for private finance purchases – thus adding to the general impression that OJEU notices successfully provide basic information about contracts procured using competitive dialogue, but do not always result in comprehensive understanding of what is being purchased, or how it is being paid for.

[30] See recital 31 to Directive 2004/18/EC, as well as the Commission Explanatory Note, n. 12 above, p. 3.

PART II

Competitive dialogue in selected Member States of the EU

3

Competitive dialogue in the United Kingdom

SUE ARROWSMITH AND RICHARD CRAVEN

1. Introduction

1.1. Scope of the chapter

This chapter examines the application of the legal rules on competitive dialogue in the United Kingdom (UK) – or, more precisely, in England, which is the largest part of the UK in terms of both population and area. As Chapter 2 explained, the UK, along with France, is one of the two 'heavy' users of competitive dialogue, and thus has extensive experience of the procedure. There has also been significant empirical research on the operation of the procedure in the UK, including work by one of the present authors on the way in which practitioners interpret and apply the law. This sheds light both on how the legal regime on competitive dialogue is used and on the perceived advantages and difficulties of the legal rules. Since domestic law merely repeats, without addition or subtraction, the legal rules in place at EU level, the study may be of interest beyond the UK.

We will see that in general competitive dialogue has been welcomed: research indicates that it is regarded by both the public and private sectors as a valuable addition to the toolbox of award procedures under Public Sector Directive 2004/18 and is considered in general to have led to an improvement on the pre-2004 approach used for awarding complex contracts.[1]

On the other hand, we will see also that the procedure is not without difficulties. Some of these stem from the legal rules that are the focus of our enquiry: we will see that in certain respects the rules are perceived as too inflexible for effective commercial procurement, and also as very uncertain. In our conclusions, we will suggest that some of the rules require clarification in line with a flexible approach, and that guidance in

[1] See section 6 below.

this direction from both the domestic government and the EU, as well as appropriate judicial development, could play an important role in improving both legal certainty and commercial efficiency. Other problems, we will see, have arisen from the way in which competitive dialogue is operated in practice, including over-use of the procedure[2] and a lack of planning and focus,[3] which have led to unnecessary costs and protracted timescales.

Against this background, the UK government recently announced that there will in future be a presumption against use of competitive dialogue as part of a general strategy to reduce the costs and timescales of government procurement, along with other initiatives relevant to competitive dialogue as well as other award procedures, such as providing better advance information to the market and better planning.[4] This may lead to reduced use of competitive dialogue in future. The announcement is welcome in that it may help curb use of competitive dialogue in cases in which open or restricted procedures are more suitable, as well as promoting improvements in its operation. However, there is a danger of throwing the baby out with the bathwater if this new policy steer should deter use in all but very exceptional cases.[5] The great flexibility of competitive dialogue makes it inherently useful in a wide variety of situations, and it is important not to overlook the fact that it is widely perceived in the UK as representing an improvement over what went before. The main ongoing challenge, in our view, is to improve its practical operation and to curb any abuse to maximise the benefits available.

The limitation of this chapter to England requires brief explanation. The UK is not a federal state and until recently the general policy-making and legislative power over public procurement for the whole country resided with the UK central government in Westminster. However, in 1998 there occurred a process of devolution, whereby various powers of legislation and policy-making were passed ('devolved') from this central government to new regional (devolved) governments for Scotland, for Wales and for Northern Ireland.[6] Under devolution public

[2] See section 4.2 below. [3] See section 5.2 below.

[4] Speech by Francis Maude, Minister for the Cabinet Office, 21 November 2011, available at www.cabinetoffice.gov.uk/news/crown-and-suppliers-new-way-working. Unless otherwise stated, all websites referred to in this chapter were last accessed on 6 December 2011.

[5] See further the argument in section 4.4 below.

[6] This was done originally under the Scotland Act 1998, the Government of Wales Act 1998 and the Northern Ireland Act 1998. The provisions applying to Wales are now largely

procurement policy in these territories became in principle the responsibility of the devolved administrations.[7] This could potentially lead to significant differences in law and policy on competitive dialogue in different UK jurisdictions. The reality, however, is different, in particular as regards the applicable legal rules. So far as concerns EU law, the government of Scotland enjoys a general power to implement EU legislation with respect to Scotland[8] and since 2004 Scotland has adopted separate legislation transposing the EU procurement Directives[9] – but these regulations are almost identical to the regulations applying in other parts of the UK.[10] For Wales, the Welsh Assembly *may* be designated as the body for implementing EU law in particular areas (Government of Wales Act 2006, s.59), but this has not happened in the area of public procurement: thus the UK Treasury retains this power for Wales. Similarly, no order has yet been made designating a Northern Ireland minister for the purposes of transposing EU law. Thus a single set of procurement rules (as discussed further below) has been adopted by the Westminster government to cover England, Wales and Northern Ireland. However, the devolved governments do have significant responsibilities for practical and strategic matters relating to competitive dialogue, which results in some policy differences. To avoid unwieldy descriptions of all the jurisdictions, this chapter focuses on England, but much of the analysis is equally relevant for other parts of the UK.

1.2. Background: organisation and regulation of public procurement in the UK

So far as the conduct of procurement is concerned, this has traditionally been carried out on the basis of a largely decentralised model, by individual central government departments and agencies, individual

contained in a later Act, the Government of Wales Act 2006, which conferred further powers on the Welsh government.

[7] See further P. Henderson, 'The Impact of Devolution on Public Procurement in the United Kingdom' (2003) 12 *Public Procurement Law Review* 175; C. Boch, 'The Implementation of the Public Procurement Directives in the United Kingdom: Devolution and Divergence?' (2007) 16 *Public Procurement Law Review* 410.

[8] Scotland Act 1998, s. 53 and Sched. 8, para. 15.

[9] Scottish Statutory Instrument 2006 No. 1, the Public Contracts (Scotland) Regulations 2006 and Scottish Statutory Instrument 2006 No. 2, the Utilities Contracts (Scotland) Regulations 2006.

[10] See further Boch, n. 7 above.

local authorities (municipalities) and other public bodies (such as universities): each generally makes purchases to meet its own requirements. There are also, however, many co-operative initiatives, enabling entities to take advantage of economies of scale from joint purchasing, and/or of the expertise of specialised purchasing agencies.

As regards general policy and regulatory issues, responsibility in England rested until recently with the Office of Government Commerce (OGC) but in 2011 this agency was integrated into the Efficiency and Reform Group within the Cabinet Office in central government and no longer has a separate identity.[11] The functions of the former OGC are now exercised to a greater or lesser degree by the Government Procurement Service in the Cabinet Office. An important function of the former OGC was issuing extensive guidance on procurement policy for central government and – important in the present context – issuing guidance for the whole public sector on interpreting and applying legal rules, including those deriving from EU law. This guidance of the old OGC has, as we will see, substantially influenced the approach to competitive dialogue. However, it appears that the Cabinet Office may not in future produce guidance to the same extent, and centralised guidance on interpretation of the legal rules may in future play a less important role. The provision of general guidance and other activity relating to aspects of value for money in central government public procurement has, in addition, been undertaken centrally by the Treasury as part of its function of managing public expenditure,[12] and, as we will see below, the Treasury has also been involved in work on competitive dialogue.[13]

So far as concerns the *general approach* to regulating individual contracting authorities, in many countries domestic rules on public procurement contracts, and especially rules governing tendering, have been enacted into law, and sometimes aggrieved firms, as well as other interested parties, have a right to enforce the rules. In contrast, however, the UK, in implementing its domestic procurement objectives (such as

[11] The remit of the Cabinet Office in general is to ensure effective development, co-ordination and implementation of policy and operations across government departments and to ensure the Civil Service provides effective and efficient support.

[12] General guidelines–such as the principle of using competition unless there are good reasons not to do so–are set out in HM Treasury, *Managing Public Money* (2011), in Ch. 4, Annex 4.4, available at www.hm-treasury.gov.uk/psr_mpm_index.htm.

[13] See section 3 below.

value for money and sustainability),[14] does not have a long-standing tradition of regulating through detailed rules that are legally binding or enforceable.[15] Rather, the government has instead relied on the judgment of individual contracting authorities and officials, who have traditionally been given significant discretion, and has preferred to focus on outcomes obtained, rather than compliance with rules, to measure success. This policy is supported by an emphasis on development of professional training and skills.[16] This is particularly the case in central government; here, rules directed at value for money and other objectives have been applied through administrative directions and guidelines from the Treasury, the former OGC, the Cabinet Office and other relevant authorities. In principle, these are *not enforceable* by aggrieved firms. Further, direction from these central authorities often has not taken the form even of non-binding *requirements* (directions) to act in a certain way, but merely the form of *suggestions* (guidance) on how to act, which leaves the ultimate decision to each individual purchasing authority. Another facet of traditional procurement rules in the UK is the fact that the content of even these 'soft' norms (i.e. non-binding and/or unenforceable rules) is often quite basic and lacking in detail. Thus the rules leave it to individual contracting authorities to fill out the precise details of how they ought to act in conducting procurement procedures.

The traditional character of the procurement regime has, however, been altered significantly by accession to the EU, which occurred in 1973. After accession there was initially a considerable period of delay in which – reflecting the UK's traditional approach to procurement regulation – the EU procurement Directives were given effect only by

[14] See, for example, the six objectives of OGC procurement activities stated at http://webarchive.nationalarchives.gov.uk/20110822131357/www.ogc.gov.uk.

[15] See generally C. Turpin, *Government Procurement and Contracts* (London: Longmans, 1989), *passim*; and S. Arrowsmith, *The Law of Public and Utilities Procurement* (2nd edn, London: Sweet & Maxwell, 2005), Ch. 2.

[16] See HM Treasury, *Setting New Standards: A Strategy for Government Procurement* (Cm 2840, 1995); and A. Erridge, 'Innovations in Public Sector and Regulated Procurement', Ch. 12 in A. Cox (ed.), *Innovations in Procurement Management* (Boston, Lincolnshire: Earlsgate, 1996); N. Deverill, *Change and Innovation in Government Procurement*, Ch. 13 in Cox (ed.), above; and, recently, HM Treasury, *Transforming Government Procurement* (January 2007), section 2.4, available at www.hm-treasury.gov.uk/d/government_procurement_pu147.pdf. The last report led to the development of the Government Procurement Services (GPS) Skills Frameworks: see http://webarchive.nationalarchives.gov.uk/20110822131357/www.ogc.gov.uk/learning_and_development_procurement_skills_and_competences.asp.

central government guidance indicating the need to follow these rules, and not in a manner compliant with EU obligations, which require these rules to be given a binding and enforceable character in domestic law.[17] However, in the early 1990s the UK finally complied with its obligations and transposed the procurement Directives through secondary legislation in the binding form of Ministerial regulations with specific rights of enforcement for economic operators.[18] Since the EU procurement Directives cover a large part of the regulatory space available in public procurement,[19] at least for major contracts, the effect has been to subject this activity to significant formal regulation in a manner alien to the traditional UK approach.

However, to the extent permitted by EU law, the UK has retained its traditional approach: it has regulated procurement by law only to the minimum extent required by the Directives and has not imposed further obligations on contracting authorities. Thus all choices permitted to Member States under the Directives are left to contracting authorities themselves: they have a free choice between the Directives' procedures – open, restricted or negotiated, and competitive dialogue – and over use of framework agreements, auctions and dynamic purchasing systems, subject only to the restrictions in the Directives themselves. The law also generally allows entities the full choice allowed by the Directives on *how* to structure those procedures and techniques – for example, it allows free choice on what selection or award criteria to use within the freedom allowed by the Directives. Further, the Westminster government has not adopted specific legal rules to regulate contracts outside the Directives, including those that are subject to obligations of transparency and non-discrimination under the TFEU: it has merely issued guidance drawing attention to these obligations.[20] As we will see in section 3, the approach to competitive dialogue in the UK merely reflects this traditional approach to procurement regulation and its general manifestation in the transposition of EU procurement rules rather than other possible considerations, such as reluctance to regulate a novel procedure.

[17] Case C-433/93, *Commission* v. *Germany* [1995] ECR I-2303.

[18] On the history of implementation, see Arrowsmith, n. 15 above, Ch. 3.

[19] See S. Arrowsmith, 'The Past and Future Evolution of EC Procurement Law: From Framework to Common Code?' (2006) 35 *Public Contract Law Journal* 337.

[20] OGC, *Procurement Policy Note 10/03* (16 September 2003); and also OGC, *Procurement Policy Note* 03/06 (31 July 2006). On the position in Scotland, see Boch, n. 7 above.

The EU Directives applicable as of July 2011 have been transposed for England, Wales and Northern Ireland, through two sets of regulations, which came into force on 31 January 2006 and repealed and replaced the previous regulations implementing the EU procurement rules. These are:

(1) the Public Contracts Regulations 2006,[21] implementing the Public Sector Directive 2004/18 and also the Remedies Directive 89/665; and
(2) the Utilities Contracts Regulations 2006,[22] implementing the Utilities Directive 2004/17 and the Utilities Remedies Directive 92/13.

These regulations transposed into national law the new obligations imposed by the Directives and at the same time also provided for the increased flexibilities allowed, including by adding competitive dialogue as an award procedure. They have been amended on several occasions, notably by the Public Contracts (Amendment) Regulations 2009 (SI 2009 No. 2992) and the Utilities Contracts (Amendment) Regulations 2009 (SI 2009 No. 3100), which introduced the amendments required by Directive 2007/66/EC on remedies and related matters.

It is a further important feature of the national procurement regulations (in line with a broader government policy in implementing EU measures) that the procurement Directives have been transposed mainly by copying out the Directives' text,[23] avoiding offering *interpretations* of its provisions. This avoids the legal errors that might arise in interpretation: there is particular potential for such errors because of the complex and ambiguous nature of the Directives and the unpredictable nature of decisions of the CJEU. Thus, as stated by the OGC, in commenting on its draft of the regulations, 'we have avoided any unnecessary elaboration, or any elaboration which risks being at odds with the meaning of the directive'.[24] Only in very limited respects do the regulations seek to

[21] Public Contracts Regulations 2006, SI 2006 No. 5.

[22] Utilities Contracts Regulations 2006, SI 2006 No. 6.

[23] For the exceptions to this approach and a more detailed analysis of the UK approach to transposition, see S. Arrowsmith, 'Implementation of the New EC Procurement Directives and the Alcatel Ruling in England and Wales and Northern Ireland: A Review of the New Legislation and Guidance' (2006) 15 *Public Procurement Law Review* 86.

[24] OGC, Consultation Document, *Draft Regulations Implementing the New Public Sector and Utilities Procurement Directives* (June 2005), available at http://webarchive.nationalarchives.gov.uk/20110822131357/www.ogc.gov.uk/index.asp, at 2.1. For a formal statement of this policy as a reflection of the government's more general policy towards EU law, see Regulatory Impact Assessment: Public Contracts Regulations 2006, at 2.2.

clarify the meaning of the Directives (for example, by specifying to some extent which domestic bodies are within the concept of a contracting authority): instead, the government has used guidance to indicate any views it wishes to convey on interpretation.

As already observed, one function of the former OGC was to issue guidance for the whole public sector, including on interpreting EU procurement law and on conducting procedures in practice under the EU rules. It issued a series of guidance notes when the Directives were implemented, covering the key new provisions,[25] and later supplemented these with further guidance, including on competitive dialogue, as we will see below. However, it needs to be noted that, following the General Election in 2010, the new government, which took office in May 2010, indicated that previous guidance (which has now been removed to an archive) was being revised and updated and did not necessarily reflect *current* policy.[26] In practice, there has been little activity in producing guidance since that time, the main exception being the issuing by the Cabinet Office of a limited number of procurement policy notes to address new issues.[27] This may indicate that, as we have noted above, centralised guidance will no longer be given such a significant role in the future as in the past in helping authorities interpret the EU rules.

We can also note that, in the UK, a starting point of the law on government contracts in general is that, as regards both their formation and contents and their execution, these are in principle subject to the ordinary private law of contract that applies also to contracts between private persons and companies, and that that law is administered by the ordinary courts. However, there are many exceptions where specific rules have been developed in both case law and legislation to take account of the special governmental context[28] including, in some cases, controls over tendering procedures.

Proceedings relating to violations of EU procurement law are generally brought in England and Wales before the High Court, with the possibility of appealing decisions thereafter to the Court of Appeal and (in very rare cases, subject to leave being granted) to the Supreme Court.[29] These

[25] The OGC guidance is now archived at http://webarchive.nationalarchives.gov.uk/20110822131357/www.ogc.gov.uk.

[26] See the archive in n. 25 above.

[27] Available at www.cabinetoffice.gov.uk. These notes were formerly issued by OGC.

[28] On special rules in government procurement, see Arrowsmith, n. 15 above, Ch. 2.

[29] This took over from the House of Lords as the highest court in the UK in 2009.

are courts of general jurisdiction hearing all kinds of legal proceedings, although procurement proceedings before the High Court are (according to the subject-matter and choice of the parties) sometimes heard by specialist judges, in particular in the Administrative Court or the Technology and Construction Court of the Queen's Bench Division of the High Court or in the Chancery Division of the High Court (which has particular expertise in EU law matters).

An important feature of the legal background in the UK is that there is still little litigation and case law in comparison with other Member States – reported case law (covering almost all litigation in the field) has increased from one or two cases a year when EU law was first implemented to only around fifteen to twenty a year at present (although still gradually increasing).[30] The main reasons for this found in a research project conducted by Pachnou in 2000–1 were, first, the high cost of legal proceedings and, secondly, a general perception by suppliers that procedures were fair combined with a desire to avoid a culture of litigation that could disrupt the process; the fear of retaliation by contracting authorities was also a factor but a less significant one.[31] There has been speculation as to whether this position might change as a result of the recent strengthening of remedies in Directive 2007/66. Anecdotal evidence from lawyers suggests many more queries being raised and challenges being made, but this is not yet reflected to any great extent in reported cases.

The general absence of case law to develop legal interpretations means that government guidance can play a significant role in guiding practice.[32] It is also noteworthy that, although such guidance is not a formal source of law, it may be (and often is) consulted in applying the basic principle of interpretation of legislation in the UK which is to establish the meaning of the words in context.[33] The courts have referred to procurement guidance to inform their views on the meaning of the

[30] These figures are based on the authors' own count. In 2010, for example, the authors have counted exactly twenty reported cases involving EU procurement law issues. Procurement cases that do not involve any EU procurement issues are very rare.

[31] D. Pachnou, 'Bidders' Use of Mechanisms to Enforce EC Procurement Law' (2005) 14 *Public Procurement Law Review* 256.

[32] See P. Braun, 'Strict Compliance versus Commercial Reality: The Practical Application of EC Public Procurement Law to the UK's Private Finance Initiative' (2003) 9 *European Law Journal* 575, discussed further in, section 3.2 below.

[33] See *Risk Management Partners* v. *Brent London Borough Council* [2009] EWCA Civ 490 (CA).

procurement regulations, simply citing and adopting the views in national guidance with little discussion, even when the rules merely transpose directly effective requirements of EU law without modification.[34]

2. The background: complex procurement prior to competitive dialogue

Prior to the introduction of competitive dialogue for contracts covered by the Directives, the award procedures legally available to contracting authorities were simply the open procedure, the restricted procedure and the negotiated procedure as they existed at that time in the Directives. As explained in section 1, in accordance with the UK's general approach to the procurement Directives, these procedures were provided for in domestic legislation in the same form as they appear in the Directives and made available on the same grounds. Thus it was in principle left to each contracting authority to choose which of these procedures to use for its complex contracts and how to operate that procedure, provided, of course, that the authority operated within the parameters of the Directives themselves.

As will be explained below, a major group of contracts for which competitive dialogue is currently used comprises privately financed infrastructure (PFI) contracts for, for example, schools, hospitals, prisons and roads.[35]

Empirical research by Braun[36] found that in the 1990s these contracts were awarded using the competitive version of the negotiated procedure – but using a specific structured form of that procedure. This procedure involved using a broad output specification; submission of initial offers by those selected to negotiate – which were used as the basis for

[34] See, for example, *DeVilbiss Medequip Ltd* v. *NHS Purchasing and Supply Agency* [2005] EWHC 1757 (Ch) referring to OGC guidance on framework agreements.

[35] PFI refers to the Private Finance Initiative launched formally by the government to encourage use of private finance in infrastructure contracts. See generally P. Badcoe (ed.), *Public Private Partnerships and PFI* (looseleaf) (London: Sweet & Maxwell).

[36] Braun, n. 32 above. See also para. 2 of OGC, *Competitive Dialogue Procedure: OGC Guidance on the Competitive Dialogue Procedure in the New Procurement Regulations* (January 2006) ('OGC 2006 guidance'), available at http://webarchive.nationalarchives.gov.uk/20110822131357/www.ogc.gov.uk/documents/guide_competitive_dialogue.pdf, stating that most complex procurements such as PFI projects and complex IT contracts were awarded by the negotiated procedure prior to 2006.

discussion and in some cases to narrow down the number of those invited to submit a full offer; and then submission of final offers, as the basis for selecting the winning provider. As found by Braun, this approach represented a widespread and common practice amongst contracting authorities, steered by guidance from government policy-makers[37] but not embodied in any formal legal rules. He also found that contracts within this group that were *not* covered by the Directives because they are classified as services concessions were awarded using the same type of process (and indeed the guidance from government made no significant distinction in its policy advice between concessions and contracts governed by the Directives). Subject to what is said below concerning, in particular, the stage after selecting the winner of the competition,[38] the approach used in the UK for these contracts once it had been developed over a period of years is one that largely fits the Directive's rules on competitive dialogue and in fact has been one of the important influences on the development of those rules.[39] As the OGC notes in its guidance issued when competitive dialogue was implemented in domestic law in 2006, '[l]obbying by UK stakeholders helped to ensure that the final text fitted better [than the original draft] with existing UK PFI practice. The end result is a structured negotiated procedure which is similar in many ways to the existing practice of letting PFI contracts.'[40] The government considered prior to 2006 that the negotiated procedure was available for PFI contracts in general either on the basis that overall pricing was not possible (a basis applicable to works and services contracts) or on the ground that it was not possible to set a specification (applicable to services contracts).[41] The European Commission had concerns over whether the grounds for using the negotiated procedure covered these kinds of

[37] Treasury Taskforce, Technical Note No. 2, *How to Follow EC Procurement Procedure and Advertise in the OJEC* (1998), at 3.2. See Braun, n. 32 above, on the importance of this guidance in shaping UK practice.

[38] See section 5.9 below.

[39] This observation is based on Arrowsmith's experiences as a former member of the European Commission's Advisory Committee on the Opening Up of Public Procurement and also from informal meetings with Commission officials to discuss how the new competitive dialogue procedure should be developed.

[40] OGC 2006 guidance, n. 36 above, at 1.2.

[41] Grounds found respectively in Council Directive 93/37/EEC [1993] OJ L199/547(2)(c) (Works Directive) and Art. 11(2)(b) of Council Directive 92/50/EEC [1992] OJ L209/1 (Services Directive); and Art. 11(2)(c) of Directive 92/50. See Treasury Taskforce, Technical Note No. 2, n. 37 above, at 3.2.

contracts and initiated discussions with the UK government on this.[42] However, use of the negotiated procedure in these cases was effectively endorsed by the High Court of England and Wales (Richards J) in *R* v. *Rhondda Cynon Taff County Borough Council, ex parte Kathro*.[43]

As Chapter 2 explained (and see also section 4 below), the other single major type of contract for which competitive dialogue is used extensively in the UK is major IT contracts. There is no scientific empirical evidence on how these contracts were awarded previously. However, anecdotal evidence from lawyers active in this field suggests that these types of contracts were awarded using both restricted procedures and the negotiated procedure, with the latter being used, in particular, when (for a period) major IT contracts were awarded under the PFI approach, whereby the private sector provided up-front finance for the development and then operation of the systems over a period of several years.[44] However, lawyers advising on these projects have informed the authors that when the restricted procedure was used there was some difficulty in conducting effective procurement within the confines of that procedure, and it can also be noted that guidance issued by the former Central Computer and Telecommunications Agency on procurement of IT systems[45] promoted a very flexible view of what is permitted under the restricted procedure, including an iterative process.

More generally, it is interesting to note that, as discussed in section 3 below, since 2006 the use of the competitive form of the negotiated procedure has declined closely in line with the rise in use of competitive dialogue. This reinforces the conclusion that many contracts now awarded by competitive dialogue previously were awarded using that procedure.[46]

[42] OGC 2006 guidance, n. 36 above, at 2. No proceedings reached the CJEU, perhaps because it had been decided to address the problem they raised by introducing competitive dialogue.

[43] *R* v. *Rhondda Cynon Taff County Borough Council, ex parte Kathro* [2001] EWHC Admin 527. For discussion, see Arrowsmith, n. 15 above, pp. 564–5.

[44] The authors are grateful, in particular, to Roger Bickerstaff of Bird & Bird, who advised on many such procurements during the 1990s, and has provided information on this subject.

[45] Total Acquisition Process (TAP).

[46] And see also OGC/Treasury, *Competitive Dialogue in 2008: OGC/HMT Joint Guidance on Using the Procedure* (2008) ('OGC/Treasury 2008 guidance'), available at www.hm-treasury.gov.uk/d/competitive_dialogue_procedure.pdf, at 3.2, which states generally that '[h]istorically ... the Competitive Negotiated Procedure has been used for most UK complex procurements'.

3. Introduction to competitive dialogue

3.1. The legislation on competitive dialogue

As section 1 mentioned, competitive dialogue was introduced into domestic law for contracts covered by Directive 2004/18 by the Public Contracts Regulations 2006, from 31 January 2006. There were never any doubts that competitive dialogue would be included as a procedure for use by contracting authorities in domestic law – its inclusion, along with all the other new flexibilities of the Directive, simply reflects the general policy towards transposing the procurement Directives that allows contracting authorities the full flexibility permitted to them under EU law.[47] In fact, it was always expected that competitive dialogue would be useful and widely used in the UK for projects previously awarded by negotiated procedures, as section 4 below will elaborate. However, it is notable that all new mechanisms provided by the Directives were made available in the domestic legislation simply as a matter of general policy, without any debate as to their utility and, indeed, in the case of the dynamic purchasing system, with perhaps an expectation that it would not be much used.[48]

The approach to competitive dialogue in England so far as the legal rules are concerned also reflects the more general policy towards implementing the procurement Directives that was described in section 2 above. Thus so far as legislation is concerned, we find that the competitive dialogue procedure has been included in the regulations simply by largely repeating what is provided in the Directives, although with some reordering of the provisions. In this respect, both the grounds for use and the procedure to be followed are set out in Public Contracts Regulations 2006, regulation 18. As is the general approach to the Directives, individual contracting authorities are given full freedom both:

[47] See OGC, Consultation document, *The Approach to the Implementation of the New Public Sector Procurement Directive* (May 2004), at 3.5, stating the general intention to transpose all new provisions of Directive 2004/18 in the regulations that became the Public Contracts Regulations 2006.

[48] This has proved to be the case: see S. Arrowsmith, 'Methods for Purchasing Ongoing Requirements: The System of Framework Agreements and Dynamic Purchasing Systems under the EC Directives and UK Procurement Regulations', Ch. 3 in S. Arrowsmith and J. Tillipman (eds.), *Public Procurement Regulation in the 21st Century: Reform of the UNCITRAL Model Law on Procurement* (Eagan, MN: West, 2010).

- to use the procedure in any of the circumstances in which this is allowed by the Directives themselves; and
- to structure the procedure in any manner that is contemplated by the Directives.

There are no additional rules provided – for example, no rules beyond those of the Directive itself restricting contracting authorities' choice on how the dialogue phase should be operated, or what selection or award criteria should be used.

Also following this general approach, since competitive dialogue is not included in the Utilities Directive, it is also not included in the Utilities Contracts Regulations 2006 that transpose that Directive. Utilities can, however, follow a comparable procedure simply by operating the negotiated procedure with a notice in a manner that in practice follows the approach of competitive dialogue.

For contracts outside the Directives and contracts for Part B services, we have seen in section 1 that tendering procedures have not generally been regulated by domestic legislation: thus the detailed procedures are in principle within the discretion of individual procuring entities, though subject to guidance from government, general legal duties concerning value in procurement, and the legal constraints of the TFEU. Procuring entities are thus able to use procedures similar to competitive dialogue to award these contracts, also, if they wish and, as we will see below, sometimes do so. However, where they do so they are not subject to the detailed legal constraints applicable to the formal competitive dialogue rules that apply under Directive 2004/18 and the Public Contracts Regulations 2006.

3.2. *Case law and guidance*

So far as case law goes, reflecting the general paucity of case law in the UK that was discussed in section 1, there have been no cases interpreting the specific provisions on competitive dialogue and only one significant case relating to the competitive dialogue procedure at all (concerning the application of the general rules on disclosure of award criteria).[49] Thus the role of case law in this field has been negligible.

On the other hand, there has been important guidance from government, in particular government-wide guidance contained in the

[49] See section 5.8.2 below.

document, *Competitive Dialogue in 2008*, a joint OGC/Treasury publication of July 2008[50] (hereinafter 'OGC/Treasury 2008 guidance'). This provides both strategic guidance on the operation of the procedure, and guidance on interpreting the legal rules, drawing on the practical experience of operating the procedure in the UK since 2006. However, it is notable that the guidance stays away from pronouncing in much detail on many of the controversial and grey areas of law, preferring to deal with these matters largely by general statements of principle rather than detailed concrete examples – although it does address some of these matters, such as how many tenders must be invited at the final tender stage (see section 5 below). Government-wide guidance is also found in the earlier document, *Competitive Dialogue Procedure: OGC Guidance on the Competitive Dialogue Procedure in the New Procurement Regulations* (January 2006) (hereinafter 'OGC 2006 guidance'),[51] which was issued when the regulations were first adopted; and in the document from the OGC, *Practical Guidance on the Use of Competitive Dialogue* (July 2006).[52] There has also been guidance for specific sectors, such as guidance issued by Partnerships for Schools,[53] a body set up to administer the government's former 'Building Schools for the Future' investment programme,[54] on how to conduct a competitive dialogue procedure in the context of that programme (which involved the development of new or refurbished infrastructure for schools).[55] All this guidance is relevant to indicate how the government has guided contracting authorities during the first few years of competitive dialogue's operation. It should be reiterated here, however, that the contents of the previously published guidance do not necessarily reflect the policy of the current government that took office in May 2010.[56] It is also worth mentioning that recent

[50] OGC/Treasury 2008 guidance, n. 46 above. [51] N. 36 above.

[52] OGC, *Procurement Policy Note 04/06: Practical Guidance on the Use of Competitive Dialogue* (31 July 2006), available at http://webarchive.nationalarchives.gov.uk/20110822131357/www.ogc.gov.uk/documents/ProcurementPolicyCompetitiveDialogue.pdf.

[53] Available at www.partnershipsforschools.org.uk/library/BSF-archive.jsp.

[54] The programme was cancelled as from July 2010.

[55] See Partnerships for Schools, *Guidance Note on Classification of the Contract and Choice of Procedure under the EU Procurement Rules for the Building Schools for the Future Programme* (February 2006), and Partnerships for Schools, *BSF Guidance Note on How to Conduct a Competitive Dialogue Procedure* (January 2006), both available at www.partnershipsforschools.org.uk/library/library.html.

[56] See further, section 1.2 above.

reviews of competitive dialogue have been critical of the proliferation of guidance without a consistent approach.[57]

Especially given the previous influence of government guidance on contracting authority behaviour, as mentioned in section 2 above, it seems likely that this guidance would influence the use and conduct of competitive dialogue over the first few years of the procedure. It is clear from the qualitative research conducted by Craven into UK practice on competitive dialogue, which is explained in section 3.4 below, that guidance has indeed played an important role in steering contracting authorities towards particular interpretations, or in giving them confidence in applying a particular interpretation in areas of uncertainty. Thus, for example, fifteen interviewees in Craven's study cited statements by the OGC in 2006[58] and the OGC and Treasury in 2008[59] indicating that the competitive negotiated procedure was not generally available for PPP projects as a key influencing factor in the decision to procure certain projects under competitive dialogue rather than the negotiated procedure,[60] even if they did not always share this interpretation of the law. Also, fifteen interviewees stated that they gain comfort in areas of uncertainty when actions are supported by domestic guidance. For instance, a perceived generous interpretation of the scope for change after identifying a preferred bidder was given as an illustration of an area where comfort had been taken from the OGC/Treasury 2008 guidance.

In addition to the non-binding guidance, policy-makers may, within their sphere of influence, shape the practical operation of competitive dialogue. In particular, where a contracting authority must obtain approval at different stages of the procurement process, there may be strong pressure on an authority to run a procurement process in line with the approving body's preferred interpretation of the law (for example, as evidenced in guidance). Ten of those interviewed by Craven commented that in certain sectors, notably schools and hospitals, the approvals process enabled higher regulatory bodies to dictate conduct

[57] HM Treasury, *HM Treasury Review of Competitive Dialogue* (November 2010) ('2010 Treasury review'), available at www.hm-treasury.gov.uk/d/ppp_competitive_dialogue.pdf; Cabinet Office, *Accelerating Government Procurement – Management Summary of the Findings of a 'Lean' Study to Investigate Waste and Inefficiencies in Government's Procurement Process* (February 2011), available at www.cabinetoffice.gov.uk/sites/default/files/resources/lean-study-accelerating-government-procurement.pdf.

[58] OGC 2006 guidance, n. 36 above, section 2.

[59] OGC/Treasury 2008 guidance, n. 46 above, section 3.

[60] See further section 3.3 below.

under the competitive dialogue. In the specific context of the 'Building Schools for the Future' programme, before concluding the contract with the preferred bidder authorities were required to obtain 'Final Business Case' approval from Partnerships for Schools, which involved showing that the authority had followed the procurement rules.[61]

3.3. *The extent of use of competitive dialogue*

As we have seen in section 2, PFI contracts – the largest group of contracts currently awarded using competitive dialogue – were awarded prior to 2006 mainly by a structured process under the negotiated procedure with a notice, which fits substantially into the new competitive dialogue framework and influenced the way in which competitive dialogue was designed. It had long been perceived in the UK that there was need for a procedure for awarding PFI contracts that was more flexible than the open and restricted procedures and that if – as the Commission maintained – the negotiated procedure was not legally available a new procedure was needed. Further, it was widely considered that the restricted procedure was unsatisfactory for awarding certain other types of complex contracts for which authorities were currently using it in the absence of any suitable alternative. The perceived need for the new procedure combined with the fact that competitive dialogue reflected to a significant extent existing national practice for many complex contracts (both those awarded under the Directives and major contracts outside the Directives) clearly created a situation that was likely to be receptive to the use of competitive dialogue.

However, this does not give the whole picture, since there were also some concerns from the outset[62] over the 'fitness for purpose' of competitive dialogue, notably because of the potentially high costs for both parties of more than one firm being required to prepare a complete final tender. Thus it was by no means a foregone conclusion that contracting authorities would abandon the previous practice of using the negotiated procedure (though in a very structured form) for PFI contracts. Given

[61] See Partnerships for Schools, *Final Business Case Guidance (For Approval to Procure a LEP to Deliver Investment in the Secondary School Estate)* (January 2007), available at www.partnershipsforschools.org.uk/library/library.html, at 1.2.

[62] See, for example, Arrowsmith, n. 15 above, Ch. 10; 4ps, *Competitive Dialogue* (February 2007), available at http://test.4ps.gov.uk/UserFiles/File/Publications/competitive%20dialogue%204ps%20guidance%20vis10.pdf, p. 3. On this issue, see section 5 below.

this last point, it is important to mention that a strong steer towards the new procedure for PFI contracts in which the negotiated procedure would previously have been used was given to contracting authorities by government guidance.[63]

The position has in fact been that the UK has indeed – as anticipated – become a significant user of competitive dialogue. Thus, as de Mars and Craven explained in Chapter 2, the UK, along with France, is one of two Member States that can be categorised as 'heavy users': there were 1,390 contracts notices placed for competitive dialogue by UK authorities in the period 2006–9 (compared with 1,446 for France), with the number remaining fairly steady in 2007–9 (367 in 2007, 375 in 2008 and 368 in 2009).[64] More recent figures also reflect the same picture: figures from the OJEU show fifteen procedures in the UK in April 2011, twenty-nine in March and forty-four in February (a total of eighty-eight), as compared with thirty-five, twenty-five and twenty-one (a total of eighty-one) in the same months in 2009. As we will explain further in section 4, it appears that competitive dialogue has in its first few years of operation to a significant extent indeed replaced the negotiated procedure for certain types of procurement, in particular PFI contracts, and also that this development has been influenced by the government's guidance. However, there are certain factors that may lead to changes in the near future, considered briefly in section 4.

3.4. *Empirical research on competitive dialogue*

This chapter draws on several studies which explore the practical operation of competitive dialogue.

The first is a qualitative study sponsored by the Economic and Social Research Council (ESRC) and Bevan Brittan LLP,[65] which was conducted by Craven, one of the present authors. Throughout 2010, four years on from the UK transposition of competitive dialogue, Craven conducted semi-structured interviews with key actors in the practical operation of competitive dialogue in the UK in the specific context of Public–Private Partnerships (PPP). PPP was defined for this purpose as 'a risk-sharing relationship between the public and private sectors based upon a shared aspiration to bring about a desired public policy

[63] See section 4 below. [64] See Table 3.1 below.

[65] Under the 'CASE' PhD studentship scheme of the ESRC.

outcome',[66] thus encompassing PFI (as described above) and also other non-PFI public–private relationships, such as the contracting out of public services and contractual and non-contractual joint ventures. As we saw in Chapter 2, the vast majority of projects procured under competitive dialogue are PPPs in some form and thus the research represents a fairly comprehensive study of UK competitive dialogue. Interviewees comprised legal advisors with experience of advising UK contracting authorities on the competitive dialogue process, in-house procurement officers or legal advisors with experience of procuring PPP projects under competitive dialogue, and senior figures from government departments and other organisations, the remit of which includes public sector policy-making responsibilities with respect to the operation of competitive dialogue. The project's aim was to examine the way in which the legal framework for competitive dialogue is applied in the specific context of PPP procurement in the UK, and actors' perceptions of that framework. It sought to identify: perceived positive aspects of the framework in facilitating best practice; perceived problems, including any legal uncertainty and constraints on best practice; strategies to conduct the process within the constraints; and the factors that influence compliance and approach to legal risk. The research explored procurement practice with respect to PPP projects in the whole of the UK; however, for the purposes of this chapter and for the reasons outlined in section 1, only the findings from interview subjects based in England will be presented. An initial scoping survey of UK contracting authorities revealed that in these complex procurements it was most common for external legal advisors to play a lead role in the running of the competitive dialogue process; hence, the bulk of interviews were made up of external legal advisors (thirty-three).[67] However, eleven interviews were also conducted with in-house contracting authority procurement officers/legal advisors,[68] and three interviews were also conducted with those involved in setting policy for contracting authorities more broadly.

HM Treasury has also completed a review of complex procurement generally under competitive dialogue, which was published in November

[66] Institute of Public Policy Research, *Building Better Partnerships* (London, 2001), p. 40.

[67] These were mainly selected by reference to www.chambersandpartners.com/UK and the individual websites of law firms; however, so as not to neglect different perspectives, the study included seven law firms not listed in Chambers, identified using www.lawsociety.org.uk and firms' individual websites.

[68] These interviewees were identified through contract notices advertised in the OJEU.

2010 (hereinafter the 2010 Treasury review).[69] The objective of the review, undertaken with accountancy firm PricewaterhouseCoopers LLP, was to examine the way in which competitive dialogue has been undertaken in practice and the impact this has had on complex procurement in the UK.[70] Unlike Craven's study, this was not confined to PPP projects. The review brings together desk-based research, survey data, and information gathered from a number of roundtable discussions with groups of key stakeholders. Although providing little detail on research method, the review is stated to have involved two surveys: one project-specific and one general. According to the review, the project-specific survey targeted individuals from the public sector team on each individual competitive dialogue procurement identified by initial desk-based research, and the general survey was Internet-based and open to all individuals with an interest in competitive dialogue.[71] The roundtable discussions covered issues raised by the surveys and allowed stakeholders, such as central government commercial directors, PPP programme managers, academics, infrastructure bidders, IT bidders, legal advisors, financiers and central government/local authority representatives, to share their views.[72]

Further research into the operation of competitive dialogue has been published by the Confederation of British Industry (CBI),[73] an organisation representing UK businesses, in the 2008 report, *Actions Speak Louder Than Words: Unlocking the Full Potential of Competitive Dialogue*[74] (hereinafter the 2008 CBI study). Again, this document lacks a detailed explanation of method; however, it is said to have been prepared with advice from a range of government departments, procurers and suppliers, including the Treasury, the OGC, Partnerships UK, the Society of Procurement Officers in Local Government and the CBI's Public Services Strategy Board.[75] This provides, in particular, a view of competitive dialogue from the perspective of bidders, focusing on improvements considered necessary to reduce bidder costs and increase confidence in the private sector.

Finally, most recently, the Cabinet Office conducted a review of the process of competitive dialogue, *Accelerating Government Procurement*,[76]

[69] 2010 Treasury review, n. 57 above. [70] *Ibid.*, at 1.4. [71] *Ibid.*, at 1.7.

[72] *Ibid.*, at 1.8. [73] See www.cbi.org.uk.

[74] CBI, *Actions Speak Louder Than Words: Unlocking the Full Potential of Competitive Dialogue*, CBIBRIEF (May 2008).

[75] *Ibid.*, p. 1.

[76] See *Accelerating Government Procurement*, n. 57 above, and the related Cabinet Office, *Lean Procurement Diagnostic Findings* (December 2010), available at www.cabinetoffice.gov.uk/resource-library/sme-procurement.

in November/December 2010 as part of a more general 'Lean review', announced on 1 November 2010, to identify and rectify wasteful practices in the procurement process.[77] This was carried out in conjunction with industry and included workshops and some individual interviews with suppliers.[78] The findings reinforced many key points identified in the earlier government reviews and work is currently ongoing to address these points.

4. Scope of the competitive dialogue procedure in law and practice

4.1. The legal provisions

As regards the scope for using competitive dialogue in domestic law for procurements covered by the Public Sector Directive, this is dealt with in regulation 18(1) and (2) of the Public Contracts Regulations 2006. These provisions largely mirror the wording on scope in Articles 1(11)(c) and 29(1) of the Public Sector Directive 2004, the meaning of which was discussed in this respect in section 4 of Chapter 1. Thus it is provided that the competitive dialogue may be used where, under regulation 18(2), 'a contracting authority wishes to award a particularly complex contract and considers that the use of the open or restricted procedure will not allow the award of that contract'. A 'particularly complex contract' is defined as a contract where the contracting authority 'is not objectively able to (a) define the technical means [in accordance with the requirements for a precise specification in the open or restricted procedures[79]] capable of satisfying its needs or objectives, or specify the legal or financial make-up of the project, or both' (regulation 18(1)). To date there has been no domestic case law interpreting these provisions.

4.2. Government guidance and use of the procedure in practice

As we have seen in Chapter 1 and in section 3.3 above, the UK has so far been in practice a significant user of competitive dialogue, with 1,390 contract notices in the period since implementation in 2006 up to December 2009, and the evidence from early 2011 shows that use is

[77] See www.cabinetoffice.gov.uk/news/plans-open-government-small-businesses.
[78] On the methodology, see *Accelerating Government Procurement*, n. 57 above, section 3.
[79] Regulation 9(7), (8) and (9) of the Public Contracts Regulations 2006.

fairly steady at the same level. According to the government, the use of competitive dialogue since 2006 represents 2.6 per cent of all government procurements in the UK and the UK is the highest user of any Member State in percentage terms.[80] However, it is also pertinent to note at this point that, as mentioned in section 1, the government has recently announced an intention to shift away from this procedure that could reduce this figure in future. This development is considered separately in section 4.4. below.

As also seen from Chapter 1, of the 1,390 contract notices up to December 2009, a majority related to one of two main sectors.[81] One is infrastructure (27 per cent of total notices for competitive dialogue) covering, *inter alia*, housing (the largest single sector with 28 per cent of infrastructure notices), education (with 16 per cent of such notices), non-residential area development (7 per cent), transport (6 per cent) and health (4 per cent). The majority of the infrastructure projects involved private sector finance (39 per cent), whilst in 4 per cent the possibility of private sector finance was left open, and in another 31 per cent it was not clear whether or not private finance was involved; thus privately financed infrastructure projects are clearly a major part of projects awarded using competitive dialogue. The other main sector covered by the notices was ICT (25 per cent of total notices for competitive dialogue).[82] As Chapter 1 also explains, however, competitive dialogue has been used for a wide variety of other projects, including facilities management and maintenance, and, by way of further specific examples, nursery services, provision of fairground attractions, bar and catering services, printing and mailing services, double glazing, design and production of UK passports, the supply of low-carbon and electric-powered vans, and the supply of bullet-proof vests.

Data from notices in the OJEU show that use of the competitive dialogue procedure in the UK as a whole has been closely paralleled by a decline in the use of the negotiated procedure with a notice. See Figure 3.1.

These figures tend to suggest that competitive dialogue is now being used for many projects that would previously have been procured under the negotiated procedure – including infrastructure projects under PFI which, as we have explained in section 3, were previously generally

[80] *Lean Procurement Diagnostic Findings*, n. 76 above, p. 12.

[81] The data in this paragraph are taken from Ch. 2 of the current volume.

[82] See Ch. 2, section 5.4.1.

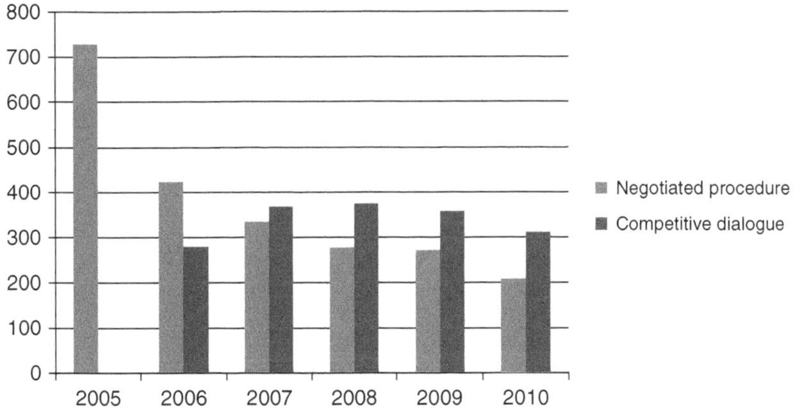

Figure 3.1 Number of contract notices for negotiated procedures and competitive dialogue in the United Kingdom, 2005–2010

awarded using the negotiated procedure with a notice, despite the European Commission's reservations on the legality of this practice.

This is in line with a strong policy steer given by the government since competitive dialogue was introduced in domestic law towards use of that procedure for PFI projects (and other complex projects) when the negotiated procedure with a notice would previously have been used. Essentially, the position adopted following introduction of competitive dialogue was that the negotiated procedure with a notice was not available for many of these projects and that the new competitive dialogue procedure should be used instead. Thus in its 2006 guidance the OGC emphasised that the previous general practice of awarding complex projects under the negotiated procedure 'will not be possible with the availability of the competitive dialogue procedure':[83] the negotiated procedure is to be used only in 'very exceptional circumstances'.[84] The guidance gives as an example of an exceptional case in which a negotiated procedure might still be used a project let prior to the introduction of competitive dialogue for the upgrading and long-term maintenance of parts of the London Underground undertaken using finance of this kind, which was the first ever project of this kind[85] – and

[83] OGC 2006 guidance, n. 36 above, section 2. [84] *Ibid.*, section 2.

[85] Although the guidance also emphasises, in para. 2, that the mere fact that the contracting authority itself is undertaking a complex procurement for the first time does not justify use of the procedure, as is clearly correct: see section 4 below.

which the Commission assumed in a Decision on state aid relating to the same project had been let correctly under the negotiated procedure.[86] In the OGC/Treasury 2008 guidance, this message generally encouraging limited use of the negotiated procedure was affirmed, with the addition of the following warning:

> Any contracting authority using the negotiated procedure should clearly set out the justification in writing, after seeking advice from its commercial department, legal team and lawyers and/or external professionals as appropriate before advertising the contract notice in the OJEU. Contracting authorities should be aware that the European Commission may scrutinise any use of the negotiated procedure.[87]

The government did not expressly articulate the reasons why it considered that the negotiated procedure was no longer available for such projects where its previous guidance took a different view. However, this seems likely to have been influenced by a sense that the courts might take a different approach to the availability of the negotiated procedure after introduction of competitive dialogue, as well as a view that the adequacy of competitive dialogue made it no longer necessary to push for a broad interpretation of the negotiated procedure at EU level – not surprising given that, as we have explained, the competitive dialogue mirrored to a significant degree, and was influenced by, the UK's practice in operating the negotiated procedure for PFI projects. Whilst some commentators expressed doubts over the suitability of competitive dialogue because of the strict conditions and uncertainty at the final tender stage and beyond, the government's official view was that the new procedure was a suitable one. It is also perhaps relevant that a standardisation of approach and documentation for many types of infrastructure project had been developed on the basis of initial experience with PFI projects, which had contributed to doubts over the availability of the negotiated procedure for many of these projects even in the years prior to the adoption of competitive dialogue.

Craven's empirical research[88] also suggests that there has been a switch from using the negotiated procedure for PPP projects, including PFI, to the competitive dialogue procedure, and also indicates that the government guidance above has strongly influenced this switch: fifteen

[86] Decision of the Commission in Case N 264/2002, *London Underground Public Private Partnerships*, Decision of 2 October 2002 [2002] OJ 309/15.

[87] OGC/Treasury 2008 guidance, n. 46 above, box 3.2. [88] See section 3.4 above.

interviewees cited the policy statements of the OGC[89] and Commission to have significantly influenced the choice of award procedure away from competitive dialogue towards the negotiated procedure, and many had chosen competitive dialogue because of this guidance even though they did not in fact agree with the narrow interpretation put forward regarding the continued availability of the negotiated procedure.

As mentioned in section 3.2, ten interviewees in Craven's research reported instances where a procuring contracting authority lacked full control of its procurement process, as government or a higher regulatory authority would dictate the precise conduct of the process. In this regard, one interviewee discussed how a contracting authority may have little choice but to procure under competitive dialogue instead of the negotiated procedure:

> [I]f they are projects that are government funded then the agency requires you to use competitive dialogue or you are not going to get the funding; so, whatever we say is quite irrelevant ... Authorities really do not have much control of the process, particularly not on [the 'Building Schools for the Future' programme]. Although it is their OJEU notice and their procurement, you would not think so. There is more scope for using the negotiated procedure where there is an authority doing something by itself ... where there is no PFI.

As only one English legal advisor interviewed mentioned what might be seen as the mandatory use of competitive dialogue for certain procurements, the prevalence of such a situation is unclear.

We have so far considered the guidance and evidence on use of competitive dialogue as an alternative to the *more* flexible negotiated procedure. Another issue is, however, whether it is legitimate to use competitive dialogue rather than the *less* flexible open or restricted procedures.

In this respect, it can be noted that both the OGC/Treasury 2008 guidance[90] and the OGC's 2006 guidance[91] appear to concur with the legal interpretation offered by Arrowsmith when competitive dialogue was first introduced,[92] which also seems to be accepted by the

[89] See OGC 2006 guidance, n. 36 above, section 2; and OGC, *Procurement Policy Note*, n. 52 above, p. 3.

[90] OGC/Treasury 2008 guidance, n. 46 above, at 3.5, stating that technical complexity can exist 'where the Contracting Authority cannot ... determine which of several possible solutions would best satisfy its needs'.

[91] OGC 2006 guidance, n. 36 above, section 5.

[92] Arrowsmith, n. 15 above, pp. 633–4.

Commission,[93] namely, that the procedure can be used in principle when the procuring entity cannot otherwise determine what is the *best* technical solution to satisfy its needs, rather than being confined to cases in which it is not possible to set a specification at all. This interpretation was also shared almost unanimously by the interviewees in Craven's study. Of course, as discussed in Chapter 1, there is, however, a wide variation possible in the way that such a test is interpreted and applied in practice, and such a variation in approach was seen in the approach of interviewees. It can also be noted that a significant majority of interviewees in Craven's research regarded competitive dialogue as a standard procedure in the sense that its availability was to be interpreted broadly whilst only ten of those interviewed regarded competitive dialogue to be an exceptional procedure, viewing its availability narrowly.

A number of interviewees in Craven's study specifically commented that competitive dialogue was now being used to procure projects that would previously have been tendered under the restricted procedure for lack of any alternative but in an 'awkward' way, since the restricted procedure was not suitable for such projects. It seems such an approach can help achieve a better solution than would have been obtained before. Thus competitive dialogue can be seen not only to bring a greater degree of control and transparency into projects previously let under the negotiated procedure but also better-value procurement for other projects.

As regards use for specific types of contracts, the 2006 OGC guidance suggests specifically that the existence of technical complexity in the sense just defined may occur in certain IT contracts.[94] The 2006 OGC guidance – in common with guidance from the Commission[95] – also suggest specifically that PFI projects involving provision of services may provide examples of projects that are complex because of legal or financial uncertainty,[96] and fifteen of the interviewees in Craven's research also considered that legal or financial complexity could be found in PPP projects. However, thirteen also questioned whether the latter was always the case with projects for which highly standardised documentation has been developed, such as schools, hospitals and waste disposal. Eight of the thirteen, however, considered that complexity may arise from elements of the project other than the standardised documentation; for example, technical complexity may exist for many such projects because of issues specific to the project. This was, in particular,

[93] See Ch. 1, sections 4.4 and 4.5. [94] OGC 2006 guidance, n. 36 above, section 5.
[95] See Ch. 1, section 4.4. [96] OGC 2006 guidance, n. 36 above, section 6.

the view of interviewees for high-technology areas like ICT and waste: according to one London-based lawyer, for example, 'with ICT projects there is inevitably going to be a sufficient amount of bespoking, e.g. the need for interfacing, interconnectivity with other complex systems'. Complexity was also considered by interviewees concerned with this area to exist with regeneration projects, as explained by one lawyer:

> [I]t is self-evident that there are a number of ways for the authority to achieve its objective of getting investment into an area or getting obsolete or redundant land or assets back into economic circulation. There could be different blends of end user, different configurations of infrastructure, different constructional techniques (all of which have their respective pros and cons), different contractual models, different funding models, and different commercial models. The possibilities are numerous and that is what the competitive dialogue was invented to deal with.

A handful of interviewees expressing doubts over the legal/financial complexity of certain standardised PPP projects considered that, with infrastructure, *technical* complexity could exist, for example, because of possible wide variations in design that will benefit from discussion between the parties; or because it is necessary (for example, with hospitals and schools) to discuss whether the best solutions will be those offering rebuilding on the same site, refurbishment or the use of new sites. In other words, whilst the EU and domestic guidance suggests that complexity in PPP contracts is legal or financial, some of those operating the procedure have tended to see it more in the technical aspects of these projects. PPP and IT contracts are, in fact, as we have just seen, the two most common types of project for which competitive dialogue is actually used, and this use is also supported by the Commission's own guidance and the recitals to the Public Sector Directive.[97] However, it is clear that competitive dialogue cannot be used automatically for projects simply because they fall into these categories – it is necessary to consider on the facts of each case whether the conditions for use are met,[98] and this may be particularly necessary in the case of the 'standardised' type of projects.

[97] See the discussion in Ch. 1, section 4. And see also the 2010 Treasury review, n. 57 above, at 2.33, stating that large-scale IT projects, hospital and prison PFI projects and urban regeneration partnerships are amongst the 'obviously complex' projects for which use of competitive dialogue was observed.

[98] A point reinforced by government guidance on the need for documentation of the justification for using the procedure: see further below.

As for the use of competitive dialogue for projects other than PFI and IT, some of the projects mentioned in Chapter 1 as using this procedure, such as design and production of UK passports, do appear possibly to be of a complex nature – although it is difficult to tell based solely on the information on the notices. However, both the 2008 CBI study[99] and the 2010 Treasury review expressed concerns that UK authorities may be using competitive dialogue where the contract is not in fact sufficiently complex for the conditions for use to be met. Thus the 2010 review states:[100]

> We were concerned to note [some projects using competitive dialogue] which were not so obviously complex, for example purchasing annual insurance policies, occupational clothing, and detergents, printing a local government newsletter and obtaining cleaning services for a single school . . . Our review has indicated that contracting authorities are increasingly viewing Competitive Dialogue as the default process for all but the most straightforward procurements.

The recent Cabinet Office study, *Accelerating Government Procurement*, considered that in almost 30 per cent of 210 instances analysed for the study use of competitive dialogue was 'neither necessary nor helpful'.[101]

Apart from the question of whether the procurement is sufficiently complex, a further condition for use is that use of the open or restricted procedure will not allow the award of that contract; and the 2010 review has thus sought to emphasise that competitive dialogue cannot be considered a default procedure even for contracts that are complex.[102]

In this connection, it is notable that the OGC/Treasury 2008 guidance advises authorities to document the justification for using competitive dialogue with regard to both the applicable legal conditions for use – that is, stating both why the project is considered particularly complex *and* why the open or restricted procedure cannot be used.[103] The 2010 review reaffirms this message and goes one step further, suggesting that authorities should include the justification document in the published procurement documentation.[104] It suggests that work on investigating carefully the justification for using competitive dialogue will not only ensure that competitive dialogue is used only when it is really not

[99] 2008 CBI study, n. 74 above, p. 3.
[100] 2010 Treasury review, n. 57 above, at 2.34–2.35.
[101] *Accelerating Government Procurement*, n. 57 above, at 4.5.
[102] 2010 Treasury review, n. 57 above, at 2.40.
[103] OGC/Treasury 2008 guidance, n. 46 above, at 5.1.5.
[104] 2010 Treasury review, n. 57 above, at 2.45.

possible to produce a specification that will enable effective use of a restricted procedure but also that if competitive dialogue is used the authority's requirements are as focused as possible.[105] The 2010 Treasury review[106] did in fact find some evidence of contracting authorities already engaging with the market prior to launching a procedure in order to establish whether the proposed approach and specifications would be acceptable to bidders so as to allow use of the restricted procedure. The 2008 CBI study also emphasises the importance of authorities undertaking sufficient work to establish the parameters of acceptable solutions, to avoid bidders wasting costs in proposing solutions under competitive dialogue that are not acceptable – and suggests that authorities undertaking this work might then conclude that the project could in fact be awarded under a different procedure.[107] The study cites the waste sector as one in which it considers competitive dialogue to be over-used, suggesting that solutions proposed by bidders are often not acceptable to the public and that more public consultation is often needed before commencing any award procedure.[108]

The 2010 review suggests that one reason for use of competitive dialogue when it is not justified might be the absence of guidance on use of other procedures as compared with competitive dialogue;[109] and guidance on use of the other procedures is currently being prepared.

Another consideration that influences the choice of competitive dialogue rather than less flexible procedures is that the legal risk of such a choice is relatively low. Twenty-four interviewees in Craven's study[110] perceived there to be a low risk of legal challenge, since an aggrieved bidder would have at most three months from publication of the contract notice in which to bring a challenge and was unlikely to wish to challenge the choice of procedure at that initial point; sixteen of these interviewees perceived the risk of challenge for the possible unlawful use of competitive dialogue to be lower than procuring under the restricted procedure where the need for negotiation might arise and lead to violation of the rules against negotiation. These findings are consistent with previous findings of Braun, who found similar factors to have influenced the decision to use negotiated rather than restricted procedures for PFI projects prior to the introduction of competitive dialogue.[111]

105 *Ibid.*, at 2.43. 106 *Ibid.*, at 3.8. 107 2008 CBI study, n. 74 above, pp. 3–4.
108 *Ibid.*, p. 3. 109 2010 Treasury review, n. 57 above, at 2.38–2.40.
110 The other interviewees did not comment specifically on this point.
111 Braun, n. 32 above.

It is not clear how far competitive dialogue can be used simply because the particular contracting authority does not itself have experience of the relevant type of project – that is, to what extent the test of use is an objective rather than subjective one.[112] It is interesting, however, that several of Craven's interviewees (seven) suggested that in practice use of the procedure for certain projects did sometimes depend on the contracting authority's own experience of the type of project in question.

Whilst, on the one hand, there appears to be some over-use of competitive dialogue, as just discussed, on the other hand evidence suggests that in some cases contracting authorities seek positively to avoid using the procedure. In this respect, twenty-one interviewees in the research by Craven spontaneously stated in response to questions on the relationship between the competitive dialogue and other procedures that for various reasons – commonly a perception that the procedure is excessively costly, time-consuming and/or complex – they, or certain clients, would try to avoid using competitive dialogue wherever possible and award what they considered to be complex contracts under another procedure. Eighteen of the interviewees indicated that this would mainly be the restricted procedure. However, it should be mentioned that some of the negative perceptions of competitive dialogue that led to this approach were based on experiences of the procedure – such as procedures operated with unfocused dialogue[113] – that were not in line with what is widely considered good practice; and also that a number of the interviewees indicated that quite extensive dialogue had been conducted within the 'restricted procedures' used.

Finally, as we have seen in section 3.1, under the legal regime that applies procuring entities are free to use a procedure similar to competitive dialogue for contracts that are outside the Public Sector Directive: for entities covered by the Utilities Directive this can be done by using the competitive negotiated procedure and structuring it in a manner similar to competitive dialogue, whilst for contracts not covered by either Directive procuring entities are generally free to structure their procedures as they wish, subject to their Treaty obligations. There is evidence that the procedure as set out in the Directive is used as a model for some non-covered contracts in practice, although it is not clear how widespread this practice is. Thus Craven's empirical research found five instances where contracts for Part B services or concession contracts had been advertised

[112] See Ch. 1, section 4.5. [113] On this, see section 5.6 below.

in the OJEU to be awarded under competitive dialogue, or where competitive dialogue was expected for an upcoming procurement of such a contract (sometimes reserving the right to depart from the competitive dialogue legal framework where necessary, or stating that the authority is not voluntarily submitting to the Public Contracts Regulations 2006). There were also two cases where the procurement was structured in accordance with the legal rules on competitive dialogue, but the procurement was not advertised as a competitive dialogue procurement; for example, one of these procurements was advertised as a negotiated procedure, but was structured as a competitive dialogue and employed the same terminology as would be expected under a competitive dialogue.

4.3. *On the threshold: a shift in policy for the future?*

This, then, is the picture so far. However, as already mentioned, it seems that the UK is on the threshold of a shift in policy on use of competitive dialogue: as mentioned in the introduction to this chapter, the Cabinet Office recently announced that there will be a presumption against use of competitive dialogue as part of a drive to reduce procurement costs and timescales.[114] This followed on from the recent 'Lean review' of government procurement, mentioned above, which indicated that reforms will be undertaken to reduce reliance on competitive dialogue in favour of more use of open or restricted procedures, to curb the over-use identified in the review which was considered to result in unnecessarily long and complex procedures.[115]

It is difficult to predict precisely what impact this change will have. However, against the background set out above and the current work on guidance on use of open and restricted procedures referred to above, it can certainly be expected that competitive dialogue will to some extent be replaced by these two procedures. Given the evidence of over-use, some change in this direction would seem to be a welcome development.

However, it is possible that the recent policy announcement has also been influenced by negative perceptions of competitive dialogue that have arisen because of poor practice by many contracting authorities in operating the procedure even in cases in which it *is* appropriate. To the extent that this is the case, there is a danger of throwing the baby out

[114] Speech by Francis Maude, Minister for the Cabinet Office, 21 November 2011, available at www.cabinetoffice.gov.uk/news/crown-and-suppliers-new-way-working.

[115] *Accelerating Government Procurement*, n. 57 above.

with the bathwater in moving away from use of competitive dialogue. The great flexibility of competitive dialogue makes it inherently a useful procedure for many kinds of projects if operated in a suitable way: at its simplest, it can be a procedure very similar to the restricted procedure but allowing for discussions with suppliers to secure improved solutions, whilst it also allows the possibility for a sophisticated procedure for the most complex and novel situations. It is important not to lose sight of the fact that the procedure itself is inherently a useful one and that its introduction is widely seen in the UK as representing an improvement over what went before. Thus it might be argued that a more appropriate response to some of the problems with the procedure is not to curb its use to too great an extent, but to focus on improving the way in which it is applied to maximise the benefits available. Issues relating to improving the practical operation of competitive dialogue in order, *inter alia*, to reduce cost and delay, are considered further in section 6 below.

It should also be noted that some reservations have arisen as to whether competitive dialogue, rather than the negotiated procedure, is appropriate for some of the projects for which it has been used and whether the interpretation emphasising availability of the negotiated procedure in government guidance is in fact correct, especially in light of funding difficulties with using the competitive dialogue that have emerged in the recent financial crisis. Thus several interviewees in Craven's study raised these points in the context of PFI projects, and two of the policy-makers interviewed mentioned that a shift back towards the negotiated procedure might be anticipated – although formal government guidance has not changed at the time of writing. According to one policy-maker interviewed by Craven, the availability of the negotiated procedure is an area that is being looked at due to a perception that domestic contracting authorities may be being placed at a disadvantage to procurers in certain other Member States where a more liberal interpretation of the grounds for using the negotiated procedure may be prevalent:

> Maybe we are too cautious in not using the negotiated procedure more; some other countries have done [that] . . . Ireland has done that . . . There are uneven approaches around the EU. Probably the UK is at the more cautious end of the spectrum and there are other countries taking a more robust approach. Are we labouring under a slight disadvantage compared to other countries? . . . The EU is looking at how competitive dialogue has worked out in practice; there may be an opportunity for them to provide greater clarity there.

As regards the countries studied for the present volume, it can be noted that Germany made significant use of the negotiated procedure with a notice for complex contracts and continues to do so, but its use in the other countries studied appears quite limited.[116]

It is possible that a move away from competitive dialogue could thus also see a shift towards greater use in future of the negotiated procedure with a notice. If that were to occur, however, it would be important to take measures to ensure that an appropriate balance is still maintained between flexibility and the discipline of relatively complete final offers – a discipline which has been seen by many practitioners as an important advantage of competitive dialogue over the approach adopted under the negotiated procedure prior to 2004. This issue is discussed in sections 5.7 and 5.8 below.

5. Operation of the competitive dialogue procedure

5.1. *Introduction*

As we have seen in section 2, the legal rules on competitive dialogue set out in the Public Contracts Regulations 2006 allow contracting authorities the full flexibility provided by the Directive itself in deciding how to structure and operate a competitive dialogue procedure. However, as we will see, practice under competitive dialogue in many respects very much resembles past UK practice under the negotiated procedure:[117] that is to say, a limited number of bidders will be invited to dialogue/negotiate the contract with the contracting authority and the number will be whittled down further over the course of one or more formal bidding stages. However, the requirements in competitive dialogue for formal close of dialogue and complete final tenders and the restrictions placed on negotiations with the preferred bidder have limited the extent to which past practice under the negotiated procedure can continue under competitive dialogue, and this is reflected in a corresponding change to UK practice at this stage of the procedure.

The most common structure for a competitive dialogue process in the UK,[118] mapped against the Articles of the Public Sector Directive that govern the relevant stages (as outlined in Table 1.1 in section 2.4 of Chapter 1) is set out in Table 3.1. This will be referred to at various points in the analysis below.

[116] See Ch. 1, section 4, and the references there.

[117] On this practice, see Braun, n. 32 above; Arrowsmith, n. 15 above, Ch. 8.

[118] Based on the study by Craven outlined in section 2.3 above.

Table 3.1 *Competitive dialogue procedure: the approach in the United Kingdom for PFI projects*

1. ADVERTISING Phase	Contract notice in OJEU
2. SELECTION Phase(technical and/or professional ability; economic and financial standing; Article 45 criteria) Articles 44–52	Suitability (qualification)
	Selection of candidates to tender from suitable ones
3. AWARD Phase (choice of lowest price or most economically advantageous tender) Article 53	Dialogue Phase (i) Outline proposals from, for example, three to seven participants (often no or limited financial information) ('Invitation to Submit Outline Solutions' (ISOS)) (ii) Authority chooses, for example, two or three participants to submit further proposals (iii) Discussion of proposals with the two or three chosen (iv) Submission of detailed financial and technical proposals from the chosen two or three ('Invitation to Submit Detailed Solutions' (ISDS)) (v) Further discussions if required (vi) 'Dry-run' of the final tender stage (applied in some cases only)
	Submission of final tenders by two or three bidders
	Clarification, supplementation or fine-tuning of final tenders
	Choice of lowest price or most economically advantageous tender (and notification to all tenderers)
4. POST-TENDER Phase	Clarification and confirmation stage with 'preferred bidder'
5. STANDSTILL Phase	✓
6. CONCLUSION of contract	✓
7. POST-CONTRACT	Contract award notice

5.2. *The planning stage and drafting of the descriptive document*

5.2.1. The importance of planning and government guidance on planning

As with the Directive, the stages of competitive dialogue prior to publication of the contract notice are not regulated in detail in the domestic regulations, but are subject only to general principles, such as equal treatment.

It has become apparent, however, that an effective planning and preparatory stage is essential for an effective competitive dialogue procurement. Indeed, the need for this is one of the key lessons that has emerged for procuring entities from the first few years of experience of competitive dialogue in the UK. Thus the 2008 CBI report identified inadequate planning as a key problem to be addressed in the management of competitive dialogue,[119] and the 2010 Treasury review concluded – on the basis of its surveys and roundtable discussion – that this is in fact 'the most influential' stage of a competitive dialogue procedure.[120] The importance of this stage is confirmed by Craven's study, in which virtually all interviewees explicitly mentioned this. Work indicated in this study as being important before formally commencing the procurement with a contract notice (although this can vary between projects and sectors) included: organisational preparation within an authority (including internal governance and resourcing for the negotiations);[121] planning of the procedure itself in terms of, for example, the number, nature and timing of the phases; development of the requirement; identification of issues for the dialogue; and development of documentation and criteria (selection and award criteria).

One major reason that careful planning is necessary is to limit costs. Bidder costs, increased by the need to develop their bids more fully whilst in competition under competitive dialogue than under previous practice with the negotiated procedure,[122] along with higher procurement costs for contracting authorities – for example, from having to undertake detailed dialogue with multiple bidders for much longer under competitive dialogue[123] – have been a major concern in the

[119] 2008 CBI study, n. 74 above, pp. 1 and 3–4.

[120] 2010 Treasury review, n. 57 above, at 3.3.

[121] The OGC/Treasury 2008 guidance, n. 46 above, advises also of the need to ensure an understanding of the procedure within the procuring entity, especially the limited flexibility after close of dialogue: see *ibid.*, at 5.1.1.

[122] See section 5.7.3 below. [123] Again, see section 5.7.3 below.

UK.[124] Planning to limit costs is important not only for its own sake but also, with supply side costs, to help ensure that there is adequate competition. High bid costs in the later stages of the procurement, may make suppliers selective about which contracts to bid for (an even greater concern in the recent economic recession) and poor planning is likely to raise the costs of participation still further. Research by the National Audit Office relating to April 2004–May 2006 already suggested that potential bidders in fact look at the quality of procurement documentation in determining the adequacy of preparation and deciding whether or not to bid for a project;[125] and interviewees in Craven's study also indicated that bidders often assess an authority at the outset to judge whether it is prepared and organised and likely to run a cost-effective procurement.

One aspect of planning, which impacts on both cost and legal risk, is the need to limit the risk of legal challenge and of re-running aspects of the procedure in order to ensure legal compliance. Several interviewees in Craven's study emphasised the importance of this. One aspect of this, that has been the subject of a procurement policy note by the OGC, as well as being highlighted in the 2008 OGC/Treasury guidance, is the need for sufficient knowledge at the time of the contract notice to specify the project in a way that is both sufficiently certain and sufficiently flexible: this issue is discussed further in section 5.4.2 below.

Despite its importance, however, according to the findings of the 2010 Treasury review, in practice the planning and preparation phase of the procurement 'is often the most neglected and poorly executed part of the process'.[126] That projects have often proceeded in the past without adequate planning and preparation is also borne out by Craven's study: whilst recognising the importance of planning and preparation, seventeen interviewees discussed how, for a variety of reasons – such as political pressure to reach the 'milestone' stage of using a contract notice, time pressures on completion, and pressures on resources – sufficient upfront work often may not take place in practice. The 2010 Treasury review also noted specifically that 'frequently' there is pressure to

[124] See section 6 below.
[125] National Audit Office, *Improving the PFI Tendering Process* (8 March 2007), Report by the Comptroller and Auditor General, HC 149 Session 2006–2007, available at www.nao.org.uk/publications/0607/improving_pfi_tendering.aspx, p. 13.
[126] 2010 Treasury review, n. 57 above, at 3.3.

commence the formal part of the award procedure (presumably the contract notice) too early.[127]

Whilst the 2006 guidance from OGC, which is brief and focused mainly on the issues regulated by specific detailed rules, did not mention the planning phase, the OGC and Treasury guidance of 2008 emphasised the importance of this stage of competitive dialogue.[128] Further, its importance is being recognised by the fact that the Efficiency and Reform Group of the Cabinet is currently preparing guidance specifically on this subject.[129] Thus a change in practice towards more careful planning and preparation may be one of the key changes that can be expected in the future operation of the procedure.

A particular concern noted in the 2010 Treasury review, and also in the CBI's paper of 2008,[130] is that certain entities neglect preparatory work, viewing the dialogue phase of competitive dialogue as 'an opportunity to take advantage of "free consultancy" from the market'.[131] To address this concern, the 2010 Treasury review makes a big push for what it terms 'targeted dialogue'.[132] This is essentially a situation where a procuring entity only permits bidders to engage in dialogue with it on a limited number of pre-defined issues – necessitating work upfront to ensure that any issues not up for negotiation will be acceptable to the private sector. This is considered further at section 5.6.3 below.

The 2008 guidance also mentions the importance of ensuring affordability and a robust business case before proceeding with a formal award procedure.[133]

5.2.2. Consultations with the market

Engagement with the market is one important part of the planning and preparation stage referred to above. The 2010 Treasury review found in its roundtable meetings a 'strong consensus' on both the demand and supply side on the fact that early engagement is essential[134] – and concluded in general terms that earlier and more focused engagement would 'significantly' improve both the award procedure and its outcomes.[135] There are several (related) reasons for undertaking such engagement.

[127] *Ibid.*, at 3.2. [128] OGC/Treasury 2008 guidance, n. 46 above, para. 5.1.
[129] 2010 Treasury review, n. 57 above, para. 39. [130] 2008 CBI study, n. 74 above, p. 4.
[131] 2010 Treasury review, n. 57 above, at 3.6. [132] *Ibid.*, at 3.30–3.32.
[133] *Ibid.*, at 5.1.1. [134] 2010 Treasury review, n. 57 above, at 3.5. [135] *Ibid.*, at 3.4.

First, as we have already seen in section 4, engagement with the market can be relevant for deciding whether to use the competitive dialogue procedure in the first place. As already mentioned, in considering use of the procedure, the 2010 Treasury review[136] found some evidence of authorities using market engagement in this context, to establish whether the proposed approach and specifications would be acceptable to bidders so as to allow use of the restricted procedure.

Secondly, market consultation can be useful to gauge interest in the project, providing an opportunity to take steps to ensure that adequate interest exists (for example, by addressing perceived barriers to participation) if it appears that there may not be sufficient competition. The OGC/Treasury 2008 guidance[137] and the CBI's 2008 study both recommend consultations for this purpose, with the 2008 guidance suggesting methods such as market research and publication of a Prior Information Notice (PIN) as possible approaches for this purpose.[138] The 2010 Treasury review found strong evidence of consultation for this purpose being carried out in practice.[139]

Another reason for approaching the market is for help in scoping the project and developing technical requirements. This appears to be one of the most difficult areas for procuring entities to deal with. There is a dilemma, in that it can be easier to obtain more detailed and helpful information through detailed dialogue with a limited number of participants than in a very broad consultation, but that this may give rise to a risk of violation of the (rather uncertain) equal treatment principle, as discussed in Chapter 2. It is notable that the OGC guidance of 2006, the OGC/Treasury guidance of 2008 and the 2010 review do not offer guidance on the legal issues that arise here or on the specific practices that might be followed, except that the 2010 review document does comment briefly that procuring entities may have been 'overly cautious' in this respect.[140] This may be an area that the 2010 review had in mind when recommending earlier and more focused engagement, as mentioned above.

According to the 2010 Treasury review, there was little evidence of engagement with suppliers to help identify achievable outcomes or to define scope[141] (leading to the above comment that procuring entities

[136] *Ibid.*, at 3.8. [137] OGC/Treasury 2008 guidance, n. 46 above, at 5.1.8– 5.1.9.

[138] *Ibid.*, at 5.1.8. The 2008 CBI study, n. 74 above, suggests that PINs are under-used and are a useful method for ensuring sufficient preparation time for the market also.

[139] 2010 Treasury review, n. 57 above, at 3.7. [140] *Ibid.*, at 3.5. [141] *Ibid.*, at 3.7.

may have been overly cautious although without providing further details of suggested practice). However, Craven's study revealed evidence of this use of market consultation. However in view, *inter alia*, of the legal risks, the study found that practitioners take different approaches. Of twenty-one interviewees who spoke in detail about this,[142] whilst seven signalled a preference for technical dialogue with a limited selection of suppliers to ensure meaningful dialogue, eleven interviewees expressed the need for great caution and highlighted the legal difficulties in conducting technical dialogue with a small selection of potential suppliers. Those choosing to undertake technical dialogue with a small group sought to ensure that such dialogue was as transparent as possible – in particular by documenting discussions heavily and releasing publicly all information made available by the authority during discussions, which was considered to reduce the legal risk involved.

In a speech of 21 November 2011,[143] the Cabinet Office minister, Francis Maude, announced an intention both to provide greater advance notice to the market on forthcoming projects[144] and to enhance dialogue by engaging more in informal talks with potential suppliers in advance of formally launching procurement – referring specifically to the 'myth' that dialogue with suppliers is prohibited under EU law.[145] This may possibly herald a push towards a less cautious approach towards supplier engagement than is seen in the current practice of some contracting authorities. However, the exact form and impact of any such policy in this area remains to be seen.

5.3. *Confidentiality of information and solutions*

Article 29(3) of Directive 2004/18 deals specifically with confidentiality in competitive dialogue, as discussed in section 5.3 of Chapter 1. According to regulation 18(21)(c) of the Public Contracts Regulations 2006, which implements Article 29(3) almost *verbatim*, throughout a competitive dialogue procedure, the contracting authority must 'not reveal to other participants the solutions proposed or any confidential information communicated by a participant without the participant's agreement'.

[142] Many of the legal advisors interviewed were not brought in to advise at this stage and thus did not comment.

[143] N. 4 above.

[144] See the text of the speech, n. 4 above, for initiatives already launched.

[145] *Ibid.*

We may begin by noting that a fear of 'cherry-picking' or of merging different solutions from different bidders appear to be a real fear in the private sector: the 2010 Treasury review of competitive dialogue found that 55 per cent of public sector respondents considered bidders to have a 'considerable' or 'very considerable' fear that this is an active issue.[146] However, the review considered that the problem was not in fact 'rife' in practice and that authorities are in fact giving due regard to confidentiality.[147] From a private sector perspective, the CBI report stresses the critical importance of bidder confidentiality[148] and the report recommends a high level of preparation on confidentiality issues, noting policy statements and internal codes of conduct as beneficial. The report also suggests that it is good practice for the contracting authority to draw bidders' attention to statements of confidentiality at each dialogue meeting.[149]

It appears that at a general level a common practice has in fact developed towards dealing with these issues. According to this practice, as found in Craven's study,[150] the descriptive documents will explain at the outset that bidders must mark up any specific information provided that they regard as confidential if they want to ensure that the information is not shared with other bidders. Where a procuring entity disagrees with a bidder about the confidential nature of certain information, the authority will warn the bidder before sharing and, if agreement cannot be reached, give the bidder the option of withdrawing the information. Such advance agreement is mentioned as 'one potential mechanism' for dealing with confidentiality in the OGC/Treasury 2008 guidance[151] and appears to be almost without exception the approach that is adopted. Craven's study found that, using this approach, disagreements over confidentiality tended to be resolved amicably in practice. However, it should also be mentioned that the existence of the legal rules in the Directive seem not to have been sufficient by themselves for some bidders: seven interviewees explained that the private sector often insists upon the contracting authority and its staff signing up to formal – sometimes quite complex – confidentiality agreements to reflect the understandings reached on confidentiality of certain information.

[146] 2010 Treasury review, n. 57 above, para. 4.24. [147] *Ibid.*, paras. 4.25–4.26.
[148] 2008 CBI study, n. 74 above, p. 10. [149] *Ibid.*
[150] Eighteen interviewees (only one interviewee put forward a different approach).
[151] OGC/Treasury 2008 guidance, n. 46 above, p. 19.

We saw in Chapter 2 that the Directive is not entirely clear as to whether it protects information through an 'EU-level' standard of confidentiality which may go beyond that of domestic law. Since disagreements over confidentiality have tended to be amicably resolved without apparent need for detailed discussion of applicable legal standards, few interviewees in Craven's study could speak in great depth about their understanding of the appropriate standard of confidentiality (and several legal advisors commented that this is a matter for intellectual property experts within their law firm, who would advise if the issue arose but were not involved on a regular basis). However, to the extent that comments were offered by interviewees, divergent approaches were revealed to interpreting this provision: thirteen considered bidders tend to regard a greater amount of information as confidential under the Directive than would be the case under domestic law and authorities tend to defer to bidder assessments; whilst eight considered that in the event of a dispute the confidential nature of information should be assessed against domestic law standards, such as the law of confidence and the Freedom of Information Act 2000 (which allows access to government information on request).[152]

Regulation 18(21)(c) of the Public Contracts Regulations 2006, repeating Article 29(3) of the Public Sector Directive, allows a contracting authority to share confidential information where it has obtained the agreement of the bidder concerned. However, few interviewees in Craven's study had experience of situations where such agreement had been obtained where it was accepted that the information was of a confidential nature and thirteen interviewees specifically stated that they had never needed to seek such agreement, suggesting that this situation is a relatively rare occurrence. Although, as we saw in Chapter 1 (see section 5.3 of that chapter), the Commission has suggested that 'agreement' to share will exist if this is stipulated by the contracting authority as a condition of participation, Craven's study found that it was very rare to do this since it would not be acceptable to bidders: whilst two interviewees had included 'agreement to share' as a condition of participation in the contract notice, the others had not done so. Further, very few interviewees had experience of seeking agreement to share a bidder's confidential information on a case-by-case basis. However, four explained how agreement had been obtained through negotiation; and

[152] Freedom of Information Act 2000.

four interviewees spoke of getting agreement in return for payment. Two interviewees spoke about how public open days were held during the dialogue stage where bidders' solutions were on display; in these cases, bidders had been made aware of this requirement at an early stage and did not object to it.

From a legal perspective, it is also worth noting here that, although there are no specific comparable provisions on confidentiality in relation to the Directive's other award procedures, the government guidance suggests that the same confidentiality requirements apply across all award procedures.[153]

5.4. *Advertising requirements (contract notice etc.)*

5.4.1. The legal rules and practice on advertising

In accordance with the UK's general approach to implementation, the Public Contracts Regulations 2006 (regulation 18(4)) impose exactly the same advertising requirements as those of the Public Sector Directive (Articles 35 and 36), namely, to publish contract notices in the OJEU, with no further additions in the legislation itself – for example, there are no *legal* requirements for advertising in any particular national publication.

However, since March 2011 central government bodies such as government departments have also been required to publish online, through a new service, 'contractsfinder',[154] opportunities for all contracts of a value above £10,000, in pursuit of a more general government policy on transparency in procurement.[155] In accordance with domestic tradition of regulating in general only to the extent essential under EU law, this requirement is imposed only by administrative instructions and not by law. In addition, contract notices published by *all* national authorities in the OJEU – central and local – are now automatically published each

[153] OGC/Treasury 2008 guidance, n. 46 above, at 5.2.11.

[154] www.contractsfinder.businesslink.gov.uk. This is a free service provided by government and includes the possibility of registering for email alerts on relevant opportunities.

[155] See generally Cabinet Office, Guidance Note, *Transparency – Publication of Tender Documentation* (December 2010, updated February 2011), available at www.cabinet-office.gov.uk/resource-library/guidance-transparency, at 3.9; and see OGC, *Procurement Policy Note – Published Guidance on Implementing Requirements for Greater Transparency in Central Government Procurement and Contracting*, available at http://webarchive.nationalarchives.gov.uk/20110822131357/www.ogc.gov.uk/documents/PPN_2_11_Transparency_PPN_%282%29.pdf.

day in the contractsfinder database as well. This means that in practice there will be found in this national database, as well as the OJEU, at least: (i) all notices for competitive dialogue projects covered by the contract notice requirements of Directive 2004/18 and (ii) notices for competitive dialogue-type procedures run by central government for projects that are not fully covered by the Directives, such as those for Part B services or concessions.

Other means of advertisement have also been used in some other cases – for example, some local authorities advertise projects locally, and for specialist projects notices may occasionally be placed in trade-specific publications.

Anecdotal evidence[156] suggests that, in the past few years prior to the advent of contractsfinder and the new transparency policy, it has been quite common to advertise competitive dialogue projects using the OJEU only. The OJEU was widely considered inadequate as a sole means of advertising major projects when it was not available online, but since the advent of free online availability was often considered sufficient as a means to notify tenderers and attract sufficient competition. In practice, the systems that some authorities used meant that the advertisements also appeared on national portals such as the former supply2gov portal (now replaced by contractsfinder). However, previously, including for many of the projects covered by the empirical work referred to in this chapter, the OJEU has often been the sole or main means of notifying the market of opportunities.

5.4.2. Legal issues in drafting notices

The main legal issue of significance that has arisen in the UK in relation to contract notices has concerned the description of the subject-matter. In a competitive dialogue, the precise details of what is to be procured are not clear at the outset. Thus it may be particularly difficult to draft a notice that provides for adequate flexibility but is also sufficiently precise to give a sufficient indication of the subject-matter of the contract both to meet the legal requirement for a sufficient description of that subject-matter[157] and to attract the most appropriate bidders. This is even more difficult when there has been inadequate planning and preparation. As Chapter 1 explained (see sections 5.2 and 5.4 of that chapter), EU law

[156] We are grateful, in particular, to Susie Smith, former partner and now consultant with Bevan Brittan LLP, for providing information on advertising practices.

[157] Case C-423/07, *Commission* v. *Spain*, judgment of 22 April 2010.

requires that, if a project in the end differs materially from the project as described in the contract notice, the changed project constitutes a new procurement[158] and there is a danger that a new notice may be needed if the original notice does not sufficiently cover the final project. The difficulty of drafting suitable notices was mentioned by a few interviewees in Craven's study, some of whom mentioned that problems arose, in particular, when contracting authorities drafted notices without legal advice, and considered that it was important to get legal advice on the wording of notices. The problems arising in this respect were highlighted when in 2008 the Commission commenced infraction proceedings against the UK in relation to a situation where a UK authority had allegedly not included in a contract notice a reference to all the types of services which were included in the final contract in a PFI project, which the Commission considered should have been done to ensure that the contract awarded was not materially different from that advertised.[159]

These proceedings led to the publication in April 2009 of an OGC policy note[160] advising authorities to ensure that contract notices cover the totality of the likely requirement. According to the policy note:

> it is better to include ... potential requirements, with suitable caveats, than it is to award a contract which covers material elements not specified in the contract notice. Where the specific details of the requirement are not certain at the time of the contract notice, the contracting authority should provide a suitably broad or generic description in Section II.1.5 of the Notice and quote appropriately high-level CPV codes in Section II.1.6.[161]

In August 2009, Treasury guidance also addressed the issue of contract notices in the specific context of PFI contracts in view of the turbulent market conditions.[162] As the financial crisis worsened and the provision of private finance to fund projects became less and less secure, it was considered advisable for authorities to 'draft the OJEU notice and other tender documents as widely as possible to ensure that alternative

[158] Case C-454/06, *pressetext Nachrichtenagentur* v. *Austria* [2008] ECR I-4401. This applies also for non-priority services contracts: Case C-91/08, *Wall AG* v. *Stadt Frankfurt am Main and Frankfurter Entsorgungs- und Service GmbH*, judgment of 13 April 2010.

[159] OGC, *Procurement Policy Note – The Need to Ensure Published Contract Notices Are Accurate and Cover the Complete Requirement*, Action Note 03/09 (8 April 2009).

[160] *Ibid.* [161] *Ibid.*, para. 8.

[162] HM Treasury, *Application Note – PPP Projects in Current Market Conditions* (28 August 2009), available at www.hm-treasury.gov.uk/d/market_dislocation_280809.pdf.

financing solutions can be accommodated'.[163] The note expired on 31 August 2010; however, according to HM Treasury, some of the note's principles remain relevant with the above statement amended as follows: '[t]o reduce the risk of infringing procurement procedures, the OJEU notice and tender documents should be drafted sufficiently broadly to allow for the possibility of public sector financing and funding, including capital contributions'.[164]

5.5. *The selection phase: choosing the candidates to participate in the dialogue*

Regulation 18(10)–(14) implements the rules of the Public Sector Directive concerned with the selection of candidate to participate in the dialogue, simply stating what is required by the Directive itself. The key requirements of the Directive relating to selection were outlined in section 5.5 of Chapter 1.

Thus, where there is a sufficient number of qualifying firms, a contracting authority may, using objective and non-discriminatory criteria, choose a limited number (minimum or maximum) to invite to take part in the dialogue phase of the process (regulation 18(12)). The authority must take a minimum of three qualifying firms through to dialogue, provided this is sufficient to ensure genuine competition (regulation 18(12) and (13)).

The OGC/Treasury 2008 guidance does not provide authorities with an ideal number of firms to invite to dialogue, stating that this is a matter of professional judgment depending on the specifics of each individual procurement; however, it is explained that, in assessing whether there is a sufficient number to ensure genuine competition, authorities should consider: 'the number of bidders, the likely strength of those bidders, bidders' interest in the project, and bidders' desire to complete the procurement process'.[165]

This general 2008 guidance sets out the balance a contracting authority must strike in deciding on bidder numbers: invite too few firms and there is a risk of reducing the range of potentially innovative solutions and competitive intensity; invite too many firms and there is a risk that

[163] *Ibid.*, at 2.3.

[164] See HM Treasury, *Public Private Partnerships: Technical Update 2010*, PPP Policy Update (2010), available at www.hm-treasury.gov.uk/d/ppp_technical_update.pdf, section A6.

[165] OGC/Treasury 2008 guidance, n. 46 above, at 5.2.7.

some firms, who could have enhanced competition, might drop out because of the perceived limited chances of success.[166] The guidance also makes reference to the important practical problems associated with inviting too many firms to dialogue, namely, the strain placed on contracting authority resources and also the consequent stretching of the time taken for the procedure[167] (although the guidance notes also the need to take into account that selection itself involves use of resources).[168] The Partnerships for Schools guidance recommended that up to eight bidders be selected to take part in dialogue.[169] Craven's study found that in practice the number of bidders invited to dialogue in the context of PPP projects typically ranges from three to seven, whilst the *Accelerating Government Procurement* study found typically seven participants in the dialogue in the procedures it studied.[170] That study in fact considered that savings should be made by taking fewer suppliers into the dialogue, but concluded that this could be facilitated by providing better feedback to suppliers to enable them to decide to drop out themselves, where appropriate, at an earlier point than at present.[171]

In a long competitive dialogue procedure, various changes can occur to a bidder's circumstances, potentially impacting upon selection decisions from both a legal and practical perspective. For example, a bidder's financial standing may deteriorate or there may be a change in the make-up of a consortium (including because a member becomes insolvent) which may impact upon, in particular, financial standing or technical capability. This may make it unsatisfactory from a practical point of view to continue with that bidder or may raise legal issues over whether the bidder should be allowed to continue in the procedure.[172] Thirteen interviewees in Craven's study highlighted that for these reasons it is necessary to keep qualification and selection decisions under review throughout the procedure; for instance, documentation issued at each stage of the dialogue might require bidders to notify the contracting authority of any material changes in circumstance.

[166] *Ibid.*, at 5.2.7. [167] *Ibid.*, at 5.2.8. [168] *Ibid.*, at 5.2.8.

[169] *How to Conduct a Competitive Dialogue Procedure*, n. 55 above, para. 13.

[170] *Lean Procurement Project Diagnostic Findings*, n. 76 above, p. 20. [171] *Ibid.*

[172] For example, if with the different membership the consortium would not have scored sufficiently highly in the selection process to be selected for dialogue, it might be argued that the equal treatment principle requires that a reselection take place.

5.6. *The dialogue phase*

5.6.1. Structure of the dialogue phase

In structuring the dialogue phase of the procedure, the Public Contracts Regulations 2006 give contracting authorities the full freedom of the Directive, the rules of which were outlined in this respect in section 5.6 of Chapter 1. Thus, where there is sufficient interest, the contracting authority must invite a minimum of three firms to the dialogue (regulation 18(12)), the aim of which must be to identify and define the means best suited to satisfying the authority's needs (regulation 18(20)). Under regulation 18(21), during the dialogue phase the contracting authority may discuss all aspects of the contract with participants, and, according to regulation 18(21), the authority may conduct the dialogue phase in successive stages in order to reduce the number of solutions to be discussed during dialogue.

So far as practice is concerned, Craven's study found from the descriptions of twenty-four interviewees that in competitive dialogue procurements for PPP projects there was a common structure of award procedure generally resembling the structure adopted in the UK prior to the introduction of competitive dialogue when awarding PFI projects under the negotiated procedure,[173] although with important modification to take account of the specific legal requirements of competitive dialogue (no alternative descriptions of the process at all were put forward for projects that prior to 2006 would likely have been procured under the negotiated procedure). Based on Table 3.1 in section 5.1 above, this process can be summarised as follows:

(i) Outline proposals from, for example, three to seven participants (often no or limited financial information) ('Invitation to Submit Outline Solutions' (ISOS)).
(ii) Based on the outline proposals, authority chooses, for example, two or three participants to submit further proposals.
(iii) Discussion of proposals with those chosen under (ii).
(iv) Submission of detailed financial and technical proposals from those chosen under (ii) ('Invitation to Submit Detailed Solutions' (ISDS)).

[173] As to which, see section 2 above. The OGC/Treasury 2008 guidance, n. 46 above, acknowledges that equivalent stages to those set out below, invitation to submit outline proposals and invitation to negotiate, were pre-2006 usual practice under the negotiated procedure for PFI: at 5.2.22 and 5.2.23.

(v) Further discussions if required.
(vi) 'Dry-run' of the final tender stage [applied in some cases only].

Thus, typically, a limited number of bidders will be invited to participate in dialogue – as noted above, three to seven is typical for PFI projects. The number of bidders participating is then often reduced, if needed, over the course of one or more formal bidding stages, so that often only two or three bidders will be involved in detailed dialogue and submit final tenders. As we will see at section 5.6.2 below, this reduction is done in practice based mainly on award criteria relating to the technical nature of the different solutions offered by different bidders and commercial issues – although we will see that consideration is also sometimes given even at dialogue stage to the financial aspects of different solutions offered.

The level of detail in which proposals are considered will often increase as the dialogue progresses. Thus, a common approach is for there to be an outline solutions stage (often referred to as the ISOS (Invitation to Submit Outline Solutions) stage) early on in the dialogue, which may be followed by a detailed solutions stage (often referred to as the IDIS (Invitation to Submit Detailed Solutions) stage),[174] as is discussed further below. Typically, the number of bidders might be reduced from five to seven down to two to three using these outline solutions alone, as shown in Table 3.1 above, although in some cases the ISDS stage is also used to reduce bidder numbers.

Practice does, however, vary according to the nature of the project and response of the market. Thus it is sometimes the case, for example, that the two bidding stages referred to above – ISOS and ISDS – will be held but they will not be used with a view to reducing participants but simply to enable participants to improve their offers.

The 2008 guidance from the OGC and Treasury on conducting competitive dialogue does not recommend any specific way to structure the dialogue, since this will vary from project to project, but sets out the process above as one possible way of operating. However, one important piece of guidance provided by the 2010 Treasury review is that the selection of bidders to go forward to the final tender stage should be made early. According to the review: 'Experienced public sector professionals who attended the roundtable expressed a strong consensus view that one of the most significant lessons they would take into their next

[174] OGC/Treasury 2008 guidance, n. 46 above, at 5.2.21–5.2.23.

Competitive Dialogue was the importance of down-selecting early.'[175] This was also a significant finding of Craven's study: twenty interviewees spoke of the importance of this point.

Craven's study also found that a common practice in PFI procurement prior to the formal closing of the dialogue is to require bidders to submit 'dry-run' final tenders – fully detailed and costed proposals, which are in content equivalent to final tenders but which are not actually treated as final tenders for the purpose of the Directive/Regulations. This stage is also shown in the list above and in Table 3.1. This practice helps to ensure that no problems emerge in the final tenders, given that the lawful scope for adjustment after the formal final tender stage (both before and after choosing the preferred bidder) is both limited and uncertain (as discussed in sections 5.7.4 and 5.8 below). Further discussions on the content of these submissions might then be held if needed – for example, to consider how aspects of the full proposals that are not considered satisfactory to the authority can be amended or to correct any misunderstandings that might render a bid non-compliant. The authority will then formally close the dialogue and call for final tenders in the sense of the legislation, which are the fully detailed and costed proposals in binding form. This final tender process is examined at section 5.8 below. Although, however, the above practice of holding a 'dry run' final tenders stage prior to formal close of dialogue was raised spontaneously in ten interviews and some interviewees referred to such a practice as being 'well established' and 'widespread', the study does not indicate with any certainty quite how prevalent this practice is. According to one lawyer, the practice is more common amongst risk-averse authorities because of the legal comfort gained, whilst others (who might take a more flexible approach to what can be done after the final tender stage)[176] regard it as unnecessary.

Under the approach described above, bidders are often eliminated during the dialogue on the basis of the merits of, *inter alia*, the detail of the solutions that they offer. As explained in Chapter 1, the question has been raised as to whether the Directive permits authorities to adopt a procedure whereby participants themselves are eliminated from the procedure during the dialogue phase, or whether it is necessary that anyone invited to participate in the dialogue should be allowed to submit a final tender based on one of the other solutions presented;

[175] 2010 Treasury review, n. 57 above, at 3.18.

[176] As to which, see section 5.7 below.

but it was suggested there that that is very clearly contemplated in the Directive and, indeed, is assumed to be the main approach by which competitive dialogue will be operated.[177] Clearly, this UK practice above assumes the possibility of eliminating bidders based on all aspects of their solutions, both technical and financial, and this view is also implicit in the OGC's 2008 guidance and stated by the CBI in its 2008 report.[178]

Craven's study revealed no general structure for complex contracts other than those procured under PFI programmes – for example, complex IT contracts. It seems from the responses of those interviewees with the most experience of using competitive dialogue outside of PFI programmes that the structure of the award procedure very much depends upon the specifics of the procurement, such as market size, likelihood of bidders dropping out, cost of bidding and complexity of dialogue. However, as with PFI procurement, it seems that some kind of staged approach to dialogue, with formal submission of bids prior to close of dialogue, is commonly adopted.

In line with the Directive, in competitive dialogue the Regulations do not require a contracting authority to draw up a detailed technical specification against which bidders will submit final tenders; however, if it wishes, it is possible for an authority to do so. The OGC/Treasury 2008 guidance simply explains that final tenders will usually be based on the solutions that were presented during the dialogue phase.[179] In the UK, it is most common for bidders to develop their individual solutions with the contracting authority separately from other bidders and to base final tenders on the solutions developed over the course of the dialogue. According to seventeen interviewees, usually the authority will do this by requiring bidders to tender against output-based specifications, which are drawn up broadly enough to allow for each bidder's solution. In terms of the models of dialogue outlined in Chapter 1 (see section 5.6.3 of that chapter) this represents the 'own-solutions model' or – where changes are made to the specifications during the dialogue (for example, to add or delete certain requirements) – the 'hybrid' model. It appears that other approaches are less common: four interviewees explained how bidders tendered against a single detailed technical specification (the 'designated solutions model' referred to in Chapter 1); and three interviewees described how bidders tendered against separate detailed specifications.

[177] See Ch. 1, section 5.6.2.2. [178] 2008 CBI study, n. 74 above, p. 8.
[179] OGC/Treasury 2008 guidance, n. 46 above, at 5.4.3.

In relation to variant bids (regulation 10), government guidance indicates that a contracting authority is free to invite submission of variant bids under competitive dialogue.[180] Thus the 2009 Treasury application note, *PPP Projects in Current Market Conditions*, advises authorities to consider funding variants to encourage bidders to explore options that may be developing in the funding markets.[181] The issue of variant bids was not addressed in detail in Craven's study but several interviewees mentioned that variants are sometimes used in practice, including technical variants. Thus the authority may sometimes specify the ideal solution from its initial point of view and challenge bidders to better it or, if this is not possible, to depart from it as little as possible. The legality of variants in competitive dialogue under the Directive was discussed in section 5.7.5 of Chapter 1.

We can note that, although the legal rules are clear that authorities may reduce solutions during dialogue, they are not clear on whether or not this *must* always be done on the basis of formal bids.[182] The domestic guidance from government is also silent on this issue. Craven's study shows that domestic practitioners take different views on this legal issue but that a formal process is followed in practice in the context of PPP procurement. Thus, of twenty-two interviewees addressing the question, fourteen stated that they interpreted the legal rules to mean that any elimination must be made on the basis of a formal process (and it can be noted that the CBI report suggests that elimination must be done on the basis of written submissions).[183] On the other hand, ten interviewees considered that a formal bidding process was not needed. However, of these ten, six stated that a formal process was invariably adopted in practice to minimise legal risk – something that we have already noted in outlining the general structure of the dialogue phase above.

We should finally note in this section that the CBI's 2008 report recommends that it is important for the contracting authority to provide a rapid process for review and feedback to bidders on novel ideas raised during the dialogue stage, to avoid bidders wasting costs developing solutions that are not attractive to the authority; this was considered an important issue by CBI members that had participated in competitive dialogue procedures.[184]

[180] *Ibid.*, at 5.4.1.
[181] *PPP Projects in Current Market Conditions*, n. 162 above, at 3.7.
[182] See the discussion in, section 5.6 below.
[183] 2008 CBI study, n. 74 above, p. 8.
[184] *Ibid.*

5.6.2. Award criteria for the reduction of bidders/solutions

As we have seen, in many (although not all) projects, an approach is adopted whereby the number of participants is reduced during the dialogue phase, in practice through formal submissions. There can, in fact, be considerable commercial pressure from the private sector participants on contracting authorities to reduce the number of bidders involved in a competitive dialogue as quickly as possible, and this is generally a primary purpose of the ISOS stage: authorities can save bidders that are unlikely to succeed from incurring the high costs of fully developing a solution. Nevertheless, because in the early stages of dialogue bidders' solutions are unlikely to be presented and discussed in the same level of detail as they are in relation to the final tender stage, there is the potential for unfairness both in eliminating bidders who might ultimately have been the best bidder and in eliminating bidders for not meeting certain minimum criteria but without full information.

One aspect of the law that is unclear is the extent to which the information used to eliminate solutions at the ISOS stage may differ in detail from the submissions at the final tender stage. Another, related, legal question is how far the criteria, and weightings for the criteria, that are used to eliminate bidders or solutions, may differ between the dialogue stage and the point at which the winner is chosen based on the final tenders (see section 5.6.5 of Chapter 1).

This issue arises in the UK, in particular, in the context of consideration of financial information and criteria. These are clearly important in all projects for choosing the winner at the final tender stage. However, until technical solutions are fully developed it is difficult to compare the relative merits of different bids by reference to financial criteria since the financial aspects cannot yet be clearly established.

In this respect, both guidance and practice take the view that it is lawful and also efficient procurement practice to use different criteria and/or weightings of the criteria at different stages of the process. In this respect, the OGC/Treasury 2008 guidance encourages authorities at the ISOS stage to focus on only technical solutions and key commercial issues, such as allocation of risks under the project.

So far as financial criteria are concerned, the guidance advises that bidders submit (non-binding) indicative costs only where there are concerns about the likely affordability of potential solutions.[185] It is

[185] OGC/Treasury 2008 guidance, n. 46 above, at 5.2.22.

advised that financial aspects are then considered only to the extent that bidders might be eliminated if it does not appear that basic affordability criteria are met; bidders will not, however, be eliminated on the basis that their solutions as offered appear likely to be relatively costly in comparison with others. Thus financial criteria may be used only to a very limited extent at this stage, in comparison with the final tender stage.

On the basis of twenty-seven interview responses, Craven's study found that it is most common in practice for contracting authorities, in line with guidance, to look at financial elements of the solution extensively only at later stages of the dialogue and to vary award criteria accordingly. In adopting this practice, interviewees differed in relation to how they presented the evaluation of bids in formal terms; however, generally these approaches resulted in the same outcome, namely, the non-application, or more limited application, of certain award criteria at earlier stages of the process than at later stages. This was presented sometimes by applying a weighting of 0 per cent to financial award criteria at the earlier stage, sometimes by automatically giving bidders full marks for financial criteria, and sometimes simply by not using the financial award criteria at the earlier stage. It was explained by ten of these interviewees that they specify weightings as a range, such as 0 per cent–70 per cent, in the descriptive documents and then vary the weighting within that range at different stages of the procedure, some describing how the precise weighting to be applied at each stage is set out upfront.

On the other hand, six interviewees considered it to be high-risk behaviour, from a legal perspective, not to apply at the outline solutions stage the full set of award criteria (including the financial criteria) and weightings that are to be used at the final tender stage. However, whilst considering all the criteria may be considered to increase one type of legal risk, namely, that arising from using different criteria, using exactly the same criteria at each stage creates another to the extent these criteria are applied on the basis of limited information.

Six other interviewees explained how in practice, although they will look at sufficient areas of bids to enable full application of the headline award criteria with the same weightings at all stages of the dialogue, the award criteria below that level (sub-criteria) would be tailored to the level of detail in which solutions are being considered at a particular stage.

5.6.3. Meetings

During dialogue in a procedure in which bidders will each bid against their own solutions, bidders will generally meet with the contracting authority separately to discuss and develop their own individual solution(s). This dialogue with each individual bidder may be broken down into several streams of dialogue meetings (in particular, involving a technical stream, a commercial stream and a legal stream).[186] This practice can result in organisationally complicated procedures that are difficult to manage and involve numerous costly meetings, particularly when coupled with a strict interpretation of the equal treatment rules, as discussed below.

Essentially mirroring Article 29(3) of the Directive, regulation 18(21)(b) provides that, during the dialogue, contracting authorities 'shall ensure equality of treatment among all participants and in particular, shall not provide information in a discriminatory manner which may give some participants an advantage over others'. Many interviewees in Craven's study[187] were critical of how they had seen equal treatment interpreted under the legal rules on competitive dialogue, often in such a way as to lead to some dialogue stages being run in an overly structured manner. For example, often meetings are set at the outset of dialogue and held whether needed or not and each bidder receives an equal number of meetings, which are equal in length and only involve discussion of pre-identified issues. Some of these interviewees did not feel the equal treatment rules required such an inflexible approach.

Lengthy and costly dialogues, often caused by an excessive number of meetings, as well as requests for information that is not relevant to evaluation, are a common criticism of competitive dialogue.[188] As mentioned in section 5.2, HM Treasury is now promoting greater adoption of 'targeted dialogue' and the safeguarding of standard form contracts during dialogue in order to encourage more efficient competitive dialogue procurement. Twenty-one participants in Craven's study spoke of how they had already adopted such a targeted approach in practice. However, it should be noted that several of these interviewees had experienced some difficulty with this approach in that it removed flexibility for negotiating on matters, such as certain contract terms,

[186] 2008 CBI study, n. 74 above, p. 8. Twenty-four interviewees in Craven's study also described conducting dialogue in this way.

[187] Fourteen indicated this (others did not comment).

[188] See, for example, 2008 CBI study, n. 74 above, pp. 1 and 11; and 2010 Treasury review, n. 57 above, at 3.24. Sixteen interviewees in Craven's study also commented that they considered expensive and time-consuming meetings to be a major source of the problems with competitive dialogue.

that were unacceptable to some bidders, and clearly successful targeted dialogue requires very sound preparation and knowledge of the market.

5.7. *Final tender stage*

5.7.1. General

Under regulation 18(24), again effectively repeating what is stated in the Directive, an authority may continue the dialogue phase until it can identify one or more solutions capable of meeting its needs. At this point, the authority must formally close the dialogue phase, inform each bidder that that phase of the procedure is now over and request each bidder to submit a final tender (regulation 18(25)).

We have already seen above that it is common to structure the dialogue phase into a series of formal bidding phases which are used to eliminate some bidders, and to conclude the dialogue phase itself with the submission of fully detailed and costed proposals from those remaining in the competition *before* formally closing the dialogue. This is done not for the purpose of further elimination but to ensure that all issues that might arise for discussion have already been covered before entering into the final tender phase. This may mean that the final tender stage merely involves a formal confirmation of the documentation already submitted (perhaps with limited modification) as representing the binding legal tender. The operation of the final tender stage itself needs to be seen in this context.

5.7.2. Number of bidders

The rules on the number of bidders at the final tender that apply under Directive 2004/18 itself were discussed in section 5.7.2 of Chapter 1.

As with the Directive, the Regulations, although providing that a minimum of three firms must be invited to participate in dialogue itself, do not explicitly state the minimum number of bidders that is required at the final tenders stage, simply providing that authorities must 'ensure the number of economic operators to be invited to participate at the final stage is sufficient to ensure genuine competition to the extent that there is a sufficient number of economic operators to do so' (regulation 18(23)).

In practice, according to thirty-five interviewees in Craven's study, soliciting final tenders from two to three bidders appears to be the most common approach in PPP projects. When competitive dialogue was first introduced, there was some debate in the UK over whether two may ever be a sufficient number of tenderers to invite at the final tender stage.[189] This has been an important issue in the UK because of the high cost of submitting final tenders: it is widely considered that in some procedures it is difficult to attract a competitive field, or to ensure that bidders will continue to the final tender stage, if more than two must always be invited in the final stage as well as being wasteful of resources. However, the practice referred to above suggests that it is regarded as legally adequate, and this is also the view taken in the 2008 OGC/Treasury guidance (stating that 'at least two bids from credible bidders' are required)[190] and the Partnerships for Schools guidance.[191] This does not, of course, mean that two should be invited in every case: as is emphasised in the 2008 OGC/Treasury guidance,[192] what is sufficient for genuine competition will depend on the facts of each case, such as whether those invited are actually likely to follow through by submitting tenders – for example, as the guidance points out, more bidders may be needed in a market that is developing rather than mature. It was suggested in Chapter 1 (see section 5.7.2 of that chapter) that the Directive does indeed allow for the possibility of inviting two bidders only in appropriate circumstances.

Although taking two or three bidders only to final tenders is quite common, however, it is also not uncommon to invite more than that number: indeed, the 2010 Treasury review found that 15 per cent of survey respondents had taken six bidders to the final tender stage – which the review considered a 'worryingly high percentage',[193] given the implications for costs and timescales.

5.7.3. Completeness of final tenders

Using the same language as the Directive (Article 29(6)), regulation 18(25) states that final tenders must contain 'all elements necessary for the performance of the project'. In addition, as with Article 29(7) of the Directive, the Regulations limit the work that may be undertaken once the bidder with the most economically advantageous tender has been selected (the 'preferred bidder'):

[189] This legal issue is discussed at Ch. 1, section 5.7.2.
[190] OGC/Treasury 2008 guidance, n.46 above, at 5.4.4.
[191] *How to Conduct a Competitive Dialogue Procedure*, n. 55 above, p. 7.
[192] OGC/Treasury 2008 guidance, n. 46 above, at 5.4.5.
[193] 2010 Treasury review, n. 57 above, at 3.19.

the contracting authority may request the participant identified as having submitted the most economically advantageous tender to clarify aspects of that tender or confirm commitments contained in the tender provided that this does not risk distorting competition or causing discrimination (regulation 18(28)).

Both provisions referred to in the paragraph above clearly had the potential to impact heavily on UK procurement practice in relation to PFI, and there was some concern about this when the competitive dialogue procedure was introduced. Under the negotiated procedure, PFI practice consisted of early identification of a preferred bidder followed by significant negotiation with just the preferred bidder, either for the purpose of completing the details of the bidder's offer or to amend provisions of the offer on the basis of which selection as preferred bidder was made.[194] Although the negotiations with the preferred bidder took place under little, if any, competitive tension, such practices were considered by some to be commercially justifiable on the basis that only one bidder need incur the high costs of fully developing its solution. This practice was accepted by the Commission in the *London Underground* case referred to above.[195]

Although there is legal uncertainty over precisely what may be done at the preferred bidder stage in a competitive dialogue in both key respects – completion of the tender and amendment of the tender – what has always been clear is that the legal rules that govern the final tender stage in competitive dialogue limit the extent to which authorities may finalise issues only at the preferred bidder stage – and that they preclude authorities from following the same practice at this stage that was adopted under the negotiated procedure. As anticipated, this has clearly led in practice to increased costs. Thus, as is discussed further in section 6 below, costs of losing bidders appear to have doubled from those incurred under the negotiated procedure for similar projects, and public sector costs have also increased, attributed by those involved to the need for final tenders to be submitted by more than one bidder.

On the other hand, it is generally considered that there are benefits to value for money in the final deal as a result of the increased discipline in negotiations and the fact that negotiations are conducted under competitive pressure. This was one of the key reasons highlighted by the Treasury review in its conclusion that competitive dialogue achieves

[194] See Braun, n. 32 above. [195] *London Underground*, n. 86 above.

better value for money than the old negotiated procedure,[196] as discussed in section 6 below. Twenty-two interviewees in Craven's study who commented on this point also considered that there were significant benefits in this respect. However, the overall benefits of competitive dialogue in this respect are not undisputed: twelve of Craven's interviewees suggested that the benefits in this respect were actually limited or non-existent and that any benefits were outweighed by the higher costs of the process.

Clearly, the balance of costs and benefits in this respect of operating under competitive dialogue rather than the negotiated procedure are currently affected by how the rather uncertain legal rules that govern this stage are applied in practice. In future, this practice may, of course, change, in light of clarification of the legal position.

So far as the requirement for complete tenders is concerned, the OGC/Treasury 2008 guidance suggests that there are still some issues that can be resolved once a preferred bidder has been identified, but only if the authority has 'good cause' to leave them until that point.[197] The guidance suggests that such good cause could lie *either* in the practical impossibility of addressing matters before then *or*, significantly, in considerations of cost-effectiveness.[198] Although noting that each case needs to be dealt with in the context of the specific procurement, the guidance then offers some specific examples that might be best dealt with once a preferred bidder has been identified,[199] namely: full details of subcontracts; detailed planning applications; financial swap rates; and design detail – endorsing the suggestion in the guidance issued by Partnerships for Schools that Royal Institute of British Architects Stage D design should be sufficient for the purpose of selecting a preferred bidder and that Stage E can be completed with the preferred bidder before the contract is signed.[200] Whilst the 2008 guidance does not offer any principles of interpretation, these examples indicate very much less flexibility than under the negotiated procedure with a notice.

[196] 2010 Treasury review, n. 57 above, at 1.10.

[197] OGC/Treasury 2008 guidance, n. 46 above, box 5.8. [198] *Ibid.*

[199] *Ibid.* It is stated at the top of box 5.8 that these issues could be relevant either after receiving final tenders or at the preferred bidder stage (and the box appears in the, section on clarifying, specifying and fine-tuning, prior to the separate section of the guidance on the preferred bidder); but in fact all but one of the examples are then tied specifically to the preferred bidder stage.

[200] OGC/Treasury 2008 guidance, n. 46 above, box 5.8.

The Partnerships for Schools guidance references the argument of Arrowsmith[201] in favour, also, of a flexible interpretation of the work that can be undertaken post-tender under a competitive dialogue,[202] suggesting that from a legal perspective the requirement to include all elements in the final tender should be interpreted in light of the greater need in complex projects to leave some matters of detail open, which again suggests that this might arise for reasons of both practicality *and* cost.[203] In the context of school PFIs, the Partnerships for Schools guidance adds the following to the above OGC and Treasury list: detailed site surveys, investigation of legal title, lender due diligence, completion of the performance mechanism, and finalisation of the financial model.[204]

Craven's study on PPP procurement examined both understanding of the law and experiences of its practical operation in this important area.

So far as the law is concerned, the great majority of interviewees (nineteen of twenty-nine) set forth a strict literal interpretation of the requirement for complete final tenders. These interviewees suggested that final tenders are required to be at a very high stage of development, for example, so that it is possible to conclude the contract immediately after the selection of the most economically advantageous tender. In comparison, only four interviewees adopted a more flexible interpretation of the law at this stage as requiring final agreement only on points that are material, in the sense that the content of bids on these matters could potentially affect the ranking of bids. Six interviewees declined to offer any interpretation in view of the obvious uncertainty in the law.

There was, however, more of a divergence of approach in practice. Thus, regardless of their interpretation of the law, most interviewees (twenty-two) indicated that, when running competitive dialogue procedures, a strict literal approach as set out above was not actually followed. The examples that interviewees adopting a reasonably flexible approach in practice gave of matters that may be left to be finalised after the close of the dialogue stage generally corresponded with those matters listed in the Partnerships for Schools guidance and the 2008 OGC/ Treasury guidance mentioned above. It was, however, highlighted, by four different interviewees that it was not possible to generalise about

201 Arrowsmith, n. 15 above, pp. 650–2.
202 *How to Conduct a Competitive Dialogue Procedure*, n. 55 above, para. 34.
203 *Ibid.*, para. 34. 204 *Ibid.*, para. 35.

the matters that would be left to be resolved just with the preferred bidder, as this would vary depending upon the nature of the procurement – for example, the cost for bidders, the practicalities, and the extent to which any matters had the potential to have a material impact on price or the risk/reward balance in the sense that it might affect the ranking of bidders.

According to the twenty-two interviewees not adopting a strict approach to the requirement for final tenders in practice, a flexible approach was adopted because it was either not possible or not desirable – for example, because bidders would not be prepared to incur certain costs at risk, because bidders may be unco-operative, or because of time or (internal) cost pressures necessitating a premature close of dialogue. Nevertheless, according to ten of these 22 interviewees, matters were in practice being brought to a fuller conclusion than they might have been under the negotiated procedure. Likewise, the 2010 Treasury review concluded that competitive dialogue has successfully addressed the issue of protracted post-preferred-bidder discussions.[205] However, four interviewees expressed a contrary view on this point, indicating that practice may perhaps differ to some extent.

On the other hand, fourteen interviewees did actually adopt a strict approach and a further eight interviewees, although not engaging in or advising upon such practices themselves, stated an awareness of the existence of such strict approaches in practice.

Thus, whilst a large majority of interviewees appear to take a strict interpretation of the law, this was not necessarily carried through in the way that they operated in practice. However, Craven's findings do indicate that a strict approach is reasonably prevalent. Different reasons were put forward to explain the reason for taking a strict approach. Eleven interviewees argued that the strict approach was caused by the uncertainty of the legal rules coupled with the risk of legal challenge that was perceived to exist should incomplete bids lead to post-tender negotiations. Clearly, the risk of legal challenge of such conduct is high, since the bidder(s) remaining in the competition have at that point invested significant resources in the process and also have much to gain from a successful challenge, especially (as is often the case) if bids are close. Five interviewees also mentioned that it was often seen to be to the benefit of contracting authorities to require a high degree of bid development

[205] 2010 Treasury review, n. 57 above, at 3.34.

whilst bidders are still in competition. Also, nine interviewees commented that full bid development prior to close of dialogue was often a result of business case authorisation requirements under certain investment schemes (for example, the Building Schools for the Future and NHS Local Investment Finance Trust programmes).

It is evident from the CBI research[206] and the 2010 Treasury review that the approach actually adopted to the requirement for complete final tenders is a concern for bidders – despite the fact that it appears from Craven's study that for commercial reasons authorities do not always follow even what they believe to be required for full legal compliance. According to the 2010 Treasury review, '[d]isproportionate amounts of bid costs are being incurred by bidders prior to the closure of dialogue on procurements where an overly prudent approach is taken'.[207] This tends to indicate that a strict legal interpretation is very much out of line with the practicalities of effective procurement in complex projects; and that even the more pragmatic approach applied in the UK practice does not adequately meet the commercial concerns of bidders.

The legal position that applies under the Directive in this respect was discussed further in section 5.7 of Chapter 1, where it was suggested that a flexible approach should indeed be taken to this issue in light of the realities of complex procurement.

5.7.4. Clarification, specification and fine-tuning of tenders

After final tender submission but prior to the identification of the most economically advantageous tender, under regulation 18(26), as with Article 29(6) of the Directive, the contracting authority may request a participant to clarify, specify or fine-tune a tender, provided such clarification, specification, fine-tuning or additional information does not involve changes to the basic features of the tender or the call for tender when those variations are likely to distort competition or have a discriminatory effect. The meaning of this provision in the Directive, and the legal uncertainty that it has engendered, were discussed in section 5.7.4 of Chapter 1.

206 2008 CBI study, n. 74 above, p. 11.

207 2010 Treasury review, n. 57 above, at 3.38. The review assumes that this results from the approach adopted to the concept of specifying, clarifying and fine-tuning bids, which governs the situation prior to selecting the preferred bidder, but in practice this section discusses the situation after appointment of the preferred bidder.

The OGC/Treasury 2008 guidance simply states that the legal meaning and interpretation of 'clarify, specify or fine-tune' are ultimately matters for the courts to determine, and shies away from providing any detailed understanding of the terms which could be 'potentially misleading'.[208] However, the 2008 guidance does explicitly steer authorities towards the Commission's view[209] that the phrase is to be interpreted 'narrowly'.[210] Indeed, the guidance appears to endorse the view that what may be done at this stage is comparable to what may be done in open or restricted procedures.[211] Thus, according to the domestic guidance, 'there is no scope for the contracting authority to seek to change any of the final bids due to them being unacceptable, or to respond to late changes in its requirements. Bidders cannot reopen discussions with the contracting authority at this stage and non-compliant bids will not be acceptable.'[212] The 2008 guidance does not, however, consider the difficult question of what scope there is for correcting errors in tenders, including errors that render a tender non-compliant, which may be more likely in complex procurement and in respect of which a more flexible approach might be needed than with more formal tendering, as discussed in Chapter 1.[213] It is also interesting that the guidance quoted above specifically rejects the possibility of allowing changes to tenders to respond to late changes in the authority's requirements: it can be argued that this is one case in which changes might be appropriate (at least if arising from external circumstances and submitted in another formal round of tendering) as allowing such changes seems preferable to negotiating changes only with the preferred bidder.

The Partnerships for Schools guidance apparently adopts a more flexible approach so far as general principles are concerned, taking the view that there is more flexibility than in formal procedures:

> These conditions would rule out, for example, most instances of pricing changes – other than those resulting from changes imposed on the process by outside factors. The scope is not as wide as under the competitive negotiated procedure. However, it should still be interpreted in the context of a procedure which has been specifically designed to deal with 'particularly complex projects' and which therefore demands a greater degree of flexibility than would be permitted, for example, under the open or restricted procedures. It should be noted that the Commission resisted

[208] OGC/Treasury 2008 guidance, n. 46 above, at 5.4.7.
[209] See Ch. 1, section 5.7.4.
[210] OGC/Treasury 2008 guidance, n. 46 above, at 5.4.8.
[211] *Ibid.*, at 5.4.8.
[212] *Ibid.*, at 5.4.9.
[213] See Ch. 1, section 5.7.4.

> any wider wording and so it can be expected to adopt a narrow interpretation of the words 'clarify, specify and fine tune'.[214]

The Partnerships for Schools guidance goes on to provide examples of circumstances that may give rise to a need to clarify specify or fine-tune tenders.[215] This guidance suggests that it is possible to discuss and clarify contractual issues, provided the issues do not affect matters of principle or the basic features of a bidder's proposal. The guidance also takes the view that there is probably some scope to correct inconsistencies or errors under 'clarification' or 'fine-tuning', to bring tenders into compliance or to correct the tender, even when the intended content of the tender is not clear. The guidance even argues that under 'fine-tuning' there may be some scope for minor improvements to tenders[216] – something that does not seem to be contemplated in the OGC/Treasury guidance. According to the guidance, under 'specification' or 'fine-tuning' the authority may be able to request that bidders provide further information and additional details because, for example, these were not originally requested or because the information provided by bidders is not sufficiently detailed. Finally, it is considered that where, due to unforeseen circumstances, it is necessary for the authority to make changes to specifications or requirements, there may be limited scope to do so under 'fine-tuning' – which again, as we have seen, is a different approach to that taken in the OGC/Treasury guidance of 2008 (although the present authors would take the view that this is much less risky if done through a formal re-tender).

Craven's study found that, in agreement with the interpretation of the Commission, now also reflected in the OGC/Treasury guidance of 2008, twenty of the forty interviewees who discussed the point adopted a narrow interpretation of the scope of this provision, as offering the same, or even less flexibility than is available under the similar stage of the restricted procedure. However, twelve interviewees spoke of regulation 18(26) as being more flexible than the open or restricted procedures. So far as actual practice under regulation 18(26) is concerned, the study found no clear picture. According to the experiences of fifteen interviewees, there is in fact often very little need for clarification, specification and fine-tuning at this stage because of the dialogue that has taken place preceding submission of final tenders which, as we saw

214 *How to Conduct a Competitive Dialogue Procedure*, n. 55 above, para. 31.

215 *Ibid.*, para. 32. 216 *Ibid.*, para. 32.

above, may include a 'dry run' final tender stage before closing the dialogue. However, thirteen interviewees, explained that in their practical experience conduct at this stage sometimes went beyond mere clarification (for example, to allow amendments if bidders have not included things that the authority would like to see included that were referred to in the dialogue).

Also, the lack of clarity surrounding the provision was flagged in eight interviews. These eight interviewees explained how, because of the uncertainty in the law, conduct would often depend upon practical considerations, such as the risk of legal challenge. Two interviewees explained how in practice authorities used this uncertainty to their advantage by adopting a narrow or broad reading of the provision depending on its particular circumstances.

5.8. *Procedure following the selection of the winning tender or preferred bidder*

5.8.1. Introduction

Corresponding almost identically with the wording of Article 29(7) of the Directive, regulation 18(28) of the Public Contracts Regulations 2006 provides that an authority may request the participant identified as having submitted the most economically advantageous tender – commonly referred to in the UK as the 'preferred bidder'[217] – to clarify aspects of that tender or confirm commitments contained in the tender provided that this does not have the effect of modifying substantial aspects of the tender or the call for tender and does not risk distorting competition or causing discrimination. The relevant provision of the Directive and the legal uncertainty that it involves have been discussed in Chapter 1 in section 5.8 of that chapter.

As we have already mentioned, the question of what can be done under this provision once the preferred bidder is appointed is an important issue in the UK. The rules on this matter crucially affect the extent to which previous practice adopted in the UK in PFI contracts can continue under the competitive dialogue procedure, with implications for bid costs that could have an effect on the availability of competition for complex procurements. The uncertainty surrounding the work that can be left open in terms of completing a tender after final tenders was

[217] OGC/Treasury 2008 guidance, n. 46 above, para. 5.5.

discussed in section 5.7.3 above on the standard of completeness required of final tenders. This section concerns the related matter of changes to a preferred bidder's tender or the call for tender after the preferred bidder has been chosen.

Previous UK practice, as we have seen, was to leave substantial matters open for negotiation after appointment of the preferred bidder, and the possibility of this, as well as external events, giving legitimate cause for quite extensive changes to the bidder's offer or the project terms seemed to be accepted by the Commission in the *London Underground* state aid case[218] – at least in the context of particularly innovative and complex procurement. As Chapter 1 also explained, the legal provisions affecting change in competitive dialogue as set out above are highly ambiguous as regards the possibility for changes, not least because of the apparent inconsistency involved in, on the one hand, apparently permitting merely 'clarification and confirmation' whilst, on the other, apparently allowing certain changes that do not modify 'substantial' aspects of the tender or call for tender. Whilst it does seem clear that the scope for change is less than that allowed for in PFI practice under the old negotiated procedure, the exact scope for change, if any, is far from evident from the provisions.

Craven's study of the operation of competitive dialogue revealed a number of reasons why in the procurement of a complex contract, particularly when the procurement spans a long period of time, the issue of change may be a very real one in practice. These include that matters have not been sufficiently covered during the dialogue phase; mistakes in tenders (such as costing errors); or mistaken assumptions by bidders (for example, in relation to ground conditions). Other reasons relate to developments on the contracting authority side; for example, changed requirements resulting from political change within the authority, or spending cuts that make a project unaffordable without a reduction in scale.

Yet other reasons arise from external factors – for example, lenders' requirements on due diligence. These were by far the most common source of changes identified by interviewees in Craven's study, with twenty-two mentioning this. Four interviewees in the study noted the problems with private lenders (such as banks) being reluctant to fully engage in the procurement process until the client had some guarantee

[218] *London Underground*, n. 86 above.

of success, due to the costs for banks doing so. According to these interviewees, lenders' due diligence post-dialogue invariably gave rise to changes to tenders/requirements, raising the level of legal risk. In view of the difficulty with lenders, ten interviewees explained attempts to address the problem. These include, for example, getting lenders (or shadow lenders if there is to be a funding competition) to attend dialogue meetings; getting bidders, as a condition for submitting a final bid, to submit a letter signed by the lender to the effect that there are no additional points on the contract the lender wishes to raise; investigating the expectations of lenders pre-procurement; and funding competitions (discussed by one policy-maker). Despite the above attempts, only two of the thirty interviewees expressed the opinion that the situation with respect to lender engagement in competitive dialogue procurement was satisfactory. The reluctance to incur unnecessary cost and a lack of interest in the procurement rules were cited as reasons for this. In addition, nineteen interviewees recognised that, due to the volatile funding market caused by the recent financial crisis, even when banks do fully engage and give sufficient financial terms to a bidder, it is unlikely that a bank will be able to hold to those terms through to financial close (potentially a year or more down the road). Two interviewees (including one policy-maker) described how, after a period of 'good behaviour', in recent years the situation with lenders was deteriorating. Statements conflicting with the opinion of these two interviewees were expressed, but due to the limited numbers involved, it is difficult to say with any certainty how representative their views are.

It is also the case that detailed planning applications tend to be left to the preferred bidder phase,[219] and any planning conditions may necessitate changes to a preferred bidder's solution which in turn, as noted by the OGC/Treasury 2008 guidance, could result in changes in the price and other terms of the tender.[220]

The recent global financial crisis and UK recession have increased the significance of the issue of post-tender change, in particular in that after appointment of the preferred bidder consortium members or subcontractors may become insolvent or lenders may withdraw funding. As mentioned above, this has also affected the willingness of banks to adhere to offered funding terms right through to contract close.

219 Planning authorities will often refuse to process more than one full application for the same site.

220 OGC/Treasury 2008 guidance, n. 46 above, at 5.5.14.

The findings of the study concerning the interpretation and application of the rules on change to these kinds of situations will now be discussed, following consideration of the guidance issued by the domestic government on this subject.

5.8.2. Domestic guidance

The OGC/Treasury 2008 guidance on the scope for change at the preferred bidder stage commences with a clear statement that '[t]he Contracting Authority does not have the flexibility under Competitive Dialogue, which it previously had under the Negotiated procedure, to negotiate changes to final bids'.[221] It also acknowledges the problem of legal uncertainty.[222] In this context, the guidance seeks to offer some practical advice, which is realistic about the demands of complex procurement, without giving a firm view on the appropriate legal interpretation:

> The challenge for the contracting authority ... is to balance the legal requirements with the need to achieve contract signature while operating in a world where change can occur between the closure of the dialogue phase and contract signature.[223]

It can be argued that this guidance, referring to the need to 'balance' the legal requirements with commercial concerns, implicitly endorses the possibility that the realities of efficient practical procurement cannot realistically be combined with the strict legal requirements. However, this may not be the intention: rather the intention is perhaps simply to seek and promote – in an area of recognised uncertainty – a legal interpretation that balances the transparency objectives of the legislation with the interests of effective procurement in terms of an efficient procedure and value for money.

The guidance, first, offers the view that certain changes are *not* permitted: these are changes that could have been anticipated and dealt with at the dialogue stage *and* changes directly under the authority's control.[224] There are some situations that would clearly fall within these concepts: for example, should an authority decide towards the end of dialogue that one or more bidders' designs are no longer acceptable for, say, environmental reasons, because of a change to the political environment, it is clearly not possible to leave negotiating any necessary changes

[221] *Ibid.*, at 5.5.7. [222] *Ibid.*, at 5.5.11.
[223] OGC/Treasury 2008 guidance, n. 46 above, at 5.5.8. [224] *Ibid.*, at 5.5.9.

until after final tenders and appointment of the preferred bidder. However, it might be open to debate whether a change of political control of a local authority during the preferred bidder period would fall within these categories.

Where the need for possible changes *in the future* is already recognised at the dialogue stage, the guidance suggests that, in order to mitigate risk of legal challenge, it may be appropriate for authorities to develop transparent mechanisms to allow changes to be handled in a pre-agreed manner.[225] It appears that as, it is submitted, with changes made once a contract has been concluded, developments dealt with under such provisions with a sufficient degree of precision or with objective external determination (for example, by an arbitrator) of how they should be addressed might be regarded either as not constituting changes but a mere implementation of the existing tender, or as being changes that are not material.[226] Possibly this could enable the authority to make provision even for changes that are within its own control.

As regards the, not uncommon, case of changes outside the control of the contracting authority that also could not reasonably have been predicted or anticipated, the guidance recognises the uncomfortable position that arises given the uncertainty over what changes are permitted combined with the adverse consequences for commercial procurement if changes cannot be made without redoing the procurement: '[The contracting authority] will not want to risk legal challenge, but the consequences of cancelling the procurement process could also have serious implications for all parties.'[227] The guidance suggests that, in these cases, the parties might 'define some broad categories of potential change and outline how they might be dealt with if they occur'.[228] An example given is the imposition of planning conditions when a decision on planning permission is taken after selection of the preferred bidder[229] – which itself can be predicted as a source of change, although the nature of the change cannot be predicted. This could require changes to the preferred bidder's design for infrastructure, a type of change which might be such that if it had been made earlier it would have affected who was selected as preferred bidder. Another

[225] *Ibid.*, at 5.5.12.

[226] Something that could be relevant for drawing the line between permitted and non-permitted changes, as discussed below.

[227] OGC/Treasury 2008 guidance, n. 46 above, at 5.5.13.

[228] *Ibid.*, at 5.5.14.

[229] *Ibid.*, at 5.5.14.

example of an unanticipated change beyond the authority's control that could be given is provided by the London Underground project referred to earlier – in that project the terrorist attacks of 11 September 2001 in the United States occurred during the preferred bidder stage, greatly increasing the perceived risk of terrorism on the underground system and requiring changes to the risk allocation terms under the contract (although these changes were not likely to have affected the outcome of the bidding process). On dealing with these kinds of unforeseen changes outside the authority's control, the guidance concludes in general terms:

> Provided that the contracting authority and the preferred bidder could not have better managed things to avoid this situation, it would not be in anyone's interests for the procurement to fail because of such an event. So, for practical reasons, the contracting authority may decide to allow some consequential change, provided the change results directly from such an event and is limited to that which is needed to respond to the event.[230]

This appears to combine a cautious approach to interpreting the legal rules with a pragmatic approach to applying them that does not expect full legal compliance – or at least not *certain* compliance in areas of uncertainty – where this would involve disproportionate commercial problems. In the current authors' view, the principle of proportionality in fact justifies a less cautious interpretation of the law that would allow the contracting authority to go ahead with the preferred bidder under the conditions referred to in the guidance, even if the change has a material effect on the competition – but we will see below that a more cautious view of the law is in fact widely taken in practice.

The Partnerships for Schools guidance, whilst accepting like the OGC that the scope for change is 'significantly' more limited in competitive dialogue than in the corresponding phase of the negotiated procedure, considers that regulation 18(28) – like regulation 18(26) on clarifying, specifying and fine-tuning at the final tender stage – 'should still be interpreted in the context of a procedure which has been specifically designed to deal with "particularly complex projects" and which therefore demands a greater degree of flexibility than would be permitted, for example, under the open or restricted procedures'.[231] Citing

[230] *Ibid.*, at 5.5.15.

[231] *How to Conduct a Competitive Dialogue Procedure*, n. 55 above, para. 37.

Arrowsmith's *The Law of Public and Utilities Procurement*,[232] according to this guidance, if the change is necessary for good external reasons it should be possible to adjust the preferred bidder's solution to take these factors into account – subject, of course, to the proviso that the change does not have the effect of modifying substantial aspects of the tender and does not risk distorting competition or causing discrimination.[233] This offers clearer and more straightforward guidance than the OGC/Treasury document for dealing with external events – it suggests that the problems addressed in the OGC/Treasury guidance can in fact largely be dealt with within the confines of the current law.

5.8.3. Interpretation and application in practice

It is very clear that, in line with expectations when competitive dialogue was introduced, the extent of changes made in practice at the preferred bidder stage in competitive dialogue is very much less than the changes made when using the negotiated procedure for projects prior to 2006. As reported in the 2010 Treasury review, the Public Accounts Committee had found that a full one-third of project teams had made changes at the preferred bidder stage under the competitive negotiated procedure – but the review found in its own research that both the time period at the preferred bidder stage and the practice of making changes 'appears to be very much reduced',[234] considering this a favourable outcome. Clearly, as we have mentioned, this reduces the scope of negotiation without competitive tension that might impact adversely on value for money, as well as delay that can be caused by negotiations without competitive pressure at this stage. This was one of the main benefits of the competitive dialogue procedure highlighted by the Treasury in its review, as discussed further in section 6 below.

As with the issue of completeness of tenders, Craven's study sought to establish more precisely both how policy-makers and practitioners actually interpreted the legal rules on scope for change and how they operated these rules in practice.

In terms of legal interpretation, in light of the uncertainty involved, interviewees tended to respond to questions on the scope for change by outlining differing degrees of change and the level of legal risk, or to present their answers as an interpretation that they could be comfortable with to back up a contracting authority's argument that a change is

[232] *Ibid.* [233] *Ibid.*, para. 38. [234] 2010 Treasury review, n. 57 above, at 3.34.

legitimate. This is because, according to all of the seventeen interviewees that addressed the point, any change after the appointment of the preferred bidder, however minor, carries some degree of legal risk. Thus according to some interviewees, a small change that does not affect the award scoring is low risk, whereas a change (or accumulation of minor changes) that affects scoring but does not change the award decision involves a higher risk of challenge; and the risk is raised further if the changes do not *improve* the preferred bidder's score.[235] It was seen as very high risk to allow changes that, had they been known about earlier in the process, would have resulted in different decisions or attracted different bidders. Eighteen interviewees considered that legally the most they would be comfortable with was an interpretation of regulation 18(28) to cover a change that affects the preferred bidder's score to the detriment of the contracting authority but would not impact on the award decision. These interviewees emphasised the need for a strong justification, such as the change being due to external factors outside the authority's control, to make a change of any kind. Thirteen interviewees viewed the law as narrower than the interpretation of the above eighteen interviewees.

Many interviewees referenced cases, such as *pressetext*[236] and the European Commission's *London Underground* Decision on state aid[237] as providing a useful indication of what is permitted.

Rather than dissecting the legal rules, however, interviewees tended to emphasise the uncertainty of the law balanced with practical considerations. There are several options open when a necessary change occurs at the preferred bidder stage: the authority can adopt a flexible interpretation of the law, conclude the contract with the preferred bidder, and hope losing bidders do not challenge; it can rewind the process (for example, re-run the final tender stage); it can award the contract to the second placed bidder; it can restart the process; or it can put the process on hold. Each option has advantages and disadvantages. Twenty-two interviewees explained how in practice there are a number of pressures upon contracting authorities, minimisation of legal risk being just one of them. Thus a number of factors will be taken into account, which include, *inter alia*, the severity of the breach (that is, the degree of the change); the likelihood of challenge; the possibility of restarting or otherwise rewinding the process; the legal risks associated with

[235] Four interviewees raised this last point.

[236] Case C-454/06, *pressetext*, n. 158 above.

[237] *London Underground*, n. 86 above.

rewinding the process; and the costs and delay of restarting or otherwise rewinding. There are also other factors, such as personal relationships with bidder teams.

The route actually taken will thus very much depend upon the specific circumstances. However, in view of its convenience, and practical and legal difficulties associated with other options, in most circumstances a contracting authority is likely to go ahead with the change and conclude the contract with the preferred bidder. This was expressly stated in fifteen interviews, with there being no interviewees making statements to the contrary. For a competitive dialogue to be restarted after preferred bidder appointment would be very rare, as stated by eleven interviewees (there were no interviews where an alternative view was put forward). Indeed, no interviewees expressed experience of such an occurrence at the preferred bidder stage. As discussed by fourteen interviewees, there are a number of practical factors that dissuade authorities from restarting. The most significant factor appears to be the waste of time and money for both the authority and bidders. Other factors mentioned by interviewees include the need to keep to timescales, political embarrassment for the authority and professional embarrassment for individuals, and the possibility that the preferred bidder might litigate to recover wasted costs.

If there is a necessary change at the preferred bidder stage, and the authority is not legally comfortable concluding the procurement, rewinding the process, by re-running the final tender stage or even reopening the dialogue stage, is, from a cost perspective, the next best option. Eight interviewees had practical experience of this for example, in cases where the preferred bidder was not capable of delivering its tender without changes to its tender. However, legal difficulties were identified with rewinding a competitive dialogue process. How does the authority decide how far back to rewind? How does the authority ensure compliance with equal treatment (particularly where losing bidders have been debriefed)? Is it legally possible to re-open the dialogue phase? UK guidance fails to address these issues. There may also be similar practical difficulties as those associated with restarting (such as timetable slippage). In view of these problems, according to seven interviewees, an authority is only likely to consider rewinding the process where there is a real likelihood of legal challenge and not just an abstract risk.

It can finally be noted that the Treasury review reported that 86 per cent of those responding to its general survey reported at least minor difficulties for projects because of the limited room for manoeuvre under the legislation at the preferred bidder stage (and 49 per cent of those surveyed in a survey of specific projects for the report), and 15 per cent of those responding to the Treasury survey reported 'considerable' difficulties.[238] However, there is no indication of how wide these different respondents perceived the room for manoeuvre to be.

5.8.4. Reserve bidder

Prior to the introduction of competitive dialogue, UK authorities procuring complex projects under the negotiated procedure would commonly, in order to maintain some competitive pressure when appointing the bidder with the most economically advantageous tender as the preferred bidder, invite the runner-up to be a reserve preferred bidder.[239] If the contracting authority was unable to reach contract close with the preferred bidder, the authority could offer the reserve bidder the opportunity to take the preferred bidder's place.

There is nothing in either the Regulations or the Directive disallowing the practice of maintaining a reserve bidder under the negotiated procedure or the competitive dialogue. The 2006 OGC guidance discourages the use of reserve bidders, citing recital 31 of the Directive: 'competition should not be distorted or restricted ... by involving any tenderer other than the one selected as the most economically advantageous tenderer'.[240] There is, however, somewhat of a mixed message on this point: 2006 4ps guidance expressly endorses the use of reserve bidders 'wherever possible'.[241]

Only a limited number of interviewees (five) had experience of maintaining a reserve bidder or had advised upon it. If preferred bidder negotiations were to break down, the legal possibility of taking up negotiations with the second placed bidder without re-running the final tender stage was recognised as uncertain, and sending a reserve bidder letter out was said to not make this less of an issue. According to

[238] 2010 Treasury review, n. 57 above, at 3.37.

[239] Treasury Taskforce, Technical Note No. 4, *How to Appoint and Work with a Preferred Bidder* (2007), available at http://webarchive.nationalarchives.gov.uk/+/www.dh.gov.uk/en/Aboutus/Procurementandproposals/Publicprivatepartnership/Privatefinanceinitiative/InvestmentGuidanceRouteMap/DH_4132888, p. 12.

[240] OGC 2006 guidance, n. 36 above, at 10.1.

[241] 4ps, *A Map of the PFI Process Using Competitive Dialogue* (June 2006), available at http://test.4ps.gov.uk/PageContent.aspx?id=2&tp=&s=2&title=&Sector=0&-searchbtn=Go&x=38&y=16, p. 18.

interviewees, there are also the practical difficulties – for example, the reserve bidder may not be prepared to be kept on hold and is likely to shift its focus to competitions for other contracts.

5.9. The standstill period

As explained in section 5.9 of Chapter 1, EU procurement law requires a standstill period between notifying the contract award decision to losing tenderers and conclusion of the contract, resulting first from the *Alcatel*[242] case and later from legislation in Directive 2007/66 (amending the Public Sector Remedies Directive 89/665/EEC). In the UK, a standstill was introduced into the Public Contracts Regulations 2006 based on *Alcatel* and then amended in 2009 in light of Directive 2007/66 with the new rules applying to procedures beginning on or after 20 December 2009.[243] The main difference is that, from 2009, more information than before must be provided in the notice.

As Chapter 1 explained,[244] there is uncertainty surrounding the correct timing of the EU standstill obligations – whether these should be applied at the time of the selection of preferred bidder or just before the contract is signed.

In this respect, the OGC's 2006 guidance (before the 2009 amendment) suggested that standstill should occur at the time of preferred bidder selection, before the authority engages in a stage of clarification and confirmation of commitments.[245] However, the OGC's 2008 guidance took a different view, indicating that the standstill period should occur when all material matters have been resolved ('i.e. there will be no further changes that will modify the terms under which the contract will be concluded').[246]

In Craven's study, interviewees were asked about both their interpretation of the law and their experience in actually operating the standstill period. Divergent views were expressed on the legal requirement. Seemingly in line with the 2008 OGC and Treasury guidance, fourteen interviewees argued that the law required the standstill at the time of the decision to award the contract, which was not on

[242] Case C-81/98, *Alcatel Austria v. Bundesministerium für Wissenschaft und Verkehr* [1999] ECR I-07671.

[243] Now found in regulation 32A.

[244] Ch. 1, section 5.9.

[245] OGC 2006 guidance, n. 36 above, Annex A.

[246] OGC/Treasury 2008 guidance, n. 46 above, at 5.5.6.

identification of the preferred bidder, but at a later point closer to contract signature – for example, when all substantive issues had been resolved and it is more certain that the authority will conclude the contract with the preferred bidder. An alternative interpretation from ten interviewees was that the standstill obligation was to be applied immediately following identification of a preferred bidder. Differing slightly from the above two views, five interviewees explained that compliance required that the standstill requirement take place not immediately on identification of the preferred bidder, but after the authority has gone through internal sign-off and is ready to formally announce the selection of the preferred bidder. A further five interviewees regarded the law as unclear.

As regards practice, there was again variation. In this respect, twelve interviewees – a clear majority – described practice as generally being to notify losing bidders at the time the preferred bidder is identified and to apply the standstill period at this time only. A key reason given for this related to legal risk (to avoid having the requirement 'hanging over you' during preferred bidder clarifications).

Six interviewees described the standstill period taking place in practice after the authority's internal approval processes and with the formal announcement of the preferred bidder. Nine interviewees stated that practice varies from procurement to procurement between the standstill taking place at identification of preferred bidder, taking place close to contract close or being applied at both times. It is interesting that, although most interviewees (fourteen) interpreted the law to require a standstill at a point close to contract close after conclusion of all substantive discussions, only nine of these (not including interviewees who stated that practice varies) did actually apply a standstill at contract close. The interviews are not clear on the reasons for this slight discrepancy.

No English interviewees considered that a formal standstill requirement needed to be complied with twice in law: on identification of the preferred bidder and on conclusion of the contract. However, two interviewees described how in practice, although not necessarily applying two standstill periods, a notice would be sent out at both points, this being regarded by these two interviewees as the safest approach in terms of legal risk (a 'belt and braces' approach). However, others expressly stated that they did not adopt such an approach for fear of raising suspicions of non-compliant conduct with the second notification.

5.10. Payments for costs of participation

Mirroring Article 29(8), regulation 18(29) states that a contracting authority has the option to make payments to bidders. Government policy, expressed in the OGC/Treasury 2008 guidance, is for a strong presumption against such payments.[247] The guidance notes, however, that this needs to be looked at on a case-by-case basis, as issues such as participation concerns may provide a justification for payments in certain cases.

Prior to competitive dialogue, payment of bid costs, although recognised as possible, played little if any role in UK PFI procurement practice under the negotiated procedure.[248] Despite concern over the high cost of participating in competitive dialogue, thirty-eight interviewees in Craven's study stated that they had no practical experience of such payments. Only one interviewee described a situation where they had been involved in a competitive dialogue process where payments were made to bidders – and in this case the payments were merely of a token £1,500.

5.11. Award criteria

5.11.1. Introduction

Having considered above the different stages of the award phase that lead to choosing the preferred bidder, it is useful to consider separately some general points relating to the award criteria used for making that choice. The explicit rules on this, requiring use of the most economically advantageous tender criterion and formulation and disclosure of the main criteria, are set out, as we saw in Chapter 1,[249] in Article 53 of the Directive. As Chapter 1 also explained, the rules on disclosure of award criteria have been supplemented by CJEU case law, which gives rise to some uncertainty in its application, and there are other areas of uncertainty relating to award criteria.[250] Craven's research found that uncertainty over what the law requires in relation to award criteria is a major area of concern of those involved in competitive dialogue. This is particularly so because of the high level of legal risk. Challenge is considered likely, since bids are often very close – a consequence of using the dialogue stage to align bids with the authority's preferences – and

[247] *Ibid.*, box 5.1. [248] Arrowsmith, n. 23 above, p. 108. [249] Ch. 1, section 5.6.5.
[250] Ch. 1, section 5.6.5.

bidders reaching the dialogue phase, especially the end of that phase, have invested significant resources in the process.

We have already considered at section 5.6.2 above one issue on award criteria, namely, the use of different award criteria and/or weightings during different phases of the dialogue and between dialogue and the final tender stage. Below we consider other key issues.

5.11.2. Formulation and disclosure of award criteria

Following the Directive, regulation 18(27) of the Public Contracts Regulations 2006 requires use of the most economically advantageous tender basis for the award, regulation 30(2) requires advance formulation and disclosure of the award criteria to be used for choosing this and regulation 30(3) requires advance formulation and disclosure of their weightings. As Chapter 1 explained,[251] CJEU case law also requires under the transparency principle advance disclosure of other material used to make the award such as, under certain conditions, sub-criteria used and their weightings where they may affect tenders. Prior to and during the period of the research, this CJEU case law on disclosure was applied in several domestic cases, in some of which contracting authorities were found to be in violation of the disclosure rules.[252] According to Craven's research, uncertainty over how these disclosure rules apply to specific cases has been one important source of concern in practice.

Since Craven's research, the disclosure rules have been applied by the courts in the specific context of a competitive dialogue procedure, in *Mears* v. *Leeds City Council*.[253] This case concerned an award procedure by Leeds City Council for a contract for improvement and refurbishment of social housing. Mears had been invited to participate in the dialogue but, following an assessment of outline submissions based on the stated award criteria under regulation 30, had not been invited into the second stage of dialogue. Mears complained of inadequate advance disclosure of the criteria used and of their importance and application.

The first complaint concerned a table used to evaluate the relevant criteria. This identified various quality criteria and listed 'questions' that

[251] Ch. 1, section 8.6.5.

[252] For example, in *McLaughlin and Harvey* v. *Department of Finance and Personnel (No. 2)* [2008] NIQB 91 and [2011] NICA 60; *Lettings International* v. *Newham London Borough Council* [2007] EWCA Civ 1522 and Silber J [2008] EWHC 1538 (applying the Court of Appeal ruling).

[253] *Mears* v. *Leeds City Council (Second Judgment)* [2011] EWHC 1031.

tenderers had to answer relating to each criterion. No weightings were stated for the criteria or for the matters covered by each individual question. The evaluation was actually done by giving a mark out of ten for each question, meaning that the total marks (and hence weighting) for each criterion depended on the number of questions under that criterion (for example, if there were three questions the total marks were 30). The marks for the criteria ranged from 30 to 110 (eleven questions). The court considered that each of the questions in practice represented specific quality criteria or sub-criteria that could have affected tenders; thus the council was required to disclose the weightings given to each.

Mears also complained that the council had not disclosed the 'model answers' (given to the evaluators) to the questions. These were documents indicating matters that the tenderers should have addressed – although, as the court found, each question could give rise to a broad range of different responses that would address each question. The court concluded that these model answers did not need to be disclosed in full since they did not in general introduce new criteria or sub-criteria or effectively introduce weightings. Rather, they merely contained material that a reasonably well-informed and diligent tenderer could foresee would need to be covered in the answer.

However, in two cases the model answers did operate in practice to do this, and should have been disclosed. This applied in the case of:

(i) A question asking for details of staff and of management training and development arrangements. The model answer indicated that tenderers should provide a list of staff. The court considered that this did not reasonably respond to the question – it could not have been foreseen that the question envisaged providing such a list. This introduced a new element since, according to the court, the quality of services could be affected by the staff used, and this could have affected tenders.[254]

(ii) A question asking for a description of the policy of lone-workers and the measures to ensure the suitability of operatives sent to the homes of vulnerable customers. The model answer referred to staff safety and the court considered that it effectively gave this matter (as

[254] There was no discussion of the extent to which the possibility of using information on staff to judge the quality of the services likely to be provided is precluded by the CJEU judgment in Case C-532/06, *Emm. G. Lianakis* v. *Dimos Alexandroupolis and others* [2008] ECR I-251 (as to which, see section 5.11.4 below): the court simply assumes that this is lawful.

opposed to safety of customers) a weighting that was unclear from the question.

It was relevant to the conclusion on these two points that the model answers were intended to be a template against which tenders would be judged, rather than simply being non-prescriptive guidance to the evaluators.

In the present authors' view, this decision provides suitable guidance on the kind of material that must be disclosed that will be useful for many complex procurements. It remains to be seen how far this latest case law is considered to clarify the disclosure issue by those operating the procedure in practice.

As well as the kind of material that must be disclosed if used in the evaluation, another legal and practical issue for competitive dialogue, as mentioned in Chapter 1,[255] is the required timing of disclosure in an iterative procedure. In particular, should all criteria, weightings and other information used be drafted and disclosed fully prior to the start of the award process or may this material be developed as the process unwinds – for example, by using broad award criteria for outline submissions and adding more detailed sub-criteria for assessing more detailed submissions later in the dialogue phase or at final tender stage? Craven's research revealed that practice in England is fairly evenly divided between the two approaches in the context of PPP projects with a slight majority – twenty-three interviewees as against eighteen – favouring the latter rather than the former approach in their practice (and taking the view that this approach is permitted by law).

5.11.3. Change to award criteria during the procedure

Another area of legal uncertainty discussed in Chapter 1[256] is the extent to which award criteria and other matters, such as sub-criteria, or the weightings of criteria and sub-criteria, may be *changed* from those set and disclosed. (This is a different question from whether the criteria may be expanded in more detail without, however, changing them, which was discussed above.) It was suggested that changes may in fact be made under certain conditions, including that they are not material in the sense that they may have affected the outcome – but the precise legal position is a matter for debate.[257]

[255] Ch. 1, section 5.6.5. [256] Ch. 1, section 5.6.5. [257] Ch. 1, section 5.6.5.

Craven's research revealed that a significant majority (twenty-two of thirty interviewees who expressed a view) considered that there was scope for variation of some kind provided that the variation was not 'material'. Fourteen interviewees of the twenty-two interviewees were not specific about the extent to which changes to award criteria were permitted but simply indicated that change was permitted where relevant conditions, such as non-materiality, were met. Seven interviewees spoke only about the possibility of changes to sub-criteria, whilst five spoke merely of the possibility for changes to be made to advertised weightings (one stating that, whilst award criteria could not be changed, it was possible to vary weightings).

5.11.4. The relationship between selection and award criteria

A further issue important for complex procurement and thus (although not exclusively so) for competitive dialogue is the extent to which contracting authorities may use at the award stage criteria that involve assessing matters also considered at the selection stage, such as experience of tenderers or their personnel. This possibility has been considered doubtful by some, following the decision of the CJEU in *Lianakis*.[258] However, as the literature has explained, the meaning of this decision in this respect is far from clear.[259]

Craven's research indicated that, in England, an overwhelming majority of those operating the procedure – twenty-two of twenty-six interviewees – take a flexible view of the law as allowing consideration of matters such as experience,[260] *provided that these are actually used to assess the value of the tenderer's offer* (for example, in terms of how it will affect the quality of the service provided). The other four interviewees explicitly endorsed a very narrow view that no overlap exists at all between matters that may be considered at the selection stage and at the award stage.

[258] *Lianakis*, n. 254 above.

[259] See, in particular, S. Arrowsmith (ed.), *EU Public Procurement Law: An Introduction*, at 6.7.2.6; P. Lee, 'Implications of the Lianakis Decision' (2010) 19 *Public Procurement Law Review* 47; S. Treumer, 'The Distinction between Selection and Award Criteria in EC Public Procurement Law – A Rule without Exception?' (2009) 18 *Public Procurement Law Review* 103.

[260] The interviews did not, however, explore whether this applied merely to experience of the tenderer's personnel at the award stage, or also to the experience of the tenderer itself. On this distinction, see Lee, n. 259 above.

It is also interesting that many legal advisors commented that there was a general lack of awareness within many staff in contracting authorities of the existence of any kind of legal distinction between selection and award criteria.

6. Competitive dialogue in the UK: the legal rules in context

It is finally relevant in this chapter to consider briefly other research on competitive dialogue in the UK which places in context the legal rules that have been the focus of this study. In particular, the 2008 report by the CBI, the 2010 study by HM Treasury and the study by Craven referred to above all provide a useful overall perspective on the procedure.

The CBI report, as explained, provides a valuable perspective from bidders, in particular highlighting issues that can adversely affect the costs of participation and bidder confidence. Published in 2008 and thus covering the initial years of competitive dialogue, this report concluded that the procedure is potentially capable of delivering effective public services *but* only if managed well – and that there were concerns amongst consultees that few authorities were managing it well at that time, resulting in lengthy procedures and high bid costs.[261]

The later Treasury review of 2010 similarly reported that 'both the public and private sectors believe the Competitive Dialogue procedure has been a positive addition to the procurement spectrum'.[262] The Treasury review also went further than the CBI report in this respect in concluding specifically that the new procedure has *improved* outcomes in terms of value for money.[263] The review reported that 78 per cent of respondents to its general survey believed that outcomes had improved, or improved 'significantly', from those under the negotiated procedure. The review highlights a number of reasons for this, as indicated by a 'general consensus' of consultees.[264] These include 'maintenance of competition', apparently referring to the existence of competition up until tenders are complete, as discussed at sections 5.7.3 and 5.8 above; the discipline imposed on this process leading to the close of the dialogue; and avoidance of the 'scope and price' creep found with the negotiated procedure. These are closely related aspects of competitive dialogue which derive from the legal

[261] 2008 CBI study, n. 74 above, p. 1. [262] 2010 Treasury review, n. 57 above, at 1.10.
[263] *Ibid.*, at 4.3. [264] *Ibid.*, at 1.10.

requirements for complete final tenders and limited change after identifying the preferred bidder, as compared with the negotiated procedure. On the other hand, it is worth mentioning again here[265] that the interviewees for Craven's study were not unanimously of the view that competitive dialogue is beneficial overall: a significant minority considered that the higher procedural costs for public and private sectors outweigh the benefits of maintaining competition throughout the process.

Whilst concluding that competitive dialogue is, overall, beneficial, the Treasury, like the CBI, also emphasised, however, that this is the case only when the procedure is operated 'appropriately'[266] and – like the CBI – expressed concerns over the impact on costs and timescales when this is not the case.[267]

So far as costs are concerned, the 2010 Treasury review found that 86 per cent of respondents to its survey perceived that costs had increased, or increased significantly, as compared with the costs incurred under the competitive negotiated procedure, with 55 per cent of contracting authorities consulted being also of this opinion.[268] Private sector parties at the roundtable discussions held as part of the Treasury review indicated that costs for losing bidders had increased from 2–3 per cent of the contract under the negotiated procedure to 5–6 per cent under competitive dialogue (with the costs of the winner remaining around the same).[269] Craven's study also found a consensus that costs for losing bidders had increased significantly. Public sector costs had also increased, something also confirmed by Craven's study. According to the 2010 Treasury review, these were represented mainly by administrative support and evaluation costs but were not generally quantified. The review recommended this be done[270] in order to reveal true costs[271] and to help reduce both costs and timescales. The recent Cabinet Office study, *Accelerating Government Procurement*, found that monthly bid costs for complex procurement in the public sector were almost twice that for private sector projects,[272] and suggested potential total cost reductions achievable across suppliers in

[265] See section 5.7.3 above. [266] 2010 Treasury review, n. 57 above, at 1.10.
[267] See generally *ibid.*, at 2.15; and also the specific discussion below.
[268] 2010 Treasury review, n. 57 above, at 4.7. [269] *Ibid.*, at 4.11. [270] *Ibid.*, at 4.10.
[271] *Ibid.*, at 4.8.
[272] £130,000 for the public sector projects as against £70,000 for private sector projects: *Lean Procurement Diagnostic Findings*, n. 76 above, p. 14.

competitive dialogue of £3.5 million per procedure,[273] with a potential reduction of £400,000 in costs for the authority itself.[274]

Related to the issue of cost (since longer procedures are more costly) is that of timescales, which was a concern highlighted by all the studies above. There is no clear data on how the time taken for competitive dialogue procedures compares with the time taken for similar projects under the old negotiated procedure: however, most interviewees in Craven's study who commented on the issue considered that the negotiated procedure was quicker for comparable projects (nine interviewees, one estimating that the negotiated procedure was around 30 per cent quicker) with three considering the two procedures comparable, and none suggesting that competitive dialogue was more rapid. Time scales reported by interviewees ranged from nine months to thirty-three months, with one suggesting that twenty-two to twenty-four months is a typical length. The Cabinet Office study, *Accelerating Government Procurement*, found competitive dialogue procedures to take – presumably based on the average for its own sample – 429 working days, and suggested that this could be reduced by up to as much as 70 per cent.[275] It can also be noted that the 2010 Treasury review concluded that cancellation and delay were problems in light of the costs involved to suppliers[276] – 10 per cent of respondents had been involved in procurements subject to cancellation or delay and this was mainly due to policy or other changes to requirements. As mentioned, the Cabinet Office is currently working on ways to reduce timescales significantly, including on standardisation towards more lean processes, and removing blockages such as lengthy approvals processes,[277] and has issued guidance to central government that requires publication of procurement timescales as a step toward controlling them.[278]

One problem with high participation costs and lengthy or delayed procedures is that potential bidders may be deterred. Both the 2010 Treasury review[279] and Craven's study found this to be the perception amongst those operating the procedure, and Craven's study also found this to be increasingly so during the economic recession and as the costs

[273] *Accelerating Government Procurement*, n. 57 above, section 2. [274] *Ibid.*
[275] *Ibid.* [276] 2010 Treasury review, n. 57 above, at 4.17–4.20.
[277] *Accelerating Government Procurement*, n. 57 above, section 6.
[278] *Transparency – Publication of Tender Documentation*, n. 155 above.
[279] 2010 Treasury review, n. 57 above, at 2.17 and 3.11.

involved are better understood. Nineteen interviewees specifically mentioned the difficulty of attracting bidders and preventing drop-outs, with several commenting that it is a more significant problem with lower value projects. The costs involved also appear to create more of a barrier to participation for small or medium-sized firms than for large ones – the former sometimes simply lack the depth of resources, as well as the skills and knowledge, to participate.[280]

Craven's study found a consensus that the increase in costs for both public and private sectors was due mainly to the requirement for completing offers prior to the final tender stage, requiring losing bidders to undertake more work than before and for the public sector to undertake extensive negotiations with more than one bidder. However, whilst to a large extent increased costs are an inevitable consequence of the legal rules on competitive dialogue (as compared with those of the negotiated procedure), it is also clear that there is scope for reducing those costs within the parameters of the current law by more efficient practice. The issues identified in this respect are very similar in the Treasury review, the CBI report and Craven's study.

One major concern is inadequate preparation, sometimes leading to inappropriate use of the procedure, and inadequate documentation – issues that have been discussed at section 5.2 above. The Treasury review of 2010 acknowledged this as a major concern,[281] and all interviewees in Craven's study agreed that a significant amount of work was required prior to issuing the contract notice. The CBI report specifically stressed the need to put in place the full team,[282] along with internal policies and procedures for delivery and all background and policy information on the project, *prior* to the contract notice.[283] The report specifically recommended that the gateway review process, a peer review process for evaluating major government projects at key decision points,[284] should include a specific stage for competitive dialogue to check for adequate preparation prior to the contract notice.[285] This is often done in practice, although there have as yet been no formal changes to the relevant processes and documentation.

280 *Ibid.*, at 2.17. 281 *Ibid.*, at 3.9–3.15. 282 2008 CBI study, n. 74 above, pp. 5–6.
283 *Ibid.*, p. 2.
284 The process is applied to projects in central government, local government and the health sector. See further the information at http://webarchive.nationalarchives.gov.uk/20110822131357/www.ogc.gov.uk/what_is_ogc_gateway_review.asp.
285 2008 CBI study, n. 74 above, p. 6.

The CBI report also highlighted the importance of a well-resourced procurement team with adequate expertise in legal, financial and technical aspects, as well as commercial negotiating skills.[286] As regards resourcing, the report considered it important that contracting authorities have access to public sector professionals with previous experience of competitive dialogue.[287] The 2010 Treasury review likewise acknowledged both lack of skills[288] and inadequate resourcing in the public sector as a problem, noting that three-quarters of respondents to its survey considered that the public sector did not adequately resource the process (although two-thirds of the public sector itself considered that the resource used was sufficient).[289] The Treasury report also identified the high cost of buying in skills from the private sector as a problem,[290] emphasising the need to ensure transfer of skills from private advisors. The resource-intensive nature of the process is highlighted by the fact that 59 per cent of those surveyed reported a need to bring in additional internal resources for award procedures using competitive dialogue and 59 per cent a need for external resources.[291] The problem of lack of capability in the public sector itself and over-reliance on external advisors was identified also in the Cabinet Office study, *Accelerating Government Procurement.*[292]

Another way in which it appears costs can be significantly reduced is by a more efficient approach to meetings, particularly during dialogue. Aspects of this subject were considered in section 5.6.3 above, where it was explained that an over-cautious interpretation of the equal treatment principle is one reason for problems, but that these problems are not caused solely by legal issues. We have already mentioned that to address the problem of excessive cost of meetings the Treasury is promoting a more focused approach to dialogue, and the Treasury report also emphasises the importance of a clear timetable and plan for meetings (noting also that strict adherence to the timetable was the most common recommendation for improvement made by consultees).[293] Another common cause for complaint revealed in all three studies is that contracting authorities seek too much information in dialogue.[294]

[286] *Ibid.*, pp. 5–6. [287] *Ibid.*, p. 6. [288] 2010 Treasury review, n. 57 above, at 2.08.
[289] *Ibid.*, at 2.22–2.29. [290] *Ibid.*, at 2.20–2.21. [291] *Ibid.*, at 2.24.
[292] *Accelerating Government Procurement*, n. 57 above, section 4; and see also the speech of Francis Maude, n. 4 above, which indicates specific justification will now be needed to use consultants for procurement generally.
[293] 2010 Treasury review, n. 57 above, at 3.26.
[294] 2008 CBI study, n. 74 above, at p. 8; 2010 Treasury review, n. 57 above, at 3.43–3.44.

In this respect, the Treasury has recommended that less detailed information should be requested and it should be explained in each case why information is needed and how it is linked to the award criteria.[295]

As the potentially high costs of competitive dialogue become known, it has become clear, as the 2010 Treasury review indicates, that the ability of authorities to attract a good level of competition increasingly depends on efficient operation of the procedure. Thus, as the review states, private sector contractors are examining the level of preparation and the skills and resources to be devoted to the project before deciding whether to participate,[296] and it is important for authorities to demonstrate to the market that these are adequate.

It is important to highlight that, as the CBI report acknowledges, many of the concerns above are not new and might not be wholly attributable to competitive dialogue itself[297] – the CBI study focused on how competitive dialogue itself might be improved, rather than comparing that procedure with what has gone before. However, given the inevitable costs inherent in competitive dialogue in the first place, experience so far has shown that eliminating unnecessary procedural costs is particularly important for this procedure.

We have seen above that the issue of supplier costs is also to be addressed following the 'Lean review' of government procurement by greater use of the speedier and less costly open or restricted procedures when these are appropriate;[298] and that in November 2011 the government announced that in future there will even be a presumption against use of competitive dialogue in order to reduce procurement costs and timescales. However, although some shift will be beneficial, there are likely to be many situations in which the flexibility of competitive dialogue, in one of its many various forms, will offer the best approach. A significant effort to address the practical problems discussed in this section is thus of great importance to ensure that full advantage is taken of the commercial opportunities offered by the flexibility of competitive dialogue. It would be most unfortunate if the failure of some contracting authorities to follow good practice when using competitive dialogue was to have a wider effect of discouraging its use in suitable cases.

[295] 2010 Treasury review, n. 57 above, at 4.46. [296] *Ibid.*, at 3.14.
[297] 2008 CBI study, n. 74 above, p. 2.
[298] *Accelerating Government Procurement*, n. 57 above.

7. Concluding remarks

We have seen that the UK has so far been a heavy user of competitive dialogue.[299] Thus competitive dialogue has been used frequently for contracts covered by the Public Sector Directive, and in this respect has replaced the competitive negotiated procedure for many complex contracts as well as being used for some contracts that would previously have been awarded through the restricted procedure when that procedure was not really suitable.[300] There is also evidence of a procedure modelled on competitive dialogue being used for contracts outside, or not fully covered by, the Directive.[301] This extensive use of competitive dialogue is not surprising given that it is to an extent inspired by the previous practice for awarding complex contracts in the UK and – apart from the tighter rules on final tenders and changes at preferred bidder stage – largely accommodates that practice, and given the fact that the UK pushed strongly for the introduction of the new procedure.[302]

The level of use of competitive dialogue suggests that it is considered a useful addition to the Directive and we have seen that this is borne out by studies on the operation of the procedure in its early years. Its introduction has provided greater legal certainty for authorities needing a flexible approach, given the doubts over the availability of the negotiated procedure for many complex contracts and the limited suitability of the restricted procedure. Further, as we have seen in section 6, competitive dialogue, when effectively operated, is widely regarded as beneficial when compared with previous practices under the negotiated procedure, insofar as it provides for more competition and discipline at the end of the process. On the other hand, for both the public and private sector the procedural costs are high both in absolute terms and in comparison with the negotiated procedure.[303] Whilst most of those operating the procedure consider that the benefits obtained outweigh these higher costs, this is not, however, the universal view.[304]

To some extent, as identified in various pieces of research, the high costs of competitive dialogue are attributable to factors unconnected with the legal rules, notably poor planning and preparation,[305] inadequate resourcing of the procedure,[306] excessive scope and length of

[299] See section 4.2 above. [300] Section 4.2 above. [301] Section 4.2 above.
[302] See Ch. 1, section 2.3. [303] Section 6 above.
[304] Section 5.7.3 and section 6 above. [305] Section 5.2 and section 6 above.
[306] Section 6 above.

meetings,[307] and demands for unnecessary information.[308] We have seen in section 6 that the Treasury review of 2010 and the 'Lean review' have made recommendations to address these issues and work on this is ongoing; and it is clear that authorities that do not operate the procedure efficiently are facing increased scrutiny by the private sector and may find attracting bidders difficult. It is also the case, as we have seen, that unnecessary costs arise from over-use of the procedure.[309] This last problem seems likely to be curbed by reforms that will follow from the recent 'Lean review' of government procurement, resulting in the government's November 2011 announcement of an intention to reduce use of competitive dialogue.[310] It is to be hoped that this latter development will, however, focus on reducing inappropriate use of the procedure, and that for cases in which competitive dialogue *is* appropriate attention will remain focused on making the procedure work in an efficient manner rather than on pushing authorities towards the use of inherently less suitable procedures.

We have seen, in addition, that for those cases in which competitive dialogue *is* appropriate there are also some problems with the legal rules themselves. These have been the main focus of the present study.

First and foremost, as discussed, research indicates that the main reason for the higher level procedural costs compared with the negotiated procedure is the requirement for complete tenders from more than one bidder at the final tender stage: the process of finalising a detailed tender increases costs for losing bidders as well as for contracting authorities because of the need for extensive engagement with more than one bidder.[311] We have seen that there is some legal uncertainty over what the 'complete tender' requirement involves and that its interpretation and practical application does differ between practitioners;[312] and these differences will clearly affect the balance of costs and benefits. However, there does seem to be a general consensus that, however the provision is applied, participation costs will remain high.

Whilst, however, some additional costs are inevitable and possibly justified by the benefits of greater competition, a better balance might possibly be struck between costs and benefits than at present by limiting the detail required in tenders. It appears that this is possible to achieve within the current rules by a sensible interpretation. One approach, for example, might be to require bidders to complete only details that are

[307] Section 5.6.3 and section 6 above. [308] Section 6 above. [309] Section 4.2 above.
[310] Section 4.3 above. [311] Section 5.7.3 above. [312] Section 5.7.3 above.

reasonably likely to affect the outcome of the competition; this would hardly increase the risk of abuse of negotiations to favour national suppliers, which is the main concern of the EU rules, or – from a national perspective – undermine value for money. The view that a better balance can be struck within the current legal framework is reflected in the conclusion of the 2010 Treasury review that bid costs are disproportionate because of an 'overly prudent' application of the rules – although the review does not offer a clear analysis of the meaning of the legal provisions. Such an approach is clearly supported by the principle of competition underlying the Directive, given the impact of high bid costs on the breadth of competition for competitive dialogue projects.

Legal uncertainty is also a problem in this area, as with many aspects of competitive dialogue. Both the problems that this uncertainty causes and the achievement of a more flexible practice could usefully be addressed in the short term by suitable guidance which, as we have seen from the studies by Craven and Braun, has significant practical influence.[313] Guidance from the Commission that reflects the practical reality of effective procurement of complex projects, as well as further guidance from the domestic government, would be welcome in this respect.

A second important area of legal difficulty revealed by the research is that of accommodating changes to the project that are beyond the authority's control, especially those arising during the preferred bidder period. This is again an area in which those operating the law consider the rules unclear and adopt different interpretations.[314] Many authorities take quite a cautious view of change at the preferred bidder stage, considering that any change affecting scoring involves an element of legal risk, even if it does not affect the outcome.[315] However, in contrast with the rather prudent application of the rules relating to completeness of tenders, Craven's study has shown the actual practice in relation to change has been pragmatic,[316] in view of the need for changes and the high costs of rewinding the procedure. Thus, the response in most cases has been to make the desired change despite the legal risks. The study has in this respect highlighted an important mismatch between the realities of effective commercial procurement and a strict interpretation of the law and – it is submitted – the need for a flexible approach to interpretation. In this respect, as with the requirement for complete tenders, both

[313] See sections 2 and 4.2 above. [314] Section 5.8 above. [315] Section 5.8 above.
[316] Section 5.8 above.

the problem of legal uncertainty and the need for a flexible approach can, it is submitted, be addressed to a significant degree by guidance at both domestic and EU level. In the present authors' view, this should, at the very least, permit changes due to external circumstances whenever the change would have been unlikely to affect the outcome[317] – and possibly even changes that might have done so when this is justified by application of the proportionality principle.

Legal uncertainty combined with a lack of appetite for legal risk, at least on the part of some practitioners, has also meant that the operation of competitive dialogue is not always efficient in other respects. One problem area identified, for example, is the application of equal treatment in the context of meetings: we saw that a legally cautious approach has exacerbated the significant problem of excessive meetings during dialogue.[318] Perceptions of the principle have also affected practice in a manner that is arguably detrimental to efficient procurement in relation to technical dialogue prior to the formal dialogue phase: this has led some practitioners to eschew in-depth consultations with a small group of suppliers even though others consider this invaluable.[319] Another difficult area concerns the possibility for developing or changing at different phases of the procedure the criteria and/or weightings that are used to eliminate bidders or solutions. Here, it seems that legal risk may deter some practitioners from adopting an approach that many regard as good commercial practice, namely, one that allows for some variation.[320] In these areas interpretative guidance could again play a useful role in steering procuring entities towards flexible practices when these are needed for effective procurement.

Other areas of legal uncertainty also exist, including over the meaning of the rules on confidentiality[321] and on the scope for adjusting or completing final tenders between submission and award.[322] In both respects, practitioners have developed practical strategies to deal with uncertainty. Thus, in the former case, the issue has been dealt with by obtaining explicit agreement from suppliers on what is regarded as confidential,[323] whilst in the latter the need for adjustments is removed to some extent by holding a 'dry run' of the final tender stage.[324] However, in these areas and others, there is still scope for guidance to remove legal uncertainty and assist with resolving practical

[317] See Ch. 1, section 5.8.
[318] Section 5.6.3 above.
[319] Section 5.6.3 above.
[320] See section 5.11 above.
[321] Section 5.3 above.
[322] See section 5.7.4 above.
[323] See section 5.3 above.
[324] Section 5.7.4 above.

difficulties – provided again, however, that that guidance supports an approach that is in tune with the realities of complex procurement.

In conclusion, UK experience of competitive dialogue indicates that it is a valuable addition to the toolbox of award procedures in the Public Sector Directive. However, measures can be taken to improve its practical effectiveness. Whilst some of these, such as better planning and resourcing, do not relate directly to the legal rules, others relate to the legal rules themselves. Research shows that guidance from policy-makers is influential in steering the behaviour of contracting authorities and thus could play a valuable role in improving practice. In this respect, it will be unfortunate if, as seems likely from current evidence, the Cabinet Office does not continue the work of the former OGC in providing detailed guidance on the legal interpretation of EU rules. In the longer term, however, judicial interpretation that is founded on an appreciation of the realities of complex procurement could perhaps make the most important contribution to effective development of the procedure. The present study has helped to identify the key areas of concern from a legal perspective, and it is hoped that the information provided can be utilised for effective development of the soft law and case law in the future.

4

Competitive dialogue in France

SYLVIA DE MARS AND FRÉDÉRIQUE OLIVIER

1. Introduction: regulation of public procurement in France

France has regulated state purchasing through hard law since 1833, when the first rules on state purchasing were introduced. Formal legal rules regulating public procurement existed from the early nineteenth century onwards, but the rules applicable to central government and non-central government were only consolidated in 1964, when the first Code des Marchés Publics (CMP, Public Procurement Contracts Code) entered into force.

The 1964 CMP contained rules for central government purchasing (Books 1 and 2) and non-central government purchasing (Books 3 and 4), and consisted of several hundred Articles that were frequently changed by amending decrees. As a founding member of the EU, from 1971 onwards the French government had to consider how the EU procurement Directives would fit in with this detailed and complex national legal approach.

The French government has attempted to integrate the EU requirements into the existing French national rules, supplementing them with additional rules and rewording them where and when appropriate. This approach to implementation, however, has become more difficult as the EU rules have become more detailed. To illustrate, transposition of the 1971 Works Directive[1] and the 1977 Supplies Directive[2] was accomplished by amending only a few provisions in the French CMP.[3] By contrast, the 1988 amended Works Directive[4] and Supplies

[1] Council Directive 71/305 of 21 July 1997 concerning the co-ordination of procedures for the award of public works contracts [1971] OJ L185.

[2] Council Directive 77/62 of 21 December 1976 co-ordinating procedures for the award of public supply contracts [1977] OJ L13/1.

[3] L. Richer, *Droit des Contrats Administratifs* (7th edn, Paris: LGJD, 2010), p. 357; see also Décret No. 79-98 du 12 janvier 1979 relatif à la mise en concurrence de certains marchés publics de travaux et de fournitures dans le cadre de la CEE.

[4] Directive 89/440 (amending Directive 71/305) [1989] OJ L210/1.

Directive[5] resulted in an entirely new fifth chapter in the CMP, dealing with 'European procurement'.[6]

Even this added chapter did not make the French CMP fully compliant with the EU requirements. Not all bodies considered 'public bodies' under the EU rules were considered public bodies under the CMP, which, for example, excluded specific French bodies such as mixed economy companies (categorised as 'private persons' in French law) or, for instance, the French National Bank (Banque de France) from its application.[7] To fully comply with EU law, a new law was introduced in 1991, to apply the EU rules to these relevant public bodies.[8] To date, these 'public bodies' are still regulated by separate pieces of legislation (namely, Ordinance No. 2005-649 of 6 June 2005) and have not been brought into the CMP.

Even more changes were required when additional and revised EU rules in 1993 made the 1964 CMP overly complex and difficult to use, and so, in 1996, the French government began work on a project to produce a new, simplified CMP. After five long years, in 2001, a new CMP was finally produced (Decree No. 2001-210 of 7 March 2001).[9] This CMP was both more compact and clarified numerous provisions. It also simplified procurement processes by introducing higher thresholds of application for formal procurement procedures, and focused on improving access for small and medium-sized enterprises (SMEs). The CMP made some important changes to the procurement procedures; most notably, it made *appel d'offres* (open or restricted procurement on the basis of 'most economically advantageous tender' basis) the default procurement procedure.[10]

The European Commission, however, found that the new CMP violated the Directives in a number of ways: importantly, certain types of

[5] Directive 88/295 (amending Directive 77/62) [1988] OJ L127/1.

[6] Décret No. 89-236 du 17 avril 1989 modifiant le code des marchés publics; and Décret No. 90-824 du 18 septembre 1990 modifiant le code des marchés publics.

[7] P. Valadou, 'Contracts of "Mixed Economy" Companies and Competitive Procedures in France' (1992) 1 *Public Procurement Law Review* 376, at 376.

[8] Loi No. 91-3 du 3 janvier 1991 relative à la transparence et à la régularité des procédures de marché et soumettant la passation de certains contrats à des règles de publicité et de mise en concurrence.

[9] See, for more information, Numéro special: Réforme du code des marchés publics (2001) 4 (avril) *Revue Contrats et Marchés Publics*, a special edition of *Revue Contrats et Marchés Publics* dedicated to the 2001 reform of the CMP.

[10] F. Olivier, 'L'appel d'offres rénové' (2001) 4 (avril) *Revue Contrats et Marchés Publics* 24, at 24.

contracts were excluded from formal tendering procedures where the Directive did not permit this, and the Directives' thresholds and publicity requirements were improperly implemented.[11]

On account of the Commission's complaint, another new CMP was produced in 2004. This CMP was more ambitious than the 2001 version; it was drafted to be very similar to the EU Directives, and liberalised public procurement regulation significantly by giving more freedom to individual contracting authorities.[12]

At the same time that the 2004 CMP was drafted, Directive 2004/18 was being debated in the EU. A key part of the proposals for the 2004 Directive was the introduction of a new procedure: competitive dialogue. In light of these proposals, the 2004 CMP introduced competitive dialogue[13] into French public procurement law – before the 2004 Directive had entered into force or had been transposed in France.

Unfortunately, the 2004 CMP was both the subject of a Commission complaint[14] and did not fully implement the rules of the 2004 Directive. In this context, a final revised CMP was produced in 2006. It contains rules on both contract award and contract execution for procurement covered by the Directives and procurement that falls below the Directive's thresholds but would otherwise be covered. An important point to make about the 2006 CMP is that it largely copies out the EU Directives *verbatim*, and has replaced pre-existing national rules on some subjects (such as framework agreements) with the EU rules;[15] this is a very different approach to implementing EU requirements than that previously adopted by France, where national rules were changed only insofar as this was needed for EU law compliance.

Currently, public procurement in France is regulated by the instruments set out in Table 4.1. Generally, it is also worth noting that the

[11] For details, see the Commission Press release IP/02/1507 of 17 October 2002.

[12] See, for more information, Reforme du code des marchés publics (2004) 2 (février) *Revue Contrats et Marchés Publics*; an issue of *Revue Contrats et Marchés Publics* dedicated to the 2004 reform of the CMP.

[13] P. Delelis, 'Le dialogue compétitif' (2004) 2 (février) *Revue Contrats et Marchés Publics* 46.

[14] See Commission Press Release IP 04/162 of 4 February 2004; the complaint focused on the CMP's failure to adhere to a 'minimum number invited' to a restricted procedure, and failure to comply with advertising requirements set out by *Telaustria* for Part II-B services by allowing these to *always* be awarded without publicity.

[15] See L. Folliot-Lalliot, 'The French Approach to Regulating Frameworks under the New EC Directives', Ch. 4 in S. Arrowsmith (ed.), *Reform of the UNCITRAL Model Law on Procurement: Procurement Regulation for the 21st Century* (Eagan, MN: West, 2010).

Table 4.1 *French public procurement laws applicable to central government purchasing*

Current (relevant) applicable legislation	Subject matter
CMP 2006 (last amended in September 2009)	Works, supplies and services procurement (regardless of contract value) of all 'public sector' bodies, excluding bodies that have special & exclusive rights.
Law No. 91-3 of 3 January 1991 (cancelled by Ordinance No. 2005-649 of 6 June 2005)[a]	Public bodies covered by the EU Directives but not covered by the CMP; works concessions. The procedural rules for contracts covered by these pieces of legislation are detailed in Decree No. 2005-1742 of 30 December 2005[b] and Decree No. 2005-1308 of 20 October 2005.[c]
Ordinance No. 2004-559 of 17 June 2004 on the *contrats de partenariat* (as modified by Law No. 2008-735 of 28 July 2008[d] (which has substantially modified and improved the PPP regulatory framework) and Law No. 2009-179 of 17 February 2009[e] (which, in part, has attempted to make *contrats de partenariat* more attractive and adapted to user needs, so as to stimulate their award during the global economic crisis)	Public Private Partnership (PPP) contracts that are covered by the EU Directives (depending on value); these are known in France as *contrats de partenariat.* The procedural rules for contracts covered by these pieces of legislation are detailed in Decree No. 2005-953 of 9 August 2005,[f] Decree No. 2005-1740 of 30 December 2005[g] and Decree No. 2009-243 of 2 March 2009.[h] Some *circulaires* have also been issued as guidelines on how to best use the *contrats de partenariat* legal framework; particularly relevant is the Circulaires of 29 November 2005, which contains explanations of how to use competitive dialogue to award these contracts.

Notes:

[a] Ordonnance No. 2005-649 du 6 juin 2005 relative aux marchés passés par certaines personnes publiques ou privées non soumises au code des marchés publics.

[b] Décret No. 2005-1742 du 30 décembre 2005 fixant les règles applicables aux marchés passés par les pouvoirs adjudicateurs mentionnés à l'article 3 de

Notes to Table 4.1 (*cont.*)

l'Ordonnance No. 2005-649 du 6 juin 2005 relative aux marchés passés par certaines personnes publiques ou privées non soumises au code des marchés publics.

[c] Décret No. 2005-1308 du 20 octobre 2005 relatif aux marchés passés par les entités adjudicatrices mentionnées à l'article 4 de l'Ordonnance No. 2005-649 du 6 juin 2005 relative aux marchés passés par certaines personnes publiques ou privées non soumises au code des marchés publics.

[d] Loi No. 2008-735 du 28 juillet 2008 relative aux contrats de partenariat.

[e] Loi No. 2009-179 du 17 février 2009 pour l'accélération des programmes de construction et d'investissement publics et privés.

[f] Décret No. 2005-953 du 9 août 2005 portant modification du Décret No. 2004-1145 du 27 octobre 2004 pris en application des articles 3, 4, 7 et 13 de l'Ordonnance No. 2004-559 du 17 juin 2004 sur les contrats de partenariat et L.1414-3, L.1414-4 et L.1414-10 du code général des collectivités territoriales.

[g] Décret No. 2005-1740 du 30 décembre 2005 modifiant le Décret No. 2004-1145 du 27 octobre 2004 pris en application des articles 3, 4, 7 et 13 de l'Ordonnance No. 2004-559 du 17 juin 2004 sur les contrats de partenariat et modifiant l'article D.1414-1 du code général des collectivités territoriales.

[h] Décret No. 2009-243 du 2 mars 2009 relatif à la procédure de passation et certaines modalités d'exécution des contrats de partenariat passés par l'Etat et ses établissements publics ainsi que les personnes mentionnées aux articles 19 et 25 de l'Ordonnance No. 2004-559 du 17 juin 2004.

CMP 2006 imposes obligations of equal treatment, non-discrimination, and transparency as well as freedom to contract on all national procurement procedures, regardless of their value, in order to open up public procurement to competition.

Procurement contracts are treated as administrative contracts in France, and are hence subject to administrative law; consequently, the relevant courts that deal with procurement disputes are administrative courts and tribunals, with the Conseil d'Etat acting as the highest court of appeal. France sees hundreds of procurement disputes go to court every year. An added interesting fact is that the Conseil d'Etat has frequently been involved in disputes about the validity of the non-EU rules in the CMP, and has on occasions struck down parts of the French legislation.

2. The background: complex procurement prior to competitive dialogue

As Chapter 1 has discussed (see section 3 of that chapter), the competitive dialogue procedure was introduced on account of a European-wide demand for a greater possibility for contracting authorities to enter into a dialogue with bidders on complex contracts in public sector contract awards.

In light of this perceived need, France had, in its pre-2004 legislation, a procedure comparable to competitive dialogue in place: neither the freely available open/restricted procedure in the form in which they had been generally implemented in the French legislation, nor the negotiated procedure was perceived as suitable to procure certain types of complex projects. The French legislator therefore introduced a new national procedure, considered as a variant of the EU's restricted procedure, which gave more flexibility than the more general version of the restricted procedure that had been adopted in the French legislation. This French approach of introducing a separate procedure in legislation for complex procedure can be contrasted with the approach taken to many complex contracts in the UK (see section 2 of Chapter 3), which developed a practice similar to that of competitive dialogue through its practice in operating the negotiated procedure, steered by government guidance.

This French 'complex procurement' procedure, referred to as *l'appel d'offres sur performances* (literally, a 'call for tenders on performance'), was first introduced by Decree No. 93-733 of 27 March 1993[16] and retained in the 2001 CMP, in Article 36.[17] This procedure was first proposed in a report from the Commission on the Prevention of Corruption.[18]

Article 36 of the 2001 CMP described the procedure as follows:

> [T]he *appel d'offres sur performance* is a procedure by which contracting authorities define a descriptive document, taking the form of *verifiable results to obtain* or of *needs to satisfy*. Means to obtain these results or to satisfy these needs are proposed by each candidate in his tender.[19]

[16] Décret No. 93-733 du 27 mars 1993.

[17] Richer, *Droit des Contrats Administratifs*, n. 3 above, pp. 462 *et seq.*

[18] La commission de prévention de la corruption, *Rapport de la commission de prévention de la corruption* (Documentation française: 1993); the rapport is known as the 'Rapport Bouchery'.

[19] La procédure d'appel d'offres sur performances est une procédure par laquelle la personne responsable du marché définit un programme fonctionnel détaillé, sous la forme de résultats vérifiables à atteindre ou de besoins à satisfaire. Les moyens de

Such a procedure enabled the contracting authority to ask for both detailed solutions to its problems and the details of execution of the proposed projects, for either all of or part of its recognised needs.

In 2001, the new Code des Marchés Publics restricted the availability and scope of the procedure. It first of all put in place a new definition of the procedure that aimed to stop contracting authorities from being able to combine various proposed solutions into a 'preferred' solution without their consent. Such a prohibition can also be found in the 2004 Directive; the French legislation on the *appel d'offres sur performances* in this respect may have influenced the phrasing of the Directive.

Secondly, the procedure under the 2001 CMP could be used by contracting authorities only in two cases:

(1) when they were not able to define the means to satisfy their needs; or
(2) when they were not able to identify technical or financial solutions available.[20]

Since, as we have noted, the *appel d'offres sur performances* was intended as a specific variant of the restricted procedure, there are many aspects of the procedure that are more similar to the restricted procedure than to competitive dialogue or to the even more flexible negotiated procedure, as can be seen from Table 4.2. Competitive dialogue, on the other hand, clearly is not a 'variant' of the restricted procedure, including in that it gives contracting authorities the opportunity to organise free discussions with candidate tenderers, and candidate tenderers submit proposals and solutions before submitting 'final tenders'.

As we have already noted in section 1 above, when the CMP was revised in 2004, the old *appel d'offres sur performances* was simply replaced by competitive dialogue. In the years since then, as Chapter 2 explains in detail, competitive dialogue has been used on a steadily increasing basis in France, while a decline in the use of the negotiated procedure has also been observed (see section 4.5 below). This may show that the EU's competitive dialogue procedure has in fact replaced both *appel d'offres sur performances* and the negotiated procedure, either completely or in part.

parvenir à ces résultats ou de répondre à ces besoins sont proposés par chaque candidat dans son offre.

[20] Comments on use of the procedure for these two grounds could be found in the 'Instruction pour l'application du code des marchés publics du 28 août 2001', an explanatory memorandum accompanying the 2001 CMP.

Table 4.2 *A comparison between the French 'appel d'offres sur performances' procedure and competitive dialogue*

Procedure	Minimum number of candidates required to be invited to participate?	Is it possible to discuss outline offers with the candidates?	Is there a possibility to reduce the number of bidders during the procedure?	Availability of procedure
France: *appel d'offres sur performance*	5 (as with restricted procedure)	No: initial bid submission and subsequent 'clarify/specify/fine-tune'	No	When contracting authority cannot identify means to meet its needs; cannot assess the technical or financial solutions available.
EU/France: competitive dialogue	3	Yes; proposals submitted during the dialogue (before final tenders) can be discussed	Yes, through eliminating 'solutions'	'Particularly complex contract' (where contracting authorities cannot identify the means to meet its needs or cannot assess technical/financial solutions available). For PPP, when technical/legal/financial complexity prevents contracting authorities from identifying the means necessary to meet its needs.

Table 4.2 outlines the French *appel d'offres sur performances* and compares it to competitive dialogue. The table reveals that, when it comes to the wording of the competitive dialogue provisions in the Directive, the French procedure appears to be a precedent to some degree for, *inter alia*, the concept of a 'particularly complex contract' and what can be done post-bid submission (clarifying, specifying and fine-tuning).

Generally, competitive dialogue offers more flexibility than the French adaptation of the restricted procedure ever did, first, because it is an autonomous procedure (rather than a variant of the restricted procedure), and, secondly, because it allows greater discussion, fewer bidders to be involved, and bidders to be eliminated in stages.

3. Introduction to competitive dialogue in France

Competitive dialogue was first made available in France in anticipation of the 2004 Directive (in the 2004 CMP, which entered into force on 10 January 2004), before the Directive was even finally adopted on 31 March 2004. It was then included in the 2006 CMP through transposition of the 2004 Directive.

As noted in section 2 of this chapter, there were similarities between competitive dialogue and the pre-existing French procedure called *l'appel d'offres sur performances*, both designed to help contracting authorities in the procurement of complex contracts where the means to satisfy their needs were not known. As we have mentioned, the latter procedure was repealed following the 2004 introduction of competitive dialogue.

The difference between the current rules and the 2004 CMP's provisions is that below the Directive's thresholds (for services and supplies contracts) and between €230,000 and €5.9 million (for works contracts), competitive dialogue in France could be used freely. Above the Directive's thresholds, however, competitive dialogue could only be used when the requirements of complexity for the contract, fixed by the CMP (and the Directive), were met. This ability to 'freely' use competitive dialogue, however, no longer exists (see section 4.1.1).

Currently, competitive dialogue is first of all found in the CMP, where it is made available to both central government and non-central government authorities. It is also available in the CMP regardless of the value of the contract, and can thus be used for both contracts covered by the Directive and contracts below the Directive's thresholds.

Secondly, there are additional rules in place outside of the CMP that also transpose the competitive dialogue procedure. As section 1 explained, the CMP does not cover all contracting entities to which the EU rules apply. Consequently, competitive dialogue is also included in Ordinance No. 2005-649 and Decree No. 2005-1742, which contain the rules on 'private and public law' bodies that are not subject to the CMP but subject to the EU procurement rules.

Furthermore, competitive dialogue has been made available for the procurement of other public contracts that are principally covered by the Directive (depending on their value), namely:

(1) *Contrats de partenariat.* These are public–private partnership (works and/or services) contracts that follow a design-build-finance-operate (DBFO) structure. Relevant for our discussion is the Ordinance that contains the rules for *contrats de partenariat*, which is Ordinance No. 2004-559. The provisions of this Ordinance relevant to local public authorities have been integrated in the Local Authorities Code (Code Général des Collectivités Territoriales, Arts. L.1414-4 to L.1414-7), which now contains almost the same rules for the procurement of *contrats de partenariat* (in Book IV, Title 1, Chapter 4).

(2) *Baux emphytéotiques hospitaliers* (BEH), long-term leasehold contracts for the provision of hospital infrastructure. Public 'land' is leased to a private party at a 'peppercorn' rent, on the condition that the private party builds (and possibly maintains) public facilities. The rules on using competitive dialogue to award these types of contracts are found in the Public Health Code (Code de la Santé Publique, Article L.6148-5).

(3) *Baux emphytéotiques administratifs* (BEAs), long-term leasehold contracts granted by central government, which grant permits over public land coupled with the obligation to build facilities which the state will then rent with the benefit of an early purchase option. This structure of purchasing, referred to as AOT/LOA (*autorisation d'occupation temporaire/location avec option d'achat*; authorisation for temporary occupation/location with option to buy), has been awarded for the construction and management of prisons and facilities to be used by the judiciary, the police and the *gendarmerie.* The rules on using competitive dialogue to award these types of contracts are found in the General Public Property Code (Code Général de la Propriété des Personnes Publiques, Article L.21222-15) and Decree No. 2004-18 of 6 January 2004.[21]

[21] Décret No. 2004-18 du 6 janvier 2004 pris pour l'application de l'article L.34-3-1 du code du domaine de l'Etat.

In all these pieces of legislation, the Directive's rules on competitive dialogue are copied out nearly *verbatim*. The procedure can thus be used with all the flexibility offered by the Directive for all contracts covered by these pieces of legislation and by all contracting authorities covered by these pieces of legislation – although it should be stressed here that competitive dialogue has *not* been made available for bodies operating in the utilities sector.[22]

The approach to transposition taken is striking in light of the general approach to French procurement legislation prior to 2004, where most EU requirements were supplemented with complex and additional national-level rules, and wholly separate 'national' procedures such as *l'appel d'offres sur performance* existed. The 2004 Directive's provisions replace this pre-existing procedure and are transposed with very few changes or additions; there are slight differences in wording between the CMP's provisions on the one hand, and those in secondary pieces of legislation on the other, but these do not alter the substance of the rules.

Thus far, the French administrative courts have seen a few, but not an overwhelming number of cases on competitive dialogue. Most of the disputes concerned problems with the award decisions (such as whether the best tenderer was indeed awarded the contract), although, in at least two instances, the Conseil d'Etat specifically considered the CMP provisions on competitive dialogue (see the discussions in section 5).

There is some guidance issued on competitive dialogue by the French government, generally summarising the provisions in the CMP; such guidance is found for instance in the Guide de Bonnes Pratiques[23] issued in 2009 to elaborate on the rules in the CMP. Of more interest is the guidance issued in 2007 by the Mouvement des Entreprises de France (French Confederation of Business Enterprises, MEDEF), which considers practical approaches to competitive dialogue and thus goes beyond the scope of either the EU or French legislative provisions.[24]

Other guidance material has also been produced:

[22] These are also covered by the CMP and Ordonnance No. 2005-649, but in wholly separate 'chapters' – and competitive dialogue has not been transposed into these 'chapters'.

[23] Circulaire du 29 décembre 2009 relative au Guide de bonnes pratiques en matière de marchés publics (JO No. 0303, 31 décembre 2009).

[24] MEDEF, 'Guide du dialogue compétitif' (March 2007), http://archive.medef.com/medias/files/114468_FICHIER_0.pdf.

(1) *Charte du dialogue compétitif.*[25] This document considers the use of competitive dialogue for public purchasing in the case of complex projects. It was prepared by the Assembly of French Départements, the Association of French Mayors (AMF), the Association of French Regions, the French Institute for PPP (l'Institut de la gestion déléguée (IGD)) and the Support Office for the Implementation of Contrats de Partenariat (la Mission d'appui à la réalisation des contrats de partenariat (MAPPP)).
(2) The MAPPP itself has also issued guidance documents, importantly, 'Les Contrats de partenariat et l'intangibilité des groupements candidats'[26] (addressing the question of what happens when a consortium changes membership during a competitive dialogue) and 'Gestion de la fin du dialogue compétitif'[27] (a note addressing the management of the end of the competitive dialogue procedure, once the dialogue has closed).
(3) Finally, the French government has issued a Circular on 29 November 2005[28] which discusses use of competitive dialogue for awarding PPP contracts.

In terms of use of competitive dialogue, we have seen in Chapter 2 that, in the years up to 2010, France has been the heaviest user of the competitive dialogue procedure. In the years from 2006 to 2009, France saw 1,446 competitive dialogue procedures. It is also worth noting in terms of absolute numbers that the figures of use have increased moderately in each year examined. Section 4 will discuss French use of competitive dialogue in more detail.

4. Scope of the competitive dialogue procedure in law and practice

4.1. *Legal rules on the scope of competitive dialogue*

4.1.1. The CMP

The CMP 2006's provisions on competitive dialogue are found in Articles 36 and 67 (last modified by Decree No. 2008-1355 of 19 December 2008,

[25] IGD, 'Charte du dialogue competitive' (18 January 2007).
[26] MAPPP, 'Les contrats de partenariat et l'intangibilité des groupements candidats' (February 2009).
[27] MAPPP, 'Gestion de la fin du dialogue compétitif' (October 2006).
[28] Circulaire du 29 novembre 2005 relative aux contrats de partenariat à l'attention des collectivités territoriales (JORF No. 291 du 15 décembre 2005, p. 19271).

Article 4), and, minor word changes aside, do not generally differ greatly from those found in the Directive.

Article 36 defines the competitive dialogue procedure as a procedure through which a contracting authority manages a dialogue with selected candidates with the aim to define or develop one or several solutions adapted to satisfy its needs and on which basis participants in the dialogue will be invited to present a tender; it is available only when contracts are 'particularly complex'.[29] The CMP's definition of 'particularly complex', in Article 36, provides that competitive dialogue is available where contracting authorities are objectively not capable of defining, *alone and in advance*, the technical means to satisfy their needs.[30] This potentially widens the scope of availability of the procedure from the wording of the Directive, which does not qualify 'objective incapability' by the phrase 'alone and in advance'; however, the actual effect of this change in wording has not yet been examined by either the French courts or the CJEU.

It is worth recalling that, until 19 December 2008, competitive dialogue *could* be freely used (i.e. without a requirement for particular complexity) below the thresholds of the Directive under the CMP. This, however, is no longer possible, bringing the CMP's provisions even more closely into line with those in the Directive.

The permitted scope of competitive dialogue under the Directive itself was discussed in Chapter 1, in section 4 of that chapter. Although the general approach in the French provisions is simply to repeat the wording of the Directive, the CMP contains two interesting additions to the rules contained in the Directive.

First, while the Directive refers to the possibility to make bid payments in complex procurement in the abstract, the French CMP in Article 67 contains a further instruction on how to operate bid payments. This provision will be discussed further in section 5.9.

A second addition relates to coverage of the procedure. The CMP contains provisions applicable to specific *types* of contracts; an example of this is the so-called *marchés de conception-realisation* procedure which applies to public works contracts that contain both a design and a build element. These generally are awarded using a modified restricted

[29] S. Lagumina and L. Deruy, 'L'ordonnance relative au contrat de partenariat: Dépasser la polémique' (2004) 36 (septembre), BJCP 348.

[30] Art. 36, para. 1: 'Le pouvoir adjudicateur n'est objectivement pas en mesure de définir seul et à l'avance les moyens techniques pouvant répondre à ses besoins.'

procedure (discussed in Article 69 of the CMP), but Article 69(II) also indicates that, where such a 'design and build' contract relates to the restoration of buildings and the conditions for use of competitive dialogue are met, the competitive dialogue procedure may be used instead. It is worth emphasising that France did not have to make competitive dialogue available for *marchés de conception-realisation*, which are (as mentioned) otherwise awarded using a restricted procedure (compatible with the Directive).

Thirdly, it is worth highlighting that the provisions on competitive dialogue in the CMP apply to contracts both above *and below* the Directive's thresholds. Use of competitive dialogue for below-threshold contracts is, as of 19 December 2008, subjected to the same rules as those that apply to above-threshold contracts (see section 1).

However, the CMP also makes a different and far more flexible procedure available for below-threshold procurement. This procedure, called the *procédure adaptée*, allows for unrestricted negotiation as part of the award process (conditional upon respect for the principles of equal treatment and transparency, satisfied by a requirement to inform candidates of the form of negotiation due to take place). We can see that the *procedure adaptée* offers greater flexibility than competitive dialogue as described in Article 67 of the CMP.

The fact that the *procédure adaptée* can be used freely below the Directive's thresholds suggests that, while competitive dialogue is available for below-threshold contracts, it is likely that it will not be used frequently (except when, for complexity reasons, the contracting authority cannot draft specifications to meet its needs); however, this does not preclude that the *procédure adaptée* can potentially be modelled on competitive dialogue in a more flexible form.

It is here also helpful to delineate the differences between the negotiated procedure, as implemented in the CMP 2006, and the competitive dialogue procedure. Admittedly, both procedures are similar in the sense that they permit discussions between contracting authorities and candidates – but there are substantial differences as well. The negotiated procedure, in the CMP 2006, requires formal tenders at the first step and then permits negotiation on these tenders prior to contract award; competitive dialogue, on the other hand, arranges for discussions to take place before the issuing of formal 'final' tenders, and then severely limits what can be done after these have been issued (as required by the Directive: see sections 5.7 and 5.8 of Chapter 1).

Finally, some public works contracts that are subject to both the CMP 2006 and Law No. 85-704 of 12 July 1985[31] (the Law on Public Works Control (LOI MOP), dealing with the situation where a private party acts as project manager for a public building project) may not be awarded by competitive dialogue under the CMP.[32]

4.1.2. AOT/LOA and BEH

Article 12 of the Decree No. 2004-18 permits AOT/LOA types of leasehold contracts to be concluded using competitive dialogue if they are sufficiently complex. The definition of complexity is identical to that found in the CMP (see section 4.1.1 above). In outlining the competitive dialogue process, Articles 12 and 13 of Decree No. 2004-18 copy out the CMP 2006 provisions on competitive dialogue without changes.

BEH contracts, on the other hand, can be awarded using competitive dialogue on the basis of the rules contained in Ordinance No. 2004-559 on *contrats de partenariat*; Article L.6148-5 of the Public Health Code refers readers to Article 7 of the Ordinance if the project meets the Ordinance's definitions of 'complexity'. The rules applicable to *contrats de partenariat* will be discussed in section 4.1.4 below.

4.1.3. Ordinance No. 2005-649

As discussed in section 3 above, competitive dialogue is also made available to bodies covered by the Directives but not covered by the CMP (such as 'private law' bodies that exercise public functions). Again, the wording of the Ordinance applicable to these contracts is largely identical to both the wording of the CMP and the Directive.

Here, too, the procedure is principally made available to contracts both above and below the Directive's thresholds. However, the conditions for use for contracts that fall below the Directive's thresholds are phrased very differently in the 2005 Ordinance than they are in the CMP.

[31] Loi No. 85-704 du 12 juillet 1985 portant sur les relations entre la maîtrise d'ouvrage publique et la maîtrise d'œuvre privée.

[32] Under the LOI MOP, certain types of projects (for example, for 'buildings') require very exacting project specifications before they can be concluded; this conflicts with the idea of a 'particularly complex contract', which (as discussed) is a contract where exact specifications cannot be set. In other cases, such as complex building/infrastructure projects (e.g. the building of a sewage disposal plant), the LOI MOP (under Art. 10) permits consultation on various elements of technical design; here, competitive dialogue is permissible.

Contracting authorities covered by these rules, rather than the CMP, do not have to use any of the 'formal' procedures (i.e. the EU procedures) for procurement below the Directive's thresholds.[33] It is stated that, *unless a formal award procedure is used* for contracts below the threshold, only very limited contract specifications are required.[34] As there is full freedom to use a 'non-formal' procedure to award below-threshold contracts under the Ordinance, it would seem that contracting authorities are free to use an 'amended' version of competitive dialogue that does not necessarily comply with any requirements on complexity or has less rigid rules on, for instance, negotiation after submission of bids.

4.1.4. Contrats de partenariat (Ordinance No. 2004-559)

As mentioned in section 3, *contrats de partenariat* in France are subject to separate legislation. Ordinance No. 2004-559 sets out the rules to be followed when awarding this particular type of public–private partnership (PPP) contract.[35] These PPP contracts are works and services contracts in EU terms – depending on their value, these may thus be covered by the Directive. The concept of 'PPP', however, does not cover works or services concession agreements, which are regulated in separate pieces of legislation and are procured using more flexible procedures than competitive dialogue.[36]

The standard method of procurement of PPP contracts set out in this Ordinance is the 'dialogue'. The process of the 'dialogue' is nearly identical to competitive dialogue as presented in the CMP and the Directive; it is also available for *contrats de partenariat* regardless of their value. However, there are some differences.

[33] The detailed procedural rules applicable to contracting authorities covered by Ordonnance No. 2005-649 are found in Décret No. 2005-1742 du 30 décembre 2005 fixant les règles applicables aux marchés passés par les pouvoirs adjudicateurs mentionnés à l'article 3 de l'ordonnance No. 2005-649 du 6 juin 2005 relative aux marchés passés par certaines personnes publiques ou privées non soumises au code des marchés publics.

[34] Art. 10 of Décret No. 2005-1742.

[35] Relevant provisions for local government (which are identical) are, as of 2009, found in the Local Authorities Code. See Loi No. 2009-179 du 17 février 2009 pour l'accélération des programmes de construction et d'investissement publics et privés (1), which moved the provisions from the Ordonnance to the local authorities code.

[36] See Loi No. 93-122 (n 575) and Ordonnance No. 2009-864 (n 598).

One of these is the conditions for use. All potential *contrats de partenariat* are subject to a prior assessment of several conditions: the complexity and urgency of the project and any potential benefits from using the *contrats de partenariat* contract form are assessed before contracts can even be advertised as *contrats de partenariat.*

When the *contrats de partenariat* is found to be a justifiable choice of contract on the basis of the legal and financial complexity of the project, the contracting authority *must* use the competitive dialogue procedure under the rules of the Ordinance (Article 7).

As most *contrats de partenariat* will be legally and financially complex, availability of competitive dialogue is almost inherent to these contracts; if *contrats de partenariat* are *not* legally or financially complex, they can only be awarded in the event of urgency (using the restricted procedure).

A further point of note is that a modification to the 2004 Ordinance by a 2008 Act has made the negotiated procedure with a notice freely available for the procurement of PPP contracts below a certain threshold (set by decree).[37] The negotiated procedure is more flexible than competitive dialogue, meaning that competitive dialogue may not formally be used for these below-threshold contracts in practice.

On the subject of when *contrats de partenariat* are complex enough to warrant use of competitive dialogue for award, the MAPPP outlines a few scenarios:[38] for instance, complexity arises from uncertainty about the final funding structure of the proposed project and how risk can be optimally set between the private and public sectors (the MAPPP notes that this is frequently a difficulty for inexperienced local authorities that engage in complex purchasing), or from trying to minimize public expenditure by forcing the private sector to develop the land on which the public infrastructure is meant to be built.

[37] The actual rules on this are in Art. 5 of Décret No. 2009-243 du 2 mars 2009 relatif à la procédure de passation et à certaines modalités d'exécution des contrats de partenariat passés par l'Etat et ses établissements publics ainsi que les personnes mentionnées aux articles 19 et 25 de l'ordonnance No. 2004-559 du 17 juin 2004. The Décret indicates that the negotiated procedure can be used for below-EU threshold contracts as long as the primary goal of the contract is to conceptualise and/or build a public work that meets the needs that the public authority has set out; if this is not the goal, the negotiated procedure becomes available below €133,000.

[38] MAPPP, 'Urgence, complexité et efficience économique' (28 septembre 2010).

4.2. *Guidance on use of the procedure*

The Ministry of Economics (MinEFE)[39] and the 'Bercy Colloc'[40] (for non-central government) websites offer numerous guidance documents on competitive dialogue which reiterate the rules in either the CMP or the Directive, but do not expand on them. This is also the case for the 2009 Guide de Bonnes Pratiques issued alongside the CMP, which discusses the content of Article 67 but does not elaborate on it greatly. More useful are the guidance pieces issued by the MAPPP, mentioned in section 3 above, which offer more focused and detailed information on the use of the procedure.

Also interesting is the guidance provided by MEDEF, mentioned in section 3 above. This guidance clearly illustrates the different conditions for use of competitive dialogue for public contracts on the one hand, and *contrats de partenariat* on the other. It further offers significant advice on the practical operation of a competitive dialogue procedure for either of these types of contracts; all these guidance documents will be discussed in section 5, where appropriate.

4.3. *Use of the procedure in practice*

As Chapter 2 discussed, France saw 1,430 competitive dialogue contract notices between 2006 and 2009; this excludes any contract notices advertised under the 2004 CMP, which also made competitive dialogue available.

Chapter 2 also revealed that most contract notices originated from local government authorities and bodies operating in the health sector. It was seen that competitive dialogue has been predominantly used for the award of ICT contracts relating to medical imaging and patient files; it has also commonly been used for the purchasing of public lighting installations and 'urban furniture' in local communities, explaining why these two authorities were the heaviest users of the procedure. Interestingly, France has not used competitive dialogue for infrastructure nearly as much as the UK has done (see Chapter 2), nor has it advertised the same kinds of infrastructure projects. While hospital construction was quite common, housing and schools projects were not discovered in these notices.

[39] www.minefe.gouv.fr/directions_services/daj/marches_publics/presentation-mp/marches_publics.htm.

[40] www.colloc.bercy.gouv.fr/colo_struct_marc_publ/index.html.

Finally, Chapter 2 showed that 9 per cent of all contracts advertised as competitive dialogue procedures were *contrats de partenariat*; this made *contrats de partenariat* by far the most common PPP-type contract structure that was awarded using competitive dialogue.

4.4. *Availability for contracts not covered by the Directives*

As we have already seen in section 4.1, the main pieces of legislation covered in this chapter make competitive dialogue available for contracts below the Directive's thresholds. In all three cases, the competitive dialogue procedure is again only available for 'particularly complex' contracts; however, public bodies covered by Ordinance No. 2005-649 can also use non-formal procurement procedures, and thus retain the option of modelling an award process on competitive dialogue without formally using competitive dialogue. Similarly, *contrats de partenariat* can be awarded using the negotiated procedure below the Directive's thresholds – but contracting authorities could opt to use some of the structure of competitive dialogue when using the negotiated procedure for these contracts.

Generally, it is worth highlighting that competitive dialogue has not been made available in legislation for concession agreements (see section 4.1.3) or utilities contracts, regardless of whether they are covered by the CMP or by Ordinance No. 2005-649. Concession agreements can be awarded using more flexible procedures than competitive dialogue, possibly suggesting that there is no need to introduce competitive dialogue for these contracts. Similarly, utilities contracts can freely be awarded using the negotiated procedure, which is also more flexible than competitive dialogue.

4.5. *Decline of the negotiated procedure?*

Despite the fact that in France competitive dialogue was introduced as a replacement for the *appel d'offres sur performances* procedure rather than as an alternative to the negotiated procedure as it was elsewhere, the introduction of competitive dialogue may have had an effect on use of the negotiated procedure as well.

A search of contract notices on the Tenders Electronic Daily (TED) website suggests that, during the years 2006–9, use of the negotiated procedure with a notice for public contracts *not awarded by utilities* has decreased:

Table 4.3 *Use of the negotiated procedure for the award of public contracts in France*

Year	Number of negotiated procedure notices
2006	2,878
2007	2,604
2008	2,271
2009	1,746

In considering these figures, it must be considered that their reliability depends on the accuracy of contracting authorities in completing contract notices – for instance, a utility that does not indicate that it is a utility would be filed as 'other' and be counted in these figures. However, even considering that there may be a slight margin of error (consisting of 'counted' utilities), these figures do show that use of the negotiated procedure from 2006 onwards is strongly declining. This may or may not be related to the introduction of competitive dialogue – the increase in use of competitive dialogue discussed in Chapter 2 of about 100 notices per year do not match up to the almost 1,000-notice decrease for negotiated procedures that we see between 2006 and 2009.

Some possible explanations for these numbers can be offered, however. First, regarding availability of the negotiated procedure itself, each successive revision of the CMP has made the procedure less available – by 2006, the conditions for its use have become quite stringent (both through legislation and case law interpretations). An added factor here is that the thresholds of recent CMPs have increased significantly, making more flexible procedures (such as the *procédure adaptée*) more generally available. These factors together may have reduced interest in the use of the negotiated procedure.

Secondly, it is worth noting that competitive dialogue itself is very often used for contracts that cover exceptionally long periods or need to be periodically renewed; this may account for the gradual (rather than sharp) increase of competitive dialogue.

5. Operation of the competitive dialogue procedure

5.1. Introduction

As discussed in section 4, the provisions on the competitive dialogue process found in the CMP and in the Ordinances do not differ greatly from those in the Directive. In terms of scope and flexibility, all provisions offering flexibility in the Directive are retained; similarly, restrictions in the Directive – such as the need for a 'particularly complex contract' – are also retained for procurement below the thresholds of the Directive.

The procedural rules that govern competitive dialogue under the Directive itself were discussed in section 5 of Chapter 1 of this book. The main steps of the procedure in France follow those of the Directive, as repeated in the French legislation:

(1) The procedure commences with an advertising process and the selection of the candidates admitted to the competitive dialogue.
(2) Secondly, the dialogue itself is organised. In practice, the authors' experience with working with the procedure has revealed that this is often done using several phases, and with the possibility to eliminate some proposed solutions and candidates as the dialogue continues (as is permitted, but not required, by the legal rules).
(3) Thirdly, the end of the dialogue is announced alongside an invitation to submit final offers.
(4) Finally, the contract is awarded and finalised with the winning tenderer.

There is no awareness among either author of this chapter of a 'standard' approach to competitive dialogue in practice beyond the skeletal procedure outlined above.

5.2. *The planning stage and drafting of the descriptive document*

Much like the Directive (see section 5.2 of Chapter 1), French legislation does not comment on the subject of planning or preparation. Planning for a competitive dialogue is left to the discretion of individual contracting authorities by law; the authors are not aware of any standard practice in the planning stage, and consequently cannot comment on this issue generally. The MEDEF guidance also does not address planning or preparation significantly, only noting that it would be desirable for the contracting authority to appoint a project manager to oversee the entire dialogue process as it can take a number of months to complete.[41]

[41] MEDEF, n. 32 above, p. 9.

5.3. *Confidentiality of information and solutions*

As further discussed in section 5.3 of Chapter 1, Article 29(3) of Directive 2004/18 prohibits contracting authorities from sharing candidates' solutions or their other confidential information without candidates' consent. All three relevant pieces of legislation cite Article 29(3) on confidentiality of information and solutions without making any additions. The issue of confidentiality has thus far not been considered in case law concerning competitive dialogue.

The MEDEF guidance recites both Article 29 and the relevant Articles in national legislation that cite these principles; it also stresses that contracting authorities should ensure that intellectual property is protected at all costs, as otherwise bidders will not participate in the process. MEDEF recommends that the contracting authority involved in a competitive dialogue thus ensures strict confidentiality of all solutions and keeps separate, documented records of all parts of the dialogue (both written submissions and oral submissions).[42]

In practice, two main principles apply to the maintaining of confidentiality:

(1) First, there is a general principle of confidentiality that applies to the entire dialogue process. Generally, the contracting authority will ask anyone participating in the competitive dialogue process to sign a non-disclosure agreement.
(2) Secondly, there is the added obligation for the contracting authority not to combine solutions from different candidates without their permission (i.e. the ban on 'cherry-picking'). French companies, through MEDEF and other professional federations, have been lobbying to include an express prohibition of cherry-picking practices in the French rules. Where contracting authorities opt to draft a 'common solution' on the basis of various proposed solutions and have tenderers bid on this, this has to be done with the permission of the candidates (see section 5.5).

It is generally understood by contracting authorities that the burden of taking measures to preserve confidentiality falls on the contracting authorities, as non-compliance could result in an illegal contract award. To date, there have been no reported problems of contracting authorities failing to adhere to the ban on cherry-picking.

[42] *Ibid.*, p. 10.

5.4. *Advertising requirements (contract notice etc.)*

The requirements on advertising competitive dialogue procedures under the Directive were noted in section 5.4 of Chapter 1. The CMP's advertising rules[43] (for all contracts, including those awarded by competitive dialogue) are significantly more onerous than those listed in the 2004 Directive, with different outputs being mandatory at different values from €4,000 upwards. Above €4,000, some form of advertising is mandatory but the location of the advertisement can be chosen freely by the contracting authority. Between €90,000 and the EU thresholds, all contracts *have* to be advertised in either the French *Bulletin Officiel* (Official Journal) for public contracts, or in a different journal accustomed to receiving 'legal notices'. From January 2010 onwards, these contracts also have to be advertised on the contracting authority's purchaser profile (on the Internet).

Above the EU thresholds, all contracts have to be advertised in the *Bulletin Officiel*, the OJEU and on the purchaser profile. It should be emphasised that the described rules apply to *all* contracts covered by the CMP – there are thus no specific rules for advertising competitive dialogue contracts.

Contracts covered by Ordinance No. 2005-649 are again subject to a different rule; here, advertising is mandatory in the event a 'formal procedure' is used, and advertising has to take place in the OJEU.[44] This is again irrespective of award procedure, but does apply to competitive dialogue contracts. It is noted that contracts may also be advertised in other (additional) journals to the OJEU, but this is not made mandatory as it is under the CMP.

Contrats de partenariat have to generally be advertised in such a way as to provide genuine (and sufficient) competition – below the EU thresholds this is left to the contracting authority to determine on the basis of the value and nature of the contract. All *contrats de partenariat* above the EU thresholds for services and supplies have to be advertised in the OJEU and the *Bulletin Officiel*. Publication in additional journals is also permitted.[45]

Advertising, in France, is deemed to be especially important in competitive dialogue because of the absence of rules on how to organise the dialogue. The contract notice thus provides the framework that will have to be adhered to throughout the procedure.

[43] Art. 39 of the 2006 CMP. [44] Art. 16(II) of Décret No. 2005-1742.
[45] Art. I of Décret No. 2009-243.

For *contrats de partenariat* and *baux emphytéotiques hospitaliers*, it is particularly important to set out appropriate award criteria in the contract notice; imperative criteria are the global cost of the proposed tender, performance requirements, and how much of the contract is to be set aside for SMEs. Here, contracting authorities can also specify that they are looking for particular elements, such as innovative tenders.

A final point is that, in France, the notices used to advertise competitive dialogue contracts generally comply with both national (CMP) and EU standards (Directive) for contract notices, regardless of the value of the contract.

5.5. *The selection phase: choosing the candidates to participate in the dialogue*

The rules under the Directive on selecting candidates to participate in the dialogue were discussed in section 5.5 of Chapter 1 above. In France, for both public contracts and *contrats de partenariat*, the national legislation retains the Directive's provisions on the minimum number of candidates to be invited into the dialogue – this is kept at three in all three sources of legislation.[46] As noted, the rules on operating a dialogue do not differ between contracts covered and not covered by the Directive in any of these pieces of legislation, and consequently there is no scope for inviting fewer candidates into the dialogue for low-value procurement.

Interestingly, the CMP also indicates that a maximum can be set in the contract notice; however, Ordinance No. 2004-559 is silent on this issue of setting a 'maximum'.

While the legislation thus generally insists on at least three candidates, the courts have recognised that this may not always be feasible. Key here is *Société Heli Union*,[47] in which, out of nine interested parties, seven were invited to participate in the dialogue; however, five did not respond to this invitation, and so the contracting authority ended up conducting the dialogue with just two parties. One of the non-selected parties claimed this was contrary to the Ordinance No. 2004-559, as other *suitable* tenderers were available. The Tribunal rejected this argument, as the contracting authority itself had complied with the requirements of

[46] Art. 67(1) of the 2006 CMP; Art. 23(III) of Décret No. 2005-1742; Art. 6 of Ordonnance No. 2004-559.

[47] TA Versailles, 22 janvier 2008, *Société Heli Union*, req. No. 0800043.

the Ordinance by inviting more than three tenderers; the fact that they failed to respond to the invitations did not place fault with the contracting authority.

Selection criteria in all three cases are those listed in the Directive,[48] for contracts both above and below the Directive's thresholds. Interestingly, in the original CMP 2006, Article 67 contained a provision that permitted reserving a certain number of spaces for SMEs that met the selection criteria in a competitive dialogue – but this provision was struck from the CMP in 2007, as the Conseil d'Etat considered it was contrary to the principle of equal treatment, as the requirement of 'being an SME' was not always related to the subject of the contract, as is required by Directive 2004/18.[49] Implicitly, the Conseil d'Etat appears to have argued that this would not have been an acceptable selection criterion on the basis of technical or financial ability, as required by the Directive.

In practice, contracting authorities normally fix the maximum number of candidates at five to keep the benefits of a genuine competition, and at the same time to maintain the efficiency of the dialogue and a strategic position until the end of the dialogue. The selection criteria applied are generally, first, those relating to professional and technical ability, and, secondly, those relating to economic and financial ability to realise the project. Another interesting quality of competitive dialogue as it operates in France is that there is full room in the legislation for the composition of a consortium to change during the competitive dialogue procedure.

For non-central government procurement covered by the CMP, evaluation of both the candidates and the tenders is performed by a standing local tender commission, composed of public officials elected to the commission (Article 22 of the CMP). This requirement to use a standing tender commission also existed between 2004 and 2008 for central government procurement covered by the CMP, but was abolished by Decree No. 2008-1355 in an effort to encourage faster and more flexible procurement to help France out of economic recession.

[48] Art. 67(IV) of the 2006 CMP; Art. 23(II) of Décret No. 2005-1742; for contrats de partenariat, Décret No. 2009-243 in fact lists the evidence that contracting authorities can request in order to examine candidates – but the items requested correspond to those permitted by Directive 2004/18.

[49] CE, 9 juillet 2007, *Syndicat EGF-BTP et autres*, No. 297711.

Of historical interest is that Article 24 of the 2004 CMP added that, in the case of competitive dialogue, one-third of the tender commission would be appointed by the contracting authority on the basis of having expertise in competitive dialogue; these 'competitive dialogue experts' would have advisory rights in non-central government procurement, and voting rights in central government procurement. This provision was not carried over into the 2006 CMP, for reasons that are not known.

5.6. *The dialogue phase*

The rules that govern the dialogue phase of competitive dialogue under the Directive were discussed in section 6 of Chapter 1. All three pieces of legislation in France retain the full freedom of the Directive in setting out the dialogue phase. Changes are only found with regard to the provisions on bid payments, which will be discussed in section 5.10 below.

In France, a document that aims to structure the dialogue is sent to the candidates at the same time as the descriptive document (when candidates are invited to the dialogue). This document is called the *Règlement de consultation* (Regulation of the Consultation) and it contributes to both informing the candidates of the process and keeping the dialogue process transparent.

The descriptive document generally needs to contain the information on the project required by the Directive (i.e. 'specifications' on the basis of functional performance and requirements). It is notable that, under the CMP, the contracting authority can also restrict the subject of the dialogue to only a part of a project by delimiting the descriptive document.

Guidance from the Mission d'appui à l'investissement hospitalier (Support Office for Hospital Investment, MAINH)[50] on *bail emphytéotique hospitalier* proposes the following content for the descriptive document:

(1) presentation of objectives and challenges of the project;
(2) functional definition of the contracting authority needs, tasks to be accomplished by the economic operator and constraints of the project;
(3) results and requirements to reach; and
(4) solutions to be proposed by the candidate.

[50] MAINH, 'Le Guide BEH' (février 2005), pp. 65–6.

The Conseil d'Etat has ruled that no substantial modification of the descriptive document and thus of the contracting authority's basic needs is possible during the dialogue (by analogy with the *appel d'offres sur performances*).[51]

France has not introduced any limit to the duration of the dialogue phase; however, the perception in practice appears to be that it is most efficient to let the dialogue run for a sufficient amount of time (between twelve and twenty-four months). There is anecdotal evidence of some *contrats de partenariat* procurements that have been signed after only nine months of dialogue, but this is generally seen to be a very short time – and not in the best interests of the project.

As no changes are made from the Directive, the possibility to reduce the number of solutions (not rephrased to read 'participants' in any French legislation) has also been retained for both public contracts and *contrats de partenariat*.[52] The legislation does not discuss the possibility of reducing down to only two 'solutions' or candidates, and thus does not clarify the Directive's wording in this respect; however, in practice, competitive dialogue procedures have sometimes finished with only two participants.

In terms of assessing solutions at this stage, the French legislation retains the wording of the Directive: it merely notes that solutions can be reduced by reference to the award criteria listed in the contract notice or the descriptive document.[53]

The French courts have shed only minimal light on how award criteria are to be used during the competitive dialogue process, by considering in a case whether or not award criteria can be *elaborated* on (as opposed to changed) after the conclusion of the dialogue phase.

The case in question[54] asked whether or not the Local Authorities Code was in violation of the Directive by explicitly permitting the contracting authority to clarify how it would apply its award criteria post-dialogue phase. The Conseil d'Etat concluded that the Code was not in violation, as long as the award criteria themselves and their weightings were not altered from those announced in the contract

[51] CE, 4 avril 2005, *Commune Castellar*, No. 265784, noted by A. Ménéménis (2005) *Droit Administratifs*, comm. 102; Olivier, n. 10 above.

[52] Art. 67(VI) of the 2006 CMP; Art. 40(II) of Décret No. 2005-1742; Art. 7(I) of Ordonnance No. 2004-559.

[53] *Ibid.*

[54] CE 29 octobre 2004, *M. Sueur et autres*, No. 269814-271119-271357-271362.

notice, and also that any clarifications were communicated to participating tenderers in a transparent and non-discriminatory fashion as required under CJEU jurisprudence.[55] The Conseil d'Etat referred to the wording of Article 29 of the Directive, and indicated that, prior to submission of final tenders, nothing in the Directive itself precluded a clarification that did not change the award criteria or their weightings.[56]

Even though this does not directly address the issue, this judgment does suggest that the French courts would not permit actual changes to be made to specified criteria – though there may be some scope to specify these further as the dialogue process goes on. On the other hand, the French courts have not yet touched at all the question of whether different criteria or weightings can be used at different stages of elimination, where this intended approach is specified at the outset and remains unchanged during the procedure.

Contracting authorities generally organise two stages of dialogue. Thus there is generally one or several initial proposals per candidate, known as *proposition prévisionnelle sommaire* (PPS, provisional summary proposals) in stage one, and one or several intermediary proposals (often called *propositions prévisionnelles détaillées* (PPDs, provisional detailed proposals)) in stage two, before the final tender after closing the dialogue.

Practice has also revealed use of two different types of dialogue. Thus one style of competitive dialogue used in France revolves around merging candidate offers before the final tender stage so that all candidates propose final tenders on the same solution, making for an easier comparison between bids for the contracting authority. However, this type of dialogue is not as commonly used as the other type, whereby each bidder develops and evolves individual solutions. Comparing tenders is acknowledged to be more difficult in this scenario, but it is deemed to be more in line with the 'spirit' of competitive dialogue (which acknowledges that different solutions may be equally viable for fulfilling the contracting authority's needs).

[55] See Case C-331/04, *ATI EAC Srl e Viaggi di Maio Snc and others* v. *ATCV Venezia SpA and others* [2005] ECR I-10109; and Case C-532/06, *Emm. G. Lianakis AE and others* v. *Dimos Alexandroupolis and others* [2008] ECR I-251.

[56] See also the position of the Commission, in European Commission, *Explanatory Note – Competitive Dialogue – Classic Directive*, available at http://ec.europa.eu/internal_market/publicprocurement/docs/explan-notes/classic-dir-dialogue_en.pdf.

5.7. *Final tender stage*

The procedural rules that govern the final tender stage of competitive dialogue under the Directive itself were discussed in section 5.7 of Chapter 1 of this book. As noted in sections 5.5 and 5.6 of the present chapter, the French legislation copies out the Directive's provisions on both the number of candidates needed in the dialogue and how to reduce the number of solutions during the dialogue phase. It thus offers no clarification on whether or not it is possible to retain only two bidders during the final tender stage, or how to choose these. However, case law by the French administrative tribunals suggests that, where no candidates are 'suitable' at this stage (perhaps because their solution clearly does not meet the authority's needs), it may be possible to invite only two candidates to submit a final tender.

Also interesting on this point is MEDEF guidance, which indicates that 'foreign experience' with competitive dialogue suggests that retaining two candidates is possible. It does not go so far as to actually recommend using less than three, however, and instead says that a maximum of three candidates is appropriate at the final tender stage.

On choosing the winning bid, the French legislation states that the winning bidder is the one with the most economically advantageous offer on the basis of the award criteria listed in the contract notice or the descriptive document. All provisions here generally correspond to those in the Directives,[57] though it can be added that *contrats de partenariat* have three mandatory award criteria:[58] the global price of the bid; performance objectives defined in terms of the contract specifications; and how much of the contract is contracted out to SMEs. Other award criteria permitted by the Directive can also be used, but these are not required.

As mentioned in section 5.4, all non-central government public tenders covered by the CMP, including those awarded using competitive dialogue, are awarded by a 'tender commission', but, as of the 2006 CMP, this commission no longer requires members with particular expertise in competitive dialogue.

Under Article 50 of the CMP and Article 21 of Ordinance No. 2005-649, variant submissions are permitted so long as the contracting authority indicates this in the contract notice; the

[57] Arts. 67(VIII) and 53 of the 2006 CMP; Art. 24 of Décret No. 2005-1742.

[58] Art. 8(I) of Ordonnance No. 2004-559.

provisions on variants are identical to those in the Directive. However, variants are not commonly used in practice. Ordinance No. 2004-559 on *contrats de partenariat*, on the other hand, is silent on the issue of variant submissions. Without any rules governing their availability, it is unclear if variants are available for *contrats de partenariat* awarded by competitive dialogue.

Regarding completeness of final tenders, the French legislation again offers no clarification of what is in the Directive – it notes that tenders shall contain all elements required and necessary for the performance of the contract.[59] Case law (regarding either competitive dialogue or the preceding *appel d'offres sur performances*) has offered no opinions on this issue. The MEDEF guidance states that the purpose of the dialogue is to fix 'the performance, payments, penalties and interests' of the winning bidder – but seems to suggest that these should be fixed to a reasonable standard.[60] As an example, it notes that an exceptional level of detail of design in final tenders on building work cannot be deemed to be required.

All three relevant pieces of legislation also retain the option to 'clarify, specify or fine-tune' final tenders, although in the case of *contrats de partenariat*, this is rephrased to read 'clarify, specify, complement or perfect'.[61] It is unlikely that these word changes would result in a difference as to what is permitted. Regardless, it can be noted that changes such as these do not clarify the Directive's original position, and do not make it obvious what types of changes are permitted at this stage. MEDEF offers no explanations on this point; it merely recites, as the pieces of legislation do, that none of the changes at this stage can result in a basic change to the project.

Under the CMP, as is permitted under the Directive in Article 30(1)(a), if there are no regular or acceptable tenders submitted at the final tender stage, the competitive dialogue will be declared 'interrupted' and will be discontinued. Contracting authorities may then re-advertise the contract using either competitive dialogue, the open/restricted procedure, or the negotiated procedure with a notice (provided that the contract terms are not substantially altered).

59 Art. 67(VII) of the 2006 CMP; Art. 40(III) of Décret No. 2005-1742; Art. 7(I) of Ordonnance No. 2004-559 (which has slightly different wording, but does not result in greater clarification of what is meant by 'complete').

60 MEDEF, n. 32 above, p. 23.

61 *Ibid.*

5.8. *Procedure following the selection of the winning tender or preferred bidder*

As noted, the French legislation places no restrictions on the duration of the dialogue. Contracting authorities are thus free to close the dialogue and invite final tenders when they see fit.

The CMP, in Article 67, as well as both Ordinances (Ordinance No. 2004-559 in Article 8(II) and Decree No. 2005-1742 (containing the rules for contracts covered by Ordinance No. 2005-649) in Article 40(IV)) retains a possibility for the winning bidder to clarify or confirm his commitments; the wording used is identical to that of the Directive. The legal position under the Directive itself in this respect was discussed in section 5.8 of Chapter 1.

Interestingly, Article 13 of Law No. 2009-179 of 17 February 2009 – dealing with acceleration of public construction and investment in light of the global economic crisis – permitted (until the end of 2010) contracting authorities to adjust the financial aspects of final tenders (such as, *inter alia*, funding arrangements, but *not* price) for *contrats de partenariat*. Contracting authorities relying on this possibility had to advertise it in the contract notice; the period during which adjustments could take place were set (with a deadline) by the contracting authority and the intended winning bidder. The legislation did not indicate if there were limitations to the amounts or types of adjustments made possible, though it can be observed that conditions of transparency and equal treatment would both have applied to any changes made, as per Article 3 of Ordinance No. 2004-559. As of 1 January 2011, the period in which these 'financial tender adjustments' were permitted has lapsed, as the legislation providing them was introduced to temporarily stimulate the French economy during the economic downturn in 2009. However, they could be reintroduced by new legislation at any time.

It is unclear to what extent this possibility is compatible with the restrictions on modifying final or winning tenders set out in Article 29 of the Directive; however, thus far, the Commission has not complained about the (temporary) existence of these rules.

5.9. *The standstill period*

The French legislation contains no specific rules regarding the standstill period for competitive dialogue. The general rules on the standstill are found in Article 80 of the CMP and Article 46 of Decree No. 2005-1742 (containing the rules for contracts covered by Ordinance No. 2005-649) and Article 9 of Ordinance No. 2004-559 (for *contrats de partenariat*). These simply state that there will be at least a sixteen-day[62] delay between notification of unsuccessful bidders and the signing of the public contract if tenderers are notified by post, and eleven days if notified electronically. In both situations, the standstill commences at the point when unsuccessful bidders have actually received, in writing, the news that they have been unsuccessful.

5.10. Payments for costs of participation

The CMP and both Ordinances mention the possibility of paying for participating in the dialogue; however, the wording used is significantly different from that in the Directive on this point. Where the Directive indicates that contracting authorities may specify payments to participants in the dialogue (see section 5.10 of Chapter 1), Article 67(X) of the CMP and Article 40(V) of Decree No. 2005-1742 (containing the rules for contracts covered by Ordinance No. 2005-649) instead state that the contract notice or descriptive document can specify that a 'premium' will be allocated either to all participants in the dialogue, *or to those whose proposals were the subject of discussion, or to those whose bids were ranked highest*. This provision is illustrative – it offers additional suggestions on when bid payments may be useful – but also seems limiting in nature, in that it strongly suggests that only these three types of bid payments can be extended.

Article 7(I) of Ordinance No. 2005-449 also states that a contracting authority may decide (and state in the contract notice/descriptive document) on extending bid payments to either those whose proposals were discussed or those whose bids were ranked highest – but adds that, in the event where the public authority's demands require a significant investment for the candidates that participated in the dialogue, a bid payment *must* be made. There is thus a difference drawn here between *contrats de partenariat*, which are presumed to require heavy investment from bidders, and regular public contracts awarded by competitive dialogue.

The MEDEF guidance[63] adds to this that the 'Manual of Application' issued with the 2006 CMP indicates that it may be in the best interest to

[62] Décret No. 2009-1456 du 27 novembre 2009 relatif aux procédures de recours applicables aux contrats de la commande publique.

[63] MEDEF, n. 32 above, p. 25.

provide bidders with payments to participate in a competitive dialogue, as the procedure can result in significant costs and investments for the bidders. The knowledge that the costs of their participation will be reimbursed will thus, according to the Manual, result in the greatest possible competition, as bidders are more likely to participate in the procedure. These provisions have been retained in the 2009 Guide de Bonnes Pratiques, in section 13.

The guidance further offers suggestions on how much the bid payment should be – it states, for instance, that research costs in large infrastructure bids can amount to about 3 per cent of the total cost of the work if continued to the end of the dialogue. The guidance then adds, however, that, in making payments, it should be considered that the longer a participant stays in the dialogue, the more costly the process will be for them – and the value of bid payments should be adjusted accordingly.[64]

French policy generally thus seems to heavily encourage bid payments so as to get the best possible results from the dialogue process, both in participation and in quality of solutions. In practice, bid payments are paid regularly and their value is normally substantial.

6. Concluding remarks

The French legislation has taken a very proactive and positive approach to implementing competitive dialogue. We have seen that, as early as 2004, French legislation enabled use of the procedure and, by 2006, when the Directive was due for implementation, competitive dialogue could be used to award public contracts as well as PPP-style contracts.

The French government has issued significant guidance on the use of the procedure; some of the more specific guidance on how to manage consortia and how to manage the end of the competitive dialogue process is particularly useful.

The freedom offered by the Directive is generally retained in the legislation; additions found in the rules stated are explanatory and helpful, such as the additional rules on how to operate bid payments in competitive dialogue. The general approach to the procedure is to give contracting authorities the freedom to act in their best economic interest, provided that they abide by the general principles

[64] *Ibid.*

of non-discrimination, transparency and equal treatment during the process of the dialogue.

Practice reveals substantial use of the procedure and only minimal hints of a 'standardised' approach; instead, the basic qualities of the competitive dialogue are highlighted in legislation and in guidance and contracting authorities otherwise adjust the procedure as they deem fit. Most competitive dialogue procedures appear to focus on deciding between individual solutions proposed by the separate candidates, although legislation does permit bidding on one final solution if contracting authorities prefer this.

A final interesting point was France's 'economic crisis' policy with regard to *contrats de partenariat* of allowing more substantial adjustment to final tenders on their financial elements (although, as we have seen, this is no longer in force). This policy – its legality under Article 29 of the Directive notwithstanding – appears to be reflective of the general French approach to implementing competitive dialogue: it has been made available to award those contracts where it is most likely to result in efficient procurement, with as much flexibility as is needed to get the best possible procurement results.

5

Competitive dialogue in Germany

MARTIN BURGI

1. Introduction[1]

In reporting the German experience with the competitive dialogue procedure, this introductory section seeks to provide an overview of the general approach to public procurement regulation in Germany. The section will highlight German procurement history and also deal with the most important questions in relation to transposition of and conformity with EU procurement law. Section 2 of the chapter looks at the German procurement structures available to handle complex procurement projects prior to the installation of the competitive dialogue. Section 3 then concentrates on the competitive dialogue procedure and provides an analysis of its use in practice and the approach of the German courts. Throwing light on the regulatory framework, section 4 mainly deals with the question whether the requirements set by Directive 2004/18 regarding the scope of the procedure have been implemented correctly by national legislature. Section 4 also discusses the availability of the procedure for public contracts falling outside the scope of the Directive. Section 5 provides an overview of key issues relating to the operational side of the procedure by considering briefly how these

[1] On competitive dialogue in Germany, see generally M. Burgi, 'Die Vergabe von Dienstleistungskonzessionen in Deutschland: Verfahren, Vergabekriterien, Rechtsschutz' (2005) *Neue Zeitschrift für Baurecht und Vergaberecht* 610; F. L. Hausmann, in H.-P. Kulartz, F. Marx, N. Portz and H.-J. Prieß (eds.), *Kommentar zur VOB/A* (Cologne: Bundesanzeiger Verlag, 2010); H. Kaelble, in M. Müller-Wrede and S. Amelung (eds.), *Vergabe und Vertragsordnung für Leistungen VOL/A Kommentar* (2nd edn, Cologne: Bundesanzeiger Verlag, 2010); J. Kramer, 'Gleichbehandlung im Verhandlungsverfahren nach der VOL/A' (2005) *Neue Zeitschrift für Baurecht und Vergaberecht* 138; M. Müller-Wrede, in M. Müller-Wrede (ed.), *Sektorenverordnung – SektVO, Kommentar* (Cologne: Bundesanzeiger Verlag, 2010); M. Opitz, 'Wie funktioniert der wettbewerbliche Dialog? – Rechtliche und praktische Probleme' (2006) *VergabeR* 451; H. Pünder, in H. Pünder and M. Schellenberg (eds.), *Vergaberecht Handkommentar* (Baden-Baden: Nomos Verlag, 2011).

problems and topics are dealt with in practice, legislation and jurisprudence. Finally, section 6 offers some concluding remarks.

It is of immense importance to first provide an introduction to the broader context of the German approach to public procurement law. The current German procurement system must be viewed as the result of a long and controversial legislative process in which various amendments and reforms have taken place over the years. This might be the reason why German procurement law tends to be much more complex than in many other EU Member States. Furthermore, it must be said that the German system does not only create problems for foreign academics or foreign tenderers, but it equally establishes obstacles for national practitioners and procurement experts. The complexity of the German system is primarily rooted in the fact that the law on the award of the contract is based on three different legal acts – the GWB,[2] the VgV[3] and three procurement regulations, the VOL/A, the VOB/A and the VOF[4] – constituting the so-called 'cascade variant'. Although the provisions therein are partly of a public and partly of a civil (private) law character, public procurement law is generally attached to civil law, and the norms for the *execution* of the contract are entirely governed by civil law in the shape of the German Civil Code (BGB) and the VOB/B and VOL/B.[5] Another basic feature of the elaborate and rather intricate German procurement law is the dichotomy between public procurement law applicable for public contracts above the thresholds and that applicable to contracts below the threshold, to which a different regulatory framework applies. In line with this complicated German

[2] Act against the Restraints on Competition (GWB) of 26 August 1998, BGBl. I, 2546, amended and promulgated on 15 July 2005 (BGBl. I, 214), last amended on 22 December 2010, BGBl. I, 2262.

[3] Public Procurement Regulation (VgV) of 9 January 2001, amended and promulgated on 11 February 2003 (BGBl. I, 169) and last amended via regulation on 9 May 2011 (BGBl. I, 800).

[4] Contracting rules for the award of public service contracts, public work contracts and contracts for professional services (VOL/A, VOB/A, VOF). Regulation for the award of public service contracts (VOL/A) of 31 July 2009, BAnz. No. 155a of 15 November 2009; Regulation for the award of public work contracts (VOB/A) of 20 September 2009, BAnz. No. 196a of 29 December 2009, corrected on 19 February 2010, BAnz. No. 32 of 26 February 2010; Regulation for the award of contracts for professional services of 18 November 2009, BAnz. No. 185a of 8 December 2009.

[5] Procurement Regulation for the execution of public works and public service contracts (VOB/B, VOL/B).

approach to substantive law, comparable peculiarities can be detected in the German remedies system as well.

With the Federal Republic of Germany being one of the founders of the EU, procurement law in Germany has always been markedly influenced by EU law, especially since the EU began to enact the procurement Directives, as explained in Chapter 1. As a result of these developments at EU level, Germany opted to integrate a second section into its three pre-existing procurement regulations, in order to transpose European requirements.

Prior to 1998, German public procurement law and its review system was exclusively part of budgetary law. With the procurement regulations being only of an administrative character and conveying neither subjective nor enforceable rights, the German approach of transposing the procurement Directives was heavily criticised by the European Commission. Having identified Germany's non-compliance with European secondary law, the Commission initiated proceedings against the Federal Republic pursuant to what was then Article 234 EC (Article 267 TFEU). Ultimately, the Second Act amending Public Procurement Law (Vergaberechtsänderungsgesetz), adopted in 1998, led to the renunciation of the so-called budgetary solution and the implementation of §§ 97–129 into the GWB. Since then, the fourth part of the GWB, containing all important procurement provisions for public contracts above the EU thresholds, has granted bidders subjective and enforceable rights. The procedural rules for the award of public contracts above the thresholds were also written down in the three procurement regulations, which now enjoy the status of law due to the so-called norm reference technique: it is via the Public Procurement Regulation that the three procurement regulations are considered 'law'.

The consequence of the approach adopted was that all public contracts *not* reaching the EU thresholds were still governed by budgetary law. The consequence of this was that the application of procurement law provisions as enshrined in the procurement regulations was only optional and not obligatory for these procurements.

After the elaborate reform of 1998, the institutions of the EU triggered a new phase of reorganisation of the procurement framework in Germany with the enactment of Directive 2004/18 and Directive 2004/17 (see Chapter 1, section 2.1). The German legislature transposed the EU's requirements in a timely manner with, *inter alia*, the adoption of the Act to Accelerate the Realisation of Public–Private Partnerships

(ÖPP-Beschleunigungsgesetz)[6] in September 2005. In parts, the German system is a mere *verbatim* copy of the Directive's text,[7] avoiding errors in interpretation during transposition. At the same time, the three procurement regulations were also revised again in order to establish a more transparent, competitive and innovation-friendly procurement system whilst at the same time increasing the effectiveness of review mechanisms available. It remained, however, a basic feature of the German system that independent professional services as well as public works and supply contracts were each governed by an independent regulation, although Directive 2004/18 explicitly sought to consolidate the rules for all kinds of public contracts. Adding to the revision of the procurement regulations in general, the German rules were adapted to the newly installed EU thresholds.[8]

Although these developments ensured conformity with EU law for the most part, the German approach was still criticised as being too bureaucratic and complex, and not sufficiently user-friendly. This led to reform in 2009. Once again, the reform attempts in Germany were largely influenced by developments at the EU level. This time, the pressure for reform came from the revision of the Remedies Directives through Directive 2007/66. According to the EU rules on remedies, Member States are explicitly required to ensure effective and rapid review mechanisms. Member States must ensure that diverse and adequate means are provided to prevent, correct or set aside unlawful award decisions. As Chapter 1 explained (see section 2.1 of that chapter), these rules were strengthened by Directive 2007/66, and this resulted in the German legislature making important amendments to the GWB.

First, in addition to transposing Article 26 of Directive 2004/18, allowing contracting authorities to insert secondary criteria (such as environmental and social criteria) when awarding public contracts, Germany also took account of the fundamental changes made to the Remedies Directive.[9] The transposition of the Directive's requirements through the enactment of the German law on the modernisation of

[6] See ÖPP-Beschleunigungsgesetz of 1 September 2005, BGBl. I, 2676.

[7] A. Klimisch and C. Ebrecht, 'Stellung und Rechte der Dialogteilnehmer im wettbewerblichen Dialog' (2011) *Neue Zeitschrift für Baurecht und Vergaberecht* 203.

[8] Regulation of 23 October 2006, BGBl. I, 2334.

[9] Covering the implementation of the standstill period and ineffectiveness, and making available effective review mechanisms for the *de facto* award.

public procurement law of 4 September 2009 has resulted in a modern and almost exemplary German remedies system.

Furthermore, the competent legislative bodies worked on modernising, simplifying and amending the three procurement regulations, which entered into force simultaneously with the enactment of the newest version of the VgV in June 2010. In the past, the content of Directive 2004/17 on procurement by utilities had always been integrated into sections 3 and 4 of the procurement regulations. However, as part of the comprehensive reform, the rules for public entities operating in the water, energy and transport sectors were transferred into an independent regulatory regime, the so-called sector ordinance (*Sektorenverordnung*), and entered into force in autumn 2009. It should not go unnoticed, however, that the current version of this ordinance on utilities does not provide any specific rules for postal services.

In case of interpretational problems, helpful guidance is provided mainly by case law (at national as well as EU level), as well as through additional material produced by the bodies that are responsible in Germany for the enactment, revision and design of the procurement regulations[10] (although this material mainly concerns more general issues rather than providing guidance on competitive dialogue specifically) and by legal experts.

Germany's regulatory regime on public procurement is frequently criticised as being too complex and inflexible. Even after the latest reform, further basic changes are expected, especially regarding the review framework, as effective remedies are only available for contracts exceeding the EU threshold values.[11] The budgetary solution that was described above still applies for all contracts below the thresholds, with the consequence that the bidders' rights in respect of these contracts are not enforceable (although there is currently some discussion in Germany that, controversially, enforceability might, in fact, exist).

[10] For public work contracts this is the German Committee for the award of public works contracts (DVA) and for service contracts it is the Committee for the award of public service contracts (DVAL), whilst the VOF has been enacted under the leading auspices of the Federal Ministry of Economics and Technology, the Ministry of Transport, Construction and Urban Affairs and the German Committee for Drafting the Regulation on Contract Awards for Independent Professional Services (VOF). The relevant bodies are mostly staffed equally with representatives of big contracting authorities, head organisations on the municipal level, and head organisations in economy and technology.

[11] M. Burgi, 'Streitbeilegung unterhalb der Schwellenwerte durch "Vergabeschlichtungsstellen": Ein Vorschlag zu aktuellen Reformdiskussion' (2010) *VergabeR* 403 *et seq.*

Despite limited gaps, suggestions of incompatibility with EU law and its lamented inflexibility, the procurement system worked out by the German legislator over the years is very elaborate. Due to the complexity of the general procurement system as well as the overall high-quality review system, Germany has a very elaborate case law in comparison with some other EU Member States (such as the UK). On the basis of the data available, it appears that the review cases deal with approximately 1,200 award procedures each year.[12] Apparently, however, contracting authorities do not infringe procurement law as often as one might presume bearing in mind the complexity of procurement law: in Germany, about two-thirds of the cases are decided in favour of the contracting authorities.

2. The background: complex procurement prior to competitive dialogue

The competitive dialogue procedure was integrated into German procurement law in September 2005 as an innovative procedure, allegedly introducing more flexibility and enriching the State's purchase of goods and services, in the sense that extremely complex projects, such as those involving public–private partnerships, can be handled appropriately and successfully. As will be explained in further detail in section 4 below, prior to the introduction of competitive dialogue, complex procurement projects were mostly awarded by recourse to the negotiated procedure, relying on the grounds that (i) overall pricing was not possible (works and services contracts) and (ii) it was not possible to set a specification (services contracts) – grounds which apply under both Directive 2004/18 and its predecessors.[13] As we will see, this former practice of using the negotiated procedure with a notice to award complex contracts still remains applicable – even though competitive dialogue has now taken over for a few of these procurements.

[12] See the newest data on the frequency and success rate of primary legal review procedures published by the Federal Ministry of Economics (BMWi), available at http://forum-vergabe.de.

[13] Grounds found respectively in Council Directive 93/37/EEC [1993] OJ L199/547(2)(c) (Works Directive) and Art. 11(2)(b) of Council Directive 92/50/EEC [1992] OJ L209/1 (Services Directive); and Art. 11(2)(c) of Directive 92/50. See the discussion in Ch. 1 above.

3. Introduction to competitive dialogue

In Germany, the competitive dialogue procedure was incorporated into legislation as part of the Act to Accelerate the Realisation of Public–Private Partnerships in September 2005. Being perceived as one of the most important novelties of the legislative package, this new procedure was the only aspect of Directive 2004/18 that was introduced by the Federal Republic of Germany by the deadline for the transposition of the Directive.[14] Prior to the latest reform, competitive dialogue was defined in § 101 V GWB and § 6a VgV. As a result of the latest comprehensive rearrangement of the legal rules on public procurement, competitive dialogue is now enshrined in § 101 IV GWB and after its deletion from the VgV it is now explicitly part of the procurement regulations (§§ 3 VII VOL/A-EC, § 3a IV VOB/A). As Germany decided to take an approach that closely follows the wording of the Directive in order to reduce the risks of incorrect transposition, the content of the relevant provisions are largely a *verbatim* copy of Article 29 of Directive 2004/18.[15] Consequently, the German provisions give rise to the same legal problems, and contain grey areas, to the same extent as the Directive.

For the time being, competitive dialogue is only available for particularly complex contracts falling within the scope of the Public Sector Directive. The inability to specify the means of satisfying their needs or assessing which solutions are available on the market arises mainly in the case of public–private partnerships (PPPs). Most PPP projects in Germany are handled with recourse to the competitive dialogue procedure, while most other projects are awarded by means of the negotiated procedure due to a lack of legal clarity.

Bearing in mind the lack of clarity in the Directive, contracting authorities strive for further information and assistance regarding the interpretation of the procedural rules. Guidance on how to conduct the procedure is provided only to a very limit extent by the jurisprudence: the case law regarding competitive dialogue is not very elaborate due to the rudimentary use of the procedure in practice.[16] But the longer the procedure exists,

[14] M. Burgi and B. Ruhland, 'Das Grünbuch der EG-Kommission zu öffentlich-rechtlichen Partnerschaften (ÖPP) und die Vergaberechtsreform' (2005) *VergabeR* 1.

[15] Klimisch and Ebrecht, n. 7 above, p. 203.

[16] See VK Rheinland-Pfalz of 21 July 2009, VK 1-41/09 (2009) ZfBR 720 L, highlighting the novel character of the competitive dialogue procedure and indicating that comprehensive case law is not yet available.

the more cases will be dealt with by jurisprudence and therefore it is expected that further interpretations will be available sometime in the future. The novelty of the procedure explains why most cases are of recent origin (2008 and 2009). Adding to the limited number of cases at national level, very little guidance has been received from the CJEU also.

Having provided an Explanatory Note on competitive dialogue, as explained in Chapter 1, it is mostly the European Commission that provides important strategic guidance.[17] Of course, due to the paucity of case law and the lack of clarity regarding the provisions, legal writers contribute to giving advice on how the dialogue phase should be operated, on how to structure the procedure or to correctly interpret its circumstances and requirements. Besides guidance from the Commission, case law and legal writers, a task force[18] associated with the so-called Public–Private Partnership initiative in North Rhine-Westphalia (NRW) and monitoring mechanisms to successfully handle the realisation of PPPs produced a code of best practice solutions for contracts relating to engineering in 2007. This document embraces important problems arising within the procurement process, among them being problems connected with the use of competitive dialogue.

4. Scope of the competitive dialogue procedure in law and practice

4.1. Introduction

As already mentioned, the wording of the German provisions relating to the competitive dialogue procedure do not differ much from the wording of Article 29 of the Public Sector Directive. Therefore, the procedure is available for all contracts falling within the scope of the Directive. As long as government contracts exceed the relevant EU thresholds, contracting authorities are allowed to award contracts via the competitive dialogue procedure.

In accordance with § 101 IV GWB, contracts awarded on the basis of the most economically advantageous tender might be awarded by use of

[17] European Commission, *Explanatory Note – Competitive Dialogue – Classic Directive*, available at http://ec.europa.eu/internal_market/publicprocurement/docs/explan-notes/classic-dir-dialogue_en.pdf.

[18] PPP Task Force of the Federal Ministry of Economics and Technology, the Ministry of Transport, Construction and Urban Affairs, *PPP im Hochbau Vergabeleitfaden*, 18 October 2007, available at https://broschueren.nordrheinwestfalendirekt.de/?s=Public%20Private%20Partnership.

the competitive dialogue procedure where they are 'particularly complex contracts'. The concretising rules in the procurement regulations define a public contract as particularly complex if the purchasing body is either objectively unable to define the technical means capable of satisfying the purchaser's needs and objectives or incapable of specifying the legal or financial conditions of a project.[19] The above definitions lack clarity even more than their European equivalent[20] since, unlike the Public Sector Directive in recital 31, German law does not provide for any further clarification, explanation or examples.[21] Hence, it is difficult to fully understand what these definitions are intended to cover and German practitioners must have recourse to the European provisions, discussed in Chapter 1 (see section 4 of that chapter) to interpret them.

4.2. *Technical complexity*

The first alternative of § 3a IV No. 1 VOB/A and § 3 VII S. 1 VOL/A-EC refers to the inability of the contracting authority to define the 'technical means' for meeting its needs. This rather nebulous term is not explicitly defined but may be interpreted by referring to Article 1(9) of Directive 2004/18/EC and specifying 'technical means' through a cross-reference to Article 23(3).[22] From that reference it is submitted that it follows that the contracting authority must be technically unable to formulate a functional specification and as a consequence is obliged in each individual case to prove that the technical problems cannot be solved by either using a functional specification or a technical dialogue according to recital 8 of Directive 2004/18/EC prior to the actual procurement procedure.[23]

[19] See § 3a IV No. 1 a, b VOB/A and § 3 VII S. 1 VA-EG/A-EC.

[20] For a critique of the European definitions of a 'particularly complex contract', see S. Treumer, 'Competitive Dialogue' (2004) 13 *Public Procurement Law Review* 178.

[21] In the legislative history of the law (see BT-Drs. 15/5668, p. 11) similar considerations as in recital 31 of the classical Directive can be found though.

[22] That cross-reference is capable of being misunderstood: 'Technical means' is not a synonym for the 'technical specifications' as understood from Art. 23(3)(a) of Directive 2004/18/EC. The latter is explicitly not referred to. Therefore, 'technical means' has a separate meaning in the form of a 'definition borrowing': see C. Schwabe, *Wettbewerblicher Dialog, Verhandlungsverfahren, Interessenbekundungsverfahren* (Baden-Baden: Nomos Verlag, 2009), p. 111.

[23] See Schwabe, n. 22 above, p. 111; H. Pünder and I. Franzius, 'Die Auftragsvergabe im wettbewerblichen Dialog' (2006) *Zeitschrift für deutsches und internationales Bau- und Vergaberecht* 20, at 21.

4.3. *Legal or financial complexity*

The second parts of the definition of what constitutes a particularly complex contract in section 3a IV No. 1 VOB/A, § 3 VII S. 1 VOL/A-EC do not provide much clarification, either. The terminology used is very vague and raises further questions. For the purpose of interpretation, German practitioners must again have recourse to recital 31 of the Public Sector Directive which offers at least some guidance by mentioning examples.[24] The examples given are concerned with matters often, though not exclusively, awarded by means of public–private partnerships. In the European Commission's view competitive dialogue is particularly well adapted to award public–private partnerships.[25] Unfortunately though, the Directive does not make that explicitly clear.[26] In Germany, that conclusion can be drawn from the legislative history of the transposition of the competitive dialogue procedure into national law. According to the explanatory statement regarding the law, the new and flexible procedure 'is especially designed for public–private partnerships'.[27] Of course, the term 'financial or legal complexity' does not limit the procedure to public–private partnerships, and in addition it should be highlighted that not every public–private partnership automatically qualifies as being particularly complex. For example, ambitious efforts have been made (by several so-called PPP Task Forces)[28] in Germany to standardise contracts and conditions for certain public–private partnership

[24] 'The implementation of important integrated transport infrastructure projects, large computer networks or projects involving complex and structured financing the financial and legal make-up of which cannot be defined in advance' (recital 31 of Directive 2004/18/EC).

[25] For an overview of the suitability of the competitive dialogue procedure for public–private partnerships, see M. Burnett, 'Conducting Competitive Dialogue for PPP Projects – Towards an Optimal Approach' (2009) 4 *European Public Private Partnership Law Review* 190 *et seq.*; R. Burbulla, 'Die Ausschreibung von ÖPP-Projekten' (2008) *Neue Juristische Online-Zeitschrift* 211 *et seq.*; M. Müller and G. Brauser-Jung, 'Öffentlich-Private-Partnerschaften und Vergaberecht – Ein Beitrag zu den vergaberechtlichen Rahmenbedingungen' (2007) *Neue Zeitschrift für Verwaltungsrecht* 884 *et seq.*; A. Kus, 'Die richtige Verfahrensart bei PPP-Modellen, insbesondere Verhandlungsverfahren und wettbewerblicher Dialog' (2006) *Vergaberecht* 851 *et seq.*; and M. Knauff, 'Im wettbewerblichen Dialog zu Public Private Partnership?' (2005) *Neue Zeitschrift für Baurecht und Vergaberecht* 249 *et seq.*

[26] See Schwabe, n. 22 above, p. 114. [27] See BT-Drs. 15/5668, p. 2.

[28] See, for example, the website of the PPP task force of North Rhine-Westphalia, www.ppp.nrw.de; and M. Burgi, R. Unbehauen and R. Cablitz, in *Rechtliche und praktische Hinweise für die Vergabe von ÖPP-Beratungsleistungen, ÖPP-Initiative NRW* (April 2009).

projects, and some model contracts for complete public–private partnership projects were drafted. If a certain degree of standardisation of a 'typical' public–private partnership project (for example, the building and maintenance of schools) has been achieved, the project might still be complex but not *particularly complex* in terms of the relevant provisions in the procurement rules.[29] For that reason, a case-by-case analysis is needed to assess whether the envisaged public–private partnership project is legally or financially of a particularly complex nature or not. If not, the project might be conducted via an open or restricted procedure.

4.4. *Applicability to contracts below the thresholds*

Below the thresholds for the application of Directive 2004/18, the German legislation does not provide either for the competitive dialogue procedure itself or for any comparable procedure. Although complex public contracts falling below the threshold values may not be awarded by way of competitive dialogue, contracting authorities may use a procedure resembling that of the negotiated procedure that is provided for in Articles 30 and 31 of the Directive (*freihändige Vergabe*). Again, the negotiated procedure and its equivalent for contracts below the thresholds are used frequently in any event due to their providing more flexibility and legal certainty in comparison with the novel competitive dialogue procedure.

4.5. *Applicability to concession contracts and contracts within the scope of the Utilities Directive*

As well as contracts below the thresholds, it is interesting to consider the position of concession contracts and whether they may be awarded through recourse to competitive dialogue. Another important question of applicability relates to contracts within the scope of the Utilities Directive 2004/17.

As regards the first topic, separate rules apply concerning public works and public service concessions. Whereas public works concessions are equated with traditional public works contracts with the consequence

[29] See D. Drömann, 'Wettbewerblicher Dialog und ÖPP-Beschaffungen – Zur "besonderen Komplexität" sogenannter Betreibermodelle' (2007) *Neue Zeitschrift für Baurecht und Vergaberecht* 751, at 753 *et seq.*

that procurement rules apply,[30] this is not the case with public service concessions as they are not considered typical public contracts.[31] Nevertheless, as section 2.1 of Chapter 1 explains, contracting authorities have to pay heed to the fundamental freedoms as enshrined in the TFEU.[32]

As far as concerns contracts falling within the scope of the Utilities Directive 2004/17, the competitive dialogue is not envisaged as a possible form of procedure in formal terms.[33] This is mainly due to the fact that the Utilities Directive itself does not explicitly list the dialogue procedure among the possible award procedures. In this respect, as in others, the relevant German law, the SektVO (Sector Ordinance), merely restates the provisions under the Directive itself. This fact, however, does not hinder a procuring entity from applying the negotiated procedure and modifying its rules in such a way that it parallels the structure and patterns of the competitive dialogue.[34] No information is available on whether this happens in practice.

4.6. *Application in practice*

Although the new procedure has started to be widely used in the EU and has been praised as a novelty, Germany seems to be exceptionally reluctant to use the procedure in comparison with some Member States.[35] In comparison with contracting authorities in Germany's European neighbours, contracting authorities in Germany seemingly have demonstrated an unwillingness to employ competitive dialogue. With reference to the data presented in Chapter 2, in Germany about 129 contract notices relating to the competitive dialogue have been published in total from 2006 to 2009, documenting Germany's status as a regular user of this new procedure. Based on the Tenders Electronic Daily (TED) data

[30] Schwabe, n. 22 above, p. 94; K. Gnittke and S. Rude, in O. Hattig and T. Maibaum (eds.), *Praxiskommentar Kartellvergaberecht* (Cologne: Bundesanzeiger Verlag, 2010), § 99 GWB, para. 127.

[31] Gnittke and Rude, n. 30 above, § 99 GWB, para. 77; OLG Düsseldorf of 23 May 2007, VII-Verg 50/06; OLG München of 2 July 2009, Verg 5/09 (see Art. 17 of Directive 2004/18).

[32] Case C-324/98, *Telaustria Verlags* v. *Telekom Austria* [2000] ECR I-10745, paras. 60 *et seq.*; Case C-231/03, *Consorzio Aziende Metano (Coname)* v. *Comune di Cingia de' Botti* [2005] ECR I-7287, para. 28.

[33] T. Maibaum, in O. Hattig and T. Maibaum (eds.), *Praxiskommentar Kartellvergaberecht* (Cologne: Bundesanzeiger Verlag, 2010), § 101 GWB, para. 38.

[34] BR-Drs. 16/10117, p. 20; Maibaum, note 32 above, § 101 GWB, para. 38.

[35] See Ch. 2 above.

covering the period from 1 June 2009 to June 2011, a total of 3,687 contract notices relating to competitive dialogue procedures have been published in the OJEU. Despite the fact that Germany represents the largest economy within the EU, only 109 competitive dialogue procedures took place in Germany. In contrast, contracting authorities in Germany published in the OJEU approximately 11,440 negotiated procedures (compared with 47,657 in the EU as a whole), 59,396 open procedures (509,644 in the EU) and 2,227 restricted procedures (53,618 in the EU).[36] A reason for the reluctance to use competitive dialogue seems to be that the procedure does not provide as much flexibility as the negotiated procedure, and creates several legal problems regarding its applicability and scope. Another reason for the relatively rare use of the procedure by German procurement bodies might be the bureaucracy and legal uncertainties generally involved with newly installed procedures as well as the successful long-term experience with the negotiated procedure.

Mirroring the cautious German approach in practice, the procedure has also provoked controversial reactions in German literature. Some authors regard the implementation of the procedure as being rather rudimentary;[37] others consider it an excellent way to conduct complex procurement projects;[38] while quite a few legal writers prefer a more ambivalent and diversified view.[39]

The data outlined above show clearly that the negotiated procedure is still frequently used. In fact, the scope of the two procedures designed to handle complex procurement contracts potentially overlap. As we have seen, competitive dialogue is admissible if a contracting authority is objectively unable to define the technical means or to specify the legal or financial conditions of a project. At the same time, the conditions for using the negotiated procedure may be met because contract specifications cannot be established with sufficient precision or overall pricing is not possible due to the complex nature of the works, supply

[36] Tenders Electronic Daily, supplement to the OJEU, available at http://ted.europa.eu (1 June 2009 to 22 June 2011).

[37] J. Ruthig, 'Vergaberechtsnovelle ohne Gesetzgeber – Zum deutschen Vergaberecht nach Ablauf der Umsetzungsfrist – Teil I' (2006) *Neue Zeitschrift für Baurecht und Vergaberecht* 137, at 141.

[38] W. Heiermann, 'Der wettbewerbliche Dialog' (2005) *Zeitschrift für deutsches und internationales Bau- und Vergaberecht* 766 *et seq.*

[39] Pünder and Franzius, n. 23 above, 20; A. Fritz, 'Erfahrungen mit dem Wettbewerblichen Dialog in Deutschland' (2008) *VergabeR* 379, at 382.

or service contract in question (Article 30(1)(b) and (c) of Directive 2004/18).[40] These are the two grounds that have generally been relied on to invoke the negotiated procedure with a notice to award complex contracts in Germany, both before and after Directive 2004/18. Therefore, the relationship between the two procedures has been one of the most discussed problems within public procurement law in Germany. Some authors have argued for the supremacy of the competitive dialogue procedure on the ground that it would be devoid of meaning for complex public contracts if the contracting authority could freely choose between the negotiated procedure and the competitive dialogue.[41] In addition, the primacy of competitive dialogue has been justified by recourse to the more competitive character of the dialogue procedure.[42] However, within the course of the procurement reform of 2009, the German legislature confirmed the prevailing opinion in German legal literature based on the clear wording of Article 29 of Directive 2004/18, that contracting authorities are free to choose between the two procedures, as long as the defined requirements set out by the relevant provisions (for competitive dialogue, the existence of a particularly complex contract) are met. In its reasoning for the 2009 reform, the German legislator switched the order of the two procedures in the GWB to clarify unequivocally that neither of the two procedures enjoys priority over the other.[43]

Against this background, the installation of the competitive dialogue in Germany did not result in this procedure replacing the negotiated procedure as the relevant procedure for dealing with complex procurement projects.

Despite the general reluctance to use the procedure in practice, some prominent examples in Germany have shown that the way for a more frequent use of the competitive dialogue has been paved regardless, predominantly for successfully carrying out complex urban development contracts. Some of the most outstanding projects

[40] H. Kaelble, in M. Müller-Wrede and C. Benz (eds.), *ÖPP-Beschleunigungsgesetz* (Cologne: Bundesanzeiger Verlag, 2006), p. 49, para. 41.

[41] E. Reimnitz, *Der neue Wettbewerbliche Dialog, Eine Alternative zum Verhandlungsverfahren unter Berücksichtigung von Public Private Partnership-Modellen* (Frankfurt am Main: Peter Lang Verlag, 2009), p. 232; Klimisch and Ebrecht, n. 7 above, p. 203.

[42] Kaelble (2006), n. 40 above, p. 49, para. 42.

[43] Competitive dialogue was moved from section 101, para. 5, GWB to section 101, para. 4, GWB and took the place of the negotiated procedure which was in turn shifted to section 101, para. 5, GWB (see BMWi, I B 3-2605 13/I of 3 March 2008, p. 19).

conducted via the new procedure were the construction of a new 3,500-seater football stadium in Mainz,[44] an ambitious city development project in Hanau (near Frankfurt),[45] the reconstruction of the State of Brandenburg's Parliament building[46] and a document management system for the city of Osnabrück.

5. Operation of the competitive dialogue procedure

5.1. Introduction

Bearing in mind that the German legislation mainly followed the wording of the Public Sector Directive when transposing the new procedure into national procurement law in 2005, the operation of the competitive dialogue through contracting authorities in Germany is very much aligned to the rules and conditions set out in the Directive. The scope of the competitive dialogue procedure, as we have seen, can be extracted from § 101 IV GWB, while the actual procedural rules are laid down exclusively in the procurement regulations (§ 3 VII VOL/A-EC, § 3a IV VOB/A).

Briefly covering the flow of the competitive dialogue procedure under German legislation, German writers have noted that the new procedure is divided into four main phases: the publication phase, followed by the selection phase, followed by the dialogue phase, leading ultimately to the award phase.[47] As legislation does not provide further guidance on the structure of the competitive dialogue, many issues which are unclear at the European level (see Chapter 1) remain unclear on the national level as well.

The following remarks embrace each of the relevant procedural phases by highlighting legal problems and uncertainties as well as giving a brief overview of the solutions developed by practitioners, case law or legislation in Germany.

[44] OLG Koblenz of 24 April 2009, 1 Verg 2/09.

[45] See the website of the project, available at www.wettbewerblicher-dialog.de.

[46] OLG Brandenburg of 7 April 2009, Verg 14/08 (2010) *Neue Zeitschrift für Baurecht und Vergaberecht* 71 *et seq.*

[47] H. Schröder, 'Voraussetzungen, Strukturen und Verfahrensabläufe des Wettbewerblichen Dialogs in der Vergabepraxis' (2007) *Neue Zeitschrift für Baurecht und Vergaberecht* 216, at 220; Pünder and Franzius, n. 22 above, p. 20; and Fritz, n. 39 above, p. 20. There is an alternative view which prefers a three-phase operation of the dialogue procedure: see Kus, n. 25 above, p. 857.

5.2. *The planning stage and drafting of the descriptive document*

The competitive dialogue procedure starts with the publication of a contract notice in the OJEU[48] (on the contract notice, see further section 5.4 below). Sometimes it is advisable for contracting authorities to place a notice in advance to consult the market, especially if a contracting authority finds itself in the planning and preparation stage for exceptional projects such as PPPs or privatisations. However, it should be emphasised that there is no obligation to do market research.

5.3. *Confidentiality of information and solutions*

Following Article 29(3) of the Public Sector Directive, as discussed in section 5.3 of Chapter 1, contracting authorities must ensure equality among all tenderers and must take care that solutions as well as confidential information are not revealed to other participants or communicated without agreement.[49] Having failed to enshrine a general principle of confidentiality, Germany provides only for confidentiality rules which are exclusively part of the competitive dialogue regime. The scope of the German norms in transposition go a bit further than the European rules suggest in the sense of providing that solutions shall neither be communicated to other participants nor passed on to third parties. The prohibition on communicating solutions or other confidential information to third parties is rooted in the contracting authority's obligation to use the information passed on by the tenderers in confidence only within the concrete procurement procedure.[50] Thereby, the German legislation effectively protects the interest of the participating enterprises in ensuring that their solutions are not illegally used in other projects to the benefit of others.

It is a great concern of operators that contracting authorities act in compliance with the provisions mentioned. Therefore, contracting authorities are asked to handle the information and solutions passed on during the competitive dialogue in a trustworthy manner and this is also the reason why dialogue generally has to be conducted 'behind closed doors' and separately with the different candidates. While the

[48] The rules for publication in the OJEU are laid down in European Regulation No. 1564/2005 providing a standard form.

[49] VK Brandenburg of 22 August 2008, VK 19/08, VERIS, p. 7, 8.

[50] See § 3a IV No. 3 S. 4 VOB/A.

conduct of the dialogue in secret raises the suspicion of arbitrariness, the outlined *modus operandi* runs contrary to the natural interest of public authorities in getting best value for money and purchasing high-quality and innovative products and services. By passing on information and solutions proposed within the dialogue phase to the bidders with the lowest prices, the contracting authority could ensure that the lowest-price candidates also have access to the technically best and most innovative solutions.[51]

Under the German system, confidential information must not be passed on to participants or third parties irrespective of the concrete form of communication (oral or written) or whether the passing on happened intentionally or unintentionally, by omission, due to implied behaviour or hints. Despite this far-reaching interdiction, it is not entirely clear yet what information is 'confidential'. Without doubt, information that is publicised openly does not need to be protected through the rules governing competitive dialogue. Conversely, information falling within the scope of copyright law or patent law definitely needs to be protected as well as business secrets or the business relations of an enterprise.[52] Mirroring the rules on the law on inspection of files (§ 111 II GWB), some authors argue for protecting all information that is subject to the right to inspect files. This parallel, however, is not convincing as the law of confidentiality protects solely the bidders whereas the procedural law of file inspection protects bidders and contracting authorities alike.[53] Some legal writers argue that, in order to reduce these uncertainties, bidders must declare the confidentiality of the information passed on.[54]

Of course, as envisioned by Article 29(8) of Directive 2004/18, contracting authorities might compensate bidders for sharing their ideas and know-how. In fact, the payment clause is a great incentive for entities to reveal their innovative solutions, share confidential information and thereby contribute substantially to the optimal operation of the procedure.

As briefly mentioned above, the confidentiality rule requires that information is never shared without the consent of the bidders in the sense of §§ 182 *et seq.* BGB. In the present author's view and according to some German literature on the subject, public authorities are not

[51] VK Brandenburg of 22 August 2008, VK 19/08, VERIS, p. 7, 8.

[52] Schwabe, n. 22 above, p. 220 (giving further references). [53] *Ibid.*

[54] Heiermann, n. 38 above, p. 774; Schwabe, n. 22 above, p. 220.

entitled to select the participants only on the condition that they agree to the disclosure of information;[55] although the European Commission and some legal experts hold that view in order to solve the problem of conflicting party interests,[56] this idea of the consent working as an 'entrance ticket' to the dialogue procedure would run counter to the purpose of the confidentiality rules which is to protect bidders from having their solutions revealed. Otherwise, bidders could only participate in a competitive dialogue if they allow the use of their information.

Finally in this section, some legal authors in Germany propose to solve some of the confidentiality-related problems by installing a neutral body akin to a 'mediator' that is competent to moderate and conduct the dialogue.[57] Contracting authorities, bidders and the general public would equally benefit from this suggestion, as it helps to increase confidence in a fair procedure, helps to reduce long and costly review procedures, and ensures that procurement projects are finished on time and with the purchase of the best solution.

5.4. *Advertising requirements*

As already mentioned above and according to § 12a II No. 1 in conjunction with § 12a III No. 1 lit. a VOB/A, the competitive dialogue procedure must be advertised through a contract notice in the OJEU. German law does not add anything to the requirements of EU law in this respect. As permitted under EU law and in accordance with EU requirements (as outlined in section 5.4 of Chapter 1),[58] it is possible for the purchasing body to publicise its intention to award a contract via the competitive dialogue in other media such as daily newspapers, other official publications or websites.[59]

According to § 3 VII lit. a VOL/A-EC, § 3a IV No. 2 VOB/A, the contracting authority is asked to set out its needs and requirements in the contract notice and/or in a descriptive document. In Germany, a debate about the correct understanding of the terminology used has

[55] Opitz, n. 1 above, p. 451; Schwabe, n. 22 above, p. 223.

[56] See Ch. 1, section 5.3; and T. H. Schneider, *Der Wettbewerbliche Dialog im Spannungsverhältnis der Grundsätze des Vergaberechts* (Berlin: Duncker & Humblot, 2009), pp. 178 *et seq.*; S. Rechten, 'Die Novelle des EU-Vergaberechts' (2004) *Neue Zeitschrift für Baurecht und Vergaberecht* 366, at 368; Pünder and Franzius, n. 22 above, p. 20; Commission Explanatory Note, n. 17 above, p. 7.

[57] Schneider, n. 56 above, pp. 208 *et seq.*; Schwabe, n. 22 above, pp. 225 *et seq.*

[58] See § 12a II No. 5 VOB/A. [59] See *ibid.*

arisen. To be more concrete, the difference between 'needs' and 'requirements' has been unclear. Some authors hold the opinion that needs are performance-related whereas requirements relate to the suitability of the enterprises.[60] Others see the difference in the fact that the needs cover all aspects of the contract which need to be further clarified in the course of the dialogue.[61]

In addition to the obligation to set out the needs and requirements of the subject-matter of the contract, contracting authorities must mention in the notice the award criteria,[62] outline which documents and evidence are required by the enterprises in order to attest their suitability, and publicise the criteria for the selection of the participants in the dialogue.[63] Furthermore, it is obligatory to draft (broadly) the intended structure and course of action regarding the dialogue phase (number of dialogue rounds planned and successive reduction of participants), communicate all time limits set (for example, the time limit for the application to participate or to hand in final offers) and ultimately set out the maximum number of participants to be invited to take part in the dialogue.[64]

Guidance on how to best formulate the contract notice or the descriptive documents can be sought from the best practice solutions in the form of standardised contracts and conditions produced by the PPP Task Forces,[65] for example. Most of this material focuses on special projects and provides concrete model drafts for procurement projects in specialist fields. More general advice and helpful guidelines can be extracted from academic texts on either the competitive dialogue or the law of public–private partnerships.[66]

5.5. *The selection phase*

The selection phase covers the rules for choosing the candidates to participate in the dialogue, and was discussed in section 5.6 of Chapter 1. According to Article 29(3) of Directive 2004/18, the contracting

[60] See Schröder, n. 47 above, p. 220.
[61] Schwabe, n. 22 above, p. 171, with further references.
[62] Kaelble (2006), n. 40 above, p. 53, para. 54.
[63] Klimisch and Ebrecht, n. 7 above, p. 203.
[64] See § 3 VII lit. a VOL/A-EC.
[65] See, for example, the website of the PPP task force of North Rhine-Westphalia, www.ppp.nrw.de (28 February 2010). See Model Law on Public Private Partnerships in the consultancy service sector.
[66] See Schwabe, n. 22 above; and M. Müller-Wrede (ed.), *ÖPP-Beschleunigungsgesetz* (Cologne: Bundesanzeiger Verlag, 2006).

authority is to open the dialogue with the candidates selected in accordance with the relevant provisions of Articles 44–52. Article 44 states that, although the public body is generally free to limit the number of suitable candidates within the procedure, the minimum number of participants shall not be less than three and shall be sufficient to ensure that genuine competition takes place.

Interestingly, the German provisions transposing the Directive in this respect (§ 3a IV No. 3 VOB/A, § 3 VII lit. a, b VOL/A-EC) do not explicitly mention that the selection of the candidates has to mirror the Directive's usual selection rules. Nonetheless, the criteria used to structure the procedure in the competitive dialogue remain the same as in the other award procedures.[67] The German selection system indirectly refers to Article 44 of the Public Sector Directive, insofar as § 3 VII lit. a, b VOL/A-EC permits contracting authorities to specify the maximum number of candidates that are to be invited to the dialogue and that the minimum number of candidates shall not go below three. Thereby, effective competition in the sense of Article 44(2) is ensured.

In German procurement practice, most contracting authorities tend to limit the number of participants and reduce the number of operators during the negotiations for reasons of procedural efficiency.[68] In fact, judging by statistical data[69] covering the time period from 1 January 2009 to 1 July 2011, in sixty-four competitive dialogue procedures only three public entities refrained from successively reducing the number of participants. In these procedures twenty-five purchasers invited three to five tenderers to take part in the dialogue. The data also reveal that some entities (seven entities) preferred to invite a maximum of six tenderers, a smaller number envisioned inviting three to eight (four entities) and that most entities do not go above seven or eight candidates. In the sixty-four procedures, one entity envisaged a number between five and fifty, while three other entities set ten as the maximum number.

Concerning the character and nature of the criteria applicable to limit the number of candidates, problems have surfaced that are not fully resolved. Some legal writers in Germany are of the opinion that the criteria for the selection of the candidates are the same as for the assessment of suitability. According to these writers, bidders that are 'more suitable' than others can be invited to participate in the

[67] Klimisch and Ebrecht, n. 7 above, p. 203.
[68] Pünder, n. 1 above, § 101 GWB, para. 56.
[69] See Tenders Electronic Daily (TED), n. 36 above.

dialogue.[70] Others hold the view that the selection criteria are of an autonomous character.[71] As required by the Directive, they must, of course, in any case be non-discriminatory and objective.

5.6. *The dialogue phase*

After choosing the participants in the competitive dialogue, the contracting authority enters into the actual dialogue, in which all aspects of the contract can be discussed in order to identify and define the means best suited to satisfying the purchaser's needs as set out in the contract notice and/or the descriptive document. Within the dialogue, according to the explicit provisions of Article 29 of the Directive, the equality of treatment of all tenderers needs to be ensured so that no one tenderer is given an advantage over its competitors.

The German provisions transposing the Directive's provisions on the dialogue phase do not contain any requirements additional to those of the Directive itself. Consequently, the options for the scope of discussions enjoyed under national law equate with the options provided for by European law, as were discussed in section 5.6 of Chapter 1. It rests within the margin of discretion of the public authority how the procedure is conducted, which aspects are negotiated and to what extent, provided that the fundamental procurement principles are met.[72]

As neither Article 29 of the Directive nor German procurement rules require the submission of solutions before entering into dialogue, the contracting authority might choose to hold a preliminary meeting before negotiating the orally presented solutions. Alternately, bidders might also initially be asked to submit written essentials as the basis for further negotiations.[73]

As discussed in section 5.6 of Chapter 1, one issue in European procurement law is that of whether a successive reduction of *tenderers* (rather than simply solutions) is possible or not, and this problem has arisen in Germany. Recently, a court in Germany has had the first opportunity to decide on this matter. Without giving explanation, the Higher Regional Court of Koblenz found no legal objections to the

[70] Schneider, n. 56 above, p. 140; Ruthig, n. 37 above, p. 141.

[71] Schwabe, n. 22 above, p. 188; Kaelble (2006), n. 40 above, p. 58, para. 69.

[72] Schwabe, n. 22 above, p. 236; Knauff, n. 25 above, p. 292; VK Brandenburg of 22 August 2008, VK 19/08.

[73] Schwabe, n. 22 above, p. 257.

successive reduction of candidates in subsequent dialogue phases. Furthermore, the court ruled that neither the principle of transparency nor other basic principles of procurement law obliges the purchaser to inform candidates why he or she achieved poor results with respect to a certain award criterion and was therefore in danger of not being selected for the next phase. As also argued in Chapter 1, the view of the present author is that this decision deserves approval because, by paying heed to the economic interests of the contracting authority in structuring the procedure effectively, both European and German procurement provisions clearly provide for such a proceeding (see Articles 29 IV and 44 IV of Directive 2004/18; and § 3a IV No. 4, 5 VOB/A and § 3 VII lit. c VOL/A-EC) on the condition that such an option is sufficiently publicised beforehand.

It has also been a frequent matter of debate which concrete methods of structuring the dialogue phase are admissible under national law. Some legal experts prefer the dialogue to be conducted in a linear manner, meaning that the contracting authority can enter into the dialogue with only the best bidder,[74] in the sense of the participant submitting the best bid in an indicative bid process seeking solutions (which can involve very detailed bids). This view is mainly based on the wording of § 3a IV No. 4 requiring that the dialogue shall end the moment 'the solution' or no appropriate solution is found. Furthermore, this opinion is supported by pages 8 and 9 of the Commission's Explanatory Note, which states that a dialogue need only be conducted via parallel discussions 'insofar as there are enough solutions or suitable candidates'.[75] Nonetheless, better arguments advocate the parallel conduct of the dialogue phase.[76] According to Article 44(2) of the Public Sector Directive, a genuine competition needs to be ensured, meaning that the number of participants in the dialogue should not go below three. Furthermore, the contracting authority is envisioned to enter into dialogue with the chosen candidate*s* (Article 29(3)). Likewise, Article 29(5) requires that the dialogue shall continue until the solution or *solutions* are identifiable so that a contracting authority is not entitled to negotiate with only one, namely, the best bidder.

[74] Kramer, n. 1 above, p. 138; K. Willenbruch, 'Die Praxis des Verhandlungsverfahrens nach §§ VOBA § 3a Nr. 1 VOB/A und VOL/A' (2003) *Neue Zeitschrift für Baurecht und Vergaberecht* 424, at 422.

[75] Commission Explanatory Note, n. 17 above.

[76] Schwabe, n. 22 above, p. 260, with further references.

It should be noted that the view of some German writers has been that the reduction of solutions does not *per se* match the elimination of a candidate from the procedure; in other words, candidates taking part in a competitive dialogue procedure are generally free to submit more than just one solution on the basis of the information set out in the contract notice and/or the descriptive documents, and that, if one of the solutions is eliminated from the ongoing award procedure, other solutions submitted by the same candidate might still remain in the competition.[77] However, participation without a solution is not possible.

As the rules of confidentiality oblige the contracting authority to use the information passed on by the tenderers only with the consent of the bidder (cf. § 3 VII VOL/A-EC), as discussed in section 5.3 above, the trend in Germany is that contracting authorities mainly abstain from obtaining the bidder's consent as most participants are not inclined to give away their knowledge without being sufficiently compensated, fearing that their immediate opponents might win the contract instead or that their know-how and ideas might also be used in other projects. Further, as some legal experts stress, complex projects can definitely be handled without having any need to combine different solutions.[78] The more diverse the solutions are, the more know-how is invested, and in the end the contracting authority is able to award a more economic tender compared to levelling all solutions by means of cherry-picking.[79]

5.7. *Final tender stage*

The stage following the dialogue phase is the final tender stage. This phase as it applies under the Directive was discussed in section 5.7 of Chapter 1. It begins with the contracting authority's official declaration that the dialogue phase is over because either a suitable solution or suitable solutions have been identified or it is clear that no appropriate solution fulfilling the purchaser's needs can be found. The declaration of the dialogue being terminated might also be combined with the invitation to submit final offers. As provided in Article 29(6) of the Directive,

77 Klimisch and Ebrecht, n. 7 above, p. 207. See also OLG Brandenburg of 7 May 2009, Verg W 6/09 (2009) *Neue Zeitschrift für Baurecht und Vergaberecht* 734.

78 Schneider, n. 56 above, p. 198, 199. For a more critical view, see Kaelble (2010), n. 1 above, § 3 EG, para. 289 f.

79 Schwabe, n. 22 above, p. 219.

the latter must contain all elements required and necessary for the performance of the contract.

Under the German system, there has been much confusion regarding the correct interpretation of the provisions governing the moment of termination of the dialogue phase. According to § 3a IV lit. a VOB/A, the dialogue shall end if the contracting authority identifies one solution. On the basis of this, as we have seen in section 5.6 above, some authors argue that the dialogue phase needs to be terminated the moment just one solution meets the needs of the purchaser irrespective of the suitability of all other solutions under discussion.[80] With a view to the Directive's wording and the public service contract provision set out in § 3 VII lit. d VOL/A-EC, requiring the contracting authority to continue the dialogue until *the solution or solutions* are identifiable that are capable of meeting its needs, in the author's view this opinion cannot be justified.

Most procurement experts stress that the contracting authority is not obliged to publicise adjusted specifications as a basis for the final tenders. Although this might help to improve the comparison of all final tenders submitted, it would also put the principle of confidentiality at risk as the specifications might tend to combine the confidential solutions of the participants in the dialogue.[81]

Another frequently discussed problem relates to the question of the degree of completeness and finality required by the final tenders. The rules that apply in these respects under the Directive were discussed in sections 5.7 and 5.8 of Chapter 1. Contrary to the other procurement procedures, the competitive dialogue allows for intense discussion of the solutions, as this procedure allows for the iterative development of the best solution.[82] However, once the dialogue phase is concluded, the tenders need to be complete and finalised as regards their content. This is made clear by the fact that the final tenders shall contain *all* elements required and necessary for the performance of the contract. Further, it explicitly follows from Article 29 of Directive 2004/18 and §§ 3a VOB/A, VOL/A-EC that the tenders must not be basically changed after their

[80] Opitz, n. 1 above, p. 451; Heiermann, n. 38 above, p. 766. For a different opinion, see Hausmann, n. 1 above, § 3a VOB/A, para. 72; T. Stickler and A. Kallmayer, in K. D. Kapellmann and B. Messerschmidt (eds.), *VOB Teile A und B, VgV* (3rd edn, Munich: C. H. Beck Verlag, 2010), § 3a VOB/A, para. 40.

[81] Schwabe, n. 22 above, pp. 287, 289.

[82] VK Brandenburg of 22 August 2008, VK 19/08, VERIS, p. 7, 8.

submission. The provisions set out only allow for clarification, specification and additional information. It can be noted that the German provisions transposing Article 29(6) of the Public Sector Directive do not even allow the fine-tuning of the finalised tenders. Most German courts and procurement law experts hold a very strict view concerning the interpretation of the rules on clarification and provision of additional information, as the Directive clearly states that all kinds of changes should be banned if they are likely to distort competition or have a discriminatory effect.[83] Even the potential impact of a change suffices to justify the ban on further dialogue. Other opinions in Germany, however, are based on the generally flexible character of the competitive dialogue and argue for a wider understanding of the provisions, advocating the admissibility of post-tender negotiations within the competitive dialogue.[84] In the present author's view, given the wording of the Directive, the first line of argument seems much more persuasive. The view of the courts is largely reflected in practice, as most contracting authorities avoid further contact with tenderers after the tenders have been submitted. They tend to risk further contact only if it is clear from the contents of the tenders that the tenders are not very close so that the impact of negotiations is not harmful to competition. However, if the bids are closely matched, most contracting authorities consider it unwise to risk negotiations and thereby also risk being challenged in a review procedure in light of the evidently restrictive approach practised by the review bodies.

One last relevant point related to the stage when final tenders are submitted within the competitive dialogue concerns the possibility of submitting variants which need to be assessed on the same award criteria as the final tenders. Neither the European Directive nor the German provisions answer this question directly. Nevertheless, it can be argued that variants can be submitted in the competitive dialogue procedure as much as in any other procedure. First, Article 24 of Directive 2004/18 is not designed to govern only variants within certain procedures while eliminating the benefits of variants for the competitive dialogue

[83] Heiermann, n. 38 above, p. 775; S. Verschuur, 'Competitive Dialogue and the Scope for Discussion after Tenders and Before Selecting the Preferred Bidder – What Is Fine-tuning, Etc.' (2006) 15 *Public Procurement Law Review* 336, at 327; Schwabe, n. 22 above, p. 311.

[84] A. Kullack and R. Terner, 'EU-Legislativpaket: Die neue "klassische" Vergabekoordinierungsrichtlinie – 2. Teil' (2004) *Zeitschrift für deutsches und internationales Bau- und Vergaberecht* 348.

procedure. Secondly, it is one of the basic features of the new procedure that more than just one solution can be developed and discussed during the dialogue phase. It would run counter to the flexibility, innovation-friendliness and openness of the dialogue procedure if bidders were able to submit several solutions while being disallowed from submitting a final tender and one (or more) variants.[85] Thirdly, the wording of Article 29 of Directive 2004/18 and the German equivalents allows for the interpretation that *all* tenders of one candidate are included in the term 'final tenders', so that tenders and variants may be submitted to the same extent.[86] Some German experts have argued that variants are of rather minor importance within the competitive dialogue procedure.[87] Their view is based on the fact that the dialogue phase itself already allows for sufficient discussion and for the submission of several different and innovative solutions,[88] so that it is difficult to differentiate between main tenders and variants at least within the dialogue phase. Statistical data, however, show that approximately 50 per cent[89] of contracting authorities permit bidders to submit variants in case they need optimal solutions to be presented that they have not thought about and that were not discussed during the dialogue.

After the final tenders are opened, the contracting authority assesses all offers submitted on the basis of the award criteria laid out in the contract notice and/or the descriptive document. In the view of German authors, the award criteria and their weighting (in descending order of importance) cannot be changed in the course of the procedure as this would involve a serious risk of 'steering' the procedure in favour of one or other bidders.[90] On this basis, contracting authorities often design the award criteria in a rather rudimentary manner. This is a method suitable for ensuring that contracting authorities can compare greatly varying solutions and assess which tender is most economically advantageous

[85] Also, see the opinion expressed in the Commission Explanatory Note, n. 17 above, p. 6, para. 14.

[86] On the other hand, the phrase 'their final tenders' could also mean all tenders that are submitted by all candidates. This interpretation would lead to a ban on variants as they are not explicitly permitted.

[87] Schwabe, n. 22 above, p. 198, 199.

[88] Schwabe, n. 22 above, p. 199.

[89] In sixty-four dialogue procedures (1 January 2009 to 1 July 2011), thirty-three contracting authorities allowed for variants: see the Tenders Electronic Daily, n. 36 above.

[90] Schwabe, n. 22 above, p. 200, 201; VK Düsseldorf of 11 August 2006, VK-30/2006-L; OLG Jena of 26 March 2007, 9 Verg 2/07.

without needing to modify or amend the award criteria. Sometimes, however, contracting authorities tend to sharpen their award criteria with additional (less) important criteria. In addition, they sometimes prefer to attach different importance to the award criteria depending on the relevant stage of the dialogue. Lest infringements of the principle of transparency and non-discrimination occur in consequence of these approaches, contracting authorities follow the advice of law firms specialising in this field by sufficiently indicating the specifying criteria in advance (at the latest with the invitation to participate) and their intention of applying them either at the end of each dialogue round or, alternatively, at the very end of the dialogue phase.

As outlined in section 5.6.5 of Chapter 1, at the end of the procedure it is the most economically advantageous tenderer that wins the contract.

5.8. *Procedure following the selection of the winning tender or preferred bidder*

In transposing Article 29(8) of Directive 2004/18, § 3 VII lit. e S. 2, § 3 VOL/A-EC and § 3 IV No. 5 (1) VOB/A in identical terms permit the contracting authority to approach the economically most advantageous tenderer in order to seek further clarification or to seek confirmation of certain commitments. The meaning of Article 29(8) under the Directive and the approach in some other Member States was discussed in section 5.8 of Chapter 1.

Parallel to the legal problem of the admissibility of post-tender negotiations after the final tender stage, German courts and legal experts prefer a very strict application of the norms allowing for communication with the best bidder.[91] Under the relevant legal provisions, as we saw in Chapter 1, clarification and further information is only possible provided that the communication between the parties does not lead to basic changes to either the tender or the call of tender and does not impact competition or cause discrimination. As these provisions were designed to prevent procurement projects collapsing due to unfulfilled financing commitments issued by banks, and not to generally improve the content of the tenders, the restrictive approach is, in the experience of the current author, generally accepted in German practice. Today, confirmations by third parties concerning the financing of a project, guarantee

[91] Ruthig, n. 37 above, p. 214; Kaelble (2006), n. 40 above, para. 165.

letters of official bodies or other important documents and authorisations might be confirmed pursuant to § 3 VII lit. e S. 2, § 3 VOL/A-EC, 3 IV No. 5 (1) VOB/A. Furthermore, small changes and amendments that are not relevant for the award decision are considered admissible as well, as these do not affect competition or cause discrimination.[92]

Nonetheless, some authors prefer a broader interpretation of the German provisions in question.[93] Their arguments are based mainly on the fact that, according to the wording of the German provisions, communication is only banned if it is actually capable of distorting competition and is verifiably discriminatory. According to their view, the potential danger alone cannot suffice to uphold the restrictive interpretation of the provisions.

Due to the supremacy of EU law, however, the German provisions must be interpreted in light of Directive 2004/18 and under Article 29(8). Any form of communication is banned that 'risks' the distortion of competition and causation of discrimination. From this perspective, it can be argued that the Directive in its current shape does not allow for further communication even with the best bidder.

In the experience of the current author based on talking to practitioners in the field, contracting authorities thus abstain from further discussions with the most economically advantageous bidder unless the discussions refer to issues without relevance for the selection of the most economically advantageous tender. Instead, it is primarily the dialogue phase plus – though only rarely – the stage where clarifications can be made, that are used to discuss all relevant problems.

5.9. *The standstill period*

Due to the fact that the differentiation between the contract award decision and the conclusion of the contract is unknown to the German procurement system and the contract award decision coincides with the conclusion of the contract, any kind of review mechanism taking effect before the conclusion of the contract is immensely important in German

[92] This is also accepted as lawful by the authors cited in the note below.

[93] Stickler and Kallmayer, n. 80 above, § 3a VOB/A para. 52 f.; Kus, n. 25 above, p. 862; Schneider, n. 56 above, p. 178. See also the wording of § 3 VII VOL/A-EC and § 3 IV No. 5 VOB/A, which states that discussions that 'have the effect' of distorting competition are unlawful as opposed to discussions 'likely' to distort competition regarding discussions after the submission of bids. The authors quoted base their statement for a wider interpretation mainly on the wording of the German provisions.

procurement law. One of the most important review mechanisms brought along with the amending Remedies Directive 2007/66 is the standstill period. By definition, the standstill period means that the contracting authority should refrain from awarding and concluding the contract in order to enable effective review procedures.[94]

A standstill period was expressly included in Directive 2007/66 because the absence of such a period was previously one of the most lamented weaknesses of the Remedies Directives. In particular, an adequate period should elapse between the decision to award a contract and its conclusion. There are several reasons why a certain period should apply before the conclusion of the contract finally takes place. First, the award of the contract, or at least its conclusion, is *irreversible* (*pacta sunt servanda*) which is why legal action should be taken as early as possible in order to prevent a probably illegal conclusion of a contract.[95] The contract cannot be concluded unless this period has elapsed. Secondly, the applicant bidder or candidate is given sufficient time to think thoroughly about his chances, intentions and risks of initiating a review procedure which is time-consuming and costly.

In Germany, § 101 lit. a I S. 3–5 GWB – largely geared to the wording of the relevant provisions of Directive 2007/66/EC – generally govern the standstill period irrespective of the type of award procedure used. Therefore, a particular provision governing the details of the standstill period in competitive dialogue is not found in German procurement law.

As the duration of the standstill period lies in a Member State's discretion, Germany enjoys the freedom to exceed or maintain the minimum standstill period as envisioned in Directive 2007/66/EC. In transposition of the standstill period provided for in Article 2 of the Remedies Directive and the idea anchored in recital 5 of Directive 2007/66, the duration of the standstill period is dependent on the chosen means of communicating the information about which undertaking is to be awarded the contract. A contract may not be concluded before the expiry of a period of fifteen calendar days with effect from the day

[94] Case C-81/98, *Alcatel Austria AG and others, Siemens AG Österreich and Sag-Schrack Anlagentechnik AG* v. *Bundesministerium für Wissenschaft und Verkehr* [2009] ECR I-07671.

[95] S. Hertwig, *Praxis der öffentlichen Auftragsvergabe* (4th edn, Munich: C. H. Beck, 2010), p. 151; E. Brauer, 'Das Verfahren vor der Vergabekammer' (2009) *Neue Zeitschrift für Baurecht und Vergaberecht* 297.

following the date on which the notification and information on the relevant decision has been sent to the respective tenderer or candidate. If fax or electronic means are used, however, a ten-day period applies, again taking effect from the day following the date on which the information about the contract award decision was sent. According to § 101a I S. 4 GWB, the actual receipt of the information is not relevant; rather it is the dispatch of the notification.[96] Therefore, the standstill period in the competitive dialogue begins to run the moment the contracting authority informs all dialogue candidates who have also been invited to submit final tenders that their final tenders have not been chosen and the reasons for the decision are communicated as well.

Bidders who have not yet been lawfully excluded during the different stages of the competitive dialogues and candidates having an interest in the award whose subjective rights are infringed (§ 97 VII GWB) are deemed to be concerned pursuant to § 107 II GWB, meaning that they are entitled to initiate a review procedure.

If the contracting authority awards the contract without adhering to the standstill obligation, bidders are entitled to initiate a review procedure for ineffectiveness (§ 101b I No. 1 GWB). If the standstill period elapses, the contract can officially be awarded, ensuring legal clarity and legal certainty.[97]

5.10. *Payments for costs of participation*

Article 29(8) of the Public Sector Directive grants Member States the freedom to adopt provisions relating to the compensation for costs of participation in the competitive dialogue. Germany decided to provide for this possibility within the two procurement regulations, VOL/A and VOB/A. According to § 3a IV No. 5 (2) VOB/A, § 3 VII lit. f VOL/A-EC, a

[96] M. Dreher and J. Hoffmann, 'Die Informations- und Wartepflicht sowie die Unwirksamkeitsfolge nach den neuen §§ 101 a und 101 b GWB' (2009) *Neue Zeitschrift für Baurecht und Vergaberecht* 218.

[97] Dreher and Hoffmann, n. 96 above, p. 218. Art. 2(b) of Directive 2007/66/EC allows for certain derogations from the generally binding standstill period. Germany does not regulate this topic explicitly. Notwithstanding this, the analysis of § 101a II GWB contains valuable hints that the standstill period need not be complied with in exceptional circumstances. As information is not required in case of a negotiated procedure without prior negotiation (extreme urgency), the duty of preliminary information does not apply. Further, if the information is not sent at all, the standstill period cannot begin to run. Thus, the rules of the standstill period do not apply in cases of extreme urgency. All in all, the German rules transposing are fully compatible with European law.

contracting authority is obliged to appropriately compensate all participants asked to submit sketches, drafts, drawings, calculations, diagrams or building plans. Only participants able to present the required documents in time need to be compensated for their extra workload.

It remains unclear what sums need to be paid in order to 'appropriately' compensate the bidders as the Directive does not comment on this issue but opens up a wide margin of discretion. In German literature, some authors suggest that fixed sums might be paid or sums in accordance with the German HOAI,[98] a German legal framework for the payment of architects and engineers. Since the tenders and solutions discussed in the competitive dialogue procedure are wide in range and very diverse regarding their content and the workload involved, fixed sums would certainly not be appropriate for every candidate. What is clear, however, is that the bidders are neither compensated for the value of their ideas or solutions nor for the handling and mere processing of the tenders.[99]

Because of these uncertainties, and in light of the fact that the contracting authority is under German law obliged to compensate the participants concerned, it is advisable that either the German legislature or German courts provide for some clarity on this point.

5.11. *Time limits*

The Higher Regional Court of Brandenburg[100] has had to decide upon an interesting question which had not been considered previously in either the German literature or case law. During the beginning of the dialogue phase for the award of the reconstruction of the parliament building of the State of Brandenburg, several suggestions for the reconstruction of the facades of the building were submitted. One alternative envisaged the reconstruction of historic elements while another version comprised a contemporary solution. During the dialogue phase the public authority informed the tenderers about its final decision in favour of the historic version and asked the tenderers to submit their tenders on that (the historic) basis within one month. The plaintiff, having only submitted a contemporary solution, argued that one month was not

[98] H. Ollmann, 'Wettbewerblicher Dialog eingeführt' (2005) *VergabeR* 685, at 689.
[99] Schwabe, n. 22 above, p. 266.
[100] OLG Brandenburg of 7 May 2009, Verg W 6/09 (2009) *Neue Zeitschrift für Baurecht und Vergaberecht* 734 *et seq.*

sufficient for him because he needed essentially more time – at least a few months – to adapt his solution to the new requirements. The public authority rejected that request but extended the time limit for all tenderers to almost three months. The plaintiff did not regard the new time limit as sufficient, and took the matter to review, claiming a violation of the principle of equality and seeking extension of the time limit for another three months. The court rejected the claim on all grounds and made clear that the chosen procedure did not violate the principle of equal treatment. The court pointed out that the public authority is not responsible for balancing or adjusting any differences between the tenderers in each dialogue sub-phase. On the contrary, it would constitute discrimination against the tenderers that had submitted the preferred solution if they had to wait for the other tenderers.[101] The court went on to state that deadlines set by the contracting authority must be appropriate, but that this clearly does not mean that deadlines have to be convenient for the slowest tenderer.

Contracting authorities will no doubt welcome this decision as it strengthens their discretion in designing the competitive dialogue procedure. For that reason the judgment deserves to be commended despite critique from one source that claims that the contracting authorities must also give slow tenderers the chance to catch up with the other tenderers in order for the former to have a realistic chance of winning the award.[102] This view, it is submitted, misconceives essential characteristics of the new procedure, which is primarily supposed to find innovative solutions through *competition*.

6. Conclusion

In Germany, the competitive dialogue procedure cannot be regarded entirely as a success story yet. This is partly due to the German provisions providing only limited guidance on the new procedure and partly due to the fact that as yet there is only a limited amount of case law. In consequence, public authorities are wary of judicial review and stick to the established and flexible negotiated procedure instead. Although the possibilities for the negotiated procedure under national law are restricted as well so that the decision to use this procedure is no less

[101] *Ibid.*, at p. 736.

[102] T. Mösinger, 'Gleichbehandlung der Teilnehmer im Wettbewerblichen Dialog' (2009) *Neue Zeitschrift für Baurecht und Vergaberecht* 695 *et seq.*

risky than the acceptance of errors within the competitive dialogue, authorities mainly prefer the negotiated procedure nonetheless. This does not mean that contracting authorities award contracts directly without competition in order to reduce the risk of a review procedure in the sense that the procedure is less likely to be challenged. Contracting authorities in Germany still adhere to procurement rules – but they prefer to use the flexible negotiated procedure. This is mainly due to the fact that there is more clarity and guidance from both literature and case law on how to interpret its conditions and on how to best organise the procedure as the negotiated procedure has been in existence quite a long time. In addition, critical voices in literature stressing the problems and questioning the suitability of the competitive dialogue procedure have had their effect on the procurement approach of many public entities. Finally, the competitive dialogue is only available in case of a particularly complex contract and most contracts awarded in Germany do not fulfil this requirement, while there are more prerequisites allowing for the use of the negotiated procedure.

The first decisions and judgments available on competitive dialogue seem to follow a flexible approach and to strengthen the discretion and creativity of contracting authorities. This margin of discretion combined with the paucity of guidance, creates several risks, but also offers benefits for both the public and the private sector. Thus, courageous academics and practitioners, possibly influenced by the success story of dialogue procedures in the UK and the United States, may wish to point out the potential of this new procedure in terms of improved value for money – for example, by way of selecting and analysing best practice examples.

6

Competitive dialogue in Denmark

STEEN TREUMER

1. Introduction: regulation of public procurement in Denmark

Denmark is a constitutional monarchy with a parliamentary system of government. It has a state-level government[1] and local government in ninety-eight municipalities. Denmark became a member of the European Union in 1973. Competitive public procurement has been common at least from about 1850,[2] even though the field was not regulated by laws specific to public procurement before 1966 when an Act on tenders concerning private and public works came into force.[3] However, it followed from Danish administrative law principles that tenderers should be treated equally and that the contracting entities should behave in an economically responsible manner.

The EU public procurement Directives were initially transposed into national law by Circulars in Denmark.[4] However, this approach to the implementation of the Directives was changed in 1990 when an Act implemented the public procurement Directives of that time.[5] The current public procurement Directives are implemented by Decrees.[6]

[1] This includes five independent regional state administrations that handle state tasks in areas where it is considered to be an advantage that administration and related contact between authorities and citizens are taken care of at the regional level. These institutions come under the Ministry for the Interior and Social Affairs as far as budget and organisation is concerned.

[2] See R. Nielsen, *Udbud af Offentlige Kontrakter* (4th edn, Copenhagen, 2010), p. 55. The first Danish examples of competitive public procurement are known from around 1750. The procedure was oral and public until around 1850 and concerned procurement for the church and the army. The development of the early Danish procurement system appears to have been inspired by France: cf. A. H. Pedersen, *Licitation* (Copenhagen, 1955), pp. 22–4.

[3] Cf. Licitationsloven. Act No. 216 of 8 June 1966.

[4] Circular No. 214 of 4 October 1974 on Public Works; and Circular No. 101 of 19 June 1978 on Supplies.

[5] Act No. 366 of 8 June 1990.

[6] Decree No. 936 of 16 September 2004 with subsequent amendments implements the Utilities Directive 2004/17; and Decree No. 937 of 16 September with subsequent

As explained in Chapter 1 (see section 2 of that chapter), the Directives leave considerable discretion to the Member States and thereby room for national regulation of the field of public procurement. In some Member States the national legislator has used this discretion to a wide extent, whereas the approach in other Member States has been cautious and the supplementary regulation at national level has been limited. The Danish system of public procurement regulation clearly falls into the latter category. The text of the Directives was maintained when they were implemented and the legislator thereby in all essential points refrained from making any changes to the text of the public procurement Directives. § 1 of the Decree implementing the Public Sector Directive simply states that contracting entities shall observe the provisions in the Directive and Annex 1 to the Decree reproduces the Public Sector Directive without any changes.

This method of implementation ensures that Danish interpretations are as closely linked to the EU sources of law on the competitive dialogue procedure as they can possibly be. The disadvantage is that the lack of clarity linked to the wording of the Directives is mirrored in the relevant Danish laws and that Denmark does not take advantage of the opportunity to supplement the regulation of the Directives where appropriate. It is possible that the above-mentioned Decrees will be replaced by a public procurement Act and the above-mentioned approach will be changed: the intention is that Denmark will also fill in gaps and regulate the field covered by the public procurement Directives to a wider extent than has been seen previously.[7] It is likely that the Danish legislator will consider the competitive dialogue procedure in the course of this process.

Public works procurement falling outside the scope of the public procurement Directives is regulated in an Act[8] which takes an approach very similar to the one found in the Directives. Services and goods falling below the thresholds of the Directive are also partially covered by this Act where their value exceeds DKK500,000 (about €75,000).

amendments implements the Public Sector Directive 2004/18. The legal basis of these Decrees is Act No. 600 of 1992 that authorises the relevant ministers to implement the public procurement Directives.

7 See the strategy of Minister Brian Mikkelsen on public–private co-operation published on 11 January 2011 at www.oem.dk/publikationer/2011/strategi-til-fremme-af-offentlig-privat-samarbejde.

8 Decree No. 1410 of 7 December 2007.

The contracts concluded by public bodies are subject to private law even though they are concluded by public bodies. The Danish legal system does not recognise the category of 'administrative contracts' and there are no criteria in place for categorising contracts as such. There is also no public contracts code but instead a general Contracts Act. The latter Act deals with both the formation and execution of the contract.

It should be stressed that public procurement law is given a high priority in Danish society[9] and the interpretation of the law is rather formalistic and restrictive in comparison with the situation in some Member States, including the UK. In other words, there is very high emphasis on equal treatment and transparency in Danish public procurement practice, and the guidance from the European Commission is normally followed in practice and case law.

The Danish market is also very transparent with alert competitors who benefit from one of the most efficient enforcement systems in the EU. The Danish enforcement system goes further than required by the Remedies Directives and EU law on various points.[10]

The new Act on Enforcement of the Public Procurement Rules from 2010[11] fundamentally changed the division of work between the bodies involved in enforcement of the public procurement rules. Until the above-mentioned Act entered into force, aggrieved tenderers and a number of other entities had a free choice between the Complaints Board for Public Procurement and the ordinary courts when they sought a formal settlement of a dispute. It now follows from the Act on the Enforcement of the Public Procurement Rules that complaints cannot be submitted to the ordinary courts during the standstill period. The Complaints Board for Public Procurement has become the obligatory first-instance body in procurement disputes in most cases.[12]

The Complaints Board has the power to grant interim measures, the power to establish that the rules have been violated and the power to issue set-aside orders to contracting authorities. It can also declare a

[9] Ever since the landmark case of Case C-243/89, *Commission* v. *Denmark* [1993] ECR I-3353.

[10] See S. Treumer, 'Enforcement of the EU Public Procurement Rules: Danish Regulation and Practice', in S. Treumer and F. Lichère (eds.), *Enforcement of the EU Public Procurement Rules* (Copenhagen: DJØF Publishing, 2011).

[11] Act No. 492 of 12 May 2010 on the Enforcement of the Procurement Rules with subsequent amendments.

[12] With the exceptions mentioned in § 5(2) and § 5(3) of the Act.

contract ineffective and award damages. The latter competence is remarkable and atypical in both a Danish and a European context. The award of damages is normally exclusively a matter for the ordinary courts in Denmark and the Complaints Board is an administrative body. The Complaints Board did not have the competence to award damages when it was established in the early 1990s but the legislation was changed in 2000 so that the Board became vested with the power to award damages for infringements of the EU public procurement rules.[13]

As just noted, the Complaints Board for Public Procurement is an administrative body and not a part of the judiciary. However, the Complaints Board is chaired by judges and it can make references for preliminary rulings to the Court of Justice of the European Union. The other members of the Board are experts in fields of relevance to the functioning of the Board – that is, public procurement, law and utilities, as envisaged in § 9 of the Act on the Enforcement of the Public Procurement Rules.

It is only in exceptional cases that the rulings of the Complaints Board are appealed before the ordinary courts, which happens in about 10 per cent of procurement cases, and only a couple of cases have been brought directly before the ordinary courts since the establishment of the Complaints Board. The number of complaints has increased over the years and considerably in recent years. The Complaints Board received only about 15 complaints around the year 2000 but 84 complaints in 2008,[14] 115 in 2009 and 182 in 2010. The Complaints Board has played a significant role in developing public procurement law and frequently bases its rulings on the principles of equal treatment of tenderers and the principle of transparency.

The Danish Competition and Consumer Authority (hereinafter the surveillance authority) can also deal with complaints concerning alleged infringements but *cannot* issue a binding order in the field of public procurement. However, it can instead bring a case before the Complaints Board if a contracting authority does not comply with the recommendations of the surveillance authority. This has allowed the surveillance authority to function as an easy, and also rather informal, alternative to

[13] See S. Treumer, 'Increased Effectiveness of Public Procurement Remedies in Denmark' (2000) 9 *Public Procurement Law Review* NA 120, for an analysis of the change of the legislation and its background.

[14] Cf. the preparatory works to the Act on the Enforcement of the Public Procurement Rules.

the Complaints Board for Public Procurement. Furthermore, it has ensured that disputes can be resolved at a relatively low level in many instances. The potential for a complaint of the surveillance authority to the Complaints Board has helped in reality to 'convince' many contracting authorities and it is not necessary to enter into the more formal, costly and time-consuming dispute before the Complaints Board for Public Procurement or the ordinary courts. However, the resources of the surveillance authority are now primarily used for other tasks. Contracting authorities have also recently been more unwilling than previously to suspend the tender procedures until the surveillance authority has had a chance to look into the substance of the complaint. The alternative dispute settlement is to a large extent dependent on the willingness of contracting authorities to suspend the procedures, and, if this willingness is not present, the complainants must then normally bring the case before the Complaints Board for Public Procurement if they wish to have their complaint considered. It can be added that only on rare occasions has the surveillance authority in fact used its standing to refer a complainant to the Complaints Board, and with a very low success rate.

2. The background: complex procurement prior to competitive dialogue

Unlike some other Member States, such as France,[15] Denmark did not legislate for specific tender procedures in order to be able better to handle complex contracts. Complex procurement prior to the introduction of competitive dialogue has typically followed the standard procedures, with restricted procedures being applied most frequently in this respect.

There have not been, and still there are not, a significant number of negotiated procedures with a notice in Denmark,[16] and the clear majority of procedures of this type concern contracts covered by the Utilities Directive. However, there is anecdotal evidence that at least some contracting authorities have interpreted the reasons for access to negotiated

[15] France is an interesting example as it introduced a specific procedure for complex contracts in its national regime before the introduction of competitive dialogue in the EU system. See Ch. 4, section 4.

[16] The number of procedures was about 200 for a number of years. Currently, it appears that the number is increasing.

procedures without prior publication in a rather flexible manner. It is not possible on the evidence available to assess whether this implies that the public procurement rules have been violated or to assess the extent of any possible problems. The fact that there have been only a few complaints where it was subsequently established that the contract in question was directly illegally awarded might indicate that circumvention has not been widespread. Nevertheless, this is only an indication: in particular, it should be borne in mind that direct illegal award is difficult to track and that the previous enforcement regime in the field of EU public procurement law did not provide competitors with a real incentive to bring a case of this type.[17]

Design contests have also to some extent been used for procurement of complex contracts. The number of design contests has been, and still is, relatively low in Denmark.[18] The design contest is currently normally used for contracts relating to public works but has also to some extent been used for IT contracts, primarily around ten years ago.

3. Introduction to competitive dialogue

Denmark was the first Member State to fully implement the Public Sector Directive: the Danish law entered into force on 1 January 2005 and created the legal basis for the application of the competitive dialogue procedure as of this date. As mentioned in section 1 of this chapter the Danish legislator has essentially implemented the exact wording of the Public Sector Directive. There are no changes or additions to the regulation of the competitive dialogue procedure in the Danish legislation.

There was no debate on whether competitive dialogue should be implemented as it appeared obviously appropriate to ensure increased flexibility in Danish public procurement practice. Competitive dialogue procedures are not similar to procedures previously used in national law and contracting authorities covered by the Public Sector Directive are not used to operating tender procedures with widespread negotiations. As pointed out in section 2, the use of negotiated procedures is

[17] The competitor will typically not be able to obtain damages and an illegal direct award has in many Member States not traditionally led to a termination of the contract: see S. Treumer, 'Towards an Obligation to Terminate Contracts Concluded in Breach of the EC Public Procurement Rules: The End of the Status of Concluded Public Contracts as Sacred Cows' (2007) 16 *Public Procurement Law Review* 371.

[18] On average, about thirty a year for the past five years. Currently, it appears that the number is increasing.

exceptional in Danish procurement practice for contracts covered by the Public Sector Directive.

The use and operation of competitive dialogue have been challenged in various cases in Denmark and consequently there is Danish case law on competitive dialogue – in contrast with the situation in most Member States so far. The case law is of general interest as the cases concern fundamental issues of interpretation, including the field of application of competitive dialogue. This case law is considered in further detail in sections 4 and 5 of this chapter.

The Danish Competition and Consumer Authority issues guidance on the public procurement rules and the guidance issued on the EU public procurement rules covers tendering procedures, including competitive dialogue.[19]

Denmark is one of the smaller Member States of the EU with a population of about 5.5 million. Despite the country's small size, the new competitive dialogue procedure has been applied around fifty times,[20] which is relatively frequent taking into consideration the size of the Danish market and the limited number of inhabitants. Several of these procedures have concerned public–private partnerships.

The analysis in this chapter is based – in addition to traditional legal research methods – on in-depth studies of the Danish notices on competitive dialogue in the OJEU (TED), interviews with practitioners who have been involved in competitive dialogue procedures as civil servants working for contracting authorities, employees of tenderers and the advisors of both parties.[21] In addition, due account has also been taken

[19] See www.kfst.dk.

[20] In the period 1 January 2005 to 15 June 2011. These data take into account the fact that a number of notices concern the same contract that has been tendered out twice; notices concerning the same contract have been counted as one.

[21] The author wishes to thank the following for their co-operation: Søren Staugaard Nielsen, Attorney and Business Manager, Rambøll Management Consulting; Casper Schmidt, Attorney and Manager, Rambøll Management Consulting; Tina Braad, Partner, Holst, Advokater; Kurt Bardeleben, Partner, Lett Advokatt; Jens Bødtcher-Hansen, Partner, Kammeradvokaten Advokatfirmaet Poul Schmith; Tom Holsøe, Partner, Kammeradvokaten Advokatfirmaet Poul Schmith; Simon Evers Kalsmose-Hjelmborg, Partner, Bech Bruun; Jesper Fabricius, Partner, Accura; Annemette Thorgaard, Senior Manager, Accura; René Offersen, Partner, Lett advokatfirma; Claus Berg, Partner, Viltoft; Bo Tarp, Administrative Head of Department, Road Directorate; Lotte Hummelshøj, Partner, Nielsen Nørager law firm; Henrik Ryberg, Project Director, Cowi; Frans Dupont, Cowi; Sameer Kohli, Lægemiddelstyrelsen; Peter Dann Jørgensen, Bender von Haller Dragsted; Poul Thorup, Hovmøller & Thorup; and Mads Steffensen, Odense Municipality.

of a number of reports and presentations made by contracting authorities and tenderers that have experience with competitive dialogue.[22]

4. Scope of the competitive dialogue procedure in law and practice

The conditions for the use of competitive dialogue in Danish law are identical to the conditions outlined in the Public Sector Directive, as were discussed in section 4 of Chapter 1.

It should be stressed that competitive dialogue in Danish legal theory is perceived as a procedure with a limited area of application and it appears to be commonly accepted that the grounds for its use as set out in the Directive must be interpreted strictly.[23] Taking into account also that the procedure has been applied relatively frequently in Danish procurement practice, it is not surprising that there have been several challenges to the use of competitive dialogue in Danish case law.

The first case of general interest was the ruling of 8 January 2008, *WAP Wöhr Automatikparksystem GmbH and Co. KG* v. *Ørestadsparkering A/S* from the Danish Complaints Board for Public Procurement.[24] In this case, a contracting entity – Ørestadsparkering A/S – had applied the competitive dialogue procedure to a project for the design and execution of automatic parking facilities. Five companies were qualified but only two tenderers, both German, took part in the final stages of the competitive dialogue procedure. The contracting authority had allowed variant bids[25] and a variant bid was considered the economically most advantageous tender. The tenderer that was not awarded the contract

[22] Including an article on experience with competitive dialogue by A.-M. Falch and F. Pedersen, *Erfaringer med udbudsformen 'konkurrencepræget dialog'-set fra en udbyders perspektiv* (Nordjyllands Amt, 2005), available at www.udbudsportalen.dk; and an extensive paper on the experiences of the Palaces and Properties Agency (Slots – og Ejendomsstyrelsen) of the Ministry of Finance, *Erfaringsnotat om udbud i konkurrencepræget dialog*, available at www.ses.dk.

[23] See S. Troels Poulsen, P. Stig Jakobsen and S. Evers Kalsmose-Hjelmborg, *EU Udbudsretten* (2nd edn, Copenhagen, 2011), p. 360; Nielsen, n. 2 above, p. 145; J. Fabricius, *Offentlige indkøb i praksis* (Copenhagen, 2010), p. 181; R. Offersen, *Udbudsprocessen* (Copenhagen, 2010), p. 27; M. Steinicke and L. Groesmeyer, *EU's udbudsdirektiver med kommentarer* (2nd edn, Copenhagen: Jurist- og Økonomforbundets Forlag, 2008), p. 329, J. Fabricius and R. Offersen, *EU's udbudsregler i praksis* (Copenhagen, 2006), p. 146. See also S. Treumer, 'Competitive Dialogue' (2004) 13 *Public Procurement Law Review* 178; and S. Treumer, 'The Field of Application of Competitive Dialogue' (2006) 15 *Public Procurement Law Review* 307.

[24] The author assisted the lawyer of the contracting authority in the complaints case.

[25] This was also challenged by the complainant. See section 5.7 of this chapter.

complained shortly after the award of the contract and argued, *inter alia*, that the contracting authority had violated Article 29 of the Public Sector Directive because the grounds for use of the competitive dialogue procedure were not fulfilled.

The Complaints Board introduced its ruling by emphasising that there are as yet no rulings from the Court of Justice on the issue and then commented on the implications of the wording in recital 31 of the preamble to the Public Sector Directive. It is provided in this recital that 'contracting authorities which carry out particularly complex projects may, without this being due to any fault on their part, find it *objectively impossible* [emphasis added] to define the means of satisfying their needs or of assessing what the market can offer in the way of technical solutions and/or financial/legal solutions'. The Board held that, even given the wording of this recital,[26] there is in fact no reason to assume that the possibility of using competitive dialogue is limited to circumstances where it is absolutely impossible to use traditional tender procedures,[27] as the complainant had argued. The Board added that a consideration in a preamble may cast light on the interpretation to be given to a legal rule but it cannot in itself constitute a legal rule, as provided by Case C-215/88, *Case Fleischhandels-GmbH*.[28] This part of the ruling is important as the interpretation on this point appears to deviate fundamentally from the approach of the Complaints Board in the subsequent ruling of 14 April 2008, *Damm Celluar Systems A/S mod Økonomistyrelsen*, which is further commented on below.

The Board then went on to clarify that it follows from Article 29(1) of the Public Sector Directive that the contracting authorities enjoy a certain limited discretion, as envisaged in the provision: 'Member States may provide that where contracting authorities *consider* [emphasis added] that the use of the open or restricted procedure will not allow the award of the contract, the latter may make use of the competitive dialogue procedure.' The Board then emphasised the fact that there was

[26] See further the discussion in Ch. 1, section 4, on the grounds for using competitive dialogue, including the comments on the wording of recital 31.

[27] Open procedures and restricted procedures.

[28] Case C-215/88, *Case Fleischhandels GmbH* v. *Bundesanstalt für landwirtschaftliche Marktordnung* [1989] ECR- I-2789. See S. Treumer, 'Technical Dialogue and the Principle of Equal Treatment: Dealing with Conflicts of Interests after Fabricom' (2007) 16 *Public Procurement Law Review* 99, at 103, regarding this case and the recitals on the access to technical dialogue in the public procurement Directives, the wording of which is misleading.

no experience with automatic parking facilities in Denmark[29] even though the complainant and the winning tenderer had several years of experience abroad. Finally, the board underlined that the complexity of the task had been increased by requirements relating to the design and to the functionality[30] and that even two rounds of technical dialogue and many solutions had not led to the winning bid. As mentioned above, a variant bid was considered the economically most advantageous, which is rather surprising taking into consideration the extent of dialogue in the tender procedure. On this basis, the Complaints Board held that the contract in question was 'particularly complex' and that the conditions for the use of the competitive dialogue procedure had been fulfilled.

It appears relevant to mention that the contracting authority also had documented the frequent use of competitive dialogue procedures in the UK and France and had used the practice there as an argument for a flexible approach in the concrete case. The Complaints Board did not comment on this argument. Nevertheless, it cannot be excluded that this part of the argumentation might have had some bearing on the case and that interpretation in other Member States could influence the balancing of interests in a concrete case at national level.

A few months later, the Danish Complaints Board for Public Procurement again had the opportunity to consider a challenge to the use of the competitive dialogue procedure, which led to the ruling of 14 April 2008, *Damm Celluar Systems A/S mod Økonomistyrelsen*. The ruling on the use of competitive dialogue was subsequently declared invalid by the Court of Appeal[31] due to a procedural error. The case was consequently sent back to the Complaints Board which then rendered a new ruling. Unsurprisingly, the Complaints Board confirmed its position in the new ruling of 27 April 2010, *Damm Cellular Systems A/S mod Økonomistyrelsen*. This ruling was also appealed and the case is currently pending before the ordinary courts. The remarks in the following discussion concern the original ruling of 14 April 2008; it is particularly interesting to compare this ruling and the ruling of 8 January 2008, *WAP*

[29] The complainant had argued that it was relevant to consider the general experience related to automatic parking facilities and not only the Danish experience with such facilities.

[30] The automatic parking facility was required to function in an area with heavy traffic which increased the requirements as regards the speed at which the facility could be operated. Usually automatic parking facilities are placed in areas without heavy traffic.

[31] Ruling of 29 June 2009 from the Court of Appeal (Østre Landsret 15. afd. No. B-2542-08).

Wöhr Automatikparksystem GmbH and Co. KG againt Ørestadsparkering A/S from the Complaints Board for Public Procurement.

The contract in question concerned the creation and operation of a national radio-based telecommunications network for ten years. Three tenderers were qualified and the tenderers were given seven possibilities of submitting provisional bids during the competitive dialogue procedure. The complainant in the case raised a number of issues. One of them was the allegedly unjustified use of the competitive dialogue procedure; it was argued that the contract was not particularly complex. The members of the Complaints Board did not agree and the two lay members overruled the President of the Complaints Board in the concrete case. The President found the use of the competitive dialogue procedure justified on very special grounds,[32] but the majority held that the conditions for the use of competitive dialogue were not fulfilled as the contracting authority knew of the relevant technical needs and requirements. These members also added that the contracting authority had not argued that the legal and/or financial make-up of the project caused problems.[33] Finally, these two members of the board remarked that competitive dialogue must be interpreted as an exceptional procedure which can only be applied when other possibilities are not present, as provided in recital 31 of the preamble quoted above. This interpretation given by the two lay members of the Complaints Board in the current case was clearly literal and contrary to the interpretation of the Complaints Board in the first ruling of 8 January 2008. It is submitted that the approach in the ruling of 14 April 2008, *Damm Celluar Systems A/S mod Økonomistyrelsen* is based on a misunderstanding of the legal value of a recital in the preamble as a source of law. As noted above, a recital casts light on the interpretation to be given to a legal rule but it cannot in itself constitute a legal rule – be taken literally – as clarified by the CJEU. The approach in the concrete case appears to be too restrictive and fundamentally different from the approach taken in the ruling of 8 January

[32] One of the tenderers had obtained the right to certain radio frequencies prior to the award and these rights made it very difficult to create a level playing field. The President of the Complaints Board concluded that a competitive tender procedure was the sort of tender procedure that gave the best opportunities of ensuring equal treatment of the tenderers.

[33] However, this was not correct: cf. the ruling of the Court of Appeal mentioned in n. 31 above. The contracting authority had argued that the legal and/or financial make-up of the project had influenced the choice of competitive dialogue as the tender procedure.

2008, *WAP Wöhr Automatikparksystem GmbH and Co. KG* v. *Ørestadsparkering A/S*.

Later that year, the Danish Competition and Consumer Authority[34] (hereinafter the surveillance authority) considered a complaint of 12 September 2008 concerning a tender for an IT system which led to a statement from the Authority of 9 December 2008, *Kolding Kommunes udbud af it-system til Jobcenter Kolding*. The complainant again argued that the use of competitive dialogue was unfounded as the contract was not a 'particularly complex' contract. The contracting authority was a municipality with limited experience in procuring IT systems and the municipality had admitted that *to a certain extent* it was objectively possible to establish the technical means. However, the surveillance authority did not find it proven that it was 'objectively impossible' to define the technical means. Furthermore, the surveillance authority also considered whether the contracting authority could use the competitive dialogue procedure because it would not be able to determine which of several possible solutions would be best suited to satisfying its needs. The use of competitive dialogue on this ground was considered unjustified. The surveillance authority did not find it proven that the contracting authority had tried to identify the possible solutions with the aim of establishing the technical means that fulfilled the needs of the contracting authority. Nevertheless, the authority accepted as a matter of legal principle that competitive dialogue can be used for identifying the *best* means and made a reference to the Explanatory Note of the European Commission in this context.

Finally, the surveillance authority emphasised that the fact that the contracting authority had not previously tendered out a contract concerning IT services to the specific entity in question was not of importance for assessing the complexity of the contract. It could be questioned whether this pure rejection of the lack of experience as a relevant circumstance is correct on the basis that it is relevant to consider the actual level of experience and expertise held by the contracting authority in question.[35] The Explanatory Note from the Commission supports this

[34] Called the Competition Authority in 2008, but now the Competition and Consumer Authority.

[35] See Ch. 1, section 4; and also A. Brown, 'The Impact of the New Procurement Directive on Large Public Infrastructure Projects: Competitive Dialogue or Better the Devil you Know?' (2004) 13 *Public Procurement Law Review* 160; S. Arrowsmith, *The Law of Public and Utilities Procurement* (2nd edn, London: Sweet & Maxwell, 2005), p. 634; and Treumer, n. 23 above, p. 314.

interpretation as it underlines that the concept of objective impossibility is not an abstract concept and that account needs to be taken of the capacity of the contracting authority concerned.[36]

The use of competitive dialogue was also challenged in another case before the Complaints Board for Public Procurement leading to the ruling of 14 September 2009, the consortia *Vision Area* v. *Københavns Bymuseum*. In this case, the use of competitive dialogue was not considered to be a violation of the EU public procurement rules. The project was clearly very special even though a similar project had been carried out by a service provider in New Zealand. The same service provider participated in the competitive dialogue procedure in Denmark and was finally awarded the contract some time after the complainant had brought the case before the Danish Complaints Board for Public Procurement.

Finally, the scope of competitive dialogue was also considered in the ruling of 1 November 2010, *P-Nordic* v. *Aalborg Kommune*. The contract was of a relatively modest value[37] and concerned a change of machines for parking charges. The Board considered the use of the procedure to be unjustified in the concrete case and emphasised that the requirements relating to complexity are strict. The Board also emphasised that the contracting authority only enjoys a limited discretion as to whether the conditions for the application are fulfilled and that the contracting authority carries the burden of proof for this. The Board also explicitly took into account that a similar contract had been tendered simultaneously by another municipality using an open procedure.

The risk of legal challenge to the use of the competitive dialogue procedure appears to be high in Denmark and it is hard to predict the outcome of the cases based on the limited case law. As a consequence, several practicing lawyers warn clients against using competitive dialogue. The Danish case law leaves one with the impression that there is disagreement on whether the field of application should be interpreted in a restrictive or flexible manner. However, the restrictive approach seems to be dominant.

The guide from the Danish Competition and Consumer Authority on the EU public procurement rules, mentioned in section 3, also covers the

[36] See European Commission, *Explanatory Note – Competitive Dialogue – Classic Directive*, available at http://ec.europa.eu/internal_market/publicprocurement/docs/explan-notes/classic-dir-dialogue_en.pdf, section 2.1.

[37] It follows from the ruling that the highest bid was about €1 million.

conditions for use of competitive dialogue, but the guidance on this point is limited to less than one page. A few examples of hypothetical usage are given and the basic conditions are outlined. The text is straightforward but corresponds in essence to what can easily be deduced from the text of the Public Sector Directive. However, some remarks on 'impossibility' in the guide are interesting. It is stressed that this concept is absolute and that the type of contract in question 'in general must be difficult to describe'. It is also pointed out that it must be taken into consideration whether a contracting authority easily can buy external assistance to draw up the specifications.[38]

As regards the overall picture of use in practice, we can note that the competitive dialogue procedure has been applied about fifty times between 1 January 2005 and 15 June 2011, as mentioned in section 3. Several of these competitive dialogue procedures have concerned public–private partnerships (PPPs). This is remarkable as PPPs are rare in Danish public procurement practice. Another interesting fact is that ten contracting authorities have organised more than 50 per cent of the Danish competitive dialogue procedures. The majority of these ten authorities are state authorities but a few of them are regional/local authorities.

Complex contracts for which competitive dialogue has been used are typically larger public works or ICT contracts.[39] About 50 per cent of Danish competitive dialogue procedures have related to ICT contracts and close to 40 per cent related to public works. Only a very limited number of complex services that have been the subject of competitive dialogue procedures are not linked to ICT contracts. The contract value for contracts awarded using competitive dialogue is typically very large but occasionally contracts with a relatively low value of around €1 million or even less are seen to be awarded using this procedure.

Several Danish competitive dialogue procedures have related to PPPs even though the clear majority of Danish competitive dialogue projects are not linked to PPPs. This is noteworthy as the European Commission

[38] This is clearly a more restrictive approach than is taken in the French implementation of the requirement for a particularly complex contract where emphasis is put on whether the contracting authority 'alone and in advance' can draw up the specifications: see Ch. 4, section 4.

[39] This is in accordance with the general trend in the Member States: see Ch. 1, section 4.6.2, and generally Ch. 2.

in its Explanatory Note on Competitive Dialogue indirectly invited use of the procedure in the area of PPPs: the Commission stated in this Note that competitive dialogue may become relevant due to legal or financial complexity 'very, very often in connection with projects of Public–Private Partnerships'.[40] This statement indicates a wider scope for the competitive dialogue than one would immediately assume on the basis of the wording of the Public Sector Directive. It can be added that the above-mentioned guide from the Danish surveillance authority limits itself to stating that legal or financial complexity, for instance, can be present in cases relating to PPPs.

Competitive dialogue appears not to be used for contracts that are not within the scope of the Public Sector Directive because the contracts are below the thresholds, concessions contracts or contracts that are covered by the Utilities Directive.[41] The use of competitive dialogue in a formal sense for contracts covered by the Utilities Directive would appear not to be justified because the European legislator did not create a legal basis for its use in this sector. Nevertheless, as discussed in section 4 of Chapter 1, it would be possible to construct a procedure very similar to competitive dialogue and to label it as a negotiated procedure. The use of competitive dialogue is also not ruled out by the EU public procurement rules for contracts outside the scope of the Public Sector Directive, notably services concessions and also contracts below the Directive's thresholds. The use of a procedure similar to competitive dialogue would therefore appear to be an option in theory. However, it is unlikely that Danish contracting authorities will consider it relevant to use the costly, time-consuming and lengthy competitive dialogue procedure for contracts below the thresholds.[42] It could, on the other hand, perhaps be relevant for some Annex II B services or services concessions.

Competitive dialogue appears not to have had any impact on the use of the other tender procedures that previously were used for complex contracts. However, it has to be kept in mind that the total number of Danish competitive dialogue procedures is limited to about fifty from the time the procedure was introduced in Denmark until 15 June 2011.

[40] See Commission Explanatory Note, n. 36 above, section 2.3.

[41] However, there appears to have been one exception in Danish practice. For the general trend in European practice, see Ch. 1, section 4.6.2.

[42] Several of the interviewees pointed out that this would be irrelevant.

5. Operation of the competitive dialogue procedure

5.1. Introduction

The Danish legislator has allowed practitioners considerable discretion in organising the competitive dialogue procedure, equivalent to that outlined in the Public Sector Directive. There are no changes of or additions to the regulation of the competitive dialogue procedure in the Danish legislation. The contracting authorities have therefore the privilege of interpreting the rules without the confusion that could be caused by the introduction of competitive dialogue into a national legal system.

The reader should be aware that the nature of evidence relied on in the following section differs to a considerable degree. Some statements are based on scientific empirical research that indicates clearly that practitioners address the issue in a specific manner. This is, for instance, the case when it comes to the position of variants, as considered in section 5.7, or practice on selection where it is possible to establish the practice on the basis of tender notices in the OJEU (TED). Other areas, for example payment for costs of participation as discussed in section 5.10, or structuring of the dialogue phase as discussed in section 5.6, are more complex and difficult to analyse. Analysis of these issues relies on several sources such as tender notices that might contain relevant information, interviews, reports and presentations on experiences with competitive dialogue, and anecdotal evidence. As a consequence, the empirical findings and statements on these issues are more uncertain and dependent on the reliability of the various sources applied. It can be added that some of the interviewed sources were unable or unwilling to reveal the identity of the procedures and/or contracting authorities involved.

5.2. The planning stage and drafting of the descriptive document

The Public Sector Directive does not establish requirements for the planning stage and for the drafting of the descriptive document except to provide that contracting authorities can set out their needs and requirements in a descriptive document instead of in the contract notice.

Public procurement is to a wide extent professionalised in Denmark in the sense that the administrator in charge of a given tender procedure often will be a graduate with prior experience and responsibility in the field. This tendency is enforced when it comes to more complex tender procedures such as competitive dialogue that often will involve a team of administrators assisted by external advisors, be it lawyers or management consultants. It is therefore customary in a Danish context that the contracting authority has invested considerable time and money in the planning stage of a competitive dialogue procedure. The descriptive document will therefore often be of high quality and contain very detailed information.

5.3. *Confidentiality of information and solutions*

The Danish provisions on confidentiality of information and solutions with regard to competitive dialogue are identical to the provisions in the Public Sector Directive. As we have seen in section 5.3 of Chapter 1, it is provided in Article 29(3) that the contracting authorities may not reveal to the other participants solutions proposed or other confidential information communicated by a candidate participating in the dialogue without his or her agreement. Furthermore, it follows from Article 29(6) that the contracting authority shall ask the participants in the procedure to submit their final tenders on the basis of the solution or solutions presented and specified during the dialogue. From this follows that so-called 'cherry-picking' is not allowed unless the participant agrees and that each participant must submit a bid based on its own proposal for a solution. The contracting authorities can specify prices and payments to the participants in the dialogue as provided for in Article 29(8), which is likely to make it easier to get the agreement of the firms involved to cherry-picking.

As will be further explained in section 5.6 below, the dominant model in Danish public procurement practice is to conduct the dialogue with all qualified tenderers and to let all participants bid after the tender specifications have been revised. At least some tenderers involved in Danish procedures have initially hesitated because they feared that the contracting authorities would not respect the confidentiality of information and solutions. However, the organisation of the procedures in question have not led to any subsequent case law on the issue and the interviewed tenderers have generally not considered that the confidentiality rules have been violated in the procedures in which they participated.

It is an unsettled issue of EU public procurement law whether a contracting authority can insert a tender condition in the contract notice or descriptive document to the effect that the participants must accept that the contracting authority may share its solution with the other participants in the competitive dialogue.[43] Such a tender condition is not common in Danish public procurement practice. It can be added that it is also not common to get consent to cherry-picking based on payments to the participants in the competitive dialogue made as contemplated in Article 29(8) of the Public Sector Directive.[44]

5.4. *Advertising requirements (contract notice etc.)*

The advertising requirements correspond to those outlined in the Public Sector Directive (as set out in section 5.4 of Chapter 1) and there is no requirement to advertise in places additional to the OJEU. However, it is seen in Danish practice that contracting authorities advertise competitive dialogue procedures also on their websites. The contract notices are typically very informative and it is common to find relatively elaborate descriptions of the contract and its background. In addition, many tender notices contain information going beyond what is legally required.

5.5. *The selection phase: choosing the candidates to participate in the dialogue*

As we have seen in section 5.5 of Chapter 1, it follows from Article 44(3) of the Public Sector Directive that the authority must take a minimum of three qualifying firms through to the dialogue. As also explained in Chapter 1, the generally applicable rules, which are outlined in section 5.5 of Chapter 1, on the selection phase can be found in Articles 44–52 of the Public Sector Directive. These rules are well-known from practice with regard to the other types of tender procedures in the EU public procurement regime.

It is common Danish practice to limit the number of participants to three, four or five in competitive dialogue procedures. This entails that reduction of the field of potential competitors normally takes place at an early stage in the procedure before the dialogue phase has even started. The number of applicants to participate has in Danish practice been

[43] See further on this issue Ch. 1, section 5.3, which also contains references to the position in other Member States.

[44] See section 5.10 of this chapter. This is also not common in European practice: see Ch. 1, section 5.10.

relatively limited: there have typically been around five to ten applicants in competitive dialogue procedures.[45]

The criteria for selecting from the qualified applicants have typically been linked to the ordinary selection criteria where the aim of the latter is to identify the qualified applicants. The ordinary selection criteria or some of them are most frequently applied in a relative manner in the sense that the contracting authority selects the best qualified based on their experience, financial standing etc. However, in some of the procedures the contracting authority has used an alternative approach aiming at composing a field of prospective tenderers designed to result in the best possible competition. The contracting authority will aim at achieving the best blend looking at a variety of elements such as experience and size of the company. It may, for example, select some because they are experienced and others because they are newcomers in the market.

It should be added here that some Danish competitive dialogue procedures have failed, or at least have been terminated, due to lack of competition.[46] The typical reaction to lack of interest and applications from qualified firms has been to re-tender the contract.[47] A similar problem has not been reported from other Member States covered by the current study.[48] A possible explanation for this could be the differences in the market structure or differences in the approach to advertising the contract. Another explanation could be that this situation is not perceived as a problem and that the contracting authorities in other Member States therefore possibly tend to continue the procedure instead of re-tendering the contract.[49]

5.6. *The dialogue phase*

As regards the conduct of the dialogue phase of competitive dialogue, the full freedom of the Public Sector Directive has been maintained. This is a consequence of the way the Danish legislator implemented the procedure according to which the exact wording of the Directive has been maintained.

[45] The number of applicants is typically close to five.

[46] This applies to at least five procedures, equivalent to about 10 per cent of the initiated procedures. The number of applicants is in general low, as pointed out above.

[47] This is not the reaction in all Member States: see Ch. 1, section 5.5.

[48] The issue is therefore not discussed in further detail in Ch. 1.

[49] It follows from Art. 44(3) of the Public Sector Directive that the contracting authority may continue the procedure by inviting the candidate(s) with the required capabilities where the number qualified is below the minimum number.

It should be emphasised that it appears that Danish contracting authorities do not use a model where the tenderers have explicitly consented to cherry-picking. There do not appear to be any cases where the authority openly and without keeping the solutions confidential has cherry- picked the best elements of the various solutions and used them as the foundation for the drafting of substantially modified tender specifications – that is, has used the designated solution model described in section 5.6.2 of Chapter 1.

The dominant Danish model involves conducting the dialogue in a confidential manner with all qualified tenderers, subsequently to modify the tender specifications, and then to let all tenderers bid on the basis of the revised tender specifications. This model is the so-called hybrid model that was set out in section 5.6.2 of Chapter 1. The preferred solution is typically drafted in broad terms with emphasis on functionality and any changes of the draft specifications are often minor and not substantial. In some instances there has even not been any need for changes to the original draft specifications. This approach is taken in order to assure the tenderers that the ban on cherry-picking has not been violated and in order to allow room for variations in the individual solutions discussed in the dialogue. Nevertheless, it is obvious, as pointed out by some of the interviewed advisors to contracting authorities, that cherry-picking may potentially take place to some extent when the model mentioned above is applied.

It is noteworthy that the organisation of the procedures in question have not led to any case law on the issue and that the interviewed tenderers in general have not considered that the ban on cherry-picking has been violated in the procedures that they have participated in. This can probably to some extent be explained by the fact that the legal advisors to the contracting authorities have been fully aware of the potential pitfalls and that they have done their best to ensure respect for the ban on cherry-picking.

Nevertheless, at least some tenderers involved in Danish procedures have initially hesitated and have feared that the contracting authorities would not respect the confidentiality of information and solutions. One tenderer also pointed out that a contract concluded with a competitor obviously contained elements inspired by its own submitted solution. This seems to be an exception, however, and the Danish contracting authorities appear to have balanced the conflicting interests in a manner that, in general, is considered appropriate by tenderers.

It can be added that the interests of tenderers can be fundamentally different depending on the model of contracting chosen by the contracting authority.[50] If the hybrid model mentioned above is applied, in such a case the tenderer has as a starting point an interest in ensuring as much influence on the drafting of the common solution as possible, as this presumably will give the tenderer a clear competitive advantage. In such a situation, the tenderer can be expected to be willing to submit highly detailed information on its preferred solution. In this sense, the situation is fundamentally different from the 'own-solutions model' that was described in section 5.6.2 of Chapter 1, where there are Chinese walls between the discussed solutions and where the final tender is strictly based on the individual solutions as discussed with the contracting authority. The tenderers in the latter situation will be concerned that the contracting authority respects confidentiality. The background for this is that the tenderers typically will fear that the contracting authority will pass on their innovative ideas to the competitors to their own competitive disadvantage.

Contracting authorities may provide for the procedure to take place in successive stages in order to reduce the number of solutions to be discussed during the dialogue stage, as permitted under Article 29(3) of the Public Sector Directive. The dominant interpretation in Danish legal theory has been to consider that rejecting a solution can also/must also involve rejecting the participant,[51] which Chapter 1 suggested reflects the position under the Directive.[52]

The Danish contracting authorities interviewed for our study had the same understanding of the provisions on elimination of solutions. It is noteworthy that more than 50 per cent of the Danish contracting authorities have provided for the procedure to take place in successive

[50] See Ch. 1, section 5.6.2, on the variety of models seen in European practice and described in the literature.

[51] See Troels Poulsen, Stig Jakobsen and Kalsmose-Hjelmborg, n. 23 above, p. 363; Offersen, n. 23 above, p. 28; Steinicke and Groesmeyer, n. 23 above, p. 329; S. Troels Poulsen and S. E. Kalsmose-Hjelmborg, 'Hvor meget konkurrence skal der være i konkurrencepræget dialog? – om afvejningen af markedsåbning om offentlige ordregiveres behov inden for rammerne af EU's udbudsdirektiv' (2007B) *Ugeskrift for Retsvæsen* 34; S. Treumer, 'Competitive Dialogue', n. 23 above, p. 180. J. Fabricius, n. 23 above, p. 184, essentially limits himself to stating that the issue is unsettled and disputed. For a contrary point of view, see J. Fejø, in J. Fejø and S. Treumer (eds.), *EU's Udbudsregler – implementering og håndhævelse i Norden* (2006), p. 25.

[52] See Ch. 1, section 5.6.3.2, and the references there.

stages and for elimination of solutions in this process. However, it is interesting that in practice it is only in exceptional cases that use is actually made of this option in the award procedure. Contracting authorities abstain from a formal elimination of participants for a variety of reasons. This kind of elimination is typically seen as very difficult and as exposing the contracting authority to legal challenge.[53] Furthermore, Danish contracting authorities typically do not want to limit competition more than strictly necessary and as the number of qualified applicants fairly often turns out to be low they choose not to eliminate some participants. As pointed out by some interviewees, there is also the obvious risk of eliminating potentially the best tenderer based on a weak foundation. One of those interviewed also reported that the contracting authority in question had considered it as an internal success criterion that they did not have to eliminate participants because they were all considered serious and committed. Many contracting authorities have deliberately not provided for any possibility of eliminating participants, for the same reasons.

It can be added that some contracting authorities, however, indirectly squeeze participants out of the competition instead of formally eliminating them. One way of doing this is to inform the participant that its solution is a long way from meeting the authority's preferences. Another approach is to establish or clarify requirements that are very difficult for the participant to meet.[54]

One issue that was considered in detail in Chapter 1 is the extent to which there is any possibility for changing or developing the award criteria and sub-criteria during the procedure, and also whether different criteria can be used at different stages. This issue was discussed in detail in section 5.6.5 of Chapter 1.

As a general rule, Danish contracting authorities do not either change or develop the award criteria for choosing the economically most advantageous tender during the award procedure. (An example of development could be that a contracting authority has used broad award criteria such as quality and aesthetic criteria and then subsequently has explained the understanding of these concepts in further detail or that it has added sub-criteria during the dialogue.) Several

[53] The contracting authorities feared that the concrete assessment leading to elimination would be challenged. The interviewees did not expect that the legality of the elimination of participants as such would be questioned.

[54] The same phenomenon is seen in Spain: see Ch. 8, section 5.6.2.

of those interviewed explained that they had abstained from changing the criteria because this was assessed as involving a significant risk of legal challenge even though the dialogue sometimes had made it apparent that some changes would be relevant. However, the award criteria or sub-criteria have been changed in at least a couple of cases and also developed further from the stated criteria in several cases.

The legality of *development* of award criteria was examined in the ruling of 8 January 2008, *WAP Wöhr Automatikparksystem GmbH and Co. KG* v. *Ørestadsparkering A/S* from the Danish Complaints Board for Public Procurement. It followed from the tender notice in that case that the award was to be based on the most economically advantageous tender and the award criteria were specified in the notice as 'technical issues' and 'economical [*sic*] issues'. The weighting of the award criteria also followed from the tender notice and was 60 per cent for the technical issues and 40 per cent for the economic issues. The award criteria were not changed but the contracting authority specified sub-criteria to the criteria during the dialogue and in a final version of the criteria after the conclusion of the dialogue.[55] It appears undisputed that the evaluation of the bids by the contracting authority had been based on these criteria.

The complainant challenged the development of the sub-criteria during the tender procedure with explicit reference to the Explanatory Note on Competitive Dialogue from the European Commission. As discussed in Chapter 1 (see section 5.6.5 of that chapter), the Note states that the 'the award criteria (and the order of their importance) may not be changed during the tender procedures (that is, at the latest after the transmission of the invitations to participate in the dialogue) for obvious reasons of equal treatment'.[56]

The Complaints Board rejected the complaint on this point. The Board stated that it had only been possible to establish the final version of the sub-criteria after the dialogue phase. The Board added that the contracting authority did not appear to have misled the tenderers during

[55] The tender documentation forwarded during the selection phase also considered the award criteria and established a different range of sub-criteria for the award criterion of 'technical issues'. Likewise the contracting authority established a range of criteria on technical issues for evaluating the outcome of the dialogue meetings.

[56] See the Commission Explanatory Note, n. 36 above, section 3.1, p. 6.

the process by establishing 'entirely different'[57] sub-criteria and that the evaluation strictly had followed the established criteria. Whether or not this approach is in compliance with EU law is an issue of debate that is discussed further in section 5.6.5 of Chapter 1, where it was suggested that such development of the award criteria in a competitive dialogue procedure is in fact compliant with EU law.

5.7. *Final tender stage*

The rules governing the final tender stage under the Public Sector Directive were discussed in section 5.7 of Chapter 1.

It is common Danish practice to invite three of the participants to submit a bid even though there have also been several procedures where four or five have been invited to submit final bids. As we have seen in section 5.6 above, it is common for contracting authorities to announce that elimination of solutions will take place during the dialogue stage but formal elimination in that stage is not common in practice. The number of potential bidders is instead typically reduced already at the selection phase prior to the start of the dialogue phase, as explained in section 5.5 above. There are a few procedures in which contracting authorities have only received two final bids, but this appears to have been because there has only been a limited number of applicants and/or because some of the tenderers have chosen to withdraw from the tender procedures. The award criteria are typically not specified in the tender notice and the contracting authorities most frequently establish three to five criteria. Price typically has a weight of 25–50 per cent.

There is one example of a contracting authority that announced that it would apply the criterion of 'the lowest bid' without this being legally challenged. This was a violation of one of the conditions outlined in Article 29(1) of the Public Sector Directive as it is mandatory to base the award on the principle of 'the economically most advantageous tender'.

As commented on in further detail in Chapter 1,[58] there is some debate over whether variants are permitted in a competitive dialogue procedure. However, a careful examination of the Danish tender notices on competitive dialogue procedures reveals that contracting authorities frequently have allowed variants. The fact that variants frequently are contemplated by contracting authorities in Danish competitive dialogue

[57] 'Ganske andre' in Danish. [58] See Ch. 1, section 5.7.5.

procedures is highly surprising as one would expect that there was no need of variants in procedures where the tenderers 'may discuss all aspects of the contract with the chosen candidates during this dialogue', as permitted under Article 29(3) of the Public Sector Directive.

The legality of variants in competitive dialogue procedures was considered in the ruling of 8 January 2008, *WAP Wöhr Automatikparksystem GmbH and Co. KG* v. *Ørestadsparkering A/S*, from the Danish Complaints Board for Public Procurement, previously mentioned in section 2.1 of this chapter. The contracting authorities had allowed variants in the tender procedure and complied with the standard requirements for use of variants as set out in Article 24 of the Public Sector Directive. The variant tender of one of the tenderers was considered the economically most advantageous tender and the authorisation of variant bids and the acceptance of such a bid was challenged by the complainant as incompatible with the tender procedure of competitive dialogue. Curiously enough, the complainant had also submitted a variant at the final stage of the tender procedure.

The ruling of the Complaints Board on this issue was laconic, which is unusual. The Board merely stated that there is no basis for the assumption that there is a ban on variants in competitive tender procedures and the complaint was therefore rejected on this point. This interesting issue has already been considered further in section 5.7.5 of Chapter 1, where it was suggested that variants can indeed be authorised in competitive dialogue procedures,[59] even if their use may seem surprising.

In Denmark, tenders may be clarified, specified and fine-tuned in accordance with the provisions of Article 29(6) of the Public Sector Directive, which has been implemented into the Danish legislation with exactly the same wording. The meaning of this provision in the Directive was discussed in section 5.7.4 of Chapter 1. So far there has been no Danish case law on the meaning of clarification, specification and fine-tuning. The interviewed representatives of contracting authorities have consistently stated[60] that tenders have not, or have only to a very limited

[59] It was also submitted that it is probably not in accordance with the principle of equal treatment of tenderers to allow variant bids in procedures where the contracting authority has conducted the procedure in stages with elimination of participants. As pointed out above, the eliminated participants will not get the extra chance of being awarded the contract by submitting a variant bid, in contrast with the position of tenderers that are invited to submit a final tender; cf. Art. 29(6).

[60] However, a few of the interviewees had been engaged in dialogue to an extent exceeding the usual standard for the open procedure and restricted procedure.

extent, been clarified, specified or fine-tuned and that their approach has corresponded to the approach in the standard tender procedures (the open and restricted procedures). In addition, representatives of tenderers did not in general have the impression that the contracting authorities had extended the dialogue beyond the limits outlined in Article 29(6) of the Public Sector Directive.

However, it is noteworthy that the background for this approach was not that the contracting authorities considered a wider dialogue as excluded in law but that they considered a more flexible approach as giving rise to too great a risk of legal challenge or as being unnecessary. As pointed out by some interviewees, there was essentially no need for extended dialogue because the issues had been fully discussed during the dialogue phase.

5.8. Procedure following the selection of the winning tender or preferred bidder

The possibilities that apply between selection of the winning tender and conclusion of the contract are outlined in the provisions of Article 29(7) of the Public Sector Directive, as discussed in section 5.8 of Chapter 1, and these have been applied exactly in the Danish legislation. It is sometimes seen in Danish public procurement practice that there is a timespan of some months between the award and the conclusion of the contract with regard to complex contracts and this is also the case for some competitive dialogue procedures.

It is not possible to determine the degree of changes and modifications that take place without a thorough knowledge of the concrete procedures, which is not available to the author. However, it can be said that the clear majority[61] of the interviewed parties representing contracting authorities submitted that modifications of substantial elements of the contract did not take place, even though several stated that some clarification had taken place. It should be added that representatives of the tenderers also generally had the impression that the contracting authorities had not extended the dialogue beyond the limits outlined in Article 29(7). However, at least with regard to ICT contracts, elements

[61] However, there were exceptions. An advisor to a contracting authority considered it highly questionable whether the flexible approach in the concrete case was in compliance with the limits on competitive dialogue. A tenderer also considered that parts of its solution had been integrated into the concluded contract with another tenderer.

of a more technical nature are sometimes deliberately left for the final stage between award and conclusion of the contract in order not to waste the time of all bidders.

It is interesting that the general perception appears to be that the contracting authorities have complied with legal restrictions on dialogue with the winning tenderer. However, the fact that there is sometimes a considerable timespan between the award and the conclusion of the contract could be an indication of a high level of clarification and negotiation in the concrete cases. Nevertheless, the conclusion of the contract could be delayed for other reasons, for instance formalities relating to the financing of public works.[62] It appears that Danish contracting authorities in general have not modified substantial elements of the contract and therefore have complied with the limitation on the dialogue in Article 29(7) of the Public Sector Directive. However, it should be stressed that this assumption is not based on an analysis of the contract documents relating to Danish competitive dialogue procedures but primarily on interviews with practitioners.

5.9. *The standstill period*

Competitive dialogue procedures are covered by the standard provisions on the standstill period. The provisions on the standstill period can be found in the new Danish Act on the Enforcement of the EU public procurement rules which implemented Remedies Directive 2007/66. The issue of when the standstill notice must be given in accordance with EU law for competitive dialogue procedures that are subject to this explicit standstill provision is examined in section 5.9 of Chapter 1.

It is not obvious from EU public procurement law whether there is a requirement for a standstill period for a competitive dialogue procedure *not* covered by the Directive. It follows from the preparatory works to the Danish Act on the Enforcement of the Public Procurement Rules that it is not obligatory to observe the rules on standstill if the contract is excluded from the Public Sector Directive (or Utilities Directive) under the Danish legislation.[63] It can be argued, however, that a standstill

[62] The latter was the case in at least one of the cases where there was a considerable time span between award and the conclusion of the contract.

[63] Section 2.2 of the remarks to the Proposal for an Act on Enforcement of the Procurement Rules of 27 January 2010 and sections 2 and 3.5 of the Note from the Ministry of Economics and Business of 6 January 2010 to the Danish Parliament on the Act. It is

period is also mandatory outside of the scope of the Public Procurement Directives.[64]

5.10. *Payments for costs of participation*

It is stated in Article 29(8) of the Public Sector Directive and provided also in the Danish legislation that contracting authorities may specify prices and payments to the participants in the dialogue. It has not been common Danish procurement practice to specify prices or payments to participants in tender procedures even though this is sometimes done with regard to public works contracts.[65] The above-mentioned provision therefore contemplates a different approach from the traditional one. Danish contracting authorities appear to have been reluctant to pay tenderers for their participation in competitive dialogue procedures. The background for this has for instance been a lack of political will or that this was not considered relevant because participation in the procedure in itself was already of value to the firms in question. Several of the interviewees also stated that there is clearly no tradition for payments to tenderers with regard to ICT contracts and that tenderers in this field do not expect to be paid.

However, there are a few examples of payments for participation in competitive dialogue procedures on public works in the Danish practice. Examples of payments for participation in competitive dialogue procedures in relation to ICT contracts have not been found even though the cost of preparing such bids are normally considerable. Nevertheless, suppliers in the ICT market do in fact appear to be in favour of payments for participation in the dialogue.[66] In some of the procedures there has been a fee for participation in the dialogue and an additional fee for submitting a tender in compliance with the tender conditions. The fee has in all instances been symbolic in the sense that it has only covered a

specified in section 2 of the note that the new Act as a rule follows the minimum requirements in the Remedies Directive 2007/66.

[64] See C. Risvig Hansen, 'Pligt til annoncering af offentlige kontrakter – uden effektiv håndhævelse af reglerne?' (2011) *Ugeskrift for Retsvæsen* B101. See also Treumer, n. 10 above; and Ch. 1, section 5.9.

[65] On other Member States, see Ch. 1, section 5.10.

[66] See the report of IT-Branchen on development of ICT-contracts for the state: 'Statslige IT-nyudviklingsprojekter' with the subtitle 'Rapport udarbejdet af en arbejdsgruppe under IT-Branchens Digital Forvaltning Udvalg', p. 7. The report was finished in 2009 and can be found at www.itb.dk.

relatively modest part of the real costs of participation. The payment has been up to DKK 2.5 million (about €337,000) to the tenderers in one case and about €135,000 in a couple of other cases. Even though this amount in itself is relatively high,[67] it should be stressed that the real costs of participation were estimated to be eight to ten times higher by several of the parties involved in the concrete procedures. The interviewed representatives of contracting authorities that have used payments considered that this had been worthwhile, relevant and, in addition, highly appreciated by the tenderers involved.

It can be added that these payments have not been presented as, or considered as, a payment for acceptance of cherry-picking in any of the Danish cases covered by the current study. This is noteworthy as the dominant model of organising competitive dialogue in Denmark may easily lead to a kind of cherry-picking. However, this does not appear in general to be problematic for contracting authorities and tenderers for the reasons outlined in section 5.6 of this chapter.

5.11. *Assessment of the experience with competitive dialogue in practice*

Danish contracting authorities that have experience with competitive dialogue have a very positive assessment of the results in general. They frequently recommend use of the procedure to others and several have applied the procedure more than once. Ten contracting authorities have organised more than 50 per cent of the Danish competitive dialogue procedures as mentioned in section 4 of this chapter.

Danish contracting authorities emphasise that the competitive dialogue procedure leads to more value for money. The procedure increases competition and the final contract fits much better with the needs of the contracting authority than usual. However, it has also been mentioned that competitive dialogue clearly requires more resources than traditional tender procedures and that the procedure tends to be of longer duration.

Tenderers emphasise that they obtain better understanding of the requirements of the contracting authority than usual, but have also highlighted that it requires significant resources to participate in a competitive dialogue at all stages of the procedure. Some tenderers have

[67] Compared with, for example, the only reported payment in the UK which was a token £1,500: see Ch. 3, section 5.11.

considered that it is too costly to participate and that contracting authorities should have limited the number of firms participating in the dialogue even further. This has also been the case in procedures where five participants were allowed to submit final bids. Other tenderers stress that the dialogue ensures a more efficient use of the time spent on the project than would be the case without the dialogue phase.

6. Concluding remarks

The Danish experience with competitive dialogue is of special interest in a European context for various reasons. First, Denmark was the first Member State that implemented the Public Sector Directive and the Danish law entered into force on 1 January 2005 and created the legal basis for the application of the competitive dialogue procedure as of this date. Furthermore, the Danish method of implementation of the Public Sector Directive ensures that Danish interpretations are as closely linked to the EU sources of law on the competitive dialogue procedure as they can possibly be. Section 1 of the Decree implementing the Public Sector Directive simply states that contracting entities shall observe the provisions in the Directive, and Annex 1 to the Decree is the Public Sector Directive without any changes.

Secondly, use of competitive dialogue has been challenged in various cases in Denmark and consequently there is significant case law on competitive dialogue, contrary to the situation in most Member States so far.[68] As this case law relates to fundamental issues concerning competitive dialogue, in particular its field of application,[69] it is of general interest.

Thirdly, Denmark is one of the smaller Member States of the EU with a population of about 5.5 million. However, the new competitive dialogue procedure has been applied about fifty times, which is relatively frequent considering the size of the Danish economy and in comparison with the tendencies in many other Member States where the approach to the new procedure clearly has been more hesitant.[70]

Fourthly, the Danish market is also very transparent, with alert competitors, and benefits from one of the most efficient enforcement systems in the EU. The Danish enforcement system goes further than required by the Remedies Directives and EU law on various points. The Danish

[68] See Ch. 1. [69] See section 4 above. [70] See generally Ch. 2.

experience is therefore also a good illustration of what happens when the state of law is uncertain on fundamental aspects of the law and the risk of legal challenge is high: contracting authorities hesitate to make use of the options provided for in the legislation. As a consequence, many contracting authorities appear to have abstained from using competitive dialogue in Denmark even though they considered it relevant. Contracting authorities have also not operated the procedure with the full flexibility envisaged by the European legislator. The latter applies for instance to the issue of clarification, specification and fine-tuning of tenders[71] and to eliminating participants on the basis of their submitted solutions.[72] Nevertheless, several Danish contracting authorities have accepted the risk linked to the use of competitive dialogue and have even been running the competitive dialogue with features that are debatable, for instance by allowing variants[73] and modifying the award criteria.[74]

Danish practitioners – be they representatives of contracting authorities or tenderers – that have experience of competitive dialogue tend in general to speak highly of the procedure, and they are generally in favour of widening the scope of the procedure. However, not all are in favour of a more frequent use of competitive dialogue. For example, the trade association of ICT suppliers in Denmark has stated that the procedure should only be applied in situations where it would really be beneficial and in situations where the financial value of the contract can justify the exceptional amount of time invested in a competitive dialogue procedure.[75] It will be interesting to see whether the current revision of the Public Sector Directive will lead to a widening of the scope of the procedure.

[71] See section 5.7. [72] See section 5.6. [73] See section 5.7. [74] See section 5.6.
[75] IT-Branchen, n. 66 above, p. 7.

7

Competitive dialogue in Portugal

PEDRO TELLES

1. Introduction: regulation of public procurement in Portugal

Portugal is not a federal state, but has a national government (accountable to the national parliament) and two regional governments (accountable to the relevant regional parliament) that also have legislative powers.[1] All public procurement legislation relevant for competitive dialogue has been enacted by the national parliament, and this chapter will focus on legislation produced at this level.

Portugal is a civil law state with a long tradition in regulating public procurement. Procedures for awarding contracts, legal regimes applicable to their performance and review mechanisms have existed since the nineteenth century and have led to the progressive development of a national public procurement framework. This framework is part of the country's body of administrative law, which has its own sets of rules and principles.

Portugal acceded to the EU in 1986 and has improved and updated its existing procurement framework in accordance with each successive round of procurement Directives. National laws have been restructured, reworded and adapted to accommodate each round of Directives. Currently, the bulk of public procurement rules are part of the Public Contracts Code of 2008.[2] This law has transposed into national legislation Directives 2004/17, 2004/18 and 2005/51. The approach has generally been to introduce many changes from the text, *not* simply to 'copy and paste' its contents, and Portuguese law does not generally give procuring entities the full flexibility possible under the Directives.

[1] Art. 228/2 of the Portuguese Constitution entitles regional parliaments to legislate in the field of public procurement. The Regional Parliament of the Azores has approved two Regional Decree-Laws (34/2008/A and 15/2009/A) introducing changes to the procurement framework applicable in the region, neither being relevant for competitive dialogue.

[2] This has been the first time the procurement legal framework has been codified under a single law, although some areas were not included, such as public–private partnerships.

Competitive dialogue is one of the areas in which significant changes can be identified in the transposition.

The Public Contracts Code of 2008 is the main body of law regulating both award procedures and contract performance.[3] Although it is a recent law, the Public Contracts Code has already been amended by Decree-Laws 34/2009, 223/2009 and 278/2009.

Judicial administrative courts have exclusive power to address any issues arising from public procurement award procedures or contract performance. Litigation in public procurement is fairly common in Portugal. A search for 'public procurement litigation' in a database[4] holding information on cases in appeal courts yielded 270 entries since 2005.[5]

Courts in Portugal do not have formal legal power in developing public procurement law, as their effect is binding only on the participants and not third parties. However, a string of high-profile situations where the Financial Audit Court[6] has refused to approve certain public–private partnership contracts has raised the profile of judicial decisions in this area, and these may be factored in by contracting authorities when procuring.

2. The background: complex procurement prior to competitive dialogue

Before the entry into force of the Public Contracts Code, contracting authorities would carry out complex procurement through various means, such as using the open or restricted procedures, design contests or the locally developed open procedure with a negotiation phase.

[3] Although, in the case of the latter, it only covers contracts that are deemed to have an administrative nature. Public works are textbook examples of administrative contracts, as they establish what has been deemed traditionally as an 'administrative relationship' between the state and the private sector, where the former is entitled to extra powers such as a unilateral change power. Private contracts are the ones that do not establish such an administrative relationship according to the Public Contracts Code of 2008. Their performance remains regulated by private law such as the Civil Code.

[4] Available at www.dgsi.pt, in Portuguese only.

[5] This database covers only appeal courts (Central and Supreme Court) and not the Courts of First Instance where public procurement cases are first lodged, which implies the overall numbers to be higher. Furthermore, cases are only added to the database if authorised by the judge.

[6] 'Portugal: Recent Decisions from the Portuguese Audit Court' (2010) 1 *European Public Private Partnership Law Review* 69.

Bearing in mind the lack of use of competitive dialogue in Portugal, one can add that practice has not changed a lot with its introduction. The open procedure with a negotiation phase is specific to Portugal,[7] and thus its main features require explanation.

The open procedure with a negotiation phase was created during the 1990s for the award of concessions and public–private partnerships, primarily in the transport sector. At the time it did not have a legal basis but was created *ad hoc* by means of a new law every time it was to be used. It is a procedure born from the practical necessity of tendering particularly complex contracts. Furthermore, in 2003 Decree-Law 86/2003[8] stated in its Article 3 that sectoral regulations could be approved regarding the award procedure for public–private partnerships, effectively allowing the government to create the aforementioned tailor-made procedure for the award of hospital contracts, for instance. From its creation until 2008, it became the *de facto* procedure for awarding particularly complex contracts that fell *outside* the scope of the full rules of Directives 93/36 and 93/37 (predecessor Directives to Directive 200/18 dealing respectively with supply and works contracts), specifically in the transport sector. In the Public Contracts Code, this procedure was codified and included alongside the other procedures, and is still available for the award of public works and services concessions, including public–private partnerships.[9] Article 149(1) of the Public Contracts Code does not limit this new procedure to the utility sectors; however, for it to comply with Directive 2004/18 it must be interpreted as only being available for contracts not covered by the full rules of Directive 2004/18.

The procedure can be described as a two-stage procedure. At the start, companies submit a very detailed tender that is assessed according to the award criteria. The jury will then invite the number of tenderers it has set forth in the tender documents, usually two, for negotiations on the terms of the contract. This allows the contracting authority to seek improvement to the tenders in light of the needs it seeks to address as it can also with solutions offered in a competitive dialogue procedure. The tenderers are then invited to submit a best and final offer on the basis of which the winner is then chosen.

7 And the others have been explained in P. Telles, 'Competitive Dialogue in Portugal' (2010) 19 *Public Procurement Law Review* 32.

8 The revised 2006 version of this law kept this possibility open and is still in force.

9 Art. 149 of the Public Contracts Code.

It has been suggested to the author in the course of the research described in section 3 below, that as this open procedure with a negotiation phase is available today in parallel with competitive dialogue in Portugal in certain sectors, and there is around fifteen years of experience of its use, its existence is one of the major reasons for competitive dialogue's lack of uptake in Portugal in those sectors in which the two procedures are both available. As with the previous legal regime, this open procedure with a negotiation phase is still, however, only available for contracts falling outside the scope of the full rules of Directive 2004/18, in order to avoid violating the Directive. It has been used frequently in the transport sector, covered by Directive 2004/17. After the entry into force of the Public Contracts Code, this procedure was used, for example, for six contracts relating to the new high-speed train line connecting Portugal to the border with Spain.

3. Introduction to competitive dialogue

Competitive dialogue was transposed into Portugal in 2008 through the Public Contracts Code of 2008. A version of the procedure was present in a preliminary public draft of 2006. At that time, it was very close in form and shape to the procedure in the Directive itself, without many changes and subsequent additions present in the final version. After an initial public discussion in May 2006, competitive dialogue was substantially changed and eventually taken out of the private working drafts. However, a political decision was taken to keep it as part of the Public Contracts Code. The law-makers decided then to introduce a number of changes in order to adapt it to the national framework and culture.[10] The end result is a procedure the rules of which have been regulated in minute detail, beyond EU requirements. Although this follows the Portuguese tradition of regulating topics extensively, on competitive dialogue the law has gone further than is usual in the extent to which it has included features that are not present in Directive 2004/18.

The rules on competitive dialogue are divided up between three different sections of the Public Contracts Code. The scope of the procedure can be found in Part II, Title I, Chapter III, Articles 30 and 33/1, of the Public Contracts Code, in parallel with the provisions on the special circumstances in which other procedures can also be adopted.

[10] According to respondents involved in the law-making process and interviewed by the author during his research.

The general rules on the actual operation of the procedure are defined in Part II, Title III, Chapter V, Articles 214–218, of the Public Contracts Code. Article 204 of the Public Contracts Code states the subsidiary application of the restricted procedure rules: Chapter III, Articles 162–192, of the Public Contracts Code on the restricted procedure have to be taken into account. Finally, some open procedure rules are also applicable, such as those in Articles 92, 93 and 99 of the Public Contracts Code on negotiations after the tender stage and on the confirmation of commitments.

Competitive dialogue has been transposed into national law in minute detail going well beyond EU law, as the Portuguese law-makers took the decision to create a common legal framework across different procurement procedures and thus adapted competitive dialogue to be as close as possible to the more traditional procurement procedures used in the country. One should highlight the changes made to the scope of application, the impossibility of eliminating candidates and/or solutions, the need to identify a single solution and mandatorily draft a common set of specifications, and, finally, the lack of specific rules on discussions before or after the preferred bidder has been chosen. All these points are discussed further in the analysis below. Furthermore, from the submission of tenders onwards competitive dialogue operates as an open or restricted procedure. These changes are so substantial that one may even argue that the so-called 'competitive dialogue' in Portugal is a different procedure from the one established by Directive 2004/18. Even if such changes do not represent a different procedure, they do imply that only a *redux* version of competitive dialogue is allowed in Portugal, with some features or key characteristics disabled. The author would query whether it is a correct implementation of competitive dialogue when so many changes and limitations have been introduced at the national level. This argument depends, however, on the extent to which Member States are permitted to supplement the provisions of the Directive with stricter or additional rules, an issue discussed in section 2.1 of Chapter 1.

Following the national tradition of not providing government guidance on national laws, the only relevant material on competitive dialogue that might fall into the category of guidance consists of flow-charts on the national procurement portal base.gov.pt, explaining the flow of the procedure. No guidance on how to interpret the law or apply the procedure has been produced.

No instances have been registered so far of litigation concerning the implementation and use of competitive dialogue in Portugal.

The uptake of this procedure has been very limited. As of July 2011, it had been adopted a total of six times, with the first in 2007[11] and the last in July 2011. Between March 2010 and June 2011, no competitive dialogue procedures were launched. This signals a clear lack of interest from contracting authorities in competitive dialogue.

Between March 2009 and March 2010, the author conducted empirical research on the implementation of competitive dialogue in Portugal as part of doctoral research at the University of Nottingham. He carried out twenty-seven semi-structured interviews with contracting authorities and lawyers who were experts in public procurement with the aim of analysing the 'law in action' instead of only the 'law in the books'. Three of those interviews were held with contracting authorities that had actually used the procedure. In addition, the author interviewed three of the law-makers who drafted the Public Contracts Code.

4. Scope of the competitive dialogue procedure in law and practice

4.1. *Introduction*

As explained in Chapter 1, competitive dialogue may be used for the award of complex contracts, when it is impossible to define the technical, legal or financial make-up of a contract. Three major differences between the EU and Portuguese frameworks on the scope of application can be highlighted. The first is that in Portugal, the scope appears to be more limited than what is theoretically admitted by Directive 2004/18, in that the Public Contracts Code sets more demanding requirements for the use of the procedure. Secondly, the Public Contracts Code excludes the use of this kind of procedure for the award of some contracts in the utilities sector. Thirdly, in Portugal, the procedure may be used freely to award contracts of a value below the thresholds of Directive 2004/18 so long as they fulfil the substantive conditions for use.

4.2. *General rules on scope*

The general rules on the scope of application of competitive dialogue are found in the various paragraphs of Article 30 of the Public Contracts Code. From Article 30(1), it can be seen that competitive dialogue can be

[11] Before the transposition of the procedure into national legislation.

used for the award of any type of contract[12] so long as it is particularly complex and this complexity renders impossible (and not only inadequate) the use of the open or restricted procedures. This appears to limit the use of competitive dialogue in Portugal to those situations where defining the specifications is impossible. It seems the law-makers have adopted a strict approach towards the scope of competitive dialogue.

Paragraph 2 of Article 30 of the Public Contracts Code is equivalent to Article 1(11)(c) of Directive 2004/18, but does not transpose the provision *verbatim*. It explains what is deemed as a particularly complex contract. As we have seen in Chapter 1, the Directive states that a contract is particularly complex when the contracting authority is 'not objectively able' to define the technical means, legal or financial make-up of a contract, and it appears that this means that the procedure may be used when the authority is not able to define the *best* means of meeting its requirements, even if some kind of specification could be devised.[13] For the purposes of the Portuguese law, however, a contract is deemed complex if for the contracting authority it is *objectively impossible* to define either the technical solution,[14] the technical means[15] or the financial or legal make-up of the contract.[16] Therefore, it appears that, if a Portuguese contracting authority is able to define a technical solution, even if not the best solution, it may not use competitive dialogue to award the contract[17] as it is no longer impossible to define a solution. The contracting authority will have to use a procedure that may not be tailored to find the *best* solution for its needs. The author was informed by law-makers that the subtle change in wording was intentional, to send a message to contracting authorities not to over-use the procedure.

[12] This includes public works, goods and services, works and services concessions, society and public–private partnership contracts.

[13] See the discussion in Ch. 1, section 4.5.

[14] Art. 30(2)(a) of the Public Contracts Code.

[15] Art. 30(2)(b) of the Public Contracts Code.

[16] Art. 30(2)(c) of the Public Contracts Code.

[17] M. Kirkby, 'O diálogo concorrencial', in *Estudos da Contratação Pública – I* (Coimbra Editora, 2008), p. 303. Here it is suggested that the correct interpretation of the Portuguese text is to consider this limitation in light of Directive 2004/18 and the Commission's Explanatory Note on Competitive Dialogue, thus considering the legal use of the procedure in situations when the contracting authority is able to identify a solution in advance. Kirkby accepts a more liberal interpretation than is apparent in the letter of the law.

The procedure is available also if the contracting authority is unable to identify the technical means needed for the performance of the contract.[18] However, if the contracting authority is able to express the performance or functional needs it seeks to address,[19] then it is considered that it may produce technical specifications detailed enough to launch an open or restricted procedure, further reducing the potential scope of application of the procedure.

Article 30(3) of the Public Contracts Code has a provision limiting the use of the procedure to cases where the objective impossibility of defining the technical solutions, technical means, or financial or legal make up is not due to the fault of the contracting authority. This is similar to the position stated in the first part of recital 31 of the Directive 2004/18 which, as we saw in Chapter 1, states that: 'Contracting authorities, which carry out particularly complex projects may, without this being due to any fault on their part, find it objectively impossible to define the means of satisfying their needs.' While recitals of the Directives are useful to interpret the content of Articles, Portuguese law-makers opted to elevate them to the same level as the dispositions found in Article 29 of this Directive.

From the interviews carried out by the author, it is apparent that in practice leading lawyers and contracting authorities are interpreting the scope of application of the procedure very narrowly. This general view may be due to the actual letter of the law appearing restrictive or perhaps the fact that most considered Article 30 as hard to read and may be taking a conservative approach to the scope in consequence. However, the author was told by contracting authorities that actually used the procedure that they did not have any doubts that their situation fitted the rules of Article 30.

For the author, the rules on the scope of the procedure – combined with the overall restrictive interpretation from the people in the field observed in the empirical research carried out in 2010 – appears as one of the major reasons that explains the lack of use of the procedure in Portugal up to that date. Other reasons for limited use can also be identified, including reasons concerning the procedure's compatibility with the public–private partnerships rules, the existence of the open

[18] Art. 30(2)(b) of the Public Contracts Code.

[19] These are set by Art. 49(2)(c) and (d) of the Public Contracts Code. They are similar to the rules on performance and functional requirements set forth by Art. 23(2)(b), (c) and (d) of Directive 2004/18.

procedure with a negotiation phase, the lack of exclusions, the requirement for a common set of specifications and the fact that after tenders have been submitted competitive dialogue is to be run as an open procedure; and these will be detailed further in subsequent sections below.

4.3. *Rules for utilities*

As explained in Chapter 1, Directive 2004/17 does not include any reference to the possibility of competitive dialogue being used in the utilities sectors. Article 33(1) and (2) of the Public Contracts Code state that competitive dialogue cannot be used at all if the contract is directly and fundamentally connected with any activity in the utilities sectors (water, energy, transport and postal services) *and* the contracting authority is one of those mentioned in Article 7(1) of the Public Contracts Code. The state, regional or local authorities, public institutions, public foundations,[20] public associations and associations composed by one or more of these bodies are *not* mentioned in this Article. Therefore, these authorities must always follow the public sector rules even if the contract that they award is materially a contract covered by the rules of Utilities Directive 2004/17.

In consequence, only a number of contracting authorities, such as public undertakings, are actually covered by the rules of the utilities sector and thus precluded from using competitive dialogue when procuring contracts materially covered by the rules of Directive 2004/17.

4.4. *Contracts below the thresholds of Directive 2004/18*

The Public Contracts Code does not make any reference to the applicability of competitive dialogue to contracts below the thresholds of Directive 2004/18. Whereas typically award procedures in Portugal are segregated based on the value of the contract,[21] competitive dialogue has no grounds for its use based on the value of the procurement. All its grounds for use are based solely on substantive reasons. Therefore, if the contract is deemed as particularly complex and all legal conditions are

[20] With the exception of those mentioned in Law 62/2007.

[21] These procedures range from the open procedure, which is a default procedure for all contracts above a specified national threshold, to direct award, which is available for all contracts under a national specified threshold.

met, it appears that irrespective of value the procedure may be adopted. Thus contracts below the European thresholds can be tendered through competitive dialogue.

4.5. *Public–private partnerships*

The Commission has pointed to public–private partnership contracts[22] as being a prime example of the sort of contracts for which competitive dialogue might be used. We have seen in section 4.3 that competitive dialogue cannot be used in Portugal for the award of utilities contracts by certain contracting authorities.

As explained elsewhere in this chapter,[23] contracting authorities in Portugal have been used to awarding contracts not covered by the scope of the Directive 2004/18, including public–private partnership contracts through the open procedure with a negotiation phase.

In Portugal, public–private partnerships are regulated by Decree-Law 86/2003 which has not been revoked by the Public Contracts Code. The compatibility of that legal regime with competitive dialogue has been questioned, in particular due to the requirement for a thorough assessment of the technical and financial viability of the project before the formal launch of the tender to award the public–private partnership contract.[24] It is implied that if a thorough assessment is carried out in advance, then competitive dialogue is probably not needed at the procuring stage.

In addition, Decree-Law 86/2003 presupposes that the launch of the actual tender will include detailed technical specifications, precluding even further the possibility of competitive dialogue being used.[25] Therefore, it can be argued that until Decree-Law 86/2003 is updated it will not be possible to use competitive dialogue to award public–private partnerships in Portugal. However, it has also been argued that, in fact, the rules of the Decree-Law cover only the preparatory stages and not the actual procuring procedure.[26] Under this interpretation, the rules for selecting the procedure would still be the ones found in the Public

[22] On these contracts, see A. Andrade and A. S. Raquel, 'Public–Private Partnership in Portugal – The Legal Structure of the Public–Private Partnership Contract and the Peripheral Contracts' (2010) 5 *European Public Private Partnership Law Review* 46; and J. V. Branco, 'Portugal: A Closer Look at Public–Private Partnerships' (2000) 4 *European Public Private Partnership Law Review* 25, at 26.

[23] See section 2 above; and Telles, n. 7 above. [24] Kirkby, n. 17 above, p. 307.

[25] *Ibid.*, p. 307. [26] *Ibid.*, p. 310.

Contracts Code, therefore making possible the use of competitive dialogue for the award of these contracts.

The legal uncertainty regarding the compatibility of competitive dialogue with Decree-Law 86/2003 and (in the sectors for which it is relevant) the fact that the use of the open procedure with a negotiation phase has been widespread came up in the author's research as key reasons to explain the lack of use of competitive dialogue for the award of public–private partnerships in Portugal.

4.6. *Use in practice*

As stated above, competitive dialogue has been used only six times in Portugal.[27] Contracting authorities clearly are not using it as an alternative to other procedures in tendering complex contracts. It can also be noted that competitive dialogue was not used for, for example, any of the tenders launched regarding the new high-speed train line between Lisbon and the border with Spain, with the preference being instead for the open procedure with a negotiation phase.

Of the projects for which competitive dialogue has been used, four were tendered by local councils, one by a hospital and one by a public undertaking. No contracting authority has used the procedure more than once.

Two contracts were tendered for awarding bicycle-renting schemes, one for IT services (workflow management and development of an internal network), one for consultancy services and one for hospital cleaning. All of these contracts are relatively low-value contracts. While the two bicycle-renting schemes do not have an estimated value, the others were advertised with a maximum price of €200,000 to €250,000. The most recent contract launched was for the exploitation of an underground parking project and creation of an integrated payment system for all parking available in the area.

Although the numbers of competitive dialogue procedures are simply too small to conduct a detailed analysis, the absence of infrastructure or major IT projects tendered in Portugal by means of a competitive dialogue should be noted.

[27] Data from the Tenders Electronic Daily website and the Portuguese official journal, *Diário da República*.

5. Operation of the competitive dialogue procedure

5.1. *Introduction*

As is elaborated below, the rules governing the operation of competitive dialogue in Portugal contain various provisions that are not found in the Directive and were introduced to adapt it to the procurement tradition and culture in the country. Thus, candidates may be selected according to two different selection models. They can only submit one solution, and this is evaluated before the start of the dialogue. Further, the contracting authority may not exclude either candidates or solutions during the dialogue stage. The contracting authority must identify a winning solution during the dialogue stage and then draft common technical specifications for all candidates to tender against. Finally, from the moment the tenders are submitted, competitive dialogue must be operated as if it were an open or restricted procedure.

In this respect, the way that competitive dialogue has been applied in Portugal is significantly different from the way that it has been applied in other Member States, which – contrary to the approach adopted in Portugal – have generally given to contracting authorities on key points all, or nearly all, the flexibility allowed under the Directive.

5.2. *The planning stage and drafting of the descriptive document*

The Public Contracts Code is silent regarding obligations for the contracting authority at the planning stage. It is clear that the authority must provide a reasoned explanation of why it is using competitive dialogue and not another procedure, further to the point made earlier on the apparent requirement for impossibility of drafting technical specifications.

In the three interviews with contracting authorities that have used competitive dialogue in Portugal, it was found that none of the authorities formally consulted the market in preparation for the launch of the procedure.

5.3. *Confidentiality of information and solutions*

As we have seen in section 5.3 of Chapter 1, Article 29(3) of Directive 2004/18 states that: 'Contracting authorities may not reveal to the other participants solutions proposed or other confidential information communicated by a candidate participating in the dialogue without his/her agreement.' The issue of confidentiality of information is not as thoroughly regulated as other areas of competitive dialogue in Portugal. According to Article 214(3) of the Public Contracts Code, information is to be treated as confidential by the contracting authority if the candidate classifies it as confidential during the communication. It appears that all the information disclosed by a candidate as confidential will have to be immediately treated as such by the contracting authority.

It remains to be seen what happens when candidates transmit information that is clearly in the public domain and classify it as confidential. One could mention in this respect, for instance, information on a solution that has been leaked to the press and therefore made public, or information already public before the start of the procedure.

The Portuguese law has steered clear of outlining what should be considered as confidential, for instance, information protected by intellectual property laws. In addition, for information that is considered as confidential the condition of confidentiality can only be lifted if the candidate expressly allows it in writing.[28]

Article 214(3) of the Public Contracts Code appears to be drafted in injunctive terms and it seems that the contracting authority will not be able to establish through the descriptive document the forfeiture of this protection as a condition of participation in the procedure. The obligation of confidentiality is stated in strong terms in Portuguese law. Furthermore, such protection can only be lifted with written and express consent *after* the information has been transmitted to the contracting authority: this cannot be done before transmission.[29]

As an alternative to the current legal regime on confidentiality, Portuguese law-makers might have opted to extend the rules on secrecy of tenders to the dialogue stage.[30] According to Article 66(1) of the Public Contracts Code, a tenderer may generally request that the tender or parts of it are classified as secret for reasons relating to commercial, industrial, military or other types of secrecy 'in the terms of the law'. This requires that the tenderer be very specific on what he requests protection for and his request must be founded on substantial laws which protect, for

[28] Art. 214(3) of the Public Contracts Code.

[29] One of the interviewees, however, did not find a problem with the possibility of a 'blanket authorisation' condition being present in the descriptive document.

[30] These rules were first drawn to the author's notice by one of the respondents.

instance, trade secrets. In addition, the contracting authority ultimately has discretion over whether to grant or withhold the request.

Confidentiality raises another major problem specific to the way the competitive dialogue procedure is conceived in Portuguese law, as the objective of the dialogue stage is the drafting of a common set of specifications at its end. The contracting authority may face difficulties if a candidate classifies important elements of its solution as confidential and the authority wishes to include it in the technical specifications.[31]

However, although the ban on sharing confidential information is clearly present in the Public Contracts Code, for the situation in Portugal in which contracting authorities must design a common set of specifications the author would question whether the ban is as important as in the situations in which candidates end up tendering based on their own solution. If the candidate is tendering based on his own solution, then any confidential information shared with another candidate during the dialogue will have an immediate detrimental effect on the competitiveness of his own tender. In Portugal, if it is possible for the contracting authority to draft technical specifications with elements from various solutions,[32] then having a greater input into them can arguably increase the competitiveness of a candidate's tender. It must be said, however, that it is not clear if Portuguese contracting authorities are authorized to draft common technical specifications with elements from more than one solution. If specifications are to be based on a single solution, then confidentiality is as important as when candidates present tenders that develop their own solution.

Confidentiality is also key for judicial review in Portugal. In Portugal, access to documents from public bodies justifying a challenged decision is very liberal. When faced with judicial review, the public body is required by law to surrender every document relevant to the case to be reviewed by the plaintiff and the court. The issue here is what the contracting authority should do in the face of confidential material. Should it provide all the documents pertaining to the plea, including the ones that are confidential?[33] Or, should it withhold them, as

[31] See section 5.7.2 for a more detailed discussion of the topic.

[32] Again, see further, section 5.7.2.

[33] The same remarks could be made of the tender secrecy rules of Art. 66(1). These, however, are more limited and the request has to be founded in the law, whereas confidentiality under Art. 214(3) is automatic and does not need to be justified.

suggested by the CJEU's *Varec* decision?[34] Bearing in mind the author's own experience as a lawyer in the field and the answers given by lawyers interviewed, it would appear that the most sensible thing for a contracting authority to do would be to supply the documents to the court with a specific warning that some information had been considered confidential by the company. It would then be for the judge to decide either to keep them confidential or to make them available to the other parties.

5.4. *Advertising requirements*

According to Article 208(1) of the Public Contracts Code, the notice for a competitive dialogue is to be published in the national official journal, *Diário da República*. In the event that the contract to be awarded through a competitive dialogue is a public works, public works concession, goods or services contract, then the notice must always be published also in the OJEU, irrespective of the base price defined in the technical specifications.[35]

Out of the six competitive dialogue procedures launched so far, five were advertised on the Tenders Electronic Daily website.[36] One of the bicycle schemes was not advertised there, notwithstanding the fact that Article 208(2) of the Public Contracts Code requires publication in the OJEU of all competitive dialogue procedures for the award of public works, public works concession, goods or services contracts. The explanation might be that the contracting authority was not sure if it would end up with a services or a public–private partnership contract and considered that it did not have to publish it in the OJEU.

5.5. *The selection phase*

5.5.1. Introduction

Selection of candidates in Portugal is done through one of two methods, as set out below – one labelled 'complex' and the other 'simple'.

[34] Case C-450/06, *Varec* v. *Belgium* [2008] ECR I-00581, although not entirely clear, appears to value confidentiality above transparency and indicates that the review body must keep confidential the information transmitted to it. On this case, see A. Brown, 'Protection of Confidential Information in Procurement Cases before National Review Bodies: Varec vs. Belgian State (C-450/06)' (2008) 17 *Public Procurement Law Review* NA119.

[35] Art. 208(2) of the Public Contracts Code.

[36] http://ted.europa.eu/TED/browse/browseByBO.do.

Contracting authorities may freely adopt one or the other. As we will see, both have advantages and drawbacks when used in a competitive dialogue procedure.

5.5.2. Complex method

The complex method is based on a selection model founded on the criteria of best technical and financial ability (Article 181(1) and (2) of the Public Contracts Code). Contracting authorities are able to limit the number of candidates that take part in the dialogue but the maximum number has to be defined in the contract notice. The criteria for selecting the candidates must also be defined at this stage. Candidates are then ranked according to how well they are considered in respect of the defined criteria, just as with the application of award criteria to tenders.

In accordance with Article 181(3) of the Public Contracts Code, the contracting authority must select the higher ranked-candidates until it reaches the number pre-defined in the technical specifications (open and restricted procedure) or descriptive document (competitive dialogue). The contracting authority is under two obligations in respect of the qualification of candidates: to select the number of candidates previously chosen and to select in the order of the ranking. The contracting authority has no scope at this time to redefine the number of candidates or to pick a candidate deemed as suitable but classified lower in the ranking.

In addition, although the Public Contracts Code states that the minimum number of candidates to be selected may not be less than three, there is no restriction on actually carrying on with either two or even one candidate only, if that is the number that complies with the qualification requirements.

As mentioned in the introduction, both models have drawbacks. In the case of the complex model, three issues should be highlighted. First, it is very demanding for the contracting authority as it will have to develop criteria and assess the qualities of candidates for a contract for which it is yet to define the content. Article 164(1)(m)(i) expressly demands an extremely detailed selection model to be disclosed including criteria, sub-criteria, weightings, scales and mathematical formulae. The issue here is that this level of detail may not be achievable by the contracting authority when it does not know what the content of the contract will be. Furthermore, the need for this increases the bureaucracy and the timescales involved. Secondly, the fact that candidates will be excluded creates a risk for the contracting authority as it may be faced with litigation from aggrieved candidates that would delay the procedure. Thirdly, the contracting authority may end up weeding out candidates that, in the end, may be the most suitable to deliver the contract based on the technical specifications drawn up at the end of the dialogue stage. As it is forced to make a decision so early and before the technical specifications are drawn up it is possible that the best candidates will end up being excluded at this point.

So far, no contracting authority has used the complex model to select candidates in the few competitive dialogues that have taken place in Portugal. Although the numbers involved are low, they are enough to point a clear trend.

5.5.3. Simple method

The simple system of Article 179 of the Public Contracts Code entails that *all* candidates with the necessary technical and financial ability are entitled to take part in the procedure. Candidates are considered as financially able simply if a bank statement is produced in accordance with the model supplied in Annex VI to the Public Contracts Code. No rules are present on how to evaluate the technical ability of candidates.

The distinguishing feature of this system is that *all* candidates fulfilling the minimum requirements set forth by the contracting authority must be allowed to take part in the procedure and their number cannot be limited in advance. This would not be a major problem if the contracting authority could exclude candidates or solutions during the dialogue. However, as we will see in more detail in section 5.6.6, that is not the case. In consequence, if 10 candidates make the cut, all of them must be invited to take part in the dialogue stage. This will lead contracting authorities to carry out a balancing act when drafting the criteria to evaluate the technical ability of candidates. If the thresholds are set too low, the authority may be swamped with candidates. If they are too high, it may not have enough tenderers to foster competition.

One can argue that the simple system is suitable to ease and speed up the tendering of straightforward contracts. As competitive dialogue can be used only in the case of complex contracts, where the specific qualities or characteristics of the candidates may have an impact on the quality of the discussions during the dialogue stage, one may consider that perhaps the simple system is not appropriate to select the participants.

So far, all contracting authorities that have used competitive dialogue have preferred to use this model. The author was told that they preferred to engage in dialogue with a larger number of candidates than to exclude them at this point and potentially face litigation.

5.6. *The dialogue phase*

5.6.1. Introduction

As we have already mentioned, the dialogue phase of a competitive dialogue in Portugal exhibits various differences when compared with the Directive. Candidates can only submit a solution which will be assessed before the start of the procedure; no exclusions (of solutions or candidates) are admitted during the actual dialogue; and at the end of the dialogue the contracting authority must identify which of the solutions is the best one.

5.6.2. Presentation of solutions

All candidates selected are simultaneously invited to submit their solution for the dialogue.[37] The invitation must comply with certain formalities, including by identifying the procedure (including by the reference number attributed by the national and European official journals) and stating the submission deadline and what foreign languages are to be admitted in the dialogue, if any.[38]

5.6.3. Limitation to a single solution

Each admitted candidate can present only one solution,[39] in what seems to be an arbitrary limitation imposed by Portuguese law-makers. This may reduce the scope of possible solutions to be addressed during the procedure. However, one may argue that this focuses the candidates' efforts on their best solution and on improving it, and may also keep costs down since each candidate can only put resources into developing one solution. However, if only a few companies have expertise in a certain field, it could be more productive to allow them to develop and deliver more than one solution. For instance, in an IT project, a company may have two different products that may suit the contracting authority but it is limited from the beginning to choosing one to present in the competitive dialogue.

[37] Art. 209(1) of the Public Contracts Code. The solution must be drafted in Portuguese following the rules stated by Art. 62 of the Public Contracts Code for tenders in general.

[38] Art. 209(2) of the Public Contracts Code. When queried, one of the respondents said this rule was intended to provide for a position similar to that in Art. 58/1 of the Public Contracts Code. It is worth noting that the respondent then proceeded to say that, if drafting today, he or she may have had a more open opinion regarding the possibility of accepting solutions drafted in other languages.

[39] Art. 210(2) of the Public Contracts Code.

5.6.4. Exclusion of preliminary solutions

According to Article 212(2) of the Public Contracts Code, the jury for the procedure is to assess the preliminary solutions submitted and must propose their exclusion under certain conditions. Three of these conditions are merely formal[40] and only the fourth appears to be substantial. According to the fourth condition, solutions that are deemed 'obviously inadequate' to fulfil the needs of the contracting authority are to be excluded. This assessment of clear inadequacy is the only moment in the procedure at which contracting authorities are allowed to undertake exclusions. Thus, this feature may have a paramount importance for the sound application of the procedure, especially if the simple selection method was used. No rules are provided to guide the contracting authority in this process, leaving the contracting authority with a wide discretion on what is or is not 'obviously inadequate'.

5.6.5. The dialogue itself

The dialogue itself starts after candidates have been notified of the decision regarding the solution put forward.[41] The dialogue is aimed, in the Public Contracts Code, at discussing the elements present or absent in each admitted proposal and that are relevant for the drafting of detailed specifications.[42]

Dialogue is subject to a number of formalities. Minimum notification periods,[43] rules on what should be included in the minutes of meetings,[44] rules on who can be present in the meetings and is entitled to represent the candidate,[45] cautions regarding equal treatment between candidates,[46] and the ban on transmitting confidential information[47] are all present in Portuguese law.

The option to include and clearly state formalities is typical of the Portuguese legislative system in general, which tends to regulate in

[40] Such as presenting the solution after the deadline, not following certain formal rules or being drafted in a foreign language that has not been expressly accepted.
[41] Art. 212(6) of the Public Contracts Code.
[42] Art. 213 of the Public Contracts Code.
[43] Three days according to Art. 214(1) of the Public Contracts Code.
[44] Arts. 1 of(3) and 120(3) and (5) of the Public Contracts Code.
[45] Art. 214(6) of the Public Contracts Code.
[46] Art. 214(2) of the Public Contracts Code.
[47] Art. 214(3) of the Public Contracts Code.

minute detail.[48] Even so, this shows that during the transposition of competitive dialogue this procedure was not simply bolted onto an existing framework, but it was adapted to fit within national practice.

Dialogue is to be carried out until a single solution[49] best suited for the contracting authority's needs is found or all solutions are deemed unsuitable. The jury will end the dialogue and produce a report justifying its decision and submit it to the contracting authority.[50] It is up to the contracting authority to decide whether to follow the jury's recommendations.[51]

5.6.6. Impossibility of eliminating candidates during the dialogue

As Chapter 1 explained (see section 5.6.3), under Article 29(4) of Directive 2004/18, the contracting authority may provide for successive stages in the procedure to eliminate either solutions or candidates.[52] In Portugal, however, the Public Contracts Code does not provide a legal basis for successive stages in competitive dialogue. The author was told by law-makers that, although the possibility of eliminating candidates during the dialogue had been considered during the drafting of the law, in the end it was decided that Article 29(4) of the Directive did not provide a sound approach on this issue.

The consequence of its being impossible to eliminate candidates or solutions during the dialogue is that a contracting authority may have dialogue stages which start and end with a large number of candidates, leading to high costs and long timescales. This issue is particularly acute if the assessment of the economic, technical or professional ability of candidates has been done through the simple system.

As a way out, one could argue that the contracting authority and the candidate may agree to stop developing a solution. This seems reasonable, especially bearing in mind that at the end of the dialogue a

[48] Regulating what information is to be included in the minutes of meetings may seem excessive but can be explained by the way judicial review of tenders operates in Portugal. According to the Administrative Courts Process Law, the contracting authority (such as administrative bodies), when challenged by an aggrieved party, has to produce the administrative file, containing everything connected to the tender, including all decisions and minutes of meetings that led to and support such decisions.

[49] Only the singular is present in Art. 214(5)(b) of the Public Contracts Code, without a plural, contrary to what is provided in Art. 29(5) of Directive 2004/18.

[50] Art. 215(1) of the Public Contracts Code.

[51] Art. 215(2) and (3) of the Public Contracts Code.

[52] See Ch. 1, section 5.6.3.

common set of specifications will be developed. However, according to Article 215 of the Public Contracts Code, it appears that such candidates should be retained for the tender stage as they had their solution admitted at the start of the dialogue.

From the author's research it appeared that both lawyers and contracting authorities disagree with the decision taken by the law-makers of not allowing exclusions during the dialogue stage as they consider it an appropriate feature of the procedure. One should note with caution that contracting authorities can exclude candidates at the selection phase if they use the complex method, as well as at the start of the dialogue but none has done so. It is also interesting to note that in Spain, where such dialogue exclusions are allowed, contracting authorities do not apply them in practice, in contrast with the practice in some other Member States.[53]

5.7. *Final tender stage*

5.7.1. Introduction

The end of the dialogue stage and transition to the final tender stage is regulated in detail in the Public Contracts Code and these detailed regulatory rules raise a number of points. The most significant is that a common set of specifications will have to be drafted by the contracting authority. Candidates will then submit their tenders based on these specifications and not on the solution they have been developing during the dialogue stage.

5.7.2. Common set of specifications

As provided in the Public Contracts Code, at the end of the dialogue stage the contracting authority must draft a common set of specifications. Candidates will present their tenders based on those specifications and not the solution that they themselves have developed during the dialogue. It is not clear in the Public Contracts Code how the contracting authority will actually draft the technical specifications.

Under one possible interpretation, since a winning solution must be identified by the contracting authority, this winning solution must be converted into the technical specifications, without external elements

[53] *Ibid.*

from other solutions and without being further developed by the contracting authority.

Under a second interpretation, common technical specifications can be composed of elements from the winning solution and also from solutions presented by other candidates and/or developed by the contracting authority. Technical specifications of this kind will represent, in reality, the best way to fulfil the needs of the contracting authority. It should be added that the identification of the winning solution is required by Article 215 (still within section III, which regulates the dialogue stage), whereas the obligation to draft the common technical specifications is specified by Article 217 (belonging to section IV, which regulates the presentation of tenders stage) and makes no reference to the winning solution.

Irrespective of the correct interpretation, one can see the merits of the decision taken by Portuguese law-makers of identifying the winning solution and having common technical specifications drafted at the end of the dialogue stage. It makes work easier for the contracting authority as all other solutions developed by candidates are discarded. It also makes comparison between tenders easier and more transparent, facilitating external control, since they are based on the same set of specifications, just as they would be in an open or restricted procedure. More fundamentally, as the law-makers interviewed pointed out, it makes possible the very detailed award criteria evaluation model set forth in the Public Contracts Code for the open procedure to be used in competitive dialogue. For this evaluation model to be used, it is necessary that the bids are entirely comparable, something that might be harder to achieve in practice if each candidate was allowed to submit a tender based on its own solution.

From a different perspective, however, the decision to identify a winning solution and develop common specifications leads to other problems. First, it makes all (or almost all) candidates tender on a solution which is not theirs, thus creating an imbalanced field of competition, particularly if the technical specifications are based on a single solution only.[54] Secondly, it leads to the scrapping of much of the development work done during the dialogue. Thirdly, it may also lead to a reduced field of competition in the later stages of the procedure as

[54] One can argue, however, that the rules are clear from the start of the procedure and it is a fair commercial advantage for whoever develops the solution to reap the benefits of preparing a tender based on its own work.

those candidates who have not presented the winning solution (or have not contributed significantly to the winning solution), when faced with the costs of preparing a tender from scratch, may simply decide not to do so. Fourthly, candidates participating in the dialogue may simply not be competent to tender based on the common specifications – for example, if they are in a different business area – thus also reducing competition. Finally, as we have seen above when discussing confidentiality, it is difficult to ensure compliance with the rules on protection of confidential information when using this approach of developing a common set of specifications.

If the second interpretation suggested above is correct, then an extra set of issues may be raised, since it would imply that cherry-picking is possible according to the Public Contracts Code. In addition, contracting authorities may have the incentive to guide candidates during the dialogue stage to a convergent solution that will end up serving as the base for the technical specifications, especially bearing in mind the restrictions on discussions after the end of the dialogue stage, as will be discussed further below.

Whatever the correct interpretation, the option adopted by the Portuguese law-makers raises two more questions. As we have seen, the candidates carried forward to the dialogue depend on the merits of the preliminary solution they have developed and not their own ability to execute a set of specifications. This may lead to situations where candidates who were capable and interested in submitting a tender based on the specifications that are drafted at the end of the dialogue were not carried to the dialogue due to shortcomings in their own preliminary solution – and thus will not be invited to participate in the final tender stage. The Public Contracts Code is clear in stating that only candidates who had solutions admitted may be invited to participate at the tender stage. One must ask what is the difference between having the solution excluded at the beginning or at the end of the dialogue if the actual tender will not be based on it? From a competition point of view, it also makes no sense, since the Public Contracts Code is reducing the level of competition at the tendering stage. On the other hand, the law may be construed as allowing candidates who dropped out of the dialogue stage for whatever reason to come back into the procedure.[55] This may increase competition but also increases the risk of one or more

[55] As noted by one of the interviewees.

candidates with admitted solutions stalling on development to save costs, thus offloading the development cost onto other candidates.

Finally, if the objective of the dialogue is to develop a common set of specifications just as in the open or restricted procedure, why not allow any potentially able company to tender based on those specifications instead of limiting the tenders to the participants in the dialogue stage?

5.7.3. Candidates to be invited

Article 217 of the Public Contracts Code states that, if a solution to fulfil the needs of the contracting authority has been found, then the candidates who have passed the assessment of the economic, technical or professional ability of candidates and had their solutions *admitted* shall be invited to submit tenders, presumably following the technical specifications supplied by the contracting authority at that point.[56] As mentioned above, apparently, all candidates who had their solutions admitted to the dialogue will be invited to tender based on a common set of technical specifications, irrespective of their solution having been considered as viable to fulfil the needs of the contracting authority.

5.7.4. Variants

Variants are treated in the Public Contracts Code equally for all tender procedures. As required by the Directive, they are admissible only if the contracting authorised such a possibility in the technical specifications.[57] Therefore, in the competitive dialogue procedure, contracting authorities may include in the common technical specifications an authorisation for candidates to submit variants.

5.7.5. Award criteria

Even though the apparently relevant section of the Public Contracts Code is headed 'Presentation of tenders and award', no rules on the award are to be found there. Those have to be sought in the subsidiary rules applicable to competitive dialogue – that is, the rules from the restricted procedure. Since the restricted procedure also has no bespoke rules on the award phase, the rules on the open procedure are applicable.[58] The result of this is that the rules on the award are to be found in

[56] Art. 217(3) of the Public Contracts Code.

[57] Art. 59(1) of the Public Contracts Code.

[58] Art. 162(1) of the Public Contracts Code states that the rules on the open procedure are subsidiary for the restricted procedure.

Articles 139–154 of the Public Contracts Code,[59] and that, after tender submission, the rules applicable to competitive dialogue are exactly the same as those for open and restricted procedures.

To end the procedure, the contracting authority must evaluate the tenders and award the contract. Article 139 of the Public Contracts Code establishes the rules on tender evaluation, namely, the contents of the evaluation model and in particular the requirements to draft an appropriate model to find the most economically advantageous tender.[60]

5.7.6. Phase for fine-tuning etc. of final tenders prior to choosing the winner

As explained in Chapter 1, Article 29(6) of Directive 2004/18 allows for a fine-tuning phase before the choosing of a preferred bidder where limited adjustments can be made to the tenders presented by the candidates.[61]

In the rules specifically pertaining to competitive dialogue, the Public Contracts Code does not seem to allow even for small adjustments to be made. The Portuguese law, however, allows the contracting authority to request further information from tenderers in all types of procedures. Article 72 of the Public Contracts Code states that the contracting authority may request any further information it considers necessary for the analysis of the tenders. This information may not change any feature of the tender or even bring a non-compliant tender into compliance.[62] In addition, all new information supplied by tenderers will have to be made available to its competitors.[63]

One can argue that this limitation may lead to a reduced utility of the procedure, and is arguably more stringent and less flexible than intended by Directive 2004/18, as discussed in Chapter 1. However, it can also be argued that this limitation may be beneficial, since it forces the parties to discuss all issues during the dialogue stage and not procrastinate over issues hoping they will be easier to deal with later. Potentially, the lack of post-dialogue discussions may have the effect of forcing the candidates to submit very detailed and complete bids. In this case, this ban would

[59] Excluding Arts. 140–145 of the Public Contracts Code on the electronic auction; and Arts. 149–154 on the negotiation phase.

[60] Mathematical formulae should be used when possible and no data may be dependent on the tenders to be submitted by the other tenderers, thus ruling out relative qualification schemes.

[61] See Ch. 1, section 5.7.4.

[62] Art. 72(2) of the Public Contracts Code.

[63] Art. 72(3) of the Public Contracts Code.

have a beneficial effect at the project management level by avoiding what has been described as 'bid creep'[64] when discussions are allowed after the tenders have been submitted. Having detailed bids from more than one candidate could, however, increase the transaction costs of the dialogue stage and eventually dissuade candidates from submitting bids, with negative effects on competition.

Taking into consideration the impossibility of making small changes as allowed by Article 29(6) of Directive 2004/18, it seems that more significant specification changes after bids are submitted are also precluded in Portugal. For example, after the final tendering stage, the contracting authority might wish to make some changes to the specifications, such as risk allocation or the aims and objectives of an IT contract, to maximise the benefits from the procurement procedure. The Public Contracts Code is silent regarding such a possibility[65] and as it does not allow for smaller changes it seems that the possibility of accepting these changes without restarting the procedure is also precluded.

From the author's research it appeared that both lawyers and contracting authorities have considered this to be a negative innovation by the Portuguese law-makers. For them, having this phase of fine-tuning etc. would increase the procedure's perceived utility.

5.8. *Procedure following the selection of the winning tender or preferred bidder*

Article 29(7) of Directive 2004/18 also allows for a final phase with the preferred bidder[66] after he has been selected, allowing some flexibility in finishing the details and clarifying the legal obligations of both parties. As discussed in Chapter 1, however, the provision contains ambiguous wording and the exact scope of what is allowed is unclear.[67] As examples of what could be allowed one could mention changes needed to be

[64] R. Auton, 'It's Good to Talk' (2009) *Public Finance* 26, at 26.

[65] On the conclusion of the interview, one of the interviewees, again referring to the lack of negotiation culture in the country, said that the Portuguese public administration is used to dictating, not negotiating. One of the respondents also mentioned the different cultural traditions of the UK and systems based on the Napoleonic public administration such as the Portuguese system.

[66] See Ch. 1, section 5.8.

[67] S. Arrowsmith, *The Law of Public and Utilities Procurement* (2nd edn, London: Sweet & Maxwell, 2005), pp. 660–3.

carried out due to external changes of circumstances such as modifications demanded by planning authorities during the application for planning permission.[68] The Public Contracts Code does not have a specific stage for amendments and discussions specifically for competitive dialogue. Contracting authorities may discuss issues with the winning bidder at this point under the same rules as in any other procedure. The draft of Article 99, the relevant provision, appears to be more limiting in what is allowed than Article 29(7) of Directive 2004/18 but, nonetheless, leaves some room to accommodate changes needed.

Since competitive dialogue is to be used for awarding particularly complex contracts it might be argued that the maximum amount of flexibility should be present. On the other hand, this ban on extensive changes may have positive effects. At this stage, where the bidder no longer faces competition, it is in a better bargaining position and can be expected to extract concessions from the contracting authority. Not having this possibility may once more force contracting authorities and candidates to settle as many issues as possible during the dialogue stage. These issues were discussed further in section 5.8 of Chapter 1.

5.9. *The standstill period*

Under general Portuguese public law, private parties must be served with notice of all decisions having an impact on them before the final decision is taken. Thus they are served with a preliminary decision and invited to present their views on the proposed decision within a certain timeframe. This is then followed by the definitive decision if no changes are made or a new preliminary decision (and further consulting) if the public authority has changed its mind.

Applied to competitive dialogue this means that the selection of candidates,[69] the assessment of preliminary solutions, the identification of the winning solution[70] and the award decision all have to follow such a procedure.

5.10. *Payments for costs of participation*

According to Article 206(1) of the Public Contracts Code, as per Article 29(8) of Directive 2004/18, contracting authorities may specify prices or

[68] *Ibid.*, p. 662. [69] Arts. 184 and 185 of the Public Contracts Code.
[70] Arts. 146 and 147 of the Public Contracts Code.

payments to be made to candidates for the costs of participation. If the contracting authority so decides, this option must be expressly included in the contract notice or descriptive document.

The author's research found that in practice no contracting authority has actually paid the costs of participation in the competitive dialogue procedure, and one respondent that had used the procedure argued that in the current financial climate it would not be appropriate. The majority of lawyers and contracting authorities that did not use the procedure suggested that, in theory, such payments would be beneficial by fostering participation and showing the market that the contracting authority is serious about the contract, rather than merely seeking consultancy services for free.

5.11. Judicial review

So far, no instances of judicial review concerning competitive dialogue have been observed. However, during his research, the author found a widespread fear of potential judicial review challenges over the scope of application of the procedure and also its operation, on the part of both contracting authorities and lawyers.

6. Concluding remarks

As explained in the body of this chapter, the Portuguese law-makers considered it necessary to adapt the competitive dialogue procedure to fit within the national framework and approach when introducing the procedure in Portugal. This has led to the identification of a significant number of potential issues, both legal and non-legal, with competitive dialogue in Portugal. For the author, the principal cause for the lack of use of competitive dialogue in Portugal is the restricted approach taken to the scope for use, combined with the overall restrictive interpretation that was observed in the empirical research. The purposeful sampling employed ensures that such findings are extendable to the general population of those categories (public procurement lawyers, contracting authorities). That is not to say that the drafting of the scope is the only reason, as many other factors have also contributed, such as the procedure's possible lack of compatibility with the public–private partnerships rules, the existence of the open procedure with a negotiation phase, the lack of exclusions, the requirement for a common set of specifications and the fact that after tenders have been submitted competitive dialogue is to be run as an open procedure. As mentioned above, with so many changes to the procedure as it appears in the Directive one can ask whether in fact the 'competitive dialogue' procedure in Portugal is the same 'competitive dialogue' as envisaged in Directive 2004/18. From the legal text, if not the practice, it seems that what is available for contracting authorities is, at most, a *redux* version of the procedure.

In consequence of all the above, it is no surprise that there have been only six recorded cases of use of competitive dialogue in Portugal, and only one since March 2010. The lack of actual use of competitive dialogue is a clear demonstration of the lack of interest in competitive dialogue as it has been transposed into Portuguese law.

8

Competitive dialogue in Spain

PEDRO TELLES

1. Introduction: regulation of public procurement in Spain

Spain is divided into seventeen autonomous regions and two autonomous cities, each bearing devolved powers since the entry into force of the current Constitution in 1978. The national parliament can enact laws which are applicable in the whole country, whereas regional parliaments can approve laws enforceable only within each region. National laws can include both rules directly applicable in all the country or what is called 'basic legislation' – that is, legislation that leaves some room to the regional bodies for refinements. Regional authorities have thus some room to adopt specific rules under the 'basic legislation' umbrella, as long as these are not contrary to the requirements set forth at the national level. The exact content of the 'basic legislation' concept and its boundaries have been, and still are, a matter of discussion by Spanish scholars.[1]

Spain has a long tradition of regulating public procurement, having had a detailed legal public procurement framework long before acceding to the EU in 1986. After accession, Spain periodically updated its legal framework, incorporating EU rules as they came into force. Traditionally, Spain has had an extensive procurement regime that included rules on how to conduct procedures that are additional to those found in the EU Procurement Directives. Currently the bulk of legislation applicable to public procurement is contained in the Law on Public Sector Contracts (Law 30/2007, 30 October 2007) which transposes Directive 2004/18.[2] This law was updated in August 2010 to accommodate the changes introduced by Directive 2007/66 (which revised Remedies

[1] See L. C. Montaner, *Manual de Derecho Administrativo* (19th edn, Thomson Civitas, 2008), pp. 85–9.

[2] More than a year after the deadline set by the Directive itself. The Law on Public Sector Contracts has been the object of several amendments by means of Royal Decree 817/2009, Order of the Ministry of Economics and Finance 3497/2009, Royal Decree-Law 6/2010, Royal Decree-Law 8/2010, Law 14/2010, Law 15/2010 and Law 34/2010.

Directive 89/665).[3] Directive 2004/17 on utilities procurement was transposed by Law 31/2007 (30 October 2007). The transposition of Directive 2009/81 on defence and security procurement is still pending at the time of writing.

The rules on remedies were changed in 2010 with the entry into force of Law 34/2010, which amended the Law on Public Sector Contracts. The standstill obligation became mandatory for contracts over the EU thresholds – the so-called 'contracts subject to harmonised regulation'. These contracts are also now the subject of a special administrative review appeal mechanism that needs to be exhausted before a judicial review can be filed. The competent jurisdiction depends on the nature of the contract. Issues relating to the procurement *and* performance of administrative contracts, and issues relating to the procurement of private contracts of the administration are all to be taken to the administrative courts. Litigation regarding the performance of private contracts of the administration is to be taken to the judicial courts.

2. Complex procurement prior to competitive dialogue

Before the transposition of competitive dialogue, it appears from anecdotal evidence – although the author has no actual data on this – that complex procurement was carried out at least to some extent through open or negotiated procedures, and was particularly associated with public works and services concessions.

It can be noted that these last two contractual types remain popular in the country, much more so than the new public–private co-operation type of contract for which (as explained below) competitive dialogue is the default procedure in Spain.

3. Introduction to competitive dialogue

Competitive dialogue was transposed into Spanish law in 2007 through the Law on Public Sector Contracts, which did not have a public consultation phase. In the Law on Public Sector Contracts, competitive dialogue is mainly regulated in Book III, Title I, Chapter I, Section 5, Articles 163–169. A number of other Articles scattered across this law are also relevant, either directly or indirectly, to the regulation of

[3] The most recent alterations were introduced by Law 02/2011 on sustainable economy.

competitive dialogue in Spain.[4] In general, the Spanish regulation of competitive dialogue amounts to little more than copying and pasting the Directive's content into the Spanish legal text. The only remarkable novelty of the Spanish law is making competitive dialogue the default procedure for the award of public–private co-operation contracts, as discussed in section 4 below.[5]

At the time of writing this chapter, no judicial decisions on competitive dialogue have surfaced, although one judicial review and at least two administrative appeals have been filed in accordance with the legal regime in force before August 2010.

Public procurement advisory bodies are entitled to issue guidance on public procurement in Spain. A total of sixteen of these bodies exist (one national and fifteen regional). These entities can produce opinions if asked by contracting authorities, and also produce general guidance. So far, only the national body has produced guidance on competitive dialogue. This body accepted the terms of reference of a competitive dialogue procedure launched by the Finance Ministry for the refurbishment of a building as legal and to be a good basis for other contracting authorities to adopt.[6] The author was also told by a regional body that it is considering issuing general guidance on various aspects of competitive dialogue.

As of July 2011, the procedure has been used a total of eighty times in Spain, with twenty-two procedures launched since July 2010.

Between March and August 2010, the author conducted empirical research on the implementation of competitive dialogue in Spain for a doctoral degree at the University of Nottingham as part of the wider project on competitive dialogue in the EU that forms the basis of the present book, in order to establish how the legal rules have been applied and interpreted in Spain. To this end, twenty-seven interviews were undertaken, covering contracting authorities (twenty), legal experts in public procurement (four), public procurement advisory bodies (two) and a consultant. Of this total, twenty-three had direct experience of participating in competitive dialogue.

[4] Arts. 11(1), 26, 45(1), 64, 65, 66, 67, 68, 73, 75(5), 93(3), 101(3)(b), (c) and (d), 118, 119, 120, 122(2), 129(2), 130, 135(3), 147, 148, 149, 150(2)–(5), 154(a) and 296 are all relevant to competitive dialogue and will be explained in detail below when applicable.

[5] Art. 164(3) of the Law on Public Sector Contracts.

[6] www.meh.es/es-ES/Servicios/Contratacion/Junta%20Consultiva%20de%20Contratacion%20Administrativa/Informes/Archivo%20historico/Documents/Recomendaci%C3%B3n%20sobre%20modelo%20de%20CCPP.pdf.

4. Scope of the competitive dialogue procedure in law and practice

4.1. General rules on scope

According to Article 164 of the Law on Public Sector Contracts, competitive dialogue may be used when the contract is particularly complex and the open or restricted procedures do not allow for its 'appropriate'[7] award. The express inclusion of the word 'appropriate' in the Spanish law is not present in the Spanish translation of the Directive. From the letter of the law, it appears that the scope for the use of the procedure in Spain is wider than that in neighbouring Portugal.

Practice so far has confirmed a relatively flexible approach towards the scope of the procedure. From the empirical research conducted, the author concluded that contracting authorities did not entertain doubts regarding the scope of application of the procedure. Interviewees were using the competitive dialogue because they felt the procedure was the most appropriate for the need at hand and the open or restricted procedures would not have been adequate to award the contract they wanted. Therefore, they are using competitive dialogue in situations where it would be possible to use alternatives such as the open or restricted procedures but these procedures would not, however, be satisfactory.

4.2. Public–private co-operation contracts

According to Article 164(3) of the Law on Public Sector Contracts, competitive dialogue is the default procedure for the award of public–private co-operation contracts.[8]

The approach to the definition of this legal concept is not entirely clear in Article 11 of the Spanish law,[9] but these appear to be contracts under which a private entity is mandated to perform certain tasks necessary to satisfy the general interest for a period of time, with

[7] Translated by the author.

[8] On co-operation contracts in general, see L. M. Macho, 'Las formas de colaboración público-privada en el Derecho español' (2008) 175 *Revista de administración pública* 157; N. P. Salom, 'El contrato de colaboración entre el sector público y el sector privado' (2008) 18 *Revista General de Derecho Administrativo*; and C. C. Marín, 'El nuevo contrato de colaboración entre el sector público y el sector privado' (2006) 132 *Revista española de derecho administrativo* 609.

[9] This Article was recently amended by Law 02/2011, which clarifies only the entities that can adopt this contract without providing new insight on its characteristics.

payments to be made during the performance in certain situations. Co-operation contracts are now a contract type in Spain,[10] placed side by side with public works contracts,[11] public works concessions,[12] public services concessions,[13] goods contracts[14] and services contracts.[15] Public works contracts and services concessions remain in the Law on Public Sector Contracts[16] and are highly regulated and used extensively in Spain. There is, however, considerable scope for discussion on what a public–private co-operation contract is and where the boundary with concessions actually lies. Public works and services concessions remain within the scope of the Law on Public Sector Contracts[17] and are highly regulated and used extensively in Spain. For example, during 2009 Spain launched seventy-one public works and twenty-four services concession tenders (tendered by means other than competitive dialogue) and only eleven public–private co-operation contracts of any kind.[18] These numbers lead to the conclusion that the public–private co-operation contract is yet to replace public works and services concessions and is being deployed alongside them. Moreover, in the author's view, this means also that the traditional method of procuring complex contracts has not been significantly changed with the introduction of competitive dialogue.

Public–private partnerships have been used mostly in the areas of health (twelve) and energy refurbishment (seven). As examples, one can point to nine different contracts tendered for various equipment and services in the new Hospital Son Espases in Majorca or the energy refurbishment contract for the Ministry of Justice's central offices in Madrid. This last tender also includes the supply of energy for the (unspecified) duration of the contract. In the meantime, public works concessions not tendered through competitive dialogue remain popular for infrastructure contracts, particularly in the transport sector.

The fact that all co-operation contracts have to be awarded through competitive dialogue can be interpreted in two ways. It may mean that all co-operation contracts are inherently 'complex contracts' for the effect of complying with Article 164(1) and (2) and with Directive

[10] Art. 11 of the Law on Public Sector Contracts.
[11] Art. 6 of the Law on Public Sector Contracts.
[12] Art. 7 of the Law on Public Sector Contracts.
[13] Art. 8 of the Law on Public Sector Contracts.
[14] Art. 9 of the Law on Public Sector Contracts.
[15] Art. 10 of the Law on Public Sector Contracts.
[16] In Arts. 223–250 and 251–265.
[17] In Arts. 223–250 and 251–265.
[18] Numbers from a search done by the author on the Tenders Electronic Daily website.

2004/18. Alternatively, it can be interpreted as allowing the use of competitive dialogue for contracts that are not particularly complex. The first interpretation would be obvious had the law-makers opted to include reference to co-operation contracts as a further element of definition in Article 164(2), where the concept of 'particularly complex' contract is defined, and not later in a different part of the same Article. One can thus argue that the second interpretation is more logical in the face of the drafting adopted. In addition to the fact that no reference is made to Article 164(2), Article 164(3) of the Law on Public Sector Contracts makes a reference to the need to heed Article 154(a)[19] (which allows the negotiated procedure to be used after a previous open, restricted or competitive dialogue procedure has been tried but results were not forthcoming and the original conditions are not substantively changed in the new procedure) so one can also argue that the law-makers wanted co-operation contracts to be awarded exclusively by either competitive dialogue or the negotiated procedure. It appears that Spanish law-makers have arguably not acted entirely consistently with either the Commission's stance[20] or Article 29(1) of the Directive, and have considered that all public–private co-operation contracts are necessarily particularly complex.

4.3. *Contracts under the thresholds of Directive 2004/18*

With regard to competitive dialogue, the Law on Public Sector Contracts does not make a distinction between contracts above and those below the threshold of Directive 2004/18. Therefore, the procedure is in theory available for the award of all such contracts, as long as the conditions set out in Article 164 are met. In practice, the author has seen some instances where contracts below the EU thresholds have been tendered through competitive dialogue.

[19] Art. 154(a) allows the negotiated procedure to be used after a previous open, restricted or competitive dialogue procedure has been tried but the results were not successful and the original conditions are not substantively changed in the new procedure. The novelty, again, is not the negotiated procedure's use after a competitive dialogue has failed, *per se*, but the motives behind the failure that can lead to the use of the negotiated procedure. For instance, according to that Article, if the tenders were presented by candidates deemed unsuitable, the contracting authority may resort to the negotiated procedure.

[20] European Commission, *Explanatory Note – Competitive Dialogue – Classic Directive*, available at http://ec.europa.eu/internal_market/publicprocurement/docs/explan-notes/classic-dir-dialogue_en.pdf, p. 3.

4.4. *Use in practice*

As mentioned in section 3 above, the procedure has at the time of writing been used a total of seventy-three times in practice, by fewer than fifty different contracting authorities.[21] Thirty-one of these award procedures were for the award of public–private co-operation contracts, nine of these being related to different medical equipment needed by a single hospital in Majorca.

In the medical sector in general, the procedure was used at least thirteen times, by four different contracting authorities.[22] All of them appear to be public–private co-operation contracts, both for the construction and management of hospitals and for specific types of medical equipment needed.

For construction and refurbishment projects, the procedure was used at least twenty-seven times, with fifteen being public–private co-operation contracts. Out of this total, seven are IT projects related to the deployment of new networks in different areas of the country. The most expensive contract was a public–private co-operation IT contract valued at €662 million. Apart from IT projects, none of the other construction projects represent major works contracts. In fact, the most expensive construction project that is neither an IT project nor a public–private co-operation contract was the construction of an oceanic research platform in the Canaries valued at €12 million.

A more detailed analysis of the use of competitive dialogue in Spain for the period 2006–9 can be found in Chapter 2.

Based on the above analysis, it can be said in general that competitive dialogue is yet to see widespread adoption in Spain, particularly if the 'public–private co-operation contract effect' is discounted. The use of the negotiated procedure with a contract notice is still prevalent in Spain with 672 tenders launched[23] since competitive dialogue was introduced. That is not to say that all those contracts are particularly complex in nature, but the fact the negotiated procedure has been used almost ten times more than the competitive dialogue is hard to ignore. Moreover, of the 672 negotiated procedures, 426 were launched in the last twelve

[21] Data from the Tenders Electronic Daily, Spanish Official Journal (*Boletín Oficial del Estado*) and also notices found on contracting authorities' own websites.

[22] The author was told by three different respondents that other contracting authorities in the medical sector were considering adopting the procedure in the future.

[23] According to data from the Tenders Electronic Daily website.

months alone, a number 20 times greater than the number of competitive dialogue procedures launched.

From the data analysed by the author it appears that an interesting practice is developing in Spain. Contracting authorities are applying the procedure and appear overall to be satisfied with it and the challenges to project management brought by it. They do not seem to have any issues with the grounds for use. It is interesting, however, that it has not been used for transport networks.

4.5. Litigation

As mentioned in the introduction, Spain introduced a new legal regime regulating access to remedies in August 2010 with the entry into force of Law 34/2010. Therefore, it is still too soon to determine the impact of the new regulations on competitive dialogue litigation. Under the previous legal regime, however, and from the empirical research undertaken by the author, only two administrative appeals appear to have been filed. One aggrieved bidder subsequently filed for judicial review. Another contracting authority stated that all the candidates excluded before the dialogue stage asked to know the reasons for the exclusion, although none filed for either administrative or judicial review.

5. Operation of the competitive dialogue procedure

5.1. Introduction

As mentioned above, although the Law on Public Sector Contracts repeats *verbatim* the content of Directive 2004/18 in many instances, the body of practice built upon the use of the procedure in the country provides relevant insight on how the rules are actually being applied. The current section will mostly be based on the findings the author gathered from his empirical research on this matter. It should be said, however, that many issues found by the author were more of a project-management type than legal in nature, including how to organise the meetings, draft minutes, focus the discussions or extract the most value for money during the dialogue stage.

Mention should also be made here of the jury, which is the body that runs the procedure on behalf of the contracting authority. According to Article 296 of the Law on Public Sector Contracts and Article 23 of Royal Decree 817/2009, at least one-third of the members of the jury for a competitive dialogue procedure must be specially qualified on the subject at hand.[24] During the procedure itself, the jury must assess the economic, technical or professional ability of candidates, identify the solutions to carry to successive stages (if any) and identify the solution(s) most attuned to solve the contracting authority's needs. Furthermore, it will also evaluate the final tenders and request clarifications or confirmations of commitments from the bidders if appropriate. The final decision on whom to award the contract to remains with the contracting authority and not the jury.

What constitutes an especially qualified member remains to be seen and the author's research showed that contracting authorities have not changed their previous habits regarding the composition of the jury. Internal staff members are being appointed to the jury as if the competitive dialogue was just another procedure. Since the purpose of the rules appears to be to ensure that the persons running competitive dialogue are prepared to tackle the extra project management challenges raised by it, in practice this empties the rule of any relevance.[25] Furthermore, only a limited number of authorities hired external experts to assist the jury in its role. Cost was singled out as a key reason not to hire external consultants.

5.2. *Planning stage and drafting of the descriptive document*

Although the Law on Public Sector Contracts does not provide any information on pre-launch obligations, from his research the author found out that roughly half of the contracting authorities interviewed had done work in advance of the contract notice to prepare for the procedure and included a lot of detail in the descriptive document. The other half did not include much detail due to a lack of previous development work.

The first body of respondents managed to conduct the procedure and be satisfied with the result, whereas in the second answers were mixed, with success and failure rates being similar according to the contracting authorities' own perceptions of whether the procedure was successful.

Although the total number of contracting authorities covered in the study was limited (twenty) the findings suggest that carrying out work in

24 Contracting authorities are forbidden to appoint external members to the jury in other procedures.

25 As suggested also by a lawyer at the start of the empirical research.

advance in preparation for the competitive dialogue may be considered as best practice. One of the benefits pointed out by the first group was that it was easier to keep control of the procedure and to have more engaging discussions with the candidates during the dialogue as they knew the topic in more detail. Furthermore, one contracting authority that has used the competitive dialogue on multiple occasions started doing more work in advance and passing that information to candidates as it became more experienced.

5.3. *Confidentiality of information and solutions*

Confidentiality is regulated in Article 166(2) of the Law on Public Sector Contracts in similar terms to Article 29(3) of Directive 2004/18, a provision that was discussed in section 5.3 of Chapter 1. Contracting authorities have responded to this issue in various ways. A significant number argued that all information received from participants was treated as confidential, even if such protection was not asked for by candidates. Fear that companies would not take part in the dialogue if confidentiality was not given bullet-proof protection and fear of litigation were pointed to as the main reasons. A small number of interviewees even went to the extreme of making its staff and companies sign non-disclosure agreements as a means of demonstrating seriousness about the procedure.

Based on his findings on the different models of competitive dialogue adopted in Spain that will be explained in further detail in section 5.7, the author is unsure, however, if the levels of protection are as significant as is claimed by contracting authorities. Various contracting authorities are using the input from candidates during the dialogue to create a master or trunk solution that will end up as common technical specifications. When this occurs, the author feels that, for all statements of protection, the protection is only apparent, because the contracting authority is directly or indirectly sharing information. By necessity, information must be shared for the contracting authority to create this master or trunk solution.

Another group of respondents has said that confidentiality was not an issue in their procedures and that no company raised any issues. As the author did not research the views of companies themselves, doubt remains on why the companies taking part in those procedures have not raised it. On the one hand, it may be the case that companies are genuinely happy with the procedure. On the other hand, it may be a sign that companies do not know the full extent of the protection provided by

Article 166(2) of the Law on Public Sector Contracts or are even afraid of being seen as trouble makers and of being subject to black listing.[26]

Of the two cases of litigation known to the author and mentioned in section 4.5, both were related to the issue of confidential information. In the first case, the aggrieved bidder wished to be granted access to information considered to be classified as confidential by the winner. Moreover, the unsuccessful bidder argued that the award criteria were illegal. Their administrative review was unsuccessful and the aggrieved bidder has decided to file a judicial review.

In the second case, after the winner had been selected, the company allegedly wished simply to gain access to information from the winning tenderer that had been classified as confidential during the procedure. This was declined by the contracting authority and by the administrative appeal body. The company did not file subsequently for judicial review where this issue could be settled definitively. It would be interesting to see whether a court would give primacy to confidentiality or to the principle of transparency.

5.4. *Advertising requirements*

The Law on Public Sector Contracts is not clear on what should be included in the notice or the descriptive document.[27] Regarding publication of the notice, there are no specific rules applicable to competitive dialogue, so publication will be done in accordance with the general rules of the Law on Public Sector Contracts. Article 126/1 states that contracts subject to harmonised regulation[28] (that is, those which are covered by Public Sector Directive 2004/18) must be published in the OJEU. Additionally, they must also be published in the national official journal. In the event the contract is not subject to harmonised regulation, a notice must be published in the national, regional and/or local official journals.[29]

[26] D. Pachnou, 'Factors Influencing Bidders' Recourse to the European Commission to Enforce EC Procurement Law' (2005) 14 *Public Procurement Law Review* 101.

[27] The exceptions are Art. 165(2) (on the minimum number of candidates to invite for the dialogue), 166(3) (on the possibility of successive stages during the dialogue) and 167(2) (on award criteria).

[28] Arts. 13–17 of the Law on Public Sector Contracts.

[29] With the notice being sent to the Official Journal, before it is distributed to national, regional and local official journals (Art. 126(1) and (3) of the Law on Public Sector Contracts). Due to the administrative division of the country into different provinces, the official journal relevant to each case will depend on the contracting authority

5.5. *The selection phase*

The Directive's rules governing the selection phase of competitive dialogue were examined in section 5.5 of Chapter 1. In Spain, according to Articles 147–149 of the Law on Public Sector Contracts, the selection of candidates must be made in accordance with objective criteria. The permitted criteria are specified in Articles 64–68 of the Law on Public Sector Contracts. These are related to the financial and technical ability of the candidates. Whereas the financial criteria or requirements are relevant to all types of contracts (public works, goods and services), technical criteria are divided by type, as in Article 48 of the Directive 2004/18.[30] Thus in relation to competitive dialogue, the technical criteria to consider a candidate as suitable will depend on the type of contract to be awarded. Article 165(2) states that, if the contracting authority establishes a limit on the maximum number of candidates, this limit cannot be less than three. Article 149(2) states, however, that, if the number of candidates deemed suitable for selection is less than the minimum set out, the contracting authority may carry on with the procedure. In all these respects, the Spanish legislation merely repeats what is provided in Directive 2004/18 itself.

The author has seen, however, one notice clearly stating that the contracting authority sought to select between one and three candidates, contradicting what appears to be a clear legal requirement.

The author's empirical research found that contracting authorities are avoiding restricting the number of candidates in advance, perhaps due to a perception that limiting the numbers might have a negative impact on prospective participants. The consequence is that twenty or more candidates have been considered suitable and invited to take part in the dialogue in some cases. The dialogue stage was challenging, as managing discussions with a large number of companies put a drain on contracting authorities' resources and was not conducive to good dialogue.

Contracting authorities are also carrying the dialogue out with only one candidate in some circumstances. This is perceived as a sub-optimal

awarding the contract. If the contract is being tendered by an autonomous province, local authority or public body which depends on them, then the publication in the national official journal can be replaced by publication in the official regional or local journal, respectively.

[30] Regarding content, the Law on Public Sector Contracts does not differ at all from the Directive; although, from an organisational point of view, the legislator has opted to give the criteria for each type of contract its own Article, facilitating interpretation.

solution as no competitive pressure is present, but is still seen as preferable to cancelling the procedure outright. Cancelling the procedure might be seen by the tenderer as a groundless exclusion and lead to litigation, particularly because the law does not prohibit carrying on with fewer candidates than the original number.

5.6. *The dialogue phase*

5.6.1. Introduction

As in the Directive, significant scope is left in Spanish law for contracting authorities to define the dialogue stage as they see fit. It is not specified, for instance, how meetings are to be organised or what information should be included in the minutes of meetings. This is a marked departure from the tradition of Spanish procurement laws, in which extensive legal detail is usually included.

5.6.2. Successive stages

As permitted by Article 29(4) of Directive 2004/18, according to Article 166(3) of the Law on Public Sector Contracts, the dialogue phase of the competitive dialogue procedure may be divided into successive stages,[31] so as to eliminate solutions and focus the discussions on the most promising solutions.

It should be noted that the Law on Public Sector Contracts does not expressly mention elimination of *candidates* but only of *solutions*, which leads to the question of what can be excluded during the dialogue stage. In the author's view, the clear choice of *solutions* and not *candidates* as a word to determine what is being targeted for elimination should guide us on the analysis. Article 166(4), regarding the end of the dialogue, makes the distinction between finding the best 'solutions' and notifying all 'candidates' of the end of the dialogue. This makes it clear that in the law both concepts are used with different meanings. Furthermore, since Article 166(4) contains both terms, whereas in Article 166(3) only 'solutions' are mentioned, it further indicates that the Spanish lawmakers intended the elimination to target only solutions and not candidates. In consequence, the author considers that the primary target has to be the solution and not the candidate. However, this will not apply in the case in which the dialogue stage is organised in a way that calls for

[31] Art. 166(3) of the Law on Public Sector Contracts.

candidates to submit tenders based on solutions they have designed,[32] and not on common technical specifications. In this scenario, the candidate is totally dependent on his solution(s) to reach the tender stage, and, if none of the candidate's solutions are deemed acceptable, then the exclusion will imply the end of his participation in the procedure. It was suggested in Chapter 1 (see section 5.6.3) that this approach is permitted by the Directive. Article 166(3) has also some remarks about ensuring competition in what it deems the final phase, which appears to refer to the last stage of the dialogue phase in cases in which successive stages are used. Similarly to recital 41 of Directive 2004/18, this seems to mean that the contracting authority may not use successive phases during the dialogue stage to end up with a single candidate and no competition.

Formal exclusion of either candidates or solutions has not been observed in practice by the author. In practice, it appears that contracting authorities are including the possibility of excluding candidates or solutions in the descriptive document but not implementing exclusions *formally* due to widespread fear of reducing competition in the dialogue stage. One could add as a probable reason also the fear of litigation by aggrieved candidates, although this specific opinion was not expressed by respondents. This can be surmised from the fact that contracting authorities mentioned the fear of litigation as a reason for not limiting the numbers at the start of the dialogue and from the impression the author got from various answers pointing to candidates leaving the procedure of their own accord. Contrary to *formal* exclusions, what has been seen in practice is that contracting authorities are 'raising the bar' during the dialogue, updating the requirements for the solution or asking for a certain requirement to be accompanied by a specific price. Candidates are then leaving the procedure of their own accord and without any risk for the contracting authority.

5.6.3. Organisational models in the dialogue stage

5.6.3.1. Introduction During the empirical research, the author found that contracting authorities were organising the dialogue stage in a number of different ways, given that the Spanish law does not include any detailed rules on how contracting authorities should

[32] See section 5.6.3 on the different ways the procedure can be organised. In two of them, technical specifications are drawn at the end of the dialogue stage and all candidates are to tender based on those and not the solutions they have previously developed.

organise the dialogue. In the absence of legal requirements, contracting authorities are coming up with their own bespoke approaches to the dialogue stage.

The author has identified in his research three different models of organising the dialogue stage.[33] These models are defined here as: (i) own solution; (ii) crowd-sourced or common-trunk; and (iii) common-specification models. These models may not represent the full spectrum of how competitive dialogue is being used in Spain as the author did not survey every case. Furthermore, in his sample it was simply impossible to fully identify how the dialogue stage had been developed without having access to the full documentation (and eventually interview more participants). What these models do represent is a snapshot on how contracting authorities are organically devising approaches to run the competitive dialogue in Spain in the absence of clear instructions from Spanish law.

The three models can be distinguished by the existence or not of a common solution and, if the latter exists, by whether the common solution is developed early or late in the procedure.

A question is raised by the identification of multiple models that are very different for organising the dialogue stage in practice, namely, whether the principle of transparency is being adhered to if contracting authorities do not identify clearly which model will be used to organise the dialogue stage.

5.6.3.2. Own-solution model The first model, called here the own-solution model, may be described as candidates presenting tenders that are revisions of the solution proposed by the candidates themselves and developed during the dialogue stage. In this model, no common technical specifications are drafted at the end of the dialogue stage, meaning that tenders have to be assessed by reference to outputs or assessing them may prove difficult. When reading the competitive dialogue rules in Article 29 of Directive 2004/18, this is the first organisational model that springs to mind as the way of running the dialogue stage.

Although no common specifications are drafted, the author has found some cherry-picking of solutions in these instances, as solutions were being developed in parallel, with the changes suggested by the contracting authority influenced by discussions with other candidates.

[33] See Ch. 1, section 5.6.2.

5.6.3.3. Crowd-sourced or common-trunk model The second model is the crowd-sourced or common-trunk model. This model is defined by the appearance of a common development trunk during the dialogue stage. During this stage, participants contribute changes to this trunk solution that then ends up in a common technical specifications document. Since the actual development of the common solution is shared among candidates during the dialogue, each perhaps contributing some elements, the development process is similar to that which can be found in crowd-sourced projects such as Wikipedia.

One can describe the model as follows. The contracting authority has either a pre-conceived idea about a solution for its need that needs confirmation, or develops enough capabilities during the dialogue to know better what it needs. During the dialogue stage it then proceeds to request changes to the solutions presented by the candidates to fit its conception. These changes amount to an extreme situation of cherry-picking, as candidates are contributing to a common solution and not developing their own, although they appear to be doing so, without the contracting authority always telling them that that is the case. The common solution under development is thus a better match for the needs of the contracting authority than the original solutions. This progressive unifying development may take some iteration whereby the candidates end up developing ever-more-similar solutions.

When the development of the common solution reaches a satisfactory stage for the contracting authority, it closes the dialogue and sends out a common technical specification document based on that solution. When tendering, candidates will have to adhere to these common technical specifications. In consequence, their tenders share many characteristics and may also be very different from the original solutions put forward.

Out of thirty-one procedures analysed in the author's research, this model was used at least fifteen times. This represents a substantial number of cases in which this model has been deployed. In fact, in the sample analysed, it is the most common model. One may suggest as a potential reason for the recurrent use of this model the possibility that the contracting authority is merely falling into the default position of getting different inputs during the dialogue stage and trying to make sense of them in a cohesive manner, thus developing its own 'master solution' during the dialogue as a means to make sure it obtains *the* best solution for its needs.

Another possible reason for the use of this model may be the practical difficulties in keeping information coming from different sources separate, to avoid breaching confidentiality. Two respondents explained to the author that it was very hard, even when making a conscious effort, to have discussions with different companies while at the same time ensuring no confidential information was being transferred.

The author considers, however, that the opportunity of having different candidates pooling their effort to produce the best solution for the contracting authority's needs may prove to be (directly or indirectly) too good to resist.

The use of this model was first seen by the author in the procurement of innovative products. In that case, the contracting authority was asking companies to develop a new bespoke dual-use product that could replace two existing different products. It was clearly observed that the contracting authority was prompting candidates to make changes to their products during the development that rendered them very similar.

This model raises a question regarding the relevance of confidentiality during the dialogue stage. On the own-solution model, it is in the absolute interest of the candidates to keep their information as confidential as possible. In that model, all information passed from one candidate to another has the potential to benefit the second and make the former's tender less competitive. It is not clear that the same confidentiality concerns are relevant in a crowd-sourced-type of competitive dialogue. As the objective is to have a common set of specifications at the end of the dialogue stage (on which tenders will be based), the greater input a candidate can have on the specifications, the more competitive it may be in the final tender stage. In this model, it is in each company's best interest to have more information in the common specifications which are inherently public anyway. After all, assuming it was legal, what company would pass on the opportunity of influencing the tender specifications in an open procedure, for instance? Competitive dialogue allows companies the opportunity to actually influence the technical specifications of a contract *legally*, more so under this second model.

5.6.3.4. **Common specifications** The third approach seen in Spain is the common-specifications model. Under this model, contracting authorities draft a common set of technical specifications at the end of the dialogue stage. Candidates then submit tenders based on these specifications and not the solution they developed during the dialogue stage. The difference between this and the second model is that no apparent 'master solution' is developed during the dialogue stage and solutions keep their individuality. It must be said though that in some circumstances it may be hard to distinguish between this and the crowd-sourced model.

The author has observed clear cherry-picking of elements of different solutions to compose the common specifications by contracting authorities. In the sample studied by the author, this model has been used in two situations only.

5.7. *Final tender stage*

5.7.1. Introduction

According to Article 167(1) of the Law on Public Sector Contracts, candidates must submit their tenders with all the elements required for the performance of the contract. The Spanish law does not provide any guidance or explanation on what should be considered a sufficient level of detail for this requirement to be considered as fulfilled.

5.7.2. Award criteria

As with Article 29(1) of Directive 2004/18, Article 167(2) of the Law on Public Sector Contracts states that the evaluation of tenders in a competitive dialogue in Spain must be undertaken in accordance with the award criteria specified earlier in the notice or descriptive document. Furthermore, whereas recital 46 of Directive 2004/18 states that the weighting of the award criteria must be given to tenderers 'in sufficient time', in Spain all award criteria information, including weightings, must be disclosed with the notice according to Article 134(5) of the Law on Public Sector Contracts. Thus Spanish law in this respect goes beyond what is required by the Directive. As regards competitive dialogue it will mean that contracting authorities are bound from the start of the procedure to the award criteria defined at that point. Contracting authorities will not have the scope to supply only the headings of different award criteria and to define the weightings during the dialogue stage, for example to accommodate the different solutions that are developed. In practice, this restriction may make competitive dialogue slightly less flexible than it would otherwise be, in accordance with the possibilities for developing the award methodology during the procedure that were discussed in Chapter 1 (see section 5.6.5). In the face of the different organising models referred to in section 5.6.3, particularly the two models under which common technical specifications are given out to candidates at the end of the dialogue stage, one can question the logic of this limitation on a procedure like competitive dialogue.

As mentioned in section 4.5, one of the examples of litigation found by the author concerned award criteria that the aggrieved bidder considered to be illegal.

5.7.3. Variants

According to Article 133(1) of the Law on Public Sector Contracts, variants are accepted in any procedure where the award is to be based on the most economically advantageous tender approach. As we have seen in Chapter 1, competitive dialogue may only be used in conjunction with that approach and not the lowest price, thus meaning variants are allowed.

In practice, the author saw one specific case where variants were admitted, allowing the candidates to provide slightly different solutions from that set out in the common specifications drafted in that case. Due to a lack of access to the actual technical specifications during his research, the author is, however, unsure whether there were other instances where variants were admitted in practice.

5.7.4. Fine-tuning etc. prior to choosing the winning tender

Article 167(1) of the Law on Public Sector Contracts, similarly to Article 29(6) of Directive 2004/18, states the possibility of the contracting authority requesting extra information from the tenderers before selecting the winner, namely, to 'request precisions and clarifications on the tenders, fine-tuning or extra information as long as it does not change any fundamental aspect of the tender that may distort competition or have a discriminatory effect'.[34] It does not provide any further indication on what is allowed or should be done. The meaning of Article 29(6) of the Directive in this respect was discussed in Chapter 1 (see section 5.7.4 of that chapter).

Spanish contracting authorities in practice are divided on the use of this possibility. Some do not use it at all, considering that any changes to tenders after they had been opened would put in jeopardy the principle of tender stability. Others, however, have taken advantage of it but mostly to discuss minor points such as the brand (irrelevant for the

[34] Translated by the author.

actual functionality) of equipment to be supplied or to ask for clarifications to check if the tender submitted is compatible with the technical specifications. What is apparent in practice is that most contracting authorities are not taking up the possibilities made available by the Directive and the Spanish implementation. In addition, on the basis of the limited interactions observed in practice, it appears that they are simply behaving as if they had received a tender in an open procedure.

5.8. *Procedure following the selection of the winning tender or preferred bidder*

Article 167(3) of the Law on Public Sector Contracts, similarly to Article 29(7) of Directive 2004/18 (as to which see section 5.8 of Chapter 1), allows contracting authorities the possibility of having further limited discussions with the preferred bidder. The contracting authority may request for the tender to be clarified and commitments confirmed as long as it does not entail substantial modifications nor risk distorting competition or causing discrimination.

The finding of the author's empirical research was that in practice most Spanish contracting authorities refrain from entering into any sort of discussions with the winning tenderer. In practice, as noted in section 5.7 above, they appear to be running the post-submission stages as if competitive dialogue was an open procedure. Furthermore, the author was told that companies had sometimes tried to claw back some concessions made during the dialogue and in the tender submitted, trying to benefit from the lack of competition at that moment. A limited number of contracting authorities had, however, discussed topics such as financial issues or small details not covered in the bid.

5.9. *The standstill period*

The standstill period was introduced into the Law on Public Sector Contracts with the amendments of August 2010. According to Article 140(3) of this law, a minimum standstill period of fifteen days must be applied for contracts above the EU thresholds. However, this feature is not extended to contracts below the EU thresholds. Therefore, a competitive dialogue for a contract valued under the thresholds will not be subject to the standstill period.

There is, however, an exception to the general rule set out above: a public–private co-operation contract is always subject to standstill, irrespective of its value, as it is always considered to be a 'harmonised contract' for the purpose of Spanish law.[35] As we have seen, the competitive dialogue procedure is the one used for awarding these contracts.

5.10. Payments for participation costs

Article 163(2) of the Law on Public Sector Contracts, as specified expressly in Article 29(8) of Directive 2004/18 (see section 5.10 of Chapter 1), allows contracting authorities to offer money to offset the costs of participation. Contracting authorities are free to decide whether or not to do so, but under the Spanish law must mention this in the descriptive document. In the last respect, the Spanish law adds to the explicit rules of Article 29(8) of the Directive, where no mention is made of when the decision to make payments must be communicated to the candidates.

In his research, the author found no evidence of contracting authorities ever paying candidates for development costs. Budgetary concerns were mentioned as the primary reason. It was mentioned as well that not paying compensation did not have a negative impact on competition as the expected companies participated without this. One respondent acknowledged that private companies would incur higher costs in a competitive dialogue procedure than in an open procedure and decided to waive the bond that candidates must deposit at the start of the procedure. In this situation, the bond was of substantial value since the contract being awarded was a multi-million-euro project.

5.11. Creation of consortia during the dialogue

One of the points raised by contracting authorities with experience in applying competitive dialogue was the possibility of candidates creating consortia during the dialogue stage. In one case, this was allowed as the contracting authority had included a specific provision in the descriptive document and considered that it improved competition. In the other situation, the contracting authority did not allow the creation of the consortia because it would have reduced the number of candidates in the dialogue to a number it considered insufficient for competition. Furthermore, one of the public procurement advisory bodies interviewed by

[35] Arts. 13(1), 140(3) and 310 of the Law on Public Sector Contracts.

the author acknowledged the existence of the issue and considered allowing the creation of consortia to be legal as long as competition was not impaired.

5.12. *Competitive dialogue in context*

During the course of the research, the author identified a number of issues surrounding the use of competitive dialogue that are not specifically of a legal nature but which form an important part of the context in which the law must operate. They can mainly be seen as project-management-related issues.

One of the issues most discussed by interviewees was how to organise the dialogue meetings and how to deal with minutes. Contracting authorities do not know how to proceed with the organisation – for example, what is the appropriate order for candidates to take part and what content to include in the minutes (for example, the full discussion or just the key points raised).

Another issue facing contracting authorities is the need to keep candidates interested during the dialogue. The issue here is how to conduct the discussions at a level which is sufficiently detailed for the purposes of the contracting authority but at the same time ensures that candidates are not overburdened by the discussions – for example with unnecessary meetings or constant changes to solutions – or have an incentive to drop out of the procedure because the costs are becoming greater than was anticipated.

Contracting authorities were also seen to have issues over ensuring that the promises made during the discussions are kept, and over how to extract the best tender possible from candidates. During the dialogue stage, candidates are not bound by the discussions,[36] in contrast with the position when a tender is submitted. It was observed in some instances that companies that were very engaged in the dialogue stage did not actually submit a tender. When this involves large companies, this may be happening due to the company not involving in the dialogue stage the senior executives who take the decision on whether to proceed with a tender, with their involvement being delayed up to the point at which a final decision has to be taken on whether or not to commit the company to a tender. It may be a sign of companies not attaching to the dialogue

[36] Except regarding potential pre-contractual liability.

stage as much importance as they do to the final tender stage. Related to this issue, a situation has also been observed in practice where a company submitted a much better tender than anticipated in light of the discussions held during the dialogue stage. This highlights the need for contracting authorities to plan and be advised for both scenarios.

The author has also found a body of examples that can be construed as being best practice in conducting a competitive dialogue. For instance, contracting authorities that plan in advance the procedure and make an effort to supply potential candidates with all information possible at that stage tend to control procedures better and end up with a more positive perception. Examples of information that can be supplied at the start can include not only any previous insight the authority may have into the topic but also information on the procedure itself, such as how it is going to be run and the order of the meetings.

Contracting authorities should also consider defining a clear timetable for the dialogue stage, defining a date in advance to end the stage, and including milestones to be achieved during that period. In addition, good practice implies the existence of sound internal controls within the contracting authority to make sure the timetable set out is actually adhered to. Related to internal controls, a contracting authority has suggested that oral discussions outside scheduled meetings should be precluded and that all contacts should be made in writing as a means of recording what information was conveyed and to whom.

It was also observed that contracting authorities that established a multidisciplinary team to run the dialogue, bringing together lawyers, managers, technicians and other stakeholders, consistently yielded a result with which the contracting authority was satisfied. In addition, the creation of such a team allows contracting authorities to schedule meetings focused on particular topics and involving only the relevant stakeholders from the public and private sides.

Finally, it is submitted that it can be regarded as best practice to avoid discussions when no competition is present – that is, after selecting the preferred bidder – and requiring all relevant issues to be discussed during the dialogue stage. In one situation, the winning tenderer wanted to see the payment timetable changed for more preferable terms. Limiting discussions at this stage ensures that, even if they are within the scope for discussions admitted in Article 29(7) of the Directive, all topics are in reality discussed at a point when competition is present. Since the boundaries between what can and cannot be discussed are unclear and there is a significant temptation for the private party to claw back concessions given in the tender, it can be argued that it is advisable to refuse any discussions at this stage. However, it can be argued that requiring detailed discussions with all candidates during the dialogue stage may increase the transaction costs for those involved.

6. Concluding remarks

As mentioned above, so far as the legal framework for competitive dialogue is concerned, Spain has opted mainly to simply copy and paste the content of the Directive and put it into national law. The main difference from the European rules is the fact that competitive dialogue has been made the default procedure for the procurement of public–private co-operation contracts, with these contracts representing around 40 per cent of competitive dialogue procedures in Spain.

As Chapter 2 has explained, the use of competitive dialogue is far below the levels seen in, for example, France and the UK. Moreover, when compared with the number of concessions awarded in Spain by open or negotiated procedures, the number of competitive dialogue procedures is low. It seems thus that, if one excludes public–private co-operation contracts, local practice is yet to fully embrace the new procedure.

From the data analysed by the author it appears that contracting authorities that apply the procedure appear overall to be satisfied with it and do not have concerns over the grounds for using it. Furthermore, although the European Commission has argued that competitive dialogue should not be used for all public–private partnerships contracts but only in the cases where the contract is 'particularly complex', in Spain competitive dialogue is the default procedure for all public–private co-operation contracts.

As regards operation of the procedure, from the practice in Spain it has been possible to identify three distinct models of organising the dialogue stage. It is submitted that contracting authorities should identify in advance what kind of model they intend to use in the dialogue stage; otherwise, transparency may be compromised.

Another significant point is that, although according to Directive 2004/18 it is possible to exclude candidates (or at least solutions, depending on the interpretation) during the dialogue stage, in Spain this was not seen in practice. Contracting authorities do not formally exclude candidates or solutions, nor conduct successive stages. However, the way that contracting authorities organise the dialogue by demanding more from the candidates is causing some candidates to drop out of the procedure of their own accord. Contracting authorities are thus achieving exclusion of candidates without facing the risk of judicial review.

Spanish contracting authorities also appear not to entertain discussions with tenderers or the winner of the contract. On this topic, the practice found in Spain is arguably different from what might be expected from Directive 2004/18 and the Law on Public Sector Contracts. However, it may be said that this contributes to avoiding 'negotiation or bid creep' and also avoids the risk presented when making adjustments when competition is no longer present.

From a practical and project management perspective, issues that were found to arise and are worthy of consideration by other Member States using the procedure include the perceived cost of the procedure, how to organise the meetings, how to keep the candidates interested in the procedure, how to ensure adherence to the promises during the dialogue stage and how to ensure that the best possible tenders are submitted. Further, the findings in Spain concerning the information to give at the start of the procedure, the anticipation of problems, creation of multidisciplinary teams, restricting oral discussions outside of meetings and absence of discussions after tenders are submitted may also be of use to entities in other Member States.

9

Competitive dialogue in Poland

ANNA GORCZYNSKA

1. Introduction: regulation of public procurement in Poland

In Poland, as in all EU Member States, the public authorities who are the decision-making bodies regarding public spending are not the owners of the funds expended and the results of those decisions do not affect their private budget.[1] In this context, the rules regulating award procedures for public procurement contracts in Poland seek to guarantee implementation of the most important aims of the public procurement system, namely, value for money, competitiveness and efficiency in public spending.

The first public procurement regulation in Poland dates back to 1933 when the first Act on supplies and public works for the State Treasury, self-government and bodies governed by public law was adopted,[2] and this was further elaborated by an executive Regulation of 1937.[3] However, procedures for competitive procurement for the public sector were abolished in the post-war socialist period of Polish history by the Act of 18 November 1948 on supplies, public contracts and services for the State Treasury, self-government and some categories of legal persons.[4] From then until 1994, all public entities awarded contracts without the application of legal provisions (with a few exceptions of sectoral regulations adopted by ministries).

Following this socialist period, the public procurement system was then regulated again by the Act of 10 June 1994 on Public Procurement.[5] The Act was amended many times due to the obligation to align Polish legislation to the EU legal system.

[1] T. Grzeszczyk, *Podręcznik zamówień publicznych-Polskie procedury-Zarys systemu* (Warsaw: Biblioteka Menadżera i Bankowca, 1995), p. 24.
[2] Dz.U. of 1933 No. 19 item 127. [3] Dz.U. of 1937 No. 13 item 92.
[4] Dz.U. of 1948 No. 63 item 494.
[5] Dz.U. of 1994 No. 72 item 664 with amendments, entered into force 1 January 1995.

The legislation which is now in force was adopted by the Act of 29 January 2004 (the 'Public Procurement Law').[6] Since then, the Act has been extensively amended on several occasions. The most important amendments were those needed to implement the Public Sector Directive 2004/18 and the Utilities Directive 2004/17. The latest version of the Public Procurement Law, which introduced further new EU legislation, was adopted after a short delay by the Act of 7 April 2006 on amendment of the Public Procurement Law.[7] Since then, the Act has been amended several times due to implementation of the new Remedies Directive 2007/66, further harmonisation with EU law and a decision to further rationalise the Polish public procurement system.[8]

The Public Procurement Law regulates the procedures for awarding public procurement contracts, while the execution of contracts is regulated by the Act of 23 April 1964 (the 'Civil Code').[9] In addition, Article 14 of the Public Procurement Law states that the provisions of the Civil Code shall apply to actions undertaken by the awarding entity and economic operators in the contract award procedure, unless provisions of the Public Procurement Law provide otherwise.

The Public Procurement Law is accompanied by numerous executive regulations of the government and particular ministries. Currently, twelve regulations cover specific aspects of public procurement law in Poland – for example, on documents, including their form, to prove the fulfilment of the qualification criteria, and on the threshold value for the application of EU procurement rules.[10]

[6] Dz.U. of 2004 No. 19 item 177 with amendments, entered into force mainly on 2 March 2004, partly on 1 May 2004 (for example, obligation of publication of the notice in the OJEU).

[7] Dz.U. of 2006 No. 79 item 551, entered into force on 25 May 2006.

[8] Act of 11 May 2011 on amendment of the Public Procurement Law.

[9] Dz.U. of 1964 No. 16 item 93 as amended.

[10] These twelve executive regulations are: Rozporządzenie Prezesa Rady Ministrów z dnia 22 marca 2004 r. w sprawie wysokości wynagrodzenia przewodniczącego, wiceprzewodniczącego i pozostałych członków Rady Zamówień Publicznych (Dz.U. No. 49, poz. 470); Rozporządzenie Ministra Infrastruktury z dnia 18 maja 2004 r. w sprawie określenia metod i podstaw sporządzania kosztorysu inwestorskiego, obliczania planowanych kosztów prac projektowych oraz planowanych kosztów robót budowlanych określonych w programie funkcjonalno-użytkowym (Dz.U. No. 130, poz. 1389, ostatnia zm. Dz.U. z 2011, No. 42, poz. 217); Rozporządzenie Ministra Infrastruktury z dnia 2 września 2004 r. w sprawie szczegółowego zakresu i formy dokumentacji projektowej, specyfikacji technicznych wykonania i odbioru robót budowlanych oraz programu funkcjonalno-użytkowego (Dz.U. No. 202, poz. 2072 oraz z 2005 r. No. 75, poz. 664 oraz z 2011 r. No. 42, poz. 217); Rozporządzenie Prezesa Rady Ministrów z dnia 19 maja 2006 r. w sprawie

Poland became a member of the European Union on 1 May 2004. The pre-accession period and full membership in the EU required adoption of the EU procurement rules. However, in Poland many EU provisions have been reformulated and the implementation process did not involve a simple copying out of the Directives' provisions. Further, the EU provisions are usually supplemented by national provisions.

The Public Procurement Law implements the provisions of the EU public procurement legislation usually by rewording the European legislation. Article 10(1) of the Law states that the 'primary' procedures for awarding contracts are open tenders and restricted tenders. An awarding entity may also award contracts by other procedures, namely, the negotiated procedure with a notice, competitive dialogue, the negotiated procedure without a notice, the single-source procurement procedure, the request-for-quotes procedure or electronic bidding, but the application of all these procedures is restricted and possible only under the circumstances specified in the Act. The Polish literature on

rodzajów dokumentów, jakich może żądać zamawiający od wykonawcy, oraz form, w jakich te dokumenty mogą być składane (Dz.U. No. 87 poz. 605 oraz z 2008 r. No. 188, poz. 1155), które zostało uchylone z dniem 31 grudnia 2009 r.; Rozporządzenie Rady Ministrów z dnia 1 sierpnia 2006 r. w sprawie organów właściwych do występowania do Komisji Europejskiej z wnioskiem o stwierdzenie prowadzenia działalności na rynku konkurencyjnym, do którego dostęp nie jest ograniczony (Dz.U. No. 147, poz. 1063); Rozporządzenie Prezesa Rady Ministrów z dnia 25 sierpnia 2006 r. w sprawie zakresu informacji zawartych w rocznym sprawozdaniu o udzielonych zamówieniach, jego wzoru oraz sposobu przekazywania (Dz.U. No. 155, poz. 1110 oraz z 2007 r. No. 175, poz. 1226); Rozporządzenie Prezesa Rady Ministrów z dnia 2 lipca 2007 r. w sprawie trybu przeprowadzania postępowania kwalifikacyjnego na członków Krajowej Izby Odwoławczej, sposobu powoływania komisji kwalifikacyjnej, a także szczegółowego zakresu postępowania kwalifikacyjnego (Dz.U. No. 120, poz. 820); Rozporządzenie Prezesa Rady Ministrów z dnia 9 lipca 2007 r. w sprawie wielokrotności kwoty bazowej stanowiącej podstawę ustalenia wynagrodzenia zasadniczego Prezesa, wiceprezesa oraz pozostałych członków Krajowej Izby Odwoławczej (Dz.U. No. 128, poz. 885); Rozporządzenie Prezesa Rady Ministrów z dnia 9 lipca 2007 r. w sprawie wysokości oraz sposobu pobierania wpisu od odwołania oraz rodzajów kosztów w postępowaniu odwoławczym i sposobu ich rozliczania (Dz.U. No. 128, poz. 886); Rozporządzenie Prezesa Rady Ministrów z dnia 2 października 2007 r. w sprawie regulaminu postępowania przy rozpoznawaniu odwołań (Dz.U. No. 187, poz. 1327 oraz z 2008 r. No. 188, poz. 1156); Rozporządzenie Prezesa Rady Ministrów z dnia 16 października 2008 r. w sprawie protokołu postępowania o udzielenie zamówienia publicznego (Dz.U. No. 188, poz. 1154); Rozporządzenie Prezesa Rady Ministrów z dnia 30 grudnia 2009 r. w sprawie rodzajów dokumentów, jakich może żądać zamawiający od wykonawcy, oraz form, w jakich te dokumenty mogą być składane (Dz.U. No. 226, poz. 1817).

this subject[11] generally states that this whole group of procedures should be interpreted as comprising an exemption from the general rules of 'competitive procedures' (even though these procedures do in fact involve some kind of competition), that the grounds for using them shall be strictly interpreted, and that the burden for proving the grounds exist is on the contracting authority.[12]

Contracts below the thresholds for application of the EU procurement Directives are regulated by specific Polish legal solutions which are in general compliant with EU law. These contracts can be awarded by procedures such as single-source procurement and request-for-quotes.

Depending on the value of the contract, the Public Procurement Law provides for the application of more or less strict procedures for awarding contracts. The procedures for contracts below the EU Directives' thresholds are significantly simplified, with different requirements on publication of notices, wider scope for the availability of procedures, shorter tender submission dates, and a more limited remedies regime. The public procurement procedures for tenders above the thresholds are far more formalised and they fully implement the European legal rules.

The first Act on public procurement of 1994 also introduced the institutional system for public procurement in Poland which is still in force. In particular, the Public Procurement Office was set up to ensure a smooth process for the implementation of the public procurement rules. The President of the Public Procurement Office is a central government body competent for matters concerning public contracts. The President is assisted in his work by the Public Procurement Office (Article 152). The President prepares drafts of normative acts on public contracts; issues the *Public Procurement Bulletin* in its electronic version, where all the notices and publications provided for in the Act are published; publishes the list of organisations authorised to submit legal protection measures; runs, publishes and updates the list of economic operators that have become liable in damages by failing to perform a contract or by performing a contract incorrectly, when the damage has been stated by a legally valid decision of a court; ensures the functioning of the system of

[11] J. Pierog, *Prawo zamowien publicznych. Komentarz* (Warsaw: C. H. Beck, 2010), p. 252; M. Bubnowski, *Prawo zamówień publicznych. Komentarz* (Warsaw: C. H. Beck, 2007), p. 156.

[12] These last two points are rules that the CJEU has stated are to apply in cases concerned with a negotiated procedure without a notice: on this and their possible application to other award procedures under EU law, see Ch. 1. For Polish decisions, see Judgment of Supreme Court (SN) of 6 July 2001, III RN 16/01; Judgment of Supreme Administrative Court (NSA) of 28 February 2003, II SA 2064/01.

legal protection; prepares training programmes; prepares and disseminates standard criteria for assessing the substance of training; prepares and disseminates standard forms of procurement contracts, rules of procedures and other documents in the award procedure; prepares and submits mandatory reports; and seeks to ensure the uniform application of the procurement provisions, in light of the decisions of the courts and the Constitutional Tribunal, in particular by disseminating the decisions of the National Appeal Chamber, courts and the Constitutional Tribunal which refer to public procurement.

The National Appeal Chamber, operating within the structure of the Polish Public Procurement Office, was set up as an administrative body responsible for the award and execution of public procurement contracts, and it examines the appeals lodged in contract award procedures (Article 172).

The Chamber does not have judicial power, but operates as a court of arbitration. The parties and participants in an appeal procedure may lodge a complaint to the court against the Chamber's ruling (Article 198a). Any further stage of litigation is then heard by the civil courts. This National Appeal Chamber has played an important role in developing public procurement law in Poland by applying and interpreting the procurement legislation.

The number of appeals brought to the National Appeal Chamber has shown a steadily decreasing trend from 2005 (4,094 appeals), 2006 (3,077 appeals), 2007 (1,582 appeals), 2008 (1,537 appeals) and 2009 (1,985 appeals).[13] The decrease in the number of appeals is related to an increase in the fees for hearing appeals and also the limitation of the scope of remedies under the thresholds for the EU Directives.

2. The background: complex procurement prior to competitive dialogue[14]

Prior to the introduction of competitive dialogue, complex contracts exceeding the threshold of Directive 2004/18 were realised mostly by the open tender procedure. As we have seen, in the Polish legal system open

[13] Annual Report of the National Appeal Chamber 2010 (Public Procurement Office, 2010).

[14] The information is based on analysis of the statistics on the application of particular procedures prepared by the Office of Public Procurement, comments in the commentaries to the Act, interviews with contracting authorities and the author's own experience.

and restricted tender procedures can be applied in any procurement and are designated in the legislation as 'primary' procedures. The negotiated procedure with a notice was also applied for complex contracts. However, this was not very common as the application of the procedure was possible only in the strictly described and listed situations, which have been regarded as being of narrow application in Poland. Complex contracts below the value of the Directive's thresholds, on the other hand, tended to be awarded by the negotiated procedure with a notice or single-source procurement. This tendency was criticised by the Public Procurement Office, and numerous cases before the National Appeal Chamber addressed the abuse of this procedure.

3. Introduction to competitive dialogue

Competitive dialogue was introduced in 2006 by the Act on the Public Procurement Law[15] and entered into force on 25 May 2006 when Directive 2004/18[16] was transposed into Polish law. The new procedure was introduced into the Polish legal system by an amendment to the Public Procurement Law, which originally dated from 2004. Prior to that time, the procedure was not available.

The competitive dialogue procedure was transposed into the Polish Public Procurement Law by copying the general idea of the procedure presented in the Directive but with some changes and additions – for example, referring specifically to the number of participants invited to present their solutions, as discussed below. The wording of the national regulations is similar to the wording of Directive 2004/18, but also contains some differences.

In practice, in Poland, as we will see below, use of the procedure has grown steadily and it is used for quite a few projects, although not extensively – in the last two years there were nearly fifty competitive dialogue procedures each year advertised in the OJEU.

[15] Act of 7 April 2006 on Amendment of Act on Public Procurement Law, entered into force on 25 May 2006, OJ of 2006 No. 79 item 551 and No. 106, item 719.

[16] Directive 2004/18 of the European Parliament and of the Council of 31 March 2004 on the co-ordination of procedures for the award of public supply contracts, public services contracts, public work contracts [2004] OJ L134/114. See in particular Arts. 29 and 1(11)(c) and recital 31.

4. Scope of competitive dialogue procedure in law and practice

In Poland the competitive dialogue procedure has been made available for contracts both above and below the thresholds of Directive 2004/18 and the conditions for use are similar to those set out in EU law, using similar wording to Directive 2004/18.[17] The reason for this approach was to avoid misinterpretations.

However, in the utilities rules in Poland, as under the Utilities Directive,[18] the competitive dialogue is not included explicitly, due to the existing, flexible, approach which allows a free choice between the open, restricted and negotiated procedures.

In 2010, the Public Procurement Office published guidelines on the conditions for conducting public contracts awarded by negotiated procedure with a notice, competitive dialogue, negotiated procedure without a notice, single-source procurement and request-for-quotations. The guidelines (which replaced the previous version of 2006) were intended to answer the most common questions referring to the application of procedures. However, it concentrated mainly on the other award procedures, and described the competitive dialogue procedure only briefly and in general terms, merely indicating that contracting authorities are allowed to use competitive dialogue only in the circumstances admitted in the Directive.[19] The limited description of competitive dialogue appears to reflect the general tendency of reserving the procedure only for the most complex contracts. Thus contracting authorities are left to themselves to determine the best way of implementing the procedure and interpreting the legal rules.

The competitive dialogue procedure is also mentioned in one more legal regulation, namely, the Act of 19 December 2008 on Public–Private Partnerships[20] (PPPs). This Act is the second Polish regulation on public–private partnerships and replaces the former Act of 2004 (which was not applied due to the requirement for numerous economic analyses in the context of the use of PPPs). The Act on PPPs of 2008

[17] Grounding for Act on Public Procurement Law, p. 2.

[18] Directive 2004/17 of the European Parliament and of the Council of 31 March 2004 on the co-ordination the procurement procedures of the entities in the water, energy, transport and postal services sectors [2004] OJ L134/1.

[19] Guidelines on the conditions of conducting public contracts award by negotiated procedure with a notice, competitive dialogue, negotiated procedure without a notice, single-source procurement and request-for-quotes (Public Procurement Office, 2010), p. 10.

[20] Act of 19 December 2008 on Public–Private Partnership, Art. 4.

regulates the award of contracts in the framework of PPPs, the procurement of which falls under either the Public Procurement Law or the Concession Law. PPPs are broadly defined in the Act simply as involving the common realisation of an undertaking based on tasks and risk-sharing by public and private partners (Article 1(2)). The official government interpretation of the application of the Public Procurement Law to PPPs suggests that the award of PPP contracts could be realised by the application of the competitive dialogue procedure.[21] According to the Public Procurement Office's guidelines, the competitive dialogue procedure is especially suitable for PPPs due to its flexibility and wide scope of application for particularly complex contracts.[22] Thus, whilst the guidelines unfortunately do not clarify the conditions for applying competitive dialogue in Poland, the Act on Public–Private Partnership suggests this procedure as the preferred award procedure for PPPs.

According to the data provided by the Public Procurement Office and by the author's research on the notices published in the Polish official journal (*Public Procurement Bulletin*) and the OJEU, the number of procedures that have been conducted is set out in Table 9.1. And the total application of the competitive dialogue in Poland as a percentage of all award procedures is illustrated in Table 9.2.[23]

The new procedure has been used, in particular, for award procedures for complex infrastructure projects, for information and communication networks, for purchasing innovative technical equipment (for example, for hospitals), for finding new solutions for alternative sources of energy, for construction of sports facilities and for long-term development strategies for regions and cities. The procedure could potentially be applied for the complex and large-scale investments financed from the EU Structural Funds: the past few years have seen much large-scale infrastructure investment connected to the implementation of the

[21] Grounding for the application of the Act of 19 December 2008 on Public–Private Partnerships (Ministry of Economy), p. 15.

[22] Guidelines on the conditions of conducting public contracts award by negotiated procedure with a notice, competitive dialogue, negotiated procedure without a notice, single-source procurement and request-for-quotes (Public Procurement Office, 2010), p. 10. Polish practice shows that the competitive dialogue is often applied in PPP procedures and highly appreciated by contracting authorities (source: author's interviews with contracting authorities from the Silesia Region).

[23] Annual reports from 2007, 2008, 2009 and 2010 on the functioning of the public procurement system (Public Procurement Office).

Table 9.1 *Poland: competitive dialogue procedures, 2006–2010*

Year	Notices for below-threshold contracts published in the Polish Official Journal – Public Procurement Bulletin (BZP)	Notices of awarded below-threshold contracts published in the Polish Official Journal – Public Procurement Bulletin (BZP)	Notices for above-threshold contracts published in the OJEU	Notices of awarded above-threshold contracts published in the OJEU
2006	24	1	16	1
2007	49	26	28	13
2008	72	35	35	15
2009	66	38	48	12
2010	63	41	46	28
Total	276	141	173	69

Table 9.2 *Use of the different contract award procedures as a percentage of all award procedures*

Procedure	2006	2007	2008	2009	2010
Open procedure	76.81%	63.79%	70.39%	68.28%	77.94%
Restricted procedure	4.15%	1.30%	0.97%	0.79%	0.69%
Negotiated with a notice	0.47%	0.14%	0.11%	0.11%	0.13%
Negotiated without a notice	1.41%	0.54%	0.53%	0.39%	0.29%
Electronic auction	0.03%	0.05%	0.05%	0.16%	0.17%
Competitive dialogue	0.02%	0.04%	0.03%	0.02%	0.03%

principle of socio-economic cohesion in Poland as a new EU Member State, totalling more than €67 billion in the years 2007–13. Competitive dialogue could also be used in relation to the preparations for the UEFA European football championships in 2012.

Even before the introduction of competitive dialogue to the list of possible award procedures, in many complicated tendering procedures discussions on possible solutions had taken place. Analysing the opinions of contracting authorities as expressed in discussions with the author of this chapter, it is seen that they have welcomed competitive dialogue as an interesting tool for accessing actual know-how. However, often they are still not able to formulate an appropriate description of the project as is required.

So far as legal implementation is concerned, following what is provided in the Directive itself, competitive dialogue is defined in Section 3a, Article 60a, of the Public Procurement Law, which states:

> Competitive dialogue means a contract award procedure in which, following a public contract notice the awarding entity conducts a dialogue with selected economic operators, and then invites them to tender.

The grounds for using competitive dialogue are then described in Article 60b, which stipulates the conditions which have to be met, simply following the wording of the Directive itself. These conditions and their possible interpretations were discussed in section 4 of Chapter 1.

In Poland, the concept of a complex contract seems to be given a wide interpretation which allows contracting authorities to retain a margin of discretion in deciding whether it is possible to determine the technical means or legal or financial conditions of contract performance. Because of, *inter alia*, their lack of experience and the legacy of the former socialist economy, public entities are often insufficiently market-oriented or unable to formulate a precise definition of their needs, and a pragmatic approach will result in an increase in the use of competitive dialogue.

The challenges which Poland has to face as a new EU Member State, and in particular the need for extensive infrastructure projects, structural funds expenditure and investments in sport facilities, ensure a positive environment for the enforcement of the new procedure. In such projects, the contracting authority often does not realise what technical features are feasible in the context of technological perspectives or cost reduction.[24] Moreover, based on the author's experience with contracting authorities, it appears that the complexity of the contract is understood by reference to the experience of each particular

[24] S. Arrowsmith, 'An Assessment of the New Legislative Package on Public Procurement' (2004) 41 *Common Market Law Review* 1282; S. Arrowsmith, *The Law of Public and Utilities Procurement* (London: Sweet & Maxwell, 2005), pp. 629–31; A. Brown, 'The Impact of the New Directive on Large Infrastructure Projects: Competitive Dialogue or Better the Devil You Know' (2004) 13 *Public Procurement Law Review* 178.

contracting authority or at least experience in the particular sector. New solutions in construction processes, medicine, investments or IT are understood as particularly complex and thus as falling under the scope of the competitive dialogue procedure. The possibility of legal negotiations on potential solutions and a more flexible procedural approach have been welcomed by many contracting authorities. It has created the possibility for both representatives of the administration and entrepreneurs to discuss various solutions for contract execution, to access the know-how of private entities, and to ensure effective public expenditure. This flexible approach will legalise the practice that is adopted in many complicated tendering procedures where a discussion on possible solutions takes place.

5. Operation of the competitive dialogue procedure

5.1. Introduction

We can start by noting that cases on competitive dialogue before the National Appeal Chamber (NAC) and before the courts mainly arise out of problems with implementation of the procedure: these cases concern the grounds for choosing the procedure, the stage of planning and drafting the descriptive documents, selection criteria, and confidentiality of information. According to the author's own research, the number of cases on competitive dialogue brought before the National Appeal Chamber was three in 2008, six in 2009 and ten in 2010.[25] As regards judicial decisions, it can be noted that a court ruling of 2008 stated that the provisions of Directive 2004/18 on competitive dialogue are not directly effective,[26] as the Directive is not precise and unconditional on this subject.

One of the rulings before the NAC[27] concerned the creation of regional innovation strategies, where competitive dialogue was treated by the contracting authority as a contest. In its decision, the NAC

[25] Competitive dialogue cases before the National Appeal Chamber for the years 2008 to 2010 were as follows: 2008, three cases (KIO/UZP/593/2008, KIO/UZP/993/2008 and KIO/UZP/1114/2008); 2009, six cases (KIO/UZP/1204/09, KIO/UZP/1900/09, KIO/UZP/1638/09, KIO/UZP/737/09, KIO/UZP/621 i 622/09 and KIO/UZP/1093/09); and 2010, nine cases (KIO/UZP/37/10, KIO/UZP/38/10, KIO/UZP/264/10, KIO/UZP/649/10, KIO/UZP/887/10, KIO/UZP/905/10, KIO/UZP/1463/10, KIO/UZP/2010/10 and KIO/UZP/2473/10).

[26] Ruling of the District Court in Warsaw of 27 June 2008, Vca 1175/08.

[27] Ruling of the National Appeal Chamber KIO/UZP 1204/09 of 24 September 2009.

stressed the importance of the principle of equality and competitiveness as the basis of public procurement procedures. The contracting authority made a number of mistakes in the award procedure, especially in respect of the specification of the essential terms of the contract, where no conditions for assessing offers were given. In another ruling regarding the choice of a technological partner for a football stadium in Gdańsk, in the description of the subject-matter of the contract the contracting authority stipulated specific technical solutions which were deemed as limiting competition. Another issue in that case concerned a requirement for the tenderer to finance the contract in accordance with provisions stated in the contract terms which did not provide precise assessment criteria. Other NAC rulings concerned a contract for building a high-speed train system, the development of an IT system for medical data in the Silesian Voivodeship, and the consolidation and centralisation of customs and taxation systems for the Ministry of Finance. These rulings concerned both misuse of the procedure and an abuse of competition within the procedure.

As regards the conduct of competitive dialogue, Polish legislation in general repeats the provisions of the European Directive, although it also introduces some additional provisions. Thus contracting authorities must decide for themselves the structure of the procedure. This flexible approach was at first enthusiastically welcomed by contracting authorities but subsequently led to many misunderstandings and confusion. The procedure was often mistaken for simple negotiation with a notice. Unfortunately, there is also no practice of consulting the market in advance by publishing a notice informing the market about the planned application of the procedure.

The statistics published by the Public Procurement Office on the average duration of particular procedures present the competitive dialogue as a lengthy and complicated procedure. In 2008, an average competitive dialogue procedure under the threshold lasted 94 days (as compared with 36 for an open tender procedure) and for contracts above the threshold 231 days (as compared with 84 days for an open tender procedure).

5.2. *The planning stage and drafting of the descriptive document*

The planning stage of competitive dialogue is in practice connected with the decision taken within the contracting authority regarding the choice of procedure. Contracting authorities usually try to prepare the descriptive document with the help of specialists. In practice, many contracting authorities complain that the drafting of the descriptive document seems to be quite complicated. The descriptive document should contain a description of the needs and requirements of the contracting authority that is sufficient to allow the contractors to prepare to participate in the procedure. Even if in the dialogue phase the subject of the contract is specified, the descriptive document should allow the public partner to discuss all possible solutions with all economic operators.[28]

5.3. *Confidentiality of information and solutions*

The Public Procurement Law of Poland sets out in general the rules on confidentiality of information and solutions without a more detailed description of the form and scope of confidentiality requirements, which are left to the contracting authority. According to the rules of equal treatment and competitiveness, the NAC has specifically ruled that all tenderers should be treated equally with regard to protection of confidential information.[29] Confidentiality of the dialogue is also regulated in the provisions directly governing competitive dialogue which may concern all aspects of the tender. This states that without the other party's consent neither party may disclose any technical or business information connected to the dialogue (Article 60d(6) and (7)).

The Suppression of Unfair Competition Act defines trade secrets as technical, technological or organisational information which has not been disclosed to the public, or any other information of business value with respect to which the enterprise has taken the necessary action to ensure confidentiality – for example, information on unpatented inventions or know-how. Examples of trade information include data on the enterprise's markets, sales, customers and business partners, whilst organisational information may concern information on, for example, management, salaries, methods of organising work, exchange of information or documents.[30]

As Chapter 1 discussed, ensuring confidentiality of negotiations to protect tenderers' know-how in the competitive dialogue procedure may be difficult in practice, and the author's experience suggests that, despite

[28] M. Bubnowski, *Prawo zamówień publicznych. Komentarz* (Warsaw: C. H. Beck, 2007), p. 156.

[29] Ruling of the National Appeal Chamber, UZP/KIO/1093/09.

[30] W. M. Stodolak with W. Hartung, P. Laudański, W. M. Stodolak, M. Stręciwilk and M. Winiarz, *'Zamówienia publiczne po nowelizacji' pod red. Mateusza Winiarza, Oficyna Wyd* (Wrocław: Unimex, 2006), p. 216.

the legal rules that exist, entrepreneurs in Poland are concerned about this issue, including infringement of intellectual property rights.

The author's experience also suggests that some practitioners consider that only exclusion of confidentiality will facilitate open dialogue, assure competitiveness and allow the authority to find new and innovative solutions. However, as we saw in Chapter 1 (section 5.3) it is debatable whether it is possible under EU law to make waiver of confidentiality a condition of participating in a competitive dialogue procedure.

5.4. *Advertising requirements (contract notice)*

The award procedure starts with the publication of a notice setting forth the needs and requirements of the contracting authority, which must be defined in the notice and/or descriptive document. Requirements referring to notices and descriptive documents are described in Annex VII to the Directive. Article 60c(1) of the Public Procurement Law elaborates on the requirement in the Directive, stating specifically that in the case of competitive dialogue the contract notice must include:

> a description of needs and requirements of the awarding entity defined in a way that enables economic operators to prepare for participation in the dialogue, or information on the manner of obtaining such a description.

In the Public Procurement Law, requirements concerning notices for competitive dialogue – for both above- and below-threshold contracts – are the same as those for the restrictive procedure and negotiated procedure with a notice (Article 48, recital 2, of the Public Procurement Law). For contracts above the Directive's threshold, they must, of course, be published in the OJEU. A notice for a contract under the threshold of Directive 2004/18 must be published in the *Public Procurement Bulletin*, a bulletin published only in electronic form and produced by the Public Procurement Office. In the case of both above- and below-threshold contracts, the contracting authority can additionally publish a notice in national or local newspapers, or on the website or at the site of the contracting authority, but is not obliged to do so.

As the contracting authority is not able to describe the subject-matter of the tendering procedure, the notice should include a description of needs and requirements, which constitutes a descriptive document. The document should be as detailed as possible. In the case of a detailed form of description, information on how to obtain the relevant document should be presented. The requirements are regulated in Articles 22 and

24 of the Public Procurement Law and again apply to both above- and below-threshold contracts

5.5. *The selection phase: choosing the candidates to participate in the dialogue*

The Directive's rules on the selection phase of competitive dialogue were discussed in section 5.5 of Chapter 1. Under the Directive, the number of economic operators to be invited to participate in the dialogue should be specified in the contract notice and must be sufficient to ensure competition, with a minimum number of three. However, under Article 60d of the Public Procurement Law, where the contract value is equal to or exceeds the threshold, there must be at least five participants; this goes beyond the Directive and applies a more restrictive rule.[31] Poland's restrictive rules increase the tasks of the contracting authorities by obliging them to compare more solutions, which increases the costs of the procedure for the authorities. They may also mean that offers are prepared less carefully and with less realistic business plans.

As regards the approach to selection, Article 60d(3) of the Public Procurement Law specifically provides that, if the number of economic operators which comply with the qualification requirements is greater than that stipulated in the notice, the awarding entity shall invite to the dialogue those economic operators who have received the highest scores in the selection process. This does not, however, mean that precisely the same criteria must be used for qualification and selection of those qualified. Thus contracting authorities may for example, as permitted under the Directive, use more project-specific criteria for selecting whom to invite than are used for qualification – for example, by referring to experience of construction in general for the qualification stage and construction relevant to the specific project in the selection stage.

If the number of economic operators complying with the participation requirements is less than that specified in the notice, the awarding entity must invite to participate in the dialogue all economic operators which comply with the requirements (Article 60d of the Public Procurement Law).

Economic operators who have submitted requests to participate in a procedure are informed by the contracting authority of the results of the

[31] K. Polak and G. Lang, *Gazeta Prawna*, 20 January 2010.

assessment of their compliance with the qualification requirements and of their scores in the selection process, under Article 60d of the Public Procurement Law. This creates an obligation to provide information to all participants on the results of compliance with the qualification requirements.[32]

5.6. *The dialogue phase*

The rules that apply under the Directive to the dialogue phase are discussed in section 5.6 of Chapter 1. In line with EU law, selected parties will receive an invitation to participate in the dialogue, which must include various information as specified in the Directive. In the Polish literature, it is discussed whether it is reasonable to include the requirements and needs of the contracting authority in the invitation to the dialogue, as that information is already included in the notice.[33]

As we have mentioned above, the actual organisation of the dialogue is not in general regulated by Polish law in any more detail than under the Directive, and thus contracting authorities have a discretion over how the dialogue will be conducted. In accordance with this general flexibility, the Public Procurement Law does not specify any timeframe for the dialogue. The awarding entity may conduct a dialogue until it is capable of determining – by comparing the solutions proposed by economic operators, if necessary – the solution(s) that best meet(s) its needs.

It has, however, been suggested by some that there is one important respect in which the flexibility allowed under the Directive itself is not available to contracting authorities in Poland. This arises from the fact that the possibility for having different stages in the procedure in order to reduce the number of solutions being discussed, which is expressly allowed under the Directive (Article 29(4)), is not referred to expressly in Polish legislation. Thus it has been argued in the Polish literature that under Polish law the dialogue should be conducted in parallel with all the participants in the procedure.[34] Other authors, however, have argued that stages are acceptable and the contracting authority may decide to conduct the procedure in the form of an unlimited number of stages.[35]

Equal treatment, which is the most important rule in all public procurement procedures, will, however, of course, apply to competitive

[32] A. Borkowski, *Prawo zamowien publicznych* (Kolonia Ltd, 2008), p. 121.
[33] Pierog, n. 11 above, p. 256. [34] *Ibid.*, p. 258.
[35] *Zamówienia publiczne po nowelizacji*, n. 30 above, p. 216.

dialogue[36] and in the absence of explicit rules is one of the most important requirements to govern the dialogue phase. Article 7 of the Public Procurement Law states that awarding entities shall prepare and conduct contract award procedures in a manner ensuring fair competition and equal treatment of economic operators. It is particularly important to abide by this principle when exercising the wide discretionary powers at the dialogue stage.

Finally, it can be recalled that, as mentioned in section 5.3 above, without the other party's consent, *neither party* may disclose any technical or business information connected to the dialogue (Article 60d(6) and (7) of the Public Procurement Law).

5.7. *Final tender stage*

In accordance with the requirement in Article 29(6) of the Directive to inform participants of the closing of the dialogue, the awarding entity must immediately inform the participating economic operators about the conclusion of the dialogue (Article 60e of the Public Procurement Law). It will then call for final tenders.

We can note that, in an addition to what is expressly provided in the Directive for this stage, the Public Procurement Law states that, prior to the invitation to participate in the final tender stage, the awarding entity may make changes to the technical and qualitative requirements concerning the object of contract which are the object of the dialogue (Article 60e(2)). This solution has been criticised by contractors as leading to endless dialogue or regress to an earlier stage of the procedure. Contracting authorities, however, argue that this provision enables them to introduce necessary changes after the dialogue phase and thus to realise the main idea of the procedure.

As regards the actual submission of these tenders, Polish law again adds slightly to the requirements of the Directive, concerning the time limits for submitting tenders. Whilst the Directive requires that the awarding entity shall fix a time limit for the submission of tenders, taking into account the time necessary to prepare and submit the tender, Polish law states in addition that the time limit may not be shorter than ten days from the date the invitation to submit tenders is made (Article 60e(4) of the Public Procurement Law).

[36] A. Gorczynska, 'The Principles of Public Procurement in EC Law', in M. Krolikowska-Olczak (ed.), *EU Law in the System of Polish Economy* (2005), p. 23.

The Polish Public Procurement Law also states expressly that, along with the invitation to submit tenders based on the solutions proposed during the dialogue, the awarding entity must provide the essential terms of contract (Article 60e(3)). In this respect, the contracting authority possesses wide discretion concerning the invitation to submit the final bid. Thus, a specification of essential terms of contract can be very detailed or contain just a brief outline of the most important requirements and agreed elements in the solution.[37]

As we have seen above, Polish law states expressly that, prior to the invitation to submit final tenders, the awarding entity may make changes to the technical and qualitative requirements concerning the objects of contract which are the subject-matter of the dialogue. However, for the phase after the submission of final tenders, the Polish Law, in Article 60e(2), merely repeats Article 29(6) of the Directive without elaboration, stating that tenders can only be clarified, specified and fine-tuned at the request of the contracting authority, and that this part of the dialogue may not involve changes to the basic features of the tender or the call for tender which would distort competition or have a discriminatory effect. This provision was discussed in section 5.7 of Chapter 1.

We may finally note, so far as the award phase is concerned, that in practice some problems appear to have been caused by the requirement to determine the criteria for awarding the contract at the beginning of the tender procedure – particularly when in the course of a competitive dialogue the contracting authority decides that it is preferable for bids to be assessed on the basis of criteria different from the ones initially stipulated or that different percentage weightings should be given to criteria than were originally specified.[38] The author's experience in advising on projects and information obtained from interviews with contracting authorities suggests that, in practice, contracting authorities have sometimes modified the criteria or weightings accordingly in such cases. The legality of such a practice is discussed in section 5.6.5 of Chapter 1 of this book.

[37] S. Treumer, 'Competitive Dialogue' (2004) 13 *Public Procurement Law Review* 178, at 184.

[38] A. Gorczynska, 'Öffentliches Auftragswesen. Wettbewerblicher Dialog als neue Vergabeverfahren', in *Jahrbuch zum 30. Jubileum der Zusammenarbeit Universität Lodz und Justus-Liebig Universität Giessen* (Lodz-Giessen, 2008).

5.8. *Procedure following the selection of the winning tender or preferred bidder*

As we have seen in section 5.8 of Chapter 1, after the award criteria have been applied to select the most economically advantageous tender, Article 29(7) of the Directive provides that the selected tenderer may be asked to clarify some aspects of the tender or confirm commitments contained in it, provided this does not have the effect of modifying any material aspects of the tender or the call for tender, and does not bring the risk of distorting competition or causing discrimination.

5.9. *The standstill period*

In Poland, a ten-day standstill period applies as a general rule for competitive dialogue as for all public procurement procedures, with a period of fifteen days applying for contracts above the threshold of the Directive (Article 94(1) of the Public Procurement Law).

5.10. *Payments for costs of participation*

The Public Procurement Law, Article 60c(1.2), provides that the notice of procurement can include a provision on compensation for the economic operators who during the dialogue present a solution which subsequently becomes the basis for the submission of tenders.

The decision on whether to make a payment should be taken by each contracting authority independently, as legal regulations do not actually *require* any such payment. The national practice shows that payments for the costs of participation are usually not expected and are very rare. This approach follows the general idea of understanding the public procurement system as being for the benefit of the contracting authority which possesses a discretionary power in regulating the conduct of the procedure. In practice, there have been complaints by contractors about the costs of participation.

6. Concluding remarks

Competitive dialogue is a new award procedure implemented in the Polish legal system in 2006. For the most part, it has been implemented simply by copying the provisions of the Directive. However, the national provisions differ in a few respects. In particular, as we have seen, the

Polish legislation has not included an explicit provision to state that the dialogue may be conducted in stages, and the Polish literature[39] has argued that this means that this is not possible under the Polish Public Procurement Law.[40] If that is the case, then there is a major difference from the Directive. We have seen that it is also required in Poland to invite a minimum of five participants to the dialogue, whereas the Directive contemplates that three is sometimes sufficient. There are also several points on which the Polish law seeks to elaborate or supplement what is stated in the Directive – for example, by fixing a minimum time limit of ten days for submitting final tenders at the end of the dialogue.

We have seen that, as regards use of the procedure, it has been applied in Poland in practice, although not extensively, with a total of 173 procedures now advertised in the OJEU and 276 in the Polish *Public Procurement Bulletin*. It has been used, in particular, for complex infrastructure projects, for IT projects, for purchasing innovative technical solutions and for construction of sports facilities. It can be particularly useful in the case of complicated long-term contracts concluded in the form of PPPs and, as we have seen, it is indicated as the preferred mode of awarding public contracts in most commentaries on the Public–Private Partnership Act. With continued large-scale investment in the future under the EU's Structural Funds and for the purposes of the European football championships in 2012, it is possible that the importance of competitive dialogue in Poland will continue to increase.

In applying the procedure, however, some problems are caused by the generality of the procedure and by the framework nature of the legal solutions which give rise to some doubts as to how the rules should be applied in practice. As pointed out by several commentators, and as discussed in Chapter 1, the legal provisions on competitive dialogue do not lead to clarity and simplicity in the procedure,[41] and the position in this respect has been the subject of much criticism from practitioners in Poland. The main issues in Poland, which were discussed above, seem to concern the difficulty of describing the object of the contract, ensuring the confidentiality of negotiations and the extent to which negotiations are possible after awarding the contract.

[39] Pierog, n. 11 above, p. 258. [40] *Ibid.*, p. 258.

[41] See also Treumer, n. 37 above; S. Arrowsmith, 'The European Commission's Proposals on the New Directives on Public and Utilities Procurement' (2000) 9 *Public Procurement Law Review* NA 126, at NA 130.

10

Competitive dialogue in Lithuania

DEIVIDAS SOLOVEIČIKAS

1. Introduction: regulation of public procurement in Lithuania

As Lithuania is a country with a civil law system, it is natural to expect it to have a set of written legal rules that regulate the procedures for public procurement. The Lithuanian legal system is also affected by EU law, since it has been a member of the EU since 2004. The present Lithuanian legal rules on procurement mainly refer to the post-2004 EU Directives,[1] as well as international public law and treaties, such as the WTO Agreement on Government Procurement.[2]

For the most part, the legal regulation of public procurement in Lithuania does not differ much from that provided by the EU Directives. In other words, Lithuanian law mainly reproduces *verbatim* the provisions of the EU Directives without adding anything further and without excluding the legal possibilities provided for contracting authorities by the Directives. Lithuanian law on public procurement is one of the most rapidly changing areas of law in Lithuania, having been amended almost twice a year in recent years. Some of the latest amendments have introduced elements of the EU public procurement regime which the EU Directives do not refer to explicitly. For instance, Lithuanian law includes explicit provisions on in-house purchases. Although the conditions of this exception are similar to the *Teckal*[3] criteria, there are nevertheless slight differences which render the in-house concept in Lithuania specific to Lithuania. The Lithuanian law also includes bespoke provisions on confidentiality during public procurement procedures, and thorough regulation of procedures for purchases under the thresholds of EU law, as well as other bespoke features. Thus it seems

[1] Directive 2004/17 and Directive 2004/18.

[2] World Trade Organization (WTO) Agreement on Government Procurement (GPA) (1994).

[3] Case C-107/98, *Teckal Srl* v. *Comune di Viano and AGAC* [1999] ECR I-8121.

that there is a trend to regulate the public procurement area in Lithuania in a bespoke manner rather than simply to rewrite the EU Directives into national law, as well as to adjust the EU requirements to the national legal culture, which is very highly oriented towards transparency.

The main source of public procurement law is the Law on Public Procurement (LPP).[4] This was originally adopted in 1996 and has subsequently been amended numerous times in order to adapt it to EU rules. It should be mentioned that the LPP theoretically is not the source of law with the highest ranking, since according to the hierarchy of legal sources in Lithuania the Constitution, international treaties and codified laws (codes) take precedence over a legal Act. However, the provisions of the LPP are *lex specialis*, meaning that they are the primary rules in the field of public procurement and prevail over the norms of other laws, such as the norms of the civil code, if such norms conflict.[5]

The LPP contains five sections and, so far as EU law is concerned, implements the rules of Public Sector Directive 2004/18 and Utilities Directive 2004/17, as well as the rules on remedies.[6] Thus the LPP regulates all the procedures related to public procurement.

Another important source of public procurement law comprises the regulations passed and enforced by the order of the chairman of the Public Procurement Office (PPO). Some of the regulations are non-obligatory – they are recommendations only. These include, for instance, the methodological recommendations on evaluation of the qualifications of suppliers[7] and many others devoted to the unification of public procurement practice. Regulations of this type serve as useful guidelines for contracting authorities, as they provide many helpful and user-friendly templates. Sometimes there is even a tendency in the Lithuanian case law on public procurement to consider these non-obligatory regulations as prevailing requirements – that is, almost as mandatory norms.

[4] The Law on Public Procurement (Lithuanian version, Lietuvos Respublikos viešųjų pirkimų įstatymas), Žin., 1996, No. 84-2000; 2002, No. 118-5296; 2003, No. 57-2529, No. 123-5579; 2004, No. 7-130, No. 96-3520, No. 116-4321. The English version, although not the latest version, of the Law can be viewed at: www.vpt.lt/admin/uploaded/LawonPPnew.doc.

[5] See the ruling of the Court of Appeals of Lithuania of 20 July, 2007 in civil case *Möbius Bau-Aktiengesellschaft* v. *Klaipėdos valstybinio jūrų uosto direkcija*, Case No. 2A-342/2007.

[6] On all these rules, see Ch. 1, section 2.

[7] The order of the chairman of PPO of 20 October 2003 regarding the adoption of the methodological recommendations on evaluation of the qualification of the suppliers, Žin., 1 November 2003, No. 103-4623.

Another type of PPO regulation comprises those of a mandatory nature which must be followed in every procurement.

In addition, the civil code must be taken into consideration.[8] Although it is provided in Article 1.3(2) of the civil code that any *lex specialis* provisions in other laws take precedence if they regulate the same legal issues (as is the case with public procurement), nevertheless, the provisions of the code are still relevant. For instance, it is settled case law that all public contracts and procurement documents (notices, etc.) must be interpreted and applied in light of Article 6.193 of the civil code on interpretation of contracts.[9]

Despite Lithuania being a civil law country, the concept of judicial precedent is becoming stronger in national case law. Even the Constitutional Court of Lithuania acknowledged a couple of years ago that, legally, judicial precedent is a source of law and that all courts must be consistent when applying the same legal rules to similar facts in light of previous judgments.[10] Therefore, it is no surprise that public procurement is strongly affected by case law. Lithuanian case law is in fact a rich source of law on various public procurement issues. The national courts have elaborated the idea that public procurement is a matter of *ordre public*, meaning that judges must scrutinise every allegation of public procurement violations with due care so that public funds are spent wisely and legally. The courts construe the national law in light of the EU public procurement Directives and with the purpose to safeguard and fully apply the principles of equality, non-discrimination, proportionality, transparency and mutual recognition.[11]

2. The background: complex procurement prior to competitive dialogue

The notion of competitive dialogue was introduced into Lithuanian law in 2006 when Directive 2004/17 and Directive 2004/18 were transposed into national law by amending the LPP. Prior to these amendments, no

[8] The civil code of the Republic of Lithuania, Žin., 6 September 2000, No. 74-2262.

[9] See the ruling in the civil case of the Supreme Court of Lithuania of 8 July 2005, *UAB 'Supla'* v. *Vilniaus miesto savivaldybė*, Case No. 3K-3-339/2005; ruling in the civil case of the Court of Appeals of Lithuania of 3 December 2007, *UAB 'Sostinės auditoriai'* v. *VšĮ Vilniaus Žirmūnų darbo rinkos mokymo centras*, Case No. 2A-549/2007.

[10] Decision of the Constitutional Court of Lithuania of 28 March 2006, Case No. 33/03.

[11] See further D. Soloveičikas, 'Public Procurement in Lithuania: The Ongoing Development' (2009) 2 *European Public Private Partnership Law Review* 36–48.

contracting authority had ever tried to apply procedures resembling competitive dialogue. It has been a common practice for many years for most contracting authorities to use two main forms of procurement in complex projects. The first is the open procedure, which has always been available according to the LPP and is still promoted to fully guarantee the principles of transparency and non-discrimination. The second form of procurement used quite often in practice was the negotiated procedure, especially the procedure without a prior notice. Many contracting authorities tended to negotiate directly with suppliers who bid in procedures on the basis that these bids were unsuitable, allowing contracting authorities to proceed with negotiations without publication of a notice.[12] However, this type of practice has been criticised recently by the government. At present, contracting authorities are strongly encouraged to use open procedures as well as competitive dialogue to implement complex projects, such as PPPs. Government policy is that every use of negotiated procedures without a prior notice will be scrutinised and that the procedure might be overturned when the conditions for using the negotiated procedures have been interpreted too widely. National case law seems to favour this policy.[13]

Until 2010, no competitive dialogue procedures had been launched in Lithuania to the knowledge of the author and Lithuanian contracting authorities needed to be taught more on the advantages of this type of procedure and the added value it may create. Nevertheless, competitive dialogue was not overlooked by the relevant government authorities. As discussed later below, there have been specific initiatives to promote competitive dialogue for PPPs and large investment projects, in that the PPO has issued Recommendations for this, and about how competitive dialogue should be applied to these projects, if used. In the year 2010/11, there were three notices for competitive dialogue procedures published in the OJEU for Lithuania (see section 4 of Chapter 1); and, bearing in mind that PPPs are considered by the present government as a stimulus for national economic growth, there is a high chance that competitive dialogue will be increasingly used in the future in those cases in which it is available.

[12] As provided in Art. 31 of Directive 2004/18, Arts. 56 and 73 of the Law on Public Procurement of the Republic of Lithuania, Žin., 1996, No. 84-2000; 2002, No. 118-5296; 2003, No. 57-2529, No. 123-5579; 2004, No. 7-130, No. 96-3520, No. 116-4321.

[13] See the civil case ruling of the Supreme Court of Lithuania of 13 November 2009, *National Stadium Case*, Case No. 3K-3-505/2009.

3. Introduction to competitive dialogue

The procedure of competitive dialogue, including the legal description of this type of procurement, is provided in Section II of the LPP. Competitive dialogue was transposed into the Lithuanian legal system together with the other provisions of Directive 2004/17 and Directive 2004/18 and became effective from the beginning of 2006. There were no substantial discussions on how competitive dialogue should be shaped or if any additional provisions were to be added compared with the EU legislation. At the time of its implementation into the LPP, the wording of the legal text was, and still is, the same as in Directive 2004/18.

In addition to the provisions of LPP there is another very recent set of provisions that is expected to foster the use of competitive dialogue. These are the 'Recommendations on the application of competitive dialogue', which were adopted and confirmed by order of the chairman of the PPO (hereinafter referred to as 'the Recommendations').[14] As already mentioned above, generally PPO recommendations are not binding. Nevertheless, it is a common national practice for contracting authorities to refer to recommendations as if they are legally binding when executing public procurement procedures. Therefore, it is very likely that the Recommendations will be a primary source of useful information for every contracting authority considering competitive dialogue as an option.

4. Scope of competitive dialogue in law and practice

Article 50 LPP outlines the main conditions for using competitive dialogue. It is followed by Article 51 LPP which provides for the procedural requirements of competitive dialogue (publishing of a notice, award criteria, application of a staged procedure, etc.). Article 52 LPP envisages the procedure on how to apply to take part in the competitive dialogue, whilst the selection criteria and the pre-qualification requirements are regulated by Article 53 LPP. The last Article in Section IV of the LPP is Article 54, which envisages the requirements for the invitation for the

[14] The order of the chairman of PPO of 30 September 2010 No. 1S-140 regarding the enforcement of the recommendations on the application of the competitive dialogue, Žin. 2010, No. 120-6168.

candidates to take part. In these respects, Section IV of the LPP mainly repeats all the provisions of Article 29 of Directive 2004/18 almost *verbatim*.

It is important to mention that paragraph 1 of the Recommendations states that the purpose of the Recommendations is to help contracting authorities implement competitive dialogue in sophisticated PPP and investment projects. This is a very clear indication that competitive dialogue is seen as a tool for the promotion of PPP projects and their execution in Lithuania; it is indicated that this procedure provides the flexibility important for such projects. It should be mentioned that the Recommendations were adopted with the purpose of making the PPP climate more attractive for investors in Lithuania. Therefore, it can be expected that this type of procurement will be used more often.

The Recommendations are silent on whether competitive dialogue should be used only for high-value contracts or if this procedure might be applied also for procurement that has a value below the EU thresholds. The LPP also does not give any indication on this. It is usually considered that, if the LPP does not require or forbid particular actions by a contracting authority, then such actions are allowed, provided that they do not infringe the general principles of public procurement; and on this basis it can be argued that competitive dialogue is available for contracts both above and below the thresholds of the EU Directive. However, it is unlikely that contracting authorities would use competitive dialogue for procurement below the EU threshold due to the complexity of the competitive dialogue procedure.

It can also be noted that the LPP also does not give a specific indication of whether competitive dialogue, or a procedure conducted along the lines of competitive dialogue, is available for Part B service contracts, works concessions, services concessions or for contracts governed by the Utilities Directive. Since there are no explicit restrictions on its application for these contracts, again it could be argued that this type of procedure could be used under the law for those cases.

The Recommendations of the PPO are divided into four sections. The first contains the general provisions, including the purpose of the document, as well as definitions. The second section outlines the conditions for using competitive dialogue. Preparation for competitive dialogue is examined in Section III. The final section of the Recommendations

(Section IV) covers the execution of the procedure on a step-by-step basis. All sections give a detailed explanation of how competitive dialogue should operate and are drafted on the basis of the European Commission's Explanatory Note on competitive dialogue.[15]

As provided in both Directive 2004/18 (see section 4 of Chapter 1) and the LPP, competitive dialogue may be commenced when the authority is objectively unable to define the technical means for the procurement or to specify the legal or financial background. It is explained in paragraph 6.2 of the Recommendations that this will be the case when, for instance, the public partner in a PPP project does not know to what extent private partners are ready to finance the project. This line of reasoning is continued in paragraph 8, which says that competitive dialogue is recommended in cases of complex infrastructure and services projects which are organised as PPPs. The PPO recommends choosing competitive dialogue in such cases when negotiated procedures, as applied in Lithuania, do not guarantee the expected flexibility and consultations with suppliers are necessary (paragraph 9). (Lithuanian law on the negotiated procedure (both with and without a notice) requires a set of technical specifications, even though this is not envisaged by the Directive itself.[16]) Finally, there is an obligation on each contracting authority to make a thorough evaluation of whether the legal conditions to start competitive dialogue are present (paragraph 10). From the text of the Recommendations it might be concluded that authorities may not use competitive dialogue when there is a genuine possibility to prepare a precise and exhaustive technical specification.

As we have mentioned, however, despite the above legal adoption and regulation of competitive dialogue, there has been negligible use of the procedure in practice.

5. Operation of the competitive dialogue procedure

5.1. Introduction

As mentioned above, the LPP includes the same requirements for use of competitive dialogue that are provided in Article 29 of Directive 2004/18. This means that pursuant to Article 50(2) LPP the most

[15] European Commission Explanatory Note on Competitive Dialogue, CC/2005/04_rev 1 of 5 October 2005.

[16] Art. 24 LPP. There is also a strong and consistent line of case law of the Supreme Court and the Court of Appeals requiring absolute clarity in the requirements for any public procurement (see for example Court of Appeals decision in civil case *UAB 'Labostera'* v. *VšĮ Kauno Raudonojo Kryžiaus klinikinė ligoninė*, Case No. 2A-200/2008).

economically advantageous tender must be used for the award. The legislation also states that the contracting authority may establish prizes and payments to participants.

5.2. *The planning stage and drafting of the descriptive document*

Neither Directive 2004/18 nor the LPP provisions are explicit on what should be taken into consideration while preparing for the competitive dialogue procedure or drafting the descriptive document. Article 51(1) LPP merely envisages that contracting authorities must advertise their needs and requirements in the notice and/or in a descriptive document. Section III of the Recommendations, however, suggests what should be done and when. Paragraphs 12.1–12.18 outline a checklist for the preparation stage. Points to be considered by contracting authorities include: identification and provision of the information deemed as confidential, to protect the interests of both the contracting authority and the suppliers; identification and provision of the requirements related to conflict of interest so that all suppliers are aware of whether they fit these requirements and are thus not precluded from participation; essential elements of the technical specification which might lead to shaping the final result; duration of the contract; duration of the award procedure, with suitable time-frames for both the contracting authority and the suppliers; the procurement value; selection and pre-qualification criteria; the number of candidates; means of communication; the criteria for evaluation, related parameters and the methodology for their application; requirements for sub-contractors, if any; the number of the solutions that may be presented; information on whether variant bids are allowed; requirements for consortia; and stages of the contract's execution.

In addition, these paragraphs suggest that there should be a general evaluation of the market with the purpose of identifying which of the main market players are likely to bid, whether transparent and effective competition is possible, what the reputation of the contracting authority is, etc.

These paragraphs also indicate that the contracting authority should provide information related to the competitive dialogue procedure, such as the shape of the whole procedure, how many stages are predicted, what the main questions and issues are that need to be discussed with bidders, the methodology of the dialogue, when the dialogue should end, form of invitation to present a final bid, etc.

5.3. *Confidentiality of information and solutions*

There are a couple of legal provisions related to the confidentiality requirements of competitive dialogue. The first, which is the *lex specialis* and is mostly connected to competitive dialogue, is the legal requirement in Article 51(2) and (7) LPP which, following the Directive, prohibits the contracting authority from disclosing information received from suppliers without their consent or from disclosing solutions and agreements reached with the supplier during the procedure. It should be noted that under Lithuanian case law a public procurement procedure is considered as a pre-contractual legal relationship. This means that in case of breach of the confidentiality obligation the contracting authority is responsible for *culpa in contrahendo*, meaning that the aggrieved party has a right to claim damages for the breach.

The second provision on confidentiality is Article 6 LPP, which regulates confidentiality in award procedures generally and which also has to be applied during competitive dialogue. Article 6(1) LPP repeats the above-mentioned rule that the contracting authority, the procurement committee and its members, including the experts and all the other persons involved in the procedure, must not disclose confidential information that is explicitly classified and indicated as such to the contracting authority by suppliers. The law continues with the explanation that confidential information comprises commercial secrets as well as confidential aspects of the bid. In addition, Article 6(1) LPP includes a provision that has no direct origin in Directive 2004/18, which states that upon the request of bidders the contracting authority must allow bidders to familiarise themselves with the bids of the other suppliers unless the suppliers have limited the disclosure of such information. Reading those provisions of the LPP in light of the general transparency policy that is, as mentioned, a cornerstone of the present Lithuanian public procurement system, it seems that the confidentiality of proposals and bids is not considered a priority and should generally give way to transparency. Nevertheless, in practice this provision is often circumvented simply by indicating that all the information in the bid is confidential and must not be disclosed. There have been no challenges in courts yet regarding this type of action. However, the PPO recommends a more flexible approach by allowing access to as much information provided in the bids and commercial proposals as possible.

5.4. *Advertising requirements*

Article 51(1) LPP states that the contracting authority shall publish a notice of the contract in the manner set forth in Articles 22 and 23 LPP and shall make known its needs and requirements in that notice. These Articles govern advertising of contracts above the Directive's thresholds and require notices to be published in (i) the OJEU, (ii) the national official bulletin, *Valstybės žinios*, and (iii) the central public procurement information system (CPPIS). From 1 January 2012, advertising will need to be done only through the OJEU and the CPPIS.

To help contracting authorities prepare notices for above-threshold procurement, including for competitive dialogue, the PPO has published Recommendations on completing standard forms for international procurement notices.[17] In practice, the PPO scrutinises each draft notice that is submitted to it electronically and must do this within three working days of receipt. If it has any comments, which might be, for example, on selection and award criteria, it returns the notice, and the contracting authority is obliged to act on the comments in order to secure publication of the notice.

5.5. *The selection phase: choosing the candidates to participate in the dialogue*

The rules on choosing candidates to participate in the dialogue generally reproduce those in the Directive itself, which were discussed in section 5.5 of Chapter 1. Pursuant to Article 51(2) LPP, the contracting authority must open the dialogue with the candidates selected in accordance with the relevant provisions of Article 54 LPP. Thus the contracting authority is obliged first to select those suppliers who meet the selection criteria (the minimum qualification requirements) and are able to submit an appropriate proposal. Article 53 LPP also applies, and this cross-refers to Article 47 LPP which governs restricted procedures. This makes provision for limiting the number of candidates where the number of the suitable candidates is sufficient, as is allowed under the Directive, subject to the usual rules in the Directive on disclosure of criteria.

The LPP also reproduces the other rules of the Directive concerning selection of candidates, such as those concerning the number of candidates to be invited to the dialogue and criteria for selection. In addition, in Lithuania certain common requirements for the selection phase and

[17] Order of the chairman of PPO of 29 June 2006 No. 1S-37 regarding adoption of recommendations on filling the typical forms of international public procurement notices, Žin., 2006, No. 76-2953.

related recommendations are provided in the methodological guidelines for evaluation of the suppliers' qualification.[18]

5.6. *The dialogue phase*

The rules in the Directive that govern the dialogue stage were analysed in section 5.6 of Chapter 1.

Following the Directive, Article 54 LPP provides that the contracting authority shall open a dialogue with selected candidates to identify and define the means best suited to satisfying its needs.

The LPP in Article 51(3) allows the contracting authority the freedom permitted under the Directive to provide for successive stages and to reduce the number of solutions during the dialogue process. In other respects, the LPP also repeats the provisions of the Directive regarding conduct of the dialogue.

Pursuant to paragraph 25 of the Recommendations, dialogue may be operated by:

- Searching for the most suitable solution, which may incorporate aspects from all proposals. Since a contracting authority, under the confidentiality requirements, cannot without the prior consent of a candidate disclose its proposed solutions to the other participants, the contract notice or descriptive document must state that the invitation to participate in the dialogue implies consent to the disclosure of proposed solutions to other participants. This type of legal approach has not been challenged by suppliers in court nor banned or limited by the PPO. There is no case law on this issue.
- Inviting non-binding proposals, which are then adjusted to improve them as far as possible.
- Execution of the dialogue in stages: at the beginning of the dialogue the technical means will be discussed and only later are the financial issues examined.
- Starting from an initial solution provided by the contracting authority, with participants invited to comment on this solution through dialogue.

A participant whose solution has been declined during the dialogue is to be excluded from further procedures.

[18] Order of the chairman of PPO of 30 March 2009 No. 1S-25 regarding the qualifications of suppliers for the evaluation of methodological guidelines for approval, Žin., 2009, No. 39-1505.

The Recommendations also provide that there are two possible methods of implementation of the dialogue: a consultative dialogue and a research dialogue (paragraph 26). Consultative dialogue is an approach where the contracting authority, in accordance with its developed project, seeks advice from suppliers on how and by what means the specified project can be executed. In this case, the contracting authority requires from the suppliers not to provide their own projects or solutions, but to provide alternative solutions to what is conceived by the contracting authority. The research dialogue begins with the contracting authority defining its goals and desirable results, without giving details. In this case, the suppliers first submit general proposals, and those are then revised and adjusted until the most appropriate option is defined.

Pursuant to Article 51(7) LPP, the contracting authority must prepare minutes of the dialogue, which must be signed by the chairman of the procurement committee and the authorised representative of the participating suppliers.

Prior to choosing the best offer, the contracting authority may also carry out a number of specified steps (paragraph 27 of the Recommendations). These are: resolving any remaining unclear provisions of the contract; defining what constitutes the main aspects of the proposals and narrowly defining circumstances under which the main elements of the proposals may be modified; defining the scope of possible amendments of the proposals under certain circumstances; and ensuring that the explanation, clarification and correction of the proposals is made only on the initiative of the contracting authority.

According to Article 51(6) LPP, the award criteria may not be modified during the procedure.

5.7. *Final tender stage*

Article 51(5) LPP repeats the rules of the Directive concerning the submission of final tenders and the possibility, subject to conditions, of clarifying, specifying and fine-tuning those tenders. These provisions in the Directive were examined in section 5.7 of Chapter 1.

Article 51(6) LPP, following the Directive, then provides that the contracting authority shall assess the tenders received on the basis of the award criteria laid down in the contract notice or the descriptive document and shall choose the most economically advantageous tender. As we have seen in Chapter 1, there is a view of the Directive that in some circumstances two may be a sufficient number of tenders to invite to the final tender stage, and that this is sometimes done in practice. However, it can be noted that in Lithuania the law provides that the contracting authority must invite offers from no fewer than three bidders (Article 53(2) LPP).

The legislation also provides that a bidder may present only one bid to the contracting authority.

5.8. *Procedure following the selection of the winning tender or preferred bidder*

The provisions of the Directive that govern the procedure following identification of the best tenderer were examined in section 5.7 of Chapter 1.

Again following directly the wording of the Directive, in its Article 29(7), the LPP provides that, at the request of the contracting authority, the supplier identified as having submitted the most economically advantageous tender may be asked to clarify aspects of the tender or confirm obligations contained in the tender, but these changes may not result in modifying the material aspects of the tender or of the call for tender (Article 51(6) LPP).

The Recommendations in paragraph 32 specifically provide that material changes to the proposal shall be changes to the conditions of the final bid, such as those on: the payment mechanism and payment schedule; the pricing rules and the final price; the scope of the contract; the duration of the contract and the contract performance schedules; the site, method and conditions; and technical specifications etc.

5.9. *The standstill period*

Article 18(9) LPP provides generally that a public contract cannot be concluded before the expiry of a standstill period and this general provision is applicable to competitive dialogue without any specific application. A particular feature of the Lithuanian provision is that a standstill is applied when the value of the public contract does not exceed LTL 10,000 (excluding VAT) in cases of procurement excluded from the scope of the Directives. This will be relevant for competitive dialogue if that procedure is ever operated for excluded contracts.

5.10. Payments for costs of participation

Article 50(4) LPP provides that the contracting authority may establish prizes and payments to participants taking part in competitive dialogue. Such prizes and payments shall compensate at least part of the costs incurred due to the preparation of proposals (solutions) (paragraph 11 of the Recommendations). A goal of such payments is to encourage more candidates to participate in competitive dialogue.

It is very rare that a contracting authority compensates suppliers in this way in Lithuania. There is, however, no experience yet in this respect in relation to competitive dialogue itself.

6. Concluding remarks

As we have seen, competitive dialogue can be used in Lithuania on the basis of the same legal conditions which are provided in Directive 2004/18. In contrast with the position in some other Member States, the procedure has not been taken up in practice in any significant way. However, sound preparation has been made for its implementation by Recommendations from the PPO that will serve as guidelines for contracting authorities interested in trying this method of procurement.

There is also a clear indication that its use is likely to be in the context of PPP and large investment projects, which will usually involve procurement above the thresholds of Directive 2004/18.

11

Competitive dialogue in Italy

GABRIELLA M. RACCA AND DARIO CASALINI*

1. Introduction: regulation of public procurement in Italy

Italy has a long-standing tradition of legislation on public procurement. The first Italian legislation on award procedures for work contracts dates back to the very birth of the Italian state in 1865 and was among the first statutes issued after the creation of Italy as a national state.[1] Later, the legislation on public accountancy of 1923 regulated supplies and works procurement by imposing on public authorities a general duty of competitive tendering.[2] Such domestic legislation on public contracts pursued the goal of value for money in public expenditure and was therefore drafted from the point of view of contracting authorities that must comply with the principles of efficiency and effectiveness (Article 97 of the Italian Constitution). This approach was then merged with the European Union perspective of protection of fair competition among market operators aspiring to enter into contractual relationships with public authorities. The objective choice of the best contractor meets both the need for value for money expressed by contracting authorities and the economic operators' right to fair competition, thus contributing to the continuous improvement of the European market and quality of life.[3]

This historical legal background explains why, since the first generation of EU Directives on public procurement, Italian law has implemented the EU Directives far beyond their scope. The EU Directives on

* Sections 2, 3 and 5.1 to 5.7 were written by Gabriella M. Racca; all the other sections were written by Dario Casalini.

[1] Law No. 2248 of 20 March 1865, Annex F, Law on Public Works.

[2] RD No. 2440 of 18 November 1923; A. Massera and M. Simoncini, 'Basics of Public Contracts in Italy', *Ius Publicum Network Review – Report* (2011), available at www.ius-publicum.com.

[3] The rules of public contracts were originally imposed in order to ensure the ethics of the public administration: G. M. Racca, *La responsabilità precontrattuale della pubblica amministrazione tra autonomia e correttezza* (Naples: Jovene, 2000).

public procurements have always been implemented through statute law and further amended in compliance with the next generation of EU law. European provisions are usually transposed literally with the same wording, mainly as regards principles and definitions, the rationale being to avoid setting corresponding domestic concepts that might turn out to be misleading. In addition to these literal transpositions, the Italian legislator drafts very detailed rules to limit contracting authorities' discretion in undertaking procurement.

EU Directives 2004/17 and 2004/18 have been implemented in Italy by means of Legislative Decree No. 163 of 13 April 2006 (Public Contracts Code, hereinafter PCC) and its executive regulation DPR No. 207 of 5 October 2010, which together form a body of legislation of more than 600 sections. The executive regulation entered into force only very recently, on 8 June 2011. The PCC and its executive regulation deal with the award as well as the execution of the contract. In principle, contract performance is governed by the ordinary rules (private law) applicable to contractual relationships, as defined in the Italian Civil Code. Nonetheless, many rules departing from private law (as set out in the Italian Civil Code) govern contract performance – for example, concerning subcontracting, variants, payment mechanisms, and intermediate and final inspections – as these are compulsory legal provisions that cannot be derogated from by either party. Any failure by economic operators during the performance phase may also involve a breach of rules on competition since the contract performed may not correspond with the one awarded under the rules on competition in awarding contracts.[4]

The Italian Republic 'recognises and promotes local autonomies' (Article 5 of the Italian Constitution) and, in addition to the state, 'is composed of the Municipalities, the Provinces, the Metropolitan Cities [and] the Regions' which are 'autonomous entities having their own statutes, powers and functions' (Article 114 of the Constitution). The state has exclusive legislative competence on competition rules and, consequently, on public contracts.[5] At various times, the regions have filed claims before the Constitutional Court to assert their competence

[4] R. Cavallo Perin, G. M. Racca and G. L. Albano, 'The Safeguard of Competition in the Execution Phase of Public Procurement', *Quaderni Consip*, VI (2010), www.consip.it; G. M. Racca, 'Collaborative Procurement and Contract Performance in the Italian Healthcare Sector: Illustration of a Common Problem in European Procurement' (2010) 19 *Public Procurement Law Review* 119.

[5] Art. 117, § 2, lett. e, l, m and s, of the Italian Constitution.

on matters concerning public contracts, namely, contracts below EU thresholds (Const. Court No. 401/2007), specification of requirements on in-house provision (Const. Court No. 439/08), definition of awarding procedures and regulation of contract performance (Const. Court No. 411/08), extension of public contracts (Const. Court No. 320/08), design and planning (Const. Court No. 221/2010) and exclusion of abnormally low tenders (Const. Court No. 160/2009). However, the Constitutional Court has denied regional competence on such matters on the basis that they all relate to competition issues and has left to the regions only a limited discretion in the choice of the composition and functions of the jury and on the effects of work contracts over city planning (Const. Court No. 401/07). This discretion must be exercised in compliance with EU and national principles. In addition, local authorities (municipalities, provinces, and metropolitan cities) are accustomed to issuing regulations concerning award procedures for public contracts below the thresholds of the EU Directives.

Taking account of local authorities and other public bodies covered by EU rules on public procurement, in Italy there are several thousand contracting authorities, each procuring without any supervision other than judicial review and the application of the regulatory provisions laid down by an independent national authority, as described further below.

As regards the former, judicial review of public contract award procedures falls within the jurisdiction of administrative courts (Regional Administrative Tribunals (TAR) and the Consiglio di Stato as court of appeal). Jurisdiction over public contracts litigation has been historically divided between the administrative courts, for disputes concerning the award procedure, and the ordinary courts (tribunals, court of appeal, Cassazione), for disputes regarding contract performance once the contract commences. After the implementation of Directive 2007/66 amending the EU rules on remedies for contracts governed by the procurement Directives, the administrative courts can declare the award void and the contract ineffective,[6] whereas the ordinary courts maintain the competence over disputes arising during the performance phase,[7] except for the application of special public law rules in this phase (such

[6] Art. 133, Administrative Trial Code; Cass., ord. 5 March 2010, No. 5291; Cass., S. U., ord. 10 February 2010, No. 2906; Cons. Stato, V, 15 June 2010, No. 3759.

[7] Cons. Stato, VI, 26 May 2010, No. 3347; Cons. Stato, V, 1 April 2010, No. 1885; Cass., S. U., 11 January 2011, No. 391.

as special public law rules on sub-contracting).[8] Whenever ineffectiveness is deemed to be inappropriate, the administrative courts may impose on contracting authorities the alternative penalties of fines and contract shortening.

Litigation in Italy has dramatically increased in the last decade, with several thousand legal actions on public procurement being brought each year before the administrative courts.[9] The courts have been playing a significant role in developing public procurement law and strengthening and standardising its enforcement. However, the need to reduce the growth in litigation, caused mainly by a lack of relevant professional skills within contracting authorities and consequently a lack of trust in their procuring activities, led the Italian government to add a new disposition to the PCC to penalise 'rash lawsuits' in 2011. Whenever 'the judicial decision is based on obvious reasons or well-established case law' Italian judges can now condemn the losing party (either the contracting authority or the contractor, but normally the latter as a reckless plaintiff) to pay a fine, the amount of which is between two and three times the court fees.[10]

In addition to judicial review, Italian law envisages the institution of the Italian Authority for the Control over Public Contracts (Autorità di vigilanza sui contratti pubblici). This has the task of monitoring both the award and the execution of public contracts. The Authority's activities are funded by the state, the awarding authorities and, partly, by bidders.[11] Every bidder has to pay a fee to participate in an award procedure: the payment of the fee is a mandatory requirement of the procedure, which will be set aside for non-compliance.[12] The Authority submits proposals to the government for legislative amendments to the

[8] Cons. Stato, IV, 24 March 2010, No. 1713.

[9] There were an average of 3,000–4,000 legal actions every year, amounting to 4 per cent of the overall number of award procedures: M. Lipari, 'Le cause e la casistica del contenzioso amministrativo', speech at the conference 'Gare pubbliche ed efficiente gestione delle risorse' held at LUISS, Rome, on 8 February 2011.

[10] Art. 246-bis, PCC, added by Art. 4, Law Decree No. 70 of 13 May 2011, which became Law of 12 July 2011, No. 106.

[11] G. M. Racca, 'Public Contracts', *Ius Publicum Network Review – Report* (2011).

[12] Arts. 6 and 8, PCC; Art. 1, § 67, Law No. 266 of 2005, provides that the Italian Authority for the Control over Public Contracts, in order to cover the costs of their activity, defines annually the amount of the fees to be paid by the public and private entities subject to its supervision, as well as the method of collection (for the amount of the fee, see the Resolution of the Italian Authority for the Control over Public Contracts of 15 February 2010).

PCC and gives opinions on the correct interpretation and implementation of the PCC. It also prepares an annual report for the Parliament on the award and execution of public contracts. The Authority enjoys powers of inspection and of imposing pecuniary sanctions against economic operators who are found liable for making false declarations of their own qualification requirements. The Authority may also impose fines on contracting authorities and economic operators that refuse to disclose information or provide false information. Besides these pecuniary sanctions, the Authority has the power to suspend from public contracts for a period of one to twelve months any economic operator found liable for making false declarations.[13]

2. The background: complex procurement prior to competitive dialogue

The competitive dialogue procedure in Directive 2004/18 overlaps with other award procedures specifically envisaged by the Italian national legislation for those cases in which the contracting authority is not able to define the most suitable work or service to meet its needs or has to resort to financial arrangements involving private capital. These other specific award procedures are relevant for complex contracts, raising the question of their relationship with and their distinction from competitive dialogue.

The need for a contracting authority to award a single contract with different subject-matter (design, execution, management, exploitation of works) through a special procedure was met in Italy by the so-called *appalto concorso.*[14] The use of such a procedure was a long and not always satisfactory experience which allowed the public administration (and particularly a jury of politicians and non-experts in the field) to

[13] Art. 6, § 11, and Art. 48, PCC.

[14] The expression *appalto concorso* appears for the first time in a Ministerial circular (No. 586 of 21 May 1917) and was then regulated by Art. 3, d.lgt. 6 February 1919, No. 107, and then by Royal Decree of 8 February 1923, No. 422. According to the legislation implementing Directive 93/37, this procedure was allowed only in special circumstances briefly defined by the Law (Art. 17, §§ 1 and 5, and Art. 20, § 3, Law of 11 February 1994, No. 109: i.e. particularly complex works which imply the choice between different technical solutions and whose amount is above €25 million). The entry into force of the new government regulation implementing PCC repealed the *appalto concorso* from 8 June 2011 (Art. 253, § 1-quinquies, PCC).

award contracts with a wide discretion, hence choosing a successful tenderer without a genuine competition.

In the past, the Italian *appalto concorso* allowed contracting authorities to express basic needs to be fulfilled and implemented by economic operators. The subject-matter of the *appalto concorso* included both what now in Italy is the object of an 'ideas contest' (*concorso di idee*) and the object of a design contest (preliminary, final and executive plans), along with the execution of the works. At times, it included facilities management services or the exploitation of the work in the same procurement award procedure.

In order to comply with Directive 93/37 on public works (one of the predecessors to the current Public Sector Directive 2004/18), the Italian procedure of *appalto concorso* was turned into an open or restricted procedure with prior publication of the contract notice in the sense of the EU procurement Directives. However, often it was also used to award works concessions[15] which, as Chapter 1 explained, are subject only to very limited obligations under the Directives. In other words, contracts awarded by this procedure could be structured either as a 'public works contract', whose subject-matter could be both the design and execution of works, or a 'public works concession', whose subject-matter was both the design and the execution of works and whose consideration consisted either solely in the right to exploit the construction or in this right together with payment.[16] A precondition for using this procedure was the complexity of the subject-matter and uncertainty over the technical solutions and specifications to be adopted.

However, linking three different subject elements (design services, execution of works, and facilities management services) in one award procedure made it difficult to guarantee a genuine overall competition for each element of the subject-matter. Effectively, the contract for the execution element was being awarded on the basis of limited planning and only a generic definition of the needs of the procuring entity (with the details being developed under the contract itself), and it appears that this does not comply with the requirements of the EU Directives. A further problem with the procedure was that – as just noted above – the juries were traditionally composed of politicians and not of persons having technical and professional skills related to the subject-matter of

[15] In accordance with Law No. 109 of 1994, Art. 20, §§ 1–3, now repealed.

[16] Law No. 109 of 1994, Art. 20, § 4, and now Art. 53, § 2, lett. b, PCC, and Arts. 105–116, DPR No. 207/2010, where it is provided that the contracting authority must define at least the final plan of the works.

the contract.[17] These factors undermined a correct and objective evaluation of the economic operators' proposals, and contributed to the decision to repeal it.

Overall, this procedure did not guarantee transparency and raised several issues relating to legality and fairness, due to the misuse of the wide discretion the procedure entails, as is apparent from the extensive case law.[18] After an initial period when a total separation between services procurement for planning (the ideas contest, and the design contest) and works procurement (execution) was compulsory, a new procedure similar to the *appalto concorso* was introduced by the PCC in 2006. This was labelled the *appalto integrato*.

The *appalto integrato* seems to comply better with the EU Directives as it involves an award on the basis of preliminary and final plans, and not only on the basis of limited planning and a generic definition of the needs of the procuring entity, as we have seen with the *appalto concorso*. The subject-matter of the *appalto integrato* is the drafting of the executive plan, along with the execution of public works, and it has been defined on the basis of the EU Directive's rule that assumes the possibility of awarding the design and execution of work either separately or jointly.[19] The needs previously met by the *appalto concorso* are now being pursued either through an *appalto integrato*, or through a public works concession procedure in the sense of the Directive if the right to exploit the work instead of receiving all or part of the payment is included in the contract documents.[20]

Besides using the *appalto integrato*, whenever a contracting authority is not able to define the design of a work to be performed, it can choose among specific procedures laid down by the PCC for that purpose, regardless of the threshold of the contract,[21] namely (i) the ideas contest and (ii) the design contest.

[17] Const. Court No. 453/1990 required the majority of the members of the jury to be experts in the subject-matter of the competitive tendering.

[18] Among the more than 1,000 decisions on the *appalto-concorso* procedures, see Cons. Stato, V, 10 September 2009, No. 5433; Cons. Stato, V, 21 January 2009, No. 282; Cons. Stato, V, 7 January 2009, No. 17; and Cons. Stato, IV, 26 May 2006, No. 3190. Currently, according to the PCC, public works can be performed only by means of public works procurements (including *appalto integrato*) or public works concessions: see Art. 53 PCC, implementing recital 9 of Directive 2004/18, while public works concession is defined under Art. 1(3) of Directive 2004/18.

[19] Art. 1(1)(b) of Directive 2004/18.

[20] Public works concession as defined by Art. 143 PCC.

[21] A similar procedure is found in French law, under which the so-called *marchés de définition* should apply whenever 'the public entity is unable to specify the aims and

The ideas contest (*concorso di idee*) is a services procurement, and its subject-matter is broad and imprecise since it was created in the PCC in order to provide contracting authorities with outlines of ideas which are less specific and detailed than those in a preliminary plan.[22] Furthermore, unlike the design contest, the subject-matter of the ideas contest is not limited to planning for works but may take place also for planning services and supply contracts. The best idea is purchased by the contracting authority from the economic operator in return for a prize or reward (not considered as compensation). The idea will then become the subject-matter for a design contest or a tendering procedure for design and execution. Alternatively, but only for public works contracts, the PCC allows the contracting authority to provide expressly in the contract notice the possibility of entrusting the winner of the ideas contest, if appropriate, with the task of completing the further steps of the design (preliminary, final and executive plans) by means of a negotiated procedure without publication of a contract notice.[23] This is done following the provision under Article 31(3) of Directive 2004/18[24] as implemented by the PCC, Article 57, § 4, which allows use of this negotiated procedure for negotiating the design contract when this has been provided for in the rules of an initial design contest held under the Directive's rules. It is important to note that, in accordance with what is allowed under the Directive, this procedure covers only the design element – it does not allow the award of a contract under the negotiated procedure without a notice for the *execution* of the project.

The design contest (*concorso di progettazione*) is used by contracting authorities to purchase the preliminary plan, which is the first level of design of works, amongst the three levels (preliminary, final and executive) of design defined by Italian law. This level comprises production of

performances which the contract must meet, the techniques to be used, and the human and material resources required. The purpose of such contracts is to explore the possibilities and conditions for establishing a contract subsequently, if necessary through production of a model or demonstrator. They must also enable the price level of the provisions to be estimated and calculated, as well as the different phases of the performance schedule' (Art. 73 of the French Public Procurement Code, issued by Decree of 1 August 2006, No. 2006-975). See Case C-299/08, *Commission* v. *France* [2009] ECR I-11587.

[22] Art. 108 PCC. [23] Art. 108, § 6, PCC.

[24] Art. 31(3) of Directive 2004/18 states that, 'when the contract concerned follows a design contest and must, under the applicable rules, be awarded to the successful candidate or to one of the successful candidates, in the latter case, all successful candidates must be invited to participate in the negotiations'.

a preliminary plan that covers the definition of the qualitative and functional characteristics of the works, the general framework of the needs and requirements to be met, and a report supporting the proposed solution, along with an outline of the dimensional, volumetric, functional and technological characteristics of the work to be performed.[25] The contracting authority enters into a service contract by means of the design contest. The object of the contract is the preliminary project. This must be further specified and detailed in the final plan and then in the executive plan. Whenever the contracting authority is not able to provide within its own organisation the two further stages of planning, a new procurement procedure must be issued for this purpose. Its subject-matter will be the design (development of the preliminary plan into final and executive plans) and construction (works execution).[26]

It is worth noting that the PCC expressly forbids economic operators who took part in the works planning phase or procedure to bid in the award procedure for the execution of these works. According to the case law of the Italian administrative courts, this rule is a specific instance of the general principle of equal treatment. This precludes the planner and its subsidiaries from being contractor, sub-contractor or concessionaire of the same works.[27]

The availability of these alternative traditional procedures was cited as the reason for a decision by the Italian legislator to suspend the use of competitive dialogue for contracts covered by Directive 2004/18 until June 2011, as described below. It is worth noting that the repeal of *appalto concorso* was linked to the entry into force of the new government regulation and the possibility to use competitive dialogue.[28] However, as we will see in section 4 below, competitive dialogue may improve transparency and guarantee advantages over these approaches that may lead to its use in practice in the future.

3. Introduction to competitive dialogue

As we have seen in Chapter 1, competitive dialogue is an optional award procedure under Directive 2004/18. Italy decided to implement

[25] Art. 93 PCC.

[26] Art. 109 PCC allows for a two-stage contest whose subject-matters are respectively the preliminary and the final projects.

[27] See Cons. Stato, IV, 3 May 2011, No. 2650.

[28] See Art. 253, §§ 1-quater, 1-quinquies and 3, PCC.

competitive dialogue in its Public Contracts Code.[29] However, the application of this procedure for contracts covered by Directive 2004/18 was postponed until the entry into force of the government regulation enforcing the code of 8 June 2011,[30] meaning that the possibility for using the procedure in Italy had only just come into force at the time of completing this chapter. This decision to postpone the implementation of the procedure arose out of the fact that competitive dialogue is an entirely new procedure whose implementation in Italy raised concerns over the risks of its abuse by contracting authorities – given the wide discretion it entails by the standards of Italy – and because of the consequent high risk of litigation. Thus, after implementing it, Italy suspended its application. This was done contrary to the opinion of the supreme administrative court (Consiglio di Stato), according to which the competitive dialogue is a self-executing provision of Directive 2004/18 whose enforcement in Italy does not need further regulation to be issued.[31] The provisions concerning competitive dialogue set out in the government regulation (DPR No. 207/2010) specify the suitability requirements, the essential content of the contract notice and the minimum requirements of the bid (feasibility study and plans), and provide that contracting authorities acquire the property of the preliminary plan by paying any prizes or awards to the winner.[32]

Besides the introduction of competitive dialogue for contracts covered by the Directive, since 2006, when the PCC implemented the new public procurement Directives, a kind of competitive dialogue procedure – an informal award procedure that was labelled as 'competitive dialogue' in national law – has been applied in Italy as an instrument to award public contracts that do not fall within the scope of the Directive or its full rules, such as concessions and other forms of privately financed arrangements and public–private partnerships (see below).[33] As Chapter 1 explained, these arrangements fall within the scope of EU principles only rather than the EU Directives on public contracts and, in default of detailed rules concerning the relevant awarding procedures, public authorities enjoy a wide discretion in shaping the procedure, including

[29] Art. 58 PCC. For the most recent overview on the topic, see S. Vinti, 'L'evidenza pubblica', in C. Franchini (ed.), *I contratti con la pubblica amministrazione*, vol. I (Turin: Utet, 2007), pp. 329–36; R. Invernizzi, 'Il dialogo competitivo e il dialogo tecnico', in M. A. Sandulli, R. De Nictolis and R. Garofoli (eds.), *Trattato sui contratti pubblici*, vol. III (Milan: Giuffrè, 2008), pp. 1905–40.

[30] Art. 253, § 1-quater, PCC. [31] Cons. Stato, ad. gen., 6 June 2007, No. 1750, § 5.6.

[32] Arts. 113–114 DPR No. 207/2010. [33] See section 4 below.

the possibility of using a procedure akin to competitive dialogue. Because of the suspension of competitive dialogue for contracts covered by the Directive, and its use only for those contracts outside the Directive, there has been only limited use of the procedure so far. In this respect, Tenders Electronic Daily (TED) reported thirty-four competitive dialogue procedures in Italy between 2006 and 2010: one in 2006; two in 2007; four in 2008; nine in 2009; and eighteen in 2010. Of these, nine were public works contracts, eighteen services contract and seven supply contracts.

By means of competitive dialogue, the procuring entity asks economic operators to co-operate in defining solutions that normally represent the starting point of a procedure and are expressed in the contract notice. In some way it seems that the public administration must justify its inability to make the typical discretionary choice between several lawful and valid solutions. It is unable to define the technical, legal or financial means best suited to satisfying its needs, to identify the alternative solutions and to be sure to choose the best one to serve the public interest. Italian law requires a specific statement of justification to be given concerning the complexity of the contract in order to justify the adoption of competitive dialogue.[34] The strong emphasis on 'complexity' suggests that such a statement of justification will comply with Italian law only if the prior conclusion of a previous and separate procurement of services – such as a completion of a study or an ideas contest[35] – would be unproductive,[36] since it is objectively impossible for the procuring entity even to define its needs and the specifications of a project. The Italian provisions specify this inability with some examples of complexity linked to historic-artistic, architectural and environmental aspects.[37]

[34] Art. 58, § 3, PCC.

[35] Whose subject-matter defines the needs and objectives to be finalised in a project and its execution: Art. 108 PCC.

[36] Art. 58, § 2, PCC provides that a contract can be considered 'particularly complex' when the contracting authority 'does not have, due to objective factors not depending on it, studies on the identification and quantification of their own needs or the detection of instrumental means to the satisfaction of those needs, functional, technical, managerial and financial-economic analysis and the same state of fact and of law of any intervention in its historical and possible components of art, architecture, landscape, and the components of sustainability environmental, socio-economic, administrative and technical matters'. Thus it seems to recall the European Commission's *Explanatory Note – Competitive Dialogue – Classic Directive* (2005), available at http://simap.eu.int.

[37] Art. 58, § 2, PCC: see section 4 below.

The competitive dialogue has been implemented in Italian law in compliance with the general approach to implementation of Directive 2004/18 in Italy. Thus it has been implemented largely by literal translation of the EU provisions, with a few details added, mainly to reduce its potential coverage (as explained in section 4 below). Further provisions in the PCC (Article 58) and the related regulation (Articles 113–114) also add some further provisions to the EU rules. They define the concept of legal or financial complexity of the subject-matter of the contract, set out the mandatory content of the descriptive document and the invitation to tender, provide for a feasibility study to be attached to every offer in the first phase of dialogue, and state that the final offer must contain the preliminary plan, while the successful bidder will draft the final and executive plans and execute the work.

Italy does not have a tradition of 'soft law' instruments. As far as the competitive dialogue procedure is concerned, there are no government guidelines. However, the Authority for the Control over Public Contracts in its annual report to the Parliament of 2007 provided a comparative overview on its implementation of competitive dialogue across EU Member States and some information about its rationale and correct use, frequently referring to the guidance from the Office of Government Commerce (OGC) in the UK.[38]

Because of the suspension of the application of competitive dialogue in Italy until June 2011 there is no relevant case law so far. Nevertheless, many judicial decisions concerning traditional issues in carrying out restricted and negotiated procedures seem relevant to highlight and analyse the main practical difficulties that competitive dialogue will probably bring about in Italy.

4. Scope of the competitive dialogue procedure in law and practice

Competitive dialogue is regarded by law and by scholars in Italy as an exceptional procedure for particularly complex contracts. According to the PCC, the public administration must clearly justify its inability to define the technical means needed to identify the most suitable solutions to meet its initial requirements, and to determine which of several

[38] Italian Authority for the Supervision of Public Contracts for Works, Services and Supplies, Annual Report 2007 (9 July 2008), § 8.1; on the OGC guidance, see generally Ch. 3 above.

possible solutions would best satisfy the public interest: thus 'the provision whereby the contracting authority decides to use the competitive dialogue must expressly point out the specific reasons' suitable for justifying its application,[39] sometimes even requiring the approval of the Superior Council of public works or of the Supreme Council of cultural heritage (see below).

In order to prevent abuse of the competitive dialogue procedure, the Italian national implementation also further specifies the type of reasons that must underlie the inability to identify the best solution, and also provides that they must not be attributable to the contracting authority itself and must be expressly stated in advance.

In this respect, along with stating expressly in the legislation the two situations defined by EU law for the existence of a particularly complex contract (contracting authorities are 'not objectively able to define the technical means capable of satisfying their needs or objectives' or are 'not objectively able to specify the legal and/or financial make-up of a project'), Italian law specifies that 'the contract may be regarded as particularly complex when the contracting authority, due to objective factors not attributable to it, has no data available':

(i) 'on the identification and quantification of its needs'; or
(ii) 'on the identification of the instrumental means capable of satisfying its needs', thus including a lack of knowledge: (a) of the 'functional, technical, managerial and economic-financial characteristics' of these means, (b) of 'the analysis of the actual condition and legal status of each intervention, regarding how its historical, artistic, architectural, or landscape aspects' are affected; and (c) of the 'sustainability, socio-economic, administrative and technical elements' of the project.[40]

The absence of case law on competitive dialogue in Italy means that there is no settled interpretation on whether the assessment of the impossibility of identifying the instrumental means capable of satisfying the contracting authority's needs requires conditions (a), (b) and (c) alternatively or cumulatively, and whether a lack of data concerning only one of the several aspects listed in the above-mentioned provision would be enough to prove this impossibility. We can expect a strict interpretation, but such uncertainty could deter contracting authorities from using competitive dialogue.

[39] Art. 58, § 3, PCC. [40] Art. 58, § 2, PCC.

Moreover, Italian law sets out further specific limitations on the use of competitive dialogue. One is a requirement for a prior advisory opinion of the Superior Council of public works or of the Superior Council for cultural heritage for contracts pertaining to the relevant field. Both must be given by the relevant council within thirty days after the request by the contracting authority, although after this deadline the contracting authority has the right to proceed anyway.

A further limitation, which is the most important, is that the most complex works procurements such as strategic infrastructure works and production plants[41] are excluded from the application of competitive dialogue. As we saw in sections 3 and 4 of Chapter 1, competitive dialogue was envisaged for use by the EU specifically for projects of this kind, so it is surprising that in Italy its scope has been narrowed, and is not available in cases falling within its core rationale of dealing with complex technical subject-matter.

Competitive dialogue is a formal award procedure regulated by Article 58 of the PCC and Articles 113–114 of DPR No. 207/2010 that sometimes – as we have seen and will see in the next sections – applies in situations that are outside the Directive's rules. It is applicable to:

(i) Public works, supply, service contracts and works concessions as defined by Directive 2004/18 (Article 54 of the PCC).
(ii) Public works, supply, service contracts and works concessions in the utilities sector. In this respect, Article 220 of the PCC expressly lists competitive dialogue among the tendering procedures available in the utilities sectors that are regulated by Directive 2004/17.[42]
(iii) Public contracts the value of which is below the threshold: in this respect Article 121 of the PCC extends the rule of the abovementioned Article 54 to public contracts below the threshold of the EU Directives. Competitive dialogue has been used in Italy in practice for such below-threshold contracts. However, it must be pointed out that technical, legal or financial complexity for contracts below the thresholds seems hard to prove, since Italian rules concerning below-threshold contracts are much simpler (no publication in the OJEU is required) and quicker (shorter time limits).[43]

[41] Arts. 161–205 PCC.
[42] G. Urbano and M. Giustiniani, 'Il dialogo competitivo', in M. Clarich (ed.), *Commentario al codice dei contratti pubblici* (Turin: Giappichelli, 2010), p. 406.
[43] Arts. 124–125 PCC.

In the case of other public contracts falling outside the scope of the Directives, contracting authorities are not bound to follow the formal award procedures defined by Article 58 of the PCC and Articles 113–114 of DPR No. 207/2010. However, authorities can structure the award procedures on the basis of such formal models if they choose to do so, thus ensuring compliance with EU principles under the TFEU that apply to these contracts. This is because service concessions, non-priority services (under Annex IIB of the Directive and Article 20 of the PCC) and other public contracts falling outside the scope of the Directives (for example, some private financing arrangements expressly defined by Italian law[44] because of their complex financial make-up that, mainly as regards public works, is put forward in order to pursue the maximum investment of private capital)[45] are only subject to these Treaty principles (Article 27 of the PCC) and not to detailed rules. The lack of detailed rules concerning these arrangements allows public authorities significant discretion in shaping the most appropriate award procedure, thus allowing the use of a kind of competitive dialogue procedure beyond any express legal provision.

The Italian law defines the special circumstances which allow for use of the special rules of competitive dialogue but does not tie its use to any particular form of public contract: thus it provides a legal tool suitable for any kind of public contract, including any PPP arrangement, such as concessions.[46] It has been expressly clarified by the Italian legislator,

[44] Arts. 152 *et seq.* PCC.

[45] According to European Commission, *Green Paper on Public–Private Partnerships and Community Law on Public Contracts and Concessions*, COM (2004) 327 final, section 20; and European Commission, *Mobilising Private and Public Investment for Recovery and Long Term Structural Change: Developing Public Private Partnerships*, COM (2009) 615 final, section 1, the common characteristic of any form of PPP – regardless of the establishment of a new subject (institutional PPP, involving co-operation between the public and the private sector within a distinct entity) or not (contractual PPP, in which the partnership between the public and the private sector is based solely on contractual links) – is to 'relieve the immediate pressure on public finances by providing an additional source of capital'.

[46] See C. Contessa and N. De Salvo, 'La procedura di dialogo competitivo fra partenariato pubblico/privato e tutela della concorrenza', *Urb. e appalti* (2006), p. 508; G. Pasquini, 'Il project financing e la discrezionalità', *Giornale dir. amm.* (2006), p. 1115; F. Gaspari, 'Il dialogo competitivo come nuovo strumento negoziale e la sua (asserita) compatibilità con la finanza di progetto', *Giust. amm.* (2007), p. 3; B. Raganelli, 'Il dialogo competitivo dalla direttiva 2004/18/CE al codice dei contratti: verso una maggiore flessibilità dei rapporti tra pubblico e privato', *Riv. it. Dir. Pub. Com.* (2009), p. 162.

amending the PCC, that the competitive dialogue procedure can be used for the award of a concession.[47]

We can argue that the core characteristic or even the *raison d'être* of competitive dialogue is precisely the impossibility to foretell the outcomes. Once competitive dialogue starts even on the basis of a preliminary plan, its outcomes cannot be predicted; hence the dialogue might in some cases lead the contracting authority to enter a public procurement, to issue a concession or to establish an institutional PPP without this being known in advance. Within these procedures, whenever the complexity of the subject-matter from a technical, legal or financial point of view justifies use of competitive dialogue, a competitive dialogue can be run, if necessary based on the preliminary, financial and economic plans to be specified or amended.[48]

On this view, the explicit legal exclusion of the competitive dialogue procedure for infrastructure works and production or industrial plants in Italy seems likely to turn out to be counterproductive. Strictly speaking, in this case the only available award procedure in Italy is a restricted procedure (based on a preliminary plan drafted by the contracting authority itself) to identify a general contractor, departing from the ordinary award procedures for public works procurement. This provides for a general contractor to be entrusted with the global task of performing, by whatever means, the public works; and this contractor will decide whether and how to provide the work planning, financial make-up and execution itself or through sub-contractors, and will also issue expropriation procedures if necessary. The general contractor also enjoys the power to define whether or not the consideration for the works to be carried out consists either solely in the right to exploit the work or in this right together with payment.[49]

The selection of a general contractor puts together many different services (planning, financing and execution of works) and therefore considerably reduces competition among economic operators potentially interested in carrying out only single part(s) of the whole

[47] Art. 58, § 15, PCC as amended by Legislative Decree No. 152/2008.

[48] The Italian Authority for Public Contracts in its annual report to the Parliament of 2008 states that the rules concerning the competitive dialogue are applicable, notwithstanding the suspension of its application until the entry into force of the government's secondary regulations (Art. 253, § 1-quater, PCC), in those cases in which the preliminary project needs to be either specified or modified; Urbano and Giustiniani, n. 42 above, pp. 403–6.

[49] Art. 176 PCC; P. Chirulli, 'L'affidamento a contraente generale', in C. Franchini (ed.), *I contratti con la pubblica amministrazione*, vol. II (Turin: Utet, 2007), pp. 953–81.

subject-matter. The general contractor procedure, like the competitive dialogue procedure, was specifically laid down to deal with complex contracts for which the involvement of private capital may be extremely useful. However, while the choice of the general contractor excludes competition in other potentially distinct market segments of work planning, financing and executing – since the general contractor is not generally compelled to apply EU Directives on public procurement – competitive dialogue may involve a fair and more transparent competition on every aspect of the arrangement, which could result in a more direct and efficient control of the contracting authority over the contractors' activities.

In practice, competitive dialogue has been used in Italy so far mainly for contracts outside the scope of the Directives – for example, in the public utilities sector to establish mixed capital companies entrusted with the task of providing public services to citizens. As we saw above, there were thirty-four procedures between 2006 and 2010, accounted for by the possibility for using competitive dialogue outside the scope of the Directives themselves (given that its use has been postponed for contracts covered by the Directives). The fact that the Italian legislator has not so far favoured competitive dialogue has been supported by the availability of alternative procedures, mainly for public works contracts, such as the design contest and the ideas contest discussed in section 2 above, the use of which is not limited to the specific circumstances that allow competitive dialogue. These alternatives were relied on to justify postponing the entry into force of the new procedure. However, their use might potentially be reduced by the new opportunities offered by competitive dialogue now that competitive dialogue has been brought into force more generally.

Two main differences distinguish these traditional tools from competitive dialogue. First, both the design contest and the ideas contest are affected by the traditional rigidity of ordinary procedures. They are still part of a strict tendering model in sharp contrast with the negotiation models. There is no room for manoeuvre for a flexible negotiation (dialogue) over the different possible solutions. The contracting authority is bound to select the best solution proposed as assessed through applying the award criteria only, unless the specific cases and circumstances which allow for a negotiated procedure are met.[50]

[50] Art. 56, §§ 2–3, PCC allows for negotiation after the time limit for bid submission has expired.

Secondly, competitive dialogue seems to offer relevant time and transaction costs savings in that its two-phase structure allows for a single award procedure for design and execution of public work. The subject-matter of the competitive dialogue is the 'needs and requirements' expressed by the contracting authority to be specified and implemented by the market operators during the dialogue. The competitive dialogue procedure may then end with the award of a public contract which entrusts the contractor with the tasks of both planning *and* executing works or planning *and* providing services. By way of contrast, both the design and ideas contests, as service contracts, need a further procedure in order to award a works contract. As the French experience underlines, any fragmentation of the award procedure into two separate procedures, the first for design and the second for execution, does not comply with EU Directives whenever participation in the latter is limited to the successful participants in the previous procedure without a new publication of the contract notice.[51] As the CJEU stated in Case C-299/08, *Commission* v. *France*: 'that difference by itself makes it impossible for [that] procedure . . . to be interpreted as a form of implementation of the competitive dialogue procedure.'[52] In other words, the direct awarding of linked, subsequent procurements is not compliant with EU rules. This key decision of the CJEU on the French procedure of *marchés de definition* outlines the crucial elements that could give rise to distortion of competition in Italy also.

5. Operation of the competitive dialogue procedure

5.1. Introduction

The PCC and its enforcing regulation provide detailed rules on how a contracting authority must conduct the procedure. In Italy, the set of rules for competitive dialogue is specified in the three main different

[51] In *Commission* v. *France*, n. 21 above, the CJEU stated that 'the purpose of the procedure for the award of *marchés de définition* is to award two types of contracts, namely *marchés de définition* [design contest] and *marchés d'exécution* [for works execution], the latter being awarded after being opened to competition limited to the holders of the former alone. Accordingly, economic operators who might be interested in participating in *marchés d'exécution*, but who are not holders of one of the *marchés de définition*, are discriminated against in comparison with those holders, contrary to the principle of equality, which is laid down as a principle for the award of contracts in Article 2 of Directive 2004/18.'

[52] *Commission* v. *France*, n. 21 above, para. 38 of the judgment.

phases as envisaged in Directive 2004/18, namely, the selection phase, the dialogue phase and the final tender phase.[53]

5.2. *The planning stage and drafting of the descriptive document*

In Italy, a key problem can be found in the lack of experience in carrying out the important planning and preparation activities that are often considered to be needed to make competitive dialogue successful (as discussed, for example, in Chapter 3 on the UK and Chapter 8 on Spain).[54] Another critical element to be considered is the correct and complete definition of the content of the descriptive document. The latter could have a scope that is even more broad and imprecise than the subject-matter of the Italian ideas contest (*concorso di idee*), discussed earlier, which might not give rise to satisfactory end results. Moreover, as the experience of the UK indicates, competitive dialogue requires skilled and experienced officials at all stages of the procedure and a significant input in terms of staffing, advice and support.[55]

As elaborated in section 5.5 below, the number of participants in the dialogue can be reduced to below the number of those satisfying the minimum qualification requirements by means of applying the qualitative selection criteria, but this must be planned in advance since the contract documents must in this case provide for a maximum number of participants to be invited to the dialogue.[56]

The original implementation of competitive dialogue in Italy contained a provision that allowed contracting authorities to specify in more detail at the final tender stage the award criteria as stated in the contract notice, in order to adapt them to the specificities of the solution or solutions chosen during the dialogue and admitted to the final stage. However, this has been repealed, following an infringement procedure against Italy.[57] The possibility of later specification of the award criteria was considered in Italy as not being compliant with the CJEU case law

[53] R. Dipace, 'Il dialogo competitivo', in C. Franchini (ed.), *I contratti di appalto pubblico* (Turin: Utet, 2010), pp. 622–8.

[54] See respectively Ch. 3, section 5.2, and Ch. 8, section 5.2.

[55] OGC/Treasury, *Competitive Dialogue in 2008: Joint Guidance on Using the Procedure*, § 1.14: see Ch. 3 above.

[56] Art. 55, § 6, PCC; as for the contract notice, see Art. 64, § 1, and Art. 58, § 5, PCC: see section 5.5 below.

[57] Art. 58, § 13, PCC, repealed by Law No. 152 of 11 September 2008, following the decision of EU Commission C (2008) 0108 of 31 January 2008 pursuant to infringement procedure No. 2007/2309 against Italy.

requiring the award criteria to be defined in such a way as to allow any participants to be aware of any relevant elements while drafting the offer, without later specifying 'elements which, if they had been known at the time the tenders were prepared, could have affected that preparation'.[58] Thus according to Italian law, the descriptive documents expressing the needs of the contracting authority or the contract notice must define both the suitability requirements of tenderers and the awarding criteria for both evaluating the solutions proposed during the dialogue phase *and* the final tenders stage,[59] without adding to these or developing them in any more detail prior to the final tender phase. Therefore, the PCC compels contracting authorities to use the qualitative selection criteria and the award criteria defined in the contract notice. The position under the Directive itself as regards the possibility of developing the award criteria during the procedure was considered in section 5.6.5 of Chapter 1.

The contract notice could, however, define in advance *different* criteria to be applied in each stage of the procedure (for example, criteria regarding technical merit in the first stage of the dialogue and criteria concerning aesthetic, functional characteristics and price in the second stage). Again, the position under the Directive itself in this respect was considered in section 5.6.5 of Chapter 1.

5.3. *Confidentiality of information and solutions*

As stated in the Directive, under Italian law contracting authorities 'may not reveal to the other participants solutions proposed or other confidential information communicated by a candidate participating in the dialogue without his/her agreement'.[60] Italian law does not provide any further guidance on how to protect confidential information disclosed by participants during the dialogue, leaving it to contracting authorities' discretion.

As for the Italian experience, the issues relating to confidentiality of information have been assessed by academics and practitioners only in a theoretical way, because of the lack of practical enforcement or case law.[61]

[58] See, in particular, Case C-532/06, *Emm. G. Lianakis and others* v. *Dimos Alexandroupolis and others* [2008] ECR I-251, para. 43.

[59] Art. 58, § 5, PCC; and Art. 113, § 1, DPR No. 207/2010.

[60] Art. 58, § 8, PCC, implementing the exact wording of Art. 29(3) of Directive 2004/18.

[61] S. Vinti, 'Il dialogo competitivo: troppo rigido nella fase creativa, poco regolato in quella comparativa' (2009), available at www.LexItalia.it; Raganelli, n. 46 above, pp. 164 *et seq.*

5.4. *Advertising requirements*

In Italy, the contract notice for competitive dialogue must be published in the OJEU, as required by the Directive, and is also subject to further national requirements on publication, which also apply to other award procedures. In this respect, the notice must be published in the national official journal (special series for public contracts notice) and on the websites of both the Authority for the Control over Public Contracts and the relevant Ministry. A summary of the contract notice must also be published in at least two high-circulation national newspapers and in two of the most circulated local newspapers.[62] Italian law lists the fixed content of the contract notice or the descriptive document: the needs or objectives of the contracting authority as well as the requirements for admission to the competitive dialogue, the tender evaluation criteria and the deadline for submission of the applications for participation in the procedure.[63]

5.5. *The selection phase*

The rules governing the selection phase under Directive 2004/18 were discussed in section 5.5 of Chapter 1. As regards the number of participants to be invited to the dialogue, Italian law adopts a stricter approach than required by Directive 2004/18. As we have seen in Chapter 1, this generally requires a minimum of three economic operators to be invited. In Italy, it is provided that the maximum number of participants may be limited if required for 'justified reasons of good administration'[64] (that is, to prevent overcrowding in the negotiations, which can hinder their flexibility and prolong the procedure excessively) – but, even so, the number invited cannot be less than six, insofar as there is a sufficient number to satisfy the selection requirements.[65]

As regards the requirements for selection of those to be invited, the rules on the permitted selection criteria and the disclosure of those criteria are the same as those in the Directive, the provisions of which are simply repeated in the Italian legislation.[66]

[62] Art. 66, § 7, PCC. [63] As expressly stated in Art. 58, § 5, PCC.

[64] Art. 62, § 1, PCC allows for a maximum number of economic operators to be invited only for contracts whose subject-matter is particularly complex (competitive dialogue and works contracts of a value above €40 million) as well as for the negotiated procedure with prior publication of a contract notice.

[65] Art. 62, § 2, PCC.

[66] Art. 62, § 1, PCC implementing Art. 44(3) and (4) of Directive 2004/18; see also section 5.2 above.

As required under the Directive itself, minimum levels of suitability requirements (economic and financial standing and technical or professional capacity) specified in the contract notice must be related to and proportionate to the subject-matter of the contract.[67] The relevant provisions aim to avoid the risk of unreasonably high requirements that may reduce participation and competition. The reasonableness of such qualitative selection requirements could prove to be difficult to assess, however, as the contract value and its precise subject-matter are indefinite and hence hard to define in advance.

It is also provided in the Italian legislation – in a provision that is additional to the rules in the Directive – that, if a maximum number of economic operators to be invited has been defined (according to Article 44(3) of Directive 2004/18), this number must be proportionate to the structure of the relevant supply market (that is, considering the number of economic operators who satisfy the suitability requirements), in order to ensure genuine competition.[68]

Selection of participants using qualitative selection criteria is relatively new in Italy. Economic and financial standing and technical or professional capacity have been used in the past as selection criteria suitable for reducing the number of economic operators to be invited in a tendering stage only in the context of public works, before the relevant provisions were repealed in 1995, although reintroduced in 1999.[69] The qualitative selection criteria to be applied in order to reduce the number of participants to be invited in the dialogue phase are expressly listed in Article 263 and Annex L to DPR No. 207/2010 (applicable to the restricted procedure as well as competitive dialogue, in compliance with Article 44(3) of Directive 2004/18). The relevant provisions state that the score to be assigned depends only on certain specified elements and only if they exceed the minimum selection requirements set out in the contract notice. These elements are the overall turnover of the previous financial year (at least between two and four times the contract

[67] Art. 2, § 1, Art. 73, § 3, and Art. 74, § 5, PCC.

[68] See Art. 62 and the general principle stated in Art. 57, § 6, PCC, though referring to the negotiated procedure.

[69] As for works contracts, such a provision – first included in Art. 27 of Law No. 406/1991 and then in Art. 23 of Law No. 109/1994 – was repealed by Law No. 216/1995. See Vinti, n. 29 above, pp. 332–6.

value), the list of similar works or services previously carried out, and the list of the technicians employed.[70]

5.6. *The dialogue phase*

When compared with the traditional tendering model, the flexibility of competitive dialogue is basically due to the power of the contracting authority to discuss the proposals submitted by economic operators and to ask for further amendments. This exception to the basic rule of regular tendering that prohibits amendment of offers after the time limit for their submission raises some issues as far as the principles of non-discrimination and equal treatment are concerned.

Under Italian law, the contract notice must indicate whether there is a limit to the solutions that will be discussed during the dialogue stage.[71] If this is the case, the notice must define the objective and non-discriminatory award criteria to be applied in order to select the projects admitted to the dialogue phase.[72] The Italian legislation, following the Directive,[73] requires that the contract notice or the descriptive document shall specify the award criteria chosen to determine the most economically advantageous tender along with their relative weighting or, at least, whenever the weighting is not possible for justifiable reasons, their descending order of importance. It seems inherent in competitive dialogue that these award criteria may need to be of wide application across a range of very different bids, so that they are suitable to identify the final best proposal or proposals. To that aim, the award criteria arguably need to leave a wide discretion to the awarding authority. Nonetheless, as we have seen at section 5.2 above, such award criteria can no longer be amended, modified or further specified during the dialogue as was previously envisaged in the Italian legislation, which, as we saw, has been

[70] Art. 265 of and Annex L to DPR No. 207/2010 contain the same rules as Art. 67 of and Annex F to the repealed DPR No. 554/1999, according to which half of the maximum number of participants must be selected by applying the qualitative selection criteria and the remaining half chosen by means of a public lot.

[71] Art. 58, § 9, PCC.

[72] Art. 58, § 9, PCC uses the same wording as Art. 29(4) of Directive 2004/18, which states that 'contracting authorities may provide for the procedure to take place in successive stages in order to reduce the number of solutions to be discussed during the dialogue stage by applying the award criteria in the contract notice or the descriptive document'.

[73] Art. 83 PCC implementing Art. 53 of Directive 2004/18; in this respect, Cons. Stato, adv. sect. on legislative draft, 17 September 2007, No. 3262, warns of the problems of guaranteeing genuine competition.

amended in this respect in order to comply with the European Commission's assessment during an infringement procedure against Italy.[74]

The Italian legislation allows the same freedom that is allowed by the Directive regarding the structure of the dialogue and the manner of conducting it. This means, *inter alia*, that contracting authorities may choose between two available alternatives: to run the dialogue individually with each candidate or to discuss the proposals jointly with all of them at the same time. Under the first option, the problem of how to ensure that information given is the same, or how to assure that genuine competition and non-discriminatory treatment – since the discussion will be held on the basis of different solutions – arises.[75]

The choice in this respect may depend on the subject-matter of the contract and on the expected content of the tenders. A joint dialogue would allow the public administration to assess in-depth, and compare, the quality and economic aspects of the proposals, considering the operators' experience and the added value that the dialogue would entail. The lack of mutual knowledge of other competitors' tenders[76] is a weakness of traditional tendering models in cases of complex contracts, since it increases transaction costs due to information asymmetries. Competitive dialogue was set up as a response to these failures, since it is capable of drawing public procurement into a situation of perfect information considered by microeconomics as being the ideal model of perfect competition.[77] However, the requirement of a perfect information scenario must be balanced against the need to comply with the rules on protection of confidential information and technical or trade secrets, and the risk of unauthorised 'cherry-picking' (i.e. the use of the ideas

[74] See section 5.2 above. [75] Vinti, n. 61 above.

[76] As for the ordinary tendering procedure (open or restricted procedure), the basic rule is not to disclose any of the content of tenders until the contract is awarded, to avoid hindering fair competition. Art. 13, § 2, PCC provides a time limit to information disclosure that goes far beyond Art. 6 of Directive 2004/18 concerning only the content of information and according to which 'the contracting authority shall not disclose information forwarded to it by economic operators which they have designated as confidential; such information includes, in particular, technical or trade secrets and the confidential aspects of tenders'.

[77] Assuming that all agents (contracting authority as well as bidders) are rational and have perfect information, they will choose the best solutions, and public contracting will reward those who propose the best solutions with higher rewards. Perfect information allows a contracting authority to make the best decision as long as it means in practice that the buyer knows all things, about all products, at all times.

and solutions of one of the participants by another one without that other's consent).

It can be noted that, in Italy, the breach of the equal treatment principle during a public contract procedure due to unfair leaking of information or selective communication has sometimes led to criminal convictions.[78]

As we have seen in section 5.6.3 of Chapter 1, under the provisions of the Directive the dialogue phase can be structured in successive stages in order to reduce the number of solutions to be discussed by applying the award criteria where this is provided for in advance. The same flexibility on this issue is found in the Italian legislation on competitive dialogue.[79] Therefore, during the dialogue in Italy there could be more than one application of the award criteria as defined in the contract notice: first, in order to reduce the number of solutions to be discussed during the dialogue stage, secondly, for the choice of the best solution among the final tenders (see section 5.7 below).

As we have seen in Chapter 1,[80] there are various possible approaches under the Directive as regards the development of the basis for the final tender, and these are all possible also under the flexible approach of the Italian legislation. Thus one possibility is that at the end of the dialogue phase the contracting authority will identify the best solution amongst those proposed, which represents a solution deemed suitable and effective to serve the public interest; and on the basis of this solution it will open the competition asking for the final and complete tender, thus receiving from all tenderers offers based on another tenderer's project. This approach has been labelled by one commentator in Italy as the promoter model.[81] The dialogue could eventually also entail the choice for the basis of the final tender stage of a mixed solution that includes the best elements of quality and the most innovative solutions of the various different tenders. This has been referred to in Italy as the patchwork solution.[82] There is also a third model, which has been referred to in Italy as the Chinese walls model:[83] under this approach

[78] See for collusive tendering: Cass., sect. VI, 19 January 2000, *Virgili*; and Cass., sect. VI, 28 April 1999, *Bruno*. For bribery in public contracting, see Cass., sect. VI, 12 June 1997, *Albini*; and Cass., sect. VI, 25 March 1994.

[79] Art. 58, § 8, PCC implementing Art. 29(4) of Directive 2004/18.

[80] See Ch. 1, section 5.6.3.

[81] M. Ricchi, 'Negoauction, discrezionalità e dialogo competitivo' (2007), available at www.giustizia-amministrativa.it.

[82] Ricchi, n. 81 above. [83] Ricchi, n. 81 above.

the dialogue is carried out separately to best protect confidential information and technical or trade secrets and different solutions are discussed waiving any effective comparison among them (for example, a tunnel or bridge in order to solve a transportation bottleneck; or totally different locations of solutions in a land development plan).[84] This third model appears to be the one most commonly used in practice in Italy.

It can be noted that the Italian law expressly provides for any 'specifications, clarifications, improvements or additions' by any participants during the dialogue (Article 58, § 14, PCC). This is because the negotiation that this phase entails requires an exchange of information among the parties involved to the maximum possible extent (as also applies in the negotiated procedure: Article 56, §§ 2–3, and Article 57, § 6, PCC), provided that the negotiation complies with the framework of the procedure for conducting the dialogue set out by the contracting authority in the contract documents.

Italian law provides that any solution submitted during the dialogue phase by the participants shall include its relevant feasibility study and provisional costs report.[85] These documents are obviously subject to changes and amendments during the dialogue phase. The aim of such provisions is to ensure the parties enter the final tender stage with a sufficiently precise and accurate solution to be put to tender.

5.7. *Final tender stage*

As we have seen in section 5.6.4 of Chapter 1, it is stated in the Directive, and is also repeated in the Italian legislation,[86] that the contracting authority closes the dialogue when it can identify the solution or solutions which are best suited to satisfying its needs, if necessary after comparing the solutions proposed by applying the award criteria defined in advance. It then calls for final tenders, which must contain all the elements required and necessary for the performance of the project.[87] The Italian legislation also repeats the provision stated in the Directive (as discussed in section 5.7.4 of Chapter 1) that the final tenders may be clarified, specified and fine-tuned by participants if the contracting authority so requests, provided that this does not involve changes to

[84] OGC, *UK Procurement Policy Note – Preliminary Guidance on the Application of the Public Procurement Rules to Development Agreements* (19 October 2009).

[85] Art. 113, § 2, DPR No. 207/2010.

[86] Art. 58, § 10, PCC.

[87] See Ch. 1, section 5.7.1; Art. 58, § 12, PCC.

the basic features of the tender or the call for tenders, insofar as such variations are likely to distort competition or have a discriminatory effect.[88]

The Italian legislation also contains a specific provision, not found in the Directive, stating that the final offer shall include the preliminary plan and the draft of the contract documents for contract performance.[89] The dialogue's purpose is the drafting of a preliminary plan and the winner must draft the final and executive plans in addition to defining all elements required and necessary for the performance of the work or service. Italian legislation clearly provides that the final offer will contain a preliminary plan. The winner can be asked to develop his project (into final and executive plans) and execute it, if so provided in the contract notice.[90] This will be done after the contract is concluded.

This approach differs from UK experience (as reported in Chapter 3), since, in Italy, such a possibility does not apply to the negotiated procedure,[91] thus leaving room for completing the project later only in case of competitive dialogue. However, it seems compliant with EU law[92] since the further activity (detailing the bid into final and executive plans) defined by the contract signed by the winner does not seem to risk modifying substantial aspects of the tender (that still include 'the preliminary plan and the draft of the contract documents for contract performance')[93] or distorting competition or resulting in discrimination.

5.8. *Procedure following the selection of the preferred bidder*

Once the best offer has been selected, the PCC provides for a provisional award that is subject to a positive assessment of the suitability requirements (such as the final verification of a bidder's self-certifications of his own suitability requirements) and to completion of documentation, and may be subject to approval by a controlling authority. Once these steps are completed, the provisional award to the preferred bidder is then

88 Art. 58, § 14, PCC. 89 Art. 113, § 4, DPR No. 207/2010.

90 Art. 113, § 5, DPR No. 207/2010.

91 Where bids can be modified and improved only if the procedure takes place in successive stages (Art. 56, § 4, PCC implementing Art. 30(4) of Directive 2004/18): Cons. Stato, VI, 15 June 2011, No. 3642.

92 Art. 29(6) of Directive 2004/18 requires the final tender to 'contain all the elements required and necessary for the performance of the project'.

93 Art. 113, § 4, DPR No. 207/2010.

confirmed as the final award, prior to concluding the contract. This is a general approach applicable to every award procedure, not only to competitive dialogue.[94]

On the other hand, the rule allowing the preferred bidder 'to clarify aspects of the tender or confirm commitments contained in the tender', as stated in Article 29(7) of Directive 2004/18, applies only to competitive dialogue and seems to raise many doubts concerning the future application of competitive dialogue in Italy. The clarification follows a specific request of the contracting authority and seems necessary whenever the preferred bid substantially differs from the initial offer because of its evolution during the dialogue. As we have seen, Italian law allows for any 'specifications, clarifications, improvements or additions' by any participants during the dialogue (Article 58, § 14, PCC), but following Article 29(7) it allows only for clarification of 'aspects of the tender' or confirmation of 'commitments contained in the tender' by the preferred bidder (Article 58, § 16, PCC), stating that in both cases they must 'not have the effect of modifying substantial aspects of the tender or of the call for tender and must not risk distorting competition or causing discrimination' (Article 58, §§ 14 and 16, PCC).

The meaning of Article 29(7) of the Directive was discussed in section 5.8 of Chapter 1. The simple repetition in Italy of the EU Directive's wording on this issue, together with the prohibition of such clarifications in every other procedure but competitive dialogue, do not indicate any well-established principles for defining the boundaries of what may be done at the preferred bidder stage. Comparing the slightly different expressions used in the Italian law with reference respectively to participants in the dialogue and preferred bidder, the latter seems stricter. The preferred bidder can clarify only 'aspects of the tender' or confirm 'commitments contained in the tender',[95] while any other 'specifications, clarifications, improvements or additions' – allowed in the dialogue phase – are prohibited.

The amendments to the preferred bid also raise the issue of challenge where there is a breach of Article 29(7), since it seems difficult

[94] Arts. 11–12 PCC.

[95] The European Commission in its Explanatory Note on competitive dialogue, n. 36 above, § 3.3, clearly emphasises that 'this does not entail any negotiations solely with this economic operator – amendments aimed at authorising such negotiations were proposed and rejected by the Community legislative process'.

for the interested parties to access the relevant information. Consequently, some uncertainty over the time limit for legal proceedings may also be raised.

It is submitted that further drafting of the final and executive plans[96] by the winning bidder after conclusion of the agreement as was discussed above does not amount to a clarification or confirmation of the tender in the sense envisaged by Article 29(7) but is a mere fulfilment of the obligation undertaken by subscribing to the contract.

5.9. *The standstill period and the possibility for legal challenge*

As explained in section 5.9 of Chapter 1, EU law has recently acknowledged and now provided for in legislation (in Directive 2007/66) a requirement for a standstill period between notification of the award decision and conclusion of the contract.

A general standstill provision was in fact provided for in the former Italian regulatory system, but the consequences of its derogations were not defined. Furthermore, the standstill period could be waived whenever the public administration invoked reasons of urgency.[97] Italian law implementing the EU standstill requirement laid down expressly in Directive 2007/66 does not provide for any special provision on the standstill period for the competitive dialogue procedure. The standstill period in Italy is thirty-five days, commencing with the receipt of the last notification of the final award, thus exceeding the minimum of 'at least ten days' provided by Article 2a(2) of Directive 2007/66.[98] Such a long standstill period is due to the explicit willingness of the Italian legislator to define a longer term than applies for filing legal claims before the

[96] Provided for in Art. 113, § 5, DPR No. 207/2010.

[97] Art. 10, § 7, PCC, before the implementation of Directive 2007/66 by means of Legislative Decree of 20 March 2010, No. 53; for further references, see G. M. Racca, 'Derogations from the Standstill Period, Ineffectiveness and Remedies in the New Tendering Procedures: Efficiency Gains vs. Risks of Increasing Litigation', in S. Treumer and F. Lichère (eds.), *Enforcement of the EU Public Procurement Rules* (Copenhagen: DJØF, 2011), pp. 95–102.

[98] Art. 11, §§ 10 *et seq.*, PCC. Art. 11, § 9, PCC states that the standstill period runs from the moment when the final (for example, after the assessment of bidders' documents on suitability requirements or the approval of controlling authority) contract award decision is sent to the tenderers and candidates concerned.

administrative courts against the contracting authority's decision (thirty days for public contracts).[99] This approach aims to favour the correction or revision of the award procedure: in case of legal claims, the contracting authority can thus decide to revise the procedure or part of it before the contract is signed.

The standstill period of thirty-five days is common to every procedure and must be considered together with settled Italian case law that allows lawsuits only against decisions (such as contract documents, rejection of a bidder, or a final contract award) that are effectively prejudicial to the tenderers or candidates concerned.[100] Participants in competitive dialogue can take proceedings in respect of any decision immediately prejudicial to their interests and the court can suspend the procedure or annul part of it whenever the prejudicial decision is unlawful.

These rules can delay challenges to the conduct of the dialogue phase. These rules contribute to the complexity of the competitive dialogue procedure in Italy, and, together with the risk of legal challenge already highlighted that is entailed by the multiple applications of qualitative selection and award criteria, may deter contracting authorities from using this cumbersome, costly and time-consuming procedure.[101]

5.10. *Payments for costs of participation*

The PCC allows contracting authorities to award 'prizes or incentives to the participants in the dialogue',[102] even if the dialogue terminates without award due to the fact that none of the solutions proposed is capable of satisfying the needs expressed in the contract documents.

Where a competitive dialogue is terminated without an award, however, the participants cannot receive any compensation other than the prizes provided for in the contract documents.[103]

Italian law does not specify or regulate in detail the organisation of these economic incentives for participation, which are left to the

[99] Art. 120 of the Administrative Trial Code, whereas the ordinary courts maintain competence over disputes arising during the performance phase: see section 1 above.

[100] Settled Italian case law rules out any standing requirement for challenging violations during a public contract award procedure carried out in stages (i.e. concessions, PPP): see Cons. Stato, sect. V, 1 October 2010, No. 7277, with comment of M. Mattalia, 'Project Financing, un istituto in continua evoluzione' (2011) 5 *Giurisprudenza Italiana* 1198–1208.

[101] See Racca, n. 97 above, pp. 99–102.

[102] Art. 58, § 17, PCC.

[103] Art. 58, § 11, PCC.

contracting authority's choice. The only mandatory legal provision set out in the regulation enforcing the PCC is that, whenever payments of prizes or awards are provided for, those payments must bring about the transfer of the property of the preliminary plan submitted during the dialogue.[104]

Three main alternatives are thus possible:

(i) The dialogue terminates without award and the contracting authority neither awards any prize nor compensates for the costs of participation.
(ii) The competitive dialogue concludes with an award and only the winner receives the envisaged prize (together, if applicable, with the right of execution of the project).
(iii) The competitive dialogue concludes with an award and both the winner (who may also, if applicable, have the right of the execution of the project) and participants are awarded different prizes.

Although competitive dialogue was suspended until recently – and therefore there is no experience of payments in that context – an established practice on payments to participants has been developed with regard to design contests[105] and ideas contests.[106]

Through the payment of such prizes to the winner and other deserving bidders, the contracting authority acquires the property of the relevant designs or ideas. Prizes and payments for costs of participation are used both to boost disclosure of confidential information and innovative know-how and to purchase them. The introduction of these economic incentives induces potential tenderers to participate.

6. Concluding remarks

As we saw in section 3 of Chapter 1, the origin of competitive dialogue lies in the experience of other EU Member States. One aim of competitive dialogue was to avoid a distorted use of the restricted procedure; and the European Commission was also seeking to encourage use of competitive dialogue rather than the negotiated procedure for major projects.[107] Thus the procedure was established to provide a flexible procedure for complex contracts in which the rigidity of previous

[104] Art. 114 DPR No. 207/2010. [105] Art. 99, §§ 4–5, PCC.
[106] Art. 108, §§ 1 and 4, PCC.
[107] European Commission, Explanatory Note, n. 36 above.

procedures generated inefficient outcomes, and a more structured alternative to the negotiated procedure in order to control negotiations. A key issue was the need to reconcile the interests of EU policy in the development of the best European undertakings with the active interest of Member States in keeping a certain autonomy in public contracting, including for cases of particularly complex contracts.

The competitive dialogue procedure seems an adequate procedure at a national level. However, one possible problem is that the procedure might not easily attract participation and competition at a European level between economic operators of different Member States, even with projects of considerable value. It seems obvious to say that negotiation and dialogue are easier between parties that share the same language and legal system.[108] It is unlikely that undertakings of other Member States will face the cost of a procedure that could turn out to involve significant costs and not to result in obtaining a contract. The complex Italian implementation of competitive dialogue will probably discourage both foreign and national participation, thus undermining the possibility of satisfying the Italian requirement for a minimum of six participants in the dialogue phase.

In Italy, specifically, we have seen that there was no previous experience of an award procedure of this kind. Further, since the application of competitive dialogue, although found in the Italian legislation, was suspended until very recently, it is not possible to say how this procedure will be used in practice for contracts covered by Directive 2004/18. However, we have identified in the analysis above some potential problems with the procedure. One is that the attempt to formalise and structure negotiation in detail runs the risk of not being supported by adequate public management. Another problem is that it entails the risk of numerous claims for damages filed by tenderers that in Italy go through two suitability assessments and two rounds of application of the award criteria. First, there is the evaluation of each bidder's capacity requirements; secondly, there is the reduction of the number of participants by means of applying the qualitative selection criteria to decide who will be invited to participate in the dialogue; thirdly, whenever the dialogue is carried out in successive stages, the award criteria are applied to reduce the number of solutions to be discussed; and, finally, the same award criteria are applied again to choose the best final tender. In Italy,

[108] Italian Authority for the Supervision of Public Contract for Works, Services and Supplies, Advice of 2 April 2008, No. 4.

such a highly complex system entails a real risk of frequent litigation insofar as each step of the procedure may be the object of claims and damages claims by economic operators. Each excluded participant could file a claim, and the court could either suspend the procedure, or annul it and require the contracting authority to pay damages. An Italian contracting authority considering commencing a competitive dialogue procedure needs to balance carefully the possible litigation costs in the event of a claim with the opportunities entailed by the greater flexibility involved in such a procedure. For these reasons, it may be that the procedure will not be used extensively in Italy.

On the other hand, competitive dialogue seems to offer positive possibilities from an Italian perspective, overcoming the lack of transparency entailed by the previous similar procedure of the *appalto concorso.* It introduces and promotes competition at a stage of the award procedure traditionally run in Italy directly by the contracting authorities within their own organisations, namely, the drafting of the contract documents. In the Italian experience, the informational weakness of public officials often entails a failure of public contracting and consequently high transaction costs without an efficient outcome. More specifically, the lack of adequate professional competence sometimes induces the smallest contracting authorities to improperly leave the drafting of the technical specifications of a particularly complex contract to the same economic operators who then participate in the award procedure as tenderers. Despite the issues raised by the implementation of competitive dialogue and the risks of non-objective and discriminatory awards that are presented in Italy, competitive dialogue may provide a structured, formalised and transparent procedure to define the technical specifications for complex public contracts, which will be useful to prevent the distortions that may otherwise occur at this stage and undermine the policy objectives of public contracting.

12

Competitive dialogue in the Netherlands

MARIJKE NAGELKERKE AND JACOBIEN MUNTZ-BEEKHUIS*

1. Introduction: regulation of public procurement in the Netherlands

The Netherlands is a constitutional monarchy that has been governed by codified law since the end of Napoleonic rule in 1814. Statutory law itself pre-empts the Napoleonic laws, which were introduced in the Netherlands during Napoleonic rule from 1795 to 1814. Cursory research shows that public procurement has a long-standing tradition in the Netherlands,[1] whereby relevant statutory civil law[2] on both procurement and the execution of the contract has been supplemented with a general procurement policy. Even in 1815, public procurement by means of an open procedure was declared obligatory by royal decree.[3]

Together with Germany, Luxemburg, Belgium, France and Italy, the Netherlands were one of the Founder Member States of the European Union, and EU Treaty law and secondary legislation under the relevant treaties, including the procurement Directives, have been applicable to Dutch legislation from the outset. The first Dutch law aiming to implement EU procurement provisions[4] simply declared the provisions on public procurement applicable without explicitly transferring the separate provisions into Dutch legislation.

More recently, Public Sector Directive 2004/18 was implemented in the Netherlands on 1 December 2005 when the 'Decree Tender

* The authors would like to express their appreciation for the contributions of Mr Diederik van der Staay, Consultant with the Ministry of Internal Affairs, Government Buildings Agency (Rijksgebouwendienst) and Mr Jeroen Oehler, Consultant Regional Development with the Ministry of Economic Affairs, Agriculture and Innovation, Rural Area Department.

1 One example is the tender for the barge-canal in Leiden on 27 February 1657.

2 Dutch Civil Codebook.

3 www.europeseaanbestedingen.eu/europeseaanbestedingen/europese_aanbesteding/historie_eu_aanbesteding.

4 Framework law on EEC-provisions public procurement, 31 March 1993.

Regulations for Government Procurements' (Dutch abbreviation: BAO)[5] took effect. This legislation is compulsory for all governmental procurement agencies, which includes local and other contracting authorities.[6]

At the time of writing, the Dutch government[7] has been in the process of elaborating a new law on public procurement. Initially, the law on public procurement started out as a comprehensive law. This draft, however, failed to pass the Dutch senate. Currently, the Ministry of Economic Affairs, Agriculture and Innovation is working on a second draft of the law.[8] Both drafts include provisions from Directive 2004/18 and Utilities Directive 2004/17. The second draft of the law also includes provisions to implement the Remedies Directive 89/665.[9] Currently, it is not clear to what extent the new draft either will adhere closely to the provisions elaborated in both Directives or will insert additional provisions.

Discussions, however, are difficult as the SME lobby has grave concerns about the safeguarding of their interest in public tenders. Moreover, there is an ongoing discussion on the general quality of public procurement. Initially, the legislator tried to guarantee more professionally held public tenders by drafting an extensive and comprehensive law on public procurement. A wide number of experts are of the opinion that professional procurement cannot be induced by legislation alone. Improving professional knowledge and conduct inevitably requires an extensive effort in informing, educating and training (new) personnel. Large procurement agencies[10] already have and continue to invest in professional procurement. For smaller entities such as municipalities,[11] however, this is not easy.

[5] The Dutch name for the tender legislation is 'Besluit Aanbestedingsregels voor Overheidsopdrachten' (BAO).

[6] Art. 1(9) of Directive 2004/18.

[7] Headed by the Department of Economic Affairs, Agriculture and Innovation.

[8] An additional amendment memorandum is expected in March 2011.

[9] Currently implemented by the Law on the Implementation of the Public Procurement Remedies Directives (Dutch abbreviation: WIRA).

[10] The Directorate-General of Public Works and Water Management (Rijkswaterstaat), which is the Procurement agency of the Ministry of Infrastructure and Environment; and the Government Buildings Agency (Rijksgebouwendienst), the procurement agency for non-residential buildings, currently part of the Ministry of Internal Affairs. Until September 2010, the Rijksgebouwendienst was part of the Ministry of Housing, Spatial Planning and Environment.

[11] There are over 400 municipalities in the Netherlands.

For the improvement of government procurement as a whole, a government agency, PIANOo, has been established. The focus of its activity at the moment is to assist smaller procurement agencies – for example, provinces and municipalities – in developing professional procurement practices. Currently, PIANOo is developing tender guidelines and provides for advisory services for all procurement agencies that may wish to make use of the agency. Other services offered include an extensive network where procurement agencies can swap experiences, and the provision of information on procurement issues such as competitive dialogue.

In addition to the official legislation, the ministries formerly known as Housing,[12] Infrastructure,[13] Agriculture[14] and Defence[15] have officially issued a general procurement policy on works in 2005[16] (hereinafter Procurement Policy). This Procurement Policy sets out rules on how the respective ministries and their procurement agencies will act in respect of the procurement of works that are below the thresholds of Directive 2004/18. Although there is more room to manoeuvre when procuring works below the thresholds, the Procurement Policy adheres closely to the Directive's procurement methods. Additional methods – such as limited bidding or even conclusion of contract by direct agreement for procurements below the thresholds – are possible when sufficiently justified. The respective ministries and their procurement agencies are bound to uphold these Procurement Policies when conducting government procurements.[17]

Part of the Procurement Policy is the obligation to apply the Procurement Regulations on Tender Procedures for Works 2005 (Dutch abbreviation: 'ARW 2005').[18] The ARW 2005 is a direct interpretation of the BAO that was mentioned above, with minimal additional paragraphs. The ARW 2005 is not official legislation as such. Local authorities such as provinces and municipalities are therefore free to either apply the ARW 2005 or not. Most local authorities, however, have voluntarily

[12] Full denomination: Housing, Spatial Planning and Environment.

[13] Full denomination: Infrastructure and Water Management.

[14] Full denomination: Agriculture, Nature and Fisheries.

[15] Since the transfer in government in the Netherlands in October 2010, the organisation of the Dutch ministries has been substantially reshaped and reduced.

[16] *Staatscourant* (Dutch law gazette), 25 October 2005, No. 207, p. 14. The policy of 2005 replaced the official policy of 2004.

[17] Art. 4:84 of the General Law on Administrative Provisions (Dutch abbreviation: Awb).

[18] The ARW 2005 has replaced the ARW 2004 since 1 December 2005.

taken up the use of the ARW 2005 for tender procedures as it has proved to be a worthwhile tool to comply with the provisions of the Directive. Another point of interest is that, although the ARW 2005 refers to works and not to procurements of supplies and services, procurement agencies tend to take the ARW 2005 as a basis for these procurements as well.[19]

On top of the officially published Procurement Policy 2005, the government procurement agencies have their own ambitions and policies to continually improve their procurement efforts. These policies with regard to the improvement of their efforts as a professional contracting authority aim for the implementation of an extensive training programme on subjects such as project management,[20] procurement management, public–private partnership projects,[21] and related subjects.

The overall view, however, is that neither the central government and its procurement agencies nor the local authorities are subject to rules – official or otherwise – which diverge in any substantial way from what is required under the provisions of Directive 2004/18.

Research[22] on litigation on procurement from 1 September 2004 until 31 August 2009 shows that arbitration, the district courts, the courts of appeal and the Supreme Court of the Netherlands pronounced a total of 599 judgments, with 140 of these judgments in 2009 compared with 69 in 2004. Another piece of research[23] on judgments – excluding arbitration judgments – shows 474 judgments in the period 1999–2006. These have included rulings on issues such as: the invalidity and rejection of tenders, and amending and supplementing tenders (292 judgments); transparency (248 judgments); and equality (183 judgments). Through judgments on such matters, litigation results in guidelines on how to interpret existing legislation on these subjects. As we will see in section 3 below, there has already been some litigation on the competitive dialogue procedure itself.

[19] E.g. the project for a digital personnel information system called 'P-direct', mentioned in section 2.

[20] The respective ministries have, for instance, founded the National Academy for Project Management.

[21] Training modules for PPP projects (2011) developed by the PPP Unit of the procurement agency Rijkswaterstaat of the Ministry of Infrastructure and Environment.

[22] Report on procurement litigations in the Netherlands, June 2010, instigated by the Ministry of Economic Affairs.

[23] T. van der Linden, 'Public Procurement Agencies Often Win Disputes on Public Tenders' (January 2008) *Journal on Public Procurement* (in Dutch: *TijdschriftAanbestedingsrecht*) 6.

It should be noted that in the Netherlands litigation must always be brought either before the courts or to arbitration; there is no national tender authority. It should be noted that when applying the ARW 2005 the choice of court incorporated in the provisions is the district court.[24]

2. The background: complex procurement prior to competitive dialogue

Before the implementation of competitive dialogue, complex contracts which met the stipulated grounds for use of the negotiated procedure with prior notification[25] were awarded using that procedure, with the exception of a few experimental procurements, which were held on the basis of the principles of the competitive dialogue. The experimental procedures implied are, *inter alia*, the procurement of a digital personnel information system called 'P-direct' (procedure completed in 2005) and the extension of the highway A4 between Burgerveen and Leiden (procedure completed in 2006).

These experiments were made possible because of the ARW 2004. This regulatory provision included an Article,[26] which made it possible to deviate from the established procedures[27] with the objective of realising a more efficient procurement procedure. When applying this possibility to deviate from the regular procedures, compliance with the general legislation, and in particular with the principles of the (EU) procurement legislation, is, however, paramount.

This provision was included in the ARW 2004 in order to make it possible for the four central government procurement agencies to deviate. At that time, Directive 2004/18 already included provisions on competitive dialogue. Without the possibility to deviate from the ARW 2004, procurement agencies would lack the possibility to use the competitive dialogue on the basis of the Procurement Policy, while procurement agencies not bound by the Procurement Policy would be free to apply competitive dialogue for their tenders.[28]

Until 2006, competitive dialogue and the negotiated procedure were only rarely applied. The underlying reasons for this limited use were:

[24] Art. 4.33.1 ARW 2005. [25] Art. 30 of Directive 2004/18.
[26] Art. 8.1 of the ARW 2004.
[27] Prior to 1 December 2005, restricted to the open and restricted procedure and the negotiated procedure with or without previous notification.
[28] Framework law on EEC-provisions public procurement, 31 March 1993.

(1) The limited range and strict interpretation of the grounds for use of the negotiated procedure.
(2) The possibility for using competitive dialogue applied only from 31 March 2004. Before that the stipulations in the ARW 2004 and that of its predecessor the UAR 1991 elaborated on how the negotiated procedure with a notice was to be conducted. The general approach under this procedure as elaborated in these provisions differs from the competitive dialogue as presently applied.
(3) Until the end of 2002,[29] there was a general policy to elaborate contract documents in detail and to put them out for tender on the award criterion of the lowest price. Because of this policy the number of contracts which could be defined as complex in the sense stipulated in what is now Article 30(1)(b) of Directive 2004/18 (referring to 'exceptional cases, when the nature of the works, supplies, or services or the risks attached thereto do not permit overall pricing'), thus meeting the grounds for use of the negotiated procedure were small.

Since 2006, use of both competitive dialogue and the negotiated procedure has soared.[30] The increased use of the latter case has apparently resulted from changing the way the market is approached by using different, more functionally specified contracts, meaning that the number of contracts meeting the grounds for using the procedure has increased.

3. Introduction to competitive dialogue

Competitive dialogue was implemented in the Netherlands on 1 December 2005 as part of the BAO. Simultaneously, competitive dialogue was elaborated in the ARW 2005. Before the implementation of competitive dialogue, government procurements were largely conducted by use of the open and restricted procedures. The number of negotiated procedures was relatively small in comparison, although as we noted earlier it was sometimes used for awarding those complex contracts that existed at that time.

The procedural provisions elaborated in the BAO and ARW 2005 adhere closely to the provisions in Directive 2004/18, and there are almost no legislative or other provisions on competitive dialogue and

[29] See section 4 below. [30] See Table 12.1 below.

its conduct. The lack of specific regulations concerning the conduct of competitive dialogue leads to a substantial freedom in determining the actual conduct of the procedure,[31] so long as the use and conduct of the procedure do not clash with the general principles of transparency, equality and proportionality or otherwise disturb an open and fair competition.

As competitive dialogue is not included as an award procedure in the Utilities Directive, it has not been included in the Dutch regulations on utilities.[32] The Dutch regulations on utilities do, however, specify the possibility of conducting a flexible negotiated procedure with prior notification. As the regulations on how to conduct these negotiations leave full freedom to the contracting authority it is possible to conduct a procedure similar to the competitive dialogue.

As explained in Chapter 2, in comparison with other Member States the Netherlands can be considered as a 'regular' user of competitive dialogue, with a total of eighty-four procedures using competitive dialogue between 2006 and 2009 according to the methodology used for Chapter 2.[33] The majority of the procedures using competitive dialogue in the Netherlands have concerned complex ICT contracts (23 per cent of the procedures) and contracts on infrastructure and construction (43 per cent of the procedures), many of the latter being types of project classified as public–private partnerships (PPPs) in the sense of a collaboration – usually based on contractual relations[34] – between the government or its procurement agencies and the private sector, where the two join forces in order to realise a project from both the financial and technical perspectives. As the Dutch government has focused its procurement of infrastructure and building projects on PPP, it is to be expected that further use will be made of competitive dialogue in the coming years.

The relative novelty of competitive dialogue combined with the vagueness of the provisions led to a steep learning curve for the

[31] Art. 29 and recital 31 of Directive 2004/18; Art. 29 BAO.

[32] Decree on Tenders for Special Sectors (Dutch title: Besluit Aanbestedingen Speciale Sectoren (BASS)).

[33] The figures used in section 4 below differ from those used in Ch. 2, in that Ch. 2, in comparing the procedure with its use in other Member States, excludes procedures that were abandoned, whereas the analysis in section 4 below includes those abandoned procedures.

[34] In the Netherlands, several types of contracts – for instance, a DBFM contract – are considered to be PPP contracts.

contracting authorities concerned. It may also lead one to expect a large number of legal disputes on competitive dialogue. Litigation in 2009 totalled 140 cases, while the number of judicial disputes on competitive dialogue was nine in the period 2006–10,[35] five of which were in 2009. During 2009, about 4,000 tender procedures above the thresholds were held and, according to the data collected for Chapter 2, these included twenty-eight competitive dialogue procedures.[36] This means that there were disputes in more than 15 per cent of competitive dialogue procedures compared with disputes in only about 3.5 per cent of other tender procedures, which would make the number of disputes on the competitive dialogue relatively high. Nonetheless, not much can be said of the way in which the courts will interpret the competitive dialogue procedure as in the majority of the cases points of law not exclusive to competitive dialogue were addressed, although one case[37] discusses the issue of a candidate discontinuing one of its proposed solutions.

Furthermore, there are no official guidelines on competitive dialogue in the Netherlands. At the moment, there is merely a guide on competitive dialogue, which is based on the current experience of the Government Buildings Agency, the procurement agency for non-residential buildings of the Ministry of Internal Affairs (hereinafter Rijksgebouwendienst), the Directorate-General of Public Works and Water Management, a procurement agency of the Ministry of Infrastructure and Environment (hereinafter Rijkswaterstaat) and the Ministry of Defence.[38] Use of this guide is not compulsory for any entities. Its intention is merely to provide interested parties with best practices and suggestions for possible solutions to perceived problems.

As part of the effort to improve their performance as contracting authorities, procurement agencies such as the Rijkswaterstaat and the Rijksgebouwendienst have made substantial efforts to improve their performance on competitive dialogue. To this end, a national standard contract on privately financed infrastructure has been developed and a national standard tender guideline on competitive dialogue is currently

[35] www.rechtspraak.nl/Uitspraken. [36] See Ch. 2 above.

[37] District Court of The Hague, 6 May 2010, LJN BM3705, MNO Vervat.

[38] M. Nagelkerke, J. Oehler, J. Muntz-Beekhuis and D. van der Staay, 'The Competitive Dialogue: A Guide Based on the Current Experience of the Rijksgebouwendienst, Rijkswaterstaat and the Ministry of Defence' (Rijksoverheid: The Hague, October 2009), available at www.pppinthenetherlands.nl and www.pianoo.nl.

Table 12.1 *Official notices of competitive dialogue and negotiated procedures, 2004–2010*

Year	Number of competitive dialogue	Number of negotiated procedure government tenders
2004	–	–
2005	0	11
2006	17	210
2007	16	199
2008	21	108
2009	30	93
2010	19	47
Total	103	668

Note:
[a] tender information derived from Tenders Electronic Daily.

being drafted.[39] Ways to support smaller procurement entities in the areas of PPPs and relevant complex tender procedures such as competitive dialogue are currently under consideration.

4. Scope of competitive dialogue in law and practice

The provisions on public procurement of the BAO and the ARW 2005 are not substantially different from those of Directive 2004/18. There are scant additional legislative or other provisions on competitive dialogue and its conduct.

After the implementation of Directive 2004/18 on 1 December 2005, during the period 2006–10, as shown in Table 12.1,[40] 103 competitive dialogue procedures have been launched, while in the same period 668 negotiated procedures were held. In 2005, there were no tenders based on competitive dialogue and 11 on the negotiated procedure. In the following years up to 2010, the numbers rose considerably, as shown in

39 The national format for PPP contracts is available at www.pppinthenetherlands.nl; these formats are also available in the English language. The format for the national tender guidelines will be issued on the same website in due course.

40 As mentioned in n. 34 above, the figures used for this analysis differ from those used in Ch. 2, in that Ch. 2, in comparing the procedure with its use in other Member States, excludes procedures that were abandoned, whereas the analysis in this section includes those abandoned procedures.

Table 12.1. The number of negotiated procedures rose even more spectacularly than the number of competitive dialogue procedures. The numbers have, however, dropped again in 2010.

Although extensive research on the reasons for the increased use of both competitive dialogue and the negotiated procedure is not available in the Netherlands, the most likely cause of the considerable increase seems to be the change in procurement strategy of the government after the parliamentary enquiry in 2001–2[41] on corruption in the building industry. Before the parliamentary enquiry, the government mainly focused on lowest price as an award criterion, whereas after the enquiry a shift was made to the award criterion of the most economically advantageous tender. This shift was made with a view to normalising relations with the building industry. Whereas use of the lowest price as the basis for award led regularly to clashes of interests and relations between principal and service provider, it is expected that contracts where competition can evolve around qualitative criteria will be less prone to such clashes. In order to provide such a competitive environment, the government has increased its efforts on contracts in using PPPs. Most tenders by means of both the competitive dialogue and the negotiated procedure seem to be a consequence of this changed procurement strategy.

The sudden drop in numbers of the negotiated procedure in 2010 may have been caused by the fact that the European Commission started an infringement procedure on the procurement practice for fire insurance.[42] According to the European Commission, the use of the negotiated procedure for these contracts is contrary to the provisions in Directive 2004/18. The Netherlands has complied with the Commission's reasoned opinion on these tenders. In order to ensure use of appropriate award procedures for fire insurance in the future, the state[43] will draft a guideline on tendering for fire insurance.[44]

With a total of 103 procurements by means of competitive dialogue, the Netherlands is a small user in comparison to the UK.[45] Most of the competitive dialogue procedures have been held in relation to 'design, build, finance and maintain' (DBFM) contracts, either for complex

41 Report on the parliamentary enquiry on corruption in the building industry, parliamentary paper 28 244, session 2002–3.

42 European Commission, Reasoned Opinion, IP/10/1233, 30 September 2010.

43 Under the auspices of the Ministry of National Affairs.

44 www.pianoo.nl/actueel/openbare-aanbestedingen-van-brandverzekeringen, 17 February 2011.

45 1,531 notices in the period 2006–9.

integrated infrastructure projects[46] or for complex integrated non-residential buildings.[47] The types of contracts for which the competitive dialogue has been used are diverse. Other uses of the competitive dialogue have related to: alliance contracts; concession contracts;[48] complex ICT contracts;[49] contracts for 'design and construct', 'design and build' and 'design, build and maintain' of a highly technical and complex nature;[50] maintenance contracts of a highly complex technical nature; integrated project- and area-development contracts;[51] equity participation in area development and in a publicly owned undertaking; a turnkey contract on waste processing; a research contract; a contract concerning carbon dioxide storage facilities; and the design and realisation of a sustainable energy plant.

Although most competitive dialogue procedures are held for procurements above the thresholds, there is no legal restraint on the use of competitive dialogue for procurements below the thresholds. Due to the lack of exhaustive data on the use of competitive dialogue it is difficult to estimate how many of these have actually been held. There was at least one infrastructure project for a contract below the thresholds conducted by means of competitive dialogue, by the province of North Brabant.[52] There was also a negotiated procedure in accordance with the Utilities Directive that used elements of competitive dialogue.[53]

5. Operation of the competitive dialogue procedure

5.1. Introduction

As stated above, legal provisions in the Netherlands largely follow the provisions of Directive 2004/18. Procurement agencies therefore have substantial freedom to arrange the conduct of the procedure, apart from the restrictions induced by their own policies.

[46] For example, the A15 Maasvlakte–Vaanplein road, the A12 Utrecht–Lunetten–Veenendaal road and the second Coen Tunnel.
[47] For example, the office building of the Ministry of Finance, several detention centres, tax offices etc.
[48] For example, for public transport and supplying energy.
[49] For example, for hospitals, complex office networks and e-learning facilities.
[50] For example, with highly complex mechanical engineering for hospitals and research centres.
[51] For example, the A2 Maastricht.
[52] Roundabout Gemertseweg in Laarbeek, published on 1 October 2008.
[53] The extension of the airstrip at Groningen Airport Eelde.

The procurement agencies of the central government have joined forces to exchange knowledge and best practices on competitive dialogue and PPP projects. There are similarities in conduct of the dialogue between the Rijkswaterstaat and the Rijksgebouwendienst. In view of these similarities, a national standard tender guideline is currently being drafted.[54] The tenders of the Rijkswaterstaat, however, tend to be financially larger and more elaborate than those of the Rijksgebouwendienst. Therefore, competitive dialogue as applied by the Rijkswaterstaat is taken as the basis for further elaborations in this chapter. See Figure 12.1.

5.2. The planning stage and drafting of the descriptive document

When drafting the tender documents, there are no additional obligations on the contract notice beyond the provisions of Directive 2004/18. With several complex tenders – for example, large DBFM contracts – advance notices have been issued in order to consult and/or inform the market on the upcoming tender. The use of such prior notices is part of the deliberations of the contracting authority on the procurement method of a specific project. At the moment, there is no standard approach to these consultations, although in most instances a prior information notice in the sense of Article 35 of Directive 2004/18 has been used to inform the private sector of the upcoming consultation.

These advance notices have been used, *inter alia*, for: holding a market consultation to verify the feasibility of the proposed approach to the tender; informing the market of the upcoming tender by means of the competitive dialogue, one of the goals of which is to provide the private sector with the opportunity to form consortia if needed; holding a market consultation on specific problems relating to the tender; testing the interest of the private sector for the upcoming project; and holding a market consultation on the possible scope of the project.

5.3. Confidentiality of information and solutions

Competitive dialogue was introduced in order to create a flexible procedure which not only preserves competition between economic operators but also supports the need for the contracting authority to discuss all aspects of the contract.[55] To this end, as Chapter 1 explained,

[54] See also section 3. [55] Directive 2004/18, recital 31.

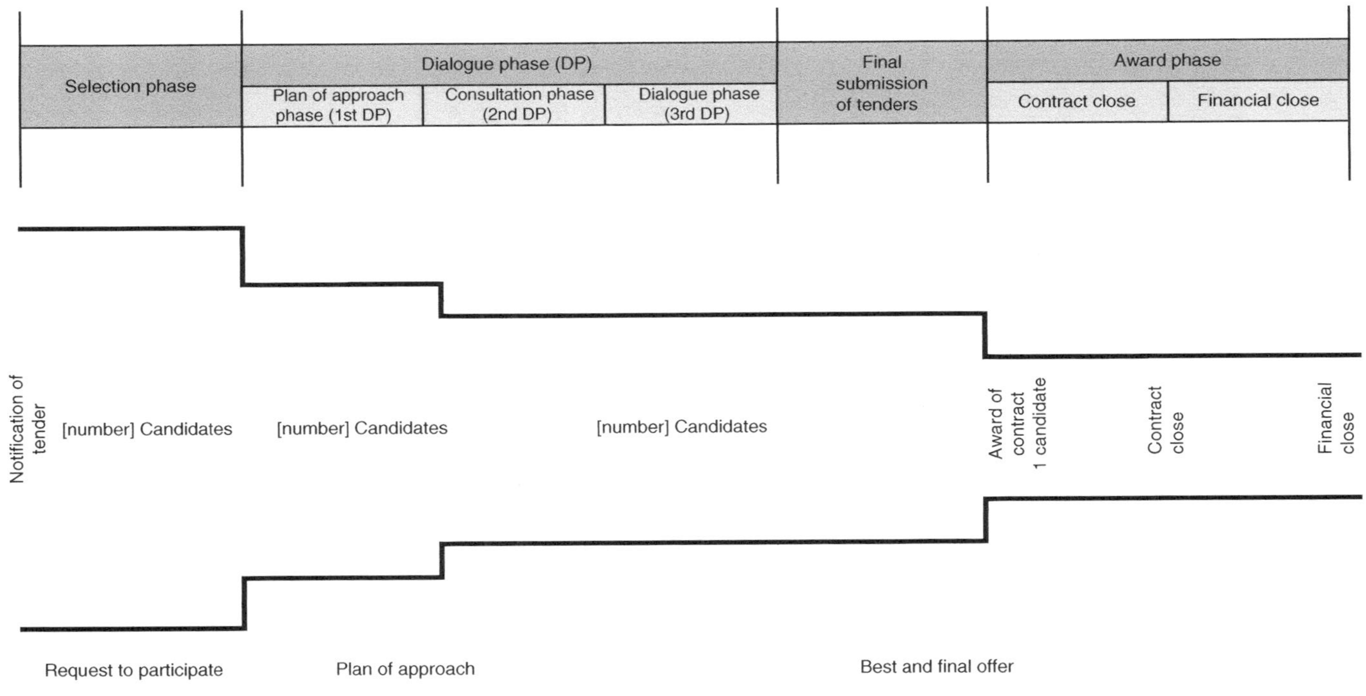

Figure 12.1 Conceptual scheme for competitive dialogue

Article 29 of Directive 2004/18[56] states that contracting authorities can open a dialogue with the aim to identify and define the means best suited to satisfy their requirements.

Concerning the conduct of the competitive dialogue, the European Commission takes in its Explanatory Note[57] as a starting point 'that the dialogue should be carried out individually with each of the candidates on the basis of the ideas and solutions of the economic operator concerned'. A tender procedure whereby the contracting authority exercises maximum openness in its conduct of the tendering process, with the additional possibility to hold a dialogue with each individual candidate separately, in itself, however, may not induce candidates to divulge their solutions to the contracting authority. In order to protect their commercial interests candidates may hold back on their ideas for creative and innovative solutions. Should these ideas reach their competitors during the tender procedure contractors may lose their competitive edge. A truly open discussion with candidates therefore will only be feasible if there are guarantees to preserve the confidentiality of solutions presented by candidates.

As section 5.3 of Chapter 1 explained, Article 29(3)[58] of Directive 2004/18 provides for addressing confidentiality for the solutions proposed or other confidential information communicated by candidates. According to the European Commission, confidentiality is also protected by the general provision on confidentiality in Article 6 of the Directive. The European Commission refers to the protection laid down by EU or national legislation on intangible property. Article 6 BAO in the Dutch legislation implementing these provisions of the Directive provides for a general obligation not to disclose confidential information provided by candidates, without prejudice to Articles 29, 35, 36 and 41 BAO and the Law on Public Access to Public Administration (Dutch abbreviation: WOB). The Dutch WOB provides for a general obligation for the public administration to provide for information on administrative affairs unless one of the restrictions provided for in Articles 10 and 11 WOB applies. Amongst other restrictions for disclosing information, Article 10, paragraph 1,

[56] Implemented in Dutch law and regulations by Art. 29, para. 4, BAO.

[57] European Commission, *Explanatory Note – Competitive Dialogue – Classic Directive* (2005), available at www.simap.eu.int.

[58] Implemented in Dutch law and regulations by Art. 29, para. 6, BAO.

WOB states that disclosure will be denied when the request for information relates to operational and production data divulged in confidence by a private party. Another reason to withhold disclosure is provided by Article 10, paragraph 2, WOB, which states that disclosure may be denied in order to prevent disproportionate advantage or damage to the private parties concerned.

Although confidentiality relating to proposed solutions is clearly provided for, it is not entirely clear what may be comprehended by the concept of 'other confidential information communicated by candidates'.[59] Is it information designated as confidential by a candidate, as Article 6 of Directive 2004/18 suggests? And, if so, how can the contracting authority ensure equal treatment of all candidates in accordance with Article 29(3)[60] when it is of the opinion that – contrary to the view of the candidate – the information is not in fact confidential? What if the situation does not involve clear-cut reasons for confidentiality, such as (1) information directly relating to a solution proposed by the candidate; (2) information directly relating to technical and/or trade secrets; or (3) information the disclosure of which would result in distortion of fair competition? How is it then to be determined if the information may be considered confidential?

In order to deal with possible differences of opinion concerning confidentiality of information, the procurement agencies, Rijkswaterstaat and the Rijksgebouwendienst, have developed a standard procedure for confidentiality issues in their tender guidelines. During the award procedure, candidates are given the opportunity to submit information relating to their upcoming tenders to discuss during the dialogue and to submit requests for information relating to the tender documents and/or their proposed solutions. Any information relating to the upcoming tenders which may give any insight into the proposed solutions of each candidate will be automatically deemed confidential. When submitting requests for information relating to the tender documents, confidentiality is not, however, a certainty and candidates and contracting authority may hold different views.

To avoid unnecessary legal disputes concerning the confidentiality or otherwise of the information concerned, the following procedure has been adopted.

[59] Art. 29(3) of Directive 2004/18; and Art. 29, para. 6, BAO.
[60] Implemented in Dutch law and regulations by Art. 29, para. 5 of BAO.

Step 1: Candidates submit their requests for information and label the request as either confidential or non-confidential.

Step 2: If the submitting candidate labels the request for information non-confidential, the contracting authority provides the requested information to all candidates equally.

Step 3: If the submitting candidate labels the request for information confidential and the contracting authority agrees with this categorisation, the contracting authority provides the requested information exclusively to the said candidate.

Step 4: If the request for information is labelled confidential by the submitting candidate and the contracting authority does not agree, the submitting candidate is requested to clarify his view on the confidentiality of the information.

Step 5: If the clarification of the candidate concerning the confidentiality of the information is satisfactory to the contracting authority, the contracting authority proceeds in providing the requested information exclusively to the said candidate.

Step 6: If the clarification of the candidate concerning the confidentiality of the information is not, however, satisfactory to the contracting authority, the contracting authority will ask the candidate to label the request for information as non-confidential.

Step 7: If the candidate agrees with the contracting authority and changes the label to non-confidential, the contracting authority proceeds to provide the requested information to all candidates equally. If necessary, the candidate concerned can rephrase its question in order to avoid any chance of inadvertently divulging confidential information.

Step 8: If the candidate, however, does not agree with the contracting authority and retains the confidentiality label, the contracting authority will ask the candidate to withdraw his request for information. Whether or not the candidate complies will, however, make no difference to the refusal of the contracting authority to provide the requested information.

In addition to the above procedure concerning requests for (non-) confidential information, the tender guideline reserves the right for the contracting authority to give general information to all candidates equally, even if the need for general information is the result of a request for information which is labelled confidential by the submitting candidate. The contracting authority will, however, enable the submitting candidate to voice his views on the phrasing of the information concerned, so that inadvertent divulging of information relating to his solution or other legitimate commercial interests can be prevented.

At the beginning of the tender, the contracting authority issues a tender guideline in which it stipulates the conditions applicable to the procedure. One of the stipulations is that candidates agree with the stipulated conduct of the procedure by simply taking part. One could argue that such an implicit agreement is forced upon the candidates, which may leave the level of agreement, including on the subject of (non-)confidentiality, debatable. In Dutch law, however, there is the principle of freedom of contract, which means that parties are free to agree or not to a commitment governed by private law. In theory, they could choose not to participate in the tender. Apart from not participating, there are other means to determine whether or not sufficient agreement exists. According to the provisions in the Remedies Directive[61] as implemented in Dutch national law through the Law on the Implementation of the Remedies Directive (Dutch abbreviation: WIRA), candidates can ask for a provisional judgment on the offending stipulation. If a potential tenderer is successful in its appeal, the contracting authority may find itself obliged to change the stipulations in the tender guideline accordingly. To succeed, such an appeal should be made at the beginning of the tender procedure when possible infringements can be corrected.[62] In a case[63] concerning a tender which fell within the scope of Directive 2004/17[64] on utilities contracts, the District Court of Arnhem considered on this issue that 'although the applicable law [i.e. Directive 2004/17 and the national implementing legislation] does not provide for a peremptory time limit, it does not handicap the possibility of the contracting authority to include a clause stipulating a peremptory time limit in the tender documents themselves'. In the case of *Alliander* v. *Headfirst*, paragraph 3.8 of the tender documents stated: 'The candidate unconditionally accepts the

[61] Directive 2007/66 of the European Parliament and of the Council of 11 December 2007 on amending Council Directives 89/665 and 92/13 with regard to improving the effectiveness of review procedures concerning the award of public contracts [2007] OJ L335/31, 11 December 2007, Art. 2.

[62] Case C-230/02, *Grossmann Air Service and Bedarfsluftfahrernehmen GmbH Co. KG* v. *Austria* [2004] ECR I-1829.

[63] District Court of Arnhem, 23 June 2011, LJN BR0127, *Alliander* v. *Headfirst*.

[64] Directive 2004/17 of the European Parliament of the Council of 31 March 2004 coordinating the procurement procedures of entities operating in the water, energy, transport and postal services sectors [2004] OJ L134/1, 30 April 2004. This Directive is implemented in Dutch legislation by means of the Decree on Tenders for Special Sectors (Dutch title: Besluit Aanbestedingen Speciale Sectoren (BASS)).

stipulations of both the tender documents and the information notices in question and all conditions therein stipulated concerning the tender procedure.' By participating in the tender procedure and not challenging the stipulation concerning the peremptory time limit *within a reasonable time after being informed of this stipulation*,[65] the complainant's request was deemed inadmissible in court.

Interestingly, there are no known cases concerning breaches of the confidentiality rules. This may be because contracting authorities are very careful during the dialogue not to leak ideas from one candidate to another. It may also be the case that cherry-picking is hard to prove when it concerns 'minor' parts of the offer of an individual candidate.

5.4. *Advertising requirements (contract notice etc.)*

Tenders above the threshold start with a notification of tender both on the official publication site Tender Electronic Daily (TED) of the European Union and the Dutch publication site, www.aanbestedingskalender.nl.[66] In practice, it suffices for contracting authorities to submit their notification of tender with the Dutch website just mentioned, as this automatically forwards notifications above the thresholds to TED. The site provides for standard forms with instructions that are in accordance with the EU notification requirements. It also provides additional information on, for example, the applicable CPV codes, and refers to other sites and authorities such as the aforementioned PIANOo,[67] which may provide information on tendering. Large procurement agencies such as the Rijkswaterstaat and the Rijksgebouwendienst have their own departments that provide similar forms and instructions for notifications of tender as the above website, and provide for specialist assistance during preparation of the tender.

5.5. *The selection phase: choosing the candidates to participate in the dialogue*

The rules governing the selection phase of competitive dialogue under Directive 2004/18 were considered in section 5.5 of Chapter 1. The selection phase starts with a notification of tender. Interested parties may

[65] The text in italics was added by the authors.
[66] A new website, www.tenderned.nl (if the upcoming pilot proves to be successful), will replace www.aanbestedingskalender.nl.
[67] See also section 4 above.

submit their request to participate within thirty-seven days, after which either all candidates that meet the selection criteria go through to the dialogue phase or a further selection is made to either five or three candidates.[68] The number and content of the selection criteria may differ in relation to the chosen market strategy of the contracting authority. In order to determine the market strategy, contracting authorities make a more or less detailed market analysis to achieve a more solid understanding of the number and nature of interested parties that may be expected to submit a request to participate. At the moment, the Rijksgebouwendienst usually reduces the number of candidates for the dialogue phase to three, while the Rijkswaterstaat reduces the number of candidates to five or – dependent on the market analysis – to a number that has not been pre-set.

In the national standard tender guideline for DBFM contracts, which is currently under development, the selection criteria are minimal. For infrastructure projects, the criteria are readiness and capability to furnish a specified amount of money, experience in project management, and experience in project financing. In tenders for non-residential buildings, there is a slightly different approach to the criteria concerning former experience: these criteria are experience in integrated contracts, and experience with a specific design. Direct experience in construction, on the other hand, is not deemed necessary.

As only the major governmental procurement agencies commit to the use of the standard tender guidelines, other contracting authorities are free to decide whether or not to comply with these provisions. The tender guidelines will be made available to all interested parties by publication on the website, www.pppinthenetherlands.nl.

5.6. *The dialogue phase*

5.6.1. General

As stated earlier,[69] the legal provisions in the BAO and ARW 2005 adhere closely to the provisions of Directive 2004/18, thus leaving contracting authorities a substantial freedom in determining the actual conduct of the competitive dialogue procedure. The major governmental procurement agencies[70] to a certain extent use a similar approach for conducting

[68] According to Art. 44(3) of Directive 2004/18, a minimum of three candidates must be invited to participate in the dialogue.

[69] See sections 3, 4 and 5.1 above.

[70] Rijkswaterstaat, Rijksgebouwendienst and the Ministry of Defence.

the procedure. The dialogue phase as used by the Rijkswaterstaat is sub-divided into three phases, namely, the plan-of-approach phase, the consultation phase and the discussion phase. The Rijksgebouwendienst also starts with a kick-off meeting as discussed in section 5.6.2, but its subsequent procedure is simplified.

During the award procedure, the contracting authorities reduce the number of candidates in various ways. It may be that the number of candidates is immediately reduced to three during the selection phase by means of previously notified selection criteria. The Rijkswaterstaat currently uses the plan-of-approach phase to reduce the number of candidates to a minimum of three by judging the submitted plans of approach on the basis of previously notified award criteria. Finally, contracting authorities may choose to reduce the number of candidates in stages, first during the selection phase and secondly during the plan-of-approach phase. When using the possibility to reduce candidates during the plan-of-approach phase, the dialogue usually starts with a maximum of five to seven candidates, depending on the size of the project and the amount of work necessary to submit and assess the plans of approach. After reduction, the dialogue, by then consisting of the consultation- and discussion phase, will be continued with a maximum of three candidates.

Although there are no exact numbers available, it is safe to say that virtually all candidates base their final bids on their own solution as discussed during the dialogue. During the award procedure, contracting authorities are focused on the confidentiality of the solutions and on guaranteeing a level playing field for all candidates. The only project where candidates were asked to divulge their solutions to the general public before submitting their final bid was the A2 Maastricht, a road construction project combined with municipal area development in the city of Maastricht. According to the conditions in the contract documents, however, cherry-picking was not allowed. Candidates were required to put in their final bids on the basis of the presented solution. The possible changes to their solutions were limited to those resulting from the reactions of the public as a consequence of the voluntary public presentation. The common platform for all candidates during the competitive dialogue is restricted to the conditions of the contract, which are issued to all candidates accordingly.

Unless the contracting authority stipulates in its tender documents that part of the solution has to be made public, the confidentiality of information relating to the solutions of the candidates will be safeguarded. Measures taken to protect confidentiality can consist of (i) using protected locations to store digital information and (ii) using methods for checks and balances before sending information to candidates or divulging information in relation to the award procedure to the general public.

Once they have been admitted to the dialogue phase, not many qualified candidates leave the competition. Once again, there are no exact numbers available, but the authors of this chapter know of only two examples. One arose in an award procedure for the Burgerveen–Leiden road project, a construction project to improve the traffic flow between The Hague and Amsterdam, where one of the five candidates dropped out of the competition, and one during the tender of the A2 Maastricht, where one of the three participants left the procedure.

5.6.2. Kick-off meeting

In several award procedures,[71] a kick-off meeting was organised at the start of the award procedure to enable candidates and the members of the project team to become acquainted with each other and for the candidates to be informed of the goals and main characteristics of the project. Additionally a visit to the project location can be organised. The kick-off meeting has no set design. It can be organised in a variety of ways: a meeting, depending on the issues to be discussed, can be convened for all the candidates at the same time, separate meetings can be convened for each candidate or a hybrid form is possible. The project A15 Maasvlakte–Vaanplein is an example of this hybrid approach to the kick-off. The kick-off for this project began with a plenary session in which the candidates received a general explanation, and an explanation of the substance of the project and the dialogue process. This plenary session was followed by sessions at theme tables, when the individual candidates were offered an opportunity to discuss specific issues in more detail.

The choice of one or other forms of a kick-off meeting depends on the objectives of the contracting authority. When the objective is restricted to ensuring that all candidates receive identical information about, for example, the project, the project's scope and objectives and the upcoming award procedure, a meeting for all candidates at the same time will

[71] E.g. the A15 Maasvlakte–Vaanplein road and the A12 Utrecht–Lunetten–Veenendaal road.

be the obvious choice. When the objective is to include an initial discussion on the possible solutions of the candidates, then a separate meeting for each candidate or a hybrid form of the kick-off meeting is more appropriate.

When organising separate kick-off meetings, the contracting authority must be alert to the fact that special attention is needed to assure the observance of the principles of equal treatment and transparency. Conversely, separate meetings offer the benefit that the meeting can address the candidate's confidential solutions and questions. If a plenary meeting is organised, candidates will probably say nothing that could be detrimental to their competitive position.

The use of a kick-off session has proven to be a successful tool to start the award procedure. Possible issues to address during a kick-off meeting[72] include: the expectations concerning the rules and parties' attitude governing the dialogue; the project's scope and objectives; the objective of the award procedure; the consultative organisation and the status of the various meetings of the dialogue team and possible sub-teams; and subjects submitted by the candidates.

5.6.3. Plan-of-approach phase (three to five candidates)

Currently a plan-of-approach phase is mainly being used for infrastructure projects. During this phase candidates are invited to submit their individual plan of approach on several critical success factors (CSFs). To this effect, the contracting authority formulates three to five CSFs on which the candidates have to base their plan of approach. Each CSF has to be elaborated to meet the conditions specified in the tender documents. If the submission does not meet the minimum requirements, it will be deemed null and void and subsequently will not be taken into consideration. Each CSF will be assessed on the basis of previously notified award criteria. Examples of CSFs during past tenders include: (1) minimisation of traffic disruption, during both the realisation and the exploitation phases of the contract; (2) project management; (3) mutual co-operation and responsibility sharing; (4) indicative price; (5) preliminary design; and (6) guaranteeing the stability of an existing engineering construction during the realisation phase of the contract.

[72] For a more extensive analysis of this subject, see 'The Competitive Dialogue: A Guide Based on the Current Experience of the Rijksgebouwendienst, Rijkswaterstaat and the Ministry of Defence', n. 18 above, para. 3.

After assessment of the submitted plans of approach, three candidates[73] will be invited to participate in the next phase of the dialogue.

The limitation on the number of CSFs is based on the experience that expanding the number of subjects to elaborate in the plan of approach does not automatically lead to better competition between the candidates. On the contrary, an inordinate number of CSFs to be elaborated in the plan of approach will have a detrimental effect on the distinctive character of each CSF. Once the requirements of the plan of approach are such that they lack the possibility for candidates to distinguish themselves from other competitors, identifying the best three plans will not only be difficult, but the formal statement of reasons for the decision may not be sufficiently conclusive. Such inconclusiveness may lead to more legal disputes.

5.6.4. Consultation phase

The consultation phase has as its objective the discussion and possible improvement of the tender documents issued by the contracting authority. The aforementioned tender documents include the contract terms on which the final offers must be based. During this phase candidates may propose amendments to the tender documents.

The question arises as to whether to give candidates complete freedom to propose every alteration possible or to limit this freedom to specific subjects. Leaving candidates complete freedom may leave ample room for creativity; however, it also leads to substantial efforts on the part of candidates. If and when the contracting authority can exclude certain topics in the tender documents as eligible for change beforehand, it is advisable to limit the possibilities of amending the tender documents to this extent. Should candidates put in substantial efforts into proposing changes, but find that these are generally rejected, this will understandably result in frustration on their part.

Other topics during the consultation phase are the final specification of the risks listed for the project and the plans for financing the contract. The assessment results of the plans of approach are also discussed with the remaining candidates. As these plans are the basis for further elaboration of candidates' tenders, the view of the contracting authority on their performance with respect to the plan of approach may be of importance to the candidates.

[73] Each candidate submits one plan of approach during this phase.

An example can be given relating to the CSF of 'mutual co-operation and responsibility sharing'.[74] In the tenders of the A12 Lunetten–Veenendaal and the A15 Maasvlakte–Vaanplein roads – both large road construction projects – this CSF was one of the CSFs to be elaborated in the plan of approach. In the plan of approach, a relatively abstract view was required initially on the management of the project with a view to supporting the contracting authority with its responsibilities – for example, in dealing with external stakeholders. The tender guidelines then stipulated that the candidates were required to further develop these views in their final offer. The guidelines also stipulated that amendments on the views as elaborated in the plan of approach could not be changed without the express authorisation of the contracting authority. This stipulation was inserted in order to prevent deterioration of what was offered in the plan-of-approach phase when the candidates put in their final offers on 'mutual co-operation and responsibility sharing'. In order to have a clear view of the requirements of the contracting authority and the possible estimation of strong and weak points in their initial plans, candidates were offered the opportunity to discuss their initial performance with the plan of approach during the consultation phase.

The consultation phase does not, however, lead to a further limitation of solutions. Thus at the end of this phase all remaining candidates will be invited to participate in the discussion phase.

5.6.5. Discussion phase[75]

During the discussion phase, the proposals of the remaining three candidates are discussed. To this end, the contracting authority proposes a schedule of subjects under discussion with the aim of clarifying the scope and target of the project. In order to further aid a more efficient dialogue process candidates are invited to render their views on the proposed schedule. If possible the contracting authority will adjust this schedule according to the wishes of candidates, although the schedule will remain similar for all parties concerned.

[74] See sections 5.6.2 above.

[75] It can be noted that in the Tender Guidelines this specific part of what the Directive refers to as the 'dialogue' ('*dialoog*' in Dutch) is also called the 'dialogue' phase ('*dialoogfase*' in Dutch). This use of the term 'dialogue' in two different senses can be confusing and thus the term 'discussion' phase is used here for this 'sub-section' of the dialogue.

In practice, contracting authorities in large and complex tenders have used the possibility to hold dialogues with teams of specialists in addition to the regular dialogues with the overall tender team. When using this possibility the contracting authority is advised to specify and communicate the respective authority of the teams of specialists in relation to the authority of the overall tender team. If it is left unclear who has the last say in matters that may bind the contracting authority, the consistency of the award procedure may be jeopardised.

If specified in the tender guidelines, the plan of approach is the subject of discussion as the elaboration of CSFs in this plan may be intended as the basis for further detailed proposals of candidates. In this case, the tender guidelines state that the candidate must continue with its submitted plan of approach. Part of the plan of approach may be, for example, a global elaboration of a preliminary design. During the discussion phase, candidates are required to submit a more detailed elaboration of this design in accordance with the requirements formulated in the tender guidelines. In addition to a further elaboration of the design, the technical requirements and desired surplus value, the listed risks and the plans for financing the contract may be amongst the subjects under review. All subjects under review are previously identified elements of the final tender to be submitted. In this way, candidates are able to refine their basic proposals and to complete them according to the contracting authority's priorities.

An interesting case on the conduct of the competitive dialogue is the case of MNO Vervat[76] (hereinafter MNO). The Dutch contracting authority Rijkswaterstaat commenced an award procedure for the expansion of the A50 highway. The tender procedure used was the competitive dialogue. MNO was one of the candidates in the dialogue procedure. In the end, the contract was awarded to another bidder. MNO disputed the award decision on the basis that the winning design significantly resembled the design MNO initially proposed but which was dropped on account of critical remarks by the contracting authority. According to MNO, the contracting authority's remarks amounted to a statement that the design did not meet the requirements in the tender specifications. The Rijkswaterstaat confirmed the fact that it had made some critical remarks on the design, but emphatically denied having stated that the design did not meet

[76] District Court of The Hague, 6 May 2010, LJN BM3705, MNO Vervat.

the requirements. The judgment of the District Court stated that MNO was unable to prove that the Rijkswaterstaat declined the design on the basis that it did not meet the requirements. The written statement of four of their employees was not sufficient evidence, as it did not match the statement of the representative of the Rijkswaterstaat. The court took into consideration that MNO had declined to make use of the possibility to formally file its design with the contracting authority during the dialogue and to file for clarification of the tender requirements, thus foregoing the possibility to acquire a written response to its proposed design. The court concluded that under these circumstances the decision to drop the design was an independent decision of MNO and therefore MNO bore the responsibility for it. The burden of this risk can only be transferred to the contracting authority if it can be proved that the decision not to continue on the proposed line of design is due to an explicit rejection by the contracting authority.

In previous award procedures, contracting authorities have applied basically two modes of operation during the discussion phase. Both methods start with an open discussion on all subjects based on drafts submitted by the candidates. Subsequently one method invites candidates to submit all finalised elements of the tender together with the final submission of tenders as a whole. The other method invites candidates to submit the finalised elements of the tender in parts during the discussion phase with a concluding submission of tender in the final submission phase. Both methods have their pros and cons. The first method leaves room to adjust or refine elements of the tender up to the final submission of tenders, while the other method may be a more manageable tender process for large projects. The latter method, however, does necessitate a sharp control of the integral procedure of the competitive dialogue. Both methods create the opportunity for candidates to test their initial proposals on acceptability and validity and to adjust these according to their findings.

Inviting the candidates to submit their final tenders concludes the discussion phase. Procurement agencies of the central government have a policy of taking at least three candidates through to the final submission of tenders, although there is no explicit legal obligation to do so. As a result of this policy, central government procurement agencies will not – as a rule – reduce the number of candidates to invite for the final tender phase to a number lower than three. The policy does not, however, exclude the possibility of deviating from this general approach when there are sufficient reasons to do so, though the likelihood of such deviations will be limited. Other contracting authorities may choose to reduce the number of solutions simply in accordance with Article 29(4) of Directive 2004/18.[77] This means that they may reduce the number of candidates to two if so desired, as long as genuine competition remains.[78]

During the phases of the tender, an element may be part of the plan-of-approach phase, the discussion phase and the final tender stage. If this is the case, the corresponding award criterion is the same through all phases of the tender. It is, however, possible that an element in, for example, the plan-of-approach phase is not part of the discussion and/or the final tender stage. As such, it is possible that the criteria used in the plan-of-approach phase (partially) differ from those in the discussion and final tender stages. For example, a contracting authority could choose to limit the elaboration of the CSF of 'mutual co-operation and responsibility sharing' to the plan-of-approach phase and merely require at the final tender stage that this element be included in the plan of approach as part of the final tender. It can also be the other way around. During the tenders for the A12 Lunetten–Veenendaal and the A15 Maasvlakte–Vaanplein roads, the CSFs required in the plan of approach were also formulated as elements to be further elaborated for the final tender stage. Further, as well as these elements of the final tender, more elements were required, which were not mentioned in the plan-of-approach phase. An example was the element of sustainability of the design and realisation of the project. The award criterion for this element was announced only at the beginning of the discussion phase.

Although there is some debate on this subject, as discussed further in section 5.6.5 of Chapter 1, the authors of the present chapter are of the opinion that the award criteria themselves may be subject to further clarification and elaboration insofar as they are made available in good time and do not lead to a substantial change to the award criteria.[79] An example of this may be the elaboration of the CSF of 'mutual co-operation and responsibility sharing' during the tenders of

[77] Art. 29, para. 7, BAO.
[78] Directive 2004/18, Art. 44(4); as to which, see the discussion in Ch. 1, section 5.7.2.
[79] Case C-532/06, *Emm. G. Lianakis and others* v. *Dimos Alexandroupolis and others* [2008] ECR I-251; Case C-496/99P, *Succhi di Frutta* [2004] PB C 79 of 18 March 2000.

the A12 Lunetten–Veenendaal and the A15 Maasvlakte–Vaanplein roads. In the plan-of-approach phase, this CSF was to be elaborated in the outlines of a basic management plan at a high level of abstraction. Candidates were required to give their view on aspects of several subjects of this basic management plan, such as stakeholder management, their vision on the realisation of the project, and the interests of the contracting authority. During the discussion phase, they were required to further elaborate this CSF into a basic management plan of a lesser degree of abstraction. As the elements of both the plan of approach and the final tender were to be assessed on the basis of an 'outstanding performance' on the part of the candidate, clarification was needed as to what this meant in both phases of the dialogue, and the clarification had to suit the extent of elaboration required of the basic management plan.

5.7. *Final tender stage*

In accordance with the policy[80] of the government procurement agencies, at the end of the discussion phase the remaining three candidates are requested to submit their final tenders. As explained earlier, during the discussion phase itself there is no further reduction of solutions on the basis of award criteria, at least not in the current practice of these procurement agencies.

In most award procedures conducted by means of competitive dialogue, the basis of the tender is a functionally specified contract. In addition to the functional specifications of the contract, candidates are given additional opportunity to distinguish themselves by offering additional quality and/or performance[81] – either by offering a better performance than strictly needed on the basis of the minimum requirements in the contract or by offering additional performance on topics as specified in the tender guideline. This method of approach is referred to as 'award on added value'.[82] For example, during tenders such as the A12 Lunetten–Veenendaal and the A15 Maasvlakte–Vaanplein roads, the opportunity was created for candidates to offer additional

[80] See section 5.6.5 above.

[81] Art. 29(1) of Directive 2004/18; and Art. 29, para. 2, BAO.

[82] A method of formulating award criteria developed by the Dutch National Knowledge Platform for Infrastructure, Transport and Public Space (CROW) (in Dutch: Gunnen op Waarde).

value in their final offer on top of the minimum requirements for specifically defined items. Sustainability of the design and realisation of the project was one of these items on which added value could be offered. Offering added value as such was not obligatory. Candidates who offered added value would, however, be granted an advantage in relation to other candidates who did not, by adding a notional amount of money to the tenders of those candidates who did not offer added value.

Although neither Directive 2004/18 nor the BAO prohibits the use of variants in competitive dialogue at the final tender stage, the ARW 2005 states in Article 4.23 that variants are not allowed. This restriction has been inserted with the view that during the dialogue there is ample opportunity to discuss various variants. Therefore, there is no further need for variants at the final tender stage. The procurement agencies of the central government whose policy is to use the ARW 2005 therefore do not use variants.[83] Procurement agencies which are not obligated to use the ARW 2005 may choose whether or not to allow variants.

On the whole, contracting authorities in the Netherlands invite candidates in a competitive dialogue to submit a tender that includes the candidate's own solution. Each tender may thus differ. There is a difference in approach in the completion of the tender procedure of the two largest government procurement agencies, namely, the Rijkswaterstaat and the Rijksgebouwendienst. The Rijkswaterstaat has an exchange of views during the dialogue on the compensation of risk that may lead to a different solution for each candidate separately; for example, one candidate may accept more risk than another, so that the risk profile of the candidates' final offers will diverge. However, the same exchange of views with the Rijksgebouwendienst usually leads to a set solution on this issue applicable for all candidates concerned. However, they both invite candidates to submit their own individual solution.

To assess the final tender, a selection of the following award criteria are used in practice: quality of the design; flexibility of the design; functionality of the design; logistics; neutralised actual value of the price; the value of the listed risks remaining with the contracting authority; the value of the specified added performance, which might include things such as the minimisation of disruption to traffic flows; the reduction of any adverse environmental impact of the project; and sustainability.

[83] See section 1 above.

The actual criteria to be used in each case are determined on the basis of the specific needs of the projects and the interests of the principal concerned which have to be met.

In accordance with Directive 2004/18, final tenders must contain all elements required and necessary for the performance of the project.[84] Once the final tenders are submitted, the scope for adjustment according to the Directive[85] is limited; but much is still unclear as to the range of the possibilities to adjust the tender after final submission, as discussed in Chapter 1.[86]

As we saw there, Directive 2004/18 allows for the candidates to be asked to clarify, specify or fine-tune their tender.[87] The limitation in the English version of that provision in the Directive is that the basic features of the (call for) tender may not be changed. The wording of this provision leaves room for different interpretations on the concept of 'basic features of the (call for) tender'. The addition of the phrase 'variations in which are likely to distort competition or have a discriminatory effect' puts the limitation into some perspective, but does not fully explain the limits to the possibility of clarifying, specifying and fine-tuning the tender.

For the Dutch version of the Directive, this part of the provision has been translated[88] into: 'the clarifications, specifications and fine-tuning may not essentially change the basic elements of the tender or the call for tender.' The phrasing 'essentially change' could suggest that changes in itself to the basic elements would be possible, just not essential ones. This lack of uniformity in the translated versions of the same provisions leads to more confusion over the precise scope of the room for adjustment of the tender at the final tender stage.

5.8. Procedure following the selection of the winning tender or preferred bidder

Once the assessment of the tenders has been completed, the contracting authority notifies the candidates of the award decision as soon as possible. In accordance with EU law, this notification must include at

84 Stated in Art. 29, para. 10, BAO.
85 Art. 29(6) of Directive 2004/18; and Art. 29, paras. 11 and 12, BAO.
86 See Ch. 1, section 5.7.4.
87 Art. 29(6) of Directive 2004/18; and Art. 29, paras. 11 and 14, BAO.
88 Art. 29(6) of Directive 2004/18; and Art. 29, para. 11, BAO.

least the grounds for the award decision with, for example, information about the characteristics and benefits of the designated tender, and the name of the successful candidate.[89] Contracting authorities such as the Rijkswaterstaat and the Rijksgebouwendienst strive for an exhaustive explanation.[90] They also provide the rejected candidates with the possibility to have a meeting in order that the authority may further explain the reasons for their rejection.

As Chapter 1 explained, under Article 29(7) of Directive 2004/18, the contracting authority may request the candidate with the economically most advantageous tender to clarify elements of the tender or to confirm commitments contained in the tender, provided that this does not have the effect of modifying substantial aspects of the tender or of the call for tender and does not risk distorting competition or causing discrimination, and this provision is simply repeated in the Dutch provision.[91] The tender rules as stated in the Procurement Directive and repeated in the Dutch BAO do not, in the authors' opinion, provide for any scope for negotiations with the successful candidate after the submission of the tender. Article 29(7) of the Procurement Directive[92] does, however, leave room to complete the documentation of the tender prior to the conclusion of the contract within the scope of the Directive. In DBFM contracts, confirmation of the commitments of the winning candidate takes place during contract close and financial close. Thus, during the contract close, the tender documents – consisting, *inter alia*, of the DBFM contract and corresponding annexes – and the final offer of the preferred bidder are united into a definitive contract. During this phase, there will usually be no need for amendments to the final offer, as the DBFM contract (which is based on a standard contract from the UK) is completed with the elements as submitted by the preferred bidder. At most, some clarification may be needed to be able to conclude an unambiguous contract as a solid basis for the realisation of the contract. After contract close, the financial close is accomplished. During this phase, the preferred bidder and its financiers conclude the financial backing of the DBFM contract. As a result of the financial close, the interest rates are fixed, for which the contracting authority shares some of the risk.

[89] Art. 41(2) of Directive 2004/18; Art. 41, para. 1, BAO; and Art. 4.29.6 ARW 2005.
[90] Art. 6 WIRA.
[91] Art. 29(7) of Directive 2004/18; Art. 29, para. 14, BAO; and Art. 4.29.3 ARW 2005.
[92] Also Art. 29, para. 11, BAO.

Contracts without the need for a financial agreement are finalised by completing the contract documents.

As long as the contract is not concluded with the winning bidder, the rejected candidates are held in reserve. Their bid bond as well as that of the winning tender must remain valid during this period. Should the winning tender for whatever reason not lead to the conclusion of the contract, the next best tenderer will be asked to step in.

The period in which contract close and financial close were concluded for the projects of the A12 Lunetten–Veenendaal and the A15 Maasvlakte–Vaanplein roads was about sixteen weeks in both cases. For the duration of this period, the rejected candidates were required to submit a bid bond in case the financial close with the preferred bidder failed. In the limited number of similar projects so far, however, there has been a wide variation in timeframes in reaching financial close – for example, financial close of the second Çoen Tunnel project took over a year, while other contracts took about six months to reach financial close. As the use of competitive dialogue in combination with DBFM contracts is becoming more of a standard procedure, the period in which financial close can be reached from the moment of selecting the preferred bidder realistically seems to be between four and six months.

5.9. *Standstill period*

After informing the rejected candidates of the reasons why their final offer has not been designated as the economically most advantageous tender,[93] a standstill period of fifteen days[94] is observed. During this time, the rejected candidates can choose to institute interim injunction proceedings to challenge the contracting authority's decision. The exclusion from the procedure of the rejected candidates is not final until the court has ruled the decision of the contracting authority legitimate or until the possibility to institute legal proceedings has passed.[95] If for some reason the contracting authority did not send a reasoned notification to the rejected candidates, the decision on the designated tender is deemed to be defective.[96] Without the reasoned notification, litigation cannot be deemed inadmissible on the basis of the expiration of the standstill period of fifteen days.

[93] Art. 6 *juncto* Art. 4 WIRA.
[94] Art. 4.30 ARW 2005; and Art. 4, para. 3, WIRA.
[95] Art. 5, para. 1, WIRA.
[96] Art. 5, para. 2, WIRA.

5.10. *Payments for costs of participation*

Before 1992, it was common practice in the Netherlands for the building industry to charge for the costs of preparing for a tender when tendering for a contract: this was done by bidders including the amount of bidders' costs in each tender, with the winning bidder then reimbursing the other bidders for the costs incurred. In order to reach agreement on the costs to be covered a price system was agreed upon, which was observed by the building industry. This practice was ended with the decision of the EU Commission of 5 February 1992 concerning the request of the union SPO[97] for a dispensation from what was then Article 85 EC; thus it was determined that this practice in the Netherlands violated EU competition law.[98] After this decision, the possibility of reimbursement for preparation costs was banned completely. The idea of reimbursing transaction costs was therefore not entirely alien to the Netherlands, although the design of the reimbursement of the transaction costs as implemented in the current procurement Directive[99] is substantially different. The transaction costs as referred to in the procurement Directive relate to a substantial effort on the side of the candidates to put in an elaborated offer, while the previous system used by the building industry before 1992 concerned merely the reimbursement of the costs of calculating the price of delivering the contract in accordance with a detailed specification (sometimes referred to as 'calculation costs'). After the implementation of Directive 2004/18, it has been a practice to at least partly reimburse candidates in a competitive dialogue for the costs they must incur to put in a tender. Procurement agencies such as the Rijkswaterstaat and the Rijksgebouwendienst consider a partial reimbursement of transaction costs fair in relation to the effort candidates must make. However, there is a difference between current practice and the old practice prior to 1992. Previously, candidates were reimbursed for calculation costs even when tendering for relatively simple contracts where all they had to do was to offer a price. However, for tenders where the efforts of candidates are limited, for example because they only have to calculate their prices or use minimal additional effort, there is no reimbursement of

[97] SPO is the Dutch abbreviation of the Union of Price System Organisations.

[98] IV/31.572 and 32.571, Construction Industry in the Netherlands (92/204) [1992] OJ L92, 7 April 1992, pp. 1–30.

[99] Specifically Art. 29(8) of Directive 2004/18; and Art. 29, para. 15, BAO.

transaction costs (in accordance with the decision of the EU Commission of 5 February 1992 on EU competition law, as mentioned above). In relation to competitive dialogue, it is the general practice to partly reimburse transaction costs for all tenders using this provision since costs are generally considerable, but no reimbursement will take place when the candidates have merely to calculate a price or when a small amount of additional effort is required – for example, in submitting a plan together with a price.

Apart from providing for a partial reimbursement, the Rijkswaterstaat and the Rijksgebouwendienst strive to reduce the transaction costs in a tender as much as possible. Notwithstanding the measures implemented to reduce the transaction costs involved in competitive dialogue, the market players taking part in the tender procedure still incur substantial transaction costs. With tenders using the competitive dialogue, which can take from one-and-a-half to two years, the transaction costs of candidates may amount to €8–9 million per candidate.

5.11. *Other issues*

In addition to policies for improving professionalism in its own procurement,[100] the Rijkswaterstaat has an active policy of involving the private sector in early stages of the public decision-making process on infrastructure for which the use of the competitive dialogue seems to be an appropriate tool. The aim of such early market involvement is to optimally profit from the knowledge and creative and innovative power of the private sector. The Rijksgebouwendienst has a similar aim to make use of the knowledge and creative and innovative power of the private sector, albeit in a somewhat different context.

In the period February–May 2011, an evaluation was held of the competitive dialogue procedure for the projects A12 Utrecht–Lunetten–Veenendaal and A15 Maasvlakte–Vaanplein roads. A brief overview of the findings show that the evaluation both highlights some examples of best practice – for example, the use of a digital Q and A tool together with a web-based data room, the use of sub-teams of specialists in addition to the dialogues held by the overall tender team and the kick-off meeting at the start of the dialogue – and makes recommendations for improvements.

[100] See also section 1 above.

The main recommendations for improvement concern a number of matters. One is the need to reduce the constraints on amending the contract and tender documents after the consultation phase. Another is the need for optimum timing of the moment and sequence for submitting the various elements of the tender; and another is the need to improve on discussing the definition and allotment of listed risks. The evaluation also recommends continuing the use of the method of submitting the finalised elements of the tender in parts during the discussion phase with a concluding submission of the tender in the final submission phase (as was discussed in section 5 above), but improving on its timing. There is also a recommendation to take special care to provide a distinctive, clear and concise formulation of the award criteria. A further recommendation is on the need to make clear-cut choices in the information placed at the disposal of the candidates. It is also recommended that there should be an examination of possible improvements concerning the financing transactions necessary for DBFM contracts.

The recommendations for improvement are not limited to the contracting authority. Thus there are several issues the candidates need to take on board, such as improving on communication skills and a more pro-active disposition.

On the basis of the recommendations in the evaluation report, the contracting authority will, in due time, assess what recommendations will be incorporated in its procurement policies and when these changes will be brought about. The results of the evaluation – with the complete report on best practices and recommendations for improvement – will in due course be made available to interested parties.[101]

6. Concluding remarks

Notwithstanding long-standing procurement practise in the Netherlands,[102] competitive dialogue is a new approach to the tendering of a project, especially as regards the tendering of PPP (mostly DBFM) projects. Since the first competitive dialogue procedures, both government procurement agencies and the private sector involved in these tenders have gone through a steep learning curve. However, knowledge

[101] Probably at www.ppsbijhetrijk.nl (Dutch language) and possibly at www.pppinthe-netherlands.nl (English language).

[102] See also section 1 above.

of both competitive dialogue and PPP is not widely available. At the moment, only the larger procurement agencies and private companies can avail themselves of sufficient potential to tackle large and complex (PPP/DBFM) tenders by means of the competitive dialogue procedure.

Currently, the applicable national rules and regulations adhere closely to the provisions of Directive 2004/18. On the one hand, this state of affairs leaves room to manoeuvre when designing the conduct of the dialogue. On the other hand, however, there is also a lot that is unclear regarding the scope of the provisions concerning competitive dialogue. One example is the room for clarification, specification and fine-tuning[103] of the final tender.[104] Future jurisprudence of the CJEU will need to clarify such ambiguities.

As to developments concerning the conduct of the competitive dialogue as described in this chapter, the results of the evaluation of the tenders of the projects A12 Utrecht–Lunetten–Veenendaal and A15 Maasvlakte–Vaanplein roads may lead to some changes, though overall the approach used for both projects has proven to be satisfactory. The Rijksgebouwendienst earlier decided to select only three candidates during the selection phase and commence the dialogue with these three. The Rijkswaterstaat may also opt for several changes in its conduct of the competitive dialogue, though the plan-of-approach phase for large and complex projects will probably remain. The Rijkswaterstaat will, however, continually try to improve on the requirements formulated in the tender documents, while for smaller and/or less complicated contracts it may also opt for selecting only three candidates during the selection phase instead of using the plan-of-approach phase to limit the number of candidates for the remainder of the dialogue as at present. The reason for this may be that the transaction costs for smaller contracts – with the use of the plan-of-approach phase – may be assessed to be disproportionate in relation to the contract value.

[103] Art. 29(6) of Directive 2004/18; and Art. 29, para. 11, BAO.
[104] See also section 5.7 above on the final tender stage.

INDEX